Explore Your World!

Interact with exciting online activities.

Journey to different parts of the world by using the dynamic online activities in this program. At PHSchool.com you're only one web code away from exciting interactivities on geography, history and culture. Use the web codes listed in the Go Online boxes to tour each region.

Here are some additional activities that you can start using today!

Medieval Times to Today Activities

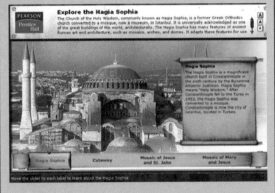

Explore the Hagia Sophia
The Church of the Holy Wisdom, commonly known as Hagia Sophia, is a former Greek Orthodox church converted to a mosque, now a museum, in Istanbul. It is universally acknowledged as one of the great buildings of the world, architecturally. The Hagia Sophia has many features of ancient Roman art and architecture, such as mosaics, arches, and domes. It adapts these features for use

Web Code	Activity
	History Interactive
lgp-8900	Explore the Hagia Sofia
lgp-8901	Learn more about the 5 Pillars of Islam
lgp-8902	Travel with Mansa Musa
lgp-8903	Travel Along the Inca Roads
lgp-8904	Tour a Maya City
lgp-8905	Explore a Chinese Ship
lgp-8906	Tour a Japanese Castle
lgp-8907	Explore Two Feudal Societies
lgp-8908	Explore the Magna Carta
lgp-8909	Explore Luther's Legacy
lgp-8910	Trade between Europe, Africa and Asia About 1700
lgp-8911	Transforming the World: The Columbian Exchange
lgp-8922	Triangular Trade
lgp-8924	Explore the Scientific Method
lgp-8925	Spreading the Word of Revolution
lgp-8929	Jazz Age
	Geography Interactive
lgp-8923	Expansion of Russia
lgp-8926	Imperialism in Africa to 1914
lgp-8927	Independent Nations of Latin America, 1844
lgp-8928	The Western Front and the Eastern Front, 1914-1918
lgp-8930	World War II in Europe and North Africa, 1942-1945
lgp-8941	The Cold War World
lgp-8942	Latin America: Economic Activity
lgp-8943	World Oil Resources and Consumption
	MapMaster
lgp-8944	The Seasons

Go Online
PHSchool.com

For: An activity on the Renaissance
Visit: PHSchool.com
Web Code: lgd-8601

Teacher's Edition

PRENTICE HALL

WORLD STUDIES

MEDIEVAL TIMES TO TODAY

In association with

DK

DISCOVERY CHANNEL SCHOOL

PEARSON

Prentice Hall

Boston, Massachusetts
Upper Saddle River, New Jersey

Program Consultants

Heidi Hayes Jacobs, Ed.D.

Heidi Hayes Jacobs has served as an education consultant to more than 1,000 schools across the nation and abroad. Dr. Jacobs serves as an adjunct professor in the Department of Curriculum on Teaching at Teachers College, Columbia University. She has written two best-selling books and numerous articles on curriculum reform. She received an M.A. from the University of Massachusetts, Amherst, and completed her doctoral work at Columbia University's Teachers College in 1981. The core of Dr. Jacobs's experience comes from her years teaching high school, middle school, and elementary school students. As an educational consultant, she works with K–12 schools and districts on curriculum reform and strategic planning.

Michal L. LeVasseur

Michal L. LeVasseur is the Executive Director of the National Council for Geography Education. She is an instructor in the College of Education at Jacksonville State University and works with the Alabama Geographic Alliance. Her undergraduate and graduate work were in the fields of anthropology (B.A.), geography (M.A.), and science education (Ph.D.). Dr. LeVasseur's specialization has moved increasingly into the area of geography education. Since 1996 she has served as the Director of the National Geographic Society's Summer Geography Workshops. As an educational consultant, she has worked with the National Geographic Society as well as with schools and organizations to develop programs and curricula for geography.

Senior Reading Consultants

Kate Kinsella

Kate Kinsella, Ed.D., is a faculty member in the Department of Secondary Education at San Francisco State University. A specialist in second-language acquisition and adolescent literacy, she teaches coursework addressing language and literacy development across the secondary curricula. Dr. Kinsella earned her M.A. in TESOL from San Francisco State University, and her Ed.D. in Second Language Acquisition from the University of San Francisco.

Kevin Feldman

Kevin Feldman, Ed.D., is the Director of Reading and Early Intervention with the Sonoma County Office of Education (SCOE) and an independent educational consultant. At the SCOE, he develops, organizes, and monitors programs related to K–12 literacy. Dr. Feldman has an M.A. from the University of California, Riverside in Special Education, Learning Disabilities and Instructional Design. He earned his Ed.D. in Curriculum and Instruction from the University of San Francisco.

Acknowledgments appear on page 297, which constitutes an extension of this copyright page.

Copyright © 2008 by Pearson Education, Inc., publishing as Pearson Prentice Hall, Boston, Massachusetts 02116.
All rights reserved. Printed in the United States of America. This publication is protected by copyright, and permission should be obtained from the publisher prior to any prohibited reproduction, storage in a retrieval system, or transmission in any form or by any means, electronic, mechanical, photocopying, recording, or likewise. For information regarding permission(s), write to: Rights and Permissions Department, One Lake Street, Upper Saddle River, New Jersey 07458.

MapMaster™ is a trademark of Pearson Education, Inc.
Pearson Prentice Hall™ is a trademark of Pearson Education, Inc.
Pearson® is a registered trademark of Pearson plc.
Prentice Hall® is a registered trademark of Pearson Education, Inc.
Discovery Channel School® is a registered trademark of Discovery Communications, Inc.
ExamView® is a registered trademark of FSCreations, Inc.

DK is a registered trademark of Dorling Kindersley Limited.

PEARSON
Prentice Hall

Prentice Hall World Studies is published in collaboration with DK Designs, Dorling Kindersley Limited, 80 Strand, London WC2R 0RL. A Penguin Company.

Cartography Consultant

DK Andrew Heritage

Andrew Heritage has been publishing atlases and maps for more than 25 years. In 1991, he joined the leading illustrated nonfiction publisher Dorling Kindersley (DK) with the task of building an international atlas list from scratch. The DK atlas list now includes some 10 titles, which are constantly updated and appear in new editions either annually or every other year.

ISBN 0-13-251660-8
2345678910   10 09 08 07

Academic Reviewers

Africa
Barbara B. Brown, Ph.D.
African Studies Center
Boston University
Boston, Massachusetts

Ancient World
Evelyn DeLong Mangie, Ph.D.
Department of History
University of South Florida
Tampa, Florida

Central Asia and the Middle East
Pamela G. Sayre
History Department,
    Social Sciences Division
Henry Ford Community College
Dearborn, Michigan

East Asia
Huping Ling, Ph.D.
History Department
Truman State University
Kirksville, Missouri

Eastern Europe
Robert M. Jenkins
Center for Slavic, Eurasian and
    East European Studies
University of North Carolina
Chapel Hill, North Carolina

Latin America
Dan La Botz
Professor, History Department
Miami University
Oxford, Ohio

Medieval Times
James M. Murray
History Department
University of Cincinnati
Cincinnati, Ohio

North Africa
Barbara E. Petzen
Center for Middle Eastern Studies
Harvard University
Cambridge, Massachusetts

Religion
Charles H. Lippy, Ph.D.
Department of Philosophy
    and Religion
University of Tennessee
    at Chattanooga
Chattanooga, Tennessee

Russia
Janet Vaillant
Davis Center for Russian
    and Eurasian Studies
Harvard University
Cambridge, Massachusetts

South Asia
Robert J. Young
Professor Emeritus
History Department
West Chester University
West Chester, Pennsylvania

United States and Canada
Victoria Randlett
Geography Department
University of Nevada, Reno
Reno, Nevada

Western Europe
Ruth Mitchell-Pitts
Center for European Studies
University of North Carolina
    at Chapel Hill
Chapel Hill, North Carolina

Reviewers

Sean Brennan
Brecksville-Broadview Heights
    City School District
Broadview Heights, Ohio

Stephen Bullick
Mt. Lebanon School District
Pittsburgh, Pennsylvania

William R. Cranshaw, Ed.D.
Waycross Middle School
Waycross, Georgia

Dr. Louis P. De Angelo
Archdiocese of Philadelphia
Philadelphia, Pennsylvania

Paul Francis Durietz
Social Studies
    Curriculum Coordinator
Woodland District #50
Gurnee, Illinois

Gail Dwyer
Dickerson Middle School,
    Cobb County
Marietta, Georgia

Michal Howden
Social Studies Consultant
Zionsville, Indiana

Rosemary Kalloch
Springfield Public Schools
Springfield, Massachusetts

Deborah J. Miller
Office of Social Studies,
    Detroit Public Schools
Detroit, Michigan

Steven P. Missal
Newark Public Schools
Newark, New Jersey

Catherine Fish Petersen (Retired)
East Islip School District
Islip Terrace, New York

Joe Wieczorek
Social Studies Consultant
Baltimore, Maryland

MEDIEVAL TIMES TO TODAY

Develop Skills

Use these pages to develop students' reading, writing, and geography skills.

Focus on History

Introduce students to the geography, history, and cultures from medieval times to today.

- Learn map skills with the MapMaster Skills Handbook.
- Practice your skills with every map in this book.
- Interact with every map online and on CD-ROM.

Maps and illustrations created by DK help build your understanding of the world. The DK World Desk Reference Online keeps you up to date.

The World Studies Video Program takes you on field trips to study countries around the world.

The *World Studies* Interactive Textbook online and on CD-ROM uses interactive maps and other activities to help you learn.

Special Features

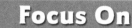

Eyewitness Technology

Detailed drawings show how technology shapes places and societies.

Target Reading Skills

Chapter-by-chapter reading skills help students read and understand social studies concepts.

Citizen Heroes

Introduce people who have made a difference in their country.

Discovery Channel SCHOOL

MAP★MASTER™

MAP★MASTER™ Interactive

Go online to find an interactive version of every MapMaster map in this book. Use the Web Code provided to gain direct access to these maps.

How to Use Web Codes:

1. Go to **www.PHSchool.com**.
2. Enter the Web Code.
3. Click Go!

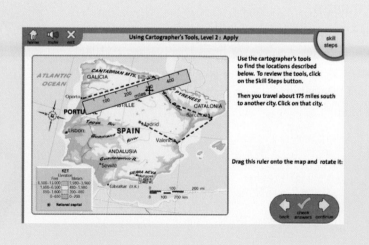

Charts, Graphs, and Tables

NCLB Implications for Social Studies

The No Child Left Behind (NCLB) legislation was a landmark in educational reform designed to improve student achievement and create a fundamental shift in American education. In the essay that follows, we will explore the implications of NCLB on social studies curriculum, instruction, assessment, and instructional programs.

Facts about NCLB

The No Child Left Behind Act of 2001 (NCLB) calls for sweeping educational reform, requiring all students to perform proficiently on standardized tests in reading, mathematics, and (soon to be added) science by the year 2014. Under NCLB, schools will be held accountable for students' academic progress. In exchange for this accountability, the law offers more flexibility to individual states and school districts to decide how best to use federal education funds. NCLB places an emphasis on implementing scientifically proven methods in teaching reading and mathematics, and promotes teacher quality. It also offers parental choice for students in failing schools.

Effects on Curriculum, Instruction, and Assessment

Since the primary focus of NCLB is on raising the achievement of students in reading and mathematics, some educators have wondered how it relates to social studies. Some teachers have expressed concerns that since NCLB does not require yearly testing of social studies, state and school districts may decide to shift resources and class time away from teaching social studies. However, NCLB considers the social studies areas of history, geography, economics, and government and civics to be core academic subjects. Many states are requiring middle grades social studies teachers to be highly qualified in history and geography in order to comply with the principle of improving teacher quality in NCLB.

NCLB sets the goal of having every child meet state-defined education standards. Since social studies educators have been leaders in the development of standards-based education and accountability through student testing over the past decade, many state and local districts have their own standards and assessments for social studies already in place. Assessment, including screening, diagnostic, progress-monitoring—including end-of-year, end-of-schooling, grade level, district, and state testing—and large-scale assessments, will continue to play a significant role in shaping social studies curriculum and instruction in the near future.

Integrating Reading into Social Studies Instruction

Due to the increased emphasis on reading and mathematics required by NCLB, social studies teachers may be called on to help improve their students' reading and math skills. For example, a teacher might use a graph about exports and imports to reinforce math skills, or a primary source about a historical event to improve reading skills. The connection between reading and social studies is especially important. Since many state and local assessments of reading require students to read and interpret informational texts, social studies passages are often used in the exams. Therefore, social studies teachers may assist in raising reading scores by integrating reading instruction into their teaching of social studies content.

Implications for Instructional Programs

The environment created by the NCLB legislation has implications for instructional programs. In keeping with the spirit of NCLB, social studies programs should clearly tie their content to state and local standards. Programs should also provide support so that all students can master these standards, ensuring that no child is left behind. An ideal instructional program is rooted in research, embeds reading instruction into the instructional design, and provides assessment tools that inform instruction—helping teachers focus on improving student performance.

Prentice Hall Response

We realize that raising the achievement level of all students is the number one challenge facing teachers today. To assist you in meeting this challenge, Prentice Hall enlisted a team of respected consultants who specialize in middle grades issues, reading in the content areas, and geographic education. This team created a middle grades world studies program that breaks new ground and meets the changing needs of you and your students.

With Prentice Hall, you can be confident that your students will not only be motivated, inspired, and excited to learn world studies, but they will also achieve the success needed in today's environment of the No Child Left Behind (NCLB) legislation and testing reform.

In the following pages, you will find the key elements woven throughout this World Studies program that truly set it apart and assure success for you and your students.

Teacher's Edition Contents in Brief

Research on Effective Reading Instruction

Why do many students have difficulty reading textbooks? How can we help students read to learn social studies? In the pages that follow, we examine the research on the challenge of reading textbooks; explain the direct, systematic, and explicit instruction needed to help students; and then show how Prentice Hall has responded to this research.

What is skilled reading?

Recent research (Snow et al., 2002) suggests that skillful and strategic reading is a long-term developmental process in which "readers learn how to simultaneously extract and construct meaning through interaction with written language." In other words, successful readers know how to decode all kinds of words, read with fluency and expression, have well-developed vocabularies, and possess various comprehension strategies such as note-taking and summarizing to employ as the academic reading task demands.

Many students lack reading skills

Sadly, many secondary students do not have solid reading skills. In the early years, students read mainly engaging and accessible narratives, such as stories, poems, and biographies. But in the upper elementary years, they shift toward conceptually dense and challenging nonfiction, or expository texts. It is no accident that the infamous "Fourth-Grade Slump" (Chall and Jacobs, 2003; Hirsch 2003)—a well-documented national trend of declining literacy after grade four—occurs during this time. The recent National Assessment of Educational Progress (NAEP, 2002) found that only 33 percent of eighth-grade students scored at or above the proficient level in reading.

Even students quite skilled in reading novels, short stories, and adolescent magazines typically come to middle school ill-equipped for the rigors of informational texts or reading to learn. They tend to dive right into a social studies chapter as if reading a recreational story. They don't first preview the material to create a mental outline and establish a reading purpose. They have not yet learned other basic strategies, including reading a section more than once, taking notes as they read, and reading to answer specific questions.

Dr. Kate Kinsella
Reading Consultant for *World Studies*
Department of Secondary Education
San Francisco State University, CA

Dr. Kevin Feldman
Reading Consultant for *World Studies*
Director of Reading and Early Intervention
Sonoma County, CA

"Even students quite skilled in reading novels, short stories, and adolescent magazines typically come to middle school ill-equipped for the rigors of informational texts or reading to learn."

The unique demands of textbooks

The differences between textbooks and the narratives students are used to reading are dramatic. The most distinctive challenges include dense conceptual content, heavy vocabulary load, unfamiliar paragraph and organizational patterns, and complex sentence structures. Academic texts present such a significant challenge to most students that linguists and language researchers liken them to learning a foreign language (Schleppegrell, 2002). In other words, most secondary students are second language learners: they are learning the academic language of informational texts!

Effective reading instruction

Research illustrates that virtually all students benefit from direct, systematic, and explicit instruction in reading informational texts (Baker & Gersten, 2000). There are three stages to the instructional process for content-area reading:

(1) before reading: instructional frontloading;

(2) during reading: guided instruction;

(3) after reading: reflection and study.

Before reading

Placing a major emphasis on preteaching, or "front-loading" your instruction—building vocabulary, setting a purpose for reading, and explicitly teaching students strategies for actively engaging with the text—helps you structure learning to ensure student success (see Strategies 1 and 2 on pages T32-T33). Frontloading strategies are especially critical in mixed-ability classrooms with English language learners, students with special needs, and other students performing below grade level in terms of literacy.

During reading

In guided instruction, the teacher models approaches for actively engaging with text to gain meaning. The teacher guides students through the first reading of the text using passage reading strategies (see Strategies 3-7 on pages T33-T35), and then guides discussion about the content using participation strategies (see Strategies 8-11 on pages T35-T37). Finally, students record key information in a graphic organizer.

After reading

During the reflection and study phase, the teacher formally checks for student understanding, offers remediation if necessary, and provides activities that challenge students to apply content in a new way. To review the chapter, students recall content, analyze the reading as a whole, and study key vocabulary and information likely to be tested.

References

Baker, Scott and Russell Gersten. "What We Know About Effective Instructional Practices for English Language Learners." *Exceptional Children*, 66 (2000):454–470.

Chall, Jeanne S. and Vicki A. Jacobs. "Poor Children's Fourth-Grade Slump." *American Educator* (Spring 2003):14.

Donahue, P.L., et al. *The 1998 NAEP Reading Report Card for the Nation and the States* (NCES 1999-500). Washington, D.C.: U.S. Department of Education, Office of Education Research and Improvement, National Center for Education Statistics, 1999.

Griggs, W.S., et al. *The Nation's Report Card: Reading 2002* (NCES 2003-521). Washington D.C.: U.S. Department of Education, Institute of Education Sciences, National Center for Education Statistics, 2003.

Hirsch, E.D., Jr. "Reading Comprehension Requires Knowledge—of Words and the World." *American Educator* (Spring 2003):10-29.

Kinsella, Kate, et al. *Teaching Guidebook for Universal Access.* Upper Saddle River, NJ: Prentice Hall, 2002.

Schleppegrell, M. "Linguistic Features of the Language of Schooling." *Linguistics and Education*, 12, no. 4 (2002): 431–459.

Snow, C., et al. *Reading for Understanding: Toward an R&D Program in Reading Comprehension.* Santa Monica, California: The Rand Corporation, 2002.

Reading Support

Putting Research Into Practice

Prentice Hall enlisted the assistance of Dr. Kate Kinsella and Dr. Kevin Feldman to ensure that the new middle grades *World Studies* program would provide the direct, systematic, and explicit instruction needed to foster student success in reading informational texts. To help students rise to the challenge of reading an informational text, *World Studies* embedded reading support right into the student text.

Embedded Reading Support in the Student Text

Before students read

- **Objectives** set the purpose for what students will read.
- **Target Reading Skill** for the section is explained.
- **Key Terms** are defined up front with pronunciation and part of speech.

During the section

- **Target Reading Skill** is applied to help students read and understand the narrative.
- **Key Terms** are defined in context, with terms and definitions called out in blue type.
- **Reading Checks** reinforce students' understanding by slowing them down to review after every concept is discussed.
- **Caption Questions** draw students into the art and photos, helping them to connect the content to the images.

After students read

- **Section Assessment** revisits the **Key Terms**, provides an opportunity to master the **Target Reading Skill**, allows student to rehearse their understanding of the text through the **Writing Activity**.

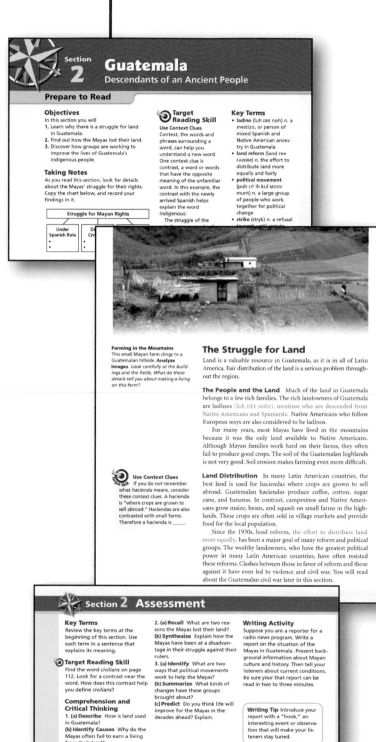

Putting Research Into Practice

World Studies offers teachers guidance in direct, systematic, and explicit reading instruction. The instructional sequence in the Teacher's Edition explicitly guides you in the use of effective strategies at each stage of the instructional process.

Reading Instruction in *World Studies* Teacher's Edition

Before Reading

Every lesson plan begins with suggestions that help you integrate frontloading strategies into your teaching. Build Background Knowledge activates and builds prior knowledge. Set a Purpose for Reading prompts students to predict and anticipate content and motivates students to engage with the text. Preview Key Terms helps students learn Key Terms to understand the text. Target Reading Skill models a reading strategy to help students gain meaning from the text. Vocabulary Builder gives teachers definitions and sample sentences to help teach high-use words.

During Reading

In the "Instruct" part of the lesson plan, you can use suggestions for getting students actively engaged in the text. Guided Instruction clarifies high-use words, applies a passage-reading strategy to promote text comprehension, and guides discussion to construct meaning. Independent Practice prompts students to reread and take notes in the graphic organizer provided to rehearse understanding.

After Reading

The lesson plan closes with specific strategies for the reflection and study phase after reading is completed. Monitor Progress checks students' note taking, and verifies students' prereading predictions. Assess and Reteach measures students' recall of content and provides additional instruction if needed. Review Chapter Content promotes retention of key concepts and vocabulary.

Integrated Reading Resources

The *World Studies* program provides instructional materials to support the reading instruction in the Teacher's Edition.

The **All-in-One Teaching Resources** provides reading instruction support worksheets, such as a Reading Readiness Guide, Word Knowledge, and Vocabulary Development.

Students can use the **Reading and Vocabulary Study Guide** (English and Spanish) to reinforce reading instruction and vocabulary development, and to review section summaries of every section of the student text.

Research on Differentiated Instruction

It's basic, but it's true—not all our students learn in the same manner and not all our students have the same academic background or abilities. As educators, we need to respond to this challenge through the development and utilization of instructional strategies that address the needs of diverse learners, or the number of children who "fall through the cracks" will continue to rise (Kame'enui & Carnine, 1998).

Providing universal access

Universal access happens when curriculum and instruction are provided in ways that allow all learners to participate and to achieve (Kinsella, et al., 2002). Teachers who teach in heterogeneous, inclusive classrooms can provide universal access by modifying their teaching to respond to the needs of typical learners, gifted learners, less proficient readers, English language learners, and special needs students. Many of these learner populations benefit from extensive reading support (see pages T14-T17).

It is also critical to properly match the difficulty level of tasks with the ability level of students. Giving students tasks that they perceive as too hard lowers their expectations of success. However, giving students assignments that they think are too easy, undermines their feelings of competence (Stipek, 1996). Therefore, it is important for a program to give teachers leveled activities that allow them to match tasks with the abilities of their individual students.

When students connect to and are engaged with the content, comprehension and understanding increase. Technology, such as online activities, can provide an ideal opportunity for such engagement. It also can be used to provide additional opportunities to access content. For example, a less proficient reader may reinforce understanding of a key concept through watching a video. A complete social studies program makes content available in a variety of formats, including text, audio, visuals, and interactivities.

> "Universal access happens when curriculum and instruction are provided in ways that allow all learners to participate and to achieve (Kinsella, et al., 2002)."

Kame'enui, Edward and Douglas Carnine. *Effective Teaching Strategies that Accommodate Diverse Learners.* Upper Saddle River, NJ: Prentice Hall, 1998.

Kinsella, Kate, et al. *Teaching Guidebook for Universal Access.* Upper Saddle River, NJ: Prentice Hall, 2002.

Stipek, D.J. "Motivation and Instruction," in R.C. Clafee and D.C. Berlinger (Eds.), *Handbook of Educational Psychology.* New York: Macmillan, 1996.

Putting Research Into Practice

Prentice Hall recognizes that today's classrooms include students with diverse backgrounds and ability levels. Accordingly, the *World Studies* program was designed to provide access to the content for all students. The program provides both the instructional materials to meet the learning needs of all students and the guidance you need to accommodate these needs.

Differentiated Instruction in the Teacher's Edition

The Teacher's Edition was designed to make it easy for teachers to modify instruction for diverse learners. Teaching strategies, provided by Dr. Kate Kinsella and Dr. Kevin Feldman, to help you modify your teaching are incorporated into every lesson plan. Specific activities help you differentiate instruction for individual students in five categories—less proficient readers, advanced readers, special needs students, gifted and talented, and English language learners. Resources are identified as being appropriate for use by each of these categories. All resources are also assigned a level—basic, average, and above average—so you know exactly how to assign tasks of appropriate difficulty level.

All-in-One Teaching Resources

Everything you need to provide differentiated instruction for each lesson, including reading support, activities and projects, enrichment, and assessment—in one convenient location.

World Studies Video Program

Students will benefit from our custom-built video program—the result of an exclusive partnership with Discovery Channel School—making content accessible through dynamic footage and high-impact stories.

Student Edition on Audio CD

The complete narrative is read aloud, section by section, providing extra support for auditory learners, English language learners, and reluctant readers. Also available is the Guided Reading Audio CD (English/Spanish), containing section summaries read aloud.

Interactive Textbook—The Student Edition Online and on CD-ROM

The Interactive Textbook allows students to interact with the content and includes reading aids, visual and interactive learning tools, and instant feedback assessments.

Differentiated Instruction

For Less Proficient Readers [L1]
Have students read the section in the Reading and Vocabulary Study Guide. This version provides basic-level instruction in an interactive format with questions and write-on lines.

Chapter 4, Section 1, **Latin America Reading and Vocabulary Study Guide**, pp. 42–44

For Special Needs Students [L1]
Have students read the section as they listen to the recorded version on the Student Edition on Audio CD. Check for comprehension by pausing the CD and asking students to share their answers to the Reading Checks.

Chapter 4, Section 1, **Student Edition on Audio CD**

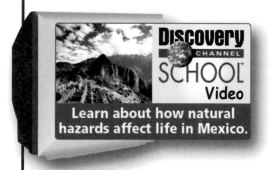

Learn about how natural hazards affect life in Mexico.

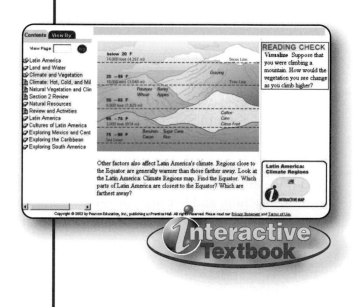

Research on Geographic Literacy

As the *Geography for Life: National Geography Standards* (1994) state, "There is now a widespread acceptance among the people of the United States that being literate in geography is essential if students are to leave school equipped to earn a decent living, enjoy the richness of life, and participate responsibly in local, national, and international affairs." A middle grades social studies program needs to help teachers produce students who are literate in geography.

Geographic literacy defined

Results for the 2001 National Assessment of Educational Progress (NAEP) Geography assessment show that the average scores of fourth- and eighth-grade students have improved since 1994. The average score of twelfth-grade students, however, has not changed significantly. In order to make the critical leap from basic geography skills to the kind of geographic literacy needed by the twelfth grade and beyond, a program must teach both geography content and geography skills, and then help students think critically. Geography content is made up of the essential knowledge that students need to know about the world. Geography skills are the ability to ask geographic questions, acquire and analyze geographic information, and answer these questions. To be truly literate in geography, students must be able to apply their knowledge and skills to understand the world.

Elements for success in middle grades

Students in the elementary grades don't always get enough training in geography. In order to help all students gain a base upon which to build middle grades geographic literacy, a program should introduce basic geography skills at the beginning of the school year.

The quality of maps is also vital to the success of a middle grades world studies program. Maps must be developmentally appropriate for middle grades students. They should be clean, clear, and accurate. Maps should be attractive and present subject matter in appealing ways, so that students *want* to use them to learn.

Another element that can lead to success is the incorporation of technology into the teaching and learning of geography, specifically the Internet. Research has shown that 8th grade students with high Internet usage scored higher in geography (NAEP, 2001).

U.S. Department of Education, Office of Educational Research and Improvement, National Center for Education Statistics, National Assessment of Educational Progress (NAEP), 2001 Geography Assessment.

Andrew Heritage
Head of Cartography
Dorling Kindersley (DK)

"Maps should be attractive and present subject matter in appealing ways, so that students *want* to use them to learn."

Putting Research Into Practice

Prentice Hall partnered with DK—internationally known for their dynamic atlases—to develop the *World Studies* program. DK's Andrew Heritage and his world-renowned cartography team designed all maps, resulting in stunning, high quality maps that are middle grades appropriate.

The MapMaster™ System

World Studies offers the first interactive geography instruction system available with a world studies textbook.

Introduce Basic Map Skills

The MapMaster Skills Handbook, a DK-designed introduction to the basics, brings students up to speed with a complete overview at the beginning of every book.

Build Geographic Literacy with Every Map

Scaffolded questions start with questions that require basic geography content and skills, and then ask students to demonstrate geographic literacy by thinking critically about the map.

Activate Learning Online

MapMaster Interactive—online and on CD-ROM—allows students to put their knowledge of geography skills and content into practice through interactivities.

Extend Learning with DK

• **DK World Desk Reference Online** is filled with up-to-date data, maps, and visuals that connect students to a wealth of information about the world's countries.

• **DK Compact Atlas of the World** with Map Master Teacher's Companion provides activities to introduce, develop, and master geography and map skills.

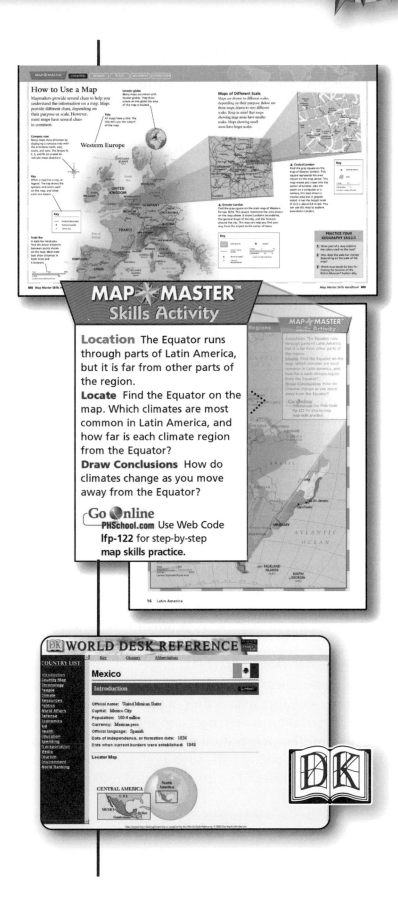

Research on Assessment

Meeting the NCLB challenge will necessitate an integrated approach to assessment with a variety of assessment tools. With the spotlight now on *improving* student performance, it is essential to use assessment results to inform instruction.

Assessments Tools for Informing Instruction

The key to success is using a variety of assessment tools coupled with data analysis and decision making. Teachers work with information coming from four kinds of assessment.

Screening assessments are brief procedures used to identify at-risk students who are not ready to work at grade level.

Diagnostic assessments provide a more in-depth analysis of strengths and weaknesses that can help teachers make instructional decisions and plan intervention strategies.

Progress-monitoring assessments (sometimes referred to as benchmark tests) provide an ongoing, longitudinal record of student achievement detailing individual student progress toward meeting end-of-year and end-of-schooling, grade level, district, or state standards.

Large-scale assessments, such as state tests and standardized tests, are used to determine whether individual students have met the expected standards and whether a school system has made adequate progress in improving its performance.

Ongoing Assessment

Daily assessment should be embedded in the program before, during, and after instruction in the core lessons. Legitimate test preparation experiences also should be embedded in the program. Test preparation involves teaching students strategies for taking tests, such as eliminating answers, reading comprehension, and writing extended response answers.

Eileen Depka
Supervisor of Standards and Assessment
Waukesha, WI

"Meeting the NCLB challenge will necessitate an integrated approach to assessment with a variety of assessment tools."

Putting Research Into Practice

Prentice Hall developed the *World Studies* program with a variety of assessment tools, including ongoing assessment in the student text.

Assessments for Informing Instruction

World Studies was designed to provide you with all four kinds of assessment.

- **Screening test** identifies students who are reading 2-3 years below grade level.

- **Diagnostic tests** focus on skills needed for success in social studies, including subtests in geographic literacy, visual analysis, critical thinking and reading, and communications skills, as well as vocabulary and writing.

- **Benchmark tests**, to be given six times throughout the year, monitor student progress in the course.

- **Outcome test**, to be administered at the end of the year, evaluates student mastery of social studies content standards.

Ongoing Assessment

- **Student Edition** offers section and chapter assessments with questions building from basic comprehension to critical thinking and writing.

- **Test Prep Workbook** and **Test-taking Strategies with Transparencies** develop students' test-taking skills and improve their scores on standardized tests.

- **Exam***View*® **Test Bank CD-ROM** allows you to quickly and easily develop customized tests from a bank of thousands of questions.

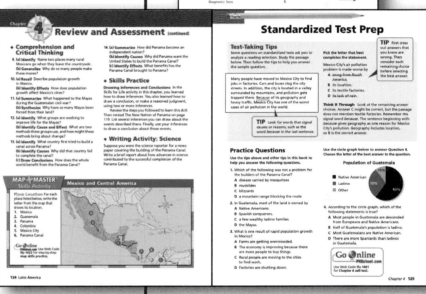

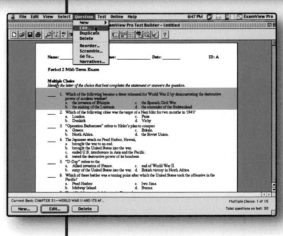

Medieval Times to Today Skills Scope and Sequence

Prentice Hall *World Studies* contains a comprehensive program of core skills. Each skill is taught in every book of the series. A Target Reading Skill is located at the beginning of each chapter and expanded upon in each section within the chapter. Core skills are also taught either in the "Skills for Life Activity" in the Student Edition, or in a "Skills Mini Lesson" in the Teacher's Edition. In addition, worksheets for the students' use in completing each skill are located in the All-in-One Teaching Resources. The chart below lists the skills covered in *Prentice Hall World Studies: Medieval Times to Today* and the page where each skill is taught.

Medieval Times to Today Analysis Skills	SE	TE
Analyzing Graphic Data	pp. 196–197, 236–237	pp. 236–237
Analyzing Images	pp. 196–197	pp. 196–197
Analyzing Primary Sources		p. 95
Clarifying Meaning	pp. 34, 36, 38, 44, 46, 52, 55	pp. 34b, 36, 44, 52
Comparing and Contrasting	pp. 188, 190, 194, 198, 200, 204, 208, 212, 214	pp. 48, 188b, 190, 198, 204, 212
Decision Making		p. 202
Distinguishing Fact and Opinion	pp. 138–139	pp. 138–139
Drawing Inferences and Conclusions		p. 234
Identifying Cause and Effect/Making Predictions	pp. 68–69, 88, 90, 95, 100, 102, 108, 110	pp. 68–69, 88b, 90, 100, 108
Identifying Frame of Reference and Point of View		p. 136
Identifying Main Ideas/Summarizing	pp. 60, 62, 65, 70, 72, 78, 81, 98–99	pp. 60b, 62, 70, 78, 98–99
Making Valid Generalizations		p. 13
Problem Solving		p. 104
Recognizing Bias and Propaganda		p. 165
Sequencing	pp. 116, 118, 120, 126, 131, 133, 136, 140, 142	pp. 81, 116b, 118, 126, 133, 140
Supporting a Position		p. 158
Synthesizing Information		p. 214
Transferring Information From One Medium to Another	pp. 16–17	pp. 16–17
Using the Cartographer's Tools		p. 39
Using Context	pp. 152, 154, 159, 161, 166, 170, 176, 180, 181	pp. 152b, 154, 161, 170, 180
Using the Reading Process	pp. 8, 10, 14, 18, 22, 26, 28	pp. 8b, 10, 18, 26
Using Reliable Information	pp. 42–43	pp. 42–43
Using Special-Purpose Maps	pp. 178–179	pp. 178–179
Using Word Analysis	pp. 220, 222, 223, 230, 234, 238, 241	pp. 220b, 222, 230, 238

Pacing Options

World Studies offers many aids to help you plan your instruction time, whether regular class periods or block scheduling. Section-by-section lesson plans for each chapter include suggested times, based on the 18-week course configuration below. Teacher Express CD-ROM will help you manage your time electronically.

Medieval Times to Today Pacing Options			12-week unit	18-week unit
Chapter 1	Section 1	The Byzantine Empire	5	8.5
	Section 2	The Beginnings of Islam	1	2
	Section 3	The Golden Age of Muslim Civilization	3.5	4
Chapter 2	Section 1	Africa and the Bantu	2	3.5
	Section 2	West African Kingdoms	1.5	2
	Section 3	East Africa's Great Trading Centers	3	4
Chapter 3	Section 1	South America and the Incas	2	3.5
	Section 2	Cultures of Middle America	1	2
	Section 3	Cultures of North America	3	4
Chapter 4	Section 1	Golden Ages of China	2.5	3.5
	Section 2	Medieval Japan	1.5	2
	Section 3	The Great Mughal Empire in India	3.5	4
Chapter 5	Section 1	Feudalism and the Manor System	1	2
	Section 2	The Church and the Rise of Cities	1	2
	Section 3	The Crusades	2	4
	Section 4	The Power of Kings	4	5
Chapter 6	Section 1	A New Age in Europe	1.5	2
	Section 2	The Age of Exploration	1.5	2
	Section 3	The Age of Powerful Monarchs	2	3.5
	Section 4	Conquests in the Americas and Africa	3.5	4
Chapter 7	Section 1	The Enlightenment	2	3.5
	Section 2	Political Revolutions	1.5	2
	Section 3	The Industrial Revolution	1.5	2
	Section 4	Nationalism and Imperialism	3	4
Chapter 8	Section 1	War and Revolution	1	2.5
	Section 2	The Postwar World	2	4
	Section 3	The World Today	3	4.5
Total Number of Days			60	90

Correlation to *Geography for Life*, the National Geography Standards

On the following pages, *Prentice Hall World Studies: Medieval Times to Today* is correlated with *Geography for Life*, the National Geography Standards. These standards were prepared in response to the Goals 2000, Educate America Act, by the Geography Education Standards Project. Participating in the project were the American Geographical Society, the Association of American Geographers, the National Council for Geographic Education, and the National Geographic Society. Concepts and skills contained in the Geography Standards are incorporated throughout the program. This correlation displays places where the standards are directly addressed.

Standard	Medieval Times to Today
The World in Spatial Terms	
Standard 1 Use maps and other geographic representations, tools, and technologies to acquire, process, and report information from a spatial perspective.	MapMaster Skills Handbook World Overview, 1:1, 1:3, 2:1, 3:1, 3:3, 4:1, 4:2, 5:1, 5:3, 6:1, 6:2, 8:3
Standard 2 Use mental maps to organize information about people, places, and environments in a spatial context.	World Overview
Standard 3 Analyze the spatial organization of people, places, and environments on Earth's surface.	1:2, 2:1, 3:1–3, 4:1, 4:3
Places and Regions	
Standard 4 Understand the physical and human characteristics of places.	1:1, 1:2, 2:1–3, 3:1–3, 5:1, 6:4
Standard 5 Understand that people create regions to interpret Earth's complexity.	2:2, 3:1–3, 6:2, 8:2
Standard 6 Understand how culture and experience influence people's perception of places and regions.	World Overview, 1:1–3, 2:1, 2:2, 3:3, 4:1, 4:2, 6:1, 6:4, 7:2, 7:4, 8:1, 8:2
Physical Systems	
Standard 7 Understand the physical processes that shape the patterns of Earth's surface.	2:1, 3:1, 3:3
Standard 8 Understand the characteristics and spatial distribution of ecosystems on Earth's surface.	2:1, 3:2, 4:3

Correlation to *Geography for Life*, the National Geography Standards *(continued)*

Standard	Medieval Times to Today
Human Systems	
Standard 9 Understand the characteristics, distribution, and migration of human populations on Earth's surface.	1:2, 1:3, 2:1, 2:3, 3:1–3, 6:2, 6:4, 7:4
Standard 10 Understand the characteristics, distribution, and complexity of Earth's cultural mosaics.	1:1–3, 2:1, 2:3, 3:1–3, 6:1, 6:4, 7:4, 8:1
Standard 11 Understand the patterns and networks of economic interdependence on Earth's surface.	1:1, 2:2, 2:3, 3:2, 4:1, 4:3, 5:2, 7:3, 8:3
Standard 12 Understand the processes, patterns, and functions of human settlement.	1:1, 1:2, 2:1, 2:3, 5:1, 6:2, 6:4, 7:4, 8:1, 8:2
Standard 13 Understand how the forces of cooperation and conflict among people influence division and control of Earth's surface.	1:2, 2:3, 4:1, 4:2, 5:1–4, 6:2, 6:3, 6:4, 7:2, 7:4, 8:1, 8:2
Environment and Society	
Standard 14 Understand how human actions modify the physical environment.	3:2, 3:3, 5:2, 6:2, 8:1
Standard 15 Understand how physical systems affect human systems.	1:2, 2:1–3, 3:1–3, 6:1, 6:2
Standard 16 Understand the changes that occur in the meaning, use, distribution, and importance of resources.	2:1–3, 3:2, 3:3, 4:1–3, 5:2, 7:3, 8:2
The Uses of Geography	
Standard 17 Understand how to apply geography to interpret the past.	1:1, 1:2, 2:1, 4:1–3
Standard 18 Understand how to apply geography to interpret the present and plan for the future.	8:3

Correlation to the NCSS Curriculum Standards

On the following pages *Prentice Hall World Studies Medieval Times* is correlated with *Expectations of Excellence*, the Curriculum Standards for Social Studies. These standards were developed by the National Council for the Social Studies to address overall curriculum design and comprehensive student performance expectations.

Standard	Medieval Times to Today
Performance Expectations 1: Culture	
• compare similarities and differences in the ways groups, societies, and cultures meet human needs and concerns • explain how information and experiences may be interpreted by people from diverse cultural perspectives and frames of reference • explain and give examples of how language, literature, the arts, architecture, other artifacts, traditions, beliefs, values, and behaviors contribute to the development and transmission of culture • explain why individuals and groups respond differently to their physical and social environments and/or changes to them on the basis of shared assumptions, values, and beliefs • articulate the implications of cultural diversity, as well as cohesion, within and across groups	3:1–3, 4:1–3, 5:1, 5:2, 5:3, 6:1–4, 7:1–4, 8:1, 8:2
Performance Expectations 2: Time, Continuity, and Change	
• demonstrate an understanding that different scholars may describe the same event or situation in different ways but must provide reasons or evidence for their view • identify and use key concepts such as chronology, causality, change, conflict, and complexity to explain, analyze, and show connections among patterns of historical change and continuity • identify and describe selected historical periods and patterns of change within and across cultures • identify and use processes important to reconstructing and reinterpreting the past • develop critical sensitivities regarding attitudes, values, and behaviors of people in different historical contexts • use knowledge of facts and concepts drawn from history, along with methods of historical inquiry, to inform decision-making about and action-taking on public issues	1:1–3, 2:1–3, 3:1–3, 4:1, 4:2, 5:1–4, 6:1–4, 7:1, 7:3, 7:4
Performance Expectations 3: People, Places, and Environment	
• elaborate mental maps of locales, regions, and the world that demonstrate understanding of relative location, direction, size, and shape • create, interpret, use, and distinguish various representations of the earth • use appropriate resources, data sources, and geographic tools to generate, manipulate, and interpret information • estimate distance, calculate scale, and distinguish geographic relationships • locate and describe varying landforms and geographic features and explain their relationship with the ecosystem • describe physical system changes and identify geographic patterns associated with them • describe how people create places that reflect cultural values and ideals • examine, interpret, and analyze physical and cultural patterns and their interactions • describe ways that historical events have been influenced by, and have influenced, physical and human geographic factors in local, regional, national, and global settings • observe and speculate about social and economic effects of environmental changes and crises resulting from natural phenomena • propose, compare, and evaluate alternative uses of land and resources in communities, regions, nations, and the world	1:1, 2:1, 2:2, 3:1–3, 4:1–3, 5:1, 5:2, 5:3, 6:1–4, 7:1, 7:3, 7:4, 8:1–3

Correlation to the NCSS Curriculum Standards *(continued)*

Standard	Medieval Times to Today
Performance Expectations 4: Individual Development and Identity	
• relate personal changes to social, cultural, and historical contexts • describe personal connections to place—as associated with community, nation, and world • describe the ways family, gender, ethnicity, nationality, and institutional affiliations contribute to personal identity • relate such factors as physical endowment and capabilities, learning, motivation, personality, perception, and behavior to individual development • identify and describe ways regional, ethnic, and national cultures influence individuals' daily lives • identify and describe the influence of perception, attitudes, values, and beliefs on personal identity • identify and interpret examples of stereotyping, conformity, and altruism • work independently and cooperatively to accomplish goals	1:3, 2:1, 2:3, 3:1–3, 5:1, 5:2, 6:1, 6:2, 6:3, 7:1, 7:3
Performance Expectations 5: Individuals, Groups, & Institutions	
• demonstrate an understanding of concepts such as role, status, and social class in describing interactions of individuals and social groups • analyze group and institutional influences on people, events, and elements of culture • describe the various forms institutions take and the interactions of people with institutions • identify and analyze examples of tensions between expressions of individuality and group or institutional efforts to promote social conformity • identify and describe examples of tensions between belief systems and government policies and laws • describe the role of institutions in furthering both continuity and change • apply knowledge of how groups and institutions work to meet individual needs and promote the common good	2:1, 3:1–3, 4:1–3, 5:1–4, 6:1, 6:3, 7:1, 7:4, 8:1, 8:3
Performance Expectations 6: Power, Authority, and Governance	
• examine persistent issues involving the rights, roles, and status of the individual in relation to general welfare • describe the purpose of government and how its powers are acquired, used, and justified • analyze and explain ideas and governmental mechanisms to meet needs and wants of citizens, regulate territory, manage conflict, and establish order and security • describe the ways nations and organizations respond to forces of unity and diversity affecting order and security • identify and describe the basic features of the political system in the United States, and identify representative leaders from various levels and branches of government • explain conditions, actions, and motivations that contribute to conflict and cooperation within and among nations • describe and analyze the role of technology as it contributes to or helps resolve conflicts • explain how power, role, status, and justice influence the examination of persistent issues and social problems • give examples and explain how governments attempt to achieve their stated ideals at home and abroad	1:1, 1:2, 2:2, 2:3, 3:1, 3:2, 4:1–3, 5:1, 5:4, 6:3, 6:4, 7:2, 7:3, 7:4, 8:1–3

Correlation to the NCSS Curriculum Standards *(continued)*

Standard	Medieval Times to Today
Performance Expectation 7: Production, Distribution, and Consumption	
• give examples of ways that economic systems structure choices about how goods and services are to be produced and distributed • describe the role that supply and demand, prices, incentives, and profits play in determining what is produced and distributed in a competitive market system • explain differences between private and public goods and services • describe a range of examples of the various institutions that make up economic systems • describe the role of specialization and exchange in the economic process • explain and illustrate how values and beliefs influence different economic decisions • differentiate among various forms of exchange and money • compare basic economic systems according to who determines what is produced, distributed, and consumed • use economic concepts to help explain historical and current events in local, national, or global concepts • use economic reasoning to compare different proposals for dealing with contemporary social issues	1:1, 2:2, 2:3, 4:1, 5:2, 5:3, 6:4, 7:3, 8:3
Performance Expectation 8: Science, Technology, and Society	
• examine and describe the influence of culture on scientific and technological choices and advancement • show through specific examples how science and technology have changed peoples' perceptions of their social and natural world • describe examples in which values, beliefs, and attitudes have been influenced by new scientific and technological knowledge • explain the need for laws and policies to govern scientific and technological applications • seek reasonable and ethical solutions to problems that arise when scientific advancements and social norms or values come into conflict	1:3, 3:1, 3:2, 4:1, 6:1, 6:2, 7:1, 7:3, 8:3
Performance Expectation 9: Global Connections	
• describe instances in which language, art, music, and belief systems, and other cultural elements can facilitate global understanding or cause misunderstanding • analyze examples of conflict, cooperation, and interdependence among groups, societies, and nations • describe and analyze the effects of changing technologies on the global community • explore the causes, consequences, and possible solutions to persistent contemporary and emerging global interests • describe and explain the relationships and tensions between national sovereignty and global interests • demonstrate understanding of concerns, standards, issues, and conflicts related to universal human rights • identify and describe the roles of international and multinational organizations	1:1, 2:1–3, 3:2, 4:1, 4:3, 6:2, 6:4, 7:1–4, 8:1–3

Correlation to the NCSS Curriculum Standards *(continued)*

Standard	Medieval Times to Today
Performance Expectation 10: Civic Ideals and Practices	
• examine the origins and continuing influence of key ideals of the democratic republican form of government, such as individual human dignity, liberty, justice, equality, and rule of law • identify and interpret sources and examples of the rights and responsibilities of citizens • locate, access, analyze, organize, and apply information about selected public issues—recognizing and explaining multiple points of view • practice forms of civic discussion and participation consistent with the ideals of citizens in a democratic republic • explain and analyze various forms of citizen action that influence public policy decisions • identify and explain the roles of formal and informal political actors in influencing and shaping public policy and decision-making • analyze the influence of diverse forms of public opinion on the development of public policy and decision-making • analyze the effectiveness of selected public policies and citizen behaviors in realizing the stated ideals of a democratic republican form of government • explain the relationship between policy statements and action plans used to address issues of public concern • examine strategies designed to strengthen the "common good," which consider a range of options for citizen action	4:1–3, 5:1–3, 6:3, 7:1, 7:2, 8:1–3

Instructional Strategies for Improving Student Comprehension

In response to today's environment of the NCLB legislation and testing reform, Prentice Hall asked Dr. Kate Kinsella and Dr. Kevin Feldman to provide specific instructional strategies you can use to improve student comprehension. Their guidance informed the development of the *World Studies* Teacher's Edition. The lesson plans in this Teacher's Edition incorporate the following instructional strategies to enhance students' comprehension.

There is no single magical strategy that will solve all of the difficulties students encounter in reading challenging content area texts. Secondary students in mixed-ability classrooms depend on teachers to use a consistent set of research-informed and classroom-tested strategies in a patient and recursive manner—not the occasional or random use of different strategies. Students will not become skillful readers of content area texts in a week or two of instruction. However, when teachers engage students in the consistent use of a well-chosen set of content reading strategies appropriately matched to the demands of the text and the students' level of knowledge, their ability to comprehend difficult grade level texts will be dramatically enhanced.

Strategy 1: Set a Purpose for Reading

This program has two types of activities designed to help students set a purpose for reading: an Anticipation Guide and a KWL chart. The two types rotate by section.

A. Anticipation Guide

Purpose: To focus students' attention on key concepts, and guide them to interact with ideas in the text

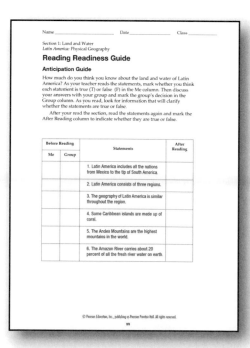

1. Distribute the *Reading Readiness Guide*. Read each statement aloud, and then ask students to react to the statements individually and in groups, marking their responses in the Before Reading column.

2. Use the worksheet as a springboard for discussing the section's key concepts as a unified class. Refrain from revealing the correct responses at this time, to avoid taking away the need for them to read the text.

3. Have students read the section with the purpose of finding evidence that confirms, disproves, or elaborates each statement in the *Reading Readiness Guide*.

4. After students finish reading, have them return to the statements and mark the After Reading column on their worksheets. Have them locate information from the text that supports or disproves each statement.

5. Discuss what the class has learned and probe for any lingering confusion about key concepts.

Instructional Strategies

B. KWL

Purpose: To engage students before, during, and after reading

The KWL worksheet guides students to recall what they **K**now, determine what they **W**ant to learn, and identify what they **L**earn as they read.

1. Distribute the *Reading Readiness Guide*. Brainstorm with the group about what they already know about the topic. List students' ideas on the board. Encourage students to generate questions at points of ambiguity.

2. Students then list pieces of information they already know and questions they want to answer in the first two columns of their worksheets.

3. As students read the section, ask them to note information that answers their questions or adds to what they know.

4. After reading, facilitate a class discussion about what the students have learned. Clarify any lingering confusion about key concepts.

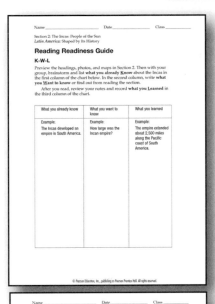

Strategy 2: Teach High-Use Academic Words

Purpose: To teach students words used often in academic texts, beyond the content-specific Key Terms

How to Do It

1. Have students rate how well they know each word on their *Word Knowledge* worksheets. Tell them there is no penalty for a low rating.

2. Survey students' ratings to decide which words need the most instruction.

3. Provide a brief definition or sample sentence for each word. (See Vocabulary Builder at the beginning of each section for definitions and sample sentences.) Rephrase your explanation, leaving out the word and asking students to substitute it aloud.

4. Work with students as they fill in the "Definition or Example" column of their *Word Knowledge* worksheets.

5. Point out each word in context as you read the chapters. Consider allowing students to earn extra credit if they use a word correctly in class discussion or assignments.

Strategy 3: Oral Cloze

Purpose: To help students read actively while the teacher reads aloud

How to Do It

1. Choose a passage and direct students to "read aloud silently using their inner voices." Be sure students understand reading is an active process, not simply a listening activity, and their job is to follow along—eyes riveted to each word, saying the words to themselves as you read aloud.

2. Tell students to be on their "reading toes," for you will be leaving out an occasional word and their task is to chorally supply the word.

3. The first few times you use the Oral Cloze, demonstrate by telling the students in advance what word you will be leaving out, directing them to read the word at the right time. Practice this a few times until they have the feel for the procedure. Leave out fewer words as students become more familiar with the Oral Cloze and require less direction to remain focused during teacher read alouds.

Instructional Strategies

Strategies for Improving Student Comprehension *(continued)*

Strategy 4: Choral Reading

Purpose: To have students attend to the text in a non-threatening atmosphere

How to Do It

1. Choose a relatively short passage.

2. Tell students that you will all read the text aloud at once. Direct students to "keep your voice with mine" as they read.

3. Read the passage slowly and clearly.

4. Have students read the text again silently.

Strategy 5: Structured Silent Reading

Purpose: To give students a task as they read silently to increase their attentiveness and accountability

How to Do It

1. Assign a section to read silently. Pose a question for the whole class to answer from their silent reading, such as the Reading Check question at the end of each subsection. Model how one thinks while reading to find answers to a question.

2. When students get used to reading to answer the Reading Check question, pose more in-depth questions, progressing from factual recall to questions that stimulate interpretive or applied thinking.

3. Teach students to ask and answer their own questions as they read. Model this process by reading a section aloud and asking and answering your own questions as you read.

4. After the students have finished reading, engage the class in a brief discussion to clarify questions, vocabulary, and key concepts.

Strategy 6: Paragraph Shrinking

Purpose: To increase comprehension during reading

How to Do It

1. Partner struggling students with more proficient students and assign a manageable portion of the text.

2. Ask one member of each pair to identify the "who or what" the paragraph is about and tell the other.

3. Have the other member of the pair identify important details about the "who or what" and tell the other.

4. Ask the first member to summarize the paragraph in fifteen to twenty words or less using the most important details. The second member of the pair monitors the number of words and says "Shrink it!" if the summary goes over twenty words.

5. Have the partners reverse roles and continue reading.

6. Discuss the reading as a class to make sure students' paragraphs have correctly hit upon the main ideas of the passage.

Strategy 7: ReQuest (Reciprocal Questioning)

Purpose: To ask and answer questions during reading to establish a purpose for reading and monitor one's own comprehension

How to Do It

1. Prepare students to read by doing the section's Build Background Knowledge, Set a Purpose for Reading, and Preview Key Terms activities.

2. Begin reading a brief portion of the text aloud. Ask and answer your own questions about the text, progressing from recall to critical thinking questions.

3. After modeling this question and response pattern with a brief passage, ask students to read the next section of the text. Tell students that they will be taking turns asking you questions about what they read, and you will answer their questions, just like you modeled for them.

4. Ask students to read the next section. Inform them that you will be asking them questions about the section and they will be answering your questions.

5. Continue to alternate between student-generated questions and teacher-generated questions until the entire designated passage has been read. As students become used to the strategy, they gradually assume more responsibility in the process.

6. When the students have read enough information to make predictions about the remainder of the assignment, stop the exchange of comprehension questions. Instead, ask prediction questions, such as, "What do you think will be discussed in the next section? Why do you think so?"

7. Assign the remaining portion for students to read silently. Then lead a wrap-up discussion of the material.

Strategy 8: Idea Wave

Purpose: To engage students in active class discussions

How to Do It

1. Pose a question or task.

2. Give students quiet time to consider what they know about the topic and record a number of responses.

3. Whip around the class in a fast-paced and structured manner (e.g. down rows, around tables), allowing as many students as possible to share an idea in 15 seconds or less.

4. After several contributions, if there tends to be repetition, ask students to point out similarities in responses rather than simply stating that their idea has already been mentioned.

Strategies for Improving Student Comprehension *(continued)*

Strategy 9: Numbered Heads

Purpose: To engage students in active class discussions

How to Do It

1. Seat students in groups of four and number off one through four (if possible, combine established partners to form groups of four).

2. After giving the discussion prompt, allow students to discuss possible responses for an established amount of time.

3. Remind students to pay close attention to the comments of each group member because you will be randomly selecting one student to represent the best thinking of the entire group.

4. Call a number (one through four), and ask all students with that number to raise their hands, ready to respond to the topic at hand in a teacher-directed, whole-class discussion.

5. Add comments, extend key ideas, ask follow-up questions, and make connections between individual student's comments to create a lively whole-class discussion.

6. Provide any summary comments required to ensure that all students understand critical points.

Strategy 10: Think-Write-Pair–Share

Purpose: To engage students in responding to instruction

How to Do It

1. **Think**—Students listen while the teacher poses a question or a task related to the reading or classroom discussion. The level of questions should vary from lower level literal to higher order inferential or analytical.

2. **Write**—Provide quiet thinking or writing time for students to deal with the question, and go back to the text or review notes. Have students record their ideas in their notebooks.

3. **Pair/Share**—Cue students to find a partner and discuss their responses, noting similarities and differences. Teach students to encourage one another to clarify and justify responses.

4. Randomly call on students to share during a unified class discussion after they have all rehearsed answers with their partners.

5. Invite any volunteers to contribute additional ideas and points of view to the discussion after calling on a reasonable number of students randomly.

6. Direct students to go back to notes and add any important information garnered during the partner and class discussions.

Strategy 11: Give One, Get One

Purpose: To foster independent reflection and peer interaction prior to a unified class discussion

How to Do It

1. Pose a thought-provoking question or a concrete task to the class.

2. Allow three to five minutes of quiet time for students to consider what they may already know about the topic and jot down a number of potential responses.

3. Ask students to place a check mark next to the two or three ideas that they perceive as their strongest and then draw a line after their final idea to separate their ideas from those that they will gather from classmates.

4. Give students a set amount of time (about eight to ten minutes) to get up from their seats and share ideas with classmates. After finding a partner, the two students exchange papers and first quietly read each other's ideas. They discuss the ideas briefly, then select one idea from their partner's list and add it to their own, making sure to accurately copy the idea alongside the partner's name.

5. When one exchange is completed, students move on to interact with a new partner.

6. At the end of the exchange period, facilitate a unified class discussion. Call on a volunteer to share one new idea acquired from a conversation partner. The student whose idea has just been reported then shares the next idea, gleaned from a different conversation partner.

Professional Development

For more information about these strategies, see the end of each chapter's Interleaf.

Objectives

- Learn how to read nonfiction critically by analyzing an author's purpose, distinguishing between facts and opinions, identifying evidence, and evaluating credibility.

Prepare to Read

Build Background Knowledge L2

Write the phrase "Don't believe everything you read" on the board. Ask students to brainstorm examples that illustrate the saying. Provide a few simple examples to get them started. (*tall tales, advertisements*)

Instruct

Reading Informational Texts L2

Guided Instruction

- Tell students that they must actively evaluate the information in most of the nonfiction they read.

- Read the sample editorial on this page aloud. Tell students that an editorial usually expresses a person's opinion. Ask students to consider why the author wrote this editorial. (*The author expresses the opinion that the proposal to build the new shopping center should have been approved.*) Ask **How might this purpose affect what the editorial says?** (*The author may present information in the best possible light to prove his or her belief.*)

- Another important step in evaluating nonfiction is distinguishing between facts and opinions. Ask each student to write one fact and one opinion, on any subject, in their notebooks. Use the Idea Wave strategy (TE, p. T35) to get students to share their facts and opinion. If students have incorrectly categorized examples, help them to see why.

Reading Informational Texts

Reading a magazine, an Internet page, or a textbook is not the same as reading a novel. The purpose of reading nonfiction texts is to acquire new information. On page M18 you'll read about some ⊙ **Target Reading Skills** that you'll have a chance to practice as you read this textbook. Here we'll focus on a few skills that will help you read nonfiction with a more critical eye.

Analyze the Author's Purpose

Different types of materials are written with different purposes in mind. For example, a textbook is written to teach students information about a subject. The purpose of a technical manual is to teach someone how to use something, such as a computer. A newspaper editorial might be written to persuade the reader to accept a particular point of view. A writer's purpose influences how the material is presented. Sometimes an author states his or her purpose directly. More often, the purpose is only suggested, and you must use clues to identify the author's purpose.

Distinguish Between Facts and Opinions

It's important when reading informational texts to read actively and to distinguish between fact and opinion. A fact can be proven or disproven. An opinion cannot—it is someone's personal viewpoint or evaluation.

For example, the editorial pages in a newspaper offer opinions on topics that are currently in the news. You need to read newspaper editorials with an eye for bias and faulty logic. For example, the newspaper editorial at the right shows factual statements in blue and opinion statements in red. The underlined words are examples of highly charged words. They reveal bias on the part of the writer.

> More than 5,000 people voted last week in favor of building a new shopping center, but the opposition won out. The margin of victory is irrelevant. Those <u>radical</u> voters who opposed the center are obviously <u>self-serving elitists</u> who do not care about anyone but themselves.
>
> This month's unemployment figure for our area is 10 percent, which represents an increase of about 5 percent over the figure for this time last year. These figures mean unemployment is getting worse. But the people who voted against the mall probably do not care about creating new jobs.

Reading and Writing Handbook

- Tell students that identifying evidence is another way to read nonfiction critically. Ask students to look again at the facts highlighted in the sample editorial. Then ask **Does the evidence presented in these facts convince you that building a new shopping center is a good idea?** (*The evidence is incomplete—the author has not shown that the new shopping center would solve the unemployment problem.*)

- Tell students that analyzing an author's purpose, distinguishing between fact and opinion, and identifying evidence are all ways to evaluate the credibility of the author. Tell students to look at the checklist for evaluating Web sites. Ask students to think about Web sites they have visited. Do those Web sites pass the checklist's test? Why or why not?

Identify Evidence

Before you accept an author's conclusion, you need to make sure that the author has based the conclusion on enough evidence and on the right kind of evidence. An author may present a series of facts to support a claim, but the facts may not tell the whole story. For example, what evidence does the author of the newspaper editorial on the previous page provide to support his claim that the new shopping center would create more jobs? Is it possible that the shopping center might have put many small local businesses out of business, thus increasing unemployment rather than decreasing it?

Evaluate Credibility

Whenever you read informational texts, you need to assess the credibility of the author. This is especially true of sites you may visit on the Internet. All Internet sources are not equally reliable. Here are some questions to ask yourself when evaluating the credibility of a Web site.

- ❑ Is the Web site created by a respected organization, a discussion group, or an individual?
- ❑ Does the Web site creator include his or her name as well as credentials and the sources he or she used to write the material?
- ❑ Is the information on the site balanced or biased?
- ❑ Can you verify the information using two other sources?
- ❑ Is there a date telling when the Web site was created or last updated?

Independent Practice

Ask students to bring in an editorial from the local newspaper, or distribute copies of an appropriate editorial. Ask students to critically assess their editorial by analyzing the author's purpose; underlining facts and circling opinions in the text of the editorial; summarizing the evidence presented in the editorial; and finally drawing a conclusion about the credibility of the editorial.

Monitor Progress

Pair students and have them share their editorial assessments. Ask them to explain the reasoning behind the conclusions they drew about the editorial's credibility. Circulate and offer assistance as needed.

Assess and Reteach

Assess Progress L2
Collect students' papers and review their assessments.

Reteach L1
If students are struggling, tell them to approach the task by asking themselves the following questions as they read a piece of nonfiction: **Why** did the author write this? **How** has the author made his or her points, using facts or opinions? **What** evidence has the author used to support the main idea? **Who** is the author, and what sources has he or she used?

Extend L3
To extend this lesson, tell students to turn to the Table of Contents in the Student Edition and pick a chapter name that intrigues them. Then, ask them to search the Internet and find two Web sites about the chapter's topic. Finally, ask them to use the checklist on this page to evaluate each Web site and compare the two in terms of credibility.

Differentiated Instruction

For Advanced Readers L3
Draw students' attention to the checklist under the heading "Evaluate Credibility." Ask students to create a similar checklist for analyzing an author's purpose, distinguishing between fact and opinion, and identifying evidence.

For Special Needs Students L1
If special needs students are having trouble making the distinction between facts and opinions, partner them with more proficient students to do the *Distinguishing Fact and Opinion* lesson on the Social Studies Skill Tutor CD-ROM.

💿 *Distinguishing Fact and Opinion,* **Social Studies Skill Tutor CD-ROM**

Reading and Writing Handbook
Step-by-Step Instruction

Objectives
- Use a systematic approach to write narrative, persuasive, expository, and research essays.

Prepare to Read

Build Background Knowledge **L2**

As a group, brainstorm all the ways that people use writing to communicate. Start them with these examples: labeling a folder, writing an email. Conduct an Idea Wave (TE, p. T35) and write students' responses on the board. Tell them that people often write to express ideas or information. Give them *Four Purposes for Writing* and tell them to keep it in their notebooks for future reference.

All in One Medieval Times to Today Teaching Resources, *Four Purposes for Writing,* p. 9

Instruct

Narrative Essays **L2**

Guided Instruction
- Tell students that narrative essays tell a story about the author's experiences. Discuss the steps listed in the Student Edition.

- Choose an event in your own life (or invent one) such as visiting friends in another city. Write your topic on the board and model how to list details. *(what the trip was like, what you did while you were there, what your friends are like)* Cross out the least interesting details.

- Think aloud as you form your topic into a sentence that conveys the main idea of your essay.

- Tell students that you will go on to flesh out the details into a colorful story.

Independent Practice
- Tell students to write a narrative essay about a recent positive experience. Have student pairs brainstorm topics.

Writing for Social Studies

Writing is one of the most powerful communication tools you will ever use. You will use it to share your thoughts and ideas with others. Research shows that writing about what you read actually helps you learn new information and ideas. A systematic approach to writing—including prewriting, drafting, revising, and proofing—can help you write better, whether you're writing an essay or a research report.

Narrative Essays

Writing that tells a story about a personal experience

1 Select and Narrow Your Topic
A narrative is a story. In social studies, it might be a narrative essay about how an event affected you or your family.

2 Gather Details
Brainstorm a list of details you'd like to include in your narrative.

3 Write a First Draft
Start by writing a simple opening sentence that conveys the main idea of your essay. Continue by writing a colorful story that has interesting details. Write a conclusion that sums up the significance of the event or situation described in your essay.

4 Revise and Proofread
Check to make sure you have not begun too many sentences with the word *I*. Replace general words with more colorful ones.

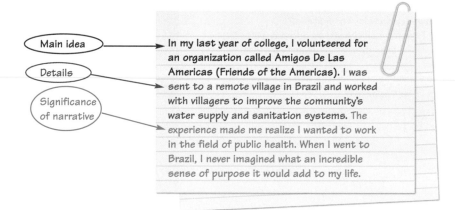

Main idea · Details · Significance of narrative

In my last year of college, I volunteered for an organization called Amigos De Las Americas (Friends of the Americas). I was sent to a remote village in Brazil and worked with villagers to improve the community's water supply and sanitation systems. The experience made me realize I wanted to work in the field of public health. When I went to Brazil, I never imagined what an incredible sense of purpose it would add to my life.

RW2 Reading and Writing Handbook

- Give students *Writing to Describe* to help them write their essays. After they have written the body of their essay, give them *Writing the Conclusion* to help them complete it.

All in One Medieval Times to Today Teaching Resources, *Writing to Describe,* p. 10; *Writing the Conclusion,* p. 11

Monitor Progress

Have students share their drafts with their partners. Give them *Using the Revision Checklist* and ask them to review their partners' papers. Urge them to provide constructive criticism and suggestions for improvement.

All in One Medieval Times to Today Teaching Resources, *Using the Revision Checklist,* p. 12

Persuasive Essays

Writing that supports an opinion or position

① Select and Narrow Your Topic

Choose a topic that provokes an argument and has at least two sides. Choose a side. Decide which argument will appeal most to your audience and persuade them to understand your point of view.

② Gather Evidence

Create a chart that states your position at the top and then lists the pros and cons for your position below, in two columns. Predict and address the strongest arguments against your stand.

③ Write a First Draft

Write a strong thesis statement that clearly states your position. Continue by presenting the strongest arguments in favor of your position and acknowledging and refuting opposing arguments.

④ Revise and Proofread

Check to make sure you have made a logical argument and that you have not oversimplified the argument.

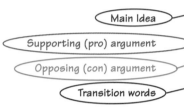

Main Idea	It is vital to vote in elections. When people vote, they tell public officials how to run the government.
Supporting (pro) argument	Not every proposal is carried
Opposing (con) argument	out; however, politicians do their best to listen to what the majority of people want.
Transition words	Therefore, every vote is important.

Reading and Writing Handbook **RW3**

Persuasive Essays L2

Guided Instruction

- Tell students that the purpose of writing a persuasive essay is to convince other people to believe your point of view. However, you must use solid, reliable evidence and arguments to make your points.

- Model the thought process by pointing out how the writer presents his or her argument in the paragraph on this page.

Independent Practice

- Tell students to write a persuasive essay about a topic that is important to them. Have students form pairs. One student in each pair should state his or her position. The other student then shares opposing arguments, which the first student should refute in his or her essay. Then the pairs switch roles.

- Give students *Writing to Persuade* to help them write their essays.

  All in One Medieval Times to Today Teaching Resources, *Writing to Persuade,* p. 13

Monitor Progress

If students are having trouble structuring their paragraphs, give them *Structuring Paragraphs* and *Creating Paragraph Outlines* to provide a framework.

All in One Medieval Times to Today Teaching Resources, *Structuring Paragraphs,* p. 14; *Creating Paragraph Outlines,* p. 15

Expository Essays L2

Guided Instruction

- Read the steps for writing expository essays with students.

- Tell students that the graphic organizer example given on the Student Edition page is for a cause-and-effect expository essay. They might use a Venn diagram for a compare-and-contrast essay and a flow-chart for a problem-and-solution essay.

- Model how to create a topic sentence from the information in the cause-and-effect graphic organizer. *(Sample topic sentence: In Mexico, several factors are causing rural families to move from the countryside to the city.)*

- Create a brief outline showing how you will organize the paragraphs in your essay.

Independent Practice

Tell students to write an expository essay based on a recent current event. Have them brainstorm ideas with a partner, then choose which type of essay best suits their topic (cause and effect, compare and contrast, or problem and solution.) Give them *Writing to Inform and Explain* and *Gathering Details* to help them start drafting their essays.

All in One Medieval Times to Today Teaching Resources, *Writing to Inform and Explain,* p. 16; *Gathering Detail,* p. 17

Monitor Progress

If students are struggling with their essays, give them *Writing a Cause-and-Effect Essay* or *Writing a Problem-and-Solution Essay.*

All in One Medieval Times to Today Teaching Resources, *Writing a Cause-and-Effect Essay,* p. 18; *Writing a Problem-and-Solution Essay,* p. 19

Research Papers L2

Guided Instruction

Go over the steps for writing a research paper carefully. Ask students to share questions about the process using the Idea Wave (TE, p. T35). Answer any questions they might have.

Expository Essays

Writing that explains a process, compares and contrasts, explains causes and effects, or explores solutions to a problem

1 Identify and Narrow Your Topic

Expository writing is writing that explains something in detail. It might explain the similarities and differences between two or more subjects (compare and contrast). It might explain how one event causes another (cause and effect). Or it might explain a problem and describe a solution.

2 Gather Evidence

Create a graphic organizer that identifies details to include in your essay.

Cause 1	Cause 2	Cause 3
Most people in the Mexican countryside work on farms.	The population in Mexico is growing at one of the highest rates in the world.	There is not enough farm work for so many people.

Effect
As a result, many rural families are moving from the countryside to live in Mexico City.

3 Write Your First Draft

Write a topic sentence and then organize the essay around your similarities and differences, causes and effects, or problem and solutions. Be sure to include convincing details, facts, and examples.

4 Revise and Proofread

Research Papers

Writing that presents research about a topic

1 Narrow Your Topic

Choose a topic you're interested in and make sure that it is not too broad. For example, instead of writing a report on Panama, write about the construction of the Panama Canal.

2 Acquire Information

Locate several sources of information about the topic from the library or the Internet. For each resource, create a source index card like the one at the right. Then take notes using an index card for each detail or subtopic. On the card, note which source the information was taken from. Use quotation marks when you copy the exact words from a source.

Source #1
McCullough, David. *The Path Between the Seas: The Creation of the Panama Canal, 1870-1914.* N.Y., Simon and Schuster, 1977.

3 Make an Outline

Use an outline to decide how to organize your report. Sort your index cards into the same order.

Outline
I. Introduction
II. Why the canal was built
III. How the canal was built
   A. Physical challenges
   B. Medical challenges
IV. Conclusion

Differentiated Instruction

For Gifted and Talented L3

Tell students that a verb is in active voice when the subject performs the action named by the verb. A verb is in passive voice when the subject undergoes the action named by the verb.

Give these examples:

Passive voice: The house is being painted by my sister and me.

Active voice: My sister and I are painting the house.

Tell students that using the active voice whenever possible will make their writing more dynamic and concise.

Introduction

Building the Panama Canal

Ever since Christopher Columbus first explored the Isthmus of Panama, the Spanish had been looking for a water route through it. They wanted to be able to sail west from Spain to Asia without sailing around South America. However, it was not until 1914 that the dream became a reality.

Conclusion

It took eight years and more than 70,000 workers to build the Panama Canal. It remains one of the greatest engineering feats of modern times.

④ Write a First Draft

Write an introduction, a body, and a conclusion. Leave plenty of space between lines so you can go back and add details that you may have left out.

⑤ Revise and Proofread

Be sure to include transition words between sentences and paragraphs. Here are some examples:

To show a contrast—*however, although, despite.*

To point out a reason—*since, because, if.*

To signal a conclusion—*therefore, consequently, so, then.*

Evaluating Your Writing

Use this table to help you evaluate your writing.

	Excellent	Good	Acceptable	Unacceptable
Purpose	Achieves purpose—to inform, persuade, or provide historical interpretation—very well	Informs, persuades, or provides historical interpretation reasonably well	Reader cannot easily tell if the purpose is to inform, persuade, or provide historical interpretation	Purpose is not clear
Organization	Develops ideas in a very clear and logical way	Presents ideas in a reasonably well-organized way	Reader has difficulty following the organization	Lacks organization
Elaboration	Explains all ideas with facts and details	Explains most ideas with facts and details	Includes some supporting facts and details	Lacks supporting details
Use of Language	Uses excellent vocabulary and sentence structure with no errors in spelling, grammar, or punctuation	Uses good vocabulary and sentence structure with very few errors in spelling, grammar, or punctuation	Includes some errors in grammar, punctuation, and spelling	Includes many errors in grammar, punctuation, and spelling

Reading and Writing Handbook **RW5**

Independent Practice

- Have students consider topics for a research paper. Give them *Choosing a Topic* to help them learn how to evaluate potential topics.

  All in One Medieval Times to Today Teaching Resources, *Choosing a Topic,* p. 20

- Once students have selected a topic, tell them they will need facts to support their ideas. Give them *Using the Library, Summarizing and Taking Notes,* and *Preparing Note Cards* to help them start their research.

  All in One Medieval Times to Today Teaching Resources, *Using the Library,* p. 21; *Summarizing and Taking Notes,* p. 22; *Preparing Note Cards,* p. 23

Monitor Progress

Give students *Writing an Introduction* and *Writing the Body of an Essay* to help them write their essays.

  All in One Medieval Times to Today Teaching Resources, *Writing an Introduction,* p. 24; *Writing the Body of an Essay,* p. 25

Assess and Reteach

Assess Progress   L2

Ask students to pick the best essay they have written so far and evaluate it using the rubric on this page.

Reteach   L1

Collect students' essays and self-evaluations. Meet with students to go over good points and areas for improvement. Revisit each type of essay as needed with the whole class.

Extend   L3

To extend this lesson, tell students there are many other different types of writing. Have them complete *Writing for Assessment* and *Writing a Letter* to learn about two more types of writing.

  All in One Medieval Times to Today Teaching Resources, *Writing for Assessment,* p. 26; *Writing a Letter,* p. 27

Differentiated Instruction

For English Language Learners   L2

To help students understand the tasks you have given them, provide them with an example of a well-executed essay from a different class or a previous year. The example essay should be well written and organized but not above grade level. You could look for and save good examples each year you teach.

MapMaster Skills Handbook
Step-by-Step Instruction

Objective
- Identify and define the five themes of geography.

Prepare to Read

Build Background Knowledge `L2`
Assign students to small groups and give them five minutes to write a definition of geography. Then write the five themes of geography on the board. Remind students that a theme is an important underlying idea. As a class, decide which parts of their definitions go under each of the geography themes. For example, "landforms" would fall under the theme of place.

Instruct

Five Themes of Geography `L2`

Guided Instruction
- Divide the text using the headings and ask students to read the pages using the Structured Silent Reading strategy (TE, p. T34). Clarify the meanings of any unfamiliar words.

- Ask students to give the relative locations of their homes.

- Mention the popularity of different kinds of ethnic foods in the United States. Ask **What theme of geography are these foods a good example of?** *(movement)* Encourage students to name other examples of the movement of cultural traditions from one region to another.

- Discuss the climate in your area. Ask **How does the environment affect how we live?** *(affects dress, travel, sports and other recreational activities, the way homes are built)*

MAP★MASTER™ SKILLS HANDBOOK

CONTENTS

Go Online
PHSchool.com Use Web Code **lap-0000** for all of the maps in this handbook.

Five Themes of Geography

Studying the geography of the entire world is a huge task. You can make that task easier by using the five themes of geography: location, regions, place, movement, and human-environment interaction. The themes are tools you can use to organize information and to answer the where, why, and how of geography.

LOCATION

1 Location answers the question, "Where is it?" You can think of the location of a continent or a country as its address. You might give an absolute location such as 22 South Lake Street or 40° N and 80° W. You might also use a relative address, telling where one place is by referring to another place. *Between school and the mall* and *eight miles east of Pleasant City* are examples of relative locations.

▲ **Location**
This museum in England has a line running through it. The line marks its location at 0° longitude.

MapMaster Skills Handbook

Differentiated Instruction

For English Language Learners `L1`
Students may find it difficult to pronounce some of the multisyllable words in this section such as *relative, environment, interaction, government, signature,* and *communicate.* Show students how to break down these words into smaller parts to help them sound out the pronunciation.

For Advanced Readers `L3`
Have students find articles in newspapers or magazines that illustrate the five themes of geography. Have students underline the relevant sections and identify the theme or themes they illustrate. Suggest that they create a bulletin board to share their examples with the class.

REGIONS

2 Regions are areas that share at least one common feature. Geographers divide the world into many types of regions. For example, countries, states, and cities are political regions. The people in any one of these places live under the same government. Other features, such as climate and culture, can be used to define regions. Therefore the same place can be found in more than one region. For example, the state of Hawaii is in the political region of the United States. Because it has a tropical climate, Hawaii is also part of a tropical climate region.

MOVEMENT

4 Movement answers the question, "How do people, goods, and ideas move from place to place?" Remember that what happens in one place often affects what happens in another. Use the theme of movement to help you trace the spread of goods, people, and ideas from one location to another.

PLACE

3 Place identifies the natural and human features that make one place different from every other place. You can identify a specific place by its landforms, climate, plants, animals, people, language, or culture. You might even think of place as a geographic signature. Use the signature to help you understand the natural and human features that make one place different from every other place.

INTERACTION

5 Human-environment interaction focuses on the relationship between people and the environment. As people live in an area, they often begin to make changes to it, usually to make their lives easier. For example, they might build a dam to control flooding during rainy seasons. Also, the environment can affect how people live, work, dress, travel, and communicate.

◀ **Interaction**
These Congolese women interact with their environment by gathering wood for cooking.

PRACTICE YOUR GEOGRAPHY SKILLS

1 Describe your town or city, using each of the five themes of geography.

2 Name at least one thing that comes into your town or city and one that goes out. How is each moved? Where does it come from? Where does it go?

MapMaster Skills Handbook **M1**

Independent Practice

Partner students and have them complete *The Five Themes of Geography.*

All in One Medieval Times to Today Teaching Resources, *The Five Themes of Geography,* p. 31

Monitor Progress

As students complete the worksheet, circulate to make sure that individuals comprehend the material. Provide assistance as needed.

Assess and Reteach

Assess Progress   L2

Have students complete the questions under Practice Your Geography Skills.

Reteach   L1

Help students create a concept web that identifies the five themes of geography. Start filling in blank *Transparency B17: Concept Web* to model how to identify information to clarify each theme. For example, under Regions students might write "share common features such as government, climate, culture." Encourage students to refer to their webs to review the themes.

Medieval Times to Today Transparencies, *Transparency B17: Concept Web*

Extend   L3

To extend the lesson, ask students to find out about any plans for new buildings, highways, or other types of construction in your area. Ask students to predict how these changes will affect the community's environment.

Answers

PRACTICE YOUR GEOGRAPHY SKILLS

1. Answers should include an example of each of the five themes that relates to your community.

2. Students' answers should provide examples of goods, ideas, or things that move into and out of your community.

Objective

- Explain how the movements of Earth cause night and day, as well as the seasons.

Prepare to Read

Build Background Knowledge L2

Remind students that while Earth revolves around the sun, it also rotates on its own axis. Review the meanings of "revolve" and "rotate" in this context. Ask students to brainstorm ways that Earth's revolving and rotating might affect their lives. Conduct an Idea Wave (TE, p. T35) to generate a list of ideas.

Instruct

Understanding Movements of Earth L2

Guided Instruction

- Read the text as a class using the Oral Cloze strategy (TE, p. T33). Explain that the illustration on pp. M2 and M3 show the information in the text visually. Clarify the meanings of any unfamiliar words.

- Ask students **How does Earth rotating on its axis cause day and night?** *(It is daytime on the side of Earth facing the sun, while the side facing away from the sun is dark.)*

- Ask **How does the tilt of Earth affect the seasons?** *(The farther away a part of Earth is from the sun's rays, the colder it is.)*

Independent Practice

Partner students and have them complete *Understanding the Movements of the Earth.*

All in One Medieval Times to Today Teaching Resources, *Understanding the Movements of the Earth,* p. 32

Understanding Movements of Earth

The planet Earth is part of our solar system. Earth revolves around the sun in a nearly circular path called an orbit. A revolution, or one complete orbit around the sun, takes 365¼ days, or one year. As Earth orbits the sun, it also spins on its axis, an invisible line through the center of Earth from the North Pole to the South Pole. This movement is called a rotation.

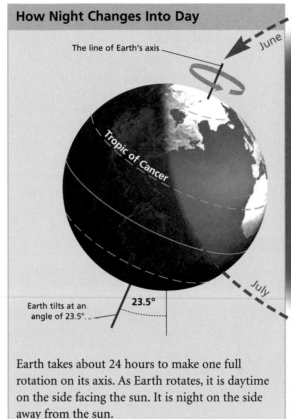

How Night Changes Into Day

The line of Earth's axis

Tropic of Cancer

Earth tilts at an angle of 23.5°.   **23.5°**

Earth takes about 24 hours to make one full rotation on its axis. As Earth rotates, it is daytime on the side facing the sun. It is night on the side away from the sun.

▼ **Spring begins**
On March 20 or 21, the sun is directly overhead at the Equator. The Northern and Southern Hemispheres receive almost equal hours of sunlight and darkness.

Equator

April
May
June
July
August
September

◄ **Summer begins**
On June 21 or 22, the sun is directly overhead at the Tropic of Cancer. The Northern Hemisphere receives the greatest number of sunlight hours.

M2 MapMaster Skills Handbook

Background: Links Across Place

Sunrise and Sunset Most people have heard the saying "The sun rises in the east and sets in the west." However, the sun does not ever actually change position. Every day, Earth rotates on its axis so that as each region faces the sun, it experiences day. The rotation continues so that as a region turns away from the sun, it experiences night. The sun stays in the same place. A person viewing sunrise or sunset is really seeing Earth's slow turn on its axis, not the sun rising or setting.

The Seasons

Earth's axis is tilted at an angle. Because of this tilt, sunlight strikes different parts of Earth at different times in the year, creating seasons. The illustration below shows how the seasons are created in the Northern Hemisphere. In the Southern Hemisphere, the seasons are reversed.

PRACTICE YOUR GEOGRAPHY SKILLS

1 What causes the seasons in the Northern Hemisphere to be the opposite of those in the Southern Hemisphere?

2 During which two days of the year do the Northern Hemisphere and Southern Hemisphere have equal hours of daylight and darkness?

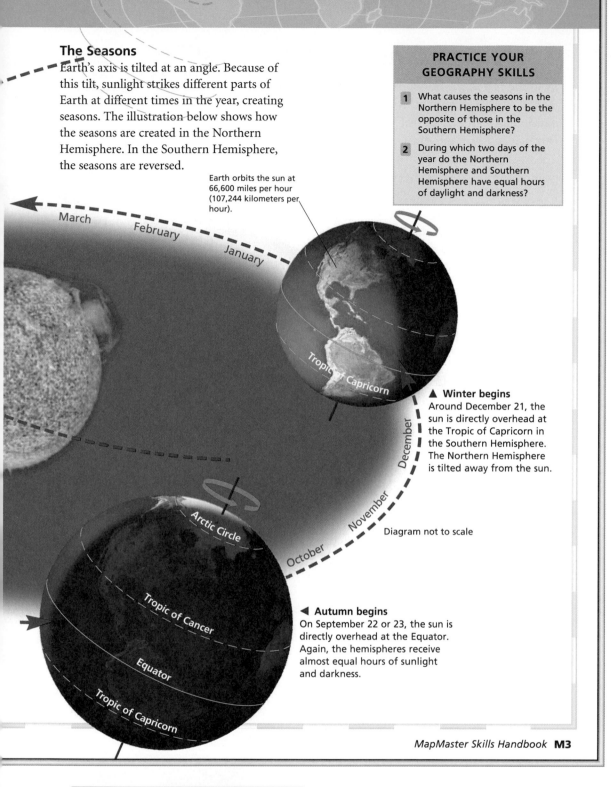

Earth orbits the sun at 66,600 miles per hour (107,244 kilometers per hour).

March
February
January
December
November
October

Tropic of Capricorn

▲ **Winter begins**
Around December 21, the sun is directly overhead at the Tropic of Capricorn in the Southern Hemisphere. The Northern Hemisphere is tilted away from the sun.

Diagram not to scale

Arctic Circle
Tropic of Cancer
Equator
Tropic of Capricorn

◄ **Autumn begins**
On September 22 or 23, the sun is directly overhead at the Equator. Again, the hemispheres receive almost equal hours of sunlight and darkness.

MapMaster Skills Handbook **M3**

Differentiated Instruction

For Special Needs Students L1

Have students act out the revolution of Earth around the sun. Assign one student the role of "the sun," and other students the roles of Earth at four different times of the year. Have them walk through a year's cycle. Show *Color Transparency LA 1: The Earth's Revolution and the*

Seasons to guide them. Ask them to simulate the tilt of Earth's axis as shown in the illustrations on pp. M2–M3.

📖 **Medieval Times to Today Transparencies,** *Color Transparency MT 1: The Earth's Revolution and the Seasons*

Monitor Progress

As students do the worksheet, circulate to make sure individuals comprehend the key concepts. Provide assistance as needed.

Assess and Reteach

Assess Progress L2

Have students complete the Practice Your Geography Skills questions.

Reteach L1

If students are having trouble understanding these concepts, create a model to demonstrate Earth's revolution. Use a foam ball to represent Earth. Insert a pencil through the ball to represent Earth's axis, labeling the ends "North Pole" and "South Pole." Draw the Equator perpendicular to the axis. Place a light source in the center of a table to represent the sun. Then tilt the ball at a slight angle and move it around the light to mimic Earth's revolution. Have students notice the point at which each pole is nearest the sun and identify what season it would be in each hemisphere.

Extend L3

To extend the lesson, ask students to consider Earth's relationship to its satellite, the moon. Ask them to research on the Internet to answer these questions: "Does the moon rotate like Earth? Does the moon revolve around Earth as Earth revolves around the sun?" To help students start their research, give them *Doing Searches on the Internet.*

All in One **Medieval Times to Today Teaching Resources,** *Doing Searches on the Internet,* p. 33

Answers

PRACTICE YOUR GEOGRAPHY SKILLS

1. The seasons are reversed in the Northern Hemisphere and Southern Hemisphere because the Earth is tilted. When one hemisphere is tilted towards the sun, the other hemisphere is tilted away from the sun.

2. September 22–23 and March 20–21

Objectives

- Understand how a globe is marked with a grid to measure features on Earth.

- Learn how to use longitude and latitude to locate a place.

Prepare to Read

Build Background Knowledge L2

Tell students that in this lesson, they will learn how to use globes. Ask students what it would be like to see Earth from a spacecraft. Discuss the shape that students would see. Then discuss why a globe is a more accurate rendering of Earth than a flat map. Point out that a globe is like a model car in that it is a small version of something larger. If a globe is available, have students examine it.

Instruct

Understanding Globes L2

Guided Instruction

- Read the text as a class using the Oral Cloze strategy (TE, p. T33). Have students study the illustrations carefully.

- Ask **What line of latitude divides the Northern and Southern Hemispheres?** *(the Equator)* **At what degrees latitude is this line?** *(0°)*

- Ask **Where do the lines of longitude come together?** *(at the North and South Poles)* **What is the name of the meridian at 0 degrees?** *(Prime Meridian)*

- Have students look at the global grid on *Color Transparency MT 3: The Global Grid.* Ask **What is the global grid?** *(a pattern of lines formed where the parallels of latitude and meridians of longitude cross)* **What continent in the Eastern Hemisphere does the 100°E meridian pass through?** *(Asia)*

  📖 **Medieval Times to Today Transparencies,** *Color Transparency MT 3: The Global Grid*

Understanding Globes

A globe is a scale model of Earth. It shows the actual shapes, sizes, and locations of all Earth's landmasses and bodies of water. Features on the surface of Earth are drawn to scale on a globe. This means that a small unit of measure on the globe stands for a large unit of measure on Earth.

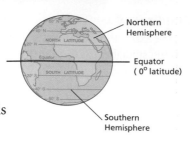

Northern Hemisphere

Equator (0° latitude)

Southern Hemisphere

Parallels of Latitude

Geographers divide the globe along imaginary horizontal lines called parallels of latitude. One of these latitude lines is the Equator, located halfway between the North and South Poles. Parallels of latitude are measured in degrees (°). One degree of latitude represents a distance of about 69 miles (111 kilometers).

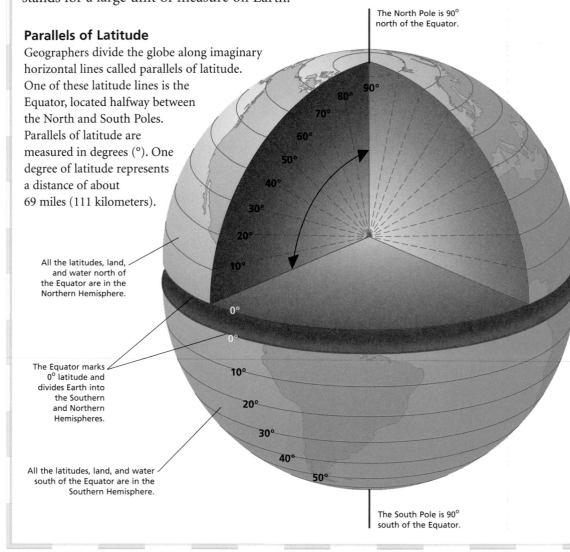

The North Pole is 90° north of the Equator.

All the latitudes, land, and water north of the Equator are in the Northern Hemisphere.

The Equator marks 0° latitude and divides Earth into the Southern and Northern Hemispheres.

All the latitudes, land, and water south of the Equator are in the Southern Hemisphere.

The South Pole is 90° south of the Equator.

M4 MapMaster Skills Handbook

Background: Links Across Time

The First Globes Historians believe that the first globe may have been made in the second century B.C. by a Greek geographer known as Crates of Mallus. The mathematician Ptolemy represented Earth as a globe in his written works in the second century A.D. In late 1492 Martin Behaim made a terrestrial globe that, although inaccurate by today's knowledge, reflected the best geographical knowledge of the time. This globe still exists and is on display in Behaim's hometown of Nuremberg, Germany.

Meridians of Longitude

Geographers also divide the globe along imaginary vertical lines called meridians of longitude, which are measured in degrees (°). The longitude line called the Prime Meridian runs from pole to pole through Greenwich, England. All meridians of longitude come together at the North and South Poles.

PRACTICE YOUR GEOGRAPHY MAP SKILLS

1 Which continents lie completely in the Northern Hemisphere? In the Western Hemisphere?

2 Is there land or water at 20° S latitude and the Prime Meridian? At the Equator and 60° W longitude?

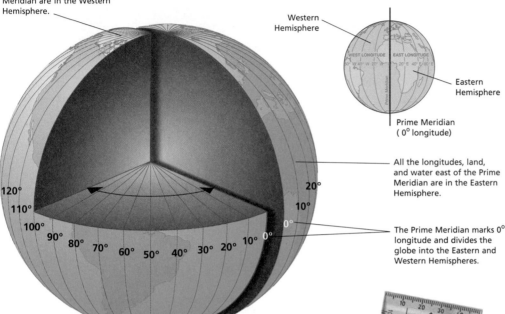

All the longitudes, land, and water west of the Prime Meridian are in the Western Hemisphere.

Western Hemisphere

Eastern Hemisphere

Prime Meridian (0° longitude)

All the longitudes, land, and water east of the Prime Meridian are in the Eastern Hemisphere.

The Prime Meridian marks 0° longitude and divides the globe into the Eastern and Western Hemispheres.

120° 110° 100° 90° 80° 70° 60° 50° 40° 30° 20° 10° 0° 20° 10° 0°

The Global Grid

Together, the pattern of parallels of latitude and meridians of longitude is called the global grid. Using the lines of latitude and longitude, you can locate any place on Earth. For example, the location of 30° north latitude and 90° west longitude is usually written as 30° N, 90° W. Only one place on Earth has these coordinates—the city of New Orleans, in the state of Louisiana.

▲ **Compass**
Wherever you are on Earth, a compass can be used to show direction.

MapMaster Skills Handbook **M5**

Differentiated Instruction

For Less Proficient Readers L1
For students having difficulty understanding the concept of a global grid, give them *Understanding Grids* and help them complete it. Then follow up with *Using a Grid*.

All in One Medieval Times to Today Teaching Resources, *Understanding Grids,* p. 38; *Using a Grid,* p. 39

For Advanced Readers L3
Have students complete *Comparing Globes and Maps.* Then ask them to make a chart showing the pros and cons of these two ways of representing Earth.

All in One Medieval Times to Today Teaching Resources, *Comparing Globes and Maps,* p. 40

Independent Practice

Have students work in pairs to complete *Understanding Hemispheres* and *Understanding Latitude and Longitude.*

All in One Medieval Times to Today Teaching Resources, *Understanding Hemispheres,* p. 34; *Understanding Latitude and Longitude,* p. 35

Monitor Progress

As students do the worksheets, circulate to make sure pairs understand the key concepts. Show *Color Transparency MT 2: The Hemispheres* to help students.

Medieval Times to Today Transparencies, *Color Transparency MT 2: The Hemispheres*

Assess and Reteach

Assess Progress L2
Have students answer the questions under Practice Your Geography Skills.

Reteach L1
Use the DK Atlas activity *Understanding Latitude and Longitude* to review these skills with students. Have students complete the activity in pairs.

All in One Medieval Times to Today Teaching Resources, *DK Compact Atlas of the World Activity: Understanding Latitude and Longitude,* p. 36

Extend L3
To extend the lesson, have students complete *Using Latitude and Longitude.* Then have students use the map and with a partner, play a game of Can You Find …? Each partner takes a turn giving the coordinates for a place on the map and the other partner must name the place.

All in One Medieval Times to Today Teaching Resources, *Using Latitude and Longitude,* p. 37

Answers

PRACTICE YOUR GEOGRAPHY SKILLS

1. Northern Hemisphere: North America; Europe; Western Hemisphere: North America; South America

2. water; land

Objectives

- Compare maps of different projections.
- Describe distortions in map projections.

Prepare to Read

Build Background Knowledge **L1**

In this lesson, students will learn ways in which cartographers depict Earth on a two-dimensional map. Remind students that if they were traveling in a spaceship, Earth would look like a globe. Ask if they could ever see the entire Earth at one time from space. Help students recognize that a flat map is the only way to see all of Earth at once.

Instruct

Map Projections **L2**

Guided Instruction

- Read the text as a class using the Choral Reading strategy (TE, p. T34). Direct students to look at the relevant maps after you read each section together. Follow up by having students do a second silent reading.

- Help students locate Greenland on the Mercator and Robinson maps. Ask **What difference do you notice in the way Greenland is shown?** *(It appears much larger on the Mercator Map.)* **How would you explain this?** *(The Mercator is a same-shape map and the shapes toward the poles are enlarged.)*

- Ask **Where does the distortion usually occur on an equal-area map?** *(at the edges of the map)*

- Have students compare Antarctica on the three projections. *(It is largest and most distorted on the Mercator map; smallest on the equal-area map; covers the entire bottom edge of the Robinson map.)*

Map Projections

Maps are drawings that show regions on flat surfaces. Maps are easier to use and carry than globes, but they cannot show the correct size and shape of every feature on Earth's curved surface. They must shrink some places and stretch others. To make up for this distortion, mapmakers use different map projections. No one projection can accurately show the correct area, shape, distance, and direction for all of Earth's surface. Mapmakers use the projection that has the least distortion for the information they are presenting.

Same-Shape Maps

Map projections that accurately show the shapes of landmasses are called same-shape maps. However, these projections often greatly distort, or make less accurate, the size of landmasses as well as the distance between them. In the projection below, the northern and southern areas of the globe appear more stretched than the areas near the Equator.

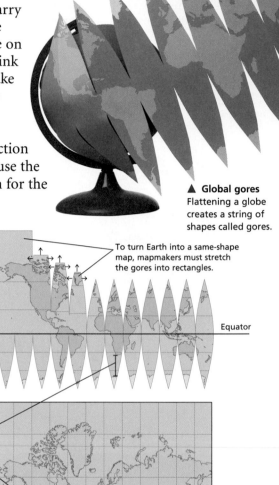

▲ **Global gores**
Flattening a globe creates a string of shapes called gores.

To turn Earth into a same-shape map, mapmakers must stretch the gores into rectangles.

Equator

Stretching the gores makes parts of Earth larger. This enlargement becomes greater toward the North and South Poles.

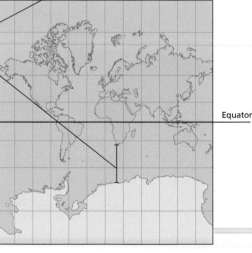

Equator

Mercator projection ▶
One of the most common same-shape maps is the Mercator projection, named for the mapmaker who invented it. The Mercator projection accurately shows shape and direction, but it distorts distance and size. Because the projection shows true directions, ships' navigators use it to chart a straight-line course between two ports.

M6 MapMaster Skills Handbook

Differentiated Instruction

For Special Needs Students **L1**

If students have difficulty understanding why distortion occurs, draw a simple picture on an orange. Then have students try to peel the orange in one piece. Challenge students to place the peel flat on a piece of paper without any tears and spaces. Talk about what happens to the drawing. Explain that mapmakers face this same challenge when drawing Earth on a flat paper.

For Gifted and Talented **L3**

Have students complete *Great Circles and Straight Lines.* Then ask them to use their completed page and a globe to explain the concept of great circles to the class.

All in One Medieval Times to Today Teaching Resources, *Great Circles and Straight Lines,* p. 42

Equal-Area Maps

Map projections that show the correct size of landmasses are called equal-area maps. In order to show the correct size of landmasses, these maps usually distort shapes. The distortion is usually greater at the edges of the map and less at the center.

PRACTICE YOUR GEOGRAPHY SKILLS

1 What feature is distorted on an equal-area map?

2 Would you use a Mercator projection to find the exact distance between two locations? Tell why or why not.

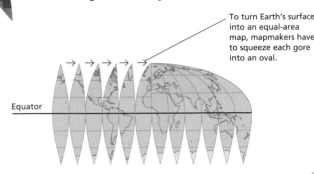

To turn Earth's surface into an equal-area map, mapmakers have to squeeze each gore into an oval.

Equator

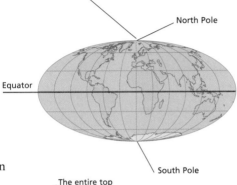

The tips of all the gores are then joined together. The points at which they join form the North and South Poles. The line of the Equator stays the same.

North Pole

Equator

South Pole

Robinson Maps

Many of the maps in this book use the Robinson projection, which is a compromise between the Mercator and equal-area projections. The Robinson projection gives a useful overall picture of the world. It keeps the size and shape relationships of most continents and oceans, but distorts the size of the polar regions.

The entire top edge of the map is the North Pole.

The map is least distorted at the Equator.

Equator

The entire bottom edge of the map is the South Pole.

Independent Practice

Have students work with partners to complete *Understanding Projection.*

All in One Medieval Times to Today Teaching Resources, *Understanding Projection,* p. 41

Monitor Progress

As students do the worksheet, circulate to make sure individuals comprehend the key concepts. Provide assistance as needed.

Assess and Reteach

Assess Progress   L2

Have students complete the Practice Your Geography Skills questions.

Reteach   L1

Use *Maps with Accurate Shapes: Conformal Maps* and *Maps with Accurate Areas: Equal-Area Maps* to help students go over the information in the lesson. Model thinking for each question and partner students to complete each page together. Circulate to provide explanations and help as students work.

All in One Medieval Times to Today Teaching Resources, *Maps with Accurate Shapes: Conformal Maps,* p. 43; *Maps with Accurate Areas: Equal-Area Maps,* p. 44

Extend   L3

To extend the lesson, ask students to complete *Maps with Accurate Direction: Azimuthal Maps.* Then have students write a sentence or two describing the different projections they have learned about.

All in One Medieval Times to Today Teaching Resources, *Maps with Accurate Directions: Azimuthal Maps,* p. 45

Background: Biography

Gerardus Mercator The Mercator projection takes its name from a Flemish geographer, Gerhard Kremer (1512–1594). Kremer, who used the Latin form of his name, Gerardus Mercator, wrote books on ancient geography and cartography. He made his first world map in 1538. In 1554 he made a map of Europe. In 1568, the first map using the Mercator projection bearing his name appeared. Mercator also began an atlas of his maps, which was finished by his son and published in 1594.

Answers

PRACTICE YOUR GEOGRAPHY SKILLS

1. shapes

2. No; the Mercator projection distorts distances.

Objective

- Identify and use the parts of a map.

Prepare to Read

Build Background Knowledge **L1**

In this lesson, students will learn about the practical aspects of maps. Ask students to name reasons that they might use a map; for example, to find directions, boundaries, distances. Conduct an Idea Wave (TE, p. T35) to generate a list of ideas. List the ideas on the board.

Instruct

How to Use a Map **L2**

Guided Instruction

- Divide the text and captions in the lesson using the headings and ask students to read the pages using the Structured Silent Reading strategy (TE, p. T34). Remind students to use the illustrations to acquire additional understanding. Refer to the list on the board, then ask students which map part (key, compass rose, scale, symbol, title) would be helpful in using a map for a specific purpose.

- Ask **What is the purpose of a compass rose?** (to show directions)

- Talk about how the three maps show different amounts of Earth's surface. Ask **Which map shows the largest area?** (Western Europe) **Which map shows the smallest area?** (Central London)

- Ask **What are some symbols that you might find on a map key?** (border, national capital, city, airport, park, point of interest)

Independent Practice

Partner students and have them complete *Using the Map Key* and *Using the Compass Rose*.

> **All in One** **Medieval Times to Today Teaching Resources,** *Using the Map Key,* p. 46; *Using the Compass Rose,* p. 47

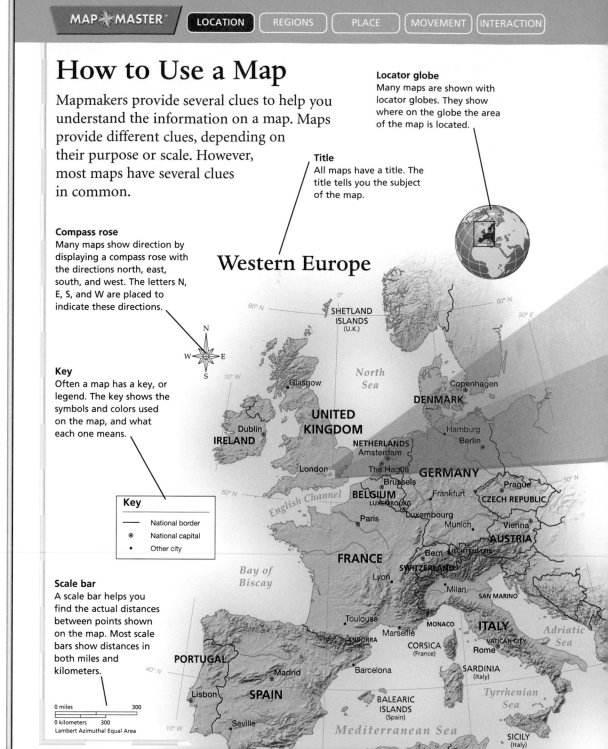

How to Use a Map

Mapmakers provide several clues to help you understand the information on a map. Maps provide different clues, depending on their purpose or scale. However, most maps have several clues in common.

Locator globe
Many maps are shown with locator globes. They show where on the globe the area of the map is located.

Title
All maps have a title. The title tells you the subject of the map.

Compass rose
Many maps show direction by displaying a compass rose with the directions north, east, south, and west. The letters N, E, S, and W are placed to indicate these directions.

Key
Often a map has a key, or legend. The key shows the symbols and colors used on the map, and what each one means.

Key

——	National border
⊛	National capital
•	Other city

Scale bar
A scale bar helps you find the actual distances between points shown on the map. Most scale bars show distances in both miles and kilometers.

0 miles   300
0 kilometers   300
Lambert Azimuthal Equal Area

Western Europe

SHETLAND ISLANDS (U.K.)

North Sea

Glasgow
Copenhagen
DENMARK
UNITED KINGDOM
Dublin
Hamburg
Berlin
IRELAND
NETHERLANDS
Amsterdam
London
The Hague
GERMANY
Brussels
Frankfurt
Prague
BELGIUM
LUXEMBOURG
CZECH REPUBLIC
English Channel
Paris
Luxembourg
Munich
Vienna
FRANCE
Bern
AUSTRIA
Bay of Biscay
SWITZERLAND
LIECHTENSTEIN
Lyon
Milan
SAN MARINO
Toulouse
MONACO
ITALY
Adriatic Sea
Marseille
VATICAN CITY
PORTUGAL
ANDORRA
CORSICA (France)
Rome
Madrid
Barcelona
SARDINIA (Italy)
Lisbon
SPAIN
BALEARIC ISLANDS (Spain)
Tyrrhenian Sea
Seville
Mediterranean Sea
SICILY (Italy)

M8 MapMaster Skills Handbook

Differentiated Instruction

For Less Proficient Readers **L2**

If students have difficulty recalling the purposes of different parts of a map, have them make a table using each part as a heading. Under each heading, help students list the important function or functions of that map part. Suggest that they refer to their table when they are working with maps.

For English Language Learners **L1**

Some of the words in the lesson, such as *symbol* and *scale,* may be unfamiliar to students acquiring English. Have students identify difficult words, look them up in the dictionary, and write sentences explaining what the terms mean.

Maps of Different Scales

Maps are drawn to different scales, depending on their purpose. Here are three maps drawn to very different scales. Keep in mind that maps showing large areas have smaller scales. Maps showing small areas have larger scales.

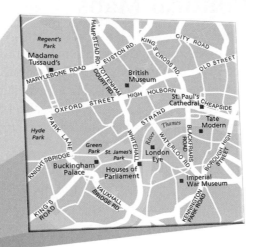

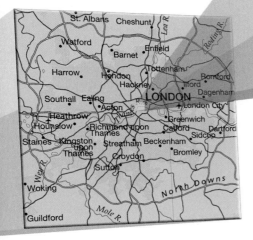

▲ Greater London
Find the gray square on the main map of Western Europe (left). This square represents the area shown on the map above. It shows London's boundaries, the general shape of the city, and the features around the city. This map can help you find your way from the airport to the center of town.

▲ Central London
Find the gray square on the map of Greater London. This square represents the area shown on the map above. This map moves you closer into the center of London. Like the zoom on a computer or a camera, this map shows a smaller area but in greater detail. It has the largest scale (1 inch represents about 0.9 mile). You can use this map to explore downtown London.

Key

■ Point of interest

▨ Park

0 miles   0.5   1
0 kilometers   1

Key

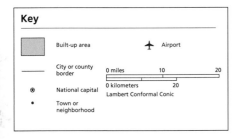

▨ Built-up area

─ City or county border

⊚ National capital

• Town or neighborhood

✈ Airport

0 miles   10   20
0 kilometers   20
Lambert Conformal Conic

PRACTICE YOUR GEOGRAPHY SKILLS

1. What part of a map explains the colors used on the map?

2. How does the scale bar change depending on the scale of the map?

3. Which map would be best for finding the location of the British Museum? Explain why.

Circulate around the room as students complete the worksheets. Make sure that individuals comprehend the material. Provide assistance as needed.

Assess and Reteach

Assess Progress L2
Have students complete the questions under Practice Your Geography Skills.

Reteach L1
Some DK Atlas Activities will be helpful in reteaching the lesson. Give students more practice using these concepts by doing the activities for *Using the Map Key, Using the Compass Rose,* and *Using the Map Scale.*

> **All in One Medieval Times to Today Teaching Resources,** *DK Compact Atlas of the World Activity: Using the Map Key,* p. 48; *DK Compact Atlas of the World Activity: Using the Compass Rose,* p. 49; *DK Compact Atlas of the World Activity: Using the Map Scale,* p. 50

Extend L3
To extend the lesson, have students complete *Comparing Maps of Different Scale* and *Maps with Accurate Distances: Equidistant Maps.*

> **All in One Medieval Times to Today Teaching Resources,** *Comparing Maps of Different Scale,* p. 51; *Maps with Accurate Distances: Equidistant Maps,* p. 52

Answers

PRACTICE YOUR GEOGRAPHY SKILLS

1. key

2. The larger the scale of the map, the smaller the distance shown on the scale bar.

3. the map of Central London; it shows the streets in more detail and includes the British Museum as a point of interest

Objective

- Understand and use political maps.
- Understand and use physical maps.

Prepare to Read

Build Background Knowledge **L1**

Tell students that they will learn about political maps and physical maps in this lesson. Explain that a political map is one that shows the boundaries and cities of an area as established by its people. Physical maps show information about the physical features of the area. These physical features would exist whether people lived in a place or not.

Instruct

Political Maps **L2**
Physical Maps **L2**

Guided Instruction

- Read the text as a class using the Choral Reading strategy (TE, p. T34) and ask students to study the map.

- Ask students to identify what river forms the boundary between Zimbabwe and South Africa. *(Limpopo River)* Then ask them to name at least two capitals on the Mediterranean Sea. *(Tripoli, Algiers, Tunis)*

- Read the text with the class and draw students' attention to the map and its key.

- Explain that sea level is the average height of the ocean's surface; sea level is at zero elevation. Ask students what color represents sea level on the map key. *(dark green)*

- Have students find the Qattara Depression. Ask **What is its elevation?** *(from 0 to 650 feet)*

- Ask **What is the difference between elevation and relief?** *(Elevation is the height of land above sea level while relief shows how quickly the land rises or falls.)*

Answers

PRACTICE YOUR GEOGRAPHY SKILLS

1. solid line, star in a circle, dot
2. Luanda

Political Maps

Political maps show political borders: continents, countries, and divisions within countries, such as states or provinces. The colors on political maps do not have any special meaning, but they make the map easier to read. Political maps also include symbols and labels for capitals, cities, and towns.

PRACTICE YOUR GEOGRAPHY SKILLS

1 What symbols show a national border, a national capital, and a city?

2 What is Angola's capital city?

Political Africa Key

— National border
- - - Disputed border
⊕ National capital
• Other city

▲ **Dakar, Senegal**
Dakar is the capital of Senegal, in West Africa. Its Presidential Palace overlooks the Atlantic Ocean.

M10 MapMaster Skills Handbook

Background: Global Perspectives

Africa's Highest Peaks Africa's two highest mountains are both extinct volcanoes that rise near the equator on the eastern part of the continent. The tallest mountain, Kilimanjaro in Tanzania, reaches 19,340 feet (5,895 m) at its highest point. Although snow covers its peaks, farmers raise coffee and plantains on the lower southern slopes of Kilimanjaro. Africa's second highest mountain is Mt. Kenya at 17,058 feet (5,199 m) located in central Kenya. Like Kilimanjaro, it is snowcapped in its highest regions. Both Kilimanjaro and Mt. Kenya are attractions for mountain climbers from all over the world.

Physical Maps

Physical maps represent what a region looks like by showing its major physical features, such as hills and plains. Physical maps also often show elevation and relief. Elevation, indicated by colors, is the height of the land above sea level. Relief, indicated by shading, shows how sharply the land rises or falls.

PRACTICE YOUR GEOGRAPHY SKILLS

1 Which areas of Africa have the highest elevation?

2 How can you use relief to plan a hiking trip?

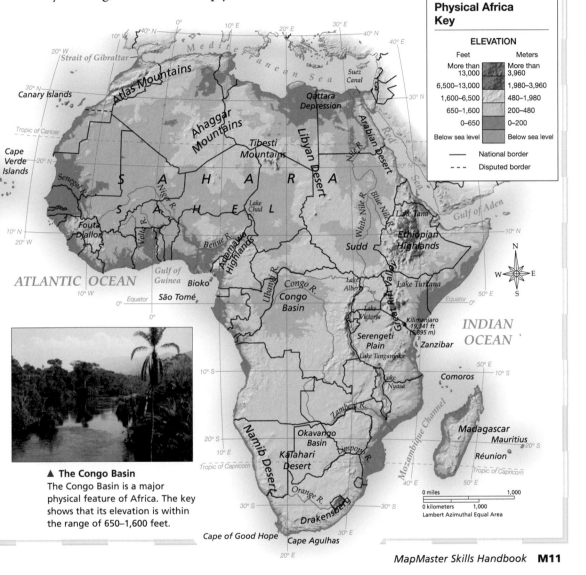

Physical Africa Key

ELEVATION

Feet		Meters
More than 13,000		More than 3,960
6,500–13,000		1,980–3,960
1,600–6,500		480–1,980
650–1,600		200–480
0–650		0–200
Below sea level		Below sea level

— National border

- - - Disputed border

0 miles 1,000
0 kilometers 1,000
Lambert Azimuthal Equal Area

▲ The Congo Basin
The Congo Basin is a major physical feature of Africa. The key shows that its elevation is within the range of 650–1,600 feet.

MapMaster Skills Handbook **M11**

Independent Practice

Have students complete *Reading a Political Map, Reading a Physical Map* and *Elevation on a Map* working with partners.

All in One Medieval Times to Today Teaching Resources, *Reading a Political Map,* p. 53; *Reading a Physical Map,* p. 58; *Elevation on a Map,* p. 59

Monitor Progress

As students complete the worksheets, circulate around the room to make sure individuals understand the key concepts. Provide assistance as needed.

Assess and Reteach

Assess Progress L2

Have students answer the questions under Practice Your Geography Skills on pp. M10 and M11.

Reteach L1

Use the DK Atlas Activities *Reading a Political Map* and *Reading a Physical Map* to review the concepts in this lesson.

All in One Medieval Times to Today Teaching Resources, *DK Compact Atlas of the World Activity: Reading a Political Map,* p. 54; *DK Compact Atlas of the World Activity: Reading a Physical Map,* p. 60

Extend L3

To extend the lesson, have students fill in the name of each country and its capital on the outline maps *North Africa, West and Central Africa,* and *East and Southern Africa.* Also, ask them to use colors and shading to indicate the Atlas Mountains, the Ethiopian Highlands, the Congo Basin, and the Namib Desert.

All in One Medieval Times to Today Teaching Resources, *Outline Map 22: North Africa,* p. 55; *Outline Map 23: West and Central Africa,* p. 56; *Outline Map 24: East and Southern Africa,* p. 57

Differentiated Instruction

For Special Needs Students L1
Reuse *Reading a Political Map* to help students understand the features of a political map. Point to the symbol for a national border in the key, then trace the borders of several countries. Invite students to trace others.

All in One Medieval Times to Today Teaching Resources, *Reading a Political Map,* p. 53

For Advanced Readers L3
Challenge students to explore the concepts of relief and elevation further by completing *Relief on a Map* and *Maps of the Ocean Floor.*

All in One Medieval Times to Today Teaching Resources, *Relief on a Map,* p. 61; *Maps of the Ocean Floor,* p. 62

Answers

PRACTICE YOUR GEOGRAPHY SKILLS

1. mountains; the areas with the purple or brown coloring
2. It can help you find out how the land rises and falls.

MapMaster Skills Handbook
Step-by-Step Instruction

Objective
- Understand and use climate maps.
- Understand and use language maps.

Prepare to Read

Build Background Knowledge **L1**
Ask students to think of as many meanings for the word *special* as they can. Tell them that maps can be special too. Ask **What do you think a special-purpose map might show?** List suggestions on the board.

Instruct

Special-Purpose Maps: Climate **L1**

Guided Instruction
- Ask students to read the text using the Structured Silent Reading strategy (TE, p. T34). Point out that the map shows Bangladesh, Bhutan, Nepal, and parts of Myanmar and Pakistan as well as India.
- Point out the map and key. Ask **What areas have a tropical wet climate?** *(area along the southern western coast; eastern part of Bangladesh)*
- Ask **What color represents an arid climate?** *(brown)*

Independent Practice
Partner students and have them complete *Reading a Climate Map.*

All in One Medieval Times to Today Teaching Resources, *Reading a Climate Map,* p. 63

Monitor Progress
As students complete the worksheet, circulate around the room to make sure individuals comprehend the key concepts. Provide assistance as needed.

Answers

MAP MASTER   LOCATION   REGIONS   PLACE   MOVEMENT   INTERACTION

Special-Purpose Maps: Climate

Unlike the boundary lines on a political map, the boundary lines on climate maps do not separate the land into exact divisions. For example, in this climate map of India, a tropical wet climate gradually changes to a tropical wet and dry climate.

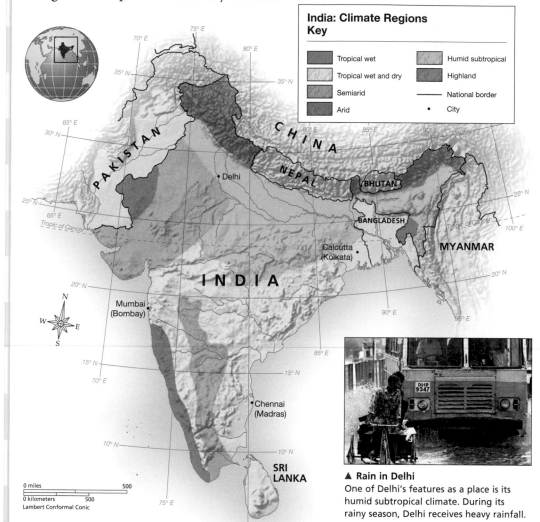

India: Climate Regions Key

- Tropical wet
- Tropical wet and dry
- Semiarid
- Arid
- Humid subtropical
- Highland
- — National border
- • City

0 miles 500
0 kilometers 500
Lambert Conformal Conic

▲ **Rain in Delhi**
One of Delhi's features as a place is its humid subtropical climate. During its rainy season, Delhi receives heavy rainfall.

Differentiated Instruction

For English Language Learners **L1**
If students are unfamiliar with words in the lesson, help them identify and look up those words in the dictionary. For example: *arid*—adj. having little or no rainfall; dry *humid*—adj. having a lot of water; damp *semi*—adj. part or partially

Follow up by having students determine the meaning of *semiarid.*

For Gifted and Talented **L3**
Give students *Reading a Climate Graph.* Ask students to compare the information in the graph with the information on the map above. Ask them to write a sentence synthesizing about the climate of Mumbai.

All in One Medieval Times to Today Teaching Resources, *Reading A Climate Graph,* p. 64

Special-Purpose Maps: Language

This map shows the official languages of India. An official language is the language used by the government. Even though a region has an official language, the people there may speak other languages as well. As in other special-purpose maps, the key explains how the different languages appear on the map.

PRACTICE YOUR GEOGRAPHY SKILLS

1. What color represents the Malayalam language on this map?

2. Where in India is Tamil the official language?

The Hindi language ▶ Hindi is the most widely spoken language in India. It is also the most popular language in Delhi.

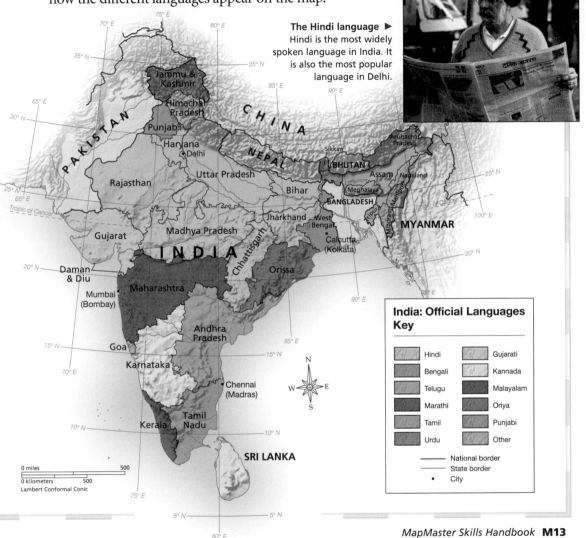

India: Official Languages Key

- Hindi
- Bengali
- Telugu
- Marathi
- Tamil
- Urdu
- Gujarati
- Kannada
- Malayalam
- Oriya
- Punjabi
- Other

—— National border
—— State border
• City

0 miles 500
0 kilometers 500
Lambert Conformal Conic

Background: Daily Life

The Hindi Language Hindi is the official language of India and is the primary language for about 300 million people. English is also spoken by many Indians and is considered the language of politics and commerce. However, the diversity of the country is reflected in the enormous number of languages spoken there, more than 1,500 in all. Ten of India's major states are organized along linguistic lines, and the Indian constitution recognizes 15 regional languages.

Special-Purpose Maps: Language   L2

Guided Instruction

- Read the text as a class. Draw students' attention to the map and its key.

- Have students consider the diversity of official languages. Ask **Why might it be important for a region to have an official language in addition to village or other local languages?** (*Communication is easier with a common language.*)

Independent Practice

Have students work with partners to read another special purpose map, *Reading a Natural Vegetation Map.*

All in One **Medieval Times to Today Teaching Resources,** *Reading a Natural Vegetation Map,* p. 65

Monitor Progress

As students complete the worksheet, circulate around the room and make sure individuals understand key concepts.

Assess and Reteach

Assess Progress   L2

Have students answer the questions under Practice Your Geography Skills on pp. M12 and M13.

Reteach   L1

Have students practice using a special-purpose map by completing *Analyzing and Interpreting Special Purpose Maps.*

⊙ *Analyzing and Interpreting Special-Purpose Maps,* **Social Studies Skills Tutor CD-ROM**

Extend   L3

Have students learn about another type of special-purpose map by completing *Reading a Time Zone Map.* Then ask students to find out the time zones in India and create their own time zone map, using *Outline Map 26: South Asia: Political.*

All in One **Medieval Times to Today Teaching Resources,** *Reading a Time Zone Map,* p. 67; *Outline Map 26: South Asia: Political,* p. 66

Answers

PRACTICE YOUR GEOGRAPHY SKILLS

1. light pink
2. southeast India

Objectives

- Learn why people migrate.
- Understand how migration affects environments.

Prepare to Read

Build Background Knowledge **L1**

Remind students that they studied the theme of movement earlier in this unit. Brainstorm with students why people move from place to place, particularly those who move from one country to another. Use the Numbered Heads participation strategy (TE, p. T36) to generate ideas.

Instruct

Human Migration **L2**

Guided Instruction

- Divide the text using the headings and ask students to read the pages using the Paragraph Shrinking strategy (TE, p. T34). Clarify the meanings of any unfamiliar words.

- Have students look at the map. Ask **From what European countries did people migrate to the Americas in the years between 1500 and 1800?** *(Portugal, Spain, France, Netherlands, England)*

- Ask **Where did the French settle in the Americas?** *(French Guiana, an island in the Caribbean [Haiti], and a region of southern North America [Louisiana])* **Which European country had the most possessions in the Americas?** *(Spain)*

- Ask **Why were some Africans forced to migrate?** *(They were imported as slaves from their homeland. Europeans wanted them to work on the land they claimed in the Americas.)*

Human Migration

Migration is an important part of the study of geography. Since the beginning of history, people have been on the move. As people move, they both shape and are shaped by their environments. Wherever people go, the culture they bring with them mixes with the cultures of the place in which they have settled.

Explorers arrive ▼
In 1492, Christopher Columbus set sail from Spain for the Americas with three ships. The ships shown here are replicas of those ships.

▲ Native American pyramid
When Europeans arrived in the Americas, the lands they found were not empty. Diverse groups of people with distinct cultures already lived there. The temple-topped pyramid shown above was built by Mayan Indians in Mexico, long before Columbus sailed.

Migration to the Americas, 1500–1800

A huge wave of migration from the Eastern Hemisphere began in the 1500s. European explorers in the Americas paved the way for hundreds of years of European settlement there. Forced migration from Africa started soon afterward, as Europeans began to import African slaves to work in the Americas. The map to the right shows these migrations.

ATLANTIC OCEAN

NEW SPAIN (Spain)
Mexico City

Caribbean Sea

Panama City

NEW GRENADA (Spain)

DUTCH GUIANA (Netherlands)

FRENCH GUIANA (France)

Amazon R.

PERU (Spain)
Lima
Cuzco

BRAZIL (Portugal)

Potosí

RIO DE LA PLATA (Spain)

Concepción

Buenos Aires

0 miles 1,000
0 kilometers 1,000
Wagner VII

Differentiated Instruction

For Less Proficient Readers **L1**
Review with students the meaning of "push" and "pull" factors in terms of human migration. Model for students how to make a table with the headings Push and Pull. Then work with students to list as many factors as they can under each heading.

For Advanced Readers **L3**
Have students complete *Analyzing Statistics.* When they have finished, have them write a paragraph explaining how economic and social statistics are related to "push" and "pull" factors.

All in One **Medieval Times to Today Teaching Resources,** *Analyzing Statistics,* p. 69

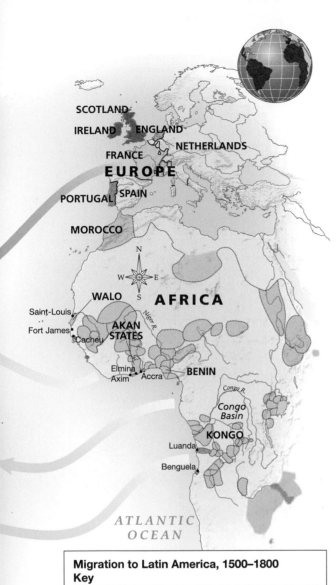

1 Where did the Portuguese settle in the Americas?

2 Would you describe African migration at this time as a result of both push factors and pull factors? Explain why or why not.

"Push" and "Pull" Factors

Geographers describe a people's choice to migrate in terms of "push" factors and "pull" factors. Push factors are things in people's lives that push them to leave, such as poverty and political unrest. Pull factors are things in another country that pull people to move there, including better living conditions and hopes of better jobs.

Migration to Latin America, 1500–1800 Key

← European migration	Spain and possessions
← African migration	Portugal and possessions
— National or colonial border	Netherlands and possessions
···· Traditional African border	France and possessions
African State	England and possessions

▲ **Elmina, Ghana**
Elmina, in Ghana, is one of the many ports from which slaves were transported from Africa. Because slaves and gold were traded here, stretches of the western African coast were known as the Slave Coast and the Gold Coast.

Independent Practice

Have students work with partners to complete *Reading a Historical Map*. Have students be ready to explain how the movement of European groups changed the map of Africa. (*Much of Africa was colonized by Europeans.*)

All in One Medieval Times to Today Teaching Resources, *Reading a Historical Map,* p. 68

Monitor Progress

As students complete the worksheet, circulate around the room to make sure individuals comprehend the key concepts. Provide assistance as needed.

Assess and Reteach

Assess Progress   L2

Have students complete the questions under Practice Your Geography Skills.

Reteach   L1

Help students make an outline of the lesson. Show *Transparency B15: Outline* as a model. Then work with students to identify the main points. Encourage students to refer to their outlines to review the material.

Medieval Times to Today Transparencies, *Transparency B15: Outline*

Extend   L3

To extend the lesson, have students complete *The Global Refugee Crisis.* Then ask them to choose a specific region on the graph and find out more about refugees from one country in that region.

Go Online
PHSchool.com **For:** Environmental and Global Issues: *The Global Refugee Crisis*
Visit: PHSchool.com
Web Code: lgd-8001

Answers

1. Brazil

2. most likely push factors because people were forced to leave; the need for workers in the Americas was a pull factor although it was the Europeans who responded to it by importing Africans as slaves

Objectives
- Understand and use a land use map.
- Learn how land use and economic structures are linked.

Prepare to Read

Build Background Knowledge [L1]

Discuss with the class the ways that people in your community are using land. For example, is all the land used for homes? How much is used for commercial purposes? What kinds? Are there farms or manufacturing facilities? Point out that communities in all parts of the world use land in different ways.

Instruct

World Land Use [L2]

Guided Instruction
- Read the text as a class using the Oral Cloze strategy (TE, p. T33). Follow up by having students do a second silent reading. Encourage students to study the map and photographs.

- Talk about the difference between commercial and subsistence farming. Have them look closely at the photographs on pp. M16 and M17. Ask **How do the tools and equipment people use differ in these types of farming?** (*Large power machines are used in commercial farming; hand tools are used in subsistence farming*) **Why might people use more land in commercial farming?** (*Machines make it possible to cultivate more land: the more land cultivated, the more sales possible.*)

- Ask **What color represents nomadic herding on this map?** (*light purple*) **In what parts of the world is this an economic activity?** (*Africa, Asia*)

- Ask **Why might some parts of the world have little or no land use activity?** (*Land and/or climate might not be suitable for farming or other activity.*)

World Land Use

People around the world have many different economic structures, or ways of making a living. Land-use maps are one way to learn about these structures. The ways that people use the land in each region tell us about the main ways that people in that region make a living.

World Land Use Key

	Nomadic herding
	Hunting and gathering
	Forestry
	Livestock raising
	Commercial farming
	Subsistence farming
	Manufacturing and trade
	Little or no activity
——	National border
- - - -	Disputed border

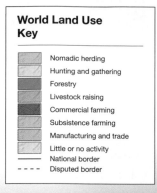

▲ **Wheat farming in the United States**
Developed countries practice commercial farming rather than subsistence farming. Commercial farming is the production of food mainly for sale, either within the country or for export to other countries. Commercial farmers like these in Oregon often use heavy equipment to farm.

Levels of Development
Notice on the map key the term *subsistence farming*. This term means the production of food mainly for use by the farmer's own family. In less-developed countries, subsistence farming is often one of the main economic activities. In contrast, in developed countries there is little subsistence farming.

▲ **Growing barley in Ecuador**
These farmers in Ecuador use hand tools to harvest barley. They will use most of the crop they grow to feed themselves or their farm animals.

NORTH AMERICA

SOUTH AMERICA

0 miles		2,000
0 kilometers		2,000

Robinson

Background: Global Perspectives

Agriculture Almost 50 percent of the world's population is occupied in agriculture. A much higher proportion of this is in developing countries where dense populations, small land holdings, and traditional techniques predominate. In areas where there is intense cultivation using people and animals but few machines, the yield is low in relation to the output of energy. In leading food producing countries such as the United States, industrial farms make use of new technology and crop specialization to increase output.

▲ **Growing rice in Vietnam**
Women in Vietnam plant rice in wet rice paddies, using the same planting methods their ancestors did.

PRACTICE YOUR GEOGRAPHY SKILLS

1 In what parts of the world is subsistence farming the main land use?

2 Locate where manufacturing and trade are the main land use. Are they found more often near areas of subsistence farming or areas of commercial farming? Why might this be so?

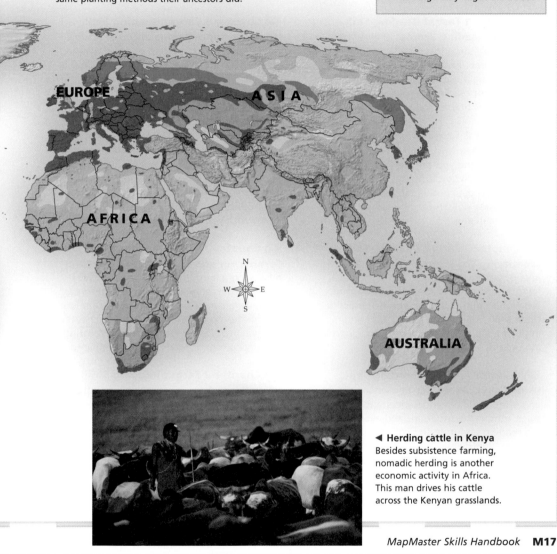

EUROPE

ASIA

AFRICA

AUSTRALIA

◄ **Herding cattle in Kenya**
Besides subsistence farming, nomadic herding is another economic activity in Africa. This man drives his cattle across the Kenyan grasslands.

MapMaster Skills Handbook **M17**

Independent Practice

Partner students and have them complete *Reading an Economic Activity Map.* Have students be ready to offer explanations for how the economic activity in Somalia might affect the lives of people there.

All in One Medieval Times to Today Teaching Resources, *Reading an Economic Activity Map,* p. 70

Monitor Progress

Circulate around the room as students complete the worksheet to make sure individuals comprehend the key concepts. Provide assistance as needed.

Assess and Reteach

Assess Progress   L2

Have students complete the questions under Practice Your Geography Skills.

Reteach   L1

Help students make a table to identify the main kinds of land use. Draw a model on the board for students to follow. Use these headings: Nomadic Herding, Forestry, Livestock Raising, Commercial Farming, Subsistence Farming, Manufacturing and Trade. Under each heading, help students write a short explanation. Then have students find one or two places on the map in their books where that activity takes place.

Extend   L3

To extend the lesson, have students complete *Reading a Natural Resources Map.* Point out that this map shows mineral resources. Then ask students to write a paragraph relating mineral resources to land use.

All in One Medieval Times to Today Teaching Resources, *Reading a Natural Resources Map,* p. 71

Differentiated Instruction

For English Language Learners   L3

Students may find it difficult to pronounce some of the multisyllable words in this section, such as *nomadic, subsistence, commercial,* and *forestry.* Model how to break down these words into smaller parts to help students sound out the pronunciation.

Answers

PRACTICE YOUR GEOGRAPHY SKILLS

1. Africa, Asia, South America

2. areas of commercial farming; both manufacturing and trade and commercial farming require equipment and technology that subsistence farmers do not have

Teaching the Target Reading Skills

The Prentice Hall *World Studies* program has interwoven essential reading skills instruction throughout the Student Edition, Teacher's Edition, and ancillary resources. In Medieval Times to Today, students will learn eight reading skills.

Student Edition The *World Studies* Student Edition provides students with reading skills instruction, practice, and application opportunities in each chapter within the program.

Teacher's Edition The *World Studies* Teacher's Edition supports your teaching of each skill by providing full modeling in each chapter's interleaf and modeling of the specific sub-skills in each section lesson.

All in One Teaching Resources The *World Studies* All-in-One Teaching Resources provides a worksheet explaining and supporting the elements of each Target Reading Skill. Use these to help struggling students master skills, or as more practice for every student.

How to Read Social Studies

Target Reading Skills

The Target Reading Skills introduced on this page will help you understand the words and ideas in this book and in other social studies reading you do. Each chapter focuses on one of these reading skills. Good readers develop a bank of reading strategies, or skills. Then they draw on the particular strategies that will help them understand the text they are reading.

Chapter 1 Target Reading Skill
Using the Reading Process Previewing can help you understand and remember what you read. In this chapter you will practice using these previewing skills: setting a purpose for reading, predicting, and asking questions before you read.

Chapter 2 Target Reading Skill
Clarifying Meaning If you do not understand something you are reading, you can use several skills to clarify the meaning of the word or idea. In this chapter you will practice these skills: rereading, paraphrasing, and summarizing.

Chapter 3 Target Reading Skill
Identifying the Main Idea The main idea of a section or paragraph is the most important point and the one you want to remember. In this chapter you will practice these skills: identifying both stated and implied main ideas and identifying supporting details.

Chapter 4 Target Reading Skill
Using Cause and Effect Recognizing cause and effect will help you understand relationships among the situations and events you are reading about. In this chapter you will practice identifying cause and effect, understanding effects, and recognizing cause-and-effect signal words.

Chapter 5 Target Reading Skill
Using Sequence Noting the order in which events take place can help you understand how the events relate to one another. In this chapter you will practice recognizing sequence signal words, identifying sequence, and making a sequence chart.

Chapter 6 Target Reading Skill
Using Context Context—the words and sentences surrounding a word—can help you understand the word's meaning. In this chapter you will practice using these context clues: definitions, synonyms, and explanations, along with your own general knowledge.

Chapter 7 Target Reading Skill
Comparing and Contrasting Comparing means examining the similarities between things. Contrasting is looking at differences. These skills can help you sort out and analyze information you are reading. In this chapter you will practice comparing and contrasting, identifying contrasts, and making comparisons.

Chapter 8 Target Reading Skill
Using Word Analysis Breaking an unfamiliar word into its parts can help you understand and pronounce it. In this chapter you will practice using prefixes and suffixes—word parts that attach to a word root and change its meaning—as well as your knowledge of word origins.

Assessment Resources

Use the diagnosing readiness tests from **AYP Monitoring Assessments** to help you identify problems before students begin to study Medieval Times to Today.

Determine students' reading level and identify challenges:

- 📄 *Screening Tests*, pp. 1–11

Evaluate students' verbal skills:

- 📄 *Critical Thinking and Reading Tests*, pp. 25–34
- 📄 *Vocabulary Tests*, pp. 45–52
- 📄 *Writing Tests*, pp. 53–60

MEDIEVAL TIMES TO TODAY

To understand today's world, we must learn about its past. Ancient civilizations laid many of the foundations for modern cultures. The people who lived in medieval times—the years between ancient and modern times—built upon those foundations but also made contributions of their own. Advances in science, technology, and the arts; new belief systems; migrations of people and ideas; developments in government and economic systems—all of these helped to shape our modern world.

Guiding Questions
The text, photographs, maps, and charts in this book will help you discover answers to these Guiding Questions.

1. **Geography** How did physical geography affect the development of societies around the world?

2. **History** How have societies around the world been shaped by their history?

3. **Culture** What were the belief systems and patterns of daily life in those societies?

4. **Government** What types of government were formed in those societies?

5. **Economics** How did each society organize its economic activities?

Project Preview
You can also discover answers to the Guiding Questions by working on projects. Several project possibilities are listed on page 246 of this book.

Medieval Times to Today **1**

Assess students' social studies skills:

- *Geographic Literacy Tests*, pp. 13–20
- *Visual Analysis Tests*, pp. 21–24
- *Communications Tests*, pp. 35–44

The *World Studies* program provides instruction and practice for all of these skills. Use students' test results to pinpoint the skills your students have mastered and the skills they need to practice. Then use *Correlation to Program Resources* to prescribe skills practice and reinforcement.

- *Diagnosing Readiness Test Correlations*, pp. 64–77

Guiding Questions

- This book was developed around five Guiding Questions about Medieval Times to Today. They appear on the reduced Student Edition page to the left. The Guiding Questions are intended as an organizational focus for the book. The Guiding Questions act as a kind of umbrella under which all of the material falls.

- You may wish to add your own Guiding Questions to the list in order to tailor them to your particular course.

- Draw students' attention to the Guiding Questions. Ask them to write the questions in their notebooks for future reference.

- In the Teacher's Edition, each section's themes are linked to a specific Guiding Question at the beginning of each chapter. Then, an activity at the end of the chapter returns to the Guiding Questions to review key concepts.

Project Preview

- The projects for this book are designed to provide students with hands-on involvement in the content area. Students are introduced to some projects on p. 246.

- *Book Projects* give students directions on how to complete these projects, and more.

  All in One Medieval Times to Today Teaching Resources, *Book Project: One Job Through the Ages,* pp. 77–79; *Book Project: Two Tales of One City,* pp. 80–82; *Book Project: The Birth of a Nation,* pp. 83–85; *Book Project: Major Migrations,* pp. 86–88

- Assign projects as small group activities, whole-class projects, or individual projects. Consider assigning a project at the beginning of the course.

Objectives

- Describe the relative locations and sizes of Earth's continents.
- Examine the elevation of Earth's land and explore Earth's oceans.
- Analyze changes in population distribution from medieval times to today.
- Explore changes in the political geography of the world.
- Investigate the Columbian Exchange.

Prepare to Read

Build Background Knowledge **L2**

Ask students to think about how the world has changed in the last 1,500 years. Tell them to preview the chapter to get ideas about what life was like in the past. Tell students that they will either confirm or revise these impressions during their study of the world from medieval times to today.

Instruct

Investigate Medieval Times to Today **L2**

Guided Instruction

- Read the introductory and Location paragraphs as a class. Have students work in small groups to answer the questions.
- Direct students' attention to the photo captions on p. 2. Then ask students to use the map to identify on which continent each pictured place is located. (*Amazon Basin—South America; Sahara Desert—Africa*)
- Have students fill in the worksheet below as they study the World Overview.

  All in One Medieval Times to Today Teaching Resources, *World Overview,* pp. 93–95

Monitor Progress

Circulate to make sure groups are communicating effectively.

Answers

LOCATION north; seven; North America, Europe, Asia's mainland; Australia, Antarctica; Europe and Asia; their histories may be interconnected.

Investigate Medieval Times to Today

The fall of the Western Roman Empire in A.D. 476 marked the end of the ancient world and the beginning of medieval times. Civilizations developed in separate regions of the world. Then new methods of travel and the ambitions of powerful leaders led to exploration and huge migrations of people.

▲ **The Sahara, Algeria**
The Sahara is the largest desert in the world. Deserts—dry areas receiving little rainfall—cover about one fifth of the world's land surface.

The World: Physical

▲ **Amazon Basin, Venezuela**
The mighty Amazon River runs through the Amazon basin, a region that contains the world's largest tropical rain forest.

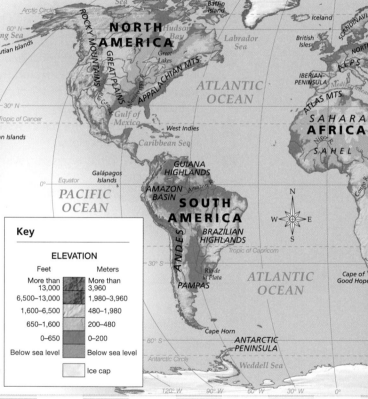

LOCATION

1 Investigate the Continents of Earth
Look at the map at the right. Find the Equator. Is most of the land on the map north or south of the Equator? How many continents are there? Which continents are entirely north of the Equator? Which continents are entirely south of it? Which two continents are part of the same landmass? How do you think being part of one landmass might have affected the history of these two continents?

Key

ELEVATION

Feet	Meters
More than 13,000	More than 3,960
6,500–13,000	1,980–3,960
1,600–6,500	480–1,980
650–1,600	200–480
0–650	0–200
Below sea level	Below sea level
Ice cap	

Mental Mapping

The Shape of the World Have students close their textbooks. Take down or cover any maps of the world that may be hanging in your classroom. Then give each student a blank piece of paper. Ask them to draw a map of the seven continents. Encourage them to draw the shapes of the continents as accurately as possible. Have them draw in any continent borders that appear on land and then label the continents.

PLACE

2 Examine Elevation

As you study the map key, remember that elevation is the height of land above sea level. What color indicates the highest elevation? Where are areas of high elevation found? What effect do you think mountain ranges might have had on human settlement and travel?

▲ **The Himalayas, Nepal**
The Himalayas contain the world's tallest peaks. This mountain range formed millions of years ago when the Indian and Eurasian landmasses collided.

PLACE

3 Explore Earth's Oceans

Does the map show more land or more water? What does that tell you about Earth? Which ocean lies between South America and Africa? Which ocean is west of the Americas? Which ocean is east of Asia? Why do you think some people say that there is just one ocean, the "world ocean"?

▲ **Kayangel Atoll, Micronesia**
Atolls, small ring-shaped coral islands that surround lagoons, dot the Pacific Ocean.

World Overview **3**

- Read the Place paragraphs. Ask students to name the landforms that make up the large area of high elevation in Asia. *(Plateau of Tibet, Himalayas, Hindu Kush, and Tian Shan)*

- Have students compare the elevation of western North America to the elevation of eastern North America. *(The western part of the continent has higher elevations than the eastern part of the continent.)* Then ask **Which mountain range makes up much of the higher elevation in the West?** *(the Rocky Mountains)*

- Ask **Around which sea can you find an area of land that is below sea level?** *(the Caspian Sea)*

- Discuss the part the oceans played in the settlement of the world. *(Explorers traveled to distant continents by sailing the world's oceans.)*

Independent Practice

Distribute *Outline Map 1: The World: Physical.* Ask students to fill in the names of the continents and oceans. Then list several of the world's major physical features on the board such as the Andes and the Gobi Desert. Ask students to locate and label them on their maps without looking in their textbooks.

All in One **Medieval Times to Today Teaching Resources,** *Outline Map 1: The World: Physical,* p. 96

Monitor Progress

Circulate to make sure students are correctly labeling their maps. Then have students reopen their books and check their maps against the map on pp. 2–3.

Differentiated Instruction

For Less Proficient Readers L1
For students who may have trouble reading the physical map of the world found on pages 2–3 of the Student Edition, distribute the DK Atlas Activities *Reading a Physical Map* and *Elevation on a Map.* Have students complete the activities in pairs.

All in One **Medieval Times to Today Teaching Resources,** *DK Compact Atlas of the World Activity 10: Reading a Physical Map,* p. 97; *DK Compact Atlas of the World Activity 11: Elevation on a Map,* p. 98

Answers

PLACE purple; in western North and South America, eastern Africa, and southern Asia; Possible answer: Mountains may have served as barriers to human travel and settlement.

PLACE more water; Earth is made up of more water than land; Atlantic Ocean; Pacific Ocean; Pacific Ocean; Possible answer: All of the world's oceans are connected; they are part of one large world ocean.

World Overview **3**

Human Settlement: A.D. 500 to Today [L2]

Guided Instruction

- Use the Choral Reading strategy (TE, p. T34) to read the Movement paragraph.

- Ask students **Which color on the map represents the most densely populated areas?** *(dark purple)* **Which color represents the most sparsely populated areas?** *(yellow)*

- Ask students to identify the only continent that has no permanent human settlements. *(Antarctica)* **Why do you think this is so?** *(Possible answer: Antarctica is located very far from the Equator, so it is very cold. It is almost completely covered by ice. Therefore, it would be difficult for humans to live there.)*

Answers

MOVEMENT Southern Asia, Europe, eastern and central Africa; southern Asia, small parts of Europe, North America, South America, and Africa; Possible answer: Southern Asia is still densley populated; North and South America's population densities have increased since people from Europe and other parts of the world began to move there.

Human Settlement: A.D. 500 to Today

MOVEMENT

4 Investigate Where People Live

The black dots on this map show where people lived in A.D. 500, when the population was much smaller than it is now. The colors show where people live today. What parts of the world were most densely populated in A.D. 500? What parts of the world are most densely populated today? Describe the change in population density in a sentence or two. Why do you think this change has occurred?

▲ **Pueblo Cave Painting, Arizona**
People who lived in the cliffs of the present-day southwestern United States left paintings like this one, which dates from around A.D. 1200.

▲ **Mayan Ruins, Guatemala**
The Mayas flourished in Mexico and Central America from about A.D. 300 to 900. Today, ruins of towns and temples provide clues to this rich civilization.

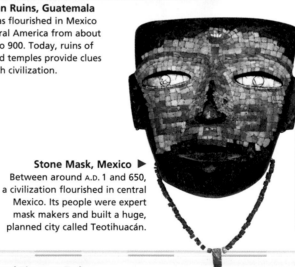

Stone Mask, Mexico ▶
Between around A.D. 1 and 650, a civilization flourished in central Mexico. Its people were expert mask makers and built a huge, planned city called Teotihuacán.

World: Population Density Key

Population per sq. mile		Population per sq. kilometer
More than 259		More than 100
52–259		21–100
24–51		5–20
Less than 24		Less than 5

- • 1 Million people in A.D. 500
- — National border
- - - Disputed border

Differentiated Instruction

For English Language Learners [L1]
Spend extra time reviewing how to read the population density map with English language learners. Point out the map key and review what a square mile is. Have students find at least one area on the map that corresponds to each density range and have them say aloud the number of people it represents as they point to the area on the map.

◀ **Hagia Sophia, Istanbul, Turkey**
The Hagia Sophia was first built as a Christian church in A.D. 537. Its architecture is a classic example of Byzantine architecture.

▲ **Songshan Pagoda, China**
Built in A.D. 520, this is the oldest Buddhist temple in China. Buddhism spread to China from India in the century after A.D. 1.

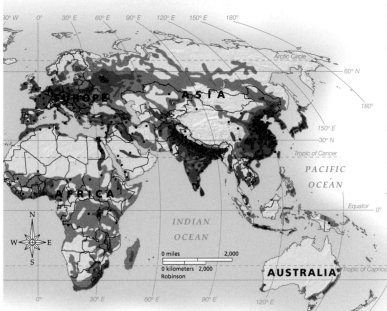

INTERACTION

5 **Consider Why People Live Where They Do**

Study the map on this page, and then look back at the physical map of the world on the previous page. Identify at least three types of places where people settled in A.D. 500. For example, did they tend to settle along the seacoasts or in the middle of continents? What natural features seem to attract human settlement? Why might these natural features be less important today than in 500?

▲ **Alice Springs, Australia**
Aborigines, or native peoples, had lived in this area long before European settlers arrived in the late 1800s.

Background: Global Perspectives

World Population Density While many of the world's largest countries in size also have the largest populations, one of the smallest countries has the highest population density. Monaco, a tiny country located southeast of France, has a population density of about 42,000 people per square mile. The area of the entire country is actually less than one square mile!

Guided Instruction (continued)

- Read the Interaction paragraph aloud as students follow along in their textbooks. Pause after each question and find the answers as a class.

- Point out the line of dots that run from north to south in northeastern Africa. Then have students find this area on the physical map on pp. 2–3. Ask **Why do you think many people lived in this area in A.D. 500?** *(The Nile River is located in this area. People probably settled along the river because they could use the water for farming and drinking.)*

- Have students continue to complete the *World Overview* worksheets.

  All in One **Medieval Times to Today Teaching Resources,** *World Overview,* pp. 93–95

Independent Practice

- Have students study today's world population by making a bar graph of the five most populated countries in the world.

- Ask students to use the DK World Desk Reference Online to identify the five most populated countries and their populations in millions. Tell students to use this information to create their bar graphs. Ask students to give the graph a title and provide labels for the x- and y-axis.

- Then display *Transparency MT 10: The World: Political.* Ask students to use this map and the map on pp. 4–5 to find which continent each country is located on.

  Medieval Times to Today Transparencies, *Transparency MT 10: The World: Political*

Monitor Progress

Make sure students are able to identify the most populated countries in the world. Check bar graphs for appropriate labels and titles. Provide assistance as needed.

Answers

INTERACTION People tend to settle along coasts. People tend to live near rivers and other bodies of water, and on plains. Possible answer: Deserts and mountains seem to discourage settlement. Possible answer: People have learned ways to adapt to more difficult environments. For example, people have learned terrace farming to grow food in mountainous areas.

The World Around 1500 L2

Guided Instruction

- Read the Place paragraph as a class. Have students work in pairs to answer the questions.

- Ask students **Other than Russia, which empire stretched across more than one continent?** *(the Ottoman empire)* Ask students to name the continents. *(Europe, Africa, and Asia)*

- Read the Movement paragraph. Ask students to look closely at the items in the Columbian Exchange. Ask students to think about the advantage and disadvantages of the exchange. *(Advantages— greater variety of food and animals; Disadvantages—spread of disease, new species of plants or animals might upset delicate balance of existing plants and animals.)*

Independent Practice

Ask students to do further research on the Columbian Exchange. Tell students to choose a continent they would like to focus their research on—North America, South America, Europe, or Africa. Have them write a brief essay explaining how the Columbian Exchange changed life on the continent.

Monitor Progress

If students are having trouble focusing their essays, encourage them to consider how the specific diseases and products listed in the diagram could affect daily life.

Answers

PLACE Today the world has defined political boundaries and country names whereas in 1500, it did not. Possible answer: These groups of people lived independently of other groups and did not seek to establish a large empire; in Europe and Southwest Asia; Inca Empire, Aztec empire, Great Zimbabwe, and Mughal India; Possible answer: The cultures in two civilizations that are close to each other might be similar, while the culture of an isolated civilization may be very different from those of other civilizations.

The World Around 1500

PLACE

6 Explore Changes in Political Geography

Look at the map below and then at the World: Political map in the Atlas. What is the major difference that you see? Notice that some areas on this map have no boundaries representing major civilizations or nations, but they do have the names of different peoples. Where are civilizations or nations close to one another? Which civilizations are isolated? What effect might nearness to other civilizations have on a culture?

▲ **Carcassonne, France**
Built in the 1200s, Carcassonne is a classic example of a medieval walled town. People still live in the town today.

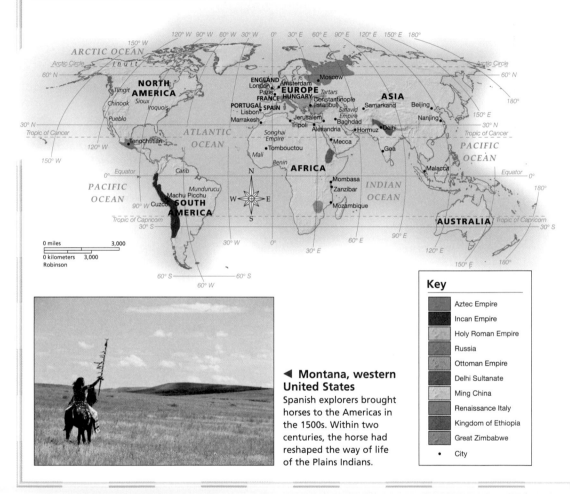

◄ **Montana, western United States**
Spanish explorers brought horses to the Americas in the 1500s. Within two centuries, the horse had reshaped the way of life of the Plains Indians.

Key

	Aztec Empire
	Incan Empire
	Holy Roman Empire
	Russia
	Ottoman Empire
	Delhi Sultanate
	Ming China
	Renaissance Italy
	Kingdom of Ethiopia
	Great Zimbabwe
•	City

Differentiated Instruction

For Advanced Readers L3

Have students read the primary sources *Morning Girl, Journal Entry,* and *Chief Joseph Surrenders* to learn more about how European exploration and settlement of the Americas affected the people who already lived in the region. Tell students to answer the questions at the end of the selections individually.

All in One Medieval Times to Today Teaching Resources, *Morning Girl,* pp. 99–101; *Journal Entry,* p. 102; *Chief Joseph Surrenders,* p. 103

MOVEMENT

7 Investigate the Columbian Exchange

When Europeans explored and settled the Americas, they brought many things with them. They also brought things from the Americas back to Europe. This movement of plants, animals, and diseases is called the Columbian Exchange. Because of trade with Africa, including the transport of enslaved Africans to the Americas, Africa also became part of the Columbian Exchange. Study the diagram at the right. Name three items from Europe that you think had an important effect on the Americas.

FROM AFRICA, ASIA, AND EUROPE TO THE AMERICAS

Coffee	Honeybee
Banana	Chicken
Citrus fruit	Sheep, Cattle
Watermelon	Horse
Peach, Pear	Chickenpox
Lettuce, Onion	Measles
Grains (wheat, barley, oats)	Scarlet fever
	Smallpox
Sugar cane	Malaria

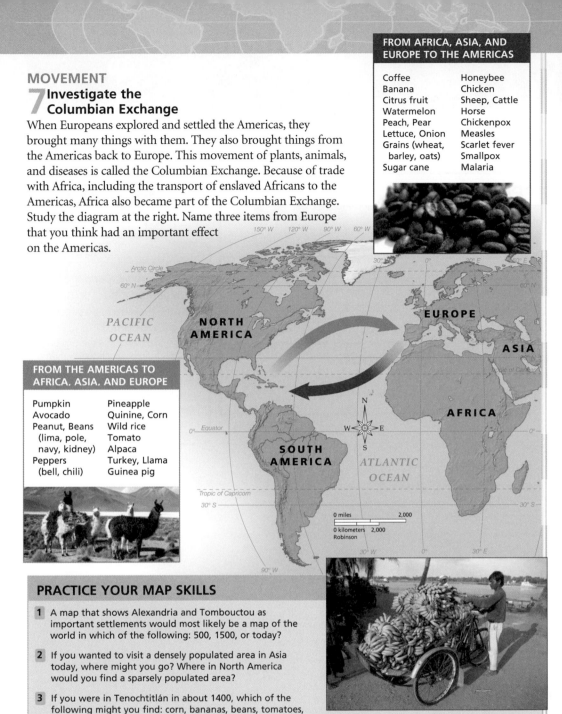

FROM THE AMERICAS TO AFRICA, ASIA, AND EUROPE

Pumpkin	Pineapple
Avocado	Quinine, Corn
Peanut, Beans (lima, pole, navy, kidney)	Wild rice
	Tomato
	Alpaca
Peppers (bell, chili)	Turkey, Llama
	Guinea pig

▲ A Latin American vendor sells bananas.

PRACTICE YOUR MAP SKILLS

1. A map that shows Alexandria and Tombouctou as important settlements would most likely be a map of the world in which of the following: 500, 1500, or today?

2. If you wanted to visit a densely populated area in Asia today, where might you go? Where in North America would you find a sparsely populated area?

3. If you were in Tenochtitlán in about 1400, which of the following might you find: corn, bananas, beans, tomatoes, or chickenpox?

PRACTICE YOUR MAP SKILLS

1. 500 or 1500

2. India or China; central and northern Canada

3. You might find corn, beans, and tomatoes, but not bananas or the chickenpox.

Assess and Reteach

Assess Progress   L2

- Have students revisit the differences they brainstormed in Build Background Knowledge. Using the information they have learned so far, ask them to confirm or revise some of their impressions. If some aspects have yet to be touched on, tell students to write them in their notebooks and look for more information as they begin their study of medieval times to today.

- Ask students to complete Practice Your Geography Skills on p. 7.

Reteach   L1

Have students begin working on *Building a Time Capsule* to learn more about what different areas of the world are like today and why it is important to know what they were like in the past.

> **Go Online**
> **PHSchool.com** **For:** Long-Term Projects: *Building a Time Capsule*
> **Visit:** PHSchool.com
> **Web Code:** lgd-8002

Extend   L3

One way of assessing student accomplishments is by having them build a portfolio of their best work. To begin their portfolios for Medieval Times to Today, have students choose one of the civilizations or nations found on the map on pp. 6–7. Then, assign a project on this civilization of nation. Students can choose what type of project they would like to do. Options include collages, stories, paragraphs, dioramas, and more.

- Give students *Writing an Outline for Research* to help them get started on their research.

All in One **Medieval Times to Today Teaching Resources,** *Writing an Outline for Research*, p. 104

Answers

MOVEMENT Possible answers: Coffee, grain, sugar cane, chicken, cattle, horses, smallpox

Byzantine and Muslim Civilizations

Overview

 Section 1

The Byzantine Empire
1. Find out how Constantinople and the Byzantine Empire became powerful.
2. Discover the achievements of the Age of Justinian.
3. Learn about the later years of the Byzantine Empire.

 Section 2

The Beginnings of Islam
1. Learn about the Arabian Peninsula, its nomadic people, and its centers of trade.
2. Find out about the life and mission of the Muslim prophet Muhammad.
3. Learn about Muslim beliefs.

 Section 3

The Golden Age of Muslim Civilization
1. Find out how the religion of Islam spread.
2. Learn about the golden age of Islam under the rule of the caliphs.

Constantinople: Capital of the Byzantine Empire
Length: 4 minutes, 44 seconds
Use with Section 1
This segment explores the city of Constantinople, which the Roman emperor Constantine named after himself in A.D. 330. The segment will show how the city's location made it important to many different cultures throughout history.

 # Technology Resources

Students use embedded Web codes to access Internet activities, chapter self-tests, and additional map practice. They may also access Dorling Kindersley's Online Desk Reference to learn more about each country they study.

Use the Interactive Textbook to make content and concepts come alive through animations, videos, and activities that accompany the complete basal text—online and on CD-ROM.

Use this complete suite of powerful teaching tools to make planning lessons and administering tests quicker and easier.

Reading and Assessment

Reading and Vocabulary Instruction

Model the Target Reading Skill

Reading Process Explain to students that reading actively will help them retain knowledge and become better readers. To read actively, students should preview the text before reading and determine a purpose for their reading. Two ways to set a purpose for reading are to predict what they will learn about, and to ask themselves questions to answer while reading. Model this skill by thinking about the chapter aloud:

"This chapter's title is *Byzantine and Muslim Civilizations.* I will be learning about two civilizations. I know that the word *civilization* contains the word *civilize,* but I'm not sure what it means. I think it has to do with societies. I'm not sure what *Byzantine* and *Muslim* mean, either. I will scan the chapter to get a better idea of their meanings before reading. Section 1 is titled *The Byzantine Empire.* From scanning the section, it seems as though this empire is related to the Roman Empire. I predict that I will learn the differences between the Byzantine and Roman Empires in this section. Section 2 is titled *The Beginnings of Islam.* I know that *Islam* is a religion. Could *Islam* and *Muslim* be related? I will keep that question in mind while I read the chapter."

Use the following worksheets from All-in-One Medieval Times to Today Teaching Resources (pp. 120–122) to support the chapter's Target Reading Skill.

Vocabulary Builder
High-Use Academic Words

Use these steps to teach this chapter's high-use words:

1. Have students rate how well they know each word on their Word Knowledge worksheets (All-in-One Medieval Times to Today Teaching Resources, p. 123).

2. Pronounce each word and ask students to repeat it.

3. Give students a brief definition or sample sentence (provided on TE pp. 11, 19, and 27).

4. Work with students as they fill in the "Definition or Example" column of their Word Knowledge worksheets.

Assessment

Formal Assessment

Test students' understanding of core knowledge and skills.

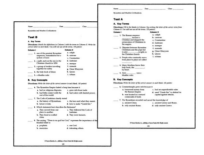

Chapter Tests A and B, All-in-One Medieval Times to Today Teaching Resources, pp. 136–141

Customize the Chapter Tests to suit your needs.

Exam*View*® Test Bank CD-ROM

Skills Assessment

Assess geographic literacy.

MapMaster Skills, Student Edition pp. 9, 27, and 32

Assess reading and comprehension.

Target Reading Skills, Student Edition, pp. 14, 22, 28, and in Section Assessments

Chapter 1 Assessment, Medieval Times to Today Reading and Vocabulary Study Guide, p. 15

Performance Assessment

Assess students' performance on this chapter's Writing Activities using the following rubrics from All-in-One Medieval Times to Today Teaching Resources.

Rubric for Assessing a Writing Assignment, p. 134

Rubric for Assessing a Newspaper Article, p. 135

Assess students' work through performance tasks.

Small Group Activity: Writing Articles About the Art of Islam, All-in-One Medieval Times to Today Teaching Resources, pp. 126–129

Online Assessment

Have students check their own knowledge.

Chapter Self-Test

Test Preparation

Screening Tests, AYP Monitoring Assessments, pp. 1–11

Diagnosing Readiness Tests, AYP Monitoring Assessments, pp. 13–63

Section 1 The Byzantine Empire

 3.5 periods, 1.75 blocks (includes Skills for Life)

Social Studies Objectives
1. Find out how Constantinople and the Byzantine Empire grew powerful.
2. Discover the achievements of the Age of Justinian.
3. Learn about the later years of the Byzantine Empire.

Reading/Language Arts Objective
Learn how to preview and set a purpose for reading.

Prepare to Read

Build Background Knowledge
Show a video about Constantinople and ask students to take notes on the important details.

Set a Purpose for Reading
Have students evaluate statements on the *Reading Readiness Guide*.

Preview Key Terms
Teach the section's Key Terms.

Target Reading Skill
Introduce the section's Target Reading Skill of **previewing and setting a purpose.**

Instructional Resources

All in One Medieval Times to Today Teaching Resources
L2 Reading Readiness Guide, p. 109
L2 Preview and Set a Purpose, p. 120

World Studies Video Program
L2 Constantinople: Capital of the Byzantine Empire

Differentiated Instruction

Spanish Reading and Vocabulary Study Guide
L1 Chapter 1, Section 1, pp. 7–8 ELL

Instruct

Constantinople at a Crossroads
Discuss Constantinople during the reign of Constantine.

The Age of Justinian
Ask questions about the early Byzantine empire and the Justinian code.

Target Reading Skill
Review **previewing and setting a purpose.**

The Empire's Later Years
Discuss the events that led to the decline of the Byzantine empire and the fall of Constantinople.

Instructional Resources

All in One Medieval Times to Today Teaching Resources
L2 Guided Reading and Review, p. 110
L2 Reading Readiness Guide, p. 109

Medieval Times to Today Transparencies
L2 Section Reading Support Transparency MT 53

Differentiated Instruction

All in One Medieval Times to Today Teaching Resources
L3 Small Group Activity: Writing Articles About the Art of Islam, pp. 126–129 AR, GT
L3 Byzantine Empress Theodora, p. 130 AR, GT
L2 Skills for Life, p. 125 AR, GT, LPR, SN

Teacher's Edition
L3 For Gifted and Talented, TE p. 12
L1 For Less Proficient Readers, TE p. 12
L1 For English Language Learners, TE p. 14
L3 For Advanced Readers, TE p. 14

Reading and Vocabulary Study Guide
L1 Chapter 1, Section 1, pp. 6–8 ELL, LPR, SN

Spanish Support
L2 Guided Reading and Review (Spanish), p. 4 ELL

Assess and Reteach

Assess Progress
Evaluate student comprehension with the section assessment and section quiz.

Reteach
Assign the Reading and Vocabulary Study Guide to help struggling students.

Extend
Extend the lesson by assigning a Book Project.

Instructional Resources

All in One Medieval Times to Today Teaching Resources
L2 Section Quiz, p. 111
L3 Book Project: Two Tales of One City, pp. 80–82 Rubric for Assessing a Writing Assignment, p. 134

Reading and Vocabulary Study Guide
L1 Chapter 1, Section 1, pp. 6–8

Differentiated Instruction

Spanish Support
L2 Section Quiz (Spanish), p. 5 ELL

Teacher's Edition
L1 For Special Needs Students, TE p. 17

Social Studies Skills Tutor CD-ROM
L1 Transferring Information from One Medium to Another ELL, LPR, SN

Key
L1 Basic to Average
L3 Average to Advanced
L2 For All Students

LPR Less Proficient Readers
AR Advanced Readers
SN Special Needs Students

GT Gifted and Talented
ELL English Language Learners

Section 2 The Beginnings of Islam

 2 periods, 1 block (includes Focus On Bedouin Life)

Social Studies Objectives
1. Learn about the Arabian Peninsula, its nomadic people, and its centers of trade.
2. Find out about the life and mission of the Muslim prophet Muhammad.
3. Learn about Muslim beliefs.

Reading/Language Arts Objective
Preview and make predictions about the text to help set a purpose for reading.

Prepare to Read	Instructional Resources	Differentiated Instruction
Build Background Knowledge Have students preview the section and think about the beliefs and origins of Islam, and write down a question they have about the religion. **Set a Purpose for Reading** Have students evaluate statements on the *Reading Readiness Guide*. **Preview Key Terms** Teach the section's Key Terms. **Target Reading Skill** Introduce the section's Target Reading Skill of **previewing and predicting**.	**All in One Medieval Times to Today Teaching Resources** L2 Reading Readiness Guide, p. 113 L2 Preview and Predict, p. 121	**Spanish Reading and Vocabulary Study Guide** L1 Chapter 1, Section 2, pp. 9–10 ELL

Instruct	Instructional Resources	Differentiated Instruction
The Arabian Peninsula Ask questions about the geography and people of the Arabian Peninsula. **The Prophet Muhammad** Discuss how Muhammad founded Islam. **Muslim Belief** Discuss different aspects of the Islam religion. **Target Reading Skill** Review **previewing and predicting**.	**All in One Medieval Times to Today Teaching Resources** L2 Guided Reading and Review, p. 114 L2 Reading Readiness Guide, p. 113 **Medieval Times to Today Transparencies** L2 Transparency B15: Outline L2 Section Reading Support Transparency MT 54	**Medieval Times to Today Transparencies** L1 Color Transparency MT 14: South Asia: Physical-Political ELL, LPR, SN **Teacher's Edition** L1 For Less Proficient Readers, TE p. 20 L3 For Advanced Readers, TE p. 22 L1 For Special Needs Students, TE p. 22 L3 For Gifted and Talented, TE p. 24 **Spanish Support** L2 Guided Reading and Review (Spanish), p. 6 ELL **PHSchool.com** L3 **For:** Long-Term Integrated Project: Building Models of Housing Around the World **Web Code:** lgd-8104

Assess and Reteach	Instructional Resources	Differentiated Instruction
Assess Progress Evaluate student comprehension with the section assessment and section quiz. **Reteach** Assign the Reading and Vocabulary Study Guide to help struggling students. **Extend** Extend the lesson by assigning an Enrichment activity.	**All in One Medieval Times to Today Teaching Resources** L2 Section Quiz, p. 115 L3 Enrichment, p. 124 Rubric for Assessing a Writing Assignment, p. 134 **Reading and Vocabulary Study Guide** L1 Chapter 1, Section 2, pp. 9–11	**Spanish Support** L2 Section Quiz (Spanish), p. 7 ELL

Key
L1 Basic to Average   L3 Average to Advanced   LPR Less Proficient Readers   GT Gifted and Talented
L2 For All Students   AR Advanced Readers   ELL English Language Learners
                                         SN Special Needs Students

Section 3 The Golden Age of Muslim Civilization

 4 periods, 2 blocks (includes Chapter Review and Assessment)

Social Studies Objectives
1. Find out how the religion of Islam spread.
2. Learn about the golden age of Islam under the rule of the caliphs.

Reading/Language Arts Objective
Preview and ask questions to help understand or remember important parts of the text.

Prepare to Read

Build Background Knowledge
Use a concept web to list words and ideas that relate to the term "Golden Age."

Set a Purpose for Reading
Have students evaluate statements on the *Reading Readiness Guide.*

Preview Key Terms
Teach the section's Key Terms.

Target Reading Skill
Introduce the section's Target Reading Skill of **previewing and asking questions.**

Instructional Resources
All in One Medieval Times to Today Teaching Resources
- **L2** Reading Readiness Guide, p. 117
- **L2** Preview and Ask Questions, p. 122

Differentiated Instruction
Spanish Reading and Vocabulary Study Guide
- **L1** Chapter 1, Section 3, pp. 11–12 ELL

Instruct

The Spread of Islam
Discuss the success of Islam.

Target Reading Skill
Review **previewing and asking questions.**

The Golden Age
Discuss how the caliphs and Muslim attitudes contributed to the advancements of the Golden Age.

Instructional Resources
All in One Medieval Times to Today Teaching Resources
- **L2** Guided Reading and Review, p. 118
- **L2** Reading Readiness Guide, p. 117

Medieval Times to Today Transparencies
- **L1** Transparency B2: Timeline
- **L2** Section Reading Support Transparency MT 55

Differentiated Instruction
Medieval Times to Today Transparencies
- **L3** Color Transparency MT Set 1: Spread of Islam AR, GT

Teacher's Edition
- **L3** For Gifted and Talented, TE p. 28
- **L1** For Special Needs Students, TE p. 29

Student Edition on Audio CD
- **L1** Chapter 1, Section 3 ELL, LPR, SN

Spanish Support
- **L2** Guided Reading and Review (Spanish), p. 8 ELL

Assess and Reteach

Assess Progress
Evaluate student comprehension with the section assessment and section quiz.

Reteach
Assign the Reading and Vocabulary Study Guide to help struggling students.

Extend
Extend the lesson by assigning a literature reading.

Instructional Resources
All in One Medieval Times to Today Teaching Resources
- **L2** Section Quiz, p. 119
- **L3** The King's Wealth, pp. 131–132
  Rubric for Assessing a Newspaper Article, p. 135
- **L2** Word Knowledge, p. 123
- **L2** Vocabulary Development, p. 133
- **L2** Chapter Tests A and B, pp. 136–141

Reading and Vocabulary Study Guide
- **L1** Chapter 1, Section 3, pp. 12–14

Differentiated Instruction
Spanish Support
- **L2** Section Quiz (Spanish), p. 9 ELL
- **L2** Chapter Summary (Spanish), p. 10 ELL
- **L2** Vocabulary Development (Spanish), p. 11 ELL

Key
- **L1** Basic to Average
- **L3** Average to Advanced
- **L2** For All Students

- **LPR** Less Proficient Readers
- **AR** Advanced Readers
- **SN** Special Needs Students

- **GT** Gifted and Talented
- **ELL** English Language Learners

Reading Background

Previewing and Prereading

This chapter's Target Reading Skill asks students to preview each section and set a purpose for reading. Students who do a brief, preliminary reading of complex material are in a strategic position to take control of their learning and comprehension. Previewing helps students consider what they already know about a topic they will be studying and gives some idea of what a text selection is about before they read it. Previewing also helps students identify the text structure and develop a mental framework for ideas to be encountered in the text. This can help them in formulating a more realistic reading and study plan.

Follow the steps below to teach students how to preview and preread.

1. Tell students that previewing will help them identify the text structure and develop a mental outline of ideas they will encounter in the text.

2. List the various text features you will be previewing in the order in which you would like students to examine them: section title, text headings, introduction, list of Key Terms, questions or tasks in the reading selection, photographs, drawings, maps, charts and other visuals in the text. Focus students' attention on some of these items, or ask them to look at all of them.

3. Prompt students to reflect after examining various text features. They may ask themselves questions such as: What is this reading selection about? What are some key words I will learn? How should I tackle this reading and divide up the task?

Applying New Words Outside the Classroom

Tell students that the vocabulary words in Chapter 1, such as *Muslim, mosque,* and *revealed,* often appear in books, newspapers, magazines, and on television. Challenge students to find real-life uses of at least three Key Terms or high-use words from the chapter. As "evidence," have students bring in a newspaper clipping with the word or write down the sentence in which the word was used during a radio or television broadcast, and include the time and date of the broadcast.

World Studies Background

Hagia Sophia

Hagia Sophia, built in Constantinople under the direction of Emperor Justinian, was the first monument with a central dome supported by pendentives, a device that enables a circular dome to be built above a square room. Originally a church, Hagia Sophia became a mosque after the Turks conquered the city in 1453. Today it is a museum and a lasting tribute to the achievements of Byzantine architecture.

Hadith

After the Quran, the most important document in Islam is Hadith, the recorded sayings and experiences of the prophet Muhammad, which together form a sort of biography. The role of Hadith in Islam is to provide authoritative rules and examples for Islamic religious and moral behavior.

Islamic Art

Although not stated in the Quran, by the mid-eighth century a formal prohibition had been made against depictions of living things—humans or animals—in Islamic art. This restriction is thought to be based on the idea that only God was believed to create life and that images of living things could become a focus for idolatry, or the worship of images other than God.

Infoplease® provides a wealth of useful information for the classroom. You can use this resource to strengthen your background on the subjects covered in this chapter. Have students visit this advertising-free site as a starting point for projects requiring research.

Use Web code **lgd-8100** for **Infoplease®**.

Guiding Questions

Remind students about the Guiding Questions introduced at the beginning of the book.

Section 1 relates to **Guiding Question** ❹ **What types of government were formed in these societies?** *(Constantine became the first Christian ruler of the Roman Empire. He moved the imperial capital to Byzantium which was renamed Constantinople. Later, Justinian, one of the greatest Byzantine emperors, collected and summarized centuries of Roman laws to form Justinian's Code. Justinian's Code became the basis for the legal systems of most modern European countries.)*

Section 2 relates to **Guiding Question** ❷ **How did each society's belief system affect its history?** *(Muhammad was the founder of the religion of Islam and became its prophet. His followers became known as Muslims. In 656, Islam split into two groups, Shiites and Sunnis.)*

Section 3 relates to **Guiding Question** ❸ **What was the pattern of day-to-day life in these societies?** *(After Muhammad's death, Islam spread west. From about 800 to 110 there was a golden age of Muslim culture. Traders from all over the world brought goods to the caliph's court at Baghdad. The work of Muslim mathematicians enabled later scientists to make discoveries in astronomy, physics, and chemistry, and Muslim writers created lasting works of literature.)*

⟲ Target Reading Skill

In this chapter, students will learn and apply the reading skill of previewing. Use the following worksheets to help students practice this skill:

All in One Medieval Times to Today Teaching Resources, *Preview and Set a Purpose,* p. 120; *Preview and Predict,* p. 121; *Preview and Ask Questions,* p. 122

Differentiated Instruction

The following Teacher Edition strategies are suitable for students of varying abilities.

Advanced Readers, pp. 14, 22
English Language Learners, p. 14
Gifted and Talented pp. 12, 24, 28
Less Proficient Readers, pp. 12, 20
Special Needs Students, pp. 17, 22, 29

Chapter 1

Byzantine and Muslim Civilizations

Chapter Preview

This chapter will introduce you to the Byzantine Empire, the religion of Islam, and the golden age of Muslim civilization.

Section 1
The Byzantine Empire

Section 2
The Beginnings of Islam

Section 3
The Golden Age of Muslim Civilization

⟲ Target Reading Skill

Reading Process In this chapter you will focus on the reading process by using previewing to help you understand and remember what you read.

▶ **Interior of a Byzantine church in present-day Turkey**

Bibliography

For the Teacher
Armstrong, Karen. *Islam: A Short History.* Modern Library, 2002.
Evans, James Allan. *The Empress Theodora: Partner of Justinian.* University of Texas Press, 2002.
Mango, Cyril A. *The Oxford History of Byzantium.* Oxford Press, 2003.

For the Student
L1 Demi, Margaret K. *Muhammad.* McElderry, 2003.
L2 Macaulay, David. *Mosque.* Houghton Mifflin/Walter Lorraine Books, 2003.
L3 Barrett, Tracy. *Anna of Byzantium.* Laurel Leaf, 2000.

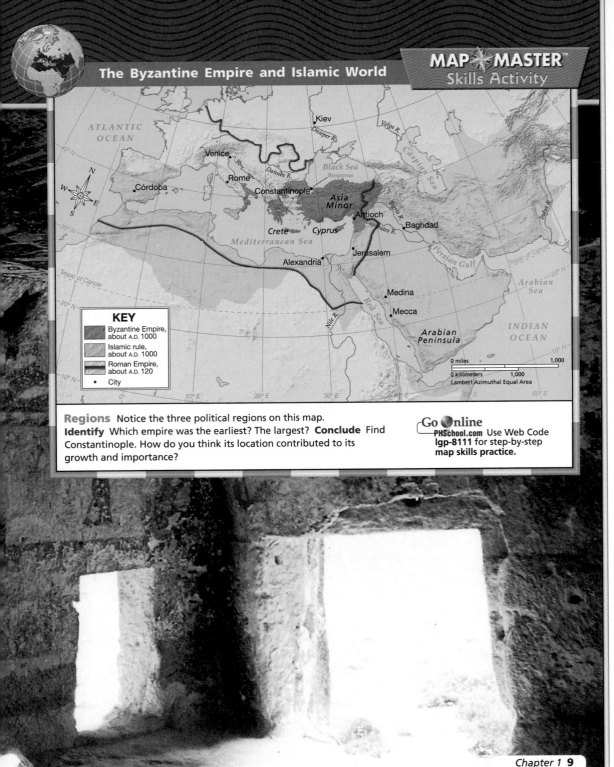

The Byzantine Empire and Islamic World

MAP★MASTER™
Skills Activity

KEY

Byzantine Empire, about A.D. 1000

Islamic rule, about A.D. 1000

Roman Empire, about A.D. 120

• City

Regions Notice the three political regions on this map.
Identify Which empire was the earliest? The largest? **Conclude** Find Constantinople. How do you think its location contributed to its growth and importance?

Go Online
PHSchool.com Use Web Code lgp-8111 for step-by-step map skills practice.

MAP★MASTER™
Skills Activity

■ Tell students to look at the map and use their fingers to trace the borders of each empire. Ask them to name the empires in order of size, from smallest to largest.

■ On the board, list all of the cities found on the map. Working in pairs, have students identify which empire or empires these cities were a part of. Then have students make a table with the information.

Using the Visual ▢L2

Reach Into Your Background Draw students' attention to the photo and its caption on pp. 8–9. Ask them to describe the church. *(It is made of stone, and decorated with carvings and paintings.)* How does this church compare with other buildings of worship they have seen? Conduct an Idea Wave (TE, p. T35) to elicit student responses.

Answers

MAP★MASTER™ **Identify** the Roman Empire; Islamic rule **Conclude** Its location on the Bosporus, between the Black Sea and Mediterranean Sea, meant that many people would have traveled through the city, eventually causing it to grow and become important.

Chapter Resources

Teaching Resources
Letter Home, p. 107
▢L2 Vocabulary Development, p. 133
▢L2 Skills for Life, p. 125
▢L2 Chapter Tests A and B, pp. 136–141

Spanish Support
Spanish Letter Home, p. 3
▢L2 Spanish Chapter Summary, p. 10
▢L2 Spanish Vocabulary Development, p. 11

Media and Technology
▢L1 Student Edition on Audio CD
▢L1 Guided Reading Audiotapes, English and Spanish
▢L2 Social Studies Skills Tutor CD-ROM
Exam*View*® **Test Bank CD-ROM**

Discovery World Studies
CHANNEL Video Program
SCHOOL

interactive Textbook

PRENTICE HALL
TeacherEXPRESS™
Plan • Teach • Assess

Section 1
Step-by-Step Instruction

Objectives

Social Studies
1. Find out how Constantinople and the Byzantine Empire grew powerful.
2. Discover the achievements of the Age of Justinian.
3. Learn about the later years of the Byzantine Empire.

Reading/Language Arts
Learn how to preview and set a purpose for reading.

Prepare to Read

Build Background Knowledge `L2`

Tell students that they will start their study of the Byzantine Empire by learning about the capital city of Constantinople. Show *Constantinople: Capital of the Byzantine Empire*. As students watch the video, ask them to write down details about the city that contributed to its success. Then conduct an Idea Wave (TE, p. T35) to have students share their responses.

Constantinople: Capital of the Byzantine Empire, **World Studies Video Program**

Set a Purpose for Reading `L2`
- Preview the Objectives.

- Read each statement in the *Reading Readiness Guide* aloud. Ask students to mark the statements true or false.

  All in One Medieval Times to Today Teaching Resources, *Reading Readiness Guide,* p. 109

- Have students discuss the statements in pairs or groups of four, then mark their worksheets again. Use the Numbered Heads participation strategy (TE, p. T36) to call on students to share their group's perspectives.

Vocabulary Builder
Preview Key Terms `L2`
Pronounce each Key Term, and then ask students to say the word with you. Provide a simple explanation such as, "A schism occurs when a group splits, or breaks away, from its main group."

Section 1
The Byzantine Empire

Prepare to Read

Objectives
In this section you will
1. Find out how Constantinople and the Byzantine Empire became powerful.
2. Discover the achievements of the Age of Justinian.
3. Learn about the later years of the Byzantine Empire.

Taking Notes
As you read this section, take notes about the Byzantine Empire's capital and rulers. Copy the concept web below and record your data in it.

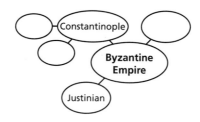

Target Reading Skill
Preview and Set a Purpose When you set a purpose for reading, you give yourself a focus. Before you read this section, look at the headings, photos, and illustrations to see what the section is about. Then set a purpose for reading, such as finding out about the city of Constantinople or the Byzantine Empire. Now read to meet your purpose.

Key Terms
- **Constantinople** (kahn stan tuh NOH pul) *n.* the capital of the eastern Roman Empire and later of the Byzantine Empire
- **Constantine** (KAHN stun teen) *n.* an emperor of the Roman Empire and the founder of Constantinople
- **Justinian** (jus TIN ee un) *n.* one of the greatest Byzantine emperors
- **Justinian's Code** (jus TIN ee unz kohd) *n.* an organized collection and explanation of Roman laws for use by the Byzantine Empire
- **schism** (SIZ um) *n.* a split, particularly in a church or religion

Greek fire being used in battle, as shown in a Byzantine manuscript

Prince Igor (EE gawr) of Kiev, which was then an important city in Russia, watched as a large force of his warships sailed across the Black Sea in A.D. 941. The prince was sure that **Constantinople**, capital of the Byzantine (BIZ un teen) Empire, would soon be his.

As his fleet drew close to the city, the prince's excitement turned to horror. Byzantine ships shot "Greek fire" at the invaders. Anything this "fire" touched burst into flames. Soon, most of Igor's fleet was ablaze. Water could not put out the flames.

Greek fire was made from a formula so secret that it was never written down. Even today, no one knows exactly how it was made, except that it contained petroleum. But this deadly weapon gave the Byzantines tremendous power throughout the Mediterranean area.

Target Reading Skill `L2`

Preview and Set a Purpose Point out the Target Reading Skill. Tell students that previewing the text helps them see what the text will be about, and setting a purpose helps give them a focus while reading.

Model previewing and setting a purpose by thinking aloud: "Previewing this section tells me that the text will be about the history of the Byzantine Empire and its rulers. My purpose for reading will be to find out who these rulers were and what contributions they made to the empire."

Give students *Preview and Set a Purpose*. Have them complete the activity in their groups.

All in One Medieval Times to Today Teaching Resources, *Preview and Set a Purpose,* p. 120

Constantinople at a Crossroads

At its height, the ancient Roman Empire controlled the lands surrounding the Mediterranean Sea. It also ruled parts of northern Europe and the region we now call the Middle East. In the centuries after Rome's power faded, these lands went through a tug of war. Two groups—the Christian Byzantines and the Muslim Arabs and Turks—developed powerful civilizations at this time. These two groups sometimes shared control and sometimes fought over the region.

Constantine and His Capital The emperor **Constantine** began his rule of the enormous Roman Empire in A.D. 306. His reign was marked by two important changes. First, Constantine became a Christian and stopped the persecution of Christians in the empire. Second, after 20 years of ruling from the city of Rome, Constantine decided to build a new imperial capital.

Constantine chose Byzantium, an ancient city founded by the Greeks, at the eastern end of the empire. He spared no expense building and fortifying his capital. In A.D. 330, Byzantium was renamed Constantinople (kahn stan tuh NOH pul), the "city of Constantine." By the early 500s, Constantinople had large markets, forums or public squares, paved roads, a cathedral, a palace, public baths, and a hippodrome or circus. An estimated half a million people lived there. Although the name of their city had changed, the people who lived there were still called Byzantines.

Fortress City
Notice the walls that protect Constantinople in the medieval painting and in the diagram of the city. The photo shows ruins of a city wall. **Infer** *Why would the aqueduct, which carried water, and the cisterns, which stored water, also be important if the city were attacked?*

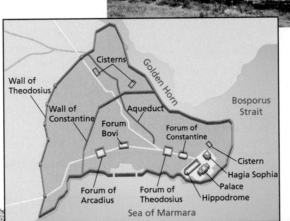

Chapter 1 Section 1 **11**

Vocabulary Builder

Use the information below to teach students this section's high-use words.

High-Use Word	Definition and Sample Sentence
reign, p. 11	*n.* period of power of a ruler During the **reign** of Constantine, the Roman capital moved to Byzantium.
imperial, p. 11	*adj.* of or related to an empire The emperor and his family lived in the **imperial** palace.
distinct, p. 14	*adj.* not alike; different The two sweaters had **distinct** styles.
regain, p. 14	*v.* to have again After resting for a while, she **regained** some of her strength.

Instruct

Constantinople at a Crossroads L2

Guided Instruction

■ **Vocabulary Builder** Clarify the high-use words **reign** and **imperial** before reading.

■ Have students read Constantinople at a Crossroads using the Structured Silent Reading strategy (TE, p. T34).

■ Ask students **What two important changes occurred during the reign of Constantine?** *(Constantine became the first Christian ruler of the Roman Empire, and he moved the imperial capital to Byzantium and renamed it Constantinople.)*

■ Have students draw a conclusion about why Constantine built his new capital at Byzantium. *(Possible answer: Constantine may have felt that the empire's center of wealth and power lay in the east. He was probably also attracted by Byzantium's location at a crossroads of trade routes.)*

Answer

Infer It would be important to protect them against attackers because the people in the city would need the water to survive.

Show students *Constantinople: Capital of the Byzantine Empire.* Ask **What was one of the disadvantages of Constantinople's location along east-west trade routes?** *(It became a constant target for invaders.)*

Guided Instruction (continued)

- Discuss with students how and why Constantinople became such a powerful city. *(The city was located right at a crossroads of major land and sea trade routes. Duties on trade goods gave the city great wealth, and the diversity of people and ideas that entered the city made it an international center of trade and culture.)*

- Ask students **What factors contributed to the fall of the western Roman Empire?** *(By A.D. 350 the western Roman Empire was already in decline; Roman armies had difficulty holding back invaders from Europe; Germanic groups were coming closer to Rome.)*

Independent Practice

Have students create the Taking Notes graphic organizer on a blank piece of paper. Then have them fill in the ovals with information they have just learned.

Monitor Progress

As students fill in the graphic organizer, circulate and make sure that individuals are choosing the correct details. Provide assistance as needed.

Gold coin from Constantinople ▶

Justinian and His Court
This work of art is a mosaic made of ceramic tiles fitted closely together.
Analyze Images *How does the artist indicate that Justinian (center) is the most important person?*

12 Medieval Times to Today

The emperors who followed Constantine continued to rule from Constantinople, in the eastern part of the empire. Over time, the Roman Empire split in two. The eastern half was by far the stronger. One reason for its strength was military. The Byzantines had the strongest army in the region. Another reason for the Byzantines' strength was trade.

Trade Constantinople was built at a major crossroads of land and sea trade routes. Find it on the map on page 9. Notice that it is located on the Bosporus. The Bosporus is a strait, or narrow passage that links two bodies of water. It connects the Black Sea and the Sea of Marmara, which flows into the Mediterranean Sea. The Bosporus also links two continents, Europe and Asia.

Goods came to Constantinople from Kiev in the north, from Egypt in the south, and across Central Asia from as far away as China. The Byzantines charged taxes on all goods that went through the city. The diverse people, goods, and ideas that poured into Constantinople made it a major center of international trade. And over time, the Byzantine Empire grew rich.

The Fall of the Western Empire Meanwhile, by A.D. 350, the western Roman Empire was already in decline. Roman armies were having difficulty holding back invaders from Europe. Germanic groups were coming closer and closer to Rome itself. In 476, a Germanic leader ousted the emperor. Historians call that event the fall of the Roman Empire.

✔ **Reading Check** Why did Constantinople become rich and powerful?

The Age of Justinian

As Rome was falling to invaders, strong fortifications and an excellent army protected Constantinople. But these were not the city's only strengths. The early Byzantine Empire had many excellent rulers who were wise as well as popular. They encouraged education and made reforms to laws and government. This kind of leadership also contributed to the strength of their empire.

The Emperor Justinian One of the greatest Byzantine emperors was **Justinian** (jus TIN ee un), whose rule began in 527. Justinian was an energetic ruler who rarely gave up on a task until it was completed. He had been born into a poor family, and he listened to the ideas of all his subjects—whether they were wealthy nobles or poor peasants.

Answers

✔ **Reading Check** The city was located at a major crossroads of trade.

Analyze Images He is in the center of the painting, in front of the other people, and is wearing a jeweled crown.

Differentiated Instruction

For Gifted and Talented　　L3
Have students learn more about the art and architecture of Islam by assigning *Small Group Activity: Writing Articles About the Art of Islam.*

　All in One **Medieval Times to Today Teaching Resources,** *Small Group Activity: Writing Articles About the Art of Islam,* pp. 126–129

For Less Proficient Readers　　L1
If students are having trouble comprehending the concepts in this section, have them read the section in the Reading and Vocabulary Study Guide. This workbook provides basic-level instruction in an interactive format with questions and write-on lines.

　📖 Chapter 1, Section 1, **Medieval Times to Today Reading and Vocabulary Study Guide,** pp. 6–8

Justinian's Code One of Justinian's most lasting contributions was a system of laws. When he became emperor, the empire was using a disorganized system of old Roman laws. Some laws even contradicted others. It was difficult to make sense of them—or to enforce them. Justinian appointed a team to collect and summarize centuries of Roman laws. The result was **Justinian's Code,** an organized collection and explanation of Roman laws for use by the Byzantine Empire. Eventually, this code became the basis for the legal systems of most modern European countries.

Byzantine Culture In addition to preserving the principles of Roman law, Byzantine scholars also kept and copied the works of the ancient Greeks. At its peak, Byzantine civilization blended Greek, Roman, and Christian influences. Later, when the empire was in decline, scholars took the ancient manuscripts and their knowledge of the rich Byzantine culture to the newly powerful city-states of Italy. In Chapter 6 you will read how these influences helped to spark the Renaissance.

✓ **Reading Check** What cultures influenced Byzantine civilization?

Citizen Heroes ★

Empress Theodora
Theodora (thee uh DAWR uh), empress of the Byzantine Empire, came from humble beginnings. Her father was a bearkeeper at Constantinople's Hippodrome, or circus. Theodora's marriage to Justinian gave her great power. Many of Justinian's decisions were made with her advice. Theodora worked to improve women's rights, and helped change divorce laws to protect women.

Hagia Sophia
It took 10,000 workers five years to build the Hagia Sophia cathedral in Constantinople. Since the fall of the empire, it has been used as a mosque. **Infer** *Why do you think Justinian built such a majestic church?*

Chapter 1 Section 1 **13**

Target Reading Skill

Preview and Set a Purpose As a follow up, have students answer the Target Reading Skill question in the Student Edition. (*The paragraph gives information about the decline of the Byzantine Empire.*)

The Empire's Later Years

Guided Instruction

- **Vocabulary Builder** Clarify the high-use words **distinct** and **regain** before reading.

- Have students read The Empire's Later Years.

- Discuss with students the events that led to the decline of the Byzantine Empire. (*After the death of Justinian, a series of wars with neighboring enemies caused a decline in trade. Also, the splitting of the Christian church further weakened the empire.*)

- Ask students to list some of the differences that led to the schism in the Christian church in 1054. (*The Byzantine emperor outlawed the use of icons; the pope disagreed with this decision and banished the emperor from the church. Many Byzantines argued that the pope did not have authority over the emperor.*)

Independent Practice

Have students complete their graphic organizers.

Monitor Progress

- Show *Section Reading Support Transparency MT 53* and ask students to check their work individually. Go over key concepts and clarify key vocabulary as needed.

  Medieval Times to Today Transparencies, *Section Reading Support Transparency MT 53*

- Tell students to fill in the last column of the *Reading Readiness Guide*. Probe for what they learned that confirms or invalidates each statement.

  All in One Medieval Times to Today Teaching Resources, *Reading Readiness Guide,* p. 109

Answer

Identify Frame of Reference Viewing icons might have helped them feel a stronger connection to their religious beliefs.

Preview and Set a Purpose
If your purpose is to learn about the Byzantine Empire, how does the paragraph at the right help you meet your purpose?

The Importance of Icons
This icon shows the Virgin Mary and the baby Jesus. The ban on icons was finally lifted in A.D. 843, and they are important in Eastern Orthodox Christianity to this day. **Identify Frame of Reference** *Why might medieval Christians have valued icons?*

14 Medieval Times to Today

The Empire's Later Years

After Justinian's death in 565, the Byzantine Empire began to decline. Later emperors had to fight wars against many neighboring enemies—including Persians and Turks to the east, Arabs to the south, and Germanic peoples to the north and west. The Byzantine Empire was shrinking in both size and power. As the Byzantines struggled to keep nearby enemies from invading Constantinople, religious and political arguments were weakening the empire from within.

A Religious Dispute Although most Byzantines were Christians, they did not practice Christianity the same way as the people in Western Europe did. Byzantine Christians rejected the authority of the pope, the leader of the church in Rome. The Byzantine emperor had to approve the choice of the patriarch, or highest church official in Constantinople. Greek was the language of the Byzantine church, while Latin was the language of the Roman church. The two branches of Christianity began to grow apart.

At that time, many Christians prayed to saints or holy people, represented by icons, or paintings of these people. In the 700s, a Byzantine emperor outlawed the use of icons, saying that they violated God's commandments. The pope disagreed, and banished the emperor from the church.

Byzantines felt that the pope did not have the authority to banish the emperor from the church. These disputes led to a schism, or split, in the Christian church in 1054. Now there were two distinct forms of Christianity: the Roman Catholic Church in the west and the Eastern (Greek) Orthodox Church in the east.

A Second Golden Age From about 900 until the mid-1000s, the Byzantine Empire experienced a final period of greatness. Trade increased and merchants came to Constantinople from as far away as Venice and Russia. Once again the population of the city grew in size and diversity.

As the economy grew in strength, so did the government. The long reign of Basil II—from 976 until 1025—was the most exceptional period of Byzantine history since the rule of Justinian. The empire regained some of the land it had lost. There was a burst of creativity in the arts.

Differentiated Instruction

For English Language Learners L1
To help students with unfamiliar vocabulary, ask them to preview the section before they read and choose five to seven words that are unfamiliar to them. Have students write each word with its part of speech and definition, and then write a sentence using the word correctly. Partner them with native English speakers to review their sentences.

For Advanced Readers L3
Encourage students to do research to learn more about Justinian's wife, Theodora. As a starting point, have students read the primary source *Byzantine Empress Theodora*.

All in One Medieval Times to Today Teaching Resources, *Byzantine Empress Theodora,* p. 130

The Fall of Constantinople During the 1000s, however, Muslim peoples to the east were also gaining power. By the late 1100s, Turks had taken the inland areas of Asia Minor away from the weakening Byzantine Empire.

The Byzantines were also threatened by Europeans. In 1171, disagreements over trade led to a war with Venice. And in the early 1200s, Constantinople was attacked by Christian crusaders. Western Christians ruled the city for 50 years. In 1261, the Byzantines regained their capital, but little was left of their empire.

In 1453, a force of about 70,000 Turks surrounded Constantinople. They came both by sea and by land, and they brought cannons to attack the city's walls. The defending force, which numbered about 7,000, held out for two months. Then the Byzantine capital—which had been a defensive fortress for more than 1,000 years—finally fell.

However, like Constantine before them, the new rulers would rebuild the city and make it an imperial capital. Renamed Istanbul, the city at the crossroads became a great center of Muslim culture and the capital of the Ottoman Empire.

✔ **Reading Check** Why did Constantinople finally fall?

The Turks Take Constantinople
The Turks dragged some of their ships overland and launched them into Constantinople's harbor. **Synthesize** *From what you know about the city's fortifications, why was this a good strategy?*

Section 1 Assessment

Key Terms
Review the key terms at the beginning of this section. Use each term in a sentence that explains its meaning.

🎯 Target Reading Skill
What was your purpose for reading this section? Did you accomplish it? If not, what might have been a better purpose?

Comprehension and Critical Thinking
1. **(a) Locate** Where was Constantinople located?

(b) Identify Effects How did its location contribute to its growth and to the strength of the Byzantine Empire?
2. **(a) Recall** What qualities made Justinian a good and successful ruler?
(b) Draw Conclusions Why was Justinian's Code so important?
3. **(a) Explain** What was the dispute that split the medieval Christian church?
(b) Draw Conclusions Why might that split have weakened the empire?

Writing Activity
Write a letter to a friend or family member from the point of view of a foreign merchant traveling to Constantinople during the reign of Justinian. Describe the city and its location as well as what you have heard about the emperor.

Go Online PHSchool.com
For: An activity on the Byzantines
Visit: PHSchool.com
Web Code: lgd-8101

Chapter 1 Section 1 **15**

Objective

Learn how to transfer information from one medium to another by using a table to write a paragraph.

Prepare to Read

Build Background Knowledge [L2]

Explain to students that the skill Using a Table to Write a Paragraph is an example of transferring information from one medium to another, or taking information presented one way and expressing it another way that better suits your purpose. Using the Idea Wave participation strategy (TE, p. T35), have students think of situations where they would use this skill. (*Possible answers: writing a report, giving an oral presentation, creating a flow chart*)

Instruct

Using a Table to Write a Paragraph [L2]

Guided Instruction

- Read the steps to using a table to write a paragraph as a class and write them on the board.

- Practice the skill by following the steps on p. 16 as a class. Model each step in the activity: identify what the table is about (*The table contrasts the same data for Istanbul in the past and today.*); identify the headings (*Characteristic, Constantinople in A.D. 540, Istanbul Today, Importance, Population, Major Religion, Sources of Wealth, Language, Challenges*); look for similarities and differences in the data (*Similarities—largest city; faced challenges of overpopulation and earthquakes; Differences—population is larger today, major religion is Islam rather than Christianity, sources of wealth are textiles, manufacturing and tourism rather than trade, people speak Turkish rather than Greek, and the challenges of disease and attack by foreigners have been replaced by pollution*); analyze the most important information, and state the conclusions. (*The differences seem more important. Possible conclusion: Although Istanbul*

Skills for Life
Using a Table to Write a Paragraph

Mr. Perez's students have just finished studying the Byzantine Empire. Now they are studying modern Turkey, which occupies some of the same land. They have learned that Istanbul is the modern name of Constantinople. Mr. Perez has asked the students to use a table of information about Istanbul and Constantinople to write a paragraph that compares the two cities.

Byzantine cup

Information—words or numbers—presented in graphs, charts, or tables is called data. When you use this type of data to write a paragraph, you are transferring information from one medium to another.

Learn the Skill

Follow these steps to write a paragraph based on data from a table.

1 **Identify the topic of the table.** First read the title. Then look at the table to get a general idea of its purpose.

2 **Identify the key pieces of information.** Headings tell the main topics. Read both across and down to understand how the data relate to the headings.

Modern Istanbul

3 **Look for similarities and differences in data.** The columns of a table often compare and contrast information.

4 **Analyze the meaning of the information.** What information seems most important? List several conclusions you can draw from the data.

5 **Write a paragraph that states and supports your conclusions.** Your main conclusion can be your topic sentence. Support it with examples from the data.

16 Medieval Times to Today

---

today has some similarity to Constantinople in A.D. 540, the city has changed greatly, particularly its size, culture, and economic activities.)

Independent Practice

Assign *Skills for Life* and have students complete it individually.

All in One **Medieval Times to Today Teaching Resources,** *Skills for Life,* p. 125

Monitor Progress

As students are completing *Skills for Life,* circulate to make sure individuals are applying the skill steps effectively. Provide assistance as needed.

Istanbul Past and Present

Characteristic	Constantinople in A.D. 540	Istanbul Today
Importance	Capital of Byzantine Empire, largest city in Byzantine Empire	Turkey's largest city
Population	About 500,000	About 10 million
Major Religion	Christianity	Islam
Sources of Wealth	Trade	Textiles, manufacturing, tourism
Language	Greek	Turkish
Challenges	Overpopulation, disease, earthquakes, attacks by foreigners	Overpopulation, earthquakes, pollution

Practice the Skill

Use the steps in Learn the Skill to transfer the information in the table above into a paragraph.

1 What is the title of the table? In your own words, state what the table is about.

2 What are the important headings? How do you find key information, such as the major religion of present-day Istanbul?

3 Note how Istanbul is similar to Constantinople and how it is different.

4 Which headings or topics represent the most important information? Are the similarities or the differences more important?

5 What is the most important thing you've learned about the two cities? Use your conclusion as the topic sentence, and support it with data from the table.

Apply the Skill

Study the table at the right, and draw a conclusion about the information in it. Write a paragraph that uses data from the table to support your conclusion.

The Christian Church Divides, A.D. 1054

Characteristic	Eastern Orthodox	Roman Catholic
Head of Church	Patriarch	Pope
Had Most Power Over Church	Emperor	Pope
Main Location	Eastern Europe	Western Europe
Language	Greek	Latin
Practices	• Priests could marry • Pope's authority was not recognized	• Priests could not marry • Pope had supreme authority

Differentiated Instruction

For Special Needs Students **L1**

Partner special needs students with more proficient readers to do Level 1 of the Transferring Information from One Medium to Another lesson on the Social Studies Skill Tutor CD-ROM together.

When students feel more confident, they can move on to Level 2 alone.

Transferring Information from One Medium to Another, **Social Studies Skill Tutor CD-ROM**

Assess and Reteach

Assess Progress **L2**

Ask students to do the Apply the Skill activity.

Reteach **L1**

If students are having trouble applying the skill steps, have them review the skill using the interactive Social Studies Skills Tutor CD-ROM.

Transferring Information from One Medium to Another, **Social Studies Skills Tutor CD-ROM**

Extend **L3**

Have students read pp. 28–30, beginning with the text under the heading The Golden Age. Working in pairs, have students create a table with information about the achievements of the Golden Age. Tables should include information about achievements in mathematics, science, and literature. Tell students to also include the key figures involved in these achievements in their tables.

Answers
Apply the Skill

Answers will vary, but students should draw a conclusion about the information in the table, and their paragraphs should include data from the table that supports their conclusions. *(Possible conclusion: There are major differences between the Eastern Orthodox and the Roman Catholic churches.)*

Section 2
Step-by-Step Instruction

Objectives

Social Studies

1. Learn about the Arabian Peninsula, its nomadic people, and its centers of trade.
2. Find out about the life and mission of the Muslim prophet Muhammad.
3. Learn about Muslim beliefs.

Reading/Language Arts

Preview and make predictions about the text to help set a purpose for reading.

Prepare to Read

Build Background Knowledge ◻L2

Explain to students that in this section they will learn about the religion of Islam. Ask students to preview the section with this question in mind: **What are the beliefs of Islam and how did the religion start?** Conduct a Give One, Get One participation strategy (TE, p. T37) to elicit responses and record them on the board. Then ask students to write one question that they hope to be able to answer after they have read the section. Be sure to revisit students' questions when reading is complete.

Set a Purpose for Reading ◻L2

- Preview the Objectives.

- Read each statement in the *Reading Readiness Guide* aloud. Ask students to mark the statements true or false.

  All in One **Medieval Times to Today Teaching Resources,** *Reading Readiness Guide,* p. 113

- Have students discuss the statements in pairs or groups of four, then mark their worksheets again. Use the Numbered Heads participation strategy (TE, p. T36) to call on students to share their group's perspectives.

Vocabulary Builder
Preview Key Terms ◻L2

Pronounce each Key Term, and then ask students to say the word with you. Provide a simple explanation such as, "Many Muslims say their daily prayers in a mosque."

Section 2 The Beginnings of Islam

Prepare to Read

Objectives

In this section you will
1. Learn about the Arabian Peninsula, its nomadic people, and its centers of trade.
2. Find out about the life and mission of the Muslim prophet Muhammad.
3. Learn about Muslim beliefs.

Taking Notes

As you read this section, keep track of the most important ideas about the beginnings of Islam. Copy the outline started below, and add to it as you read.

```
I. The Arabian Peninsula
   A. Nomadic Bedouins
      1.
      2.
   B. Mecca: A center of trade
```

🎯 Target Reading Skill

Preview and Predict Making predictions about your text helps you set a purpose for reading and remember what you read. Before you begin, look at the headings, photos, and anything else that stands out. Then predict what the text might be about. For example, you might predict that this section will tell about the origins of Muslim beliefs. As you read, if what you learn doesn't support your prediction, revise your prediction.

Key Terms

- **Muhammad** (muh HAM ud) *n.* the prophet and founder of Islam
- **nomads** (NOH madz) *n.* people with no permanent home, who move from place to place in search of food, water, or pasture
- **caravan** (KA ruh van) *n.* a group of traders traveling together for safety
- **Mecca** (MEK uh) *n.* an Arabian trading center and Muhammad's birthplace
- **Muslim** (MUZ lum) *n.* a follower of Islam
- **mosque** (mahsk) *n.* a Muslim house of worship
- **Quran** (koo RAHN) *n.* the holy book of Islam

In this miniature painting, an angel's announcement is symbolized by the blowing of a horn.

The religion of Islam (IS lahm) teaches that in about 610, the prophet **Muhammad** (muh HAM ud) went into a cave in the Arabian mountains to pray. (A prophet is a person who is regarded as speaking for God.) It is said that while Muhammad was inside the cave, he heard the voice of an angel. God told Muhammad through the angel that there was only one God, that God had created people, and that God would teach His people. The angel told Muhammad that Muhammad was to be God's messenger.

According to Islamic teaching, Muhammad was frightened and unsure that he was worthy of such an important mission. But he obeyed. God continued to send Muhammad messages, which Muhammad shared with the people of the Arabian Peninsula. These teachings formed Islam, a religion that brought great changes to the region. And in the centuries after Muhammad's death, the new religion spread to many parts of the world.

🎯 Target Reading Skill ◻L2

Preview and Predict Point out the Target Reading Skill. Tell students that making predictions about the text they are about to read will help them set a purpose for reading and remember what they read.

Model previewing and predicting by thinking aloud, using the text on p. 19 under the heading The Arabian Peninsula. "From the headings, photos, and captions on these pages, I predict that I will learn about the geography, people, and one important city of the Arabian Peninsula."

Give students *Preview and Predict.* Have them complete the activity in their groups.

All in One **Medieval Times to Today Teaching Resources,** *Preview and Predict,* p. 121

The Arabian Peninsula

In Muhammad's time, as today, much of the Arabian Peninsula was covered by desert. Although surrounded by water, the peninsula has no major rivers and receives little rainfall. Trade with neighboring peoples supported the growth of towns along trade routes. And many groups of Bedouins (BED oo inz) made their homes among the shifting sand dunes of the desert.

Nomadic Bedouins The Bedouins were **nomads,** or people who have no permanent home but move from place to place in search of food, water, and pasture. The Arabian desert yielded little food for the Bedouins or for their herds of sheep, camels, and goats. Water was also scarce—for people as well as for animals.

To make their way across the desert, the Bedouins followed traditional routes from one oasis to another. An oasis is a green area within a desert, fed by underground water. These all-important oases provided plenty of water for the nomads and their animals.

Because of their knowledge of the desert and its oases, the Bedouins also worked as guides for traders. They helped traders travel across the desert in large groups called **caravans.** These desert caravans depended on camels, which carried both people and their goods. Camels are sturdy animals with a special ability to store water for long periods.

Bedouins Today
These Bedouins in the Sinai desert of Egypt are still nomads like their ancestors. **Predict** *What kinds of events and conditions might prevent the Bedouins from continuing their traditional way of life?*

Chapter 1 Section 2 **19**

The Prophet Muhammad L2

Guided Instruction

■ **Vocabulary Builder** Clarify the high-use word **abandon** before reading.

■ With students, read about how Muhammad founded the religion of Islam in The Prophet Muhammad.

■ Ask students **Who was Muhammad?** (*Muhammad was an Arab who was born in Mecca in about 570. He became the founder of the religion of Islam and its prophet.*)

■ Ask students **What happened to Muhammad in 622?** (*He and his followers were invited to Yathrib, now Medina, where he was regarded as a prophet. This movement was called the* hijra, *or "migration," and 622 became year 1 on the Muslim calendar.*)

■ Ask students **Based on what you have learned about Mecca, why do you think the religion of Islam spread so quickly?** (*Because Mecca was a busy trading center, religious ideas, as well as goods, could travel quickly and over great distances.*)

Independent Practice
Have students continue filling in their outlines with details about Muhammad's life.

Monitor Progress
As students continue to fill in their outlines, circulate to make sure they are placing details in the same order as they appear in the text. Provide assistance as necessary.

Answer

Links to Economics

New Business Methods
From 750 to 1350, Muslims like the Arab traders shown above dominated the trade routes in Arabia and far beyond. They not only found new goods to trade, they also developed new *ways* to trade. Muslim merchants bought and sold goods on credit and set up locations for exchanging currency. To avoid carrying large sums of cash across thousands of miles, they developed a way to transfer money from one location to another—a forerunner to today's checks. Merchants could deposit funds at one location and use a letter of credit to withdraw those funds at a different location.

Mecca: A Center of Trade The oases on the Arabian Peninsula became busy trading centers. One of the most important was Mecca (MEK uh). From Mecca, great caravans traveled northwest to markets in what is now Syria. From Syria, goods could be shipped across the Mediterranean Sea to Europe. Other caravans traveled northeast from Mecca. They made a dangerous journey across the desert to markets in the area now known as Iraq. Trade was also conducted with Yemen to the south. Precious goods traded along these routes included perfume and spices, incense, expensive cloth, elephant tusks, and gold.

✓ Reading Check Why did Bedouins make good guides for traders?

The Prophet Muhammad

Muhammad was born and grew up in the trading center of Mecca. His great-grandfather had been a wealthy merchant. However, by the time Muhammad was born in about 570, his family was poor. As a young man, Muhammad worked on caravans. His job took him to distant places, including Syria, which was then part of the Byzantine Empire.

Muhammad's Mission Muhammad liked to walk in the mountains outside Mecca. Troubled by problems he saw in society, he liked to be alone to pray and think. When Muhammad was 40 years old, he first heard God speak to him through the angel in the cave. God told him that people would submit to, or agree to obey, the one true God. In time, a person who accepted the teachings of Muhammad came to be known as a **Muslim** (MUZ lum), "a person who submits." The religion of Muslims is called Islam.

Muhammad preached God's message—that all people were brothers and sisters in a community established by God—but few people in Mecca listened. They thought Muhammad's teachings threatened their old gods. They feared that abandoning their old gods would end Mecca's importance as a religious center. Many Arabs traveled to Mecca in order to pray at an ancient shrine called the Kaaba (KAH buh). People in Mecca also feared that Muhammad might gain political power.

Differentiated Instruction

For Less Proficient Readers L1
Help students visualize the routes traveled by trade caravans from Mecca by displaying *Color Transparency MT 14: South Asia: Physical-Political.* Select students to come up and trace the routes with their fingers, identifying the physical features, countries, and cities along the way.

📖 **Medieval Times to Today Transparencies,** *Color Transparency MT 14: South Asia: Physical-Political*

Muhammad in Medina In 622, Muhammad and his followers were invited to Yathrib (yah THREEB), a city north of Mecca. The people there regarded Muhammad as a prophet. This movement of early Muslims is known as the hijra (hih JY ruh), or "the migration." The year of the hijra—622 in the calendar used in the United States—became year 1 on the Muslim calendar.

After the hijra, the name of Yathrib was changed to Medina. This name means "city" and is short for "city of the prophet." Medina quickly became an important Islamic center. But Islam did not remain limited to Medina. In 630, Muhammad returned to Mecca—this time in triumph. By the time Muhammad died two years later, the new religion of Islam had spread all across the Arabian Peninsula.

✓ **Reading Check** Why did Muhammad go to Yathrib?

Muslim Belief

A muezzin (myoo EZ in), a man who calls Muslims to worship, looks out over the city and begins his loud call. The muezzin's voice echoes in all directions: "There is no god but God, and Muhammad is the messenger of God." In Arabic, the word for God is *Allah*. Five times each day, Muslims are called to worship in this way. And five times a day, every faithful Muslim stops whatever he or she is doing to pray.

Some Muslims gather in a house of worship called a **mosque** (mahsk). Others kneel outside. Wherever Muslims are in the world—in the Arabian Peninsula, in North Africa, or in the United States—they kneel in a direction that faces toward Mecca. "There is no god but God," the faithful respond, "and Muhammad is the messenger of God."

The Five Pillars of Islam Basic Muslim beliefs are expressed in the Five Pillars of Islam. These practices, shown in the table above, are the foundations of Islam. Muslims regard these pillars as sacred duties. The fifth pillar—the hajj (haj), or pilgrimage to the Kaaba—is required only of those who are able to travel to Mecca.

The Five Pillars of Islam

Pillar	Description
Declaration of Faith	Muslims must regularly declare the belief that there is only one God and Muhammad is God's messenger.
Prayer	Muslims must pray five times each day, facing in the direction of the holy city of Mecca.
Almsgiving	Muslims must give alms, or money that goes to the needy.
Fasting	Muslims must fast during daylight hours in the month of Ramadan.
Pilgrimage	Muslims must make a pilgrimage to Mecca at least one time in their lives if they are able.

■ **Chart Skills**

The photo above shows Muslim men and boys worshiping at a mosque in Brunei, in Southeast Asia. **Identify** Which pillar of Islam are they fulfilling? **Analyze Information** Which one of the five pillars would it be most difficult to fulfill? Explain why.

Guided Instruction

■ **Vocabulary Builder** Clarify the high-use words **foundation** and **descendant** before reading.

■ With students, read Muslim Belief and have them study the chart. As students read, circulate to make sure they can answer the Reading Check question.

■ Have students describe some of the aspects of Muslim prayer. (*A muezzin calls Muslims to worship with the words "There is no god but God, and Muhammad is His prophet." Muslims pray five times a day, sometimes in a mosque, but always kneeling in the direction of Mecca.*)

■ Direct students' attention to the chart on this page and discuss the Five Pillars of Islam. Ask **What are they and what do they say?** (*The Five Pillars of Islam state the basic beliefs and practices of the religion. They include declaring the belief that there is only one God and Muhammad is God's messenger, praying five times a day in the direction of Mecca, giving money to the needy, fasting during the daylight hours in the month of Ramadan, and making at least one pilgrimage to Mecca if possible.*)

Background: Daily Life

Ramadan Ramadan, the ninth month on the Islamic calendar, is also one of the holiest months for Muslims. During Ramadan, Muslims recall the revealing of the Quran to Muhammad, and atone for their sins through fasting and prayer. All able adults and older children fast from sunrise to sunset, and pray often. In the mornings, before the sun rises, Muslims eat a meal called a *suhoor*. In the evenings, Muslims break their fast with an *iftar*, or festive meal. This meal includes many courses of different kinds of food, and is usually shared with friends or family. Ramadan officially ends when the new moon is sighted. The end of Ramadan is marked with a festival called *Id al-Fitr*. Muslims observe this three-day festival with feasting and celebration.

Answers

✓ **Reading Check** Muhammad and his followers were invited to go there by the people who regarded him as a prophet.

Chart Skills Identify prayer **Analyze Information** Answers will vary, but most students will probably identify the pilgrimage to Mecca as the most difficult of the five pillars to fulfill because it involves a long and expensive journey.

Guided Instruction (continued)

- Ask students: **What is the name of the holy book of Islam?** *(the Quran)* **How is it similar to holy books in other religions?** *(It contains many kinds of writings, including stories, promises, warnings, and instructions, similar to the Torah, or Jewish holy book, and the Christian Bible.)*

- Ask students **How did Islam change the status of women in Arab society?** *(Islam taught that men and women were spiritually equal and gave women more rights.)*

- Ask students **What caused the split in Islam after the assassination of Uthman in 656?** *(One group, the Shiites, believed that the leader of Islam should be a descendant of Muhammad and the other group, the Sunnis, believed that any truly religious Muslim could lead.)*

Independent Practice

Have students complete their outlines with details from the section.

Monitor Progress

- Show *Section Reading Support Transparency MT 54* and ask students to check their graphic organizers individually. Go over key concepts and clarify key vocabulary as needed.

  📖 **Medieval Times to Today Transparencies,** *Section Reading Support Transparency MT 54*

- Tell students to fill in the last column of the *Reading Readiness Guide.* Probe for what they learned that confirms or invalidates each statement.

  All In One Medieval Times to Today Teaching Resources, *Reading Readiness Guide,* p. 113

⤵ Target Reading Skill L2

Preview and Predict As a follow up, have students perform the Target Reading Skill activity in the Student Edition. *(Answers will vary, but students should determine if their prediction is on target, and if it is not, revise it accordingly.)*

Answer

Compare that the tradition is still alive and well—perhaps even more people follow it now

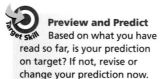

The Hajj
Muslims making a hajj to the Kaaba wear special white, seamless garments. The large photo shows a modern hajj. The small painting is from a 1410 manuscript. **Compare** *What can you conclude about this tradition by comparing the two pictures?*

🎯 **Preview and Predict** Based on what you have read so far, is your prediction on target? If not, revise or change your prediction now.

The Quran The holy book of Islam is called the **Quran** (koo RAHN). It contains the messages God revealed to Muhammad, including the rules of Islam. Many Muslims have memorized the Quran. Muslims believe that the meaning and beauty of the Quran are best appreciated in its original language. Therefore, many converts to Islam learn Arabic. This shared language has helped unite Muslims from many regions.

Like the Torah (TOH ruh), the Jewish holy book, and the Christian Bible, the Quran contains many kinds of writing, including stories, promises, warnings, and instructions. There is a reason for the similarity of the Quran to Jewish and Christian holy books. Muslims, like Jews and Christians, believe in one God. They regard Adam, Noah, Abraham, Moses, and Jesus as important people in their religious history. Muhammad saw himself as the last prophet in a long line of prophets that included all these men. Muhammad felt respect for Jews and Christians, whom he called "people of the Book."

The Role of Women Before Islam, in most of Arab society, women were not regarded as equal to men, and female children were not valued. The Quran, however, taught that men and women were spiritually equal. It also gave women more rights under the law, such as the right to inherit property and to get an education. Muslim women could not be forced to marry against their will, and they had the right to divorce.

22 Medieval Times to Today

Differentiated Instruction

For Advanced Readers L3
Working in pairs or groups, have students use the section content to create a time line that lists important dates in Muhammad's life and in the development of Islam. Encourage students to add maps to their time lines. You may wish to display students' work in the classroom.

For Special Needs Students L1
Have students read the Key Terms and their definitions, and then find each word in the text. Ask students to note how the context, or the surrounding text, helps them to better understand each word.

A Split Among Muslims You have already read about a schism that split the Christian church at the time of the Byzantine Empire. A schism, or split, also occurred among followers of Islam.

In 656, Uthman (OOTH mahn), the leader of the Muslim community, was assassinated. His death split the Muslim world in two. Muslims disagreed over who should be their rightful leader. Over the next several decades, two main groups gradually emerged on opposite sides of this disagreement.

The smaller group, called Shiites (SHEE yts), argued that the ruler should be a man who was a direct descendant of Muhammad. They believed that Muhammad's descendants would be inspired by God, just as Muhammad had been. They felt that their leader should explain the meanings of the messages Muhammad received from God, which are found in the Quran.

The larger group, called Sunnis (SOO neez), argued that any truly religious Muslim man of Muhammad's tribe could lead the community. They believed that no one man, not even the leader of Islam, should tell Muslims what God's messages meant. The Sunnis argued that a group of Muslim scholars could best explain the Quran. Today, about 85 percent of all Muslims are Sunnis.

✓ **Reading Check** What issues split the Shiites and Sunnis?

Illustrated manuscript pages from a 1500s Quran

Section 2 Assessment

Key Terms
Review the key terms at the beginning of this section. Use each term in a sentence that explains its meaning.

 Target Reading Skill
What did you predict about this section? How did your prediction guide your reading?

Comprehension and Critical Thinking
1. (a) **Note** What geographic feature covers most of the Arabian Peninsula?

(b) **Identify Effects** How did geography affect trade and settlement there?
(c) **Conclude** Why do you think the Bedouins became nomads?
2. (a) **Recall** What were the main events of Muhammad's life?
(b) **Synthesize** What are the main beliefs of Islam?
(c) **Compare and Contrast** What beliefs do Sunnis and Shiites share? Which beliefs separate them?

Writing Activity
Write a poem or a paragraph describing what it might have been like to travel in a caravan. How would it feel to ride a camel? To cross the desert? To stop for a rest at an oasis?

> **Writing Tip** Review the illustrations in this section. Then think about the sights, sounds, and smells you would expect to experience as part of caravan life. Use vivid descriptive words and phrases to describe what you see and feel.

Focus on Bedouin Life L2

Guided Instruction

- Ask students to read the text and study the art, photos, and captions on these pages.

- Ask students **What animals were important to the Bedouins and how were they used?** *(Camels provided transportation, milk, meat, hides and camel dung provided fuel for fires; the hair from goats was used to make tent panels, and goatskin was used to make bags to carry water.)*

- Have students describe some of the different responsibilities of Bedouin women and men. *(Women were responsible for making the tents and putting them up and taking them down at campsites; men herded camels and other livestock.)*

- As a class, answer the Assessment questions. Allow students to briefly discuss their responses with a partner before sharing their answers with the class.

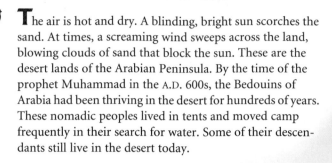

Focus On
Bedouin Life

The air is hot and dry. A blinding, bright sun scorches the sand. At times, a screaming wind sweeps across the land, blowing clouds of sand that block the sun. These are the desert lands of the Arabian Peninsula. By the time of the prophet Muhammad in the A.D. 600s, the Bedouins of Arabia had been thriving in the desert for hundreds of years. These nomadic peoples lived in tents and moved camp frequently in their search for water. Some of their descendants still live in the desert today.

Surviving in the Desert The ancient Bedouins depended upon the desert, the camel, their fellow tribe members, and the family tent. Plants gathered from the desert were used for food and medicine. Camels provided transportation, as well as milk, meat, and hides. Family members worked together to search for water and to herd their camels, goats, and sheep. The family tent sheltered the Bedouins in the harsh desert climate.

Women were responsible for the tents. They spun goats' hair into yarn to make the tent panels. When it was time to move their camp, the women took down the tents and then pitched them at the new campsite.

It was the men's job to herd camels and other livestock. Sometimes Bedouin men would raid villages or other tribes for goats, sheep, camels, and other goods.

The illustration at the right shows a Bedouin family in their tent. Bedouin women created jewelry, like the necklace shown at the top of this page.

Hospitality
Bedouin men served their guests thick, bitter coffee.

Goatskin Bag
Bags made from goatskin carried precious water.

Differentiated Instruction

For Gifted and Talented L3
Have students learn more about the way Bedouins live in the desert by completing the *Long Term Integrated Project: Building Models of Housing Around the World.* Assign students to work groups for the project.

Go Online
PHSchool.com
For: Long Term Integrated Project: *Building Models of Housing Around the World*
Visit: PHSchool.com
Web Code: lgd-8104

Bedouin Coffee Pot
The Bedouins served coffee from copper or brass pots.

Cooking
Fires were fueled by camel dung, twigs, and dry plants.

Water
Carried in goatskin bags, water came from oases and wells.

Assessment

Identify Name the four things the Bedouins depended upon most.

Analyze How did the Bedouins survive in the desert?

Independent Practice

Tell students to suppose they are a Bedouin boy or girl living in the desert of the Arabian Peninsula. Using the information from the text, art, photos, and captions on these pages, have students write a journal entry, describing what a typical day would be like. Tell students that they may also add drawings to their entries if they wish.

Answers

Assessment

Identify the desert, the camel, their fellow tribe members, the family tent
Analyze They gathered plants to use for food and medicine, raised camels, sheep and goats for a variety of uses, used tents to shelter them from the harsh climate, and obtained water from oases and wells.

Section 3
Step-by-Step Instruction

Objectives

Social Studies
1. Find out how the religion of Islam spread.
2. Learn about the golden age of Islam under the rule of the caliphs.

Reading/Language Arts
Preview and ask questions to help understand or remember important parts of the text.

Prepare to Read

Build Background Knowledge · L2
Explain that in this section students will learn about the development of Islam and the golden age of its culture. Ask students to quickly preview the headings and visuals in the section with this question in mind: **What aspects of a culture contribute to a "golden age?"** Draw a concept web on the board with "Golden Age" in the center. Conduct an Idea Wave (TE, p. T35) to generate ideas or words related to that term to fill in the concept web. Examples might include works of art or advances in science.

Set a Purpose for Reading · L2
- Preview the Objectives.
- Read each statement in the *Reading Readiness Guide* aloud. Ask students to mark the statements true or false.

  All in One Medieval Times to Today Teaching Resources, *Reading Readiness Guide,* p. 117

- Have students discuss the statements in pairs or groups of four, then mark their worksheets again. Use the Numbered Heads participation strategy (TE, p. T36) to call on students to share their group's perspectives.

Vocabulary Builder
Preview Key Terms · L2
Pronounce the Key Terms, and then ask students to say the words with you. Provide a simple explanation such as, "A caliph was a Muslim ruler, similar to a king."

Section 3

The Golden Age of Muslim Civilization

Prepare to Read

Objectives
In this section you will
1. Find out how the religion of Islam spread.
2. Learn about the golden age of Islam under the rule of the caliphs.

Taking Notes
As you read this section, jot down key events of early Muslim history and when they occurred. Copy the timeline below and use your data to complete it.

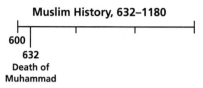

Muslim History, 632–1180

600 |

632
Death of Muhammad

Target Reading Skill
Preview and Ask Questions Before you read this section, preview the headings and illustrations to see what the section is about. Then write two questions that will help you understand or remember something important in the section. For example, you might ask, "How did Islam spread beyond the Arabian Peninsula?" Then read to answer your question.

Key Terms
- **Omar Khayyam** (OH mahr ky AHM) *n.* a Muslim poet, mathematician, and astronomer
- **caliph** (KAY lif) *n.* a Muslim ruler
- **Sufis** (SOO feez) *n.* a mystical Muslim group that believed they could draw closer to God through prayer, fasting, and a simple life

The cover of a book of verses by Omar Khayyam

Almost one thousand years ago, Persia boasted great scientists, mathematicians, and poets. One man was all three. **Omar Khayyam** (OH mahr ky AHM) was a skilled Muslim astronomer, one of the most famous mathematicians in the world, and a great poet. The poems he wrote in the Persian language are still read today. This is one of his poems:

> **When I was a child, I sometimes went to a teacher. And sometimes I taught myself, but eventually I learned The limits to all knowledge: we come into this world upon the waters, we leave it on the wind.**
>
> —Omar Khayyam

Although Khayyam writes of limits to knowledge, his was a time when mathematics, science, and poetry were all making new breakthroughs and expanding the boundaries of knowledge. It was called the golden age of Muslim civilization, and it took place across a wide geographic area.

Target Reading Skill · L2

Preview and Ask Questions Point out the Target Reading Skill. Tell students that previewing and asking questions about the text they are about to read will help them see what the section is about and understand and remember important ideas in the text.

Model previewing and asking questions using the text on pp. 28–30 under the heading The Golden Age. Think aloud: "Previewing the subheadings, photographs, and captions tell me that the text is about the golden age of Muslim culture. Two questions I can ask are: What was the golden age of Muslim culture? What were some Arab contributions to mathematics and science? I will read the text to answer these questions."

Give students *Preview and Ask Questions*. Have them complete the activity in their groups.

All in One Medieval Times to Today Teaching Resources, *Preview and Ask Questions,* p. 122

The Spread of Islam

Within 150 years after Muhammad's death in 632, Islam spread west to North Africa, and into present-day Spain. It also spread north into Persia and east to the borders of northern India and China.

Many New Converts Arab merchants traveled to many parts of Asia and North Africa and along the Mediterranean coast. Many of these traders were Muslims, and they helped to spread their new religious beliefs. Arab armies also conquered neighboring regions. This was another way that Islam spread.

In 717, the Arabs attacked Constantinople, but they were unable to take the great fortress. Even so, most Christians who lived along the eastern and southern Mediterranean eventually converted to Islam. By the 700s, Muslims had also crossed from North Africa into Spain. In 732, Arab forces were defeated by European soldiers at the Battle of Tours, in present-day France. This battle halted the Muslim advance into Christian Europe.

The Battle of Tours

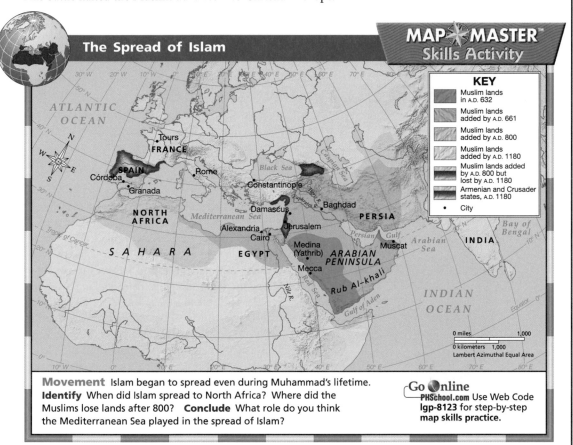

MAP MASTER™ Skills Activity

The Spread of Islam

KEY
- Muslim lands in A.D. 632
- Muslim lands added by A.D. 661
- Muslim lands added by A.D. 800
- Muslim lands added by A.D. 1180
- Muslim lands added by A.D. 800 but lost by A.D. 1180
- Armenian and Crusader states, A.D. 1180
- City

0 miles 1,000
0 kilometers 1,000
Lambert Azimuthal Equal Area

Movement Islam began to spread even during Muhammad's lifetime. **Identify** When did Islam spread to North Africa? Where did the Muslims lose lands after 800? **Conclude** What role do you think the Mediterranean Sea played in the spread of Islam?

Go Online
PHSchool.com Use Web Code lgp-8123 for step-by-step map skills practice.

Vocabulary Builder

Use the information below to teach students this section's high-use words.

High-Use Word	Definition and Sample Sentence
advance, p. 27	*n.* a movement forward The invention of computers formed a major **advance** in technology.
tolerate, p. 28	*v.* to allow My grandmother **tolerated** my drum playing, even though she did not like it.
prosperity, p. 29	*n.* wealth; success The wealthy king's followers enjoyed a time of great **prosperity**.
scholar, p. 29	*n.* learned person Professor Jones' knowledge of history made him a great **scholar** in his field.

Instruct

The Spread of Islam   L2

Guided Instruction

- **Vocabulary Builder** Clarify the high-use words **advance** and **tolerate** before reading.

- Read The Spread of Islam using the ReQuest Procedure (TE, p. T35).

- Ask students **Where did Islam spread after Muhammad's death?** *(west to North Africa and then to present-day Spain; north into Persia; east to northern India and China)* **How did this religion gain converts so quickly?** *(Muslim merchants traveled great distances, bringing Islamic ideas with them. Islam was also spread through Arab conquests of neighboring regions.)*

- Ask students **What was significant about the Battle of Tours?** *(European Christians defeated Arab Muslims, which stopped the advance of Islam into Europe, beyond Spain.)*

- Discuss with students how Arab Muslims were able to grow so powerful. *(Possible answer: Islam had united and organized the Arab peoples. Also, Islamic leaders were tolerant of other religions in their territories. After they conquered an area, there was not much resistance since people were not forced to give up their own religions.)*

Independent Practice

Have students create the Taking Notes graphic organizer on a blank sheet of paper. Then have them fill in the timeline with details they learn as they read.

Monitor Progress

As students fill in the timeline, circulate and make sure that individuals are placing events in chronological order. Provide assistance as necessary.

Answers

MAP MASTER Skills Activity **Identify** by A.D. 800; Spain, the Armenian and Crusader states, and a region along the Black Sea
Conclude Possible answer: It provided a method of transportation for reaching other areas such as Europe and North Africa.

Go Online
PHSchool.com Students may practice their map skills using the interactive online version of this map.

Preview and Ask Questions As a follow up, ask students to perform the Target Reading Skill activity in the Student Edition. *(Answers will vary, but students should ask a question, and then read the paragraph to answer their question.)*

The Golden Age `L2`

Guided Instruction

■ **Vocabulary Builder** Clarify the high-use words **prosperity** and **scholar** before reading.

■ With students, read about some of the important Arab contributions to math and science during the rule of the caliphs in The Golden Age. As they read, circulate and make sure individuals can answer the Reading Check question.

■ Ask students **Who were the caliphs?** *(a series of Muslim rulers who were Muhammad's successors)* **Why did a golden age of Islamic culture develop under their rule?** *(Under their rule, an empire developed and grew rich from trade. Traders from many parts of the world brought goods to the caliph's court at Baghdad. The caliphs were supporters of the arts.)*

■ Ask students **How did the work of Arab mathematicians influence later scientists?** *(It enabled later scientists to make discoveries in astronomy, physics, and chemistry.)*

Answers

✓ **Reading Check** Muslim rulers tolerated other faiths, while Byzantine rulers did not.

Infer He was very wealthy and wanted to impress Charlemagne.

⊙ **Preview and Ask Questions**

Ask a question that will help you learn something important from the paragraph at the right. Now read the paragraph, and answer your question.

A Royal Gift
The caliph Harun ar-Rashid presented this water jug to Charlemagne, the ruler of a Christian empire in Europe. He hoped to form an alliance with Charlemagne. **Infer** *What can you infer about Harun from this gift?*

Reasons for Success In the centuries before Muhammad, Arab peoples had not been able to conquer neighboring regions. The strong Roman Empire made invasions of these lands nearly impossible. And the later Byzantine and Persian empires successfully blocked Arabs from advancing north. So why were the Muslims successful after Muhammad's death?

By that time, the three empires that might have stopped the Arab expansion north and east were either defeated or weakened. Also, a shared religion now united the Arab peoples into one community. And once they began to work together, the Muslims quickly grew powerful.

Under Muslim Rule Unlike Byzantine leaders of the time—who did not accept different religions—Muslims tolerated other faiths. Muslim rulers allowed Christians and Jews to practice their own religions and pursue their own business affairs. Non-Muslim citizens did have fewer rights than Muslims, however. For example, they were forbidden to carry weapons and could not serve in the military. They also paid a special tax, which helped support the government.

✓ **Reading Check** Compare Muslim rulers and Byzantine rulers.

The Golden Age

The golden age of Muslim culture from about 800 to 1100 was a brilliant period of history. Great advances were made in mathematics and science, and lasting works of literature and architecture were created. Why did so much happen at that time?

The Age of the Caliphs One reason was the great wealth of the Arab world. Under Muslim rulers called **caliphs** (KAY lifs), an empire developed and grew rich. Its wealth came both from the many lands it controlled and from trade. Baghdad was the capital of the Muslim empire during the golden age. Find it on the map titled The Spread of Islam on page 27. You can see that Baghdad, like Constantinople, was a natural center for trade. With your finger, trace a route from India to Baghdad. Now trace a route from the Mediterranean Sea to Baghdad. Traders from all over the world brought their goods to the caliph's court. The caliph was considered to be Muhammad's successor, or the next person who had the right to rule.

Differentiated Instruction

For Gifted and Talented `L3`
Show students *Color Transparency MT Set 1: Spread of Islam*. Have them work in small groups to answer the following questions: Where did the Muslim Empire begin? *(Arabia)* Where did it spread? *(Europe, Africa, and other parts of Asia)* During which period did it spread into Western Europe? *(under the Umayyad caliphs, 661–750)* Describe the area that became part of the Muslim empire under the first four caliphs. *(much of Southwest Asia, including part of Persia, and the northern part of Egypt)*

 Medieval Times to Today Transparencies, *Color Transparency MT Set 1: Spread of Islam*

Harun ar-Rashid: A Powerful Caliph

Harun ar-Rashid (hah ROON ar rah SHEED) became caliph of Baghdad in 786. His rule was a time of prosperity. For 23 years, Harun ruled the world's most glamorous court. He and his favorite subjects ate off gold plates and drank from goblets studded with jewels.

Harun did not use the riches of Baghdad just for his own pleasure. He was also a great patron, or supporter, of the arts. Harun paid many skilled writers, musicians, dancers, and artists to live in Baghdad. And he lavishly rewarded those whose works pleased him. One musician is said to have received a gift of 100,000 silver pieces for a single song.

Achievements of the Golden Age

Arab scholars not only created new works but also studied history and ideas from other cultures. One scholar wrote,

> **“We should not be ashamed to acknowledge truth from whatever source it comes to us, even if it is brought to us by former generations and foreign peoples. ”**
>
> —al-Kindi

This approach led Muslim scholars to make great advances in mathematics, in science, and in literature.

Mathematics and Science Arab scholars studied both Greek and Indian mathematics. They learned about the idea of zero from Indian scholars. And they borrowed the use of the so-called Arabic numerals that we use today from India, too. The Muslim mathematician al-Khwarizme (al KWAHR iz mee) wrote a book explaining Indian arithmetic. He also made significant contributions to the development of algebra. The word *algebra* comes from the Arabic word "al-jabr." These contributions enabled later scientists to make great discoveries in astronomy, physics, and chemistry.

The famous Islamic scientist and philosopher Ibn Sina (IB un SEE nah) lived from 980 to 1037. Also known as Avicenna (ahv ih SEN uh), he organized the medical knowledge of the Greeks and Arabs into the *Canon of Medicine.*

Arab Contributions to Mathematics and Science

Medicine
The Arabs were the first to organize separate pharmacies, which sold spices, herbs, and other medicines to the public.

Mathematics
Arab mathematicians made important contributions to algebra. They studied formulas like this one. It explains how to find the length of one side of a right triangle when you know the length of the other sides.

Machines
Water-driven machines fascinated Arab scientists. Here, water falling into the cups causes the globe at the top to turn.

- Ask students **Who were the Sufis?** *(a group of Muslim poets who used poetry to teach ideas and beliefs)* **What did they teach?** *(They taught that prayer, fasting, and a simple life would draw people closer to God.)*

- Ask students **How do you think Muslim attitudes contributed to the achievements of the Golden Age?** *(Answers will vary, but should include that Muslims, unlike Byzantines, tolerated other faiths and allowed people to practice their own religions and pursue their own affairs; Arab scholars were also free to study ideas from past history and other cultures.)*

Independent Practice

Have students complete their graphic organizers with dates and details from the section.

Monitor Progress

- Show *Section Reading Support Transparency MT 55,* and ask students to check their work individually. Go over key concepts and clarify key vocabulary as needed.

  📖 **Medieval Times to Today Transparencies,** *Section Reading Support Transparency MT 55*

- Tell students to fill in the last column of the *Reading Readiness Guide.* Probe for what they learned that confirms or invalidates each statement.

  All in One Medieval Times to Today Teaching Resources, *Reading Readiness Guide,* p. 117

Differentiated Instruction

For Special Needs Students L1
Have students read the section as they listen to the recording on the Student Edition on Audio CD. Check for comprehension by pausing the CD and asking students to

share their answers to the Reading Check questions.

⊙ Chapter 1, Section 3, **Student Edition on Audio CD**

Assess and Reteach

Assess Progress [L2]

Have students complete the Section Assessment. Then administer the *Section Quiz.*

> **All in One Medieval Times to Today Teaching Resources,** *Section Quiz,* p. 119

Reteach [L1]

If students need more instruction, have them read this section in the Reading and Vocabulary Study Guide.

> Chapter 1, Section 3, **Medieval Times to Today Reading and Vocabulary Study Guide,** pp. 12–14

Extend [L3]

To learn more about the wealth and possessions of Harun ar-Rashid, have students read *The King's Wealth* and then answer the questions that follow.

> **All in One Medieval Times to Today Teaching Resources,** *The King's Wealth,* pp. 131–132

Answer

✓ **Reading Check** They taught that the world will reveal its mysteries to careful observers, and that people could get closer to God through prayer, fasting, and a simple life.

Section 3 Assessment

Key Terms
Students' sentences should reflect an understanding of each Key Term.

 Target Reading Skill
Answers will vary, but students should identify which questions helped them and what the answers to their questions were.

Comprehension and Critical Thinking
1. (a) through trade and conquest **(b)** Possible answer: All of Europe might be Muslim or under Muslim control and Europeans might also speak and write Arabic.

Literature Muslim writers created many lasting works of literature. Poetry was particularly important in the Islamic world. Poets were treated as popular musicians are today. One group of Muslims used poetry to teach their ideas and beliefs.

This group, called the **Sufis** (soo feez), were mystics who believed that they could draw close to God through prayer, fasting, and a simple life. They taught that the world will reveal its mysteries to careful observers. Sufi missionaries also helped spread Islam to Central Asia, India, and Africa south of the Sahara.

The most famous Sufi poet, Rumi (ROO mee), founded a religious group known to Europeans as the Whirling Dervishes. This group used music and dance to communicate with God. Rumi composed these verses:

> **Never think the earth [empty] or dead—
> It's a hare, awake with shut eyes:
> It's a saucepan, simmering with broth—
> One clear look, you'll see it's in [motion].**
>
> —*Rumi*

✓ **Reading Check** What did the Sufis teach?

Section 3 Assessment

Key Terms
Review the key terms at the beginning of this section. Use each term in a sentence that explains its meaning.

 Target Reading Skill
What questions helped you learn something important from this section? What are the answers to your questions?

Comprehension and Critical Thinking
1. (a) Recall Describe the two main ways that Islam spread beyond the Arabian Peninsula.

(b) Predict How might the culture of Europe be different today if the Arabs had won the Battle of Tours in 732?
2. (a) Locate Where is Baghdad located?
(b) Synthesize Information What made it a good choice for the capital of an empire?
(c) Generalize How do geography and trade contribute to a city's prosperity and power?
3. (a) Identify Name three Arab contributions to mathematics and science.
(b) Analyze How do these contributions combine borrowed knowledge and new ideas?

Writing Activity
Write a newspaper editorial either for or against the use of government money to support the arts. Use Harun ar-Rashid as one example in your argument. Begin with a statement of your position and then support it with reasons and facts.

For: An activity on Islam's golden age
Visit: PHSchool.com
Web Code: lgd-8103

---

2. (a) on the Tigris River **(b)** It was located at a major trade route crossroads. **(c)** Possible answer: A city can make money from duties or other taxes on trade goods or tolls. Trade routes bring in diverse people and new ideas, which enriches a city's culture.

3. (a) Possible answers: algebra, the "Canon of Medicine," the use of hospitals and pharmacies **(b)** Arab mathematicians and scientists expanded on existing ideas, such as Greek medical knowledge and the existing concept of zero.

Writing Activity
Use the *Rubric for Assessing a Newspaper Article* to evaluate students' editorials.

> **All in One Medieval Times to Today Teaching Resources,** *Rubric for Assessing a Newspaper Article,* p. 135

> **Go Online PHSchool.com** Typing in the Web code when prompted will bring students directly to detailed instructions for this activity.

Review and Assessment

◆ Chapter Summary

Justinian

Section 1: The Byzantine Empire

- The Roman emperor Constantine established a new capital in the eastern part of the Roman Empire. Later, Constantinople became the capital of the rich and powerful Byzantine Empire.
- Justinian, one of the greatest Byzantine emperors, organized a system of laws called Justinian's code.
- After Justinian's death, the Byzantine Empire shrank in size and power. It later enjoyed a second golden age. A schism split the Christian church into eastern and western branches.

Section 2: The Beginnings of Islam

- Although much of the Arabian Peninsula is covered by desert, important cities, such as Mecca, grew up on trade routes.
- The Muslim prophet Muhammad preached in Mecca and Medina. His teachings became the religion of Islam.
- The Five Pillars of Islam and the Quran are the basis of Muslim beliefs. A dispute among Muslims led to the split between Shiites and Sunnis.

Section 3: The Golden Age of Muslim Civilization

- After the death of Muhammad, the religion of Islam spread to many neighboring regions by both trade and conquest.
- The golden age of Islam occurred under wealthy Muslim rulers called caliphs.
- The golden age was marked by great achievements in mathematics, science, literature, and art.

Caliph's water jug

◆ Key Terms

Match each key term with its definition from the list at the right.

1. mosque
2. Constantine
3. nomads
4. caliph
5. Justinian
6. caravan
7. schism
8. Omar Khayyam

A a Muslim ruler
B a group of traders traveling together for safety
C emperor of the Byzantine Empire
D emperor of the Roman Empire
E Muslim house of worship
F a Muslim astronomer, mathematician, and poet
G people with no permanent home, who move from place to place
H a split, particularly in a church or religion

Chapter 1 **31**

─ Vocabulary Builder ─

Revisit this chapter's high-use words:

reign   abandon   tolerate
imperial   foundation   prosperity
distinct   descendant   scholar
regain   advance

Ask students to review the definitions they recorded on their *Word Knowledge* worksheets.

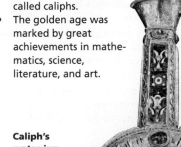 **Medieval Times to Today Teaching Resources,** *Word Knowledge,* p. 123

Consider allowing students to earn extra credit if they use the words in their answers to the questions in the Chapter Review and Assessment. The words must be used correctly and in a natural context to win the extra points.

Chapter 1
Review and Assessment

Review Chapter Content

- Review and revisit the major themes of this chapter by asking students to classify what Guiding Question each bulleted statement in the Chapter Summary answers. Form students into groups and ask them to complete the activity together. Refer to page 1 in the Student Edition for the text of the Guiding Questions.

- Assign Vocabulary Development for students to review Key Terms.

  All in One Medieval Times to Today Teaching Resources, *Vocabulary Development,* p. 133

Answers

Key Terms

1. E
2. D
3. G
4. A
5. C
6. B
7. H
8. F

Review and Assessment

Comprehension and Critical Thinking

9. (a) the eastern end **(b)** Because it was at a major crossroads of trade, it was constantly filled with diverse people, goods, and ideas, and it grew very rich. **(c)** It had the strongest army in the world and was a major center for trade.

10. (a) an organized collection and explanation of Roman laws for use by the Byzantine Empire **(b)** It helped people make sense of the laws and allowed the government to enforce them.

11. (a) when he went into a cave in the Arabian mountains to pray **(b)** Possible answer: he believed that he had been commanded by God to share his message with all people, even if some did not listen.

12. (a) holy books, the belief in one God, and many of the same important figures in their religious history **(b)** After the assassination of Uthman in 656, one group, the Shiites, believed that the leader of Islam should be a descendant of Muhammad and the other group, the Sunnis, believed that any truly religious Muslim could lead.

13. (a) in Baghdad, from about 800 to 1100 **(b)** These years produced a wealth of mathematical and scientific knowledge, inventions, and literature that were extremely valuable. It could be said that these contributions were as valuable as gold, an expensive metal.

Skills Practice

Students' paragraphs will vary, but should include a conclusion and supporting details from the table The Five Pillars of Islam on page 21.

Writing Activity: Language and Arts

Students' monologues will vary, but should be written from the point of view of one of the rulers in this chapter, and should include information about that person's life or an important event.

Use *Rubric for Assessing a Writing Assignment* to evaluate students' monologues.

All in One **Medieval Times to Today**
Teaching Resources, *Rubric for Assessing a Writing Assignment,* p. 134

Review and Assessment (continued)

◆ Comprehension and Critical Thinking

9. (a) Recall In what part of the old Roman Empire was Constantinople located?
(b) Identify Cause and Effect How did Constantinople's location affect the culture that developed there?
(c) Compare and Contrast What enabled the eastern part of the Roman Empire to survive after the western Roman Empire "fell"?

10. (a) Define What was Justinian's Code?
(b) Infer How did Justinian's Code help make the Byzantine Empire strong and successful?

11. (a) Describe How did Muhammad first receive God's message?
(b) Infer Why do you think Muhammad did not give up preaching when few people listened?

12. (a) Recall What do Muslims, Jews, and Christians have in common?
(b) Contrast How do the beliefs of Sunni and Shiite Muslims differ?

13. (a) Recall When and where did the golden age of Muslim civilization occur?
(b) Synthesize Explain in your own words why these years are called a golden age.

◆ Skills Practice

Using a Table to Write a Paragraph In the Skills for Life activity in this chapter, you learned how to use the data in a table to write a paragraph. Review the steps you followed to learn the skill.

Now review the table The Five Pillars of Islam on page 21. Use the data in the table to draw a conclusion about the topic. Write a paragraph that states your conclusion and that uses data from the table as supporting details.

◆ Writing Activity: Language Arts

A monologue is a speech by one person. In drama, a monologue is spoken directly to the audience. Choose one of the rulers you have read about in this chapter. Write a monologue that this ruler might speak in a theatrical performance. It can be about the person's whole life or about one important event. Do further research on the ruler if you wish. You may want to perform your monologue for your class.

MAP MASTER™
Skills Activity

The Byzantine Empire and the Spread of Islam

Place Location For each place or feature listed below, write the letter from the map that shows its location.
1. Rome
2. Mecca
3. Constantinople
4. Mediterranean Sea
5. Bosporus
6. Baghdad
7. Arabian Peninsula

Go Online
PHSchool.com Use Web Code **lgp-8133** for an interactive map.

Standardized Test Prep

Test-Taking Tips

Some questions on standardized tests ask you to evaluate a source for a research assignment. Read the passage below. Then use the tip to help you answer the sample question.

> Vera is writing a research paper about Justinian's Code. At the school library, she found four books that she might use.

Think It Through Even if you don't know about Justinian's Code, you can eliminate A because it is fiction—an invented story. You can also rule out C because it is about a merchant's travels, not about Justinian's Code. That leaves B and D. Justinian's Code refers to laws, not to copying Roman and Greek books. The correct answer is B.

Pick the letter that best answers the question.

Which one of the following books would be best for Vera's topic?

A ~~*Justinian's Bride*—a novel about the Empress Theodora~~

B *The Birth of Law*—a nonfiction book about the Byzantine legal system

C ~~*The Journal of Ignatius*—a firsthand account of a merchant's travels during the time of Justinian~~

D *The Rescue of Knowledge*—the story of how Byzantine scholars copied and cared for books of ancient Rome and Greece

TIP Rule out choices that don't make sense. Then choose the best answer from the remaining choices.

Practice Questions

Use the tip above and other tips in this book to help you answer the following questions.

1. Miguel's history class has been studying the Byzantine Empire. Miguel has decided to write a research paper about the empire's capital, Constantinople. He would like to find out the population of Constantinople at the time of Justinian's rule.

Which one of the following would be the best choice for this information?

A *An Atlas of Modern Turkey*—a nonfiction book that includes maps and factual data

B *Our Trip to Istanbul*—a new Web site that tells about a family's vacation to the city formerly called Constantinople

C *An Atlas of the Ancient World*—a nonfiction book that includes historical maps and other historical data

D *Population Growth of Major U.S. Cities*—a nonfiction book that includes charts and maps

Pick the letter of the word or phrase that best completes each sentence.

2. Muslims are called to worship _____.

A once a day   B four times a month

C five times a day   D once a year

3. Constantine was the first _____ to rule the Roman Empire.

A Muslim   B Jew

C Sufi   D Christian

4. The _____ links the Black Sea and the Sea of Marmara, which flows into the Mediterranean Sea.

A Bosporus   B Arabian Peninsula

C Mecca   D hijra

Go Online
PHSchool.com

Use Web Code **lga-8103** for a **Chapter 1 self-test.**

Standardized Test Prep

Answers

1. C

2. C

3. D

4. A

Chapter Overview

Overview

Section 1

Africa and the Bantu
1. Learn about the physical geography of Africa.
2. Find out about the Bantu and their movement across the continent.

Section 2

Kingdoms of West Africa
1. Learn about the trading kingdoms of the West African savanna.
2. Investigate the kingdoms of the West African rain forests.

Section 3

East Africa's Great Trading Centers
1. Learn about powerful East African civilizations whose cities included Aksum and Lalibela.
2. Find out why the coastal cities of East Africa were important.

Discovery CHANNEL SCHOOL Video

Great Zimbabwe: The Lost City
Length: 3 minutes, 30 seconds
Use with Section 3

This segment describes how cattle trade brought wealth to Great Zimbabwe, and gives possible reasons for the kingdom's decline. The segment also explores the ruins of the monument the Great Enclosure.

Technology Resources

Go Online
PHSchool.com

Students use embedded Web codes to access Internet activities, chapter self-tests, and additional map practice. They may also access Dorling Kindersley's Online Desk Reference to learn more about each country they study.

Interactive Textbook

Use the Interactive Textbook to make content and concepts come alive through animations, videos, and activities that accompany the complete basal text—online and on CD-ROM.

PRENTICE HALL
TeacherEXPRESS
Plan • Teach • Assess

Use this complete suite of powerful teaching tools to make planning lessons and administering tests quicker and easier.

Reading and Assessment

Reading and Vocabulary Instruction

⟳ Model the Target Reading Skill

Clarifying Meaning When rereading and reading ahead, students look within the text for the meaning of unfamiliar words and terms. Paraphrasing helps students restate ideas in words they better understand and remember. When summarizing, students state the main points of the passage. Model techniques for clarifying meaning by thinking aloud about this selection from page 41:

> *As the Bantu migrated, they also carried a knowledge of metalworking with them. Iron tools gave the Bantu more control over their environment than older cultures had. With strong axes, they could cut down trees and clear the land. Their sharp, iron-headed spears and arrows were powerful weapons for hunting and for warfare.*

The first sentence mentions metalworking. I'm not sure what that means. By reading ahead, I see that the next sentence clarifies the meaning. Metalworking is the creation of iron tools. I will restate the first two sentences and summarize the passage to make sure I remember the information: *As they traveled from place to place, the Bantu had an advantage over older cultures because they used iron tools to clear land, to hunt, and to control other tribes.*

Use the following worksheets from All-in-One Medieval Times to Today Teaching Resources (pp. 159–161) to support the chapter's Target Reading Skill.

Vocabulary Builder
High-Use Academic Words
Use these steps to teach this chapter's high-use words:

1. Have students rate how well they know each word on their Word Knowledge worksheets (All-in-One Medieval Times to Today Teaching Resources, p. 162).
2. Pronounce each word and ask students to repeat it.
3. Give students a brief definition or sample sentence (provided on TE pp. 37, 45, and 53).
4. Work with students as they fill in the "Definition or Example" column of their Word Knowledge worksheets.

Assessment

Formal Assessment
Test students' understanding of core knowledge and skills.

Chapter Tests A and B, All-in-One Medieval Times to Today Teaching Resources, pp. 176–181

Customize the Chapter Tests to suit your needs.
ExamView® Test Bank CD-ROM

Skills Assessment
Assess geographic literacy.
MapMaster Skills, Student Edition pp. 35, 37, 39, 58

Assess reading and comprehension.
Target Reading Skills, Student Edition, pp. 38, 46, 55, and in Section Assessments

Chapter 2 Assessment, Medieval Times to Today Reading and Vocabulary Study Guide, p. 25

Performance Assessment
Assess students' performance on this chapter's Writing Activities using the following rubrics from All-in-One Medieval Times to Today Teaching Resources.

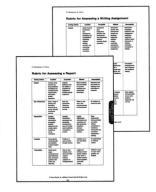

Rubric for Assessing a Writing Assignment, p. 174
Rubric for Assessing a Report, p. 175

Assess students' work through performance tasks.

Small Group Activity: Simulation: Trading Items With Silent Barter, All-in-One Medieval Times to Today Teaching Resources, pp. 165–168

Online Assessment
Have students check their own understanding.
Chapter Self-Test

Section 1 **Africa and the Bantu**

 3.5 periods, 1.75 blocks (includes Skills for Life)

Social Studies Objectives
1. Learn about the physical geography of Africa.
2. Find out about the Bantu and their movement across the continent.

Reading/Language Arts Objective
Reread and read ahead to find connections among words and sentences and to clarify unfamiliar words and ideas.

Prepare to Read	**Instructional Resources**	**Differentiated Instruction**
Build Background Knowledge Ask students to think about how geography affects travel. **Set a Purpose for Reading** Have students evaluate statements on the *Reading Readiness Guide.* **Preview Key Terms** Teach the section's Key Terms. **Target Reading Skill** Introduce the section's Target Reading Skill of **rereading or reading ahead.**	**All in One Medieval Times to Today Teaching Resources** **L2** Reading Readiness Guide, p. 148 **L2** Reread or Read Ahead, p. 159	**Spanish Reading and Vocabulary Study Guide** **L1** Chapter 2, Section 1, pp. 14–15 ELL

Instruct	**Instructional Resources**	**Differentiated Instruction**
Africa's Physical Geography Discuss Africa's tropical rain forests and savannas. **Target Reading Skill** Review **rereading or reading ahead.** **The Bantu Migrations** Discuss how scientists have researched sub-Saharan Africa and ask about their discoveries. Ask questions about the Bantu people.	**All in One Medieval Times to Today Teaching Resources** **L2** Guided Reading and Review, p. 149 **L2** Reading Readiness Guide, p. 148 **Medieval Times to Today Transparencies** **L2** Section Reading Support Transparency MT 56	**All in One Medieval Times to Today Teaching Resources** **L1** Reading a Historical Map, p. 169 ELL, LPR, SN **L2** Skills for Life, p. 164 AR, GT, LPR, SN **Teacher's Edition** **L1** For Special Needs Students, TE p. 38 **L1** For Less Proficient Readers, TE p. 38 **Student Edition on Audio CD** **L1** Chapter 2, Section 1 ELL, LPR, SN **Spanish Support** **L2** Guided Reading and Review (Spanish), p. 12 ELL

Assess and Reteach	**Instructional Resources**	**Differentiated Instruction**
Assess Progress Evaluate student comprehension with the section assessment and section quiz. **Reteach** Assign the Reading and Vocabulary Study Guide to help struggling students. **Extend** Extend the lesson by assigning a Book Project.	**All in One Medieval Times to Today Teaching Resources** **L2** Section Quiz, p. 150 **L3** Book Project: Major Migrations, pp. 86–88 Rubric for Assessing a Writing Assignment, p. 174 **Reading and Vocabulary Study Guide** **L1** Chapter 2, Section 1, pp. 16–18	**Spanish Support** **L2** Section Quiz (Spanish), p. 13 ELL **Teacher's Edition** **L1** For Less Proficient Readers, TE p. 43 **Social Studies Skills Tutor CD-ROM** **L1** Using Reliable Information ELL, LPR, SN

Key

L1 Basic to Average	**L3** Average to Advanced		LPR Less Proficient Readers		GT Gifted and Talented
L2 For All Students			AR Advanced Readers		ELL English Language Learners
			SN Special Needs Students		

Section 2 Kingdoms of West Africa

 2 periods, 1 block (includes Focus On Tombouctou)

Social Studies Objectives
1. Learn about the trading kingdoms of the West African savanna.
2. Investigate the kingdoms of the West African rain forests.

Reading/Language Arts Objective
Learn how to paraphrase to remember information.

Prepare to Read	Instructional Resources	Differentiated Instruction
Build Background Knowledge Have students generate a list of items that come from other countries through trade and think about how their lives would be different without those items. **Set a Purpose for Reading** Have students evaluate statements on the *Reading Readiness Guide.* **Preview Key Terms** Teach the section's Key Terms. **Target Reading Skill** Introduce the section's Target Reading Skill of **paraphrasing.**	**All in One Medieval Times to Today Teaching Resources** L2 Reading Readiness Guide, p. 152 L2 Paraphrase, p. 160	**Spanish Reading and Vocabulary Study Guide** L1 Chapter 2, Section 2, pp. 16–17 ELL

Instruct	Instructional Resources	Differentiated Instruction
Kingdoms of the Savanna Discuss trading centers in the Savanna. **Target Reading Skill** Review **paraphrasing.** **Kingdoms of the Forest** Discuss Ile-Ife and Benin.	**All in One Medieval Times to Today Teaching Resources** L2 Guided Reading and Review, p. 153 L2 Reading Readiness Guide, p. 152 **Medieval Times to Today Transparencies** L2 Section Reading Support Transparency MT 57	**All in One Medieval Times to Today Teaching Resources** L3 Al-Bakri Describes the Court of Ghana, Ibn Battuta Praises the Fairness of Mali's People, Leo Africanus Describes Timbuktu and Gao, pp. 170–172 AR, GT **Medieval Times to Today Transparencies** L2 Transparency MT 20: Africa: Political AR, GT, LPR, SN **Teacher's Edition** L3 For Gifted and Talented, TE p. 47 L1 For English Language Learners, TE p. 47

Assess and Reteach	Instructional Resources	Differentiated Instruction
Assess Progress Evaluate student comprehension with the section assessment and section quiz. **Reteach** Assign the Reading and Vocabulary Study Guide to help struggling students. **Extend** Extend the lesson by assigning this chapter's Enrichment activity.	**All in One Medieval Times to Today Teaching Resources** L2 Section Quiz, p. 154 L3 Enrichment, p. 163 Rubric for Assessing a Writing Assignment, p. 174 **Reading and Vocabulary Study Guide** L1 Chapter 2, Section 2, pp. 19–21	**Spanish Support** L2 Section Quiz (Spanish), p. 15 ELL

Key

L1 Basic to Average   L3 Average to Advanced   LPR Less Proficient Readers   GT Gifted and Talented

L2 For All Students   AR Advanced Readers   ELL English Language Learners

SN Special Needs Students

Section 3 East Africa's Great Trading Centers

 4 periods, 2 blocks (includes Chapter Review and Assessment)

Social Studies Objectives
1. Learn about powerful East African civilizations whose cities included Aksum and Lalibela.
2. Find out why the coastal cities of East Africa were important.

Reading/Language Arts Objective
Learn to summarize to help you remember and study what you read.

Prepare to Read	Instructional Resources	Differentiated Instruction
Build Background Knowledge Show a video about Great Zimbabwe, then lead a discussion. **Set a Purpose for Reading** Have students evaluate statements on the *Reading Readiness Guide*. **Preview Key Terms** Teach the section's Key Terms. **Target Reading Skill** Introduce the section's Target Reading Skill of **summarizing**.	**All in One Medieval Times to Today Teaching Resources** **L2** Reading Readiness Guide, p. 156 **L2** Summarize, p. 161 **World Studies Video Program** **L2** Great Zimbabwe: The Lost City	**Spanish Reading and Vocabulary Study Guide** **L1** Chapter 2, Section 3, pp. 18–19 ELL

Instruct	Instructional Resources	Differentiated Instruction
Ancient Ethiopia Discuss the rise and fall of Aksum and ask about the customs and traditions of East Africa's churches. **Target Reading Skill** Review **summarizing**. **Rich Centers of Trade** Discuss how trade centers on the southeast coast influenced the people of Africa.	**All in One Medieval Times to Today Teaching Resources** **L2** Guided Reading and Review, p. 157 **L2** Reading Readiness Guide, p. 156 **Medieval Times to Today Transparencies** **L2** Section Reading Support Transparency MT 58	**Teacher's Edition** **L3** For Advanced Readers, TE p. 55 **PHSchool.com** **L3** For: Long-Term Integrated Projects: Mapping World Trade **Web Code:** lgd-8204 AR, GT **Spanish Support** **L2** Guided Reading and Review (Spanish), p. 16 ELL

Assess and Reteach	Instructional Resources	Differentiated Instruction
Assess Progress Evaluate student comprehension with the section assessment and section quiz. **Reteach** Assign the Reading and Vocabulary Study Guide to help struggling students. **Extend** Extend the lesson by assigning a Small Group Activity.	**All in One Medieval Times to Today Teaching Resources** **L2** Section Quiz, p. 158 **L3** Small Group Activity: Simulation: Trading Items With Silent Barter, pp. 165–168 Rubric for Assessing a Writing Assignment, p. 174 Rubric for Assessing a Report, p. 175 **L2** Word Knowledge, p. 162 **L2** Vocabulary Development, p. 173 **L2** Chapter Tests A and B, pp. 176–181 **Reading and Vocabulary Study Guide** **L1** Chapter 2, Section 3, pp. 22–24	**Spanish Support** **L2** Section Quiz (Spanish), p. 17 ELL **L2** Chapter Summary (Spanish), p. 18 ELL **L2** Vocabulary Development (Spanish), p. 19 ELL

Key
L1 Basic to Average **L3** Average to Advanced
L2 For All Students

LPR Less Proficient Readers
AR Advanced Readers
SN Special Needs Students

GT Gifted and Talented
ELL English Language Learners

Professional Development

Reading Background

Pre-Teaching Vocabulary

Research literature on academic vocabulary instruction indicates that effective strategies require students to go beyond simply looking up dictionary definitions or examining the context. Vocabulary learning must be based on the learner's dynamic engagement in constructing understanding.

If students are not retaining the meaning of the Key Terms or high-use words, use this extended vocabulary sequence to engage them in learning new words.

1. Present the word in writing and point out the part of speech.
2. Pronounce the word and have students pronounce the word.
3. Provide a range of familiar synonyms (or "it's like" words) before offering definitions.
4. Provide an accessible definition and concrete examples, or "showing sentences."
5. Rephrase the simple definition or example sentence, asking students to complete the statement by substituting the word aloud.
6. Check for understanding by providing an application task/question requiring critical thinking.

Sample instructional sequence:

1. Our first word is *unique*. It is an adjective, a word that describes something.
2. Say the word *unique* after me. (Students repeat.)
3. Something *unique* is *unparalleled* or *one-of-a-kind*.
4. The word *unique* means *without an equal*; Your handwriting is *unique* because it like no one else's.
5. Many families have _____ customs and traditions for different holidays.
6. Would a product created on an assembly line be considered *unique*? Yes-No-Why? (Students answer the question.)

Simplified Outlining

In this simplified approach to outlining, students will learn to differentiate between main ideas and details. Model simplified outlining using the paragraphs under the heading *Africa's Physical Geography* on page 37 of the Student Edition. Main ideas should be assigned to Level 1. Details should be Level 2, 3, or 4.

Level 1 (Main idea): Africa's vegetation
    Level 2: (detail or support for Level 1): savanna
    Level 2: (detail or support for Level 1): Sahara
        Level 3: (detail or support for Level 2): oasis
        Level 3: (detail or support for Level 2): desert

World Studies Background

Ivory Trade

In the mid-1800s, prosperity in Europe and North America increased the demand for ivory products. This meant that traders from the north would have to travel through the Sahara to the upper Congo basin, where elephants were still abundant. This resulting upsurge in ivory trade in Central Africa greatly disrupted its people. As traders crossed the area, they raided villages and kidnapped local people to serve as workers in ivory camps or slaves in Constantinople and Cairo.

Lingua Francas

Multilingualism, the ability to speak more than one language, is important in Africa, where there are more than 800 languages spoken. However, this can make it difficult to create newspapers, radio broadcasts, and textbooks that address the various language groups. To alleviate this problem, Africans have adopted lingua francas, or "official" languages, such as Swahili, Yoruba, and even English, in distinct regions. This allows for more widespread communication between the people of Africa.

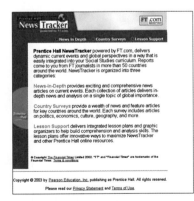

Get in-depth information on topics of global importance with **Prentice Hall Newstracker,** powered by FT.com.

 Use Web code **lgd-8204** for **Prentice Hall Newstracker.**

Guiding Questions

Remind students about the Guiding Questions introduced at the beginning of the book.

Section 1 relates to **Guiding Question ❶ How did physical geography affect the development of societies around the world?** (*Africa's physical geography has affected how its people make a living; for example, there is little farming in the deserts because of the lack of water.*)

Section 2 relates to **Guiding Question ❺ How did each society organize its economic activities?** (*West African kingdoms became rich by controlling important trade routes across the Sahara.*)

Section 3 relates to **Guiding Question ❷ How did each society's belief system affect its history?** (*Many people in Aksum, a city in ancient Ethiopia, converted to Christianity during the A.D. 300s. In the 600s, the rulers of Aksum fought with Muslims over trade routes and religious differences. Christianity in Ethiopia produced unique traditions and unusual churches that are still used today.*)

🎯 Target Reading Skill

In this chapter, students will learn and apply the reading skill of clarifying meaning to understand and remember what they read. Use the following worksheets to help students practice this skill:

All in One Medieval Times to Today Teaching Resources, *Reread or Read Ahead,* p. 159, *Paraphrase,* p. 160, *Summarize,* p. 161

Chapter 2

Civilizations of Africa

Chapter Preview

This chapter will introduce you to the early history of Africa and to some of its great civilizations.

Section 1
Africa and the Bantu

Section 2
Kingdoms of West Africa

Section 3
East Africa's Great Trading Centers

 Target Reading Skill

Clarifying Meaning In this chapter, you will focus on clarifying meaning by learning how to reread, how to paraphrase, and how to summarize.

▶ Ruins of the Great Mosque of Kilwa, in present-day Tanzania, East Africa

---

Differentiated Instruction

The following Teacher Edition strategies are suitable for students of varying abilities.

Advanced Readers, p. 55
English Language Learners, p. 47
Gifted and Talented, p. 47
Less Proficient Readers, pp. 38, 43
Special Needs Students, p. 38

Bibliography

For the Teacher
Davidson, Basil. *Africa in History.* Touchstone Books, 1995.
Oliver, R. A. and Anthony Atmore. *Medieval Africa, 1250–1800.* Cambridge University Press, 2001.
Marcus, Harold G. *A History of Ethiopia: Updated Edition.* University of California Press, 2002.

For the Student
L1 Burns, Khephra. *Mansa Musa: The Lion of Mali.* Harcourt, 2001.
L2 McKissack, Frederick L. *The Royal Kingdoms of Ghana, Mali, and Songhay: Life in Medieval Africa.* Henry Holt & Company, 1995.
L3 Bessire, Mark H. C. *Great Zimbabwe (First Book).* Orchard Books, 1999.

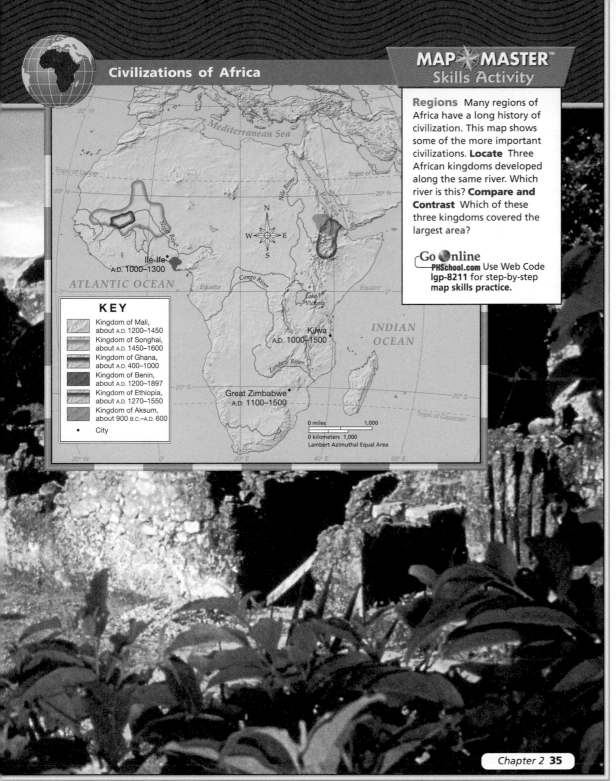

Civilizations of Africa

Regions Many regions of Africa have a long history of civilization. This map shows some of the more important civilizations. **Locate** Three African kingdoms developed along the same river. Which river is this? **Compare and Contrast** Which of these three kingdoms covered the largest area?

Go Online
PHSchool.com Use Web Code lgp-8211 for step-by-step map skills practice.

KEY

Kingdom of Mali, about A.D. 1200–1450
Kingdom of Songhai, about A.D. 1450–1600
Kingdom of Ghana, about A.D. 400–1000
Kingdom of Benin, about A.D. 1200–1897
Kingdom of Ethiopia, about A.D. 1270–1550
Kingdom of Aksum, about 900 B.C.–A.D. 600
• City

Mediterranean Sea
Tropic of Cancer
Nile River
Red Sea
Niger River
Ile-Ife A.D. 1000–1300
ATLANTIC OCEAN
Congo River
Equator
Lake Victoria
Kilwa A.D. 1000–1500
INDIAN OCEAN
Zambezi River
Great Zimbabwe A.D. 1100–1500
Tropic of Capricorn

0 miles 1,000
0 kilometers 1,000
Lambert Azimuthal Equal Area

- Have students study the map, paying particular attention to the key. Point out to students that though all of the civilizations are shown on one map, they did not exist at the same time.

- Have students copy the names of each kingdom and the dates they thrived onto a separate sheet of paper. Then have students list the kingdoms in order of the date they were founded.

Go Online
PHSchool.com Students may practice their map skills using the interactive online version of this map.

Using the Visual L2

Reach Into Your Background Draw students' attention to the caption accompanying the photograph on pp. 34–35. Ask students to list any historic ruins they have visited or read about. Then have them think about why it is important to preserve these kinds of sites. Use an Idea Wave (TE, p. T35) to help students share their thoughts.

Answers

MAP✦MASTER™ *Skills Activity* **Locate** the Niger River **Compare and Contrast** the Kingdom of Mali

---

Chapter Resources

Teaching Resources
- **L2** Vocabulary Development, p. 173
- **L2** Skills for Life, p. 164
- **L2** Chapter Tests A and B, pp. 176–181

Spanish Support
- **L2** Spanish Chapter Summary, p. 18
- **L2** Spanish Vocabulary Development, p. 19

Media and Technology
- **L1** Student Edition on Audio CD
- **L1** Guided Reading Audiotapes, English and Spanish
- **L2** Social Studies Skills Tutor CD-ROM
- *ExamView® Test Bank CD-ROM*

DISCOVERY CHANNEL **SCHOOL** World Studies Video Program

Interactive Textbook

PRENTICE HALL
TeacherEXPRESS™
Plan • Teach • Assess

Section 1
Step-by-Step Instruction

Objectives
Social Studies
1. Learn about the physical geography of Africa.
2. Find out about the Bantu and their movement across the continent.

Reading/Language Arts
Reread and read ahead to find connections among words and sentences and to clarify unfamiliar words and ideas.

Prepare to Read

Build Background Knowledge L2
In this section students will learn about Africa's physical geography and how landforms affected the Bantu people. Pose the question: **How does geography affect travel?** then have students use the Think-Write-Pair-Share participation strategy (TE, p. T36) to work together to brainstorm answers to the question. Provide a simple example to get students started.

Set a Purpose for Reading L2
- Preview the Objectives.

- Read each statement in the *Reading Readiness Guide* aloud. Ask students to mark the statements true or false.

  All in One Medieval Times to Today Teaching Resources, *Reading Readiness Guide,* p. 148

- Have students discuss the statements in pairs or groups of four, then mark their worksheets again. Use the Numbered Heads participation strategy (TE, p. T36) to call on students to share their group's perspectives.

Vocabulary Builder
Preview Key Terms L2
Pronounce each Key Term, and then ask students to say the word with you. Provide a simple explanation such as, "The migration of geese during autumn takes them from the northern to the southern region of the country."

Prepare to Read

Objectives
In this section, you will
1. Learn about the physical geography of Africa.
2. Find out about the Bantu and their movement across the continent.

Taking Notes
As you read this section, look for information about the major physical features of Africa. Copy the table below, and record your findings in it.

Physical Features of Africa	
Deserts	• •
Savannas	• •
Rain Forests	• •

Target Reading Skill
Reread or Read Ahead If you do not understand a passage, reread it to look for connections among the words and sentences. Reading ahead can also help. Words and ideas may be clarified further on.

Key Terms
- **migration** (my GRAY shun) *n.* the movement from one country or region to settle in another
- **Bantu** (BAN too) *n.* a large group of central and southern Africans who speak related languages
- **savanna** (suh VAN uh) *n.* an area of grassland with scattered trees and bushes
- **Sahara** (suh HA ruh) *n.* a huge desert stretching across most of North Africa
- **oral history** (AWR ul HIS tuh ree) *n.* accounts of the past that people pass down by word of mouth
- **clan** (klan) *n.* a group of families who trace their roots to the same ancestor

Zulu women in traditional dress in South Africa

36 Medieval Times to Today

About 4,000 years ago, many families left the places where they lived in West Africa. They would never return to their homeland. Some families had to climb over rocky hills. Others journeyed through forests or across lands baked by the sun. Mothers, fathers, and children carried everything they owned with them. After traveling for many miles, these people settled somewhere new.

No one knows exactly why they first moved. The population may have grown very quickly. If so, there may not have been enough land and resources to support all of the people. Over many years, later generations moved farther away from their original homes. They kept searching for better land for farming. Over time, their **migration** (my GRAY shun), or movement from one region to settle in another, took them across most of Africa south of the Equator. Today, their descendants number more than 200 million. The name **Bantu** (BAN too) describes both this large group of Africans and the related languages they speak.

Target Reading Skill L2
Reread or Read Ahead Point out the Target Reading Skill. Tell students that rereading and reading ahead may help them to figure out the meaning of an unfamiliar word or idea in the passage.

Model reading ahead using the last paragraph on p. 38 and the first paragraph on p. 40, in which students learn that until modern times, historians knew little about sub-Saharan Africa. By reading ahead, they learn that the lack of information was caused by the disintegration of artifacts. Students also learn that researchers are beginning to uncover new information about this area.

Give students *Reread or Read Ahead*. Have them complete the activity in groups.

All in One Medieval Times to Today Teaching Resources, *Reread or Read Ahead,* p. 159

Africa's Physical Geography

Look at the map titled Africa: Natural Vegetation. Notice the tropical rain forests that are located on either side of the Equator. They have hot, moist climates.

Surrounding these forests are bands of **savanna,** areas of grassland with scattered trees and bushes. Much of Africa is savanna. Africa's lions, zebras, and elephants live mainly on the savannas. Deserts stretch north and south of the savannas. The **Sahara** (suh HA ruh) is a desert stretching across most of North Africa. It is the world's largest desert. The Sahara is a hot, dry place of sand dunes and rocky mountains. A band of lakes, deep valleys, and rugged mountains runs north to south through East Africa.

Africa's physical geography has affected its people's ways of life. For example, there is little farming in Africa's deserts, because there is too little water. People herd cattle on the savannas, but cattle cannot survive in the rain forests. Flies and other pests in the rain forests carry diseases that are deadly for cattle.

An Oasis in the Sahara
An oasis (oh AY sis) is an area of vegetation within a desert, fed by springs and underground water. **Infer** How might oases help travelers crossing a desert?

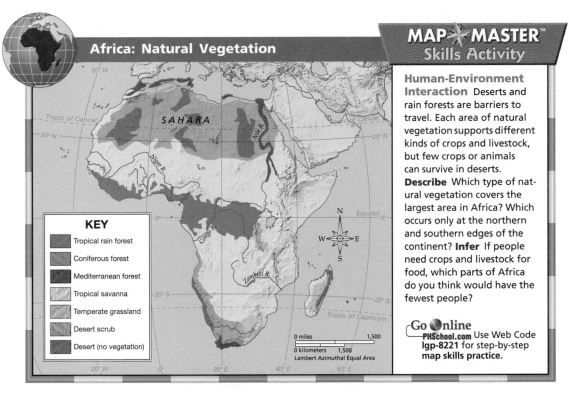

Africa: Natural Vegetation

SAHARA

Tropic of Cancer

Niger R.

Nile R.

Congo R.

Equator

Zambezi R.

Tropic of Capricorn

KEY
- Tropical rain forest
- Coniferous forest
- Mediterranean forest
- Tropical savanna
- Temperate grassland
- Desert scrub
- Desert (no vegetation)

N
W E
S

0 miles 1,500
0 kilometers 1,500
Lambert Azimuthal Equal Area

MAP MASTER™ Skills Activity

Human-Environment Interaction Deserts and rain forests are barriers to travel. Each area of natural vegetation supports different kinds of crops and livestock, but few crops or animals can survive in deserts. **Describe** Which type of natural vegetation covers the largest area in Africa? Which occurs only at the northern and southern edges of the continent? **Infer** If people need crops and livestock for food, which parts of Africa do you think would have the fewest people?

Go Online
PHSchool.com Use Web Code lgp-8221 for step-by-step map skills practice.

Vocabulary Builder

Use the information below to teach students this section's high-use words.

High-Use Word	Definition and Sample Sentence
environment, p. 38	*n.* natural surroundings Many people recycle to help keep the **environment** clean.
technique, p. 40	*n.* a way of doing something The painter's **technique** includes a special paintbrush.
traditional, p. 40	*adj.* coming from customs handed down through time She wore the **traditional** wedding dress of her culture.
adapt, p. 41	*v.* to become accustomed to a new situation He **adapted** quickly to city life after moving from a small town.

Instruct

Africa's Physical Geography L2

Guided Instruction

■ **Vocabulary Builder** Clarify the high-use word **environment** before reading.

■ Read Africa's Physical Geography using the Oral Cloze reading strategy (TE, p. T33) and have students study the vegetation map on this page.

■ Ask students **Where are Africa's tropical rain forests located?** (*on either side of the Equator*)

■ Ask students **What vegetation region is north and south of the savanna?** (*desert areas, including the Sahara*)

■ Ask students **How are Africa's people affected by geography?** (*There is little farming in the deserts because of the lack of water; people herd cattle on the savanna, but not in the rain forest.*)

Independent Practice

Ask students to create the Taking Notes graphic organizer on a blank piece of paper. Then have them complete the organizer. Briefly model how to identify which details to record.

Monitor Progress

■ As students fill in and complete the graphic organizer, circulate and make sure individuals are choosing the correct details.

■ Show *Section Reading Support Transparency MT 56* and ask students to check their graphic organizers individually. Go over key concepts and clarify key vocabulary as needed.

📖 **Medieval Times to Today Transparencies,** *Section Reading Support Transparency MT 56*

Answers

Infer An oasis would provide travelers with water and shelter from the sun.

MAP MASTER™ Skills Activity **Describe** tropical savanna; Mediterranean forest **Infer** the desert

Go Online
PHSchool.com Students may practice their map skills using the interactive online version of this map.

Target Reading Skill `L2`

Reread As a follow up, ask students to complete the Target Reading Skill activity on this page. *(Because each area of natural vegetation supports different kinds of crops and livestock, it is difficult for groups to move from one area to another.)*

The Bantu Migrations `L2`

Guided Instruction

- **Vocabulary Builder** Clarify the high-use words **technique, traditional,** and **adapt** before reading.

- Read The Bantu Migrations with students. As students read, circulate and make sure individuals can answer the Reading Check question.

- Discuss with students why it has been difficult for scientists and historians to piece together the history of sub-Saharan Africa. *(The Sahara cut off this area from Europe until modern times and materials Africans used for buildings and tools have disintegrated.)*

- Ask students **How have scientists recently uncovered new information?** *(They have gathered stories about people's past from African storytellers and modern techniques have helped scientists uncover new information.)*

Answer

✓ Reading Check It affects how they make their living; for example, there is little farming in the deserts because of the lack of water.

Reread Reread the last four paragraphs, under the heading Africa's Physical Geography, to understand how Africa's physical features might have been a barrier to movement.

The Zambezi River plunges over Victoria Falls, on the Zambia-Zimbabwe border.

Groups that share the same environment may live differently. For example, Mbuti (em BOO tee) people of Africa's rain forest live mainly by hunting animals and gathering plants, but neighboring peoples live mainly by farming.

✓ Reading Check How do Africa's physical features affect people's ways of life?

The Bantu Migrations

The physical barriers formed by lakes, forests, mountains, and rivers did not stop the movement of people across Africa. The map titled Bantu Migrations, on page 39, traces the major routes of the Bantu people. These migrations continued for more than 1,000 years. They are among the largest population movements in all of human history.

The History of Sub-Saharan Africa Historians know a great deal about North Africa's history. But they have only a sketchy knowledge of the history of Africa south of the Sahara. That area is called sub-Saharan Africa. Until modern times, the Sahara cut off this larger part of Africa from Europe. European historians have found it difficult to study sub-Saharan Africa. Today, scientists and historians are working to piece together the history of this area. In many ways, it is like solving a puzzle.

Differentiated Instruction

For Special Needs Students `L1`

Have students read the section as they listen to the recorded version on the Student Edition on Audio CD. Check for comprehension by pausing the CD and asking students to share their answers to the Reading Checks.

⊙ Chapter 2, Section 1, **Student Edition on Audio CD**

For Less Proficient Readers `L2`

Some students may have difficulty reading the historical map on p. 39. To help them develop their map skills, ask students to complete *Reading a Historical Map.*

All in One Medieval Times to Today Teaching Resources, *Reading a Historical Map,* p. 169

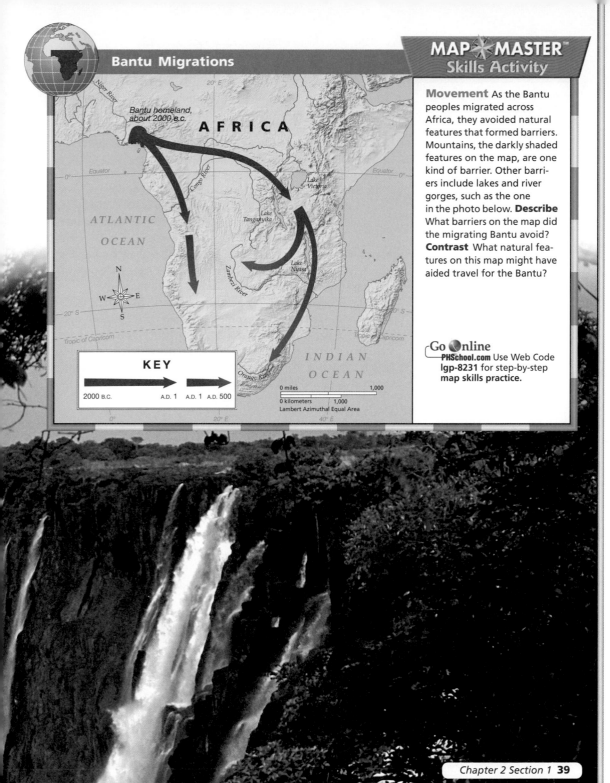

Bantu Migrations

MAP MASTER™ Skills Activity

Movement As the Bantu peoples migrated across Africa, they avoided natural features that formed barriers. Mountains, the darkly shaded features on the map, are one kind of barrier. Other barriers include lakes and river gorges, such as the one in the photo below. **Describe** What barriers on the map did the migrating Bantu avoid? **Contrast** What natural features on this map might have aided travel for the Bantu?

Bantu homeland, about 2000 B.C.

AFRICA

Niger River

Congo River

Equator

ATLANTIC OCEAN

Lake Victoria

Lake Tanganyika

Zambezi River

Lake Nyasa

Tropic of Capricorn

INDIAN OCEAN

Orange River

KEY

2000 B.C. → A.D. 1   A.D. 1 → A.D. 500

0 miles 1,000
0 kilometers 1,000
Lambert Azimuthal Equal Area

Go Online
PHSchool.com Use Web Code lgp-8231 for step-by-step map skills practice.

Chapter 2 Section 1 **39**

Guided Instruction (continued)

- Ask students **How did Bantu-speaking people meet their needs in early times?** (*They were fishers, farmers, and herders.*)

- Ask students **Why were property and positions of power passed down through the mother's side of the family in Bantu culture?** (*Many clans traced their ancestry through the mother.*)

- Ask students **Why might the Bantu have moved from their traditional homelands?** (*to search for better farmland and grazing*)

- Discuss with students how the Bantu had to change their way of living when they migrated to different environments. (*They had to learn new ways of farming and caring for livestock.*)

Skills for Life — Skills Mini Lesson

Using Cartographer's Tools

1. Teach the skill by pointing out to students that maps have features that make them easier to read. These may include a compass rose, a scale, and a map key.

2. Help students practice the skill by identifying the information that appears in the map key on p. 39. (*Bantu migration routes are shown with arrows.*)

3. Have students apply the skill by using the compass rose on p. 39 to determine in which directions the Bantu migrated. (*south, west, and east*)

Answers

MAP MASTER Skills Activity **Describe** mountains, lakes, and river gorges **Contrast** rivers and mountains

Go Online
PHSchool.com Students may practice their map skills using the interactive online version of this map.

Read the **Links Across Time** on this page. Ask students **How have the Bantu migrations affected Africans today?** (*Today more than 200 million Africans speak Bantu languages.*)

Guided Instruction (continued)

- Ask students **What did the Bantu do when they encountered other people as they moved?** (*Sometimes they joined with the group and introduced Bantu culture to them, and other times they drove away the people they met.*)

- Ask students **Why was the metalworking that the Bantu taught to others a valuable skill?** (*Iron weapons and tools could be used for hunting, defense, clearing land, and cutting trees.*)

- Ask students **What would happen when an area in which the Bantu lived became too crowded?** (*The Bantu would migrate to a new area.*)

Independent Practice

Assign *Guided Reading and Review.*

All in One **Medieval Times to Today Teaching Resources,** *Guided Reading and Review,* p. 149

Monitor Progress

Tell students to fill in the last column of the *Reading Readiness Guide.* Probe for what they learned that confirms or invalidates each statement.

All in One **Medieval Times to Today Teaching Resources,** *Reading Readiness Guide,* p. 148

Links Across Time

Bantu Languages As the Bantu speakers moved through Africa, they also spread their languages. Today, more than 200 million Africans speak Bantu languages. In fact, about 500 of the languages spoken in Africa south of the Sahara belong to the Bantu language family.

One reason this puzzle is difficult is that the wood and clay that many African peoples used for building have disintegrated. Even iron tools and weapons have not lasted, because iron rusts fairly quickly. However, modern techniques and inventions have helped scientists uncover new information. Stories told by traditional African storytellers have led to new areas of exploration. That is because these stories are often **oral history,** accounts of the past that people pass down by word of mouth.

The Bantu In early times, most Bantu-speaking peoples were fishers, farmers, and herders. Their villages were made up of families from the same **clan** (klan), or group of families who traced their roots to the same ancestor. Many of these clans traced their ancestry through mothers rather than fathers. For this reason, property and positions of power were passed down through the mother's side of the family.

The Bantu-speaking peoples moved slowly from their traditional homelands. Each generation moved a fairly short distance in their search for better farmland and better grazing. As the Bantu migrated, they entered different environments. In many places, they had to change the way they lived. For example, they learned to raise different crops or different kinds of animals.

These women in Windhoek, Namibia, belong to a present-day Bantu group, the Herero.

Background: Global Perspectives

The Columbian Exchange Just as the Bantu introduced their culture to other groups, Europeans and Native Americans exchanged many products in the late 1400s. This is called the Columbian Exchange, after Christopher Columbus, the first European to establish lasting contact between the two hemispheres. Native Americans had never before seen the horse, pig, cow, sheep, wheat, peaches, sugar, bananas, or dandelions. Similarly, maize, tomatoes, potatoes, cocoa, pineapples, tobacco, and turkeys were brought to the Eastern hemisphere for the first time. Europeans also unknowingly introduced many diseases that Native Americans had never been exposed to; many American Indians died as a result.

The Spread of Bantu Culture Often, Bantu people moved into areas where other people already lived. When this happened, they sometimes joined the groups living there. The older cultures then usually adapted to Bantu culture. For example, the Bantu introduced crops such as yams to other parts of Africa. At other times, however, the Bantu forced the people already living there to leave their homes.

As the Bantu migrated, they also carried a knowledge of metalworking with them. Iron tools gave the Bantu more control over their environment than older cultures had. With hard axes, they could cut down trees and clear the land. Their sharp, iron-headed spears and arrows were powerful weapons for hunting and for warfare.

These migrations continued over many generations, with groups moving whenever an area became crowded. In time, the Bantu had settled throughout Central and Southern Africa.

✔ **Reading Check** What kinds of skills did the Bantu carry with them?

Making Iron Tools
Bantu peoples heated rocks containing iron in furnaces to produce a lump of iron, shown above at the far left. They then gradually hammered it to shape a useful tool, such as the hoe above at the right. **Draw Conclusions** *How might iron tools have given the Bantu an advantage over people who lacked metal tools?*

Section 1 Assessment

Key Terms
Review the key terms at the beginning of this section. Use each term in a sentence that explains its meaning.

Target Reading Skill
What were you able to clarify about Africa's physical features by rereading?

Comprehension and Critical Thinking
1. (a) **Identify** Describe the main physical features of Africa.

(b) **Synthesize Information** How do Africa's physical features affect people's ways of life?
2. (a) **Recall** Over how many years did the Bantu migrations occur?
(b) **Summarize** Tell what happened when the Bantu met other African peoples.
(c) **Conclude** Why are the Bantu migrations an important part of African history?

Writing Activity
Consider the Bantu people's long history of migration and adaptation to new environments. Write a paragraph to answer the following question: What does this history suggest about the kind of people the Bantu were?

Go Online
PHSchool.com

For: An activity on the Bantu migration
Visit: PHSchool.com
Web Code: lgd-8201

Chapter 2 Section 1 **41**

Section 1 Assessment

Key Terms
Students' sentences should reflect knowledge of each Key Term.

Target Reading Skill
Answers will vary, but students should demonstrate their understanding of the skill with examples from the text.

Comprehension and Critical Thinking
1. (a) Tropical rain forests with thick vegetation and plenty of rainfall are located on either side of the Equator; the savanna is located farther from the Equator and may include lush, tall grass or short, sparse grass with some trees and bushes; desert areas, with sand dunes, rocky mountains, oases, and high temperatures, are located north and south of the savanna. (b) tropical rain forest

---

Assess Progress L2
Have students complete the Section Assessment. Administer the *Section Quiz.*

 Medieval Times to Today Teaching Resources, *Section Quiz,* p. 150

Reteach L1
If students need more instruction, have them read this section in the Reading and Vocabulary Study Guide.

📖 Chapter 2, Section 1, **Medieval Times to Today Reading and Vocabulary Study Guide,** pp. 16–18

Extend L3
Have students learn more about migrations by completing the book project *Major Migrations.*

 Medieval Times to Today Teaching Resources, *Book Project: Major Migrations,* p. 86–88

Answers

Draw Conclusions Iron tools gave them an advantage in hunting and warfare.

✔ **Reading Check** They carried knowledge of how to farm crops such as yams, and taught metalworking.

Writing Activity
Use the *Rubric for Assessing a Writing Assignment* to assess students' paragraphs.

Medieval Times to Today Teaching Resources, *Rubric for Assessing a Writing Assignment,* p. 174

Go Online PHSchool.com Typing in the Web code when prompted will bring students to detailed instructions for this activity.

2. (a) more than 1,000 years (b) Sometimes the Bantu joined other cultures and introduced aspects of their culture, such as raising certain crops and metalworking to the new groups. Other times the Bantu drove other groups away. (c) Possible answers: they are among the largest population movements in all of human history; their culture has had an impact on large parts of Africa.

Skills for Life

Objective
Learn to determine the reliability of a source.

Prepare to Read

Build Background Knowledge   L2
Define the word *reliable* for any students who are unsure of its definition, explaining that it means "trustworthy or dependable." Then ask students why it is important to be able to determine how reliable a piece of writing is. Use the Numbered Heads participation strategy (TE, p. T36) to conduct a class discussion.

Instruct

Using Reliable Information   L2

Guided Instruction
■ Read the steps to using reliable information as a class and write them on the board.

■ Practice the skill by following the steps on p. 42 as a class using the selection from *Travels in Asia and Africa 1325–1354* on p. 43. Model each step in the activity with students. They should identify when the passage was written *(the 1300s)*, decide whether more recent information would be more reliable *(it is an eyewitness account of the Sahara in the 1300s; more current sources would be needed to study the Sahara as it is today)*, examine the author's qualifications *(he saw the Sahara firsthand)*, identify any loaded language ("bitter" *and* "plagued with flies;" *these impressions could be proved true or false for the present-day Sahara)* and determine whether they think the source is reliable *(the source is probably reliable for information about Ibn Battutah's journey in the 1300s. The passage would be a good source of information if one was writing a report about travel in the 1300s. If one was writing about the present-day Sahara, a newer source of information would be better)*.

Skills for Life — Using Reliable Information

Grace was writing a paper about the Nok culture, the earliest known Iron Age culture in West Africa. She found this passage in a book called *Great Civilizations of Ancient Africa,* published in 1971. It was written by the historian Lester Brooks. Was this passage a good source for Grace's paper?

"The Nok peoples are known to have had a sophisticated agricultural society and . . . the ability to produce weapons of iron at this early time. They undoubtedly must have had relations—peaceful or otherwise—with other peoples over a wide expanse of the African interior. . . .

"But the truth . . . is that we just do not know who the Nok peoples were or how they lived. We have no written records, we have no legends or myths that explain them."

Nok statue

All books are not equally reliable. Use the skill below to help you determine how reliable a piece of writing is.

Learn the Skill
To decide whether a piece of writing is reliable, use the following steps:

1 **Look at the date of the source.** A source might have been written near the time of an event or many years later. Eyewitness accounts can tell you how an event was understood at the time it happened. Later writing may be based on respected research. New discoveries might have been made since the passage above was written.

2 **Identify the author's qualifications and purpose.** A "historian" should be a reliable source. But think about the sentence beginning, "The Nok peoples are known to have had a . . ." Who is it who *knows?* Where might this author have gotten his information?

3 **Decide whether the author has a bias.** Look for opinions, beliefs that cannot be proved. "They undoubtedly must have had relations . . ." is an opinion, not a fact. Also look for loaded words and phrases. The word *sophisticated* gives a positive impression that may or may not be accurate. Sometimes biased writers leave out information that does not support their bias.

4 **Decide how reliable the source is and why.** Consider your purpose: Are you writing about how an event seemed to the people who experienced it? Or, do you need the latest research to support your conclusions about the event?

42 Medieval Times to Today

Independent Practice
Assign *Skills for Life* and have students complete it individually.

All in One **Medieval Times to Today Teaching Resources,** *Skills for Life,* p. 164

Monitor Progress
As students are completing *Skills for Life,* circulate to make sure individuals are applying the skill steps effectively. Provide assistance as needed.

The following passage is from *Travels in Asia and Africa 1325–1354*, written by a North African merchant named Ibn Battutah. He describes a journey through the Sahara.

"[W]e passed ten days of discomfort because the water there is bitter and the place is plagued with flies. . . . We passed a caravan on the way and they told us that some of their party had become separated from them. We found one of them dead under a shrub of the sort that grows in the sand. . . ."

Practice the Skill

Read the passage above. Then follow the steps in Learn the Skill to decide if it is a reliable source.

❶ When was the passage written? Would this information be more reliable if it had been written more recently? Explain why or why not.

❷ What qualifies the author to describe the Sahara? Do you think he was an accurate observer?

❸ Identify an example of loaded language in the passage. Could this statement be proved true or false? Is it possible that the writer has left important information out of his account?

❹ Do you consider this passage a reliable source? How might your purpose in using the passage affect your decision?

Sand dunes in the Sahara

Apply the Skill

Suppose that you are writing a report on the Bantu migration. Write a brief paragraph explaining how you would find reliable sources for your report. Would you look for sources published recently or long ago? What would you want to know about the authors? How else would you decide whether or not the source is reliable?

Chapter 2 **43**

Assess and Reteach

Assess Progress L2
Ask students to do the Apply the Skill activity.

Reteach L1
If students are having trouble applying the skill steps, have them review the skill using the interactive Social Studies Skills Tutor CD-ROM.

◉ *Using Reliable Information*, **Social Studies Skills Tutor CD-ROM**

Extend L3
Have students choose a topic that interests them, such as a historical figure or a country. Have them collect a wide variety of sources, such as books from the library, articles from the Internet, and encyclopedia entries. Then have them assess the reliability of each source and write a short paper on their topic. Students may read their papers to the class and explain what kinds of sources they decided to use and why.

Answer
Apply the Skill
Students' paragraphs will vary, but should show an understanding of the skill steps.

Section 2 Step-by-Step Instruction

Objectives

Social Studies

1. Learn about the trading kingdoms of the West African savanna.
2. Investigate the kingdoms of the West African rain forests.

Reading/Language Arts

Learn how to paraphrase to remember information.

Prepare to Read

Build Background Knowledge L2

Explain to students that in this section they will learn about trading kingdoms of the West African savanna and rain forests. Using the Idea Wave participation strategy (TE, p. T35), have students generate a list of items, such as foods, which come from other countries. Ask students to discuss how their lives would be different without these items, and what they can conclude about the importance of trade.

Set a Purpose for Reading L2

- Preview the Objectives.
- Read each statement in the *Reading Readiness Guide* aloud. Ask students to mark the statements true or false.

  All in One **Medieval Times to Today Teaching Resources,** *Reading Readiness Guide*, p. 152
- Have students discuss the statements in pairs or groups of four, then mark their worksheets again. Use the Numbered Heads participation strategy (TE, p. T36) to call on students to share their group's perspectives.

Vocabulary Builder

Preview Key Terms L2

Pronounce each Key Term, then ask the students to say the word with you. Provide a simple explanation such as, "Mansa Musa ruled the kingdom of Mali in the 1300s and built it into a great trading empire."

Section 2 Kingdoms of West Africa

Prepare to Read

Objectives

In this section, you will

1. Learn about the trading kingdoms of the West African savanna.
2. Investigate the kingdoms of the West African rain forests.

Taking Notes

As you read this section, look for the main ideas and details about different African cultures. Create an outline of the section using the example below as a model.

I. Kingdoms of the savanna
  A. Ghana
    1.
    2.
  B.
II.

Target Reading Skill

Paraphrase When you paraphrase, you restate what you have read in your own words. For example, you could paraphrase the first paragraph below this way: "Thousands of people and dozens of camels carrying gold marched in a group."

As you read this section, paraphrase the information after each red or blue heading.

Key Terms

- **Mansa Musa** (MAHN sah MOO sah) *n.* a king of Mali in the 1300s
- **Mali** (MAH lee) *n.* a rich kingdom of the West African savanna
- **Ghana** (GAH nuh) *n.* the first West African kingdom based on the gold and salt trade
- **Songhai** (SAWNG hy) *n.* a powerful kingdom of the West African savanna
- **Ile-Ife** (EE lay EE fay) *n.* the capital of a kingdom of the West African rain forest
- **Benin** (beh NEEN) *n.* a kingdom of the West African rain forest

Mansa Musa, the king of Mali

Soldiers whose swords hung from gold chains rode horses decorated with gold. Hundreds of government officials marched along with the soldiers. Thousands of slaves, each one dressed in silk and carrying a staff made of gold, also accompanied the marchers. The procession included more than 60,000 people and dozens of camels, each camel loaded with many pounds of gold.

This sight greeted the astonished people of Cairo, Egypt, one day in July 1324. It was the caravan of Mansa Musa (MAHN sah MOO sah), the powerful king of Mali, in West Africa. The caravan was traveling from Mali across North Africa. Mansa Musa was performing his duty as a Muslim by traveling to the Southwest Asian city of Mecca, the holiest city of Islam. Many years later, people in Egypt were still talking about Mansa Musa's amazing visit—and about the amount of gold that he and his officials had spent.

Target Reading Skill L2

Paraphrase Point out the Target Reading Skill. Tell students that paraphrasing can help them organize information and better understand what they read.

Model paraphrasing using the text on p. 49. *(The city of Benin flourished from the 1200s to the 1600s. The mining industry, slave trade, and control of trade routes all contributed to the city's growth. The city was also a center of art, and its artists may have influenced modern western artists.)*

Give students *Paraphrase.* Have them complete the activity in their groups.

All in One **Medieval Times to Today Teaching Resources,** *Paraphrase*, p. 160

Kingdoms of the Savanna

Mansa Musa ruled **Mali** (MAH lee), a rich kingdom of the West African savanna. The kingdoms of the savanna controlled important trade routes across the Sahara. The Niger River, which flows through the region, was another important trade route. Traders traveling through these lands had to pay taxes on all their goods. This made the kingdoms rich. In return, the rulers kept peace and order throughout the land. Thus, merchants—and their caravans of valuable goods—could travel safely from one place to another.

Ghana, a Kingdom Built on Trade Salt and gold were the basis of West African trade. Most of the salt came from mines in the central Sahara. Salt was very valuable. People needed it to flavor food, to preserve meat, and to maintain good health. Salt was scarce in the rain forest region. So people from the forest region of West Africa sold gold in exchange for salt. Some gold was sold to traders on their way to North Africa. These traders returned with glass and other precious North African goods. Traders could travel hundreds of miles across the dry Sahara because their camels could travel for days without water.

The first West African kingdom to be based on the wealth of the salt and gold trade was **Ghana** (GAH nuh). By about A.D. 400, the people of Ghana took control of the trade routes across the Sahara. Ghana's location was ideal. Find Ghana on the map titled Civilizations of Africa, on page 35. Ghana was just north of the rich gold fields. Land routes south from the Sahara went through Ghana. By about A.D 800, Ghana was a major trading kingdom.

The Salt Trade in Africa
Camel caravans like the one shown at the bottom of the page carried slabs of salt from salt mines in the Sahara. Slabs of salt were traded in markets like the one below, in Mopti, Mali.
Apply Information *When traders from the forest region bought salt, what might they have offered in exchange?*

Vocabulary Builder

Use the information below to teach students this section's high-use words.

High-Use Word	Definition and Sample Sentence
independent, p. 46	*adj.* not under the control of another The United States became **independent** from Great Britain.
conquer, p. 46	*v.* to get possession of by force The ruler **conquered** all the lands south of his kingdom.
province, p. 47	*n.* a political region of a country She was born in the Canadian **province** of Manitoba.
stability, p. 48	*n.* the condition of being solid and steady This kind of sailboat is known for its strength and **stability**.

Guided Instruction

- **Vocabulary Builder** Clarify the high-use words **independent, conquer,** and **province** before reading.

- Read Kingdoms of the Savanna, using the Choral Reading strategy (TE, p. T34).

- Have students name the three kingdoms of the West African savanna. *(Mali, Ghana, Songhai)* Ask **How did they become wealthy?** *(They controlled important trade routes across the Sahara.)*

- Ask students **What resources were at the heart of West African trade?** *(salt and gold)* **Where was most of Africa's salt and gold found?** *(Salt came from mines in the central Sahara, and gold came from the forest region of West Africa.)*

- Discuss with students how Ghana became a major trading kingdom. *(Ghana began to conquer neighboring peoples and took control of trade routes across the Sahara.)*

- Ask students **Why did Ghana's power begin to fade?** *(Northern invaders overran the capital and other cities, and people fled the area. By the 1200s Ghana had broken up into a number of small states.)*

Answer
Apply Information gold

Paraphrase As a follow up, ask students to complete the Target Reading Skill activity on this page. *(Ghana was a powerful kingdom until about A.D. 1000. By the 1200s, it had broken into independent states. The area was then controlled by Mali.)*

Guided Instruction (continued)

- Discuss with students how Sundiata helped Mali become the most powerful kingdom in West Africa. *(He took control of the salt and gold trade, and conquered surrounding areas.)*

- Ask students **What was a result of Mansa Musa's trip to Mecca?** *(It created ties between Mali and the Muslim peoples of North Africa and Southwest Asia.)*

- Have students list ways in which Mansa Musa helped make Mali a center of learning. *(Possible answers: Muslims built mosques and religious leaders moved to Mali; scholars came to teach religion, arithmetic, medicine, and law.)*

- Ask students **Why do you think Mali's power began to fade after Mansa Musa died?** *(Possible answer: No strong ruler was able to take his place and hold the kingdom together.)*

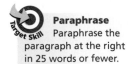

Paraphrase
Paraphrase the paragraph at the right in 25 words or fewer.

The Great Mosque at Djenné
The mosque below is in the city of Djenné, an important trading center in the kingdoms of Mali and Songhai. A mosque is a Muslim place of worship. **Analyze Images** *What does the scale of this mosque suggest about the importance of Islam to people in this region?*

Ghana's capital, Kumbi Saleh, was divided into two cities. One was the center of trade. The other was the royal city, where the king had his court and handed down his decisions. Around A.D. 1000, the power of Ghana began to weaken. Invaders from the north overran the capital and other cities. By the 1200s, Ghana had broken into small, independent states. Soon, most of the trade in the area was controlled by a powerful new kingdom, the kingdom of Mali.

The Powerful Kingdom of Mali Mali was centered in the Upper Niger Valley. Under the leadership of Sundiata (sun JAH tah), who united the kingdom about 1230, Mali took control of the salt and gold trade. Sundiata conquered surrounding areas and increased the size of the kingdom. By 1255, when Sundiata died, Mali had grown rich from trade. It had become the most powerful kingdom in West Africa. Mali continued to grow in the years after Sundiata's death.

In 1312, Mansa Musa became ruler of Mali. By this time, traders from North Africa had brought a new religion, Islam, to West Africa. Muslims, or people who practice Islam, worship one god. Mansa Musa greatly expanded his kingdom and made Islam the official religion. Mansa Musa's trip to the holy city of Mecca created new ties between Mali and the Muslim peoples of North Africa and Southwest Asia.

46 Medieval Times to Today

Background: Links Across Time

The Gold Coast The Kingdom of Ghana disappeared as a major trading empire in the 1200s. Europeans made first contact with what is now Ghana in 1471 and named the area the "Gold Coast" because of the quantities of gold found there. Great Britain later made the Gold Coast one of its colonies. In 1957, the Gold Coast achieved independence as the modern nation of Ghana. Today gold remains a major export of Ghana.

Answer

Analyze Images This large mosque suggests that Islam is very important in the region.

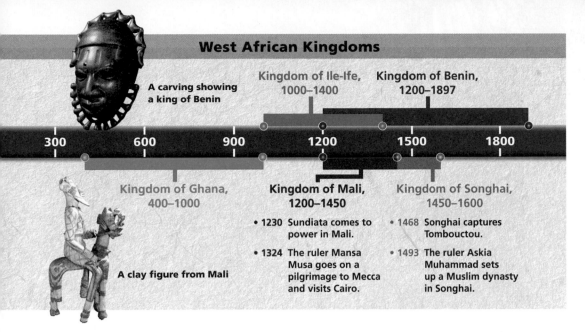

West African Kingdoms

A carving showing a king of Benin

Kingdom of Ile-Ife, 1000–1400

Kingdom of Benin, 1200–1897

300   600   900   1200   1500   1800

Kingdom of Ghana, 400–1000

A clay figure from Mali

Kingdom of Mali, 1200–1450
- 1230 Sundiata comes to power in Mali.
- 1324 The ruler Mansa Musa goes on a pilgrimage to Mecca and visits Cairo.

Kingdom of Songhai, 1450–1600
- 1468 Songhai captures Tombouctou.
- 1493 The ruler Askia Muhammad sets up a Muslim dynasty in Songhai.

During his 25-year rule, Mansa Musa used his new ties to these Muslim peoples to make Mali a center of learning. Scholars came to teach religion, mathematics, medicine, and law. In the late 1300s, however—about 50 years after Mansa Musa died— Mali's power began to fade. Raiders attacked from the north, and fighting broke out within the kingdom. Several provinces broke away and became independent. One of these former provinces became an empire in its own right. It was called Songhai (SAWNG hy).

The Rise and Fall of Songhai Songhai became the leading kingdom of the West African savanna during the 1400s. Like the rulers of Ghana and Mali, Songhai's leaders controlled trade routes and the sources of salt and gold. Songhai's wealth and power grew when it conquered the rich trading city of Tombouctou in 1468. Find Songhai on the map titled Civilizations of Africa on page 35.

In less than 100 years, however, the kingdom of Songhai began to lose power. In the late 1500s, the people of Songhai began fighting among themselves. The kingdom became weaker. And it easily fell to the guns and cannons of an army from Morocco, in North Africa. The era of the rich and powerful trading empires of West Africa was at an end.

✓ **Reading Check** Name the two most important trade items in West Africa.

■ Timeline Skills

This timeline shows five West African kingdoms. Vertical lines mark specific dates. Horizontal bars show periods of time. The kingdoms of the savanna are at the bottom of the timeline. The forest kingdoms are at the top. **Identify** Which kingdom lasted the longest? Which lasted the shortest time? **Analyze** Which forest kingdoms overlapped in time with the kingdom of Mali?

- Ask students **How was Songhai's rise as an empire similar to Ghana's and Mali's?** (*All three grew from conquests and controlled trade routes.*)
- Ask students to list the events that led to the fall of Songhai. (*The people of Songhai began fighting among themselves; the kingdom became weaker and fell to an army from North Africa.*)

Independent Practice
Ask students to create the Taking Notes graphic organizer on a blank piece of paper. Then have them fill in the outline with main ideas and details about Africa's savanna kingdoms. Briefly model how to identify which main ideas and details to record.

Monitor Progress
As students fill in the graphic organizer, circulate and make sure individuals are organizing the information correctly. Provide assistance as needed.

Differentiated Instruction

For Gifted and Talented L3
Have students read the three primary sources listed below and answer the questions that follow.

All in One **Medieval Times to Today Teaching Resources,** *Al-Bakri Describes the Court of Ghana, Ibn Battuta Praises the Fairness of Mali's People, Leo Africanus Describes Timbuktu and Gao,* pp. 170–172

For English Language Learners L1
Have English language learners use pictures to visualize the meaning of words. Pair them with more proficient students in the class and assign several words—such as *salt, agriculture,* and *journey*—from the sub-heading The Powerful Kingdom of Mali to the pairs. Have each pair draw pictures that depict the assigned words.

Answers

✓ **Reading Check** Salt and gold were the most important trade items in West Africa.

Timeline Skills Identify Benin lasted the longest—697 years; Songhai the briefest— 150 years **Analyze** Ile-Ife and Benin both overlapped with the kingdom of Mali.

Kingdoms of the Forest

L2

Guided Instruction

- **Vocabulary Builder** Clarify the high-use word **stability** before reading.

- Read Kingdoms of the Forest with students. As students read, circulate and make sure individuals can answer the Reading Check question.

- Discuss with students why there is little information about Ile-Ife and what scientists have been able to find. *(The modern town of Ife is located on top of the earlier city, trees cover sites outside of the town, rains have washed away mud buildings, and dampness has rusted iron and rotted wood and fabrics. However, scientists have discovered sculptures believed to represent powerful onis.)*

- Ask students to describe Benin's slave trade. *(Enslaved people were sold along the traditional trade routes; some worked for families in the savannah, others joined slaves from Europe and Asia in North Africa.)*

- Ask students **How was Benin a center of art?** *(Obas hired artists to make objects from bronze, brass, ivory, and copper.)*

Independent Practice

Have students complete the graphic organizer by filling in main ideas and details about Ile-Ife and Benin, in the correct order.

Monitor Progress

- Show *Section Support Transparency MT 57* and ask students to check their graphic organizers individually. Go over key concepts and clarify key vocabulary as needed.

  Medieval Times to Today Transparencies, *Section Reading Support Transparency MT 57*

- Tell students to fill in the last column of the *Reading Readiness Guide.* Probe for what they learned that confirms or invalidates each statement.

  All in One Medieval Times to Today Teaching Resources, *Reading Readiness Guide,* p. 152

48 Medieval Times to Today

Kingdoms of the Forest

Ghana, Mali, and Songhai developed on West Africa's savanna. At the same time, other kingdoms arose in the rain forests to the south of these grasslands. The peoples of the rain forests were not Muslim. They practiced religions with hundreds of different gods.

Two of the most important kingdoms of the West African forests were centered around the cities of **Ile-Ife** (EE lay EE fay) and **Benin** (beh NEEN). Both of these cities were located in the present-day nation of Nigeria. As with the kingdoms of the savanna, trade made these forest kingdoms powerful and wealthy. With their wealth and stability, these kingdoms supported larger populations than other African rain forest regions could support.

Ile-Ife: A Center of Culture and Trade

About A.D. 1000, Ile-Ife became a major cultural and trading center. The powerful leaders of this kingdom were called onis (OH neez). Traditional stories told by these people described Ile-Ife as "the place where the world was created," but historians know little about the early city or the people who lived there.

One of the reasons that we know little about Ile-Ife is that the modern town of Ife is located on top of the earlier city. Also, the region is thickly forested and damp. Trees have covered old sites outside the town, and rains have washed away old mud buildings. Dampness has also rusted iron and long since rotted wood and fabrics.

Among the most important artifacts that have survived are sculptures. Many were discovered only in the last 100 years. Scientists have dated these works of art to the years between the 1100s and the 1300s. Many of these sculptures are lifelike and may be portraits of the powerful onis of Ile-Ife.

The rain forests of West Africa have a damp climate and lush vegetation.

 Skills Mini Lesson

Comparing and Contrasting

1. Tell students that comparing means finding similarities, and contrasting means finding differences. The steps for comparing and contrasting are (1) identify what you are comparing (2) notice words that compare, such as *both*, and words that contrast, such as *but*, and (3) draw conclusions.

2. Help students compare the cities of Ile-Ife and Benin as described on pp. 48–49. *(Both were located in present-day Nigeria, both were centers of art and trade, and they shared a language and religion.)*

3. Have students contrast Ile-Ife and Benin. *(They reached the peak of their power at different times—Ile-Ife around A.D. 1000, and Benin by the 1400s.)*

Benin Rules an Empire The city of Benin dates to the 1200s. At that time, workers in the region mined copper, iron, and gold. Benin's leaders, called obas (OH buz), also sold slaves to African traders. Many of these slaves were forced to work as servants for rich families on the savanna. Others joined slaves from Europe and Asia to work in North Africa.

By the 1500s, Benin reached its greatest strength and size. The oba controlled a large army, priests, government workers, and less important local chiefs. The city of Benin ruled the trade routes along the rivers to the north and south. It became immensely rich. It ruled much of present-day southern Nigeria. Benin remained strong until the late 1600s, when the kingdom began to lose its power over the region.

Like Ile-Ife, the city of Benin also became a center of art. The obas hired skilled artists to make many beautiful objects from bronze, brass, ivory, and copper. These artists may have borrowed some cultural traditions from Ile-Ife, but the exact relationship between the two kingdoms is unclear. The artists of Benin and other West African kingdoms have in turn influenced modern artists in Europe and the Americas.

✓ **Reading Check** What were the leaders of Ile-Ife and Benin called?

Links to Art

Bronze Plaques Benin artists made bronze plaques and sculptures for the royal palaces of the obas. For example, one sculpture shows a man playing a flute and wearing an animal-skin skirt. After 1897, the British ruled this region and removed many objects. Today, hundreds of Benin plaques can be seen in museums in Europe and the United States. This plaque is about 300 years old.

Section 2 Assessment

Key Terms
Review the key terms at the beginning of this section. Use each term in a sentence that explains its meaning.

Target Reading Skill
Find the second paragraph under the heading Kingdoms of the Forest, on page 48. Paraphrase this paragraph by rewriting it in your own words.

Comprehension and Critical Thinking
1. (a) List What were the names of the three major kingdoms of the West African savanna?

(b) Identify Causes What made each of the three kingdoms rich?
(c) Apply Information What do the powerful countries of today have in common with these kingdoms?
2. (a) Recall Describe some of the art objects that the people of Ile-Ife and Benin left behind.
(b) Identify Cause and Effect Why are these objects among the few things that have survived from these cultures?

Writing Activity
Suppose that you are a foreign visitor who has traveled to the kingdom of Benin in the late 1500s. You will be allowed to meet briefly with the current oba. Write a list of five or six questions that you would like to ask him about his daily life, his kingdom, and the people he rules.

Writing Tip Be sure that your questions are worded in a way that shows respect for the powerful ruler and his kingdom. Also be sure to include a brief introduction identifying yourself and the purpose of your visit.

Chapter 2 Section 2 **49**

Links
Read the **Links to Art** on this page. Ask students **Why are many Benin plaques in the United States and in Europe today?** *(The British ruled the Benin region after 1897 and removed many objects.)*

Assess and Reteach

Assess Progress L2
Have students complete the Section Assessment. Administer the *Section Quiz.*

All in One **Medieval Times to Today Teaching Resources,** *Section Quiz,* p. 154

Reteach L1
If students need more instruction, have them read this section in the Reading and Vocabulary Study Guide.

Chapter 2, Section 2, **Medieval Times to Today Reading and Vocabulary Study Guide,** pp. 19–21

Extend L3
Have students learn more about West African culture by completing the *Enrichment* activity about folk tales.

All in One **Medieval Times to Today Teaching Resources,** *Enrichment,* p. 163

Answer
✓ **Reading Check** The leaders of Ile-Ife were called onis and the leaders of Benin were called obas.

Writing Activity
Use the *Rubric for Assessing a Writing Assignment.*

All in One **Medieval Times to Today Teaching Resources,** *Rubric for Assessing a Writing Assignment,* p. 174

Section 2 Assessment

Key Terms
Students' sentences should reflect knowledge of each Key Term.

Target Reading Skill
Student should be able to accurately paraphrase the information from the text.

Comprehension and Critical Thinking
1. (a) Ghana, Mali, and Songhai **(b)** trade in salt and gold **(c)** Possible answer: they have economies that depend on trade with other regions.
2. (a) Ile-Ife—life-like sculptures that may be portraits of the onis; Benin—bronze, brass, ivory, and copper objects that may be influenced by Ile-Ife traditions **(b)** Possible answer: The objects may have survived because some metals can stay intact over time better than other materials, and the cultures that followed the kingdoms may have appreciated and preserved the art.

Focus on Tombouctou 🔲

Guided Instruction

- Ask students to read the text and study the art, photos, and captions on these pages.

- Ask students **What items were traded in Tombouctou's markets?** *(metal wares, wood, grains, nuts, fish, camel meat, milk, water, dates, rugs, linen, precious ivory, gold, salt, and slaves)*

- Have students study the map p. 51. Ask students **Which journey do you think would be the most difficult—traveling fom Tangier to Ife, or from Taghaza to Taoudenni?** *(probably the traveling from Tangier to Ife, because it is a much longer distance)*

- As a class, answer the Assessment questions. Allow students to briefly discuss their responses with a partner before sharing their answers with the class.

Focus On
Tombouctou

From the salt mines of the Sahara, caravan leaders drove their camels through the hot desert sand. Heavily weighted with slabs of salt, the camel train headed south. Meantime, trade caravans from West Africa's gold mines traveled north. They met in the West African city of Tombouctou (tohm book TOO). In the 1500s, salt was as valuable as gold in the city's markets.

A Marketplace of Goods and Ideas Business was brisk in Tombouctou's markets. Buyers and sellers traded for metal wares and wood; grains and nuts; fish, camel meat, milk, water, and dates; rugs and linen; precious ivory, gold, salt, and even slaves.

By the mid-1500s, about 60,000 people lived in Tombouctou. Artisans such as weavers, dyers, and metalsmiths had shops in the busy city.

More than just a marketplace, this city drew scholars from all over the Islamic world to study and exchange ideas. Many people within the city spoke Arabic. Muslims could pray at three impressive dried-mud mosques.

The illustration at the right shows a market scene in Tombouctou with a mosque in the background. The illustration at the top of the page is of an ancient manuscript that was found in the city.

Background: Links Across Time

The Value of Salt In ancient times, salt was so valuable that it was traded for gold. In Ethiopia and elsewhere in Africa, salt cakes were actually used as money. But it was not necessarily the taste of salt that made it so valuable. Salt can be used as a condiment and a preservative, and could therefore preserve meat and other food items for long journeys. Also, although excessive amounts of salt can be dangerous, salt is necessary for human survival. The consequences of salt deprivation in humans can range from nausea and weakness to a coma and even death.

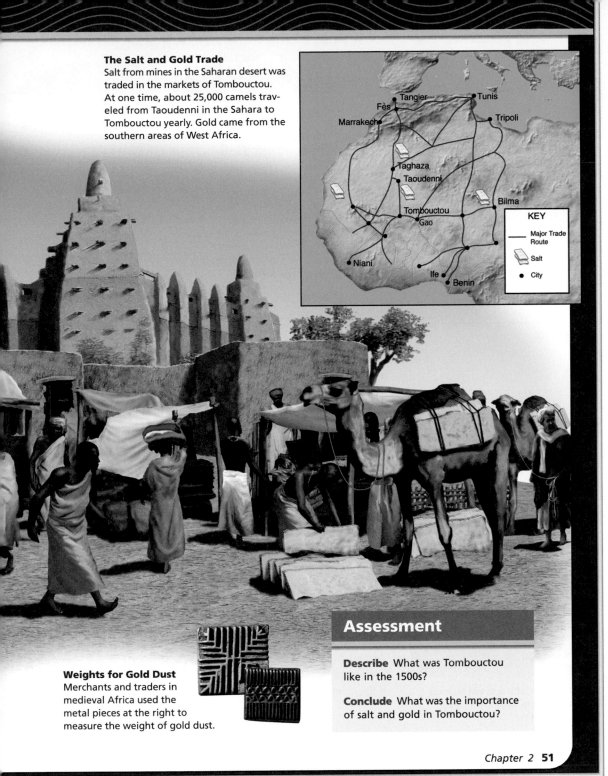

The Salt and Gold Trade
Salt from mines in the Saharan desert was traded in the markets of Tombouctou. At one time, about 25,000 camels traveled from Taoudenni in the Sahara to Tombouctou yearly. Gold came from the southern areas of West Africa.

Tangier
Tunis
Fès
Tripoli
Marrakech
Taghaza
Taoudenni
Bilma
Tombouctou
Gao

KEY
— Major Trade Route
▱ Salt
● City

Niani
Ife
Benin

Weights for Gold Dust
Merchants and traders in medieval Africa used the metal pieces at the right to measure the weight of gold dust.

Assessment

Describe What was Tombouctou like in the 1500s?

Conclude What was the importance of salt and gold in Tombouctou?

Independent Practice

Show students *Transparency MT 20: Africa: Political.* As a class, have students compare the map on page 51 with the transparency, and identify in which present-day countries the cities on the map in the Student Edition are located. Then, create a two-column table on the board, labeling one column *City* and the other *Present-day country where located.* Have students take turns coming up to the board and filling in parts of the chart.

📖 **Medieval Times to Today Transparencies,** *Transparency MT 20: Africa: Political*

Answers

Assessment

Describe By the mid-1500s, about 60,000 people lived in Tombouctou; in addition to being a marketplace, the city was filled with Islamic scholars from all over the world; many people spoke Arabic; and the city had three impressive dried-mud mosques.
Conclude The trade of salt and gold made Tombouctou an important city with a large population; this in turn attracted scholars from all over the Islamic world.

Objectives

Social Studies

1. Learn about powerful East African civilizations whose cities included Aksum and Lalibela.
2. Find out why the coastal cities of East Africa were important.

Reading/Language Arts

Learn to summarize to help you remember and study what you read.

Prepare to Read

Build Background Knowledge L2

Tell students that in this section they will learn about East Africa's trading centers, including one called Great Zimbabwe. Show the video *Great Zimbabwe: The Lost City*. Ask students to note possible reasons for the decline of Great Zimbabwe. Have students decide which theory they believe best answers the mystery and why. Use the Numbered Head participation strategy (TE, p. 36) to get students to share their opinion.

📼 *Great Zimbabwe: The Lost City*, **World Studies Video Program**

Set a Purpose for Reading L2

- Preview the Objectives.

- Read each statement in the *Reading Readiness Guide* aloud. Ask students to mark the statements true or false.

  All in One Medieval Times to Today Teaching Resources, *Reading Readiness Guide*, p. 156

- Have students discuss the statements in pairs or groups of four, then mark their worksheets again. Use the Numbered Heads participation strategy (TE, p. T36) to call on students to share their group's perspectives.

Vocabulary Builder

Preview Key Terms L2

Pronounce each Key Term, then ask students to say the word with you. Provide a simple explanation such as, "Swahili is one of the most important languages of East Africa today."

Prepare to Read

Objectives

In this section, you will

1. Learn about powerful East African civilizations whose cities included Aksum and Lalibela.
2. Find out why the coastal cities of East Africa were important.

Taking Notes

As you read this section, look for the major events in this period of East Africa's history. Copy the timeline below, and add events and dates in the proper places on it.

A.D. **100** ———————————— A.D. **1600**

🎯 Target Reading Skill

Summarize When you summarize, you review and state, in the correct order, the main points you have read. Summarizing can help you understand and study. As you read, pause occasionally to summarize what you have read.

Key Terms

- **Kilwa** (KEEL wah) *n.* one of many trading cities on the East African coast
- **Aksum** (AHK soom) *n.* an important East African center of trade
- **city-state** (SIH tee stayt) *n.* a city that is also a separate, independent state
- **Swahili** (swah HEE lee) *n.* a Bantu language with Arabic words, spoken along the East African coast
- **Great Zimbabwe** (grayt zim BAHB way) *n.* a powerful southeast African city

The ruins of the Great Mosque of Kilwa in Tanzania

52 Medieval Times to Today

The port was full of hurrying people, bobbing ships, and bundles of goods. The bright sun reflected off the water. Some traders were unloading glass beads, rice, spices, and expensive jewels carried from India. Others were bringing honey and wheat from Southwest Asia. Rich silks and fragile porcelains were also arriving after the long voyage from faraway China.

This was the bustling scene at **Kilwa** (KEEL wah), one of many trading cities along the coast of East Africa. Find Kilwa on the map titled Civilizations of Africa on page 35. Located in present-day Tanzania, Kilwa was an Islamic city with a royal palace and lush orchards and gardens. Kilwa's rulers charged taxes on all goods that entered their port. These taxes made Kilwa rich. Ibn Battutah (IB un bat TOO tah)—a famous Muslim traveler from North Africa—visited in the 1330s. He wrote that Kilwa was "one of the most beautiful and best-constructed towns in the world."

🎯 Target Reading Skill L2

Summarize Point out the Target Reading Skill. Tell students that summarizing the text will help them remember what they read.

Model the skill by reading and summarizing the last paragraph on p. 55. (*Like many medieval African kingdoms, Great Zimbabwe grew strong by trading goods such as the gold mined between two rivers of the region.*)

Give students *Summarize*. Have them complete the activity in their groups.

All in One Medieval Times to Today Teaching Resources, *Summarize*, p. 161

Ancient Ethiopia

Thousands of years ago, rich civilizations began to develop in southern Arabia and northeastern Africa along the Red Sea. By A.D. 1, the city of **Aksum** (AHK soom), located in present-day Ethiopia, was an important East African center of trade.

Aksum, a Center of Trade and Christianity Although the city of Aksum was located in the mountains about 100 miles (160 kilometers) inland, it controlled a trading port at Adulis (AD oo lis) on the Red Sea. Over time, Aksum conquered much of modern Ethiopia and southwestern Arabia. It grew steadily in strength and wealth.

The merchants of Aksum traded goods at ports as far away as India. One of the main trade goods they controlled was ivory. Ivory, the white material from elephant tusks, was highly valued for carving. As they traded goods with foreign merchants, the people of Aksum also exchanged ideas and beliefs with them.

During the A.D. 300s, King Ezana (ay ZAH nuh) of Aksum learned about a new religion—Christianity. Soon, the king became a Christian himself and made Christianity the official religion of his kingdom. Over time, most people under Aksum's rule converted to Christianity.

For several hundred years, Aksum kept its control of the major trade routes linking Africa with Europe and Asia. Then in the A.D. 600s, Muslims fought with the rulers of Aksum for control of the Red Sea trade routes. Eventually, the Muslims conquered the coastal ports. The Muslim conquest of the coast ended the trade that had given Aksum its power and wealth.

Christianity in Ethiopia
The city of Aksum, at top, remains an important religious center today. The St. Mary of Zion Church is at the right. The young priest above is holding a Coptic cross, a symbol of Ethiopian Christianity. **Compare and Contrast** *How do these images of Christianity compare to Christian imagery in the United States?*

Vocabulary Builder

Use the information below to teach students this section's high-use words.

High-Use Word	Definition and Sample Sentence
convert, p. 53	*v.* to cause someone to change a belief The preacher hoped to **convert** people to his religion.
contact, p. 54	*n.* communication or connection While on vacation, she had no **contact** with her friends.
unique, p. 54	*adj.* one of a kind He bought the painting because he liked its **unique** designs.

Ancient Ethiopia L2

Guided Instruction

- **Vocabulary Builder** Clarify the high-use words **convert, contact,** and **unique** before reading.

- Read Ancient Ethiopia using the Structured Silent Reading strategy (TE, p. T34).

- Ask students **Where was the city of Aksum?** *(in the mountains about 100 miles from the coast of the Red Sea, in what is now Ethiopia)* **How did it become a center of trade even though it was located 100 miles inland?** *(Possible answers: It controlled the trading port Adulis on the Red Sea; it conquered lands in southwestern Arabia; it controlled major trade routes linking Africa with Europe and Asia.)*

- Have students discuss how Aksum became a center of Christianity. *(King Azana learned about Christianity and made it the official religion of the kingdom during the A.D. 300s.)*

- Ask students **What was the cause of Aksum's fall from power and wealth?** *(In the A.D. 600s, Muslims fought with the Christian rulers of Aksum and gained control of the trade from the coastal ports.)*

Answer

Compare and Contrast The St. Mary of Zion Church has a different architectural style from many churches in the United States. Also, the Coptic cross, which has four arms that are all the same length, is not traditionally used in the United States.

Guided Instruction (continued)

- Ask students **Why do you think the churches of East Africa have unique customs and traditions?** *(Possible answer: Many neighboring lands had converted to Islam and mountains separated political and religious leaders from other Christians, so they developed their own customs and traditions.)*

- Ask students **What is unusual about the churches built during the rule of King Lalibela?** *(The flat rooftops of the churches are level with surrounding land.)*

Independent Practice

Ask students to create the Taking Notes graphic organizer on a blank piece of paper. Then have them add major events about ancient Ethiopia's history on the timeline, along with the corresponding dates for each event.

Monitor Progress

As students fill in the graphic organizer, circulate and make sure individuals are choosing the correct facts and dates. Provide assistance as needed.

St. George's Church, Lalibela
At top, worshipers surround St. George's Church, one of the churches that King Lalibela had carved into the rock about A.D. 1200. Above, a priest at the church's entrance.
Apply Information *How long has this church been in use?*

Lalibela and the Spread of Christianity

After Aksum had lost power, the Christian kings of the region built churches and monasteries. But these kings did not build a new capital. Instead, they moved from place to place around the kingdom. They lived in royal tents and were accompanied by thousands of citizens and servants.

Many neighboring lands converted to Islam, but present-day Ethiopia remained Christian. Cut off in their mountainous home, the Ethiopians had little direct contact with other Christian peoples. In time, their churches developed unique customs and traditions. In one such tradition, churchgoers rest their foreheads against the outside wall of a church and kiss it to show respect.

Another unique feature of the region's Christianity is a group of churches built about A.D. 1200 under King Lalibela (lah lee BAY lah). The king had his people build new churches—but not from the ground up. Instead, the people were to carve the churches down into the solid red rock. The flat rooftops of the buildings are level with the surrounding land. The churches are in a town named Lalibela in honor of the king. These fascinating churches are still used today by the Christians of Ethiopia.

✓ **Reading Check** Describe the churches of Lalibela.

Background: Links Across Time

Religion in Ethiopia Today Today, between 35 to 40 percent of Ethiopians practice the Ethiopian Orthodox religion, one of the world's oldest Christian churches. Islam is practiced by 45 to 50 percent of Ethiopians, while the remaining Ethiopians practice other religions, including traditional African religions. A small number of Ethiopians practice Judaism, but most of the country's Jews emigrated to Israel in the 1980s and early 1990s when Ethiopia was affected by war and drought.

Answers

Apply Information for about 800 years

✓**Reading Check** The churches, built almost one thousand years ago during the rule of King Lalibela, are carved from the region's solid red stone. Instead of being built from the ground up, their flat rooftops are level with the surrounding land. The churches are still used today by Ethiopia's Christians.

Rich Centers of Trade

After Muslims gained control of Indian Ocean trade, trade centers developed along the east coast of Africa. Each of these ports was a **city-state** (SIH tee stayt), a city with its own government that controls much of the surrounding land. By 1400, there were about 30 such city-states along Africa's Indian Ocean coast.

Trade thrived in East Africa because the region supplied goods such as gold and ivory that were very scarce outside Africa. In return, Muslim traders brought luxury goods that could not be found in Africa. Muslim traders from Arabia also brought their religion and language to these African city-states.

The City-State of Kilwa The merchants of Kilwa traded goods from inland regions of Africa for the foreign goods that traders brought to the port by sea. Contact between Africans and Arabs in Kilwa and other coastal city-states led to a new culture and language. Called **Swahili** (swah HEE lee), this Bantu language has words borrowed from Arabic. Swahili was spoken all along the East African coast. Most people on this coast converted to Islam.

In the 1500s, Portuguese troops sailing from Europe captured and looted Kilwa and the other coastal city-states. Portugal took over the prosperous trade routes. But the influence of Swahili culture remained. Today, Swahili is an official language in Kenya and Tanzania, and most East Africans use Swahili for business. Islam is still an important religion in the region.

Great Zimbabwe Much of the gold traded at Kilwa was mined in an inland area to the south, between the Zambezi and Limpopo rivers. This was the region controlled by the powerful southeastern African city of **Great Zimbabwe** (grayt zim BAHB way). Like other medieval African centers that you have read about, Great Zimbabwe grew rich and powerful through trade.

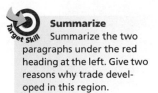

Summarize Summarize the two paragraphs under the red heading at the left. Give two reasons why trade developed in this region.

Learn about Great Zimbabwe and explore its ruins.

Mombasa Harbor, Kenya
Like Kilwa, the port of Mombasa on the Indian Ocean has a long history of trade. Wooden sailing ships like the ones below carried the trade of these city-states. **Infer** *Why were the East African city-states located along the coast?*

Chapter 2 Section 3 **55**

Assess and Reteach

Assess Progress `L2`

Have students complete the Section Assessment. Administer the *Section Quiz*.

 Medieval Times to Today Teaching Resources, *Section Quiz,* p. 158

Reteach `L1`

If students need more instruction, have them read this section in the Reading and Vocabulary Study Guide.

📖 Chapter 2, Section 3, **Medieval Times to Today Reading and Vocabulary Study Guide,** pp. 22–24

Extend `L3`

Have students learn more about how trade is conducted by completing the small group activity *Trading Items With Silent Barter.* Ask them to write a short report about the result of the barter and how they managed to communicate without talking.

 Medieval Times to Today Teaching Resources, *Small Group Activity: Trading Items With Silent Barter,* pp. 165–168

Answer

✓ **Reading Check** Trade routes may have moved, with other centers becoming more important; farmers may have overused the soil.

Section 3 Assessment

Key Terms
Students' sentences should reflect knowledge of each Key Term.

🌀 Target Reading Skill
Answers will vary, but summaries should focus on the most important ideas from the text and place them in the correct order.

Comprehension and Critical Thinking

1. (a) He became a Christian and made Christianity the official religion of the kingdom. **(b)** a group of Christian churches carved from solid red stone and built about one thousand years ago during the rule of King Lalibela **(c)** Possible answer: The churches might not have been built if King Ezana had not made Christianity the official religion of the kingdom.

2. (a) The gold traded at Kilwa was mined in Great Zimbabwe. **(b)** Possible answer: Kilwa's location as a port city along the southeast coast of Africa made it a prosperous trading center; the city of Great Zimbabwe controlled an inland area between two rivers where gold was mined and then traded.

Writing Activity
Use the *Rubric for Assessing a Writing Assignment.*

 Medieval Times to Today Teaching Resources, *Rubric for Assessing a Writing Assignment,* p. 174

Stone-walled ruins at Great Zimbabwe, in the present-day nation of Zimbabwe

Historians believe that the city of Great Zimbabwe had been founded by about 1100. Its Bantu-speaking people were the ancestors of today's Shona (SHOHN uh) people. Most people in this area were poor farmers. For those who were better off, large herds of cattle were an important form of wealth. Richest of all were the leaders who controlled the gold trade. These powerful leaders and their families lived among impressive stone-walled structures.

Great Zimbabwe thrived for hundreds of years. Historians believe that the city reached its peak before the early 1400s. By 1500, the city had fallen. Trade routes may have moved to favor other centers. Farmers also may have worn out the soil. In either case, the glory of Great Zimbabwe was not entirely lost. Its stone ruins still stand, and its history is a source of pride for the present-day nation of Zimbabwe.

✓ **Reading Check** What were two possible causes for the collapse of Great Zimbabwe?

Section 3 Assessment

Key Terms
Review the key terms at the beginning of this section. Use each term in a sentence that explains its meaning.

🌀 Target Reading Skill
Write a summary of the two paragraphs at the top of this page.

Comprehension and Critical Thinking
1. (a) Recall What change did King Ezana of Aksum make in the A.D. 300s?

(b) Identify What are some of the most famous sites in Ethiopia today?
(c) Synthesize Information How are these famous sites related to the changes made by King Ezana?
2. (a) Explain What connection was there between Great Zimbabwe and Kilwa?
(b) Analyze Information How did the locations of Kilwa and Great Zimbabwe make them powerful and rich?

Writing Activity
Study the photo of the rock-cut church of Lalibela on page 54. Write a description of this unusual church to a friend or relative. Where is it located? What does the building look like? How was it built? In what ways is it similar to or different from other buildings?

Go Online
PHSchool.com

For: An activity on historic Ethiopia
Visit: PHSchool.com
Web Code: lgd-8203

56 Medieval Times to Today

 **Go Online**
PHSchool.com Typing in the Web code when prompted will bring students directly to detailed instructions for this activity.

◆ Chapter Summary

Section 1: Africa and the Bantu
- The physical geography and natural vegetation of Africa are diverse, from tropical rain forests along the Equator to the world's largest desert.
- More than 2,000 years ago, the Bantu-speaking people of West Africa began migrating across central and southern Africa, carrying their culture wherever they went.

Section 2: West African Kingdoms
- Powerful trading kingdoms, including Ghana, Mali, and Songhai, controlled the savannas of West Africa for hundreds of years.
- The cities of Ile-Ife and Benin were important centers of trade and art in the West African rain forests.

Section 3: East Africa's Great Trading Centers
- Strong kings built lasting monuments and brought changes to the lands they ruled in present-day Ethiopia.
- City-states along the East African coast and the inland city of Great Zimbabwe grew rich from trade.

A bronze plaque from Benin

◆ Key Terms

Each statement below includes a key term from this chapter. If the statement is true, write *true*. If it is false, rewrite the statement to make it true.

1. Swahili is a language based on Portuguese, with Bantu words, that is spoken in West Africa.

2. Movement from one country or region to settle in another is called migration.

3. Mansa Musa ruled the kingdom of Mali.

4. A city-state is a city with its own government that controls much of the surrounding land.

5. The Sahara is the world's longest river.

6. Oral history is an account of the past that is passed down from generation to generation by word of mouth.

Vocabulary Builder

Revisit this chapter's high-use words:

environment	conquer	convert
technique	independent	contact
traditional	province	unique
adapt	stability	

Ask students to review the definitions they recorded on their *Word Knowledge* worksheets.

All in One Medieval Times to Today Teaching Resources, *Word Knowledge,* p. 162

Consider allowing students to earn extra credit if they use the words in their answers to the questions in the Chapter Review and Assessment. The words must be used correctly and in a natural context to win the extra points.

Review Chapter Content
- Review and revisit the major themes of this chapter by asking students to classify what Guiding Questions each bulleted statement in the Chapter Summary answers. Have students work in groups to match the statements with the appropriate questions. Conduct an Idea Wave (TE, p. T35) to share their answers. Refer to p. 1 of the Student Edition for the text of the Guiding Questions.

- Assign Vocabulary Development for students to review Key Terms.

  All in One Medieval Times to Today Teaching Resources, *Vocabulary Development,* p. 173

Answers

Key Terms

1. False. Swahili is a Bantu language, with Arabic words, spoken along the East African coast.

2. True

3. True

4. True

5. False. The Sahara is the world's largest desert.

6. True

Review and Assessment

Comprehension and Critical Thinking

7. (a) on either side of the Equator
(b) Savannas are grasslands with scattered trees and bushes. **(c)** Africa's rain forests are hot and moist, while its savannas are drier and cooler. The two climates are both capable of sustaining vegetation.

8. (a) modern techniques and oral history
(b) because historians often must piece together clues to find the whole story

9. (a) African Muslims fought the rulers of Aksum in the A.D. 600s for control of the Red Sea trade routes. **(b)** It led to further development of trade on the eastern coast of Africa.

10. (a) Ile-Ife and Benin **(b)** Possible answer: to pay tribute to the king

11. (a) Cairo **(b)** Possible answer: to rest, to trade for food and supplies

Skills Practice

Students' sentences should determine that the source is not reliable, using the skill steps they have learned.

Writing Activity: Science

Reports will vary, but should use reliable sources of information to explain how early tools and weapons were made and used. Use *Rubric for Assessing a Report,* to evaluate students' reports.

All in One **Medieval Times to Today Teaching Resources,** *Rubric for Assessing a Report,* p. 175

MAP MASTER
Skills Activity

1. D	2. G
3. A	4. C
5. B	6. F
7. E	

Go Online
PHSchool.com Students may practice their map skills using the interactive online version of this map.

Review and Assessment (continued)

◆ Comprehension and Critical Thinking

7. (a) Locate Where are Africa's tropical rain forests located?
(b) Describe What are some important features of Africa's savannas?
(c) Compare and Contrast In what ways are Africa's rain forests and savannas alike? In what ways are they different?

8. (a) List Name two things that have helped modern historians study the history of Africa south of the Sahara.
(b) Explain Why is studying this history "like solving a puzzle"?

9. (a) Summarize When and why did African Muslims fight the rulers of Aksum?
(b) Analyze Why was this fight important?

10. (a) Recall In which two rain forest kingdoms did artists make bronze sculptures?
(b) Generalize Why might an artist depict a powerful king in his or her work?

11. (a) Identify Where did Mansa Musa and his caravan stop in July 1324?
(b) Infer Why might a large caravan need to stop in the middle of a very long journey?

◆ Skills Practice

Using Reliable Information In the Skills for Life activity in this chapter, you learned how to judge whether information is reliable. Review the steps for this skill. Suppose you found the text below in a recent travel guide to Africa. Use the steps for this skill to decide whether the information is reliable. Write a sentence that explains why or why not.

"The mosque at Djenné is the most magnificent building in all of Africa. It must have been built by a powerful ruler with a strong religious faith. Every traveler to Africa should visit this mosque."

◆ Writing Activity: Science

You have read about the importance of iron tools and weapons to early peoples. Do research, using reliable sources, to find out how Africans made these early iron tools. What were the different steps in the process? What equipment did they use? What kind of tools did they make? Write a short report on your findings.

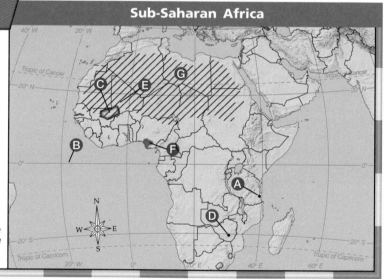

MAP MASTER
Skills Activity

Place Location For each place or feature listed below, write the letter from the map that shows its location.
1. Great Zimbabwe
2. Sahara
3. Kilwa
4. Kingdom of Ghana
5. Equator
6. Kingdom of Benin
7. Kingdom of Mali

Go Online
PHSchool.com Use Web Code lgp-8214 for an **interactive map.**

Sub-Saharan Africa

Standardized Test Prep

Test-Taking Tips

Some questions on standardized tests ask you to find main ideas. Read the paragraph below. Then follow the tips to answer the sample question.

> Imagine trading a pound of salt for a pound of gold. At today's prices, a pound of salt costs only about 50 cents, but a pound of gold is worth thousands of dollars. That has not always been true everywhere. In parts of Africa, salt was as scarce as gold in medieval times. People needed salt to preserve their food. They needed it to stay healthy, too. So they traded their gold for nearly the same weight of salt.

TIP As you read the paragraph, try to identify its main idea, or most important point. In some cases, the main idea may be stated. In other cases, such as this one, you have to add up the details to find the main idea.

Pick the letter that best answers the question.

The main idea of this paragraph is that

A today, a pound of salt costs only about 50 cents.

B in medieval Africa, salt was nearly as valuable as gold because it was needed and scarce.

C people need salt to stay healthy.

D in medieval Africa, gold was easier for traders to carry than salt.

TIP Look for key words in the answer choices or question that connect to the paragraph. In this case, two key words are *salt* and *gold*.

Think It Through The paragraph's main idea is that Africans traded gold for salt long ago, when salt was hard to get. Look at all four choices. A and C both just give details about salt. They do not compare the values of salt and gold. That leaves B and D. D gives information that is not in the paragraph. So, the correct answer is B, which is the main idea of the paragraph.

Practice Questions

Use the tips above and other tips in this book to help you answer the following questions.

1. In Africa, tropical rain forests lie along
   A Madagascar.
   B the Equator.
   C an oasis.
   D the Nile.

2. The kingdom of Mali rose to power after this West African kingdom weakened.
   A Songhai
   B Benin
   C Ghana
   D Nigeria

3. Which Christian king of East Africa had his people carve underground churches?
   A Sundiata
   B Ezana
   C Mansa Musa
   D Lalibela

Read the paragraph below, and answer the question that follows.

Medieval traders sold East African ivory in India. Ivory comes from elephant tusks. India has its own elephants, so why did Indians buy East African ivory? East African elephants have softer tusks. East African ivory is better for carving.

4. The main idea of this paragraph is that
   A ivory comes from elephant tusks.
   B Indians bought East African ivory because it was good for carving.
   C trading elephant tusks is illegal today.
   D East African elephants have softer tusks than Indian elephants.

Use Web Code lga-8201 for a **Chapter 2 self-test.**

Standardized Test Prep

Answers

1. B
2. C
3. D
4. B

Go Online PHSchool.com Students may use the Chapter 1 self-test on PH.School.com to prepare for the Chapter Test.

Overview

Section 1

South America and the Incas
1. Find out about the geography of the Americas.
2. Learn about the empire established by the Incas of South America.

Section 2

Cultures of Middle America
1. Learn about the Mayan culture of Middle America.
2. Find out about the powerful Aztec empire.

Section 3

Cultures of North America
1. Find out about the Mound Builders who lived in eastern North America.
2. Learn about the cultures of the Southwest and Great Plains.
3. Find out about the Woodland peoples of North America.

Discovery CHANNEL
SCHOOL Video

Cortés and the Aztec Empire
Length: 2 minutes, 57 seconds
Use with Section 2
This video segment describes how Cortés defeated the mighty Aztec empire.

Technology Resources

Go Online
PHSchool.com

Students use embedded Web codes to access Internet activities, chapter self-tests, and additional map practice. They may also access Dorling Kindersley's Online Desk Reference to learn more about each country they study.

Interactive Textbook

Use the Interactive Textbook to make content and concepts come alive through animations, videos, and activities that accompany the complete basal text—online and on CD-ROM.

PRENTICE HALL
TeacherEXPRESS™
Plan • Teach • Assess

Use this complete suite of powerful teaching tools to make planning lessons and administering tests quicker and easier.

Reading and Assessment

Reading and Vocabulary Instruction

⊙ Model the Target Reading Skill

Main Idea Tell students that the main idea is the most important idea in a section. All of the details in a well-written paragraph should support the main idea. Write the paragraph below, from page 73 of the Student Edition, on the board. Point out that the main idea is that Tenochtitlan was a grand city. With students, identify and underline each supporting detail.

In spite of its swampy origins, Tenochtitlán became a magnificent capital city. At its center were an open plaza and one or more towering pyramid-temples. There were schools for the sons of the nobles and large stone palaces. Raised streets of hard earth, called causeways, connected the city to the surrounding land. To supply the city with enough fresh water, the Aztecs also built aqueducts. These special channels carried spring water from distant sources to storage areas in the city.

Ask yourself aloud: What do these details have in common? *(They all support the main idea that Tenochtitlan was magnificent because of its grand structures, roads, and aqueducts.)*

Use the following worksheets from All-in-One Medieval Times to Today Teaching Resources (pp. 199–201) to support the chapter's Target Reading Skill.

Vocabulary Builder
High-Use Academic Words

Use these steps to teach this chapter's high-use words:

1. Have students rate how well they know each word on their Word Knowledge worksheets (All-in-One Medieval Times to Today Teaching Resources, p. 202).
2. Pronounce each word and ask students to repeat it.
3. Give students a brief definition or sample sentence (provided on TE pp. 63, 71, and 79).
4. Work with students as they fill in the "Definition or Example" column of their Word Knowledge worksheets.

Assessment

Formal Assessment

Test students' understanding of core knowledge and skills.

> **Chapter Tests A and B,** All-in-One Medieval Times to Today Teaching Resources, pp. 215–220

Customize the Chapter Tests to suit your needs.

> **Exam*View*® Test Bank CD-ROM**

Skills Assessment

Assess geographic literacy.

> **MapMaster Skills,** Student Edition pp. 61, 63, 80, 86

Assess reading and comprehension.

> **Target Reading Skills,** Student Edition, pp. 66, 72, 81, and in Section Assessments

> **Chapter 3 Assessment,** Medieval Times to Today Reading and Vocabulary Study Guide, p. 35

Performance Assessment

Assess students' performance on this chapter's Writing Activities using the following rubric from All-in-One Medieval Times to Today Teaching Resources.

> **Rubric for Assessing a Writing Assignment,** p. 213

Assess students' work through performance tasks.

> **Small Group Activity: Writing a Message Using Your Own Hieroglyphics,** All-in-One Medieval Times to Today Teaching Resources, pp. 205–208

Online Assessment

Have students check their own knowledge.

> **Chapter Self-Test**

Section 1 **South America and the Incas**

 3.5 periods, 1.75 blocks (includes Skills for Life)

Social Studies Objectives
1. Find out about the geography of the Americas.
2. Learn about the empire established by the Incas of South America.

Reading/Language Arts Objective
Learn how to identify main ideas while you read.

Prepare to Read

Build Background Knowledge
Have students scan the visuals in the section to determine what some of the accomplishments of ancient South American civilizations may have been.

Set a Purpose for Reading
Have students evaluate statements on the *Reading Readiness Guide*.

Preview Key Terms
Teach the section's Key Terms.

Target Reading Skill
Introduce the section's Target Reading Skill of **identifying main ideas.**

Instructional Resources

All in One Medieval Times to Today Teaching Resources
L2 Reading Readiness Guide, p. 188
L2 Identify Main Ideas, p. 199

Differentiated Instruction

Spanish Reading and Vocabulary Study Guide
L1 Chapter 3, Section 1, pp. 21–22 ELL

Instruct

Geography of the Americas
Discuss how geography and climate affected ancient peoples who lived in the Americas.

The Mountain Empire of the Incas
Discuss the accomplishments of the Incan empire and ask about the events preceding its collapse.

Target Reading Skill
Review **identifying main ideas.**

Instructional Resources

All in One Medieval Times to Today Teaching Resources
L2 Guided Reading and Review, p. 189
L2 Reading Readiness Guide, p. 188

Medieval Times to Today Transparencies
L2 Section Reading Support Transparency MT 59

Differentiated Instruction

All in One Medieval Times to Today Teaching Resources
L2 Skills for Life, p. 204 AR, GT, LPR, SN

Teacher's Edition
L1 For Special Needs Students, TE p. 65
L1 For Less Proficient Readers, TE p. 65

Medieval Times to Today Transparencies
L1 Section Reading Support Transparency MT 59 ELL, LPR, SN

Spanish Support
L2 Guided Reading and Review (Spanish), p. 20 ELL

Assess and Reteach

Assess Progress
Evaluate student comprehension with the section assessment and section quiz.

Reteach
Assign the Reading and Vocabulary Study Guide to help struggling students.

Extend
Extend the lesson by assigning a Book Project.

Instructional Resources

All in One Medieval Times to Today Teaching Resources
L2 Section Quiz, p. 190
L3 Book Project: One Job Through the Ages, pp. 77–79
Rubric for Assessing a Writing Assignment, p. 213

Reading and Vocabulary Study Guide
L1 Chapter 3, Section 1, pp. 26–28

Differentiated Instruction

Spanish Support
L2 Section Quiz (Spanish), p. 21 ELL

Teacher's Edition
L1 For Special Needs Students, TE pp. 65, 69

Social Studies Skills Tutor CD-ROM
L1 Identifying Cause and Effect ELL, LPR, SN

Key
L1 Basic to Average   L3 Average to Advanced
L2 For All Students

LPR Less Proficient Readers
AR Advanced Readers
SN Special Needs Students

GT Gifted and Talented
ELL English Language Learners

Section 2 Cultures of Middle America

 2 periods, 1 block (includes Focus On the Great Temple)

Social Studies Objectives
1. Learn about the Mayan culture of Middle America.
2. Find out about the powerful Aztec empire.

Reading/Language Arts Objective
Learn how to identify details that support a main idea.

Prepare to Read

Build Background Knowledge
Show a video and have students compare the reasons for the fall of the Aztec and Incan empires.

Set a Purpose for Reading
Have students begin to fill out the *Reading Readiness Guide.*

Preview Key Terms
Teach the section's Key Terms.

Target Reading Skill
Introduce the section's Target Reading Skill of **identifying supporting details.**

Instructional Resources

All in One Medieval Times to Today Teaching Resources
- L2 Reading Readiness Guide, p. 192
- L2 Identify Supporting Details, p. 200

World Studies Video Program
- L2 Cortés and the Aztec Empire

Differentiated Instruction

Spanish Reading and Vocabulary Study Guide
- L1 Chapter 3, Section 2, p. 23–24 ELL

Instruct

The Culture of the Mayas
Discuss the Maya's farming techniques, religion, and cities.

Target Reading Skill
Review **identifying supporting details.**

The Aztec Empire
Ask about the characteristics of the Aztec empire and discuss how the Aztecs dealt with challenges.

Instructional Resources

All in One Medieval Times to Today Teaching Resources
- L2 Guided Reading and Review, p. 193
- L2 Reading Readiness Guide, p. 192

Medieval Times to Today Transparencies
- L2 Section Reading Support Transparency MT 60

Differentiated Instruction

All in One Medieval Times to Today Teaching Resources
- L3 The Talking Stone, pp. 209–211 AR, GT

Teacher's Edition
- L1 For Special Needs Students, TE p. 72
- L3 For Advanced Readers, TE pp. 73, 76
- L2 For English Language Learners, TE p. 73
- L3 For Gifted and Talented, TE p. 76

Spanish Support
- L2 Guided Reading and Review (Spanish), p. 22 ELL

Assess and Reteach

Assess Progress
Evaluate student comprehension with the section assessment and section quiz.

Reteach
Assign the Reading and Vocabulary Study Guide to help struggling students.

Extend
Extend the lesson by assigning a Small Group Activity.

Instructional Resources

All in One Medieval Times to Today Teaching Resources
- L2 Section Quiz, p. 194
- L3 Small Group Activity: Writing a Message Using Your Own Hieroglyphics, pp. 205–208
  Rubric for Assessing a Writing Assignment, p. 213

Reading and Vocabulary Study Guide
- L1 Chapter 3, Section 2, pp. 29–31

Differentiated Instruction

Spanish Support
- L2 Section Quiz (Spanish), p. 23 ELL

Key
- L1 Basic to Average
- L3 Average to Advanced
- L2 For All Students
- LPR Less Proficient Readers
- AR Advanced Readers
- SN Special Needs Students
- GT Gifted and Talented
- ELL English Language Learners

Section 3 Cultures of North America

 4 periods, 2 blocks (includes Chapter Review and Assessment)

Social Studies Objectives
1. Find out about the Mound Builders who lived in eastern North America.
2. Learn about the cultures of the Southwest and Great Plains.
3. Find out about the Woodland peoples of North America.

Reading/Language Arts Objective
Learn how to identify details that add up to the main idea in a paragraph.

Prepare to Read	Instructional Resources	Differentiated Instruction
Build Background Knowledge Ask students preview the headings, maps, and photographs in the section to predict what they will be learning about. **Set a Purpose for Reading** Have students begin to fill out the *Reading Readiness Guide.* **Preview Key Terms** Teach the section's Key Terms. **Target Reading Skill** Introduce the section's Target Reading Skill of **identifying implied main ideas.**	**All in One Medieval Times to Today Teaching Resources** L2 Reading Readiness Guide, p. 196 L2 Identify Implied Main Ideas, p. 201	**Spanish Reading and Vocabulary Study Guide** L1 Chapter 3, Section 3, pp. 25–26 ELL

Instruct	Instructional Resources	Differentiated Instruction
The Eastern Mound Builders Ask questions about and discuss the characteristics of the North American mound building societies. **Target Reading Skill** Review **identify implied main ideas.** **Peoples of the Southwest and the Great Plains** Discuss the lives of the Anasazi, Pueblo peoples, and Plains Indians. **Peoples of the Woodlands** Ask about how Native American groups in the Northwest showed their wealth and obtained food, and discuss the Iroquois political system.	**All in One Medieval Times to Today Teaching Resources** L2 Guided Reading and Review, p. 197 L2 Reading Readiness Guide, p. 196 **Medieval Times to Today Transparencies** L2 Transparency B12: Chart/Table L2 Section Reading Support Transparency MT 61	**Teacher's Edition** L1 For English Language Learners, TE p. 82 L3 For Gifted and Talented, TE p. 82 L1 For Less Proficient Readers, TE p. 83 **Spanish Reading and Vocabulary Study Guide** L1 Chapter 3, Section 3, pp. 25–26 ELL **Spanish Support** L2 Guided Reading and Review (Spanish), p. 24 ELL

Assess and Reteach	Instructional Resources	Differentiated Instruction
Assess Progress Evaluate student comprehension with the section assessment and section quiz. **Reteach** Assign the Reading and Vocabulary Study Guide to help struggling students. **Extend** Extend the lesson by assigning an Enrichment activity.	**All in One Medieval Times to Today Teaching Resources** L2 Section Quiz, p. 198 L3 Enrichment, p. 203 Rubric for Assessing a Writing Assignment, p. 213 L2 Word Knowledge, p. 202 L2 Vocabulary Development, p. 212 L2 Chapter Tests A and B, pp. 215–220 **Reading and Vocabulary Study Guide** L1 Chapter 3, Section 3, pp. 32–34	**Spanish Support** L2 Section Quiz (Spanish), p. 25 ELL L2 Chapter Summary (Spanish), p. 26 ELL L2 Vocabulary Development (Spanish), p. 27 ELL

Key

L1 Basic to Average   L3 Average to Advanced   LPR Less Proficient Readers   GT Gifted and Talented
L2 For All Students   AR Advanced Readers   ELL English Language Learners
                                             SN Special Needs Students

Reading Background

Passage Reading Strategies

In this chapter, students will use the ReQuest strategy to read the text in Section 1. This strategy calls for students to ask their own questions while reading. Answering their own questions gives students a specific purpose for reading and helps them to monitor their own success. Model the strategy using the following passage from page 64 of the Student Edition. Read the selection aloud, and then ask and answer your own questions. Questions should progress from recall to interpretive or applied thinking.

The Incas extended their control over nearby lands through conquests, or the conquering of other peoples. Over time, many different groups came under their rule. By the 1400s, lands ruled by the Incas had grown into an empire. At its height, the Incan Empire included as many as 12 million people.

Questions:

1. How many people lived in the Incan Empire by the 1400s? *(about 12 million people)*
2. How did the Incas expand their empire? *(by conquering other peoples)*
3. Why would an empire grow through conquests? *(Once a ruling group has conquered another people, it can take over the land and establish power there, thus expanding their control and their empire.)*

Continue in this fashion, alternating between student- and teacher-proposed questions.

Mapping Word Definitions

Research shows that mapping word definitions helps students develop the ability to investigate word meanings independently and provide elaborated definitions (as opposed to simple one or two word definitions).

Model mapping word definitions by developing a graphic organizer similar to the one below for the high-use word *diverse*.

the definition (in their own words)	*different from one another*
a synonym	*different, varied*
a sentence using the word	*The people who live in North America today are diverse because they come from all over the world.*

World Studies Background

Tikal

Located in the tropical rain forests of what is now northern Guatemala, Tikal was once a major center of Mayan civilization. At its height, between 600 and 700 A.D., the city had a population of 60,000 people. Today, tourists flock to the ruins of Tikal's ceremonial center to see the remains of Mayan religious and artistic achievements, such as pyramids, temples, palaces, and plazas.

Aztec Education

For most Aztec youngsters, education began at home. Boys were taught by their fathers until they were about ten years old. After that, they were usually sent to schools either run by family groups called *calpolli* or connected with a temple. Calpolli schools gave boys general education and military training. Temple schools prepared them for the priesthood or offices of the state.

Kachinas

Kachinas play an important role in the Hopi culture. According to Hopi belief, kachinas are spirits of the dead. During the winter, the Hopi dedicate special dances and services to these spirits to ensure good harvests. Boys and girls are given carved wooden dolls to help them learn about the real kachinas.

Infoplease® provides a wealth of useful information for the classroom. You can use this resource to strengthen your background on the subjects covered in this chapter. Have students visit this advertising-free site as a starting point for projects requiring research.

 Use Web code **lgd-8300** for **Infoplease®**.

Guiding Questions

Remind students about the Guiding Questions introduced at the beginning of the book.

Section 1 relates to **Guiding Question** ❹ **What types of governments were formed in these civilizations?** *(The Sapa Inca, or emperor, owned all the land in the Incan Empire and divided it among those under his rule. He relied on government officials to help him run the empire smoothly.)*

Section 2 relates to **Guiding Question** ❸ **What was the pattern of day-to-day life in these societies?** *(Mayan life was based on farming. The Mayas grew a variety of crops including beans, pepper, and their most important crop—maize. The Mayas held religious festivals throughout the year and played games such as pok-ta-tok. Aztecs also relied on farming and built chinampas so they would have more farmland. They held religious festivals. War was a part of life in the Aztec Empire.)*

Section 3 relates to **Guiding Question** ❺ **How did each society organize its economic activities?** *(The Adena, Hopewell, Mississippians, Anasazi, and Plains Indians all traded with distant civilizations to acquire the goods they needed.)*

🎯 Target Reading Skill

In this chapter, students will learn and apply the reading skill of identifying main ideas and supporting details. Use the following worksheets to help students practice this skill:

All in One Medieval Times to Today Teaching Resources, *Identify Main Ideas,* p. 199; *Identify Supporting Details,* p. 200; *Identify Implied Main Ideas,* p. 201

⌐ Differentiated Instruction

The following Teacher Edition strategies are suitable for students of varying abilities.

Advanced Readers, pp. 73, 76
English Language Learners, pp. 73, 82
Gifted and Talented, pp. 76, 82
Less Proficient Readers, pp. 65, 83
Special Needs Students, pp. 65, 69, 72

Early Civilizations of the Americas

Chapter Preview

This chapter will introduce you to the civilizations that existed in the Americas before the arrival of Europeans.

Section 1
South America and the Incas

Section 2
Cultures of Middle America

Section 3
Cultures of North America

🎯 **Target Reading Skill**

Main Idea In this chapter you will focus on finding and remembering the main idea, or the most important point, of sections and paragraphs.

▶ **Temple of the Cross, Palenque, Mexico**

60 Medieval Times to Today

Bibliography

For the Teacher
Bakewell, Peter. *A History of Latin America.* Blackwell Publishers, 2003.
Soustelle, Jacques. *Daily Life of the Aztecs.* Dover Publications, 2002.
Zimmerman, Larry J. *American Indians: The First Nations: Native North American Life, Myth, and Art.* Duncan Baird Publishers, 2003.

For the Student
L1 Mann, Elizabeth. *Machu Picchu.* Mikaya Press, 2000.
L2 Baquedano, Elizabeth. *Aztec, Inca & Maya.* Eyewitness Books, DK Publishing, 2000.
L3 Hall, Eleanor. *Life Among the Aztec.* Lucent Books, 2004.

Civilizations of the Americas

KEY

Mayas, about A.D. 250–900

Aztecs, A.D. 1400s–1521

Incas, A.D. 1400s–1535

Mound Builders, about 700 B.C.–A.D. 1250

Anasazi, about A.D. 100–1200

Pueblo, 1200–present

Peoples of the Northwest Coast, about A.D. 500–1800

Iroquois League, 1500s–1784

• City

0 miles 1,500
0 kilometers 1,500
Lambert Azimuthal Equal Area

Northwest Coast · *Chaco Canyon* · Cahokia · *Eastern Woodlands* · *Southwest* · NORTH AMERICA · *Great Plains* · Mississippi R. · Gulf of Mexico · Tenochtitlán · MIDDLE AMERICA · Caribbean Sea · ATLANTIC OCEAN · PACIFIC OCEAN · Amazon R. · SOUTH AMERICA · •Cuzco · ANDES · Equator · Tropic of Cancer · Tropic of Capricorn

Regions The term *Middle America* is often used to describe the region of Mexico and Central America, even though this region is also part of the continent of North America. In this chapter, *North America* describes what is now the United States and Canada. **Identify** Which two civilizations were located in Middle America? **Predict** Notice the end dates for these two civilizations. What events might have contributed to their ending?

Go Online
PHSchool.com Use Web Code lgp-8321 for step-by-step map skills practice.

■ Ask students to create a table that shows which region each civilization is located in—North America, Middle America, or South America. Remind them to give the table a title.

Go Online
PHSchool.com Students may practice their map skills using the interactive online version of this map.

Using the Visual L2

Reach Into Your Background Point out the photograph on pp. 60–61 and the caption. Ask **What does the structure in the photograph tell about the past?** Ask students to think about monuments or buildings in their area that might tell about the past.

Answers

MAP★MASTER Skills Activity **Identify** Aztecs and Mayas
Predict Possible answer: conquests by Europeans

Chapter Resources

Teaching Resources
L2 Vocabulary Development, p. 212
L2 Skills for Life, p. 204
L2 Chapter Tests A and B, pp. 215–220

Spanish Support
L2 Spanish Chapter Summary, p. 26
L2 Spanish Vocabulary Development, p. 27

Media and Technology
L1 Student Edition on Audio CD
L1 Guided Reading Audiotapes, English and Spanish
L2 Social Studies Skills Tutor CD-ROM
ExamView® Test Bank CD-ROM

Discovery CHANNEL **SCHOOL** World Studies Video Program

interactive Textbook PRENTICE HALL

TeacherEXPRESS™ Plan · Teach · Assess

Objectives

Social Studies

1. Find out about the geography of the Americas.
2. Learn about the empire established by the Incas of South America.

Reading/Language Arts

Learn how to identify main ideas while you read.

Prepare to Read

Build Background Knowledge　L2

Remind students that they have learned about ancient civilizations in several parts of the world. In this section, they will learn about an ancient civilization in South America. Ask students to quickly survey the visuals in the section with this question in mind: **What might some of the accomplishments of this civilization have been?** Conduct an Idea Wave (TE, p. T35) to generate a list.

Set a Purpose for Reading　L2

■ Preview the Objectives.

■ Read each statement in the *Reading Readiness Guide* aloud. Ask students to mark the statements true or false.

■ Have students discuss the statements in pairs or groups of four, then mark their worksheets again. Use the Numbered Heads participation strategy (TE, p. T36) to call on students to share their group's perspectives.

All in One Medieval Times to Today Teaching Resources, *Reading Readiness Guide,* p. 188

Vocabulary Builder

Preview Key Terms　L2

Pronounce each Key Term, then ask students to say the word with you. Provide a simple explanation such as, "Every ten years the United States government conducts a census to count its people and learn more about them."

Section 1 · South America and the Incas

Prepare to Read

Objectives

In this section, you will
1. Find out about the geography of the Americas.
2. Learn about the empire established by the Incas of South America.

Taking Notes

As you read this section, record key points about the Incan Empire. Copy the start of the outline below, and then add more information to complete it.

> I. The mountain empire of the Incas
>   A. Growth of an empire
>   1.
>   2.
>   B.
> II.

Target Reading Skill

Identify Main Ideas Good readers identify the main idea in every written passage. The main idea is the most important, or the biggest, point of the section. It includes all of the other points made in the section. As you read, note the main idea of each paragraph or written passage.

Key Terms

• **Incas** (ING kuhz) *n.* people of a powerful South American empire during the 1400s and 1500s

• **Andes** (AN deez) *n.* a mountain chain of western South America

• **Cuzco** (KOOS koh) *n.* the capital city of the Incan Empire, located in present-day Peru

• **census** (SEN sus) *n.* an official count of people in a certain place at a certain time

• **quipu** (KEE poo) *n.* a group of knotted strings used by the Incas to record information

• **terraces** (TEHR us iz) *n.* steplike ledges cut into mountains to make land suitable for farming

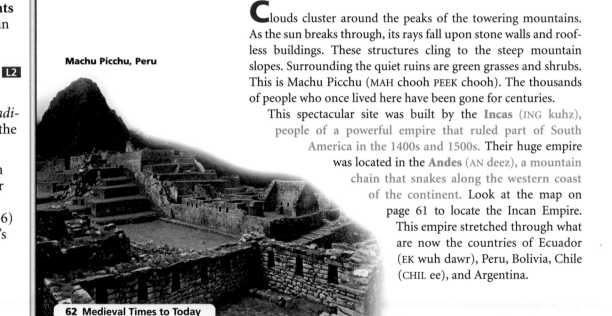

Machu Picchu, Peru

62 Medieval Times to Today

Clouds cluster around the peaks of the towering mountains. As the sun breaks through, its rays fall upon stone walls and roofless buildings. These structures cling to the steep mountain slopes. Surrounding the quiet ruins are green grasses and shrubs. This is Machu Picchu (MAH chooh PEEK chooh). The thousands of people who once lived here have been gone for centuries.

This spectacular site was built by the **Incas** (ING kuhz), people of a powerful empire that ruled part of South America in the 1400s and 1500s. Their huge empire was located in the **Andes** (AN deez), a mountain chain that snakes along the western coast of the continent. Look at the map on page 61 to locate the Incan Empire. This empire stretched through what are now the countries of Ecuador (EK wuh dawr), Peru, Bolivia, Chile (CHIL ee), and Argentina.

Target Reading Skill　L2

Identify Main Ideas Point out the Target Reading Skill. Tell students that the main idea of a section is the most important point in the section.

Model the skill by identifying the main idea of the Lasting Achievements section on p. 66. Explain that much of the main idea is stated in the introductory paragraph, and the supporting details are provided in the paragraphs that follow. *(Main idea: The Incas were amazing builders and many of their achievements still stand today.)*

Give students *Identify Main Ideas*. Have them complete the activity in groups.

All in One Medieval Times to Today Teaching Resources, *Identify Main Ideas,* p. 199

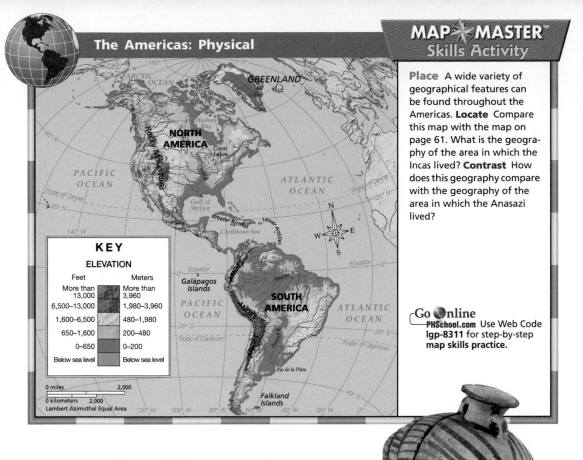

The Americas: Physical

MAP★MASTER™ Skills Activity

KEY
ELEVATION

Feet	Meters
More than 13,000	More than 3,960
6,500–13,000	1,980–3,960
1,600–6,500	480–1,980
650–1,600	200–480
0–650	0–200
Below sea level	Below sea level

0 miles 2,000
0 kilometers 2,000
Lambert Azimuthal Equal Area

Place A wide variety of geographical features can be found throughout the Americas. **Locate** Compare this map with the map on page 61. What is the geography of the area in which the Incas lived? **Contrast** How does this geography compare with the geography of the area in which the Anasazi lived?

Go Online
PHSchool.com Use Web Code lgp-8311 for step-by-step map skills practice.

Geography of the Americas

The Incas were not the first culture to develop in the Americas. Many groups had lived in the region for thousands of years. Individual cultures developed different ways of life to fit their geographic settings. Some peoples made their homes in dense forests or fertile river valleys. Other peoples lived among rocky cliffs in areas that were dry for much of the year.

Locate the mountain ranges on the map above. See which parts of the Americas are covered by plains, highland plateaus, and deserts. Also, locate the Mississippi and Amazon rivers, two of the largest river systems in the world. In North America, temperatures range from extreme cold in the far north to hot and tropical in the southern region. In South America, mountain regions are cold. Areas near sea level are hot near the Equator but much cooler in the far south.

✓ **Reading Check** Which two river systems in the Americas are among the largest in the world?

This earthenware vessel was designed to be carried on the back of a llama.

Vocabulary Builder

Use the information below to teach students this section's high-use words.

High-Use Word	Definition and Sample Sentence
dense, p. 63	*adj.* crowded closely together The **dense** fog made it hard to see the road.
complex, p. 65	*adj.* complicated; sophisticated The class invented a new game with **complex** rules.
unify, p. 65	*v.* to link together The border around the page helped to **unify** the pictures.

Instruct

Geography of the Americas L2

Guided Instruction

- **Vocabulary Builder** Clarify the high-use word **dense** before reading.

- Read Geography of the Americas with students using the ReQuest reading strategy (TE, p. T35).

- Ask **Were the Incas the first culture to develop in the Americas?** *(No.)* **How long had other groups lived in the region before the Incan culture developed?** *(for thousands of years)*

- Have students give an example of how geography could affect the kinds of homes people build. *(Possible answer: People in forests might build homes with wood while those on rocky cliffs might use stone.)*

- Ask students to describe the climates of the Americas. *(In North America temperatures range from very cold in the north to hot and tropical in the south. In South America, mountain regions are cold, and areas near sea level are hot near the Equator but cooler farther south.)*

Independent Practice

Assign *Guided Reading and Review*.

All in One **Medieval Times to Today Teaching Resources,** *Guided Reading and Review,* p. 189

Monitor Progress

Circulate and make sure students are correctly answering the questions. Provide assistance as needed.

Answers

MAP★MASTER™ Skills Activity **Locate** The Incas lived near the Andes Mountains, down South America's Pacific coast. **Contrast** The Anasazi lived inland near the Rocky Mountains, which have lower elevations than the Andes Mountains.

Go Online
PHSchool.com Students may practice their map skills using the interactive online version of this map.

✓ **Reading Check** the Mississippi and Amazon river systems

The Mountain Empire of the Incas L2

Guided Instruction

- **Vocabulary Builder** Clarify the high-use words **complex** and **unify** before reading.

- Invite students to read about the Incan empire with you. As students read, circulate and make sure individuals can answer the Reading Check question.

- Ask students **What was the capital of the Incan empire?** *(Cuzco)* **How did the Incas extend their control?** *(by conquering other peoples)*

- Discuss the role of the Inca emperor. *(He owned all the land and divided it among those he ruled. He hired government officials to help him run the empire smoothly.)*

The Mountain Empire of the Incas

At its peak, the powerful South American empire of the Incas measured 2,500 miles (4,020 kilometers) from one end to the other. This great empire grew from small beginnings over many years.

Growth of an Empire About the year A.D. 1200, the Incas settled in a small village on a high plateau in the Andes. This village, named **Cuzco** (KOOS koh), became the Incas' capital city and a center of both government and religion. In fact, the word *cuzco* means "center" in the Incan language.

The Incas extended their control over nearby lands through conquests, or the conquering of other peoples. Over time, many different groups came under their rule. By the 1400s, the lands ruled by the Incas had grown into an empire. At its height, the Incan Empire included as many as 12 million people.

Even when the empire included millions of people, it was run in an orderly way. Incan rulers had a complex system of gathering knowledge about events that happened hundreds of miles away from their capital city.

Festival of the Sun
Thousands of people gather at the ruins of an Incan fortress in Cuzco for the yearly Festival of the Sun, which celebrates the winter solstice.
Infer *How can you tell which people are part of the festival and which are just watching?*

Background: Links Across Time

Machu Picchu Located about 50 miles (80 kilometers) northwest of Cuzco, the archaeological site of Machu Picchu rises on a high ridge in the forests of the Andes Mountains. It spreads over five square miles (13 square kilometers) and overlooks the Urubamba River about 2,000 feet (610 meters) below. More than 3,000 steps link the many levels of the site. Historical evidence suggests that Machu Picchu was a retreat for Pachacuti Yupanqui, who led the Incas from about 1438 to 1471, and his family. The site includes palaces; houses for farmers, weavers, and servants; and religious monuments. Today, Machu Picchu is a major tourist attraction in Peru.

Answer

Infer The people watching the festival are dressed in street clothes and seated in chairs. Those who are taking part in the festival are dressed in bright clothing and are moving around.

Quipus in Incan Life
In the drawing below, dating from the 1500s, an official gives a noble a quipu like the one at left. The quipu may have been created hundreds of miles away. **Analyze Images** *What details in the drawing tell which person is the noble?*

- Ask students **What was the purpose of the census?** (*It was a way to keep track of everyone's responsibilities. It helped ensure that everyone paid taxes and recorded which men worked as soldiers or on public projects.*)

- Discuss the use of quipus. (*Incas created quipus to keep track of important information such as births, deaths, and harvests.*) Ask students **How do you think quipus helped to unify the Incan empire?** (*Possible answer: They were used to record statistics that were important for running the empire. The quipus were carried all over the empire and helped keep the government informed about distant parts of the empire.*)

- Ask students **How did the Incas use stone to increase farm production?** (*They used stone to create terraces on steep mountainsides, to hold the soil in place, and to build channels to carry water to farms.*)

Incan Government The Incan ruler was called Sapa Inca, or "the emperor." The people believed that their emperor was related to the sun-god. The emperor, and only he, owned all the land and divided it among those under his rule. Under the Sapa Inca was the noble class. Nobles oversaw government officials, who made sure the empire ran smoothly.

Officials used a **census,** or an official count of the people, to keep track of everyone's responsibilities. The census helped to make sure that everyone paid taxes. It recorded which men worked as soldiers or on public projects such as gold mining and road building. Farmers had to give the government part of their crops, while women had to weave cloth. In return, the empire took care of the poor, the sick, and the elderly.

The official spoken language of the empire was Quechua (KECH wuh), but the Incas did not have a written language. Instead, they invented a complex system for keeping detailed records. Information such as births, deaths, and harvests was recorded on a group of knotted strings called a **quipu** (KEE poo). Each quipu had a main cord with several colored strings attached. The colors represented different items, and knots of varying sizes recorded numbers.

Incan relay runners carried quipus across vast networks of roads and bridges to keep the government informed about distant parts of the empire. These roads also carried the Incan armies and trade caravans, both of which helped to unify the vast empire.

Differentiated Instruction

For Special Needs Students ▐L1▐
Ask students to demonstrate that they are listening and following along by having them use a piece of cardboard to underline each line of text as it is read.

For Less Proficient Readers ▐L1▐
Show *Section Reading Support Transparency MT 59* before students begin reading the section. Point out the section's key concepts to help focus students' reading.

📖 **Medieval Times to Today Transparencies,** *Section Reading Support Transparency MT 59*

Answer

Analyze Images Possible answer: The person on the right is kneeling and holding a quipu, and the person on the left is standing and seems to be wearing gold jewelry. These details would indicate that the person on the left is the noble.

Links

Read the **Links Across Time** on this page. Ask students **How do you think bridges helped spread information across the Incan empire?** *(Bridges were part of the huge network of roads that linked all parts of the empire. People traveled along this system to carry information to and from the government.)*

Guided Instruction (continued)

■ Ask **What two problems helped trigger the fall of the Incan empire before the Spanish arrived?** *(Members of the ruling family began to fight among themselves for control, and workers started to rebel against the strict government.)*

Independent Practice

Have students create the Taking Notes graphic organizer on a separate piece of paper. As they read about the Incan empire, have them fill in important headings and details on their outlines.

Monitor Progress

■ Show *Section Reading Support Transparency MT 59* and ask students to check their graphic organizers individually. Go over key concepts and clarify key vocabulary as needed.

Medieval Times to Today Transparencies, *Section Reading Support Transparency MT 59*

■ Tell students to fill in the last column of their *Reading Readiness Guides*. Probe for what they learned that confirms or invalidates each statement.

All in One Medieval Times to Today Teaching Resources, *Reading Readiness Guide,* p. 188

Target Reading Skill   L2

Identify Main Ideas As a follow-up, ask students to answer the Target Reading Skill question in the Student Edition. *(The Incas were amazing builders and many of their achievements still stand today.)*

Links Across Time

Rope Bridges This rope bridge, strung across a gorge in the Andes, is similar to those used by the Incas. A gorge is a narrow pass between steep cliffs or walls. Incan bridges were made with strong cords of braided vines and reeds. Some peoples in the Andes still make bridges from vines and reeds today. Modern steel suspension bridges in other parts of the world use the engineering principles developed by the Incas hundreds of years ago when they built their rope-and-vine bridges.

Identify Main Ideas
Which sentence states the main idea under the blue heading Lasting Achievements?

Lasting Achievements The achievements of the Incas still amaze people today. They constructed thousands of miles of paved roads, massive walls, and mountaintop buildings. And they did all this with only stone hammers and bronze chisels. Remarkably, much of what the Incas built hundreds of years ago with only primitive tools still stands today.

The Incas took advantage of their environment. They used stone—plentiful in the Andes—for many purposes. Sometimes they used enormous stones whole. At other times, they carefully broke stones into smaller blocks. First they cut a long groove into a rock's surface. Then they drove stone or wooden wedges into the groove until the rock split.

When Incan stonemasons made a wall, they made sure its large, many-sided stones fit together perfectly. After a wall was complete, the fit was so tight that not even a very thin knife blade could be slipped between two blocks. Construction without mortar, or cement, also allowed the massive stones to move and resettle during earthquakes without damaging the wall.

Among their many ingenious uses of stone was a method to increase farm production. The Andes are steep, dry, and rocky. There is little natural farmland. By building **terraces,** or steplike ledges cut into the mountains, the Incas could farm on slopes that would otherwise have been too steep. Stone terraces held the soil in place so it would not be washed away by rain. A complex system of aqueducts, or stone-lined channels, carried water to these farms. One of these aqueducts was 360 miles (579 kilometers) long.

Background: Daily Life

Incan Agriculture Despite the steep terrain of the Andes, the Incan empire was primarily agrarian. In addition to the use of terraces and irrigation systems, the Incas used fertilizers to enrich the soil. Their main food crops were potatoes, corn, quinoa (a grain), and oca (an edible root). The Incas developed a way of freeze-drying potatoes to preserve them. The Incas had no draft animals, wheels, or plows. They did have some domesticated animals including ducks, llamas, vicuña , alpacas, and dogs. In addition to food, the Incas grew cotton and used the wool of vicuña and alpacas for textiles.

The Decline of the Incan Empire The power of the Incan Empire peaked in the 1400s. After that, it lasted for less than 100 years. A number of factors contributed to the fall of the empire. Members of the ruling family began to fight among themselves for control. Also, many workers started to rebel against the strict government.

Then, in the 1530s, a Spanish conquistador (kahn KEES tuh dawr), or conqueror, named Francisco Pizarro arrived in South America. Pizarro had heard of the wealthy Incan Empire. He wanted to explore the region and conquer its peoples. The Incan emperor welcomed Pizarro. But when he and his unarmed men met the conquistador, they walked into a trap. Pizarro captured the emperor and killed his men.

The Spanish had superior weapons. They also carried diseases, such as smallpox and measles, to which the Incas had never been exposed. These diseases killed much of the Incan population. The Spanish quickly gained control of the vast Incan Empire. For decades, the Incas tried to regain rule of their land, but they never succeeded.

A wooden cup made for Pizarro shows Spanish and Incan figures.

 Reading Check Which Spanish conquistador conquered the Incas?

Section 1 Assessment

Key Terms
Review the key terms at the beginning of this section. Use each term in a sentence that explains its meaning.

Target Reading Skill
State the main idea of the first paragraph on this page.

Comprehension and Critical Thinking
1. (a) Identify Name two geographic settings in which peoples of the Americas lived.
(b) Synthesize Information What are the climates of those two regions?
(c) Infer How might the people who lived in these regions have adapted to their geography and climate?
2. (a) Recall How much land did the Incan Empire cover at its greatest extent?
(b) Explain How did the government in Cuzco keep track of distant parts of the empire?
(c) Draw Conclusions What do you think were the major problems of keeping such a large empire running smoothly? Explain your answer.

Writing Activity
If you could interview a stonemason from the Incan Empire, what would you ask? Make a list of questions you would ask in order to learn how these skilled workers accomplished so much so long ago. Then write a paragraph explaining why you want to ask the questions.

For: An activity on the Incas
Visit: PHSchool.com
Web Code: lgd-8301

Assess Progress
Have students complete the Section Assessment. Administer the *Section Quiz*.

All in One Medieval Times to Today Teaching Resources, *Section Quiz,* p. 190

Reteach
If students need more instruction, have them read this section in the Reading and Vocabulary Study Guide.

Chapter 3, Section 1, **Medieval Times to Today Reading and Vocabulary Study Guide,** pp. 26–28

Extend
Have students begin working on *Book Project: One Job Through the Ages.* Tell them they can choose one of the jobs mentioned in this section, such as soldier or stonemason, or they can choose a job from an earlier section.

All in One Medieval Times to Today Teaching Resources, *Book Project: One Job Through the Ages,* pp. 77–79

Answer

 Reading Check Francisco Pizarro

Writing Activity
Use the *Rubric for Assessing a Writing Assignment* to evaluate students' paragraphs.

All in One Medieval Times to Today Teaching Resources, *Rubric for Assessing a Writing Assignment,* p. 213

Go Online PHSchool.com Typing in the Web code when prompted will bring students directly to detailed instructions for this activity.

Section 1 Assessment

Key Terms
Students' sentences should reflect knowledge of each Key Term.

Target Reading Skill
A number of factors contributed to the fall of the Incan empire.

Comprehension and Critical Thinking
1. (a) Two of the following: dense forests, fertile river valleys, rocky cliffs, mountainous regions. **(b)** Students should use the map and the information from the last paragraph on p. 63 to describe the climate of the two regions they listed. **(c)** People would adapt by building homes suitable to the climate and utilizing available materials; by making clothing suitable for the climate; by utilizing available plants and animals; by using stone to build terraces to increase farm production.

2. (a) 2,500 miles (4,023 kilometers) **(b)** Incas recorded statistics on quipus and runners brought them to government officials. **(c)** Possible answers: It was probably difficult to maintain a large enough army to protect the entire empire from invasion. It was probably difficult to maintain control over such a large area and diverse population.

Objective

Learn how to understand cause-and-effect relationships.

Prepare to Read

Build Background Knowledge **L2**

Tell students to suppose that their school decided to cancel all school vacations. Instead, students would have to attend school year-round without any vacations. Ask students what they think the effects of such a policy would be. Conduct an Idea Wave (TE p. T35) to elicit student responses.

Instruct

Identifying Cause and Effect **L2**

Guided Instruction

- Read the steps to understanding cause-and-effect relationships as a class and write them on the board.

- Practice the skill by reading the passage and following the steps on p. 69 as a class. Model each step in the activity by choosing a condition (*Every Incan village sent a few young men and women away to work for the empire.*) and looking for possible causes. (*Villages had to pay taxes on their harvest and herds; villages could pay their taxes by having their people do special work.*)

- Then, look for clue words (*For this reason*). Finally, make a cause-and-effect diagram on the board, and summarize the cause-and-effect relationships. (*Incan villages had to pay taxes on their harvest and herds; because villages could pay their taxes by having their people do special work, every village sent a few men and women to work for the empire; in return, the Incan government gave help to the poor, the old, and the sick villagers.*)

Independent Practice

Assign *Skills for Life* and have students complete it individually.

All in One Medieval Times to Today Teaching Resources, *Skills for Life*, p. 204

Identifying Cause and Effect

Wondering why things happen is something every human being does. Why does the sun rise in the east? Why does the United States have a president and not a king? Why did the Incas build Machu Picchu? This curiosity has driven people to ask how history has shaped our world. When we ask "why" about something, we are really trying to figure out causes and effects.

A cause is something that makes an event or a situation happen. An effect is a result of a cause. When you identify cause and effect, you understand how an action or several actions led to a particular result. Causes and effects can be short term or long term.

Learn the Skill

Use these steps to understand cause-and-effect relationships.

1 **Choose one event or condition as a starting point.** Determine whether in this case it is a cause or an effect.

2 **Look at earlier events or conditions for possible causes.** Also look for clue words that signal cause, such as *because*, *so*, and *since*. Words such as *therefore*, *then*, *reason*, and *as a result* signal effects.

3 **Make a cause-and-effect diagram.** A diagram like the one above can help you understand cause-and-effect relationships. Remember that sometimes an effect becomes a cause for another effect.

4 **Summarize the cause-and-effect relationships.** Be sure to include all of the causes and effects.

68 Medieval Times to Today

Monitor Progress

As students are completing *Skills for Life*, circulate to make sure individuals are applying the skill steps effectively. Provide assistance as needed.

An Incan woman weaving

Incan Taxes

The Incas did not use money. Even so, villages had to pay taxes on their harvest and herds. To do so, they gave one third of their crops and animals to the empire. Villages could also pay their taxes by having their people do special work.

For this reason, every village sent a few young men and women to work for the empire. Some made jewelry, textiles, or pottery for nobles. Many men worked as soldiers or miners. Others built buildings or inspected roads or bridges.

In return, the government gave something back to the villages. The poor, the old, and the sick received government help.

Practice the Skill

Follow the steps in Learn the Skill to look for causes and effects in the passage above.

1 Read the passage. Find one event or condition that can serve as your starting point. Decide if it is a cause or an effect. How might the title help you?

2 What facts or conditions led to the way Incas paid taxes? What clue words in the second paragraph signal cause and effect?

3 Make a cause-and-effect diagram. Check for effects that in turn become causes for other effects. Expand your diagram if you need to.

4 Summarize the cause-and-effect relationships you have discovered.

Incan men building a fortress

Apply the Skill

Reread the two paragraphs under the heading The Decline of the Incan Empire on page 67. Use the steps in this skill to identify the causes and effects described in the passage. Make a cause-and-effect diagram or write a paragraph explaining the cause-and-effect relationships you find.

Chapter 3 **69**

Assess and Reteach

Assess Progress L2

Ask students to do the Apply the Skill activity.

Reteach L1

If students are having trouble applying the skill steps, have them review the skill using the interactive Social Studies Skills Tutor CD-ROM.

 Identifying Cause and Effect, **Social Studies Skills Tutor CD-ROM**

Extend L3

Have students turn to p. 83 and read the last paragraph under the heading The Plains Indians. Then, working in pairs, have them create a cause-and-effect diagram using the information in the text.

Answer
Apply the Skill

Answers will vary, but students should create a cause-and-effect diagram or write a paragraph explaining the cause-and-effect relationships they found in the text.

Chapter 3 **69**

Objectives

Social Studies
1. Learn about the Mayan culture of Middle America.
2. Find out about the powerful Aztec empire.

Reading/Language Arts
Learn how to identify details that support a main idea.

Prepare to Read

Build Background Knowledge L2

Tell students that they will learn about two more ancient civilizations in Middle America. Show the video *Cortés and the Aztec Empire.* Ask students to note the reasons the Aztec empire ended and to compare them to the demise of the Incan empire. Have students engage in a Give One, Get One activity (TE, p. T37) to share their ideas.

📼 *Cortés and the Aztec Empire,* **World Studies Video Program**

Set a Purpose for Reading L2

- Preview the Objectives.

- Form students into pairs or groups of four. Distribute the *Reading Readiness Guide.* Ask students to fill in the first two columns of the chart. Use the Numbered Heads participation strategy (TE, p. T36) to call on students to share one piece of information they already know and one piece of information they want to know.

All in One Medieval Times to Today Teaching Resources, *Reading Readiness Guide,* p. 192

Vocabulary Builder
Preview Key Terms L2

Pronounce each Key Term, then ask students to say the word with you. Provide a simple explanation such as, "Maize, a type of corn, has been grown for thousands of years in North America."

Prepare to Read

Objectives
In this section, you will
1. Learn about the Mayan culture of Middle America.
2. Find out about the powerful Aztec Empire.

Taking Notes
As you read this section, look for the characteristics of the Mayan and Aztec civilizations. Copy the web diagram below and record your findings for the Mayas. Then make a similar diagram for the Aztecs.

Target Reading Skill

Identify Supporting Details Sentences in a paragraph may give further details that support the main idea. These details may give examples, explanations, or reasons. In the first paragraph on page 71, this sentence states the main idea: "Thousands of years before the Aztecs built Tenochtitlán, other cultures thrived in Middle America." Note three details that support this main idea.

Key Terms
- **Aztecs** (AZ teks) *n.* a people who lived in the Valley of Mexico
- **Tenochtitlán** (teh nawch tee TLAHN) *n.* capital city of the Aztecs
- **Mayas** (MAH yuhz) *n.* a people who established a great civilization in Middle America
- **slash-and-burn agriculture** (slash and burn AG rih kul chur) *n.* a farming technique in which trees are cut down and burned to clear and fertilize the land
- **maize** (mayz) *n.* corn
- **hieroglyphics** (hy ur oh GLIF iks) *n.* the signs and symbols that made up the Mayan writing system

This page dating from the 1500s illustrates the Aztec legend. A version of it forms part of the Mexican flag today.

In about 1325, the **Aztecs** (AZ teks), a people who lived in the Valley of Mexico, began looking for a place to build a new capital. According to legend, the Aztecs asked their god of war where they should build this capital. He replied, "Build at the place where you see an eagle perched on a cactus and holding a snake in its beak."

When the Aztecs found the sign their god had described, they were surprised. The cactus on which the eagle perched was growing on a swampy island in the center of Lake Texcoco. It was an unlikely setting for an important city. But they believed their god had given them this sign, and so this was the place where the Aztecs built **Tenochtitlán** (teh nawch tee TLAHN), their capital. It would become one of the largest and finest cities of its time.

70 Medieval Times to Today

Target Reading Skill L2

Identify Supporting Details Call attention to the Target Reading Skill. Point out that supporting details provide more information about the main idea.

Model the skill by reading the first two paragraphs under The Culture of the Mayas on p. 71 and identifying the main idea and its supporting details: "The first sentence gives the main idea, that other cultures thrived in Middle America before the Aztecs did." Then read each of the following sentences and ask students if the sentences supply supporting details. *(yes)*

Give students *Identify Supporting Details.* Have them complete the activity in groups.

All in One Medieval Times to Today Teaching Resources, *Identify Supporting Details,* p. 200

The Culture of the Mayas

Thousands of years before the Aztecs built Tenochtitlán, other cultures thrived in Middle America. One of these ancient peoples, called the Olmec (AHL mek), lived along the Gulf Coast from about 1200 B.C. until about 600 B.C. The Olmec are known for their pyramid-shaped temples and huge carved stone heads.

Somewhat later, an important culture developed in parts of Central America and the Yucatán Peninsula to the north. The Yucatán Peninsula is located at Mexico's southeastern tip. These people, called the **Mayas** (MAH yuhz), established a great civilization and built many cities in this region of Middle America. The Mayas may have been influenced by Olmec culture. The Mayan way of life lasted for many centuries. Its greatest period was from about A.D. 250 until 900.

A Farming Culture Mayan life was based on farming. To grow crops, Mayan farmers used a technique called **slash-and-burn agriculture.** They first cleared the land by cutting down trees. They then burned the tree stumps, saving the ash to use as fertilizer. Finally, they planted seeds. After a few years, however, the soil would be worn out. The farmers would then have to clear and plant a new area.

Mayan farmers grew a variety of crops, including beans, squash, peppers, papayas (puh PY uz), and avocados. But their most common crop was **maize** (mayz), or corn. In fact, maize was so important to the Mayas that one of the gods they worshiped was a god of corn. And since the corn needed the sun and rain to grow, it is not surprising that the Mayas also worshipped a rain god and a sun god.

Olmec statues like this one were usually several feet tall.

Tikal—Ruins of a Great City
Tikal, located in Guatemala, was once a thriving Mayan city. The city and its surrounding areas had a population of nearly 100,000. **Infer** *Judging from the photo, what challenge probably faced Mayan farmers who lived in this region?*

Vocabulary Builder

Use the information below to teach students this section's high-use words.

High-Use Word	Definition and Sample Sentence
thrive, p. 71	*v.* to flourish; to gain in wealth and possessions The city **thrived** under new leadership.
establish, p. 71	*v.* to set up on a permanent basis Our club met to **establish** some rules for the coming year.
decline, p. 72	*v.* to weaken Business in the town **declined** after the factory closed.
equip, p. 74	*v.* to provide with the appropriate supplies for action Ty **equipped** himself with the proper pads in preparation for the football game.

Instruct

The Culture of the Mayas L2

Guided Instruction

- **Vocabulary Builder** Clarify the high-use words **thrive, establish,** and **decline** before reading.

- Read about Mayan culture with students using the Choral Reading strategy (TE, p. T34).

- Ask students **What were two cultures that thrived in Middle America long before the Aztecs?** *(the Olmec and Mayan cultures)*

- Have students describe the technique of slash-and-burn agriculture. *(First, farmers cut down trees. Then they burned the tree stumps and saved the ash to use as fertilizer. Finally, they planted seeds.)* Ask **What was a disadvantage to this way of farming?** *(It wore out the soil after a few years, forcing farmers to clear new areas for planting.)*

- Have students discuss why the Mayas worshipped a god of corn, a god of rain, and a god of sun. *(Corn was their most common and important crop. The Mayas worshipped gods of the sun and rain because these elements were important for growing corn.)*

Answer

Infer Possible answer: Mayan farmers faced the challenge of clearing the trees that grew thickly in their region.

Read the **Links to Math** on this page. Ask students **What did dots and bars stand for in the Mayan number system?** (*Dots stood for single numbers and bars stood for groups of five.*)

Guided Instruction (continued)

- Discuss the role of religion in Mayan culture. (*Religion was an important part of Mayan culture. Cities held religious festivals and ceremonies, including human sacrifices, to honor Mayan gods. Mayan priests developed a calendar to plan when to hold religious festivals.*)

- Have students describe common structures found in a Mayan city. (*Large palaces where religious and governmental leaders lived and religious temple-pyramids were located within the city. Outdoor courts where games were played could also be found in the city.*)

- Ask students to list the possible reasons that Mayans abandoned their cities. (*crop failures, war, disease, overuse of natural resources, rebellion*)

Independent Practice

Have students create the Taking Notes graphic organizer with "Mayan Civilization" in the central circle. Then ask them to fill in the circles with characteristics of Mayan civilization. Briefly model how to fill in separate pieces of information in each circle.

Monitor Progress

As students fill in the graphic organizer, circulate and make sure individuals are choosing logical details to place in the web diagram. Provide asistance as needed.

Target Reading Skill   L2

Identify Supporting Details As a follow-up, ask students to answer the Target Reading Skill question in the Student Edition. (*Today, descendants of the Mayas still live in Middle America. Many continue some of the cultural traditions of their Mayan ancestors.*)

Answer

✓ **Reading Check** They were important community leaders who developed a calendar to plan when to hold celebrations.

Links to Math

Mayan Counting The Mayas created a number system to count and record information. Dots stood for single numbers. For example, three dots in a row represented the number three. Bars stood for groups of five. Unlike our number system, which is based on 10, the Mayas' number system was based on 20. So, to record a number larger than 19, they used one large dot standing alone to represent the number 20, and more large dots for larger numbers divisible by 20. Dots and bars were used to make up the rest of the number. In the Mayan book at left, the number 29 is circled in white.

Centers of Religion and Government Mayan cities were religious and governmental centers. A different ruler commanded each city. Priests and nobles were also important community leaders. These leaders lived in large palaces within the city. Ordinary people lived on the edges of the city. Each city held great festivals to honor the many Mayan gods. The most important religious events took place at large temple-pyramids. Some of the ceremonies included human sacrifice.

Skilled mathematicians, Mayan priests developed a calendar to plan when to hold religious celebrations. The Mayas also created a system of writing using signs and symbols called **hieroglyphics.** They used these hieroglyphics to record information in books made from the bark of fig trees.

A Mayan Game Cities also had outdoor courts where a special ball game called pok-ta-tok was played. A court was about the size of a football field, and the game was a bit like soccer and basketball combined. The ball was made of hard rubber. Players tried to knock it through a stone hoop set on a wall. They could hit the ball with their elbows, knees, or hips—but not with their hands or feet. The ball could not touch the ground.

The Mayas Abandon Their Cities Around A.D. 900, the Mayas abandoned their cities, and their civilization declined. No one knows the exact reason they left. Crop failures, war, disease, or overuse of natural resources may have altered the Mayan way of life. Or people may have rebelled against their leaders. Today, descendants of the Mayas still live in Middle America. Many continue some of the cultural traditions of their Mayan ancestors.

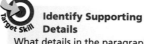

Target Skill **Identify Supporting Details** What details in the paragraph at right support the main idea that the Mayas had an important culture?

✓ **Reading Check** What did Mayan priests do?

Differentiated Instruction

For Special Needs Students   L1
Have students make a list of the Key Terms and other new words defined within the section, such as *tributes*. Then have them create flashcards with the word on one side and its definition on the other. Pair students and have them quiz each other on the definitions of the words using the flash cards.

The Aztec Empire

You have already read that the Aztecs built their new capital, Tenochtitlán, in the middle of a lake in about 1325. They had first settled in the Valley of Mexico in the 1100s. By the 1470s, the Aztecs had conquered the surrounding lands. Their large empire stretched from the Gulf of Mexico in the east to the Pacific Ocean in the west. A single powerful leader, the Aztec emperor, ruled these lands. All the people he conquered were forced to pay him tribute, or heavy taxes, in the form of food, gold, or slaves.

Waterways and Gardens In spite of its swampy origins, Tenochtitlán became a magnificent capital city. At its center were an open plaza and one or more towering pyramid-temples. There were schools for the sons of the nobles and large stone palaces. Raised streets of hard earth, called causeways, connected the city to the surrounding land. To supply the city with enough fresh water, the Aztecs also built aqueducts. These special channels carried spring water from distant sources to storage areas in the city.

As the population of Tenochtitlán grew, the Aztecs realized they needed more farmland. Their solution was to build many island gardens in the shallow lakes around the capital. These raised fields, called chinampas (chih NAM puz), were made from rich soil dredged up from the lake bottom. Trees planted along the edges prevented soil from washing away. Between the fields were canals. Farmers used the canals to transport produce by boats to a huge marketplace near the capital.

Find out how Cortés defeated the Aztecs.

Floating Gardens Today
A man poles a boat among the chinampas on the outskirts of Mexico City. **Draw Conclusions** *List some advantages and disadvantages of growing crops on chinampas.*

Chapter 3 Section 2 **73**

Show students *Cortés and the Aztec Empire*. Ask **Who and what helped Cortés defeat the Aztecs?** *(other Native Americans and diseases unknowingly carried by the Spanish to which the Aztecs had no immunity)*

The Aztec Empire L2

Guided Instruction

- **Vocabulary Builder** Clarify the high-use word **equip** before reading.

- Ask students to read The Aztec Empire. As students read, circulate to make sure individuals can answer the Reading Check question.

- Discuss the extent of the Aztec Empire. *(It stretched from the Gulf of Mexico in the east to the Pacific Ocean in the west.)* Ask **How did the Aztec emperor benefit from his conquests?** *(People he conquered were forced to pay him tributes in the form of food, slaves, and gold.)*

- Ask students to name two challenges that faced the Aztecs in Tenochtitlán. *(getting fresh water and having enough farmland)* Then ask students to describe how the Aztecs met these challenges. *(They built aqueducts to carry water from the mainland to storage areas in the city. They built chinampas, or raised fields, using rich soil from the bottom of the lake for farmland.)*

Answer

Draw Conclusions Advantages: difficult for wild animals to destroy crops, soil from the lake is very fertile; Disadvantages: farmers have to travel by boat to get to the crops, concern about soil washing away.

Differentiated Instruction

For Advanced Readers L3
Ask students to read *The Talking Stone* to learn more about the Aztec Empire. Have students work individually to answer the questions at the end of the selection.

All in One Medieval Times to Today Teaching Resources, *The Talking Stone,* pp. 209–211

For English Language Learners L2
Pair English language learners with more proficient readers to read *The Talking Stone* together. Encourage students to work together to answer and discuss the questions at the end of the selection.

All in One Medieval Times to Today Teaching Resources, *The Talking Stone,* pp. 209–211

Guided Instruction (continued)

- Ask students **Why might the Aztec civilization be described as war-like?** *(War was a constant part of life; most young men served as soldiers; their religion included prayers for victories; prisoners became either slaves or sacrificial victims.)*

- Ask **What was the largest class in Aztec society?** *(farmers)* **Why do you think this was so?** *(Possible answer: Since the empire was very large, a lot of food was needed to feed all the people.)*

- Ask students **Why do you think diseases brought by the Spanish killed so many Aztecs?** *(Possible answer: These diseases were new to the Aztecs so they had no immunity to them.)*

Independent Practice

Ask students to create a second web diagram, this time with "Aztec Civilization" in the central circle. Then have them fill in the circles with information about the Aztecs.

Monitor Progress

- Show *Section Reading Support Transparency MT 60* and ask students to check their graphic organizers individually. Go over key concepts and clarify key vocabulary as needed.

   Medieval Times to Today Transparencies, *Section Reading Support Transparency MT 60*

- Tell students to fill in the last column of the *Reading Readiness Guide.* Ask them to evaluate if what they learned was what they had expected to learn.

   All in One Medieval Times to Today Teaching Resources, *Reading Readiness Guide,* p. 192

Answer

Make Generalizations Aztecs valued their priests and, like the Mayas, relied on maize for food.

Aztec Gods and Goddesses
The Aztec God Quetzalcoatl (top) was the god of priests, and was believed to have invented the Aztec calendar. Above is the Aztec maize goddess. Both figures appear often in Aztec art.
Make Generalizations *What does the worship of gods and goddesses such as these tell you about Aztec society?*

Religion and Learning To bring about good harvests, Aztec priests held ceremonies that would win the favor of their gods. Their most important god was the sun god. Aztec religion taught that the sun would not have the strength to rise and cross the sky every day without human blood. Of course, if the sun did not rise, crops could not grow, and the people would starve. Therefore, Aztec religious ceremonies included human sacrifice. The Aztecs also prayed to their gods for victory in war. Prisoners captured in war often served as human sacrifices.

To schedule their religious festivals and farming cycles, Aztec priests created a calendar based on the Mayan calendar and their own knowledge of astronomy. The calendar had 13 periods, like months, of 20 days each. The Aztecs also kept records using hieroglyphs similar to those used by the Mayas.

Tenochtitlán had schools and a university. Boys from noble families attended these schools. They studied to be government officials, teachers, or scribes.

Aztec Society Aztec society had a strict class structure. The emperor, of course, was most important. Next were members of the royal family, nobles, priests, and military leaders. Soldiers were next in importance. Below soldiers came artisans—skilled creators of jewelry, pottery, sculpture, and other goods—and merchants. Then came the farmers. They made up the largest class of people. The lowest position in Aztec society was held by slaves, most of whom were prisoners captured in battle.

War was a part of life in the Aztec Empire, as new territory was conquered. Most young men over the age of 15 served as soldiers for a period of time. They were well trained and well equipped. Soldiers had swords and bows and arrows. For protection, they had special armor made from heavy quilted cotton. Priests and government officials did not serve in the military.

Background: Biography

Moctezuma (c. 1480–1520) Moctezuma ruled as emperor of the Aztec empire from about 1502 to 1520. During his reign there was constant warfare and unrest. When the Spanish arrived in 1519, Moctezuma believed that they were descendants of Quetzalcoatl, a legendary Aztec god. Moctezuma received the Spanish, led by Hernán Cortés, into his court. Soon, Cortés had seized Moctezuma and taken over Tenochtitlán. Moctezuma was killed in 1520. No one is sure whether he was killed by the Spanish or his subjects.

Aztec women were not allowed to work as soldiers or military leaders, though they could train to be priestesses. Most women—even women from noble families—had to be skilled at weaving. Some of the cloth they wove was used for trade. Some was used to decorate temples. The finest cloth was used to make clothing for the Aztec royal family and nobles. Before teenage girls learned to weave, they were expected to grind flour, make tortillas, and cook meals.

The End of an Empire In 1519, Spanish conquistadors invaded the Aztec Empire. Some of the peoples whose lands the Aztecs had conquered joined forces with the Spanish. Together, they fought the Aztecs and tried to overthrow the Aztec emperor, Moctezuma. The two sides waged fierce battles. Diseases carried by the Spanish spread to the Aztecs and killed many of them. In 1521, the Aztecs surrendered to the Spanish. The once-powerful Aztec Empire was at an end.

✓ **Reading Check** Describe the levels of Aztec society.

Aztec Feather Headdress
Moctezuma's head covering was decorated with feathers—an important symbol in the Aztec religion.

Section 2 Assessment

Key Terms
Review the key terms at the beginning of this section. Use each term in a sentence that explains its meaning.

Target Reading Skill
State three details that support the main idea of the first paragraph under the heading Aztec Society.

Comprehension and Critical Thinking
1. (a) **Recall** What activity was the basis of Mayan life?

(b) **Explain** How did Mayan religion reflect the importance of this activity?
(c) **Infer** What do you think is the most likely reason the Mayas abandoned their cities? Explain your choice.
2. (a) **Describe** How did the Aztec Empire expand?
(b) **Synthesize** How did the Aztecs treat the peoples they conquered in war?
(c) **Draw Conclusions** Why might some of the peoples conquered by the Aztecs have wanted to overthrow the emperor?

Writing Activity
The Mayas and the Aztecs created great civilizations. How were their cultures alike? How were they different? Write a paragraph comparing and contrasting the two civilizations.

Writing Tip First take notes on the similarities and differences. You may want to use a chart to help you organize. Be sure to write a topic sentence for your paragraph, and then support it with details from your notes.

Chapter 3 Section 2 **75**

Section 2 Assessment

Key Terms
Students' sentences should reflect knowledge of each Key Term.

Target Reading Skill
Students may cite any of the appropriate details in the paragraph.

Comprehension and Critical Thinking
1. (a) farming (b) The Mayan rain-god and sun-god were important because rain and sun were needed for growing maize.
(c) Reasons might include crop failure, war, disease, overuse of natural resources, or rebellion against leaders. Students should provide an adequate explanation for their choice.

2. (a) The Aztecs conquered other peoples. (b) Conquered peoples had to pay tributes to the emperor. Some people captured in war were used as human sacrifices. (c) Possible answer: They resented their treatment and having to pay tributes.

Assess and Reteach

Assess Progress L2
Have students complete the Section Assessment. Administer the *Section Quiz*.

All in One **Medieval Times to Today Teaching Resources,** *Section Quiz*, p. 194

Reteach L1
If students need more instruction, have them read this section in the Reading and Vocabulary Study Guide.

Chapter 3, Section 2, **Medieval Times to Today Reading and Vocabulary Study Guide,** pp. 29–31

Extend L3
To help students appreciate the accomplishments of ancient civilizations, have them complete *Writing a Message Using Your Own Hieroglyphics.*

All in One **Medieval Times to Today Teaching Resources,** *Small Group Activity: Writing a Message Using Your Own Hieroglyphics,* pp. 205–208

Answer

✓ **Reading Check** At the top was the emperor. Next were the priests, nobles, royal family members, and military leaders. Soldiers were next, followed by artisans. Next came traders, and then farmers. Slaves were in the lowest position.

Writing Activity
Use the *Rubric for Assessing a Writing Assignment* to evaluate students' paragraphs.

All in One **Medieval Times to Today Teaching Resources,** *Rubric for Assessing a Writing Assignment,* p. 213

Focus on The Great Temple

L2

Guided Instruction

- Ask students to read the text and study the art, photos, and captions on these pages.

- Ask students **Why was the Great Temple rebuilt so many times?** (*Because it was a solid, earth-filled temple, it began to sink into the soft soil of Tenochtitlán; in order to save the Great Temple, the Aztecs rebuilt it six times.*)

- Ask students **Why do you think the Aztecs rebuilt the Great Temple instead of building a new one in a different place?** (*Possible answers: It was easier and faster to rebuild the temple instead of building a new one; the area where the temple was built might have been special in some way for the Aztecs and their gods.*)

- As a class, answer the Assessment questions. Allow students to briefly discuss their responses with a partner before sharing their answers with the class.

Focus On
The Great Temple

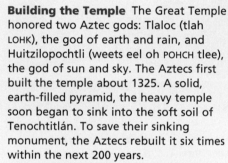

In 1521, the Spanish conquered the Aztecs and began to destroy the Aztec capital of Tenochtitlán. On the site of the ruined Aztec city, they built a new capital: Mexico City. For many years, an important piece of Mexico's past—the Great Temple of the Aztecs—remained buried under this new city. Scholars were not sure where the site of the Great Temple lay. Then in 1978, electrical workers dug up an old stone carving. Experts who studied the carving knew that it had been made by the Aztecs. The site of the Great Temple had been found.

Building the Temple The Great Temple honored two Aztec gods: Tlaloc (tlah LOHK), the god of earth and rain, and Huitzilopochtli (weets eel oh POHCH tlee), the god of sun and sky. The Aztecs first built the temple about 1325. A solid, earth-filled pyramid, the heavy temple soon began to sink into the soft soil of Tenochtitlán. To save their sinking monument, the Aztecs rebuilt it six times within the next 200 years.

The Aztecs rebuilt each new temple over the previous temple. After rebuilding, they honored their gods with human sacrifices in the temple's shrines. A figure called a chacmool, at the top left, was used to hold offerings to the gods.

The illustration at the right shows some of the temple layers. By the time the Spanish began to destroy Tenochtitlán in 1521, the Great Temple had been built seven times.

Differentiated Instruction

For Gifted and Talented   L3

Working in pairs, have students do research to learn more about other Aztec gods, such as Chalchiuhtlicue, Huixtocíhuatl, or Quetzalcóatl. Have students give a short presentation on the Aztec god they chose. Encourage students to be creative and include drawings or photos of artifacts in their presentations.

For Advanced Readers   L3

Have students do research on the Internet or in the library to learn more about the Aztec gods Tlaloc and Huitzilopochtli. Using the information they find, have students write a short essay about either of the two gods. Encourage students to be creative and include drawings or photos of artifacts related to the gods with their essays.

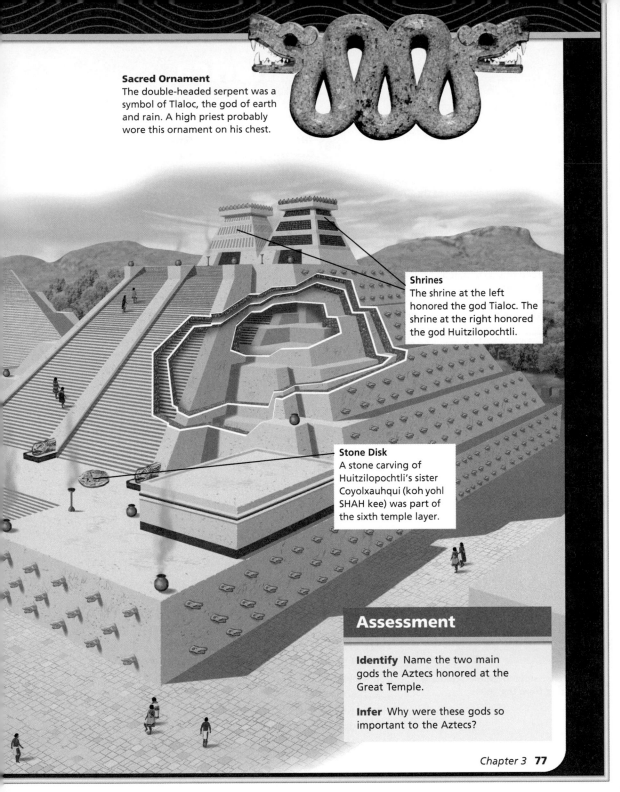

Sacred Ornament
The double-headed serpent was a symbol of Tlaloc, the god of earth and rain. A high priest probably wore this ornament on his chest.

Shrines
The shrine at the left honored the god Tialoc. The shrine at the right honored the god Huitzilopochtli.

Stone Disk
A stone carving of Huitzilopochtli's sister Coyolxauhqui (koh yohl SHAH kee) was part of the sixth temple layer.

Assessment

Identify Name the two main gods the Aztecs honored at the Great Temple.

Infer Why were these gods so important to the Aztecs?

Independent Practice

Have students do research in the library or on the Internet to learn more about other well-known religious sites in the region, such as the Temple of the Sun at Machu Picchu in Peru, built by the Incas. Working in pairs, have students create a brochure in which they list some of the history of their chosen site, as well as other important information, such as age and location.

Answers

Assessment

Identify Tlaloc, Huitzilopochtli
Infer Possible answer: The Aztecs depended on agriculture for survival, therefore they would have believed that Tlaloc, the god of earth and rain, and Huitzilopochtli, the god of sun and sky would be important to their survival. They probably believed that these gods were responsible for helping their crops grow.

Section 3
Step-by-Step Instruction

Objectives

Social Studies
1. Find out about the Mound Builders who lived in eastern North America.
2. Learn about the cultures of the Southwest and Great Plains.
3. Find out about the Woodland peoples of North America.

Reading/Language Arts
Learn how to identify details that add up to the main idea in a paragraph.

Prepare to Read

Build Background Knowledge **L2**
Review with students the ancient civilizations in Middle America they read about in earlier sections. Have students preview the headings, maps, and photographs in this section to predict what they will be learning about. Write students' predictions on the board and return to them after reading the section to assess their accuracy and make revisions as needed.

Set a Purpose for Reading **L2**
- Preview the Objectives.
- Form students into pairs or groups of four. Distribute the *Reading Readiness Guide.* Ask students to fill in the first two columns of the chart. Use the Numbered Heads participation strategy (TE, p. T36) to call on students to share one piece of information they already know and one piece of information they want to know.

  All in One Medieval Times to Today Teaching Resources, *Reading Readiness Guide,* p. 196

Vocabulary Builder
Preview Key Terms **L2**
Pronounce each Key Term, then ask students to say the word with you. Provide a simple explanation such as, "The flat land east of the Rocky Mountains makes up the Great Plains."

Section 3 · Cultures of North America

Prepare to Read

Objectives
In this section, you will
1. Find out about the Mound Builders who lived in eastern North America.
2. Learn about the cultures of the Southwest and the Great Plains.
3. Find out about the Woodland peoples of North America.

Taking Notes
As you read this section, look for information about three major Native American cultures. Copy the table below and record your findings in it. Add categories as needed.

Culture	Location	Source of Food	Type of Dwelling

🎯 Target Reading Skill
Identify Implied Main Ideas Identifying main ideas can help you remember what you read. Even if a main idea is not stated directly, the details in a paragraph add up to the main idea. For example, the details in the paragraph under the heading The Eastern Mound Builders add up to this main idea: The Mound Builders, hunters and gatherers who relied on the land's resources, became settled farmers over time.

Key Terms
- **Mound Builders** (mownd BIL durz) *n.* Native American groups who built earthen mounds
- **Anasazi** (ah nuh SAH zee) *n.* one of the ancient Native American peoples of the Southwest
- **pueblo** (PWEB loh) *n.* a cluster of Native American stone or adobe dwellings
- **kiva** (KEE vuh) *n.* a round room used by the Pueblo peoples for religious ceremonies
- **Great Plains** (grayt playnz) *n.* a mostly flat and grassy region of western North America

A Mississippian copper sculpture dating from the 1000s

Seen from above, a huge snake seems to twist and turn across the landscape. A mysterious shape—perhaps an egg?—is at its mouth. This enormous earthwork was created hundreds of years ago in what is now Ohio. Called the Great Serpent Mound, it is the largest image of a snake anywhere in the world. Uncoiled, the serpent would be about 1,349 feet (411 meters) long.

Archaeologists have found more than 1,000 earthen mounds across eastern North America. They were made by thousands of workers moving baskets of earth by hand. There are small mounds and large ones. Some contain graves, but others—like the Great Serpent Mound—do not. Most were constructed between around 700 B.C. and A.D. 1250. Today, we call the different Native American groups who built these curious and long-lasting mounds the **Mound Builders**.

🎯 Target Reading Skill **L2**

Identify Implied Main Ideas Point out the Target Reading Skill. Tell students that when a main idea is not specifically expressed, readers can combine important details to express the main idea themselves.

Model the skill by pointing out that the details in the first paragraph under The Hopewell Culture on p. 80 can be combined to express the main idea. (*The Hopewell were mound builders who lived along the Ohio and upper Mississippi rivers, appearing there about 100 years before the Adena disappeared.*)

Give students *Identify Implied Main Ideas.* Have them complete the activity in groups.

All in One Medieval Times to Today Teaching Resources, *Identify Implied Main Ideas,* p. 201

The Eastern Mound Builders

The Mound Builders lived in eastern North America. They occupied the region roughly between Minnesota and Louisiana, and between the Mississippi River and the Atlantic Ocean. The Mound Builders lived along the area's many rivers, which provided them with plenty of fish and fresh water. They hunted wild animals for food, including deer, turkeys, bears, and even squirrels. They also gathered nuts such as acorns, pecans, and walnuts to supplement their diet. Over time, these communities began to grow their own food. This meant they did not have to move as much in search of food and could form settlements.

Early Mound Builders: The Adena Archaeologists have discovered evidence of early Mound Builders who lived about 600 B.C. in the Ohio Valley. Called the Adena (uh DEE nuh), these people constructed mounds that are usually less than 20 feet high. Certain mounds were tombs that contained weapons, tools, and decorative objects in addition to bodies. Some items were made from materials not found locally, such as copper and seashells. Thus, historians believe that the Adena must have taken part in long-distance trade. Little is known about the daily life of the Adena, but they seem to have declined about 100 B.C.

Great Serpent Mound
The Great Serpent Mound snakes across Ohio's countryside.
Infer *What about the mound suggests that it may have had religious importance?*

Guided Instruction (continued)

■ Ask students **Where did the Hopewell live?** *(in North America along the Ohio and upper Mississippi rivers)*

■ Have students use the map on p. 80 to locate the different mound sites they have read about. Ask **Why do you think so many early cultures settled along rivers?** *(Rivers were a source of water for farming and drinking and a means of transportation.)*

■ Ask **Why were maize and beans so important to the Mississippians?** *(These crops could be easily dried and stored, which ensured food during times of drought or bad harvests.)*

Independent Practice

Ask students to create the Taking Notes graphic organizer on a blank piece of paper. Tell students to write the names of Native American cultures they have learned about in the first column. Then have them fill out the information in each culture's row. Display the *Chart/Table* transparency and briefly model how to choose details to complete the chart.

📖 **Medieval Times to Today Transparencies,** *Transparency B12: Chart/Table*

Monitor Progress

As students work on their organizers, circulate and make sure individuals are using the correct information. Provide assistance as needed.

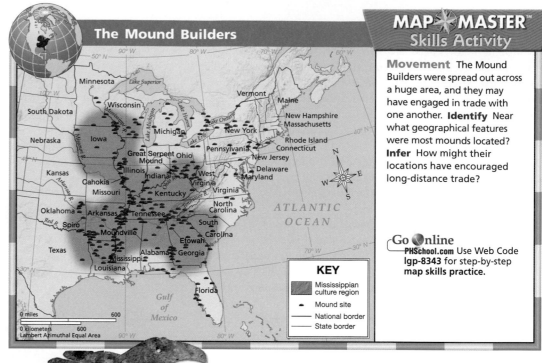

The Hopewell made figures like the copper raven (above) and the hand (bottom right), which is made of mica, a soft mineral.

MAP MASTER™ Skills Activity

Movement The Mound Builders were spread out across a huge area, and they may have engaged in trade with one another. **Identify** Near what geographical features were most mounds located? **Infer** How might their locations have encouraged long-distance trade?

Go Online
PHSchool.com Use Web Code lgp-8343 for step-by-step map skills practice.

The Hopewell Culture About 100 years before the Adena disappeared, another culture appeared along the Ohio and upper Mississippi rivers. Called the Hopewell, these peoples built larger mounds. The Hopewell did not have a highly organized society with a single ruler. Instead, they lived in many small communities with local leaders.

The Hopewell peoples grew a greater variety of crops than did the Adena. They also seem to have traded over a wider area. There is evidence that goods were traded from the Gulf of Mexico to present-day Canada and from the Rocky Mountains to the Atlantic Ocean. Hopewell sites have silver from the Great Lakes region and alligator teeth from present-day Florida.

About A.D. 400, the long-distance trade across eastern North America seems to have faded out. Also, the Hopewell stopped building new mounds. Historians are not sure why. The climate may have turned colder and hurt agriculture. The Hopewell may have suffered a severe drought or been invaded. Overpopulation is also a possible reason for their decline.

Answers

MAP MASTER™ Skills Activity **Identify** rivers **Infer** Mound Builders could travel along the river to trade goods with other civilizations.

Go Online
PHSchool.com Students may practice their map skills using the interactive online version of this map.

Background: Global Perspectives

Burial Mounds The practice of burying people in tombs covered with mounds dates to prehistoric times. These mounds are also called *barrows* or *stupa*. The Romans, Saxons, and Vikings all used barrows for the burial of important people. Stupa, used in Buddhist regions, can be found in India, Sri Lanka, Myanmar, and other Asian countries.

The Mississippians By about A.D. 700, a new and important culture called Mississippian (mis uh SIP ee un) began to flower in eastern North America. These peoples inhabited both small and large communities. Like the earlier Mound Builders, the Mississippians lived along rivers and built mounds. They, too, grew new kinds of crops. Maize and beans became important parts of their diet. Both foods are easily dried and stored in large amounts. This helped the Mississippians protect themselves against years of drought and bad harvests.

The Mississippian culture spread over a wide area in the present-day South and Midwest. During this period, long-distance trade revived. Populations increased over time, and major centers of government and religion developed. These include Moundville in present-day Alabama, and Etowah (ET uh wah) in present-day Georgia. The largest center was Cahokia (kuh HOH kee uh), located in what is now Illinois. One of Cahokia's mounds, around 100 feet tall, was the largest mound in North America.

Cahokia was a large city for its day. Historians estimate that it reached its peak about A.D. 1100. At that time, as many as 20,000 to 30,000 people may have lived there. But by 1250, the population dropped. The disappearance of the last of the Mound Builders is as mystifying as the many earthworks they left behind.

√ **Reading Check** How did the Mississippians live?

Peoples of the Southwest and the Great Plains

The mounds of the Mound Builders are not the only amazing structures built by early Native American cultures. Other peoples in North America adapted to different landscapes and climates to create distinctive structures. One of these groups created remarkable multistory homes from the available materials of the Southwest.

The Ancient Ones The **Anasazi** (ah nuh SAH zee) were an ancient Native American peoples of the Southwest. Their name can be translated as "the ancient ones." Anasazi culture began about A.D. 100. Historians think that Chaco Canyon, in present-day New Mexico, was a trading center for the region. A network of roads connected distant Anasazi villages to Chaco Canyon. Archaeologists have found tens of thousands of turquoise pieces as well as baskets, pottery, shells, and feathers in Chaco Canyon.

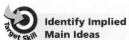

Identify Implied Main Ideas

List several details from the paragraphs under the heading The Mississippians. What implied main idea do these details support?

An archaeologist digs at Chaco Canyon, New Mexico.

Chapter 3 Section 3 **81**

🕙 Target Reading Skill   L2

Identify Implied Main Ideas As a follow-up, ask students to answer the Target Reading Skill question in the Student Edition. *(Students may list any of the details in these three paragraphs. Possible main idea: The Mississippian culture was an important culture of Mound Builders who lived along rivers in what is now the South and Midwest from about A.D. 700–1250.)*

Peoples of the Southwest and the Great Plains   L2

Guided Instruction

- **Vocabulary Builder** Clarify the high-use words **diverse, alter,** and **revive** before reading.

- Read about the Anasazi, Pueblo, and Plains Indians in Peoples of the Southwest and the Great Plains.

- Ask students **Who were the Anasazi?** *(an early Native American people who lived in the Southwest)* **What does their name mean?** *("the ancient ones")*

- Discuss the geography and climate of the Southwest. *(The soil is poor and there is little water. The winters are harsh and the summers are hot and dry.)* Ask **How were the Anasazi able to grow crops in their dry land?** *(They created a system of canals and dams.)*

- Ask **How did the Anasazi create homes that were adapted to their environment?** *(They built pueblos from adobe and stone; these dwellings stayed warm in the winter and cool in the summer.)*

- Ask **Why did the Anasazi abandon their pueblos?** *(A severe drought hit the region.)*

 Skills Mini Lesson

Sequencing   L2

1. Teach the skill by explaining that sequencing means putting things in the order in which they occurred. Tell students that making a timeline to show events in time order makes it easier to see relationships between events.

2. Help students practice the skill by putting these events in time order:

(a) Pueblo people follow Anasazi customs; (b) Anasazi culture begins in A.D. 900; (c) Anasazi abandon pueblos by A.D. 1300 *(b, c, a)*

3. Have students apply the skill by identifying a relationship between the Anasazi and the Pueblo. *(The Pueblo people modeled their culture after the Anasazi culture.)*

Answer

√ **Reading Check** They lived along rivers as farmers. They conducted long-distance trade with other groups.

Guided Instruction (continued)

- Ask **How were the Pueblo people like the Anasazi?** *(They built similar dwellings and had similar crafts; both were skilled farmers; both developed irrigation systems.)*

- Ask students **Why was sign language important to the Plains Indians?** *(Since it was understood across the region, it allowed different groups to communicate and trade.)*

- Ask students **How did the Europeans change the ways of life of the Plains Indians?** *(Europeans settled on Indian land; introduced guns, horses, railroads; brought disease; forced Native American groups from the east to move west and coexist with the groups already living there.)*

Independent Practice

Tell students to continue filling in their charts with information about the Anasazi, Pueblo, and Plains Indians.

Monitor Progress

As students work on their charts, circulate to make sure they are filling in each row with the correct information. Provide assistance as needed.

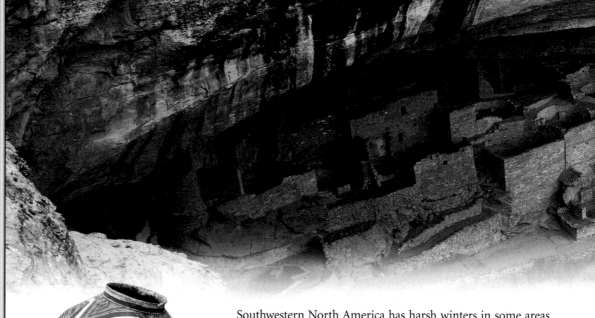

Anasazi Cliff Village
Entire villages of Anasazi people lived under the shelter of massive stone cliffs like this one in Colorado. Anasazi craftspeople decorated pottery like the jar above with black and white patterns.
Analyze Images *What might be some advantages to living under cliffs like these?*

Southwestern North America has harsh winters in some areas and hot, dry summers. The soil is mostly poor, and there is little water. To capture rainwater for their fields, the Anasazi created a system of canals and dams. This system allowed them to grow maize, beans, and squash for food. They also grew cotton for cloth.

For their homes, the Anasazi constructed **pueblos** (PWEB lohz). These clusters of stone and adobe dwellings helped to keep people warm in the winter and cool in the summer. Pueblos had thick walls, and many had high ceilings. Round rooms called **kivas** (KEE vuz) were used for special religious ceremonies. As the population grew, so did the pueblos. Some pueblos were five stories tall and had hundreds of rooms. Between 1275 and 1300, however, severe droughts hit the region. The Anasazi abandoned all their major pueblos, never to return.

Later Pueblo Peoples Anasazi customs survived among later groups who lived to the south of the Anasazi sites. They are called Pueblo peoples, or simply Pueblos. These groups also built apartment-style stone and adobe dwellings with kivas. Like the Anasazi, their crafts included weaving, basket-making, and pottery. They were also skilled farmers.

The region of New Mexico where the Pueblos lived receives only 8 to 13 inches of rain a year, but it does have rivers. The Pueblos planted corn, squash, beans, and other crops in the river bottoms near their dwellings. They relied on intensive irrigation to raise these crops. Hunting and gathering provided the Pueblos with the food they could not grow.

Differentiated Instruction

For English Language Learners L1
Students whose native language is Spanish may benefit from studying this section in the Spanish Reading and Vocabulary Study Guide.

Chapter 3, Section 3, **Medieval Times to Today Spanish Reading and Vocabulary Study Guide,** pp. 25–26

For Gifted and Talented L3
Invite students to visit the past by researching Mesa Verde National Park in the library or on the Internet. Have students use their information to plan a trip to these cliff dwellings built along canyon walls in what is now southwestern Colorado. Have students share their findings and travel plans with the class.

Answer

Analyze Images Possible answers: shaded from the hot sun, protected from invaders

The Pueblos believed in many spirits, called kachinas (kuh CHEE nuz). They wanted to please these spirits, who they believed controlled the rain, wild animals, and harvests. Many times a year, the Pueblos gathered for ceremonies that involved prayer, dancing, and singing. They also appealed to their ancestors, another type of kachina. Today the modern Pueblo peoples, including the Hopi and the Zuni, keep many of these traditions alive.

The Plains Indians West of the Mississippi River and east of the Rocky Mountains is a mostly flat and grassy region called the **Great Plains.** For centuries, this land was home to diverse groups of Native Americans called Plains Indians. Individual groups had their own languages and traditions. They used a form of sign language to trade with one another.

Some groups, such as the Mandan, were farmers. They lived in fenced villages along the Missouri River, in lodges made of earth and wood. Others, such as the Sioux (soo), followed herds of bison that roamed the plains. Dwellings such as tipis (TEE peaz)—easy to take apart, carry, and set up again—were ideal for such a lifestyle.

After the arrival of Europeans, the lives of Plains Indians changed rapidly. They had to share their land with eastern Native Americans, such as the Omaha, who had been forced west by white settlers. Newly introduced horses, guns, and railroads altered their traditions. Most groups suffered from diseases brought by Europeans and lost their land to European settlement. Many Native American cultures began to break down. Today, there is a strong effort to revive these traditional cultures.

✓ **Reading Check** How did the Sioux live?

> **Links Across**
> ## The World
>
> **The Arrival of the Horse**
> The arrival of the horse in the Americas brought major changes to the lives of many Plains Indians. Native Americans on horseback became expert buffalo hunters. They came to depend more and more on the buffalo for their existence, using the animal for food, clothing, and shelter. Many previously settled Indian groups became nomadic. They rode their horses across the plains, following the great herds of buffalo.

Differentiated Instruction

For Less Proficient Readers **L1**
Students who are less proficient readers may have difficulty absorbing the information in this section. Pair students with more proficient readers and have them create an outline of the material. Tell students to use the headings in the section as guidelines for their outlines.

Peoples of the Woodlands **L2**

Guided Instruction

- Read Peoples of the Woodlands with students. As students read, circulate to make sure individuals can answer the Reading Check question.

- Ask students **What were distinguishing symbols of wealth among Native Americans of the Northwest?** *(totem poles and potlatch ceremonies)*

- Ask **How did the people of the Northwest get food?** *(by hunting and fishing)* **In the Eastern Woodlands?** *(by hunting and farming)*

- Have students explain the Iroquois political system. *(Five nations formed a peace alliance. Each nation governed its own villages, but they all met in council to discuss issues that affected the entire group.)*

Independent Progress
Have students complete the table.

Monitor Progress

- Show *Section Reading Support Transparency MT 61* and ask students to check their graphic organizers individually.

  📖 **Medieval Times to Transparencies,** *Section Reading Support Transparency MT 61*

- Tell students to fill in the last column of the *Reading Readiness Guide.* Ask them to evaluate if what they learned was what they had expected to learn.

  All in One Medieval Times to Today Teaching Resources, *Reading Readiness Guide,* p. 196

> **Links**
> Read the **Links Across the World** on this page. Ask students **How did the introduction of the horse change the lives of many Plains Indians?** *(Plains Indians used the horse to hunt buffalo, which caused them to become more dependent on the buffalo for their survival.)*

Answer

✓ **Reading Check** They followed bison herds across the plains.

Assess Progress `L2`

Have students complete the Section Assessment. Administer the *Section Quiz*.

All in One **Medieval Times to Today Teaching Resources,** *Section Quiz,* p. 198

Reteach `L1`

If students need more instruction, have them read this section in the Reading and Vocabulary Study Guide.

📖 Chapter 3, Section 3, **Medieval Times to Today Reading and Vocabulary Study Guide,** pp. 32–34

Extend `L3`

Have students complete the *Enrichment* activity to learn more about the Iroquois.

All in One **Medieval Times to Today Teaching Resources,** *Enrichment,* p. 203

Answer

✓Reading Check It was an alliance of five Iroquois nations designed to keep the peace.

Section 3 Assessment

Key Terms

Students' sentences should reflect knowledge of each Key Term.

🎯 Target Reading Skill

See the main ideas as stated in the Chapter Summary on p. 85.

Comprehension and Critical Thinking

1. (a) Adena, Hopewell, Mississippians
(b) They built mounds, carried on long-distance trade, and grew a variety of crops.

2. (a) It has harsh winters and hot, dry summers. **(b)** They used available materials, such as sun dried adobe bricks or stone cliffs.

3. (a) totem pole—a carved, painted log stood on end that typically had images of animals carved into and painted on it; potlatch—a ceremony held by a person of high rank to show wealth **(b)** Possible answer: An elaborate totem pole with intricate carvings and paintings might signify wealth because it indicated that the owner might have had more free time to create it or could afford to pay a good artist to create it. At potlatches, people were able to show how wealthy they were by giving guests expensive gifts.

Peoples of the Woodlands

Native American groups lived in woodlands in different parts of present-day Canada and the United States. The peoples of the Northwest Coast hunted in the forests and fished in rivers full of salmon as well as in the Pacific Ocean. They lived in settlements of wooden homes. Like the Mound Builders and the Pueblos, early Native Americans of the Northwest Coast created remarkable structures. They were called totem poles.

Totem poles were carved and painted logs stood on end. They typically had images of real or mythical animals. Often the animals were identified with the owner's family line, much as a family crest is used in European cultures. Totem poles were a symbol of the owner's wealth, as were ceremonies called potlatches. At a potlatch, a person of high rank invited many guests and gave them generous gifts.

In the eastern woodlands, Native American groups such as the Iroquois (IHR uh kwoy) not only hunted in the forests but also cleared land for farms. Because the men were often at war, the women were the farmers. In the 1500s, five Iroquois nations—Mohawk, Onondaga, Cayuga, Seneca, and Oneida—formed a peace alliance. Nations of the Iroquois League governed their own villages, but they met to decide issues that affected the group as a whole. This was the best-organized political system in the Americas when Europeans arrived.

Totem pole in Vancouver, Canada

✓ Reading Check What was the Iroquois League?

Section 3 Assessment

Key Terms

Review the key terms at the beginning of this section. Use each term in a sentence that explains its meaning.

🎯 Target Reading Skill

State the main ideas in Section 3.

Comprehension and Critical Thinking

1. (a) Sequence List the three groups of Mound Builders, from earliest to latest.

(b) Compare In what ways were the three groups alike?

2. (a) Identify What is the climate of southwestern North America?

(b) Identify Cause and Effect Why did peoples of this region build pueblos rather than other types of structures?

3. (a) Define What are totem poles and potlatches?

(b) Infer How were totem poles and potlatches symbols of a family's wealth?

Writing Activity

Study the photograph of the Anasazi cliff dwellings on pages 82–83. Write a paragraph describing the site. What are the buildings like? Where are they located? What might it be like there at night or during a storm?

> **Writing Tip** Use descriptive adjectives for colors, textures, and shapes. Also include any sounds and smells you might experience there at different times of the day or year.

Writing Activity

Use the *Rubric for Assessing a Writing Assignment* to evaluate students' paragraphs.

All in One **Medieval Times to Today Teaching Resources,** *Rubric for Assessing a Writing Assignment,* p. 213

◆ Chapter Summary

Section 1: South America and the Incas

- The varied geography and climate of the Americas produced a diversity of Native American peoples and cultures.
- The Incas ruled a large, highly organized mountain empire in South America. Their accomplishments included long-lasting stone structures.

Section 2: Cultures of Middle America

- Mayan civilization was based on farming, which supported cities throughout the Yucatán Peninsula of Middle America.
- The Aztecs ruled a rich and powerful empire of diverse peoples in Middle America, from a magnificent capital called Tenochtitlán.

Aztec feather headdress

Section 3: Cultures of North America

- The Mound Builders lived along the rivers of eastern North America and built thousands of earthen mounds across the region.
- The Anasazi, and later the Pueblo peoples, adapted to the dry environment of the Southwest, while the Plains Indians farmed or followed herds of buffalo.
- Woodlands peoples of the Northwest Coast were hunters and fishers. In eastern forests, the Iroquois League was formed to bring peace to the region.

Anasazi clay vessel

◆ Key Terms

Match each term with its definition.

1. quipu
2. kivas
3. hieroglyphics
4. census
5. pueblos
6. maize
7. terraces

A corn

B an official count of people

C steplike ledges cut into mountains

D clusters of stone and adobe dwellings

E group of knotted strings used to record information

F round rooms used for religious ceremonies

G signs and symbols that made up the Mayan writing system

Chapter 3 **85**

Vocabulary Builder

Revisit this chapter's high-use words:

dense	establish	diverse
complex	decline	alter
unify	equip	revive
thrive	supplement	

Ask students to review the definitions they recorded on their *Word Knowledge* worksheets.

All in One Medieval Times to Today Teaching Resources, *Word Knowledge,* p. 202

Consider allowing students to earn extra credit if they use the words in their answers to the questions in the Chapter Review and Assessment. The words must be used correctly and in a natural context to win the extra points.

Chapter 3
Review and Assessment
Review Chapter Content

- Review and revisit the major themes of this chapter by asking students to identify which Guiding Question each bulleted statement in the Chapter Summary answers. Have students write each statement down and work in groups to determine which statement applies to which Guiding Question. Refer to page 1 in the Student Edition for the text of Guiding Questions.

- Assign *Vocabulary Development* for students to review Key Terms.

  All in One Medieval Times to Today Teaching Resources, *Vocabulary Development,* p. 212

Answers

Key Terms

1. E

2. F

3. G

4. B

5. D

6. A

7. C

Comprehension and Critical Thinking

8. (a) Incas—farming on terraces, steplike ledges cut into mountains; Aztecs—raised fields for farming in lakes, called chinampas **(b)** Both methods were based on alterations of the natural landscape. **(c)** By building terraces, Incan farmers made use of the mountainous landscape. Stone terraces prevented the soil from being washed away by rain. The Aztecs used the shallow lakes around Tenochtitlán to form their chinampas.

9. (a) Each city had its own ruler and community leaders. **(b)** The Mayas did not seek control over other peoples. **(c)** Because a civilization like the Mayas' was not organized around war and conquest, the people might find their land hard to defend against a more warlike people.

10. (a) Tenochtitlán **(b)** It was built in the middle of a lake and was connected to the mainland by causeways. It had an open plaza, towering pyramid-temples, stone palaces, aqueducts, and a huge marketplace. **(c)** Many modern capital cities have imposing structures like the Aztec pyramid-temples and stone palaces. They also have water systems that carry water from outlying sources into the city.

11. (a) in the region roughly between Michigan and Alabama, and between the Mississippi River and the Atlantic Ocean **(b)** They have learned about the Mound Builders' weapons, tools, and decorative objects, and that the Mound Builders probably engaged in long-distance trade. **(c)** The Mound Builders left no written records.

12. (a) The Great Plains are a flat and grassy region located between the Mississippi River and the Rocky Mountains. **(b)** Europeans arrived and settled on Indian land; introduced guns, horses, and railroads; brought disease; and forced Native American groups from the east to move west and coexist with the groups already living there. **(c)** They were trying to keep their land and preserve their way of life.

Skills Practice
Answers will vary.

Possible event Native American cultures began to break down (effect).

◆ Comprehension and Critical Thinking

8. (a) Describe What special farming methods were developed by the Incas and the Aztecs?
(b) Compare How were these methods similar?
(c) Analyze Information How did each method suit the geography of the region where it was used?

9. (a) Recall What type of government did Mayan cities have?
(b) Analyze Why is it not correct to call Mayan civilization an "empire"?
(c) Make Generalizations If a civilization like that of the Mayas came under attack, would it be easy or hard to defend? Explain your answer.

10. (a) Identify What city was the capital of the Aztec Empire?
(b) Describe What was this capital city like?
(c) Generalize In what ways are modern capital cities like the Aztec capital?

11. (a) Locate Where in North America are human-built mounds located?
(b) Synthesize What have archaeologists learned from studying these mounds?
(c) Analyze Why is it difficult to determine the exact use of some mounds?

12. (a) Describe Where are the Great Plains, and what are they like?
(b) Identify Cause and Effect What changes to their way of life did many Plains Indians experience, and why?
(c) Infer Why do you think some Plains Indians battled with European settlers?

◆ Skills Practice

Identifying Cause and Effect Review the steps to identify causes and effects that you learned in the Skills for Life activity in this chapter. Then reread the part of Section 3 titled The Plains Indians. Choose an event from this section, and decide if it is a cause or an effect. Look for earlier or later events that might be causes or effects. Then summarize the cause-and-effect relationships you have identified.

◆ Writing Activity: Science

Review this chapter to find out which crops were grown or collected for food by early Native Americans. Choose three crops. Do research to find out why each one might be important to a healthful diet. To which food group does it belong? What is its nutritional value? How is it different from or similar to other foods eaten by these people? Write a brief report on what you learn.

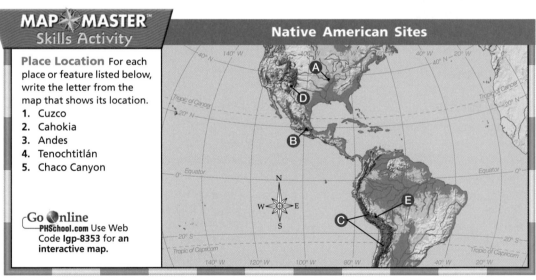

MAP MASTER™
Skills Activity

Native American Sites

Place Location For each place or feature listed below, write the letter from the map that shows its location.
1. Cuzco
2. Cahokia
3. Andes
4. Tenochtitlán
5. Chaco Canyon

Go Online
PHSchool.com Use Web Code lgp-8353 for an interactive map.

Possible causes European diseases killed many Native Americans; they lost their land to Europeans; they died in battles with Europeans.

Possible effect Today, there is a strong effort to revive Native American cultures.

Writing Activity: Science
Reports will vary but possible crops include maize, beans, squash, peppers, papayas, and avocados.

Use *Rubric for Assessing a Writing Assignment* to assess students' reports.

All in One Medieval Times to Today Teaching Resources, *Rubric for Assessing a Writing Assignment,* p. 213

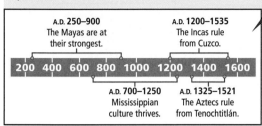

Standardized Test Prep

Test-Taking Tips

Some questions on standardized tests ask you to analyze a timeline. Study the timeline below. Then follow the tips to answer the sample question.

> **TIP** Use the lines at the beginning and end of each civilization bracket to calculate how long each civilization lasted.

A.D. 250–900
The Mayas are at their strongest.

A.D. 1200–1535
The Incas rule from Cuzco.

200 400 600 800 1000 1200 1400 1600

A.D. 700–1250
Mississippian culture thrives.

A.D. 1325–1521
The Aztecs rule from Tenochtitlán.

Choose the letter of the best answer.

Based on the timeline, which statement is true?

A Mississippian culture ended at A.D. 1100.

B The Incas ruled from Cuzco for more than 400 years.

C The Aztecs and the Incas did not live at the same time.

D Mississippian culture began to thrive about A.D. 700.

> **Think It Through** You can see that the line marking the end of Mississippian culture falls after 1200. Therefore A is incorrect. "The Incas rule from Cuzco" starts at 1200 and ends before 1600, so you can rule out B, too. The brackets on the timeline show that the Incas and the Aztecs did live at the same time. And the dates for the Aztecs, 1325–1521, overlap with the dates for the Incas, 1200–1535. So C is incorrect. That leaves only D. You can see that the line marking the start of Mississippian culture does indeed fall halfway between 600 and 800. D is the correct answer.

> **TIP** Preview the question and skim over the answer choices before you look at the timeline. Keep the questions and possible answers in mind as you study the timeline.

Practice Questions

Use the timeline above to help you choose the letter of the best answer.

1. Based on the timeline, which statement is true?
   A The Incas began to rule from Cuzco about A.D. 1000.
   B The Aztecs and the Incas did not live at the same time.
   C The Mayas were at their strongest for more than 600 years.
   D Mississippian culture lasted for only 200 years.

Choose the letter of the best answer to complete each sentence.

2. The _____ built stone and adobe dwellings close together.
   A Incas
   B Hopewell peoples
   C Anasazi
   D Adena

3. The spectacular site of Machu Picchu is located in
   A the Great Plains.
   B South America.
   C North America.
   D Lake Texcoco.

4. The _____ lived along rivers in eastern North America.
   A Mound Builders
   B Aztecs
   C Mayas
   D Pueblo peoples

Use Web Code **lga-8303**
for a **Chapter 3 self-test.**

Chapter 3 **87**

Standardized Test Prep

Answers

1. C
2. C
3. B
4. A

Go Online PHSchool.com Students may use the Chapter 3 self-test on PHSchool.com to prepare for the Chapter Test.

Assessment Resources

Use *Chapter Tests A and B* to assess students' mastery of chapter content.

All in One **Medieval Times to Today Teaching Resources,** *Chapter Tests A and B,* pp. 215–220

Tests are also available on the **ExamView®** **Test Bank CD-ROM.**

ExamView® Test Bank CD-ROM

Chapter Overview

Overview

Section **1**
Golden Ages of China
1. Learn about the Golden Age of the Tang dynasty.
2. Discover the achievements of the Song dynasty, which ruled China after the Tang.
3. Find out about Mongol rule of China.

Section **2**
Medieval Japan
1. Learn about the geography of Japan.
2. Discover the changes that occurred during the Heian period of Japanese history.
3. Find out about feudalism and the rule of the shoguns in Japan.

Section **3**
The Great Mughal Empire in India
1. Find out about the geography of the Indian subcontinent.
2. Learn about the Delhi Sultanate, a period of Muslim rule.
3. Learn about the founding and achievements of the Mughal Empire.

Kung Fu and the Shaolin Monks
Length: 5 minutes, 18 seconds
Use with Section 1
This video segment describes the origins of Kung Fu and explains how Chinese monks used Kung Fu to combat injustice and evil.

Technology Resources

Go Online
PHSchool.com

Students use embedded Web codes to access Internet activities, chapter self-tests, and additional map practice. They may also access Dorling Kindersley's Online Desk Reference to learn more about each country they study.

Interactive Textbook

Use the Interactive Textbook to make content and concepts come alive through animations, videos, and activities that accompany the complete basal text—online and on CD-ROM.

PRENTICE HALL
TeacherEXPRESS™
Plan • Teach • Assess

Use this complete suite of powerful teaching tools to planning lessons and administering tests quicker and easier.

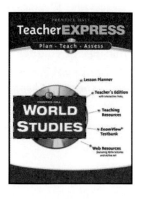

Reading and Assessment

Reading and Vocabulary Instruction

🔄 Model the Target Reading Skill

Cause and Effect Explain to students that understanding cause and effect will help them increase their understanding of the events that they read about. By identifying causes and effects, understanding that some effects are the results of multiple causes, and analyzing effects in context, students become more adept at seeing patterns both within and beyond the reading. Model this skill by thinking aloud about these statements about the Silk Road in China:

People traveling along the Silk Road introduced new ideas and goods to China.

China became a major center of trade and culture.

One of these sentences states a cause, and the other one states an effect. How will I decide which is which? Let me set up the statements in two ways, using a connection word like "because," to see which makes more sense. 1) "Because people traveling along the Silk Road introduced new ideas and goods to China, China became a major center of trade and culture." 2) "Because China became a major center of trade and culture, people traveling along the Silk Road introduced new ideas and goods to China."

My first statement makes more sense. People introducing new ideas and goods to China happened first, and caused China to become a major center of trade and culture, which is the effect.

Use the following worksheets from All-in-One Medieval Times to Today Teaching Resources (pp. 237, 238, and 239) to support the chapter's Target Reading Skill.

Vocabulary Builder
High-Use Academic Words
Use these steps to teach this chapter's High-Use Words:

1. Have students rate how well they know each word on their Word Knowledge worksheets (All-in-One Medieval Times to Today Teaching Resources, p. 240).

2. Pronounce each word and ask students to repeat it.

3. Give students a brief definition or sample sentence (provided on TE pp. 91, 101, and 109).

4. Work with students as they fill in the "Definition or Example" column of their Word Knowledge worksheets.

Assessment

Formal Assessment

Test students' understanding of core knowledge and skills.

Chapter Tests A and B, All-in-One Medieval Times to Today Teaching Resources, pp. 258–263

Customize the Chapter Tests to suit your needs.
Exam*View*®
Test Bank CD-ROM

Skills Assessment

Assess geographic literacy.

MapMaster Skills, Student Edition, pp. 89, 92, 101, 111, 114

Assess reading and comprehension.

Target Reading Skills, Student Edition, pp. 95, 102, 110, and in Section Assessments

Chapter 4 Assessment, Medieval Times to Today Reading and Vocabulary Study Guide, p. 45

Performance Assessment

Assess students' performance on this chapter's Writing Activities using the following rubrics from All-in-One Medieval Times to Today Teaching Resources.

Rubric for Assessing a Journal Entry, p. 254

Rubric for Assessing a Student Poster, p. 255

Rubric for Assessing an Oral Presentation, p. 256

Rubric for Assessing a Writing Assignment, p. 257

Assess students' work through performance tasks.

Small Group Activity: Create a Museum Exhibit About Feudalism in Japan, All-in-One Medieval Times to Today Teaching Resources, pp. 243–246

Online Assessment

Have students check their own knowledge.

Chapter Self-Test

Test Preparation

Benchmark Test 1, AYP Monitoring Assessments, pp. 141–144

88b

Section 1 Golden Ages of China

 3.5 periods, 1.75 blocks (includes Skills for Life)

Social Studies Objectives
1. Learn about the Golden Age of the Tang dynasty.
2. Discover the achievements of the Song dynasty, which ruled China after the Tang.
3. Find out about Mongol rule of China.

Reading/Language Arts Objective
Learn how to identify causes and effects.

Prepare to Read	Instructional Resources	Differentiated Instruction
Build Background Knowledge Have students preview the section and discuss the inventions of the Tang and Song Dynasties. **Set a Purpose for Reading** Have students evaluate statements on the *Reading Readiness Guide*. **Preview Key Terms** Teach the section's Key Terms. **Target Reading Skill** Introduce the section's Target Reading Skill of **identifying causes and effects.**	**All in One Medieval Times to Today Teaching Resources** **L2** Reading Readiness Guide, p. 226 **L2** Identify Causes and Effects, p. 237	**Spanish Reading and Vocabulary Study Guide** **L1** Chapter 4, Section 1, p. 28–29 ELL

Instruct	Instructional Resources	Differentiated Instruction
The Tang Dynasty Discuss achievements of the Tang Dynasty and how they affected China. **The Song Dynasty** Discuss new developments that arose in China during the Song Dynasty. **Target Reading Skill** Review **identifying causes and effects.** **The Mongols Conquer China** Discuss the Mongol Empire and contrast Mongol rule of China with rule under the Song Dynasty.	**All in One Medieval Times to Today Teaching Resources** **L2** Guided Reading and Review, p. 227 **L2** Reading Readiness Guide, p. 226 **Medieval Times to Today Transparencies** **L2** Transparency B16: Venn Diagram **L2** Section Reading Support Transparency MT 62 **World Studies Video Program** **L2** Kung Fu and the Shaolin Monks	**All in One Medieval Times to Today Teaching Resources** **L3** Writing to Inform and Explain, p. 252 AR, GT **L2** Skills for Life, p. 242 AR, GT, LPR, SN **Teacher's Edition** **L3** For Gifted and Talented, TE p. 92 **L3** For Advanced Readers, TE p. 94 **L1** For Less Proficient Readers, TE p. 94 **L2** For English Language Learners, TE p. 96 **L1** For Special Needs Students, TE p. 96 **Reading and Vocabulary Study Guide** **L1** Chapter 4, Section 1, pp. 36–38 ELL, LPR, SN **Student Edition on Audio CD** **L1** Chapter 4, Section 1 ELL, LPR, SN

Assess and Reteach	Instructional Resources	Differentiated Instruction
Assess Progress Evaluate student comprehension with the section assessment and section quiz. **Reteach** Assign the Reading and Vocabulary Study Guide to help struggling students. **Extend** Extend the lesson by assigning an Enrichment activity.	**All in One Medieval Times to Today Teaching Resources** **L2** Section Quiz, p. 228 **L3** Enrichment, p. 241 Rubric for Assessing a Journal Entry, p. 254 **Reading and Vocabulary Study Guide** **L1** Chapter 4, Section 2, pp. 36–38	**Teacher's Edition** **L3** For Gifted and Talented, TE p. 99 **Spanish Support** **L2** Section Quiz (Spanish), p. 29 ELL **Medieval Times to Today Transparencies** **L2** Transparency B15: Outline ELL, LPR, SN

Key

L1 Basic to Average   **L3** Average to Advanced

L2 For All Students

LPR Less Proficient Readers

AR Advanced Readers

SN Special Needs Students

GT Gifted and Talented

ELL English Language Learners

Section 2 Medieval Japan

 2 periods, 1 block (includes Focus On A Japanese Home)

Social Studies Objectives

1. Learn about the geography of Japan.
2. Discover the changes that occurred during the Heian period of Japanese history.
3. Find out about feudalism and the rule of the shoguns in Japan.

Reading/Language Arts Objective

Learn how to understand effects.

Prepare to Read

Build Background Knowledge
Ask students to study a map and answer questions about Japan's geography.

Set a Purpose for Reading
Have students evaluate statements on the *Reading Readiness Guide*.

Preview Key Terms
Teach the section's Key Terms.

Target Reading Skill
Introduce the section's Target Reading Skill of **understanding effects**.

Instructional Resources

All in One Medieval Times to Today Teaching Resources
- **L2** Reading Readiness Guide, p. 230
- **L2** Understand Effects, p. 238

Differentiated Instruction

Spanish Reading and Vocabulary Study Guide
- **L1** Chapter 4, Section 1, p. 30–31 ELL

Instruct

A Country of Islands
Discuss Japan's location and how its geography influences the people who live there.

The Heian Empire
Discuss the city of Kyoto and the people of the Heian Empire.

Target Reading Skill
Review **understanding effects**.

Feudalism in Japan
Ask questions about samurai and the Kamakura shogunate.

Japan and the Outside World
Discuss European influence on Japan and how the Tokugawa shogunate affected Japan's relationship with Europeans.

Instructional Resources

All in One Medieval Times to Today Teaching Resources
- **L2** Guided Reading and Review, p. 231
- **L2** Reading Readiness Guide, p. 230

Medieval Times to Today Transparencies
- **L2** Section Reading Support Transparency MT 63

Differentiated Instruction

All in One Medieval Times to Today Teaching Resources
- Rubric for Assessing a Student Poster, p. 255 AR, GT
- **L3** Small Group Activity: Create a Museum Exhibit About Feudalism in Japan, p. 243–246 AR, GT

Teacher's Edition
- **L3** For Gifted and Talented, TE p. 102
- **L1** For English Language Learners, TE p. 102
- **L3** For Advanced Readers, TE p. 103

Spanish Support
- **L2** Guided Reading and Review (Spanish), p. 30 ELL

Assess and Reteach

Assess Progress
Evaluate student comprehension with the section assessment and section quiz.

Reteach
Assign the Reading and Vocabulary Study Guide to help struggling students.

Extend
Extend the lesson by asking students to research Samurai warriors.

Instructional Resources

All in One Medieval Times to Today Teaching Resources
- **L2** Section Quiz, p. 232
- Rubric for Assessing an Oral Presentation, p. 256
- Rubric for Assessing a Writing Assignment, p. 257

Reading and Vocabulary Study Guide
- **L1** Chapter 4, Section 2, pp. 39–41

Differentiated Instruction

Spanish Support
- **L2** Section Quiz (Spanish), p. 31 ELL

Key

- **L1** Basic to Average
- **L3** Average to Advanced
- **L2** For All Students

- LPR Less Proficient Readers
- AR Advanced Readers
- SN Special Needs Students

- GT Gifted and Talented
- ELL English Language Learners

Section 3 The Great Mughal Empire in India

 4 periods, 2 blocks (includes Chapter Review and Assessment)

Social Studies Objectives

1. Find out about the geography of the Indian subcontinent.
2. Learn about the Delhi Sultanate, a period of Muslim rule.
3. Learn about the founding and achievements of the Mughal Empire.

Reading/Language Arts Objective

Learn how to recognize cause-and-effect signal words.

Prepare to Read	Instructional Resources	Differentiated Instruction
Build Background Knowledge Ask students to preview the section and think about the qualities a great ruler should have. **Set a Purpose for Reading** Have students evaluate statements on the *Reading Readiness Guide.* **Preview Key Terms** Teach the section's Key Terms. **Target Reading Skill** Introduce the section's Target Reading Skill of **recognizing cause and effect signal words.**	**All in One Medieval Times to Today Teaching Resources** **L2** Reading Readiness Guide, p. 234 **L2** Recognize Cause-and-Effect Signal Words, p. 239	**Spanish Reading and Vocabulary Study Guide** **L1** Chapter 4, Section 3, p. 32–33 ELL

Instruct	Instructional Resources	Differentiated Instruction
India's Geography **The Delhi Sultanate** Discuss the Himalayas, Muslim rule of India, and the Hindu caste system. **Target Reading Skill** Review **recognizing cause and effect signal words.** **The Mughal Empire** Ask questions about Akbar the Great and how extravagant buildings may have led to the downfall of the Mughal Empire.	**All in One Medieval Times to Today Teaching Resources** **L2** Guided Reading and Review, p. 235 **L2** Reading Readiness Guide, p. 234 **Medieval Times to Today Transparencies** **L2** Transparency B20: Timeline **L2** Section Reading Support Transparency MT 64	**All in One Medieval Times to Today Teaching Resources** **L1** Using the Map Key, p. 247 **Teacher's Edition** **L1** For Less Proficient Readers, TE p. 111 **L1** For Special Needs Students, TE p. 111 **Spanish Support** **L2** Guided Reading and Review (Spanish), p. 32 ELL

Assess and Reteach	Instructional Resources	Differentiated Instruction
Assess Progress Evaluate student comprehension with the section assessment and section quiz. **Reteach** Assign the Reading and Vocabulary Study Guide to help struggling students. **Extend** Extend the lesson by assigning a literature reading.	**All in One Medieval Times to Today Teaching Resources** **L2** Section Quiz, p. 236 **L3** Savitri: A Tale of Ancient India, pp. 248–251 Rubric for Assessing a Writing Assignment, p. 257 **L2** Word Knowledge, p. 240 **L2** Vocabulary Development, p. 253 **L2** Chapter Tests A and B, pp. 258–263 **Reading and Vocabulary Study Guide** **L1** Chapter 4, Section 3, pp. 42–44	**Spanish Support** **L2** Section Quiz (Spanish), p. 33 ELL **L2** Chapter Summary (Spanish), p. 34 ELL **L2** Vocabulary Development (Spanish), p. 35 ELL

Key

L1 Basic to Average   **L3** Average to Advanced

L2 For All Students

LPR Less Proficient Readers

AR Advanced Readers

SN Special Needs Students

GT Gifted and Talented

ELL English Language Learners

Reading Background

Discussion Ideas

One way to enrich a lesson is to encourage students to discuss the material from the chapter. Ideas for discussion must be complex enough to spark an interesting dialogue. They can relate to something students don't understand, something that seems interesting, or information students already know.

Read aloud the section The Song Dynasty on page 93 of the Student Edition and model the difference between strong and weak discussion ideas.

For example, a strong discussion idea for what you have just read might be:
I think it is more fair to hire officials based on their abilities rather than their social position or wealth.

A weak discussion idea might be:
The Song Dynasty ruled from 960 to 1276.

As students read the chapter, ask them to write down one idea that could be used to conduct an interesting discussion. Begin the class discussion by having one student present his or her idea. Monitor the discussion to ensure that an adequate number of students have had a chance to respond before you introduce another idea.

Encourage Active Participation

In this chapter, students will use an Idea Wave to share their ideas. Remind students that if their idea is closely related to another person's idea, they should acknowledge the other person's ideas when they share theirs. Below are some language strategies for active classroom participation:

> *My idea is similar to _____'s idea.*
> *As _____ already pointed out, it seems like....*
> *I don't agree with _____ because.....*

Be sure students understand that it is acceptable and desirable for them to build on their classmates' ideas, using these strategies.

World Studies Background

Jing Hao

Jing Hao, one of the most significant landscape artists in China, created most of his paintings from 910–950 A.D. Jing Hao's bold manner of using brush and ink to paint crisp lines differed from the softer techniques of other Chinese painters. In addition to his paintings, Jing Hao is thought to have written an essay describing the principles and techniques necessary for a landscape painter to work in harmony with nature.

Kyoto's Many Names

Kyoto, Japan's capital from 794 to 1868, has been known by a number of different names. *Kyoto* means *Capital City*. The city has also been called *Heian-kyo*, which means *Capital of Peace and Tranquility*, and *Miyako*, meaning *The Capital*. When Tokyo became Japan's capital in 1868, Kyoto was called *Saikyo*, or *Western Capital*.

Taj Mahal

The Taj Mahal is known as one of the finest examples of Mughal architecture. One of the main decorative features repeated throughout the complex is *pietra dura*, or inlaid semiprecious stones. These form colorful geometric and floral designs on the walls and archways of the Taj Mahal. Also, verses from the Quran are inscribed in some of the marble structures in the complex.

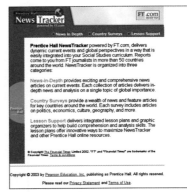

Get in-depth information on topics of global importance with **Prentice Hall Newstracker,** powered by FT.com.

Use Web code **lgd-8400** for **Prentice Hall Newstracker.**

Guiding Questions

Remind students about the Guiding Questions introduced at the beginning of the book.

Section 1 relates to **Guiding Question ④** **What types of government were formed in these societies?** *(China has been ruled by various dynasties. Mongols ruled China from 1259 to 1368.)*

Section 2 relates to **Guiding Question ①** **How did physical geography affect the development of societies around the world?** *(Because of Japan's mountainous terrain, the sea became an important transportation route for the Japanese; it protected them from invaders but also isolated them from the outside world.)*

Section 3 relates to **Guiding Question ④** **What types of government were formed in these societies?** *(The Muslim Delhi Sultanate and Mughal Empire ruled India for hundreds of years. Religious differences still divide Hindus and Muslims in India today.)*

⊙ Target Reading Skill

In this chapter, students will learn and apply the reading skill of determining cause and effect. Use the following worksheets to help students practice this skill:

All in One Medieval Times to Today Teaching Resources, *Identify Causes and Effects,* p. 237; *Understand Effects,* p. 238; *Recognize Cause-and-Effect Signal Words,* p. 239

Civilizations of Asia

Chapter Preview

This chapter will introduce you to the civilizations that thrived in China, Japan, and India during the medieval period.

Section 1
Golden Ages of China

Section 2
Medieval Japan

Section 3
The Great Mughal Empire in India

⊙ Target Reading Skill

Cause and Effect In this chapter you will focus on determining cause and effect in order to help you understand relationships among situations and events.

▶ A large stone statue of the Buddha in the Qian Qi Temple Cave, China, carved during the Tang dynasty

88 Medieval Times to Today

Differentiated Instruction

The following Teacher Edition strategies are suitable for students of varying abilities.

Advanced Readers, pp. 94, 103
English Language Learners, pp. 96, 102
Gifted and Talented, pp. 92, 99, 102
Less Proficient Readers, pp. 94, 111
Special Needs Students, pp. 96, 111

Bibliography

For the Teacher
Benn, Charles. *Daily Life in Traditional China: The Tang Dynasty.* Greenwood Publishing Group, 2002.
Jackson, Peter. *The Delhi Sultanate: A Political and Military History.* Cambridge University Press, 2004
Kure, Mitsuo. *Samurai: An Illustrated History.* Charles E. Tuttle, 2002.

For the Student
L1 Kimmel, Eric A. *Sword of the Samurai: Adventure Stories from Japan.* HarperTrophy, 2000.
L2 Dutemple, Lesley A. *The Taj Mahal.* Lerner Publications Company, 2003.
L3 Freedman, Russell. *Confucius: The Golden Rule.* Arthur A. Levine, 2002.

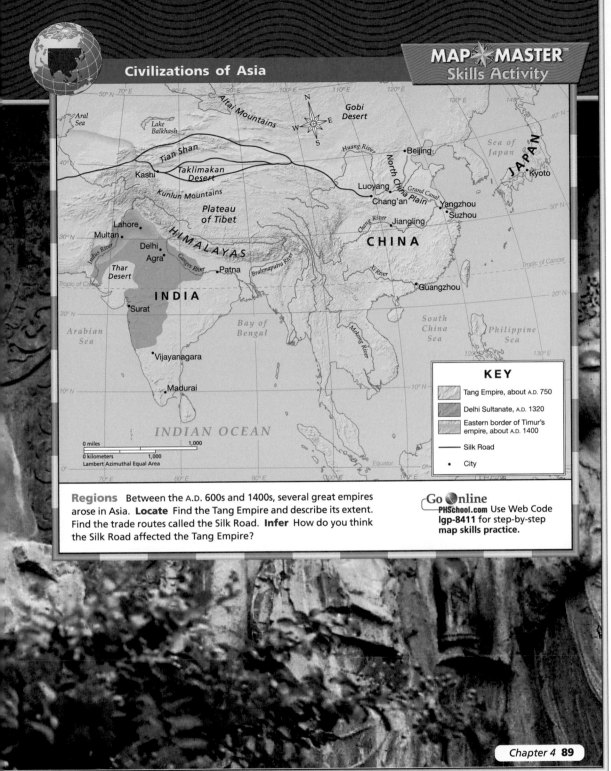

Civilizations of Asia

MAP MASTER™
Skills Activity

KEY

	Tang Empire, about A.D. 750
	Delhi Sultanate, A.D. 1320
	Eastern border of Timur's empire, about A.D. 1400
——	Silk Road
•	City

0 miles 1,000
0 kilometers 1,000
Lambert Azimuthal Equal Area

Regions Between the A.D. 600s and 1400s, several great empires arose in Asia. **Locate** Find the Tang Empire and describe its extent. Find the trade routes called the Silk Road. **Infer** How do you think the Silk Road affected the Tang Empire?

Go Online
PHSchool.com Use Web Code
lgp-8411 for step-by-step
map skills practice.

Chapter 4 **89**

MAP MASTER™
Skills Activity

- Tell students to look at the map and find the following: borders of the Tang Empire, borders of the Delhi Sultanate, eastern border of Timur's empire, and the Silk Road. Have students use their finger to trace these locations on the map.

- On the board, list all of the cities found on the map. Working in pairs, have students identify which empire or empires these cities were a part of. Then have students make a table with the information.

Go Online
PHSchool.com Students may practice their map skills using the interactive online version of this map.

Using the Visual   L2

Reach Into Your Background Draw students' attention to the photo and caption on p. 88. Lead a discussion about the challenges of carving such a large statue without the use of modern technology. Then ask students why it is important to study the art and artifacts of ancient civilizations.

Answers

MAP MASTER **Locate** The Tang Empire
Skills Activity stretched from western and central China to the eastern coast. It encompassed the Silk Road. It looks like a sideway figure eight. **Infer** It helped the Tang Empire expand by opening trade with the West.

Chapter Resources

Teaching Resources
- L2 Vocabulary Development, p. 253
- L2 Skills for Life, p. 242
- L2 Chapter Tests A and B, pp. 258–263

Spanish Support
- L2 Spanish Chapter Summary, p. 34
- L2 Spanish Vocabulary Development, p. 35

Media and Technology
- L1 Student Edition on Audio CD
- L1 Guided Reading Audiotapes, English and Spanish
- L2 Social Studies Skills Tutor CD-ROM
- *ExamView® Test Bank CD-ROM*

DISCOVERY World Studies
CHANNEL Video Program
SCHOOL

interactive Textbook

PRENTICE HALL

TeacherEXPRESS™
Plan • Teach • Assess

Section 1
Step-by-Step Instruction

Objectives

Social Studies
1. Learn about the Golden Age of the Tang dynasty.
2. Discover the achievements of the Song dynasty, which ruled China after the Tang.
3. Find out about Mongol rule of China.

Reading/Language Arts
Learn how to identify causes and effects.

Prepare to Read

Build Background Knowledge `L2`
Tell students that in this section they will learn about the Tang and Song dynasties and some of their achievements. Have students preview the photos and captions showing inventions of the Tang and Song dynasties on page 95. Using the Think-Write-Pair-Share strategy (TE, p. T36) have students identify the inventions and note whether they are still used today and where.

Set a Purpose for Reading `L2`
- Preview the Objectives.

- Read each statement in the *Reading Readiness Guide* aloud. Ask students to mark the statements true or false.

  All in One Medieval Times to Today Teaching Resources, *Reading Readiness Guide,* p. 226

- Have students discuss the statements in pairs or groups of four, then mark their worksheets again. Use the Numbered Heads participation strategy (TE, p. T36) to call on students to share their group's perspectives.

Vocabulary Builder
Preview Key Terms `L2`
Pronounce each Key Term, and then ask students to say the word with you. Provide a simple explanation such as, "In a merit system, people are hired for a job based on their ability to do a job well."

Prepare to Read

Objectives
In this section you will
1. Learn about the Golden Age of the Tang dynasty.
2. Discover the achievements of the Song dynasty, which ruled China after the Tang.
3. Find out about Mongol rule of China.

Taking Notes
As you read this section, look for similarities and differences between the Tang and Song dynasties. Copy the diagram below and record your findings in it.

Two Dynasties of China

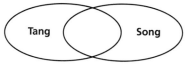

Tang   Song

⦿ Target Reading Skill
Identify Causes and Effects A cause makes something happen. An effect is what happens. Determining causes and effects helps you understand relationships among situations and events. As you read this section, think of the cultures of the Tang and Song dynasties as effects. Write their characteristics in your Taking Notes diagram. Then look for the causes of these effects.

Key Terms
- **Silk Road** (silk rohd) *n.* a chain of trade routes stretching from China to the Mediterranean Sea
- **dynasty** (DY nus tee) *n.* a series of rulers from the same family
- **Tang** (tahng) *n.* a dynasty that ruled China for almost 300 years
- **Song** (sawng) *n.* a dynasty that ruled China after the Tang
- **merit system** (MEHR it SIS tum) *n.* a system of hiring people based on their abilities
- **Kublai Khan** (KOO bly kahn) *n.* a Mongol emperor of China

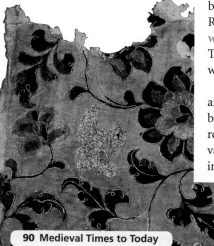

Silk from the Tang dynasty

AChinese traveler wrote, "You see nothing in any direction but the sky and the sands, without the slightest trace of a road; and travelers find nothing to guide them but the bones of men and beasts." He was describing crossing the Gobi Desert along the Silk Road. In spite of its name, the **Silk Road** was not a single road. It was a long chain of connecting trade routes across Central Asia. These routes stretched about 4,000 miles (6,400 kilometers), all the way from China to the eastern Mediterranean Sea.

For centuries, camels, horses, and donkeys carried traders and their precious goods along the Silk Road. Travelers braved blowing desert sands, cold and rocky mountain passes, and even robbers. Most of the goods they carried were small and very valuable. One—a beautiful, lightweight fabric called silk—was so important that it gave the route its name.

⦿ Target Reading Skill

Identify Causes and Effects Point out `L2` the Target Reading Skill. Tell students that a cause makes something happen, and an effect results from a cause.

Model identifying causes and effects using the second paragraph under the head The Tang Dynasty on p. 91. (*Causes—People and traders traveling along the Silk Road introduced new ideas and new goods to China;*

Chinese ideas and inventions also spread to other nations. Effect—China became an important center of trade and culture.)

Give students *Identify Causes and Effects.* Have them complete the activity in groups.

All in One Medieval Times to Today Teaching Resources, *Identify Causes and Effects,* p. 237

The Tang Dynasty

China covers much of East Asia. It is an immense land with a varied landscape. In the east are lowland and coastal regions. Fertile valleys lie along the Chang and the Huang (hwahng) rivers. To the north and west of these farmlands are great deserts and mountainous regions, including the Gobi Desert in the north and the Plateau of Tibet in the west.

Look at the map titled Tang and Song Empires on page 92. Notice that under the Tang, the land under Chinese control stretched westward into Central Asia. Peoples from these distant areas and traders traveling along the Silk Road introduced new ideas—as well as new goods—to China. In return, the Chinese traded their tea, jade, ivory, ceramics, and silk. Chinese ideas and inventions also spread to other nations. Such exchanges helped China become an important center of trade and culture.

Guarding the Silk Road
This beacon tower along the Silk Road is in western China. **Infer** Why do you think towers like this were built along the Silk Road?

Dynasties Rule China Throughout its long history, China has been ruled by many different dynasties. A **dynasty** is a series of rulers from the same family. For example, the Han dynasty ruled China from 206 B.C to A.D. 220. After the collapse of the Han dynasty, China broke up into several kingdoms, but Chinese culture survived. Buddhism spread throughout China, and the arts and learning continued to develop. In 581, the Sui (swee) dynasty came to power. The Sui ruled only until 618, but they united the north and south of China for the first time in centuries.

A Golden Age Begins In 618, the Sui dynasty was overthrown. The **Tang** came to power and ruled China for almost 300 years. The Tang dynasty was a golden age of political and cultural achievement. Under Tang rule, China grew in both area and population. Its capital, Chang'an (chahng ahn), was the world's largest city at that time. Historians estimate that it was home to about one million people. Chang'an was shaped like a rectangle and surrounded by tall walls for protection. A variety of foods, entertainment, and fine goods were available to those who lived there.

Instruct

The Tang Dynasty L2

Guided Instruction

- **Vocabulary Builder** Clarify the high-use words **fertile, estimate,** and **reform** before reading.

- Have students read The Tang Dynasty using the Structured Silent Reading strategy (TE, p. T34). As they read, circulate to make sure individuals can answer the Reading Check question.

- Ask students **What were the effects of the Silk Road on China and other countries?** (*Traders traveling along the Silk Road introduced new ideas and goods to China, and also spread Chinese ideas and inventions to other nations.*)

- Have students describe China under the Tang Dynasty. (*Under the Tang Dynasty, China entered a golden age of political and cultural achievement; China grew in area and population; the capital of Chang'an was the world's largest city, and a variety of foods, entertainment, and goods were available to those that lived there.*)

Vocabulary Builder

Use the information below to teach students this section's high-use words.

High-Use Word	Definition and Sample Sentence
fertile, p. 91	*adj.* able to produce much In order to have a good crop of vegetables, Sally planted her seeds in **fertile** soil.
estimate, p. 91	*v.* to make a general, but careful, guess We **estimated** that it would be a ten minute walk to the park.
reform, p. 93	*v.* to change, improve Steve promised to try and do better in school by **reforming** his study habits.
adopt, p. 96	*v.* to choose and follow an idea or practice I **adopted** her way of exercising because it was the most effective.

Answer

Infer Possible answers: Guards stationed in towers could serve as lookouts and protect people traveling on the Silk Road from thieves or bandits; people might also be able to use the towers for shelter.

Guided Instruction (continued)

- Ask students **What was the Grand Canal?** (*a waterway that linked the Huang and Chang Rivers*) **How did it unite the country of China?** (*It joined northern and southern China and made it possible to transport large amounts of grain grown in the south.*)

- Have students describe the teachings of Confucius. (*He wanted to bring peace and stability to China, and taught that society would be peaceful and stable if all people treated one another with respect.*) Ask students **How did his teachings affect China under the Tang Dynasty?** (*Tang Taizong, one of the rulers of the Tang Dynasty, began to reform the government according to Confucian ideas; he hired officials trained in Confucian philosophy and began giving more land to the peasants who farmed it.*)

Independent Practice

Have students create the Taking Notes graphic organizer on a blank piece of paper. Then have them fill in the "Tang" circle with details from the section they just read. Using *Transparency B16: Venn Diagram*, briefly model how to label and fill in the Venn diagram.

📖 **Medieval Times to Today Transparencies,** *Transparency B16: Venn Diagram*

Monitor Progress

As students fill in the graphic organizer, circulate and make sure that individuals are choosing the correct details and placing them in the appropriate circle. Provide assistance as needed.

Tang Taizong

The Grand Canal China enjoyed great prosperity under the Tang dynasty. One source of China's economic strength was the Grand Canal, which had been greatly extended under the earlier Sui dynasty.

The Grand Canal was a waterway that linked the Huang River and the Chang River. At more than 1,000 miles (1,600 kilometers) long, it is still the longest canal ever built. The Grand Canal helped join northern and southern China and made it possible to supply the capital with large amounts of grain grown in the south.

A Great Ruler The greatest ruler of the Tang dynasty was Tang Taizong (tahng ty ZAWNG). He began his military career at the age of 16, and helped his father establish the Tang dynasty. During his rule, from 626 to 649, he was not only a successful general, but also a scholar and historian. In addition, Tang Taizong was a master of calligraphy, the art of beautiful handwriting.

MAP✦MASTER™ Skills Activity
Tang and Song Empires

Regions Notice the difference in the areas controlled by the Tang and the Song dynasties. **Identify** Under which dynasty did China lose control of much of the Silk Road? **Infer** How might that have affected China's trade with lands to the west?

Go Online
PHSchool.com Use Web Code lgp-8421 for step-by-step map skills practice.

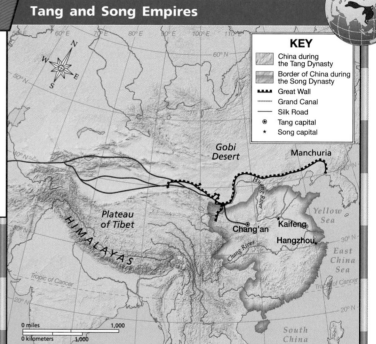

KEY
- China during the Tang Dynasty
- Border of China during the Song Dynasty
- Great Wall
- Grand Canal
- Silk Road
- ⊛ Tang capital
- ✶ Song capital

Gobi Desert
Manchuria
Plateau of Tibet
HIMALAYAS
Chang'an Kaifeng
Hangzhou
Yellow Sea
East China Sea
Tropic of Cancer
South China Sea

0 miles 1,000
0 kilometers 1,000
Lambert Azimuthal Equal Area

Answers

MAP✦MASTER™ Skills Activity **Identify** the Song dynasty **Infer** It may have hurt China's ability to travel on the Silk Road as it would have been controlled by other groups.

Go Online
PHSchool.com Students may practice their map skills using the interactive online version of this map.

Differentiated Instruction

For Gifted and Talented 〔L3〕
Have students do research in the library or on the Internet to find out more about the life and teachings of Confucius. Then have them write a short essay about Confucius with the information they have found. Tell them to make sure to include at least two

of Confucius' teachings and explain what they mean. Give them *Writing to Inform and Explain* to help get them started.

All in One **Medieval Times to Today Teaching Resources,** *Writing to Inform and Explain,* p. 252

Tang Taizong worked to strengthen law and order and his own power by promoting the teachings of Confucius (kun FYOO shus). Confucius was an ancient Chinese teacher who had taught that all people had duties and responsibilities. Confucius had wanted to bring peace and stability to China. To create this kind of society, Confucius said, all people must treat one another with respect.

Tang Taizong began to reform the government according to Confucius's ideas. The Tang government hired officials trained in Confucian philosophy. It also began land reform, giving more land to the peasants who farmed it.

✓ **Reading Check** What are some achievements of Tang Taizong?

The Song Dynasty

After 850, China's control of its westernmost lands weakened. Then fighting among different groups within China ended the Tang dynasty. Order was restored about 50 years later by the **Song** (sawng), the dynasty that ruled China from 960 to 1279.

Changes in Government At the beginning of the Song dynasty, the Chinese capital was located at Kaifeng (KY fung), along the Grand Canal. After the Song lost control of regions to the north, they moved the capital to Hangzhou (hahn JOH), near the coast.

The Song rulers made many advances in government. They expanded the **merit system** of hiring government officials. Under this system, officials had to pass tests and prove their ability to do the work. Before the Song, officials came from rich and powerful families. They were allowed to keep their positions for life even if they did not do a good job. Hiring people based on their abilities, rather than on their wealth or social position, greatly improved the Chinese government.

Improvements in Agriculture During the Song dynasty, new strains of rice and better irrigation methods helped peasants grow more rice. These two improvements allowed farmers to produce two crops a year instead of one. Food surpluses meant that more people could follow other trades or pursue the arts.

Links to Language Arts

Poems and Legends Poetry was popular and respected during the Tang dynasty. Li Bo and Du Fu were two of the greatest poets of the era. Li Bo was also famous for his adventurous life—once he was even accused of treason. His poems, however, dealt with quieter subjects, such as nature and friendship. After Li Bo died, this legend spread about his death: Li Bo was in a boat at night. The moon's reflection was so beautiful that he reached out to seize it, fell overboard, and drowned. This painting shows Li Bo at a waterfall.

The Song Dynasty   L2

Guided Instruction

- Have students learn about the achievements of the Song dynasty in The Song Dynasty.

- Ask students **What events led to the rule of the Song Dynasty?** *(After 850, China's control of its land in the west weakened, and fighting broke out among different groups. The Song dynasty restored order in China and ruled from 960 to 1279.)*

- Ask students **What is a merit system?** *(A system that hires people based on their abilities rather than their wealth or social position.)*

- Ask students **Do you think people in China agreed with the use of the merit system in hiring people? Why or why not?** *(Possible answer: People who were not from rich and powerful families probably agreed with the use of the merit system because it made it possible for them to get jobs in the government.)*

Background: Biography

Wu Hou Wu Hou (625–705), also known as Wu Zetian, was one of the most remarkable members of the Tang dynasty. Once a low-ranking member of the emperor Taizong's household, Wu used her position, personality, and ruthlessness to secure her position as empress. In spite of her dubious path to power, Wu Hou instituted policies that reformed Chinese society. One of these was her choice of associates without regard to their social standing. This led to a replacement of the military and political aristocracy with a more scholarly administration. The overall effect was to establish a more unified empire, paving the way for change in the governments of later Chinese dynasties.

Answer

✓ **Reading Check** Tang Taizong began to reform the government according to the ideas of Confucius; this meant that the government began hiring officials trained in Confucian philosophy. He also began land reform, giving more land to the peasants who farmed it.

Read the **Links to Economics** on this page. Ask students **Based on your reading, what do you think was one way that tea drinking spread from China to other areas?** (*through trade along the Silk Road*)

Guided Instruction (continued)

■ Ask students **What were the Chinese landscape paintings of the Song dynasty?** (*paintings on silk that featured peaceful scenes of water, rocks, and plants; the Chinese believed that these paintings helped both the painter and the viewer meditate*)

■ Have students name art objects made during the Song dynasty. (*Chinese landscape paintings, porcelain, and silk*) Ask students **Why were people in Asia and Europe willing to pay high prices for Chinese silk?** (*It was the best quality in the world.*)

Answer

Analyze Images Students' answers will vary, but should indicate which object they would buy and why.

Links to Economics

From China to Boston Tea drinking has been a part of Chinese culture since at least A.D. 350. The custom of drinking tea spread from China to Japan and other Asian countries, and tea became a major Chinese export crop. European countries began importing tea around 1600. The English sent tea from England to their colonies in North America. Late in the 1700s, the colonists' desire for tea—and the British government's desire to tax tea—contributed to the colonies' movement toward independence.

The Arts and Trade Chinese rulers supported many different forms of art, including music and poetry. During the Song dynasty, artists created the earliest known Chinese landscape paintings. They were painted on silk and featured peaceful scenes of water, rocks, and plants. The Chinese believed that such scenes helped both the painter and the viewer think about important forces in the natural world.

Song rulers also prized graceful art objects, such as those made from porcelain (PAWR suh lin), a white and very hard type of ceramic. Because it was first made in China, porcelain is often called *china*. For hundreds of years, Chinese craftspeople produced the finest ceramics. Because the Chinese produced the best porcelain in the world, it became an important item for trade.

Another item of great beauty and value was silk. It was so beautiful that it was called the queen of fibers. Silk comes from the cocoons of caterpillars called silkworms. For a long time, only the Chinese knew how to make silk. Even after others learned the method, Chinese silk was still the highest quality in the world. People in southwest Asia and Europe were willing to pay high prices for Chinese silk.

Chinese Ceramics
Europeans paid dearly for Song dynasty wares, such as these beautiful ceramics.
Analyze Images *If you were a European trader, which of these objects would you buy? Explain your answer.*

94 Medieval Times to Today

Differentiated Instruction

For Advanced Readers [L3]
In order to help students understand the chronological order of the dynasties in this section, have them work in pairs to create a timeline showing the dynasties and the periods in which they ruled China. Encourage students to add drawings and photos to their timelines. When students have completed their timelines, have them present their work to the class.

For Less Proficient Readers [L1]
Have students read the section in the Reading and Vocabulary Study Guide. This version provides basic level instruction in an interactive format with questions and write-on lines.

📖 Chapter 4, Section 1, **Medieval Times to Today Reading and Vocabulary Study Guide,** pp. 36–38

Inventions of the Tang and Song Dynasties

◀ Gunpowder
The Chinese invented gunpowder in the 800s. At first, they used it to make fireworks. By about 1300, however, it was being used in weapons.

◀ Compass
In the 1000s, Chinese sailors were using the magnetic compass for navigation on long voyages. At the left is a replica of a compass from the Song dynasty.

▼ Movable Type
By 1045, Chinese printers began using individual characters carved on small blocks to create a page of text. The blocks could be reused in a different order to produce various pieces of writing.

Smallpox Vaccine
As early as the 900s, the Chinese fought smallpox with a vaccine. They gave tiny doses of smallpox to healthy people so that they would develop an immunity to, or ability to avoid infection by, the deadly disease.

Printing, Books, and Learning One of the historic Song inventions was a new way to print books. For centuries, the Chinese had carved the characters of each page onto a wood block. They brushed ink over the carving and laid a piece of paper on it to print the page. Printers could make many copies of a book using these blocks, but carving the block for each page took a long time. Around 1045, Bi Sheng (bee sheng) developed a printing method that used movable type. He made many separate characters out of clay and rearranged them to make each page.

During the Song dynasty, books became less expensive. In earlier times, only the rich could buy them. With more people able to afford books, the number and kinds of books increased. More people, including women, also learned to read and write. By the 1200s, books about farming, medicine, religion, and poetry were in print. They helped to spread knowledge throughout China. This Song saying reflects the new importance of books:

> **❝To enrich your family, no need to buy good land: Books hold a thousand measures of grain. For an easy life, no need to build a mansion: In books are found houses of gold. ❞**
>
> — *A Song emperor*

✓ Reading Check What does the Song emperor's saying mean?

⊙ Identify Causes and Effects
What made it easier for people to buy books? List that as a cause. What resulted from the increase in books? List those effects.

Guided Instruction (continued)

■ Have students list the inventions of the Tang and Song dynasties in chronological order. (*gunpowder–800s; smallpox vaccine–900s, compass–1000s; moveable type–1045*)

■ Ask students **How did the widespread availability of books change life in China?** (*As books became less expensive, the numbers and kinds of books increased. Also, more people, including women, learned to read and write; and books about farming, medicine, religion, and poetry spread knowledge throughout China.*)

Independent Practice
Have students complete their graphic organizers with details about the Song dynasty.

Monitor Progress
Show *Section Reading Support Transparency MT 62* and ask students to check their graphic organizers individually. Go over key concepts and clarify key vocabulary as needed.

📖 **Medieval Times to Today Transparencies,** *Section Reading Support Transparency MT 62*

⊙ Target Reading Skill   [L2]

Identify Causes and Effects As a follow up, ask students to answer the Target Reading Skill questions in the Student Edition. (*Cause: Moveable type made books less expensive. Effects: More people learned to read and write, the number and kinds of books increased, and knowledge spread throughout China.*)

🔵 Skills Mini Lesson

Analyzing Primary Sources

1. Tell students that when they analyze primary sources they should: identify the source and main idea, separate fact from opinion, look for bias, and evaluate the source's reliability.

2. Have students practice the skill by analyzing the quotation from the Chinese traveler on page 90.

3. Apply the skill by analyzing the quotation on page 95. (*source: a Song emperor; main idea: books are worth more than material wealth; opinions: books will enrich one's life; bias: the emperor is wealthy, therefore he might say that books are more important than wealth; reliability: the speaker lived when books became more available in China*)

The Mongols Conquer China L2

Guided Instruction

- **Vocabulary Builder** Clarify the high-use word **adopt** before reading.

- Have students read The Mongols Conquer China to learn about the Mongols and their leaders.

- Ask students **Who were the Mongols?** *(nomads from Central Asia, who were fierce warriors)* **How far did their empire eventually extend?** *(across China and Korea in the east, into Russia and Eastern Europe in the west, and into the Persian Gulf)*

- Ask students **How was the Chinese government run under the Mongols?** *(The government became centralized; Mongols did not allow the old Chinese ruling class to govern, and high government positions were reserved for Mongols and even foreigners instead of Chinese.)* **How was this different from the Song Dynasty?** *(Under the Song Dynasty, people were hired based on their ability rather than their social position.)*

Independent Practice
Assign *Guided Reading and Review.*

All in One Medieval Times to Today Teaching Resources, *Guided Reading and Review,* p. 227

Monitor Progress
Tell students to fill in the last column of the *Reading Readiness Guide.* Probe for what they learned that confirms or invalidates each statement.

All in One Medieval Times to Today Teaching Resources, *Reading Readiness Guide,* p. 226

Answer

Conclude They wore armor; used swords, shields, bows and arrows; and attacked on horseback.

The Mongols Attack China
This illustration from the 1400s shows Kublai Khan's armies crossing a bridge to attack a Chinese fortress. **Conclude** *Use details in the illustration to draw conclusions about the dress, equipment, and methods of Kublai Khan's armies.*

96 Medieval Times to Today

The Mongols Conquer China
The Mongols were nomads from the plains of Central Asia, north of China. They were fierce warriors, said to "live in the saddle" because they spent so much time on horseback. By the 1200s, they were a tough military force. Under the leadership of Genghis Khan, they began forging an empire that eventually included China and Korea in the east, stretched into Russia and Eastern Europe in the west, and extended to the southwest as far as the Persian Gulf.

Kublai Khan, Mongol Ruler of China Genghis Khan had conquered all of northern China by 1215. But the southern Song empire continued to resist. It was left to Genghis Khan's grandson **Kublai Khan** to complete the conquest of China and to rule it.

Kublai Khan came to power in 1259. Within 20 years, he had toppled the last Song emperor. From his capital at the present-day city of Beijing, Kublai Khan declared himself emperor of China. He named his new dynasty *Yuan,* which means "beginning," because he intended that Mongol rule of China would last for centuries.

China Under Mongol Rule The Mongols centralized government in China. They did not allow the old Chinese ruling class to govern. High government positions were reserved for Mongols and were even given to foreigners rather than to Chinese. The Mongols also kept their own language and customs rather than adopting Chinese culture. They did, however, allow the practice of many religions.

Differentiated Instruction

For English Language Learners L2
As they read, have students identify any unfamiliar words and write them down. Divide students into pairs, and give each pair a dictionary to use. Then have the students create flashcards with the words on one side, and the part of speech and definition on the other. Students may then quiz each other on the words.

For Special Needs Students L1
Have students read the section as they listen to the recorded version on the Student Edition on Audio CD. Check for comprehension by pausing the CD and asking students to share their answers to the Reading Checks.

Chapter 4, Section 1, **Student Edition on Audio CD**

Marco Polo at Kublai Khan's Court
The Italian Marco Polo, shown kneeling before Kublai Khan, worked for the khan for 17 years. **Analyze Images** *What detail in the painting indicates that Polo is reporting to Kublai Khan?*

Visitors from all lands were welcome at Kublai Khan's court. One of these was Ibn Battutah, an African Muslim. Another was a Christian from Europe, Marco Polo. He came from Venice in present-day Italy in 1271. After returning to Europe, Polo wrote about his travels. He described the riches of Kublai Khan's palace, China's efficient mail system, and its well-maintained roads.

Marco Polo's writings sparked increased trade between Europe and China. China prospered under Kublai Khan, but not under the khans, or emperors, who followed him. In 1368, a Chinese peasant led an uprising that overthrew the foreign rulers and ended Mongol rule of China.

Explore the history of kung fu.

✓ **Reading Check** Describe Mongol rule of China.

Section 1 Assessment

Key Terms
Review the key terms at the beginning of this section. Use each term in a sentence that explains its meaning.

Target Reading Skill
What were two effects of the Mongol rule of China?

Comprehension and Critical Thinking
1. (a) **Recall** What is the Grand Canal?

(b) **Synthesize** Why was it important?
2. (a) **Identify** Describe one important change in government made by the Song.
(b) **Identify Effects** How did this change affect China?
3. (a) **Summarize** How did the Mongols conquer China?
(b) **Identify Frame of Reference** Why do you think the Mongols did not adopt Chinese customs?

Writing Activity
During the Song dynasty, printed materials became available to many more people. What would life be like today without books and other printed materials? Write a journal entry to express your thoughts.

For: An activity on Chinese inventions
Visit: PHSchool.com
Web Code: lgd-8401

Assess and Reteach

Assess Progress L2
Have students complete the Section Assessment. Then administer the *Section Quiz*.

All in One Medieval Times to Today Teaching Resources, *Section Quiz,* p. 228

Reteach L1
If students need more instruction, have them read this section in the Reading and Vocabulary Study Guide.

Chapter 4, Section 1, **Medieval Times to Today Reading and Vocabulary Study Guide,** pp. 36–38

Extend L3
To learn more about Kublai Khan, have students complete the *Enrichment* activity.

All in One Medieval Times to Today Teaching Resources, *Enrichment,* p. 241

Show students **Kung Fu and the Shaolin Monks.** Ask students **What is Kung Fu?** *(an ancient physical and spiritual discipline that promotes health and strength)*

Answers

Analyze Images He is kneeling before Kublai Khan, a sign of deference. He also appears to be presenting Kublai Khan with a document or gift.

✓ **Reading Check** The Mongols centralized government in China and did not allow the old Chinese ruling class to govern. The Mongols did not adopt Chinese culture, but allowed the practice of many religions.

Writing Activity
Use the *Rubric for Assessing a Journal Entry* to evaluate students' poems or paragraphs.

All in One Medieval Times to Today Teaching Resources, *Rubric for Assessing a Journal Entry,* p. 254

Go Online PHSchool.com Typing in the Web code when prompted will bring students directly to detailed instructions for this activity.

Section 1 Assessment

Key Terms
Students' sentences should reflect an understanding of each Key Term.

Target Reading Skill
Answers should include any two of the following: centralization of government; prohibition of the old ruling class from government posts; many religions allowed; increased trade between China and Europe.

Comprehension and Critical Thinking
1. (a) a waterway linking the Huang and Chang Rivers (b) It helped join northern and southern China and supply the capital with grain.
2. (a) They used the merit system to hire government officials. (b) The government was improved.
3. (a) by forceful conquest (b) Possible answer: the Mongols wanted their dynasty to be Mongol, not Chinese.

Objective

Learn how to make an outline.

Prepare to Read

Build Background Knowledge L2

Use the Numbered Heads participation strategy (TE p. T36) to elicit student responses to the following question: **What do you think is the best way to study for a test?** Tell students that creating an outline is one way of organizing information that they can use when they study for a test, read, or research a topic. When they create an outline, they are organizing information in an easy-to-read format.

Instruct

Making an Outline L2

Guided Instruction

- Read the steps to making an outline as a class and write them on the board.

- Practice the skill by following the steps on p. 99 as a class. Model each step in the activity by working with students to create the following outline on the board:

Title: Chinese Silk Making

I. How and when the Chinese made silk

  A. How silk is made

    1. Made by unwinding the cocoons of silkworms

    2. Process is done by hand and is long and difficult

    3. Silk strands are twisted to form yarn, and then woven into fabric

  B. History of silk making

    1. Dates back more than 3,000 years

    2. Empress His Ling Shi is said to have invented the loom to weave silk

    3. silk was expensive, only royalty and nobles could afford it

    4. because silk was so valuable, the Chinese kept the process secret

Skills for Life Making an Outline

An outline is a way to organize information. It identifies the main ideas and supporting details. You can use an outline to take notes on what you read or to plan a report that you will write.

Learn the Skill

1 **Identify the most important points or main ideas, and list them with Roman numerals.** If you are outlining a text, look for headings stating these ideas.

2 **Decide on important subtopics for each main idea, and list them with capital letters.** Indent these entries under the main ideas, as shown in the sample outline below.

3 **Use Arabic numerals to list supporting ideas or details under each subtopic.** Indent these entries. Because an outline is a type of summary, you don't have to be as detailed or complete as your source. See the sample outline below.

4 **Check your outline for balance.** Make sure that the entries with Roman numerals are the most important ideas. Check that the ideas and information listed under the main ideas support those ideas. Make sure that main topics have at least two supporting subtopics or details.

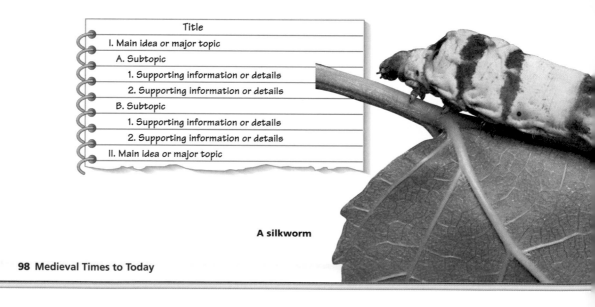

Title

I. Main idea or major topic

  A. Subtopic

    1. Supporting information or details

    2. Supporting information or details

  B. Subtopic

    1. Supporting information or details

    2. Supporting information or details

II. Main idea or major topic

A silkworm

98 Medieval Times to Today

Independent Practice

Assign *Skills for Life* and have students complete it individually.

All in One Medieval Times to Today Teaching Resources, *Skills for Life,* p. 242

Monitor Progress

As students are completing *Skills for Life,* circulate to make sure individuals are applying the skill steps effectively. Provide assistance as needed.

Women preparing newly woven silk

Practice the Skill

Suppose you are outlining an article on silk making. You want to cover two main ideas: The Chinese were the first to make silk, and silk became an important trade product for China. Use the passage at the right as the source for the beginning of your outline. Then follow the steps below to outline it.

1. What is the main idea of the passage? Make it Roman numeral I of your outline.

2. Identify at least two important subtopics, and list them with capital letters.

3. Which details support the important topics or ideas? List those with Arabic numerals under the appropriate subtopics.

4. Reread your outline to be sure you have included all the important ideas and details. Make sure your outline correctly indicates which ideas are the most important and how other ideas and details support the main ideas.

Chinese Silk Making The fabric known as silk is made from the cocoons of caterpillars called silkworms. The cocoons are unwound very carefully, to avoid breaking the fibers. This process is long and difficult if done by hand—as it was in ancient China. The silk strands are then twisted together to form yarn, which is woven into fabric on a loom.

Silk making in China dates back more than 3,000 years. It is said that the empress Hsi Ling Shi, called the Goddess of Silk, invented the loom to weave this valuable fabric. She was a patron of the silk industry, which involved tending silkworms and cultivating the mulberry trees on which the caterpillars fed. This laborious work was done by women.

Silk was so beautiful and expensive that only royalty and nobles could afford to wear it. Because the fabric was so valuable and desirable, the Chinese kept the silk-making process a secret.

Apply the Skill

Reread the portion of text titled Achievements of the Song Dynasty on pages 93–95. Make an outline of that text.

Assess and Reteach

Assess Progress L2
Ask students to do the Apply the Skill activity.

Reteach L1
If students are having trouble applying the skill steps, use the *Outline* transparency to walk through making an outline of the subsection titled The Tang Dynasty on pages 91–93. Title the outline "The Tang Dynasty," and use the blue heads as Roman numeral entries. Model how to draw information for the subtopics and the supporting details from the text.

   Medieval Times to Today Transparencies, *Transparency B15: Outline*

Extend L3
Help students prepare to study the material in Section 2 by dividing the class into four groups. Each group should be assigned one of the following subsections of information from Section 2: A Country of Islands, The Heian Empire, Feudalism in Japan, Japan and the Outside World. Each group should create an outline of the information in the subsection, and share their outline with the rest of the class by writing it on the board.

Answers
Apply the Skill

Answers will vary, but students' outlines should include appropriate information about the achievements of the Song Dynasty.

Objectives

Social Studies

1. Learn about the geography of Japan.
2. Discover the changes that occurred during the Heian period of Japanese history.
3. Find out about feudalism and the rule of the shoguns in Japan.

Reading/Language Arts

Learn how to understand effects.

Prepare to Read

Build Background Knowledge L2

Tell students that in this chapter they will read about the geography and history of Japan. Have students look at the map of Japan on page 101, and think about the following questions: **What are some of the advantages and disadvantages a nation might have if it is completely surrounded by water? How might living on an island influence the way of life for people there?** Using the Idea Wave participation strategy (TE p. T35), have students share their responses with the class.

Set a Purpose for Reading L2

■ Preview the Objectives.

■ Read each statement in the *Reading Readiness Guide* aloud. Ask students to mark the statements true or false.

   All in One Medieval Times to Today Teaching Resources, *Reading Readiness Guide,* p. 230

■ Have students discuss the statements in pairs or groups of four, then mark their worksheets again. Use the Numbered Heads participation strategy (TE, p. T36) to call on students to share their group's perspectives.

Vocabulary Builder
Preview Key Terms L2

Pronounce each Key Term, and then ask students to say the word with you. Provide a simple explanation such as, "The many islands of Japan form an archipelago."

Prepare to Read

Objectives

In this section you will

1. Learn about the geography of Japan.
2. Discover the changes that occurred during the Heian period of Japanese history.
3. Find out about feudalism and the rule of the shoguns in Japan.

Taking Notes

As you read this section, look for details about the major periods of Japan's history. Copy the table below and record your findings in it.

Japan, 794–1867	
Period	**Characteristics**
Heian period	
Rise of the samurai	
Kamakura shogunate	
Tokugawa shogunate	

Target Reading Skill

Understand Effects An effect is what happens as the result of a specific cause or factor. For example, you can see in the paragraphs on the next page that the geography of Japan has had several effects on that nation. This section also discusses how contact with the outside world affected Japan. As you read, note the effects on Japan of the contact with the Mongols and with Europeans.

Key Terms

- **archipelago** (ahr kuh PEL uh goh) *n.* a group or chain of many islands
- **Kyoto** (kee OH toh) *n.* the capital city of medieval Japan
- **feudalism** (FYOOD ul iz um) *n.* a system in which poor people are legally bound to work for wealthy landowners
- **samurai** (SAM uh ry) *n.* Japanese warriors
- **shogun** (SHOH gun) *n.* the supreme military commander of Japan

Japanese woodcut of Mount Fuji

In A.D. 882, a group of more than 100 officials sailed across the sea to Japan. They were from a kingdom in Manchuria, north of China. They carried greetings for the Japanese emperor, as well as gifts of tiger skins and honey. When the emperor heard the news, he was pleased. This visit would give the Japanese a chance to display their achievements. The emperor's name was Yozei (yoh zay ee). At the time, he was only 14 years old.

Yozei sent expensive gifts of food and clothing to the visitors. He also sent people to escort them to his capital. The officials from Manchuria had landed in the north, and the capital was far to the south. The journey over land would take five months. The Japanese quickly fixed roads and bridges along the way. When the visitors arrived, there was a celebration. Japan's nobles, government leaders, and best poets were invited. Horse races, archery, and a poetry contest took place. A great feast was held, too, with much music and dancing.

100 Medieval Times to Today

Target Reading Skill L2

Understand Effects Point out the Target Reading Skill. Tell students that effects are the result of an event or some other cause.

Model understanding effects by having students read the second paragraph on page 101. Point out the effect of Japan's geography on they way people traveled there. (*The sea became an important highway for the Japanese.*)

Give students *Understand Effects.* Have them complete the activity in their groups.

   All in One Medieval Times to Today Teaching Resources, *Understand Effects,* p. 238

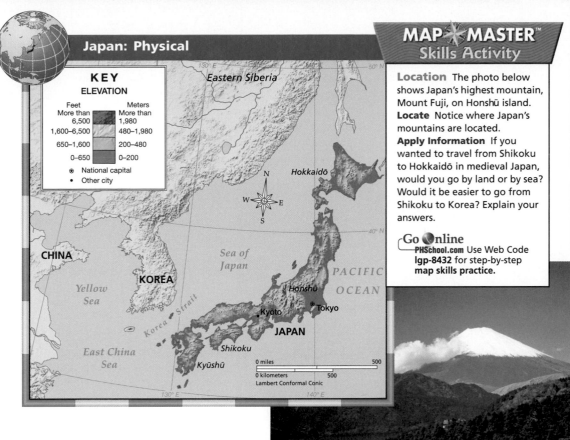

Japan: Physical

MAP MASTER™
Skills Activity

KEY
ELEVATION

Feet		Meters
More than 6,500		More than 1,980
1,600–6,500		480–1,980
650–1,600		200–480
0–650		0–200

⊛ National capital
• Other city

Eastern Siberia

Hokkaidō

CHINA

KOREA

Sea of Japan

Yellow Sea

Honshū

PACIFIC OCEAN

Kyoto

Tokyo

JAPAN

East China Sea

Shikoku

Kyūshū

Korea Strait

0 miles 500
0 kilometers 500
Lambert Conformal Conic

Location The photo below shows Japan's highest mountain, Mount Fuji, on Honshū island. **Locate** Notice where Japan's mountains are located. **Apply Information** If you wanted to travel from Shikoku to Hokkaidō in medieval Japan, would you go by land or by sea? Would it be easier to go from Shikoku to Korea? Explain your answers.

Go Online
PHSchool.com Use Web Code lgp-8432 for step-by-step map skills practice.

A Country of Islands

The visitors from Manchuria had a long trip over both land and sea to Japan. Japan is an **archipelago** (ahr kuh PEL uh goh), or chain of many islands, in the Pacific Ocean off the coast of the Asian mainland. It is about 500 miles (800 kilometers) from the coast of China but it is only 100 miles (160 kilometers) from Korea. The islands of Japan were formed by volcanoes, and earthquakes are common in the region.

Look at the map above. Notice that the islands of Japan are mountainous. The mountains make traveling by land difficult. As a result, the sea became an important highway for the Japanese—even for those traveling from place to place on the same island. On the other hand, for centuries, the sea helped to protect Japan from invaders. Over time, this isolation also led the Japanese to develop a distinctive way of life.

✓ **Reading Check** Describe Japan's geography.

Vocabulary Builder

Use the information below to teach students this section's high-use words.

High-Use Word	Definition and Sample Sentence
isolation, p. 101	*n.* a state of separation Mary did not like the **isolation** of living alone.
distinctive, p. 101	*adj.* showing a difference from others Postal workers wear **distinctive** uniforms.
related, p. 102	*adj.* connected to in some manner The fans at the football game wore shirts **related** to their favorite team.
supreme, p. 104	*adj.* highest in rank The President of the United States is the country's **supreme** leader.

Instruct

A Country of Islands L2

Guided Instruction

- **Vocabulary Builder** Clarify the high-use words **isolation** and **distinctive** before reading.

- With students, read A Country of Islands using the Oral Cloze strategy (TE, p. T33).

- Have students describe the location of Japan in relation to mainland Asia. (*It is in the Pacific Ocean off the coast of mainland Asia, about 500 miles from the coast of China.*)

- Ask students **How do the mountains of Japan influence the lives of the people who live there?** (*The mountains make travel difficult; as a result, the sea is an important highway for those traveling from place to place.*)

Independent Practice

Assign *Guided Reading and Review*.

All in One **Medieval Times to Today Teaching Resources,** *Guided Reading and Review,* p. 231

Monitor Progress

As students work on the worksheets, circulate and provide assistance as needed.

Answers

✓ **Reading Check** Japan is an archipelago in the Pacific Ocean, off the coast of mainland Asia, about 500 miles from the coast of China. The mountainous islands were formed by volcanoes, and earthquakes are common.

MAP MASTER™ Skills Activity **Locate** They are located in the center of the islands. **Apply Information** Possible answers: To travel from Shikoku to Hokkaidō in medieval Japan it would have been easier to travel by sea, since the mountains would have made travel difficult; It would be easier to travel from Shikoku to Korea, since the distance is shorter.

Go Online
PHSchool.com Students may practice their map skills using the interactive online version of this map.

Instruct

The Heian Empire L2

Guided Instruction

■ **Vocabulary Builder** Clarify the high-use word **related** before reading.

■ Together with students, learn about Japan during the years A.D. 794 to 1185 in The Heian Empire.

■ Have students describe the city of Kyoto. *(It was the capital of Japan, modeled after the city of Chang'an in Tang China; it was surrounded by walls and had mansions, marketplaces, and a palace. Most of the buildings were wooden, and fires were common; canals ran through the capital to provide water.)*

■ Ask students **How did the majority of the population, aside from the nobles, live during the Heian period?** *(They were poor and had to work hard.)* **What kind of attitude do you think they had toward the nobles?** *(Students may suggest attitudes such as fear, respect, loyalty, or resentment. Encourage them to provide reasoning to support their views.)*

Independent Practice

Ask students to create the Taking Notes graphic organizer on a blank piece of paper. Then have them fill in the "Heian Period" column with details from the section.

Monitor Progress

As students fill in their tables, circulate to make sure they are putting details in the appropriate column. Provide assistance as needed.

⟳ Target Reading Skill L2

Understand Effects As a follow up, ask students to answer the Target Reading Skill question in the Student Edition. *(The feeling of superiority set them apart from the rest of the population.)*

Answers

Infer It suggests that modern Japanese culture is a blend of old and new traditions.

✓ **Reading Check** Nobles lived in mansions and enjoyed fine architecture, literature, and beautiful gardens.

102 *Medieval Times to Today*

The Heian Empire

The emperor Yozei ruled Japan during the Heian (HAY ahn) period, which lasted from 794 to 1185. Before this time, Japan's culture—including its literature, laws, and religion—was similar to China's. But during the 800s, Japan began to develop its own traditions. In fact, official relations between the Japanese and Chinese governments ended in 894. The split would last for more than 500 years.

Modern Kyoto
The traditional Japanese pagoda, or shrine, in the foreground is still an important part of the modern, bustling city. **Infer** *What does this blend of architecture suggest about modern Japanese culture?*

An Impressive Capital: Kyoto

Heian emperors ruled from a new capital, **Kyoto** (kee OH toh). Modeled after Chang'an, the great city of Tang China, it was a rectangle of tree-lined streets. Unlike Chang'an, however, Kyoto was not surrounded by high walls. The city boasted mansions for the nobles, two marketplaces, and a palace for the emperor. Most Japanese buildings were wooden at the time, and fires were common. Kyoto's main street was very wide—to keep fires on one side from spreading to the other. Canals running through the capital also provided water to help put out any fires.

The Japanese Nobility The Heian period was a mostly peaceful time, during which Japanese culture thrived. Fine architecture, literature, and beautiful gardens all became a part of life for the nobility. Life for most of the population, however, was very different. Farmers, fishers, traders, and builders were usually poor and spent their time doing hard work.

The nobles believed that the importance of their families and their positions within the government set them apart from others. But even among the nobles, people belonged to different ranks, or classes. In fact, noblemen wore specially colored robes related to their position in society. Noblewomen were not affected by such rules because they could not hold official positions in the government.

 Understand Effects
What was one effect of the nobles' feeling of superiority?

✓ **Reading Check** How did nobles live during the Heian period?

102 Medieval Times to Today

Differentiated Instruction

For Gifted and Talented L3

Have students research a major city in Japan today. Then have students create a poster identifying vital facts about the city. *Use Rubric for Assessing a Student Poster* to evaluate students' work.

All in One Medieval Times to Today Teaching Resources, *Rubric for Assessing a Student Poster,* p. 255

For English Language Learners L1

Students may have difficulty pronouncing some of the words in this section, such as *emperor, official, surrounded, and mansions.* Encourage students to break down these words into smaller parts to help them sound out the pronunciations.

Feudalism in Japan

During the 1000s, the Japanese emperor began to lose power. He continued to rule the capital, but he had less control over the rest of Japan. At the same time, the nobles gained greater power and wealth. They owned estates, or large tracts of land, outside the capital. The work on these estates was done by peasants. This kind of economic system, in which poor people are legally bound to work for wealthy landowners, is called **feudalism.**

Samurai Warriors Rich estate owners became so independent that they often disobeyed the emperor. They even hired private armies. The nobles paid these armies to defend them, their estates, and the peasants who worked for them. The armies were made up of warriors called **samurai** (SAM uh ry).

Samurai warriors followed a strict set of rules for behavior, called *bushido* (BOO shee doh). They swore an oath to follow these rules without question. According to bushido, honor meant more than wealth or even life itself. This code said that a samurai must never show weakness or surrender to an enemy. The true samurai had no fear of death, and would rather die than shame himself. He was expected to commit ritual suicide rather than betray the code of bushido.

Prepared for War
Samurai armor was made of small scales tied with silk and leather. The painting below shows the charge of a samurai on horseback. **Analyze Images** *What do these two images suggest about samurai warriors?*

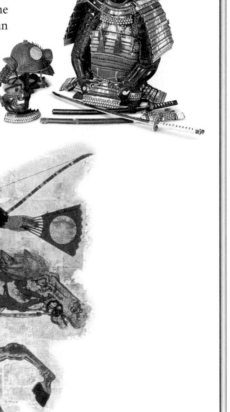

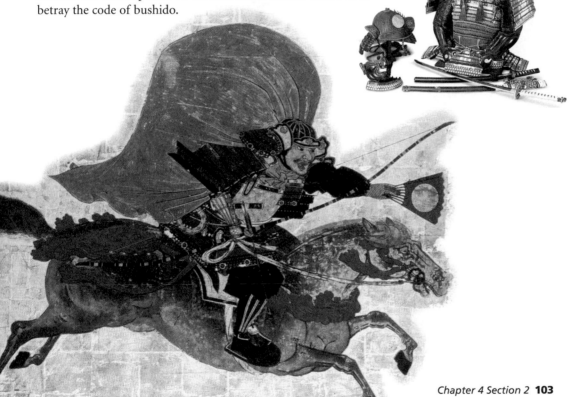

Instruct

Feudalism in Japan   L2

Guided Instruction

- **Vocabulary Builder** Clarify the high-use word **supreme** before reading.

- Read Feudalism in Japan to learn about the feudal system and samurai of Japan. As students read, circulate to make sure they can answer the Reading Check question.

- Ask students **Who were the samurai?** (*Private warriors hired by nobles to defend their estates and peasants*) **How do you think the hiring of samurai further weakened the power of the Japanese emperor?** (*Possible answer: The nobles did not have to depend on the emperor for protection; also a noble could become more powerful as he acquired a stronger samurai army.*)

- Have students discuss the idea of Bushido. Ask **How did samurai warriors think about the relationship of honor and death?** (*According to Bushido, honor means more to a Samurai than anything else. Therefore, a samurai would rather die than dishonor himself.*)

- Ask students **Who was Minamoto Yoritomo?** (*the leader of the Minamoto clan in 1192*) **How was he important to Japan?** (*He was made shogun by the emperor and set up the Kamakura shogunate.*)

Independent Practice

Have students continue filling in their tables with details about the rise of the samurai and the Kamakura shogunate.

Monitor Progress

As students continue to fill in their tables, circulate and make sure they are including all of the details in the section. Provide assistance as necessary.

Answer

Analyze Images That the Samurai were brave and skilled in creating armor to protect themselves.

Read **Citizen Heroes** on this page. Ask students **Why do you think Hideyoshi was one of the most admired heroes in Japan?** *(Possible answers: He was a fine warrior with great military skills and a skillful leader who united Japan.)*

Japan and the Outside World L2

Guided Instruction

■ Learn how Japan was influenced by Europeans in Japan and the Outside World.

■ Ask students **How did Europeans influence life in Japan?** *(They traded many items with the Japanese; European missionaries converted many Japanese to Christianity.)*

■ Have students describe what life was like in Japan under the Tokugawa shogunate. *(It was a period of peace and prosperity; the population increased; trade increased and a merchant class developed; the arts flourished.)*

Independent Practice

Have students complete their tables with details from the section.

Monitor Progress

■ Show *Section Reading Support Transparency MT 63* and ask students to check their graphic organizers individually. Go over key concepts and clarify key vocabulary as needed.

Medieval Times to Today Transparencies, *Section Reading Support Transparency MT 63*

■ Tell students to fill in the last column of the *Reading Readiness Guide*. Probe for what they learned that confirms or invalidates each statement.

All in One Medieval Times to Today Teaching Resources, *Reading Readiness Guide*, p. 230

Answer

✓ **Reading Check** The samurai became powerful as nobles relied upon them for protection rather than the emperor. Over time, the samurai grew in number and banded together under daimyos.

Citizen Heroes ★

A Peasant Warrior

Toyotomi Hideyoshi (toh yoh TOH mee hee duh YOH shee) started life as a peasant. Through hard work, he became a respected warrior. Because of his great military skills, he became a chief lieutenant in the army of a powerful daimyo. When the daimyo died in 1582, Hideyoshi took his place. A skillful leader, he went on to unite Japan. He then tried, but failed, to conquer Korea and China. Nevertheless, Hideyoshi, shown below, became one of the most admired heroes in Japan.

A New Class Gains Power Over time, the samurai warriors grew in number and formed their own clans. Each clan promised loyalty to a powerful warlord, or daimyo (DY myoh). The daimyo expected his samurai warriors to be willing to give their lives for him. As the different warlords grew in power, small wars broke out among them. Eventually the Minamoto clan became the most powerful.

In 1192, the emperor gave the title of **shogun** (SHOH gun), or supreme military commander, to the leader of the Minamoto clan. Minamoto Yoritomo (mee nah MOH toh yoh ree TOH moh) became the supreme ruler of all Japan. He set up the Kamakura (kah mah KUR ah) shogunate, a series of military dynasties.

✓ **Reading Check** How did the samurai become powerful?

Japan and the Outside World

Within a century after shogun rule began, Japan was threatened by outsiders. One group came from Mongolia, north of China. Under their fierce and brilliant leader Kublai Khan, the Mongols had already conquered China and Korea. Kublai Khan tried to invade Japan twice, and failed both times. For nearly 300 years after the Mongols were defeated in the 1200s, few foreigners came to Japan.

The Arrival of Europeans In 1543, several Portuguese ships were blown off course and landed on Japan's coast. The Japanese showed great interest in these foreigners—especially in their guns. In the years that followed, a lively trade developed between East and West. Many European traders and missionaries made the long voyage to these islands in the Pacific. And thousands of Japanese converted to Christianity. The European influence in Japan did not last long, however.

The Tokugawas Unify Japan In 1603, Tokugawa Ieyasu (toh koo GAH wah ee yay AH soo) became shogun. Ieyasu was determined to bring order to the country. To end the fighting among warring samurai bands, Ieyasu divided Japan into about 250 regions. The daimyo of each region promised to serve the shogun and swore loyalty to him. To control these local leaders, the Tokugawas required each daimyo to live in the shogun's capital, Edo (now called Tokyo), for several months every other year.

 Skills for Life **Skills Mini Lesson**

Problem Solving

1. Tell students that to solve a problem, they should identify the problem, evaluate its impact, identify possible solutions, choose a solution, and determine its effectiveness.

2. Have students read The Tokugawas Unify Japan, identify the problem faced by Tokugawa Ieyasu when he became shogun, and use the skill steps to determine how the problem was solved. *(Problem: a lack of order in the country; impact: fighting among samurai bands; solution: divide Japan into regions led by a daimyo who would swear loyalty to Ieyasu. The solution was effective.)*

3. Have students apply the skill by identifying another problem faced by Tokugawa Ieyasu, and the steps he took to solve it.

The Tokugawa shogunate ruled Japan until 1867. It was a period of peace. The economy thrived. Food was plentiful, the population increased, trade flourished inside Japan, and a merchant class developed. Cities grew, and the arts flourished. A type of Buddhism called Zen became popular in Japan. It emphasized meditation, the practice of good deeds, and reverence for nature.

Theater and poetry also thrived under the Tokugawas. Haiku—three-line poems that express a feeling or picture in only 17 syllables—were greatly admired. Plays featuring life-size puppets were popular. So was the Kabuki theater. Kabuki combines drama, dance, and music.

Japan Becomes Isolated Again At the same time, the Tokugawa shogunate was isolating Japan from foreign influences. Even Tokugawa Ieyasu had worried that Europeans might try to conquer Japan. He and the shoguns who ruled after him decided that Japan should remain isolated from Westerners. They outlawed Christianity and forced Europeans to leave. By 1638, they had closed Japan's ports, banning most foreign travel and trade. The shoguns also stopped the building of large ships that could travel long distances. For more than 200 years, the Japanese would remain cut off from the outside world.

✓ **Reading Check** How did the Tokugawas change Japan?

Kabuki Theater
Even today, men play women's roles in Kabuki theater, and many of the plays recount tales of feudal Japan.
Analyze Images *What do the elaborate makeup, costumes, and gestures suggest about Kabuki performances?*

Section 2 Assessment

Key Terms
Review the key terms at the beginning of this section. Use each term in a sentence that explains its meaning.

Target Reading Skill
What were two effects of the growing power of the daimyo?

Comprehension and Critical Thinking
1. (a) **Describe** What are the geographical features of Japan?

(b) **Identify** When did Japan start to develop its own traditions?
(c) **Identify Causes** What led to Japan's isolation?
2. (a) **Recall** What happened to the emperor and the nobles during the 1000s?
(b) **Identify Causes** What led to the establishment of shoguns?
3. (a) **Recall** How did trade develop between Japan and Europe in the 1500s?
(b) **Synthesize** How and why did the Tokugawas isolate Japan?

Writing Activity
Suppose you could interview a samurai. Write five questions that you would ask him. Then write a paragraph to introduce your interview.

For: An activity about the samurai
Visit: PHSchool.com
Web Code: lgd-8402

Assess and Reteach

Assess Progress   L2
Have students complete the Section Assessment. Then administer the *Section Quiz*.

📘 **Medieval Times to Today Teaching Resources,** *Section Quiz,* p. 232

Reteach   L1
If students need more instruction, have them read this section in the Reading and Vocabulary Study Guide.

📖 Chapter 4, Section 2, **Medieval Times to Today Reading and Vocabulary Study Guide,** pp. 39–41

Extend   L3
Have pairs of students research a specific samurai warrior. Then have each pair give an oral presentation to the class on the warrior they chose. *Use Rubric for Assessing an Oral Presentation* to evaluate students' work.

📘 **Medieval Times to Today Teaching Resources,** *Rubric for Assessing an Oral Presentation,* p. 256

Answers

✓ **Reading Check** Possible answers: They divided Japan into 250 regions; there was a good economy; there was plenty of food; the population increased; a merchant class developed; trade and the arts flourished.
Analyze Images The performances reflect a long-standing tradition of theater in Japanese culture.

Section 2 Assessment

Key Terms
Students' sentences should reflect an understanding of each Key Term.

Target Reading Skill
Small wars broke out among them; the Minamoto clan became the most powerful.

Comprehension and Critical Thinking
1. (a) Japan is an archipelago, with mountainous volcanic islands. (b) the 800s

(c) the fact that it is an island nation; the policy of Tokugawa Ieyasu
2. (a) The emperor lost power; the nobles gained power. (b) The emperor gave the title of shogun to Minamoto Yoritomo, who set up the Kamakura shogunate.
3. (a) Portuguese ships landed on Japan's coast in 1543, and the Japanese were interested in their products. (b) The Tokugawas worried that Europeans might try to conquer Japan, so they forced Europeans to leave, and outlawed foreign travel.

Writing Activity
Use the *Rubric for Assessing a Writing Assignment* to evaluate students' work.

📘 **Medieval Times to Today Teaching Resources,** *Rubric for Assessing a Writing Assignment,* p. 257

Go Online PHSchool.com Typing in the Web code when prompted will bring students directly to detailed instructions for this activity.

Focus on A Japanese Home

L2

Guided Instruction

- Ask students to read the text and study the art, photos, and captions on these pages.

- Have students describe the rules of the Tokugawa government's decree. *(Peasant men and women were not allowed to buy tea; men had to work in the fields and women at the loom; both men and women had to work at night; if a woman neglected her household duties, she must be divorced; peasants could only wear cotton or hemp.)*

- Ask students **Do you think these rules were fair? Why or why not?** *(Students' answers will vary, but most will indicate that the rules were unfair because the government prevented people from buying certain goods, and told them what to wear and how to live their lives.)*

- As a class, answer the Assessment questions. Allow students to briefly discuss their responses with a partner before sharing their answers with the class.

Focus On
A Japanese Home

In 1649, authorities of the Tokugawa government sent a decree to Japanese villages: "[Peasants] must not buy tea . . . to drink, nor must their wives. . . . The husband must work in the fields, [and] the wife must work at the loom. Both must do night work. However good-looking a wife may be, if she neglects her household duties . . . she must be divorced. Peasants must wear only cotton or hemp—no silk." This decree shows how the Tokugawa government tried to maintain a firm grip on Japanese society. Both outside and inside the home, the lives of the Japanese were guided by tradition and by law.

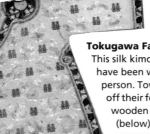

Tokugawa Fashions
This silk kimono, or robe, would have been worn by a wealthy person. Townspeople kept mud off their feet by wearing raised wooden clogs called geta (below). Peasants usually wore straw sandals.

Inside a Japanese Farmhouse The illustration at the right shows a typical farmhouse during the Tokugawa shogunate. In Tokugawa, Japan, most houses had a main room with a sunken fire pit. The family gathered around the fire pit, and sat according to rank. At night, they slept on the floor on thin mattresses, which had been stored away in cupboards during the day.

Not shown are the two back rooms. One of these was the zashiki, a formal room used for receiving guests. Inside it was a butsudan, a Buddhist altar, and a tokonoma, a recessed space decorated with a flower vase, candlestick, and incense burner. The other back room was the nando, used for sleeping and for storage. In some farmhouses, women raised silkworms on a second floor.

The illustration shows raised wood floors covered with straw mats called tatami. It was customary to remove one's shoes before stepping onto the tatami. This custom is still practiced in Japan today.

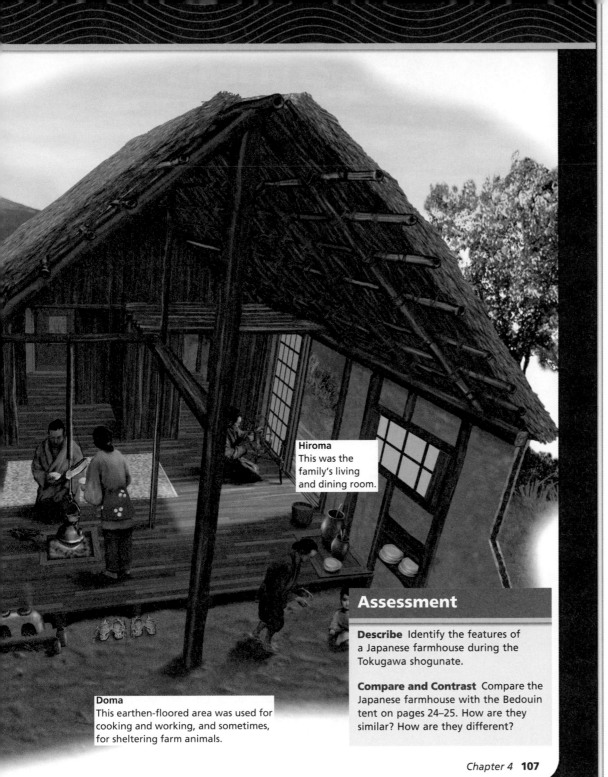

Hiroma
This was the family's living and dining room.

Doma
This earthen-floored area was used for cooking and working, and sometimes, for sheltering farm animals.

Assessment

Describe Identify the features of a Japanese farmhouse during the Tokugawa shogunate.

Compare and Contrast Compare the Japanese farmhouse with the Bedouin tent on pages 24–25. How are they similar? How are they different?

Chapter 4 **107**

Independent Practice

Have students reread the book and study the art, photos, and captions on these pages. Then have them compare their homes to the Japanese farmhouse. What things are the same? What things are different? Use the Think-Write-Pair-Share strategy (TE, p. T36) to elicit student responses.

Answers

Assessment

Describe Farmhouses had a hiroma, which was the family's living and dining room; a doma, which was an earthen-floored area used for cooking, working, and sometimes for sheltering farm animals; a zashiki, which was a formal room for receiving guests and contained a butsudan, or Buddhist altar, and a tokonoma, a recessed space with a flower vase, candlestick, and incense burner; a hando, used for sleeping and for storage. Some farmhouses had second floors where women raised silkworms. Most houses had a main room with a sunken fire pit, cupboards for storing mattresses, and raised wooden floors covered with straw mats called tatami.

Compare and Contrast Similar: both houses have large open areas for sleeping, and cooking is done outside the home but near it; different: the Bedouin tent is made of animal hair and is a temporary structure, while the Japanese farmhouse is made of wood and is a permanent structure.

Section 3
Step-by-Step Instruction

Objectives
Social Studies
1. Find out about the geography of the Indian subcontinent.
2. Learn about the Delhi Sultanate, a period of Muslim rule.
3. Learn about the founding and achievements of the Mughal Empire.

Reading/Language Arts
Learn how to recognize cause-and-effect signal words.

Prepare to Read

Build Background Knowledge **L2**
Have students preview the headings and visuals in this section. Tell them that they will be reading about some of India's great rulers. Ask students what qualities they think a good ruler should have. For example, should he or she be intelligent, compassionate, or courageous? Use the Give One, Get One strategy (TE, p. T37) to elicit answers from the class. Remind them to keep the qualities they chose in mind as they read through the section.

Set a Purpose for Reading **L2**
- Preview the Objectives.

- Read each statement in the *Reading Readiness Guide* aloud. Ask students to mark the statements true or false.

  All in One **Medieval Times to Today Teaching Resources**, *Reading Readiness Guide*, p. 234

- Have students discuss the statements in pairs or groups of four, then mark their worksheets again. Use the Numbered Heads participation strategy (TE, p. T36) to call on students to share their group's perspectives.

Vocabulary Builder
Preview Key Terms **L2**
Pronounce the Key Terms, and then ask students to say the words with you. Provide a simple explanation such as, "A sultan is a Muslim ruler, similar to a king."

Section 3 | The Great Mughal Empire in India

Prepare to Read

Objectives
In this section you will
1. Find out about the geography of the Indian subcontinent.
2. Learn about the Delhi Sultanate, a period of Muslim rule.
3. Learn about the founding and achievements of the Mughal Empire.

Taking Notes
As you read this section, look for important events in India's history, and note when they occurred. Copy the timeline below and record your findings on it.

India's History, 600–1707

600
Hindu revival begins.

Target Reading Skill
Recognize Cause-and-Effect Signal Words
Sometimes certain words, such as *because, affect,* or *as a result,* signal a cause or an effect. In this section, you will learn about invasions of India and the rise and fall of two Indian empires. Look for signal words to help you understand the causes and effects of these events.

Key Terms
- **sultan** (SUL tun) *n.* a Muslim ruler
- **caste system** (kast SIS tum) *n.* a Hindu social class system that controlled every aspect of daily life
- **Mughal Empire** (MOO gul EM pyr) *n.* a period of Muslim rule of India from the 1500s to the 1700s
- **Akbar** (AK bahr) *n.* the greatest Mughal leader of India
- **Taj Mahal** (tahzh muh HAHL) *n.* a tomb built by Shah Jahan for his wife

Timur, from an Indian manuscript

Even before Timur (tee MOOR) invaded India, people there had heard of this Mongol conqueror. He had destroyed entire cities and their populations in other parts of Asia. In 1398, he and his troops marched into northern India, in search of fabled riches. They ruined fields of crops and quickly captured Delhi (DEL ee), the capital city. Timur and his troops killed many people and took hundreds of slaves. They also carried away great treasures—pearls, golden dishes, rubies, and diamonds.

For a brief time, Delhi became part of the huge empire that Timur controlled from his capital, Samarkand (sam ur KAND). But Timur was more interested in conquering new lands than in governing those he had defeated. Not long after the Mongols invaded Delhi, they departed. Once again, a **sultan,** or Muslim ruler, took control of the city. But Delhi did not regain its command over the region, as you will see.

108 Medieval Times to Today

Target Reading Skill **L2**
Recognize Cause-and-Effect Signal Words
Point out the Target Reading Skill. Ask students to be aware of the signal words listed here.

Model recognizing cause-and-effect signal words using this sentence: *As a result, the prince defeated the sultan and went on to control the capital city, Delhi.* Identify the cause-and-effect signal words. *(as a result)*

Give students *Recognize Cause-and-Effect Signal Words*. Have them complete the activity in groups.

All in One **Medieval Times to Today Teaching Resources**, *Recognize Cause-and-Effect Signal Words*, p. 239

India's Geography

The triangular Indian subcontinent forms the southernmost part of Central Asia. A mountain range called the Himalayas stretches across the north of India. Although these mountains have helped to isolate India from lands to the north, the passes through the Himalayas have allowed some conquerors from the north to enter the subcontinent. To the west of India is the Arabian Sea, and to the east is the Bay of Bengal.

A large plain lies to the south of the Himalayas. It is dominated by major river systems, including the Indus and Ganges rivers. These rivers are fed by melting mountain snows, and much of the land here is well suited to farming. Farther to the south are highlands and plains.

✓ **Reading Check** Describe India's geography.

The Delhi Sultanate

The Mongols led by Timur were not the first people to invade India. Long before they came, India's riches had tempted others. Muslim invaders began raiding the Indian subcontinent around A.D. 1000. From 1206 to 1526, a series of sultans controlled northern India as well as parts of present-day Bangladesh and Pakistan. This period of India's history is called the Delhi Sultanate—after the capital city, Delhi.

A Hindu Revival At the time of the Muslim invasion, the region was experiencing a revival of the ancient Hindu religion. This revival had begun about A.D. 600. Hindus accept many gods, but they believe that all of these gods are just different aspects of one supreme being. Hindus also believe that social classes are part of the natural order of the universe.

In India at this time, the Hindu **caste system**—a strict system of social classes—controlled everyday life. Caste determined a person's job and status. At the top of the caste system were priests, teachers, and judges. Warriors were second. Then came farmers and merchants. The fourth class included craftspeople and laborers. Finally, there was a group of poor and powerless people who were called untouchables.

A Himalayan Mountain Pass
Even today, it is difficult to cross the Himalayas. **Infer** Why do you think modern travelers are still using pack animals rather than trucks or automobiles to cross these mountains?

Target Reading Skill

Recognize Cause-and-Effect Signal Words

As a follow up, have students answer the Target Reading Skill question in the Student Edition. (*The signal word is "caused."*)

Guided Instruction (continued)

- Ask students **What was the Hindu caste system?** (*a strict system of social classes*) **What were the different classes of the Hindu caste system?** (*Priests, teachers, and judges were at the top; warriors were second; farmers and merchants were third; craftsmen and laborers were fourth; and untouchables, who were poor and powerless, were at the bottom.*)

- Ask students **Why did conflicts occur between Hindus and Muslims?** (*Muslim culture is based on beliefs that are very different from Hindu beliefs. These beliefs led to conflicts that still exist today.*)

- Ask students **How was the Delhi Sultanate defeated?** (*A Mongol prince named Babur attacked and defeated the Sultan's army with the use of cannons and better fighters.*)

Independent Practice

Have students create the Taking Notes graphic organizer on a blank sheet of paper. Then have them fill in the time line with details they learn as they read. Briefly model how to add details using *Transparency B20: Timeline.*

📖 **Medieval Times to Today Transparencies,** *Transparency B20: Timeline*

Monitor Progress

As students fill in the time line, circulate and make sure that individuals are placing events in chronological order. Provide assistance as necessary.

Answers

✓ **Reading Check** The Mongols attacked the weakened Delhi Sultanate. They had cannons and were better fighters.

Conclude Akbar's court was made up of many men who supported him.

110 *Medieval Times to Today*

🔄 **Recognize Cause-and-Effect Signal Words** What signal word in the paragraph at the right helped you understand the conflicts between Hindus and Muslims?

Akbar Holds Court Akbar supported many kinds of artists, including those who made beautiful miniature paintings like this one. **Conclude** *What can you conclude about Akbar's court from this painting?*

110 Medieval Times to Today

The Muslims who controlled the Delhi Sultanate did not become part of Hindu society. As you read in Chapter 1, Muslim culture is based on beliefs that are very different from those of Hindu culture. These differences caused conflicts between the two groups. In fact, religious disagreements still divide the Hindus and Muslims who live in India today.

The Fall of the Delhi Sultanate In 1526, a Mongol prince named Babur (BAH bur) took advantage of the weakened Delhi Sultanate. Babur was a Muslim descendant of the Mongol conqueror Timur. Even though Babur and his troops were outnumbered almost ten to one, they attacked the sultan's army.

The sultan's forces had 100 elephants to help them fight. Babur's troops had none. But the Mongols had cannons—and they were better fighters. The prince defeated the sultan and went on to control the capital city, Delhi. A new period of India's history would now begin.

✓ **Reading Check** How was the Delhi Sultanate defeated?

The Mughal Empire

Babur founded the celebrated **Mughal Empire,** whose Muslim rulers controlled India until the 1700s. (*Mughal* is another word for "Mongol.") About 25 years after Babur's death, the empire came under the control of Babur's grandson. His name was **Akbar** (AK bahr), and he would become the greatest Mughal leader of India.

Akbar the Great When Akbar came to power, he was only 13 years old. He grew up to become a talented soldier. Through conquest, treaties, and marriage, he greatly expanded the Mughal Empire.

Akbar also encouraged the arts. He set up studios for painters at his court. He supported poets, although he himself never learned to read or write. Akbar also brought together scholars from different religions for discussions. He consulted with Muslims, Hindus, Buddhists, and Christians.

Although he was a Muslim, Akbar gained the support of his Hindu subjects through his policy of toleration. He allowed Hindus to practice their religion freely, and he ended unfair taxes that had been required of non-Muslims.

Background: Daily Life

Hinduism Dating back more than 3,000 years, Hinduism is one of the world's oldest religions. Unlike Judaism, Islam, or Christianity, Hinduism has no single founder, holy book, or system of beliefs. Hindus may worship many different lesser gods; however they are all seen as part of one being called Brahman. Brahman is believed to have the form of three major gods: Brahma, the creator; Vishnu, the preserver; and Shiva, the destroyer. Reincarnation, or rebirth, is an important belief in Hinduism. Hindus believe that after a person dies, his or her soul is reborn into another person or animal. What a person does in this life affects how he or she will be reborn in the next life. Eventually, Hindus hope to escape this cycle of death and rebirth and become part of Brahman.

MAP ✦ MASTER™
Skills Activity

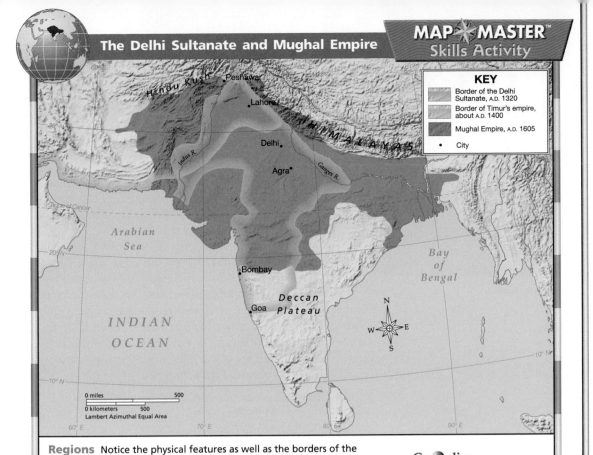

KEY

	Border of the Delhi Sultanate, A.D. 1320
	Border of Timur's empire, about A.D. 1400
	Mughal Empire, A.D. 1605
•	City

Regions Notice the physical features as well as the borders of the empires on the map. **Locate** Which empire was the oldest? Which one gained control of the mouths of India's two most important rivers? **Infer** Why do you think neither the sultans nor the Mughals extended their empires farther north?

Go Online
PHSchool.com Use Web Code lgp-8443 for step-by-step map skills practice.

Akbar created a strong central government, and he gave government jobs to qualified people, whatever their religion or caste. Hindus served as generals, governors, administrators, and clerks. These policies helped Hindus and Muslims live together more peacefully. They also strengthened Mughal power in India.

In 1605, when Akbar died, most of northern India was under his control. Akbar had ruled the Mughal Empire for 49 years, earning himself the nickname "the Great." During this long reign, his system of government had become firmly established in India. This system allowed the empire to continue developing and expanding for the next 100 years—even under rulers who were less capable than Akbar the Great.

Royal emblem from the Gujari Palace, India

Chapter 4 Section 3 **111**

The Mughal Empire L2

Guided Instruction

- **Vocabulary Builder** Clarify the high-use words **expand, extravagant,** and **rebel** before reading.

- Read The Mughal Empire to learn about Akbar the Great and other Mughal leaders.

- Ask students **How did Akbar improve relations between Hindus and Muslims?** *(He allowed Hindus to practice their religion freely and ended unfair taxes required of non-Muslims, which helped Hindus and Muslims to live together more peacefully.)*

- Ask students **What was the Taj Mahal?** *(a tomb built by Shah Jahan for his wife, Mumtaz Mahal)* **How do you think this and other extravagant buildings might have contributed to the decline of the Mughal Empire?** *(Possible answer: the buildings cost the empire a great deal of money and perhaps took too much time and money that could have been used in other areas of the empire.)*

Independent Practice

Have students complete their graphic organizers with dates from the section.

Monitor Progress

- Show *Section Reading Support Transparency MT 64.* Go over key concepts and clarify key vocabulary as needed.

  📖 **Medieval Times to Today Teaching Resources,** *Section Reading Support Transparency MT 64*

- Tell students to fill in the last column of the *Reading Readiness Guide.* Probe for what they learned that confirms or invalidates each statement.

  All in One Medieval Times to Today Teaching Resources, *Reading Readiness Guide,* p. 234

Differentiated Instruction

For Less Proficient Readers L1
Remind students that in Section 1 they read about the merit system. Ask them whether Akbar the Great used a similar system. Then have them find them reread the text under the heading Akbar the Great, and identify the sentence that tells them so. (*"Akbar created a strong central government, and he gave government jobs to qualified people, whatever their religion or caste."*)

For Special Needs Students L1
If students are having difficulty using the map on page 111, divide them into pairs and assign *Using the Map Key.*

All in One Medieval Times to Today Teaching Resources, *Using the Map Key,* p. 247

Answers

MAP ✦ MASTER Skills Activity **Locate** the Delhi Sultanate; the Mughal Empire; **Infer** The Himalayas were difficult to cross and would have prevented large armies from reaching lands to the north.

Go Online PHSchool.com Students may practice their map skills using the interactive online version of this map.

Assess and Reteach

Assess Progress L2
Have students complete the Section Assessment. Then administer the *Section Quiz*.

  All in One Medieval Times to Today Teaching Resources, *Section Quiz*, p. 236

Reteach L1
If students need more instruction, have them read this section in the Reading and Vocabulary Study Guide.

  Chapter 4, Section 3, **Medieval Times to Today Reading and Vocabulary Study Guide,** pp. 42–44

Extend L3
Have students read the story *Savitri: A Tale of Ancient India,* to see an example of Indian literature that contains Hindu gods as characters.

  All in One Medieval Times to Today Teaching Resources, *Savitri: A Tale of Ancient India,* pp. 248–251

Answer

✓**Reading Check** He spent money on expensive wars, and reversed Akbar's policies toward Hindus, causing rebellions and wars.

Section 3 Assessment

Key Terms
Students' sentences should reflect an understanding of the Key Terms.

Target Reading Skill
The words *as a result* signal a cause-and-effect relationship in the last paragraph on this page.

Comprehension and Critical Thinking
1. (a) The Himalayas are in the north; south of the Himalayas is a large plain with two great river systems, the Indus and the Ganges; the Arabian Sea is in the west, and the Bay of Bengal is in the east. **(b)** Conquerors and invaders might not have reached India.

2. (a) the period of history from 1206 to 1526 when Muslim rulers, or sultans, controlled northern India and parts of present-day Bangladesh and Pakistan **(b)** Muslims did not become a part of Hindu society, and the two cultures had many conflicts.

The Taj Mahal

The Reign of Shah Jahan More than 100 years after Akbar's death, the Mughal Empire began to fall apart. Akbar's grandson, Shah Jahan (shah juh HAHN), became emperor in 1628. Jahan spent a fortune on extravagant buildings. The most famous of these is the **Taj Mahal** (tahzh muh HAHL), a tomb for the emperor's wife, Mumtaz Mahal (mum TAHZ muh HAHL).

When his wife died, Jahan was overcome with grief. The two had been constant companions, and Jahan had asked his wife's opinion on many issues. After she died, Jahan set out to build a tomb "as beautiful as she was beautiful."

Jahan's son, Aurangzeb (AWR ung zeb), spent still more money on expensive wars. He also reversed Akbar's policies toward Hindus. Aurangzeb tried to force Hindus to convert to the Muslim faith, and he began to tax them again. As a result, many Hindus rebelled, and fighting the rebels cost still more money. After Aurangzeb died in 1707, the empire split into small kingdoms. But to this day, people from around the globe journey to see his mother's tomb—a lasting reminder of the once great Mughal Empire.

✓**Reading Check** How did Aurangzeb contribute to the decline of the Mughal Empire?

 ### Section 3 Assessment

Key Terms
Review the key terms at the beginning of this section. Use each term in a sentence that explains its meaning.

Target Reading Skill
What words in the last paragraph on this page signal cause and effect?

Comprehension and Critical Thinking
1. (a) Identify What are the major geographic features of the Indian subcontinent?

(b) Predict How might India's history have been different if there had been no mountain passes in the north?
2. (a) Define What was the Delhi Sultanate?
(b) Synthesize How did Hindus and Muslims live together in India during this time?
3. (a) Explain Why was Akbar called "the Great"?
(b) Identify Causes What caused the decline of the Mughal Empire?

Writing Activity
Suppose that Akbar is a leader under a system of government like the United States government. He is running for reelection, and you are his campaign manager. Write a short speech stating why voters should reelect him.

Writing Tip Remember to support your position with specific examples.

---

3. (a) He was a just ruler, who ruled the Mughal Empire successfully for 49 years. He encouraged the arts and persuaded Hindus and Muslims to live together more peacefully. When he died, most of northern India was under his control. **(b)** Rulers after Akbar spent money on extravagant buildings and expensive wars, and reversed Akbar's policies toward Hindus, which caused Hindus to rebel and cost the empire even more money.

Writing Activity
Use the *Rubric for Assessing a Writing Assignment* to evaluate students' speeches.

  All in One Medieval Times to Today Teaching Resources, *Rubric for Assessing a Writing Assignment*, p. 257

Review and Assessment

◆ Chapter Summary

Section 1: Golden Ages of China

Kublai Khan's court

- The Tang dynasty ruled China for almost 300 years. That period was the beginning of a golden age, during which China's territory increased, and Chinese culture and trade flourished.
- The Song dynasty, which ruled China after the Tang, expanded the merit system and promoted the spread of knowledge.
- The Mongols conquered China, and their leader, Kublai Khan, centralized China's government.

Section 2: Medieval Japan

- Japan is a mountainous island country of East Asia. The sea has provided both transportation and protection for the people of Japan.
- During the Heian period, the Japanese built a new capital and began to develop a distinctive culture.
- Warriors, called samurai, and powerful military leaders, called shoguns, took control away from the emperor. The shoguns eventually closed Japan to outsiders.

Section 3: The Great Mughal Empire in India

- The Indian subcontinent is shaped like a triangle, with mountains to the north and seas to the east and west.
- During the Delhi Sultanate, Muslim rulers called sultans ruled India.
- Mongols conquered India and established the Mughal Empire. Akbar the Great was the greatest Mughal leader.

Kabuki performer

◆ Key Terms

Define each of the following terms.

1. Silk Road
2. Tang
3. shogun
4. sultan
5. caste system
6. Kublai Khan
7. archipelago
8. samurai
9. Taj Mahal
10. dynasty

┌ **Vocabulary Builder** ┐

Revisit this chapter's high-use words:

fertile	isolation	conflict
estimate	distinctive	expand
reform	related	extravagant
adopt	supreme	rebel

Ask students to review the definitions they recorded on their *Word Knowledge* worksheets.

All in One Medieval Times to Today Teaching Resources, *Word Knowledge,* p. 240

Consider allowing students to earn extra credit if they use the words in their answers to the questions in the Chapter Review and Assessment. The words must be used correctly and in a natural context to win the extra points.

Review and Assessment
Review Chapter Content

- Review and revisit the major themes of this chapter by asking students to classify what Guiding Question each bulleted statement in the Chapter Summary answers. Form students in groups and ask them to complete the activity together. Refer to page 1 in the Student Edition for the text of the Guiding Questions.

- Assign Vocabulary Development for students to review Key Terms.

  All in One Medieval Times to Today Teaching Resources, *Vocabulary Development,* p. 253

Answers

Key Terms

1. a chain of trade routes stretching from China to the Mediterranean Sea
2. a dynasty that ruled China for almost 300 years
3. the supreme military commander of Japan
4. a Muslim ruler
5. Hindu social class system that controlled every aspect of daily life
6. a Mongol emperor of China
7. a group or chain of islands
8. Japanese warriors
9. a tomb built by Shah Jahan for his wife
10. a series of rulers from the same family

Review and Assessment

Comprehension and Critical Thinking

11. (a) Students should list any two of the following: tea, jade, ivory, ceramics, silk **(b)** They were luxury goods that were new to the people of other countries. **(c)** Traders along the Silk Road introduced new ideas and goods to China, and China became an important center of trade and culture.

12. (a) The Song began using the merit system to hire government officials. The Mongols centralized government and stopped using the merit system; instead, high government positions were reserved only for Mongols. **(b)** The Song's use of the merit system benefited China since the hiring of people based on ability improved the Chinese government. Under the Mongols, only Mongols could be part of the government; which probably angered the Chinese who lived there and weakened the government's effectiveness.

13. (a) Japan is a mountainous archipelago in the Pacific Ocean off the coast of mainland Asia; India is a triangular subcontinent in the southernmost part of Central Asia, with the Himalayas stretching across northern India and a large plain to the south of the mountains. **(b)** Because of the mountainous terrain, the sea became an important transportation route for the Japanese. It protected Japan from outside invaders but it also isolated the country. The Himalayas isolated India from the north, but mountain passes allowed some invaders to enter India and conquer it.

14. (a) a series of Japanese military dynasties **(b)** Samurai warriors formed their own clans and promised loyalty to a powerful warlord and eventually the Minamoto clan became the most powerful; in 1192 the emperor of Japan gave the title of shogun to the leader of the Minamoto clan, Yoritomo, who set up the Kamakura shogunate. **(c)** They wanted to isolate Japan from foreign influences and prevent Europeans from conquering Japan.

15. (a) Aurangazeb **(b)** Akbar had allowed Hindus freedom to practice their religion while Aurangazeb tried to force Hindus to convert to Islam. During Akbar's reign, a system of governing became firmly established in India, but after Aurangazeb's death the empire split into small kingdoms. **(c)** Under the leaders who followed Akbar, great sums of money were spent on expensive wars. During Aurangazeb's reign many

---

Review and Assessment (continued)

◆ Comprehension and Critical Thinking

11. (a) Identify Name two Chinese products that were important for trade.
(b) Explain Why were these products valued by other countries?
(c) Identify Effects How did trade in these products affect China?

12. (a) Recall How did the Song, and then the Mongols, change Chinese government?
(b) Evaluate Which changes benefited China? Which were harmful? Explain.

13. (a) Identify What are the major geographic features of Japan? Of India?
(b) Compare and Contrast How did the geography of these two places affect their history and culture?

14. (a) Define What is a shogunate?
(b) Summarize How did shoguns gain power in Japan?
(c) Identify Causes Why did shoguns ban most foreign travel and trade?

15. (a) Identify Who was the last ruler of India's Mughal Empire?
(b) Contrast How was his rule different from that of his great-grandfather, Akbar?
(c) Analyze What factors contributed to the downfall of the Mughal Empire?

◆ Skills Practice

Making an Outline In the Skills for Life activity in this chapter, you learned how to make an outline. Review the steps you followed to learn the skill. Then reread the text under the heading The Mughal Empire on pages 110–112. Make an outline of that text.

◆ Writing Activity: Science

Use encyclopedias, other reliable books, or reliable Internet sources to research one Chinese invention of the Tang or Song dynasty. Describe the invention, how it works, when and how it was invented, and why it was important. Write your findings as an essay or as an illustrated report that you can display in your classroom.

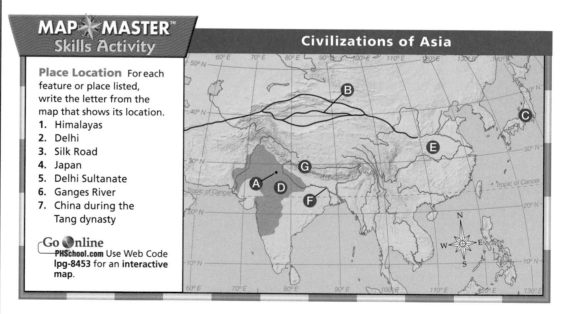

MAP MASTER™ Skills Activity

Civilizations of Asia

Place Location For each feature or place listed, write the letter from the map that shows its location.
1. Himalayas
2. Delhi
3. Silk Road
4. Japan
5. Delhi Sultanate
6. Ganges River
7. China during the Tang dynasty

Go Online PHSchool.com Use Web Code **lpg-8453** for an **interactive map.**

Hindus rebelled, and money was spent on fighting them.

Skills Practice

Making an Outline Outlines will vary, but check to make sure students have created their outlines using the proper format and have included information from the text about the Mughal empire.

Writing Activity: Science

Students' reports will vary, but should include information about a Chinese invention from the Tang or Song dynasty. *Use Rubric for Assessing a Writing Assignment* to evaluate student's reports.

All in One Medieval Times to Today Teaching Resources, *Rubric for Assessing a Writing Assignment,* p. 257

Standardized Test Prep

Test-Taking Tips

Some questions on standardized tests may ask you to identify the main topic or the topic sentence of a passage. Read the paragraph below. Then use the tip to help you answer the sample question.

> Beginning in the 1600s, the powerful shoguns of Japan outlawed Christianity. The shoguns forced Europeans to leave the country. They also closed Japanese ports to foreigners and banned foreign trade. Through their efforts to isolate Japan, the shoguns hoped to protect it from foreign invasion.

Think It Through Read all four choices. Answers A and D tell about specific actions, not broad ideas or main topics. Even though C is the first sentence of the passage, it also describes one particular action. Therefore, it is not more important than A or D. Because B summarizes the information of the other sentences, it is the correct answer.

Pick the letter that best answers the question.

Which of these sentences states the <u>main topic</u> of the passage?

A They also closed Japanese ports to foreigners and banned foreign trade.

B Through their efforts to isolate Japan, the shoguns hoped to protect it from foreign invasion.

C Beginning in the 1600s, the powerful shoguns of Japan outlawed Christianity.

D The shoguns forced Europeans to leave the country.

TIP Many paragraphs have one sentence that states the main topic. The other sentences in the paragraph all support this topic sentence. The first and last sentences are the most likely to be the topic sentence.

Practice Questions

Pick the letter that best answers the question.

1. Read the passage below. Which of the sentences that follow states the main topic of the passage?

> Hideyoshi was born a poor peasant in Japan in the 1500s. Through hard work, he became a samurai warrior. Because of his military skills, Hideyoshi was promoted to an important position working for a powerful warlord. In 1582, the warlord was killed, and Hideyoshi took his place. A skillful leader from poor beginnings, Hideyoshi became ruler of Japan.

A Through hard work, he became a samurai warrior.

B Hideyoshi was born a poor peasant in Japan in the 1500s.

C A skillful leader from poor beginnings, Hideyoshi became ruler of Japan.

D In 1582, the warlord was killed, and Hideyoshi took his place.

Read each of the following statements. If the statement is true, write _true_. If it is false, write _false_.

2. The samurai warriors of Japan followed a set of strict rules for behavior.

3. Song rulers used the merit system in Chinese government.

4. The Indian subcontinent could not be invaded from the north.

5. Akbar was a great Mughal ruler of India.

6. Japan's islands are mostly flat, and traveling by land is easy.

Use Web Code lga-8403 for a **Chapter 4 self-test.**

Chapter 4 **115**

MAP MASTER *Skills Activity*

1. G	**2.** A
3. B	**4.** C
5. D	**6.** F
7. E	

Go Online *PHSchool.com* Students may practice their map skills using the interactive online version of this map.

Standardized Test Prep

Answers

1. C

2. True

3. True

4. False

5. True

6. False

Go Online *PHSchool.com* Students may use the Chapter 4 self-test on PHSchool.com to prepare for the Chapter Test.

Assessment Resources

Use *Chapter Tests A and B* to assess students' mastery of the chapter content.

All in One **Medieval Times to Today Teaching Resources,** Chapter Tests A and B, pp. 258–263

Tests are also available on the *ExamView® Test Bank CD-ROM.*

ExamView® Test Bank CD-ROM

Use a benchmark test to evaluate students' cumulative understanding of what they have learned in Chapters 1 through 4.

Medieval Times to Today Benchmark Test 1, **AYP Monitoring Assessments,** pp. 141–144

Overview

Section 1
Feudalism and the Manor System
1. Learn when the Middle Ages were and what they were like.
2. Find out how land and power were divided under feudalism.
3. Learn how the manor system worked.
4. Discover what life was like for peasants and serfs.

Section 2
The Church and the Rise of Cities
1. Learn why the Roman Catholic Church was so important and powerful during the Middle Ages.
2. Discover the connection between an increase in trade and the growth of towns.
3. Find out what life was like in a medieval town.
4. Understand the role of culture and learning in the Middle Ages.

Section 3
The Crusades
1. Learn about the causes of the Crusades.
2. Find out about the different Crusades and what they accomplished.
3. Discover the effects the Crusades had on life in Europe.

Section 4
The Power of Kings
1. Learn about the forces that led to nation building in Europe.
2. Find out about nation building in England.
3. Discover how the Hundred Years' War affected England and France.

Feudal Life in the Middle Ages
Length: 5 minutes, 28 seconds
Use with Section 1
This video segment introduces the idea of feudalism and its effects on the relationships between lords and their servants. The segment also explores the castles and the knights who protected feudal life.

Technology Resources

Students use embedded Web codes to access Internet activities, chapter self-tests, and additional map practice. They may also access Dorling Kindersley's Online Desk Reference to learn more about each country they study.

Use the Interactive Textbook to make content and concepts come alive through animations, videos, and activities that accompany the complete basal text—online and on CD-ROM.

Use this complete suite of powerful teaching tools to make planning lessons and administering tests quicker and easier.

Reading and Assessment

Reading and Vocabulary Instruction

🔁 Model the Target Reading Skill

Sequence Explain to students that sequence is the order in which something occurs. Understanding sequence is important when reading because it allows students to recognize the order in which events in history occurred and how one event might influence another. Point out some words that are often used when describing sequence: *first, second, next, then, before, later.* You can teach this skill using the following selection from page 136 of the Student Edition:

After the capture of Jerusalem, most of the crusaders returned to Europe. Those who stayed in the Holy Land set up four Christian kingdoms. The Muslim Turks attacked these kingdoms repeatedly. European Christians then launched more Crusades to keep control of the region.

Write the selection on the board, and ask students to identify the sequence signal words as you underline them. *(after; then)* Point out that the word *after* in the first sentence refers to the fact that the return of the crusaders to Europe followed the capture of Jerusalem. Next, create a timeline on the board to show the order in which the events occurred. *(The timeline should show, in this order: capture of Jerusalem; four Christian kingdoms set up in Holy Land; Muslim Turks attack kingdoms; more crusades launched by European Christians.)*

Use the following worksheets from All-in-One Medieval Times to Today Teaching Resources (pp. 285–286) to support the chapter's Target Reading Skill.

Vocabulary Builder
High-Use Academic Words

Use these steps to teach this chapter's high-use words:

1. Have students rate how well they know each word on their Word Knowledge worksheets (All-in-One Medieval Times to Today Teaching Resources, p. 287).

2. Pronounce each word and ask students to repeat it.

3. Give students a brief definition or sample sentence (provided on TE pp. 119, 127, 134, and 141).

4. Work with students as they fill in the "Definition or Example" column of their Word Knowledge worksheets.

Assessment

Formal Assessment

Test students' understanding of core knowledge and skills.

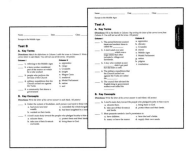

Chapter Tests A and B, All-in-One Medieval Times to Today Teaching Resources, pp. 301–306

Customize the Chapter Tests to suit your needs.
Exam*View*® Test Bank CD-ROM

Skills Assessment

Assess geographic literacy.
MapMaster Skills, Student Edition pp. 117, 119, 130, 135, 146

Assess reading and comprehension.
Target Reading Skills, Student Edition, pp. 120, 131, 136, 142, and in Section Assessments

Chapter 5 Assessment, Medieval Times to Today Reading and Vocabulary Study Guide, p. 58

Performance Assessment

Assess students' performance on this chapter's Writing Activities using the following rubrics from All-in-One Medieval Times to Today Teaching Resources.

Rubric for Assessing a Writing Assignment, p. 297

Rubric for Assessing a Newspaper Article, p. 298

Assess students' work through performance tasks.

Small Group Activity: Writing a Documentary, All-in-One Medieval Times to Today Teaching Resources, pp. 290–293

Online Assessment

Have students check their own understanding.

Chapter Self-Test

Section 1 Feudalism and the Manor System

 2 periods, 1 block (includes Focus On A Medieval Manor)

Social Studies Objectives
1. Learn when the Middle Ages were and what they were like.
2. Find out how land and power were divided under feudalism.
3. Learn how the manor system worked.
4. Discover what life was like for peasants and serfs.

Reading/Language Arts Objective
Recognize sequence signal words to help in understanding the relationships in time between ideas and events.

Prepare to Read

Build Background Knowledge
Have students preview the headings and visuals to predict what they will learn.

Set a Purpose for Reading
Have students evaluate statements on the *Reading Readiness Guide*.

Preview Key Terms
Teach the section's Key Terms.

Target Reading Skill
Introduce the section's Target Reading Skill of **recognizing sequence signal words.**

Instructional Resources

All in One Medieval Times to Today Teaching Resources
- L2 Reading Readiness Guide, p. 270
- L2 Recognize Sequence Signal Words, p. 285

Differentiated Instruction

Spanish Reading and Vocabulary Study Guide
- L1 Chapter 5, Section 1, pp. 35–36 ELL

Instruct

The Middle Ages
Discuss the time span of the Middle Ages and the major empires that existed during that time.

Target Reading Skill
Review **recognizing sequence signal words.**

Feudalism: A Kind of Government
Ask about the people who held power in the feudal system, and discuss the role of lords and vassals.

The Manor System Peasants and Serfs
Discuss the differences between feudalism and the manor system.

Instructional Resources

All in One Medieval Times to Today Teaching Resources
- L2 Guided Reading and Review, p. 271
- L2 Reading Readiness Guide, p. 270

Medieval Times to Today Transparencies
- L2 Section Reading Support Transparency MT 65

World Studies Video Program
- L2 Feudal Life in the Middle Ages

Differentiated Instruction

All in One Medieval Times to Today Teaching Resources
- L1 Lords and Vassals, p. 294 AR, GT

Teacher's Edition
- L1 For Less Proficient Readers, TE p. 120
- L3 For Gifted and Talented, TE p. 120
- L3 For Advanced Readers, TE p. 121
- L1 For Special Needs Students, TE pp. 121, 124

Student Edition on Audio CD
- L1 Chapter 5, Section 1 ELL, LPR, SN

Spanish Support
- L2 Guided Reading and Review (Spanish), p. 36 ELL

Assess and Reteach

Assess Progress
Evaluate student comprehension with the section assessment and section quiz.

Reteach
Assign the Reading and Vocabulary Study Guide to help struggling students.

Extend
Extend the lesson by assigning a Small Group Activity.

Instructional Resources

All in One Medieval Times to Today Teaching Resources
- L2 Section Quiz, p. 272
- L3 Small Group Activity: Writing a Documentary, pp. 290–293
  Rubric for Assessing a Writing Assignment, p. 297

Reading and Vocabulary Study Guide
- L1 Chapter 5, Section 1, pp. 46–48

Differentiated Instruction

Spanish Support
- L2 Section Quiz (Spanish), p. 37 ELL

Key
- L1 Basic to Average
- L2 For All Students
- L3 Average to Advanced
- LPR Less Proficient Readers
- AR Advanced Readers
- SN Special Needs Students
- GT Gifted and Talented
- ELL English Language Learners

Section 2 The Church and the Rise of Cities

 2 periods, 1 block

Social Studies Objectives
1. Learn why the Roman Catholic Church was so important and powerful during the Middle Ages.
2. Discover the connection between an increase in trade and the growth of towns.
3. Find out what life was like in a medieval town.
4. Understand the role of culture and learning in the Middle Ages.

Reading/Language Arts Objective
Identify the sequence of events to help you understand and remember them.

Prepare to Read	Instructional Resources	Differentiated Instruction
Build Background Knowledge Use transparencies to spark a discussion about medieval cathedrals. **Set a Purpose for Reading** Have students evaluate statements on the *Reading Readiness Guide*. **Preview Key Terms** Teach the section's Key Terms. **Target Reading Skill** Introduce the section's Target Reading Skill of **identifying sequence.**	**All in One Medieval Times to Today Teaching Resources** **L2** Reading Readiness Guide, p. 274 **L2** Identify Sequence, p. 286 **Medieval Times to Today Transparencies** **L2** Color Transparency MT 35: The Cathedral at Reims **L2** Color Transparency MT 36: The Cathedral at Reims: Interior	**Spanish Reading and Vocabulary Study Guide** **L1** Chapter 5, Section 2, pp. 37–38 ELL

Instruct	Instructional Resources	Differentiated Instruction
The Church in the Middle Ages Discuss the Roman Catholic Church and its influence on the people of the Middle Ages. **Eyewitness Technology** Study a diagram to learn about Gothic cathedrals. **Trade Revives and Towns Grow** Discuss how the rise in travel and growth of towns led to an increase in trade. **Life in Towns and Cities Medieval Culture** Discuss the middle class and the role of guilds in the Middle Ages. **Target Reading Skill** Review **identifying sequence.**	**All in One Medieval Times to Today Teaching Resources** **L2** Guided Reading and Review, p. 275 **L2** Reading Readiness Guide, p. 274 **Medieval Times to Today Transparencies** **L2** Section Reading Support Transparency MT 66	**Teacher's Edition** **L3** For Gifted and Talented, TE p. 128 **L1** For Less Proficient Readers, TE p. 129 **L3** For Advanced Readers, TE p. 130 **Medieval Times to Today Transparencies** **L3** Color Transparency MT 27: Western Europe: Physical-Political AR, GT **Spanish Support** **L2** Guided Reading and Review (Spanish), p. 38 ELL

Assess and Reteach	Instructional Resources	Differentiated Instruction
Assess Progress Evaluate student comprehension with the section assessment and section quiz. **Reteach** Assign the Reading and Vocabulary Study Guide to help struggling students. **Extend** Extend the lesson by assigning an Enrichment activity.	**All in One Medieval Times to Today Teaching Resources** **L2** Section Quiz, p. 276 **L3** Enrichment, p. 288 Rubric for Assessing a Writing Assignment, p. 297 **Reading and Vocabulary Study Guide** **L1** Chapter 5, Section 2, pp. 49–51	**Spanish Support** **L2** Section Quiz (Spanish), p. 39 ELL

Key
L1 Basic to Average   **L3** Average to Advanced
L2 For All Students

LPR Less Proficient Readers
AR Advanced Readers
SN Special Needs Students

GT Gifted and Talented
ELL English Language Learners

Section 3 The Crusades

 4 periods, 2 blocks (includes Skills for Life)

Social Studies Objectives
1. Learn about the causes of the Crusades.
2. Find out about the different Crusades and what they accomplished.
3. Discover the effects the Crusades had on life in Europe.

Reading/Language Arts Objective
Recognize sequence signal words to help build an understanding of the relationships between ideas and events.

Prepare to Read

Build Background Knowledge
Ask students to preview the section and write five questions to answer as they read.

Set a Purpose for Reading
Have students begin to fill out the *Reading Readiness Guide.*

Preview Key Terms
Teach the section's Key Terms.

Target Reading Skill
Introduce the section's Target Reading Skill of **recognizing sequence signal words.**

Instructional Resources

All in One Medieval Times to Today Teaching Resources
L2 Reading Readiness Guide, p. 278
L2 Recognize Sequence Signal Words, p. 285

Differentiated Instruction

Spanish Reading and Vocabulary Study Guide
L1 Chapter 5, Section 3, pp. 39–40 ELL

Instruct

Causes of the Crusades
Discuss the Crusades and the Holy Land of Jerusalem.

Target Reading Skill
Review **recognizing sequence signal words.**

A Series of Crusades
The Results of the Crusades
Compare and contrast the First and Second Crusades and discuss effects of the Crusades.

Instructional Resources

All in One Medieval Times to Today Teaching Resources
L2 Guided Reading and Review, p. 279
L2 Reading Readiness Guide, p. 278

Medieval Times to Today Transparencies
L2 Section Reading Support Transparency MT 67

Differentiated Instruction

All in One Medieval Times to Today Teaching Resources
L2 Skills for Life, p. 289 AR, GT, LPR, SN

Teacher's Edition
L1 For Special Needs Students, TE p. 135

Social Studies Skills Tutor CD-ROM
L1 Analyzing and Interpreting Special-Purpose Maps ELL, LPR, SN

Spanish Support
L2 Guided Reading and Review (Spanish), p. 40 ELL

Assess and Reteach

Assess Progress
Evaluate student comprehension with the section assessment and section quiz.

Reteach
Assign the Reading and Vocabulary Study Guide to help struggling students.

Extend
Extend the lesson by assigning an Internet activity.

Instructional Resources

All in One Medieval Times to Today Teaching Resources
L2 Section Quiz, p. 280
  Rubric for Assessing a Newspaper Article, p. 298

Reading and Vocabulary Study Guide
L1 Chapter 5, Section 3, pp. 52–54

PHSchool.com
L3 **For:** Environmental and Global Issues: Why Do Wars Begin?
  Web Code: lgd-8506

Differentiated Instruction

Spanish Support
L2 Section Quiz (Spanish), p. 41 ELL

Teacher's Edition
L1 For Special Needs Students, TE p. 139

Social Studies Skills Tutor CD-ROM
L1 Distinguishing Fact and Opinion ELL, LPR, SN

Key
L1 Basic to Average L3 Average to Advanced
L2 For All Students

LPR Less Proficient Readers
AR Advanced Readers
SN Special Needs Students

GT Gifted and Talented
ELL English Language Learners

Section 4 The Power of Kings

 5 periods, 2.5 blocks (includes Chapter Review and Assessment and Literature)

Social Studies Objectives

1. Learn about the forces that led to nation building in Europe.
2. Find out about nation building in England.
3. Discover how the Hundred Years' War affected England and France.

Reading/Language Arts Objective

Identify the order of events to help in understanding and remembering them.

Prepare to Read	Instructional Resources	Differentiated Instruction
Build Background Knowledge Discuss how the United States became a nation. **Set a Purpose for Reading** Have students begin to fill out the *Reading Readiness Guide*. **Preview Key Terms** Teach the section's Key Terms. **Target Reading Skill** Introduce the section's Target Reading Skill of **identifying sequence**.	**All in One Medieval Times to Today Teaching Resources** **L2** Reading Readiness Guide, p. 282 **L2** Identify Sequence, p. 286	**Spanish Reading and Vocabulary Study Guide** **L1** Chapter 5, Section 4, pp. 41–42 ELL

Instruct	Instructional Resources	Differentiated Instruction
Nation Building Discuss how the decline of feudalism led to the building of nations and affected the Church's power. **Target Reading Skill** Review **identifying sequence**. **Changes in England** Discuss King John and the Magna Carta. **The Hundred Years' War** Discuss the causes and effects of the Hundred Years' War.	**All in One Medieval Times to Today Teaching Resources** **L2** Guided Reading and Review, p. 283 **L2** Reading Readiness Guide, p. 282 **Medieval Times to Today Transparencies** **L2** Transparency B11: Chart/Table **L2** Section Reading Support Transparency MT 68	**All in One Medieval Times to Today Teaching Resources** **L2** Organizing Details, p. 295 AR, GT, LPR, SN Rubric for Assessing a Student Poem, p. 300 **Teacher's Edition** **L2** For English Language Learners, TE pp. 142, 150 **Spanish Support** **L2** Guided Reading and Review (Spanish), p. 42 ELL

Assess and Reteach	Instructional Resources	Differentiated Instruction
Assess Progress Evaluate student comprehension with the section assessment and section quiz. **Reteach** Assign the Reading and Vocabulary Study Guide to help struggling students. **Extend** Extend the lesson by assigning a Book Project.	**All in One Medieval Times to Today Teaching Resources** **L2** Section Quiz, p. 284 **L3** Book Project: Birth of a Nation, pp. 83–85 Rubric for Assessing a Writing Assignment, p. 297 **L2** Word Knowledge, p. 287 **L2** Vocabulary Development, p. 296 Rubric for Assessing a Report, p. 299 **L2** Chapter Tests A and B, pp. 301–306 **Reading and Vocabulary Study Guide** **L1** Chapter 5, Section 4, pp. 55–57	**Spanish Support** **L2** Section Quiz (Spanish), p. 43 ELL **L2** Chapter Summary (Spanish), p. 44 ELL **L2** Vocabulary Development (Spanish), p. 45 ELL **Medieval Times to Today Transparencies** **L1** Transparency B5: Flow Chart

Key

L1 Basic to Average	**L3** Average to Advanced	LPR Less Proficient Readers	GT Gifted and Talented
L2 For All Students		AR Advanced Readers	ELL English Language Learners
		SN Special Needs Students	

Reading Background

Question-Answer Relationships

Explain to students that there are many different types of questions. Understanding question-answer relationships can help students answer questions correctly and develop appropriate questions for initiating discussions. Give students examples of the different types of questions, referring to this chapter in the Student Edition.

Questions with:

1. Answers that are found explicitly in one or two sentences in the book. (*Example: Who were the Vikings?*)
2. Answers that are found in several different paragraphs in the book. (*Example: What were the roles of different people, such as lords, vassals, and noblewomen, under feudalism?*)
3. Answers that are not found directly in the book, but instead require you to think about what you've read. (*Example: Why do you think the Vikings did not unite the lands they settled into an empire?*)
4. Answers that are not found directly in the book and which you can answer without having read the book. (*Example: Why might a pilgrimage, or travel to a sacred place, be important to some people?*)

Divide students into teams. Have each team create examples of each type of question. Invite the teams to present the questions to the class. Before answering each question, the other students in the class should name the type of question and justify it by finding the answer in the text. Once students are comfortable with question-answer relationships, they can develop their own questions for class discussion, keeping in mind that the more interpretive type 2, 3, and 4 questions usually lead to more complex discussions.

Pattern Puzzles

One way for students to become familiar with paragraph structure is to have them complete pattern puzzles. To do this, form students into groups or pairs. Write a paragraph from the textbook on a piece of paper. Next, cut each sentence into a separate strip of paper and put the strips into an envelope. Do this with enough paragraphs to distribute to all the groups. Each group should arrange the strips into a logical paragraph. Remind students that a paragraph consists of a main idea and supporting details. The first sentence usually introduces the information in the paragraph, and the last sentence is frequently a conclusion.

World Studies Background

Geoffrey Chaucer (c. 1342–1400)

Geoffrey Chaucer was an English poet best known for his work, *The Canterbury Tales,* a poem about 17,000 lines long. He was also a courtier, diplomat, and civil servant. Chaucer invaded France with Edward III's army in 1359. He later served as a messenger during peace negotiations between England and France. In the 1370s, Chaucer was sent on a number of diplomatic missions to France and Italy.

The Beginnings of a Postal Service

Although no regulated postal service existed in the Middle Ages, kings and vassals as well as religious orders and universities needed to correspond frequently. Therefore, they set up groups of messengers to transmit information. Messenger systems improved with the increase in trade in the later Middle Ages, and corporations and guilds employed messengers to contact their customers. The travel necessary for trading was often combined with the carrying of letters. The invention of the printing press in the late 1400s increased demand for written correspondence, and some powerful families in Europe developed postal organizations. Government regulation of the postal service began in 1477, when Louis XI established the Royal Postal Service in France.

Infoplease® provides a wealth of useful information for the classroom. You can use this resource to strengthen your background on the subjects covered in this chapter. Have students visit this advertising-free site as a starting point for projects requiring research.

 Use Web Code **lgd-8500** for **Infoplease®**.

Sharing Key Concepts

Students can learn and remember key concepts and vocabulary from the chapter through discussion with their classmates. One way for students to do this is to complete an activity in which they will be sharing information with other students. After students have read through the chapter at least once, ask each student to write an explanation for one Key Term, high-use word, or concept from the chapter on an index card. Then, have students form two concentric circles so that each student is facing another. The pairs should explain the concepts from their index cards to one another. Encourage students to ask each other to elaborate upon their ideas, or to explain concepts that may be unclear. Students then trade cards and the outside circle moves clockwise one person. Repeat the process until students end up with their original cards.

Identifying Author's Craft

Knowing the author's craft, or strategy for writing, can help students understand the text. Explain that authors often present information *chronologically,* using *cause-and-effect,* or by *comparing and contrasting.* Have students choose which of these strategies was used to write each of the following sentences from the chapter:

1. *After Charlemagne's death, his empire was divided among his three sons.* (chronology)
2. *Like the men in her family, a noblewoman was often sent to other noble families for training.* (compare and contrast)
3. *The Church also held that if people* didn't *obey those rules, they would be punished after death.* (cause-and-effect)

Challenge students to determine the author's craft in other paragraphs and sections throughout the chapter.

Roger Bacon (c. 1220–1292)

The increase in learning during the Middle Ages is reflected by Roger Bacon, a medieval philosopher, scholar, and advocate of experimental science. Trained in geometry, arithmetic, music, and astronomy, Bacon was the first European to thoroughly describe the process of making gunpowder. He also developed a description of spectacles, or eyeglasses. In the late 1200s, after the pope's suggestion, Bacon created two works that attempted to scientifically explain the natural world through direct study and experimentation. Unrelenting in his quest for knowledge, Bacon wrote a number of other works, most of which remained incomplete.

Stained Glass

Stained glass windows are possibly the most remarkable elements in medieval architecture. Early medieval windows were filled with sheets of wood or marble pierced with holes into which glass, colored by mixing with metal oxides in a molten state, was inserted. Later, pieces of colored glass were connected with lead to form rich designs and symbolic pictorial compositions.

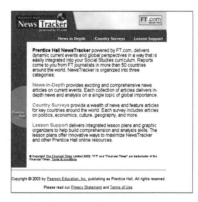

Get in-depth information on topics of global importance with **Prentice Hall Newstracker,** powered by FT.com.

Use Web Code **lgd-8505** for **Prentice Hall Newstracker.**

116h

Chapter 5

Guiding Questions
Remind students about the Guiding Questions introduced at the beginning of the book.

Section 1 relates to **Guiding Question** ④ **What types of government were formed in these societies?** *(Medieval Europeans developed a feudal system of government. Land was owned by kings or lords and held by vassals in return for their loyalty. Power belonged to those who controlled the land.)*

Section 2 relates to **Guiding Question** ③ **What was the pattern of day-to-day life in these societies?** *(Medieval towns and cities had a large middle class made up of merchants, traders, and crafts workers. Towns and cities were often overcrowded, and their lack of sanitation bred disease.)*

Section 3 relates to **Guiding Question** ② **How did each society's belief system affect its history?** *(In 1096 European Christians launched the Crusades, which were military expeditions to bring Jerusalem—a city sacred to Christians as well as Muslims and Jews—under Christian control.)*

Section 4 relates to **Guiding Question** ④ **What types of government were formed in these societies?** *(By the late Middle Ages, large parts of Europe were unifying under a single king, instead of being ruled by many nobles. Gradually, these kingdoms evolved into nations.)*

⊙ Target Reading Skill
In this chapter, students will learn and apply the reading skill of sequence. Use the following worksheets to help students practice this skill:

All in One Medieval Times to Today Teaching Resources, *Recognize Sequence Signal Words,* p. 285; *Identify Sequence,* p. 286

Differentiated Instruction

The following Teacher's Edition strategies are suitable for students of varying abilities.

Advanced Readers, pp. 121, 130
English Language Learners, pp. 142, 150
Gifted and Talented , pp. 120, 128
Less Proficient Readers, pp. 120, 129
Special Needs Students, pp. 121, 124, 135, 139

Chapter 5
Europe in the Middle Ages

Chapter Preview
This chapter will introduce you to life in Europe during the Middle Ages.

Section 1
Feudalism and the Manor System

Section 2
The Church and the Rise of Cities

Section 3
The Crusades

Section 4
The Power of Kings

⊙ Target Reading Skill
Sequence In this chapter you will focus on using sequence to note the order in which events take place. This skill will help you understand and remember those events.

▶ The medieval castle at Carcassonne, France

Bibliography

For the Teacher
Seward, Desmond. *The Hundred Years' War: The English in France 1337–1453.* Penguin USA, 1999.
Vallejo, Yli Remo. *The Crusades.* AeroArt International Inc., 2003.
Becher, Matthias. *Charlemagne.* Yale University Press, 2003.

For the Student
L1 McDonald, Fiona, and David Salariya. *How Would You Survive in the Middle Ages?* Scholastic Library Publishing, 1997.
L2 Woog, Adam. *Medieval Knight.* Gale Group, 2003.
L3 Platt, Richard and Melanie Rice. *Crusades: The Battle for Jerusalem.* DK Publishing, 2001.

Europe in 1300

NORWAY

SWEDEN

SCOTLAND

*North
Sea*

IRELAND
(England)

Copenhagen

NOVGOROD

TEUTONIC ORDER

Baltic Sea

WALES
(England)

ENGLAND

DENMARK

LITHUANIA

London

RUSSIAN
STATES

*ATLANTIC
OCEAN*

Frankfurt

HOLY

Kiev

Paris

ROMAN

FRANCE

EMPIRE

POLAND

GOLDEN HORDE

GASCONY
(England)

NAVARRE

Venice

•Budapest

HUNGARY

Black Sea

EASTERN
CHRISTIAN
STATES

PORTUGAL

ARAGON

PAPAL
STATES

VENICE

CASTILE

Rome•

Toledo•

SERBIA

BULGARIA

Constantinople•

GRANADA

MALLORCA

SARDINIA
(Aragon)

NAPLES

BYZANTINE EMPIRE

TURKISH AND
MONGOL STATES

SICILY
(Aragon)

SMALL GREEK
STATES

Mediterranean Sea

CRETE
(Venice)

CYPRUS

KEY

— Border
• City

0 miles   500

0 kilometers   500

Lambert Azimuthal Equal Area

Regions In 1300, Europe was made up of many separate kingdoms and states. **Identify** Which names on the map are familiar to you? Which are not? **Apply Information** What route might merchants traveling from Constantinople to Venice take? Which states and bodies of water would they cross?

Go Online
PHSchool.com Use Web Code
lgp-8511 for step-by-step
map skills practice.

Chapter 5 **117**

MAP MASTER™ Skills Activity

- Have students study the names of the various kingdoms shown on the map. Ask them to list the names of kingdoms that contain the names of countries that exist in Europe today.

Go Online
PHSchool.com Students may practice their map skills using the interactive online version of this map.

Using the Visual   L2

Reach Into Your Background
Have students study the photograph on pp. 116–117 and read the caption on p. 116. Discuss the location and architectural features of the castle with students. *(on top of a hill; high stone walls, small window openings)* Ask **Why do you think medieval castles would have had these features?** Conduct a Give One, Get One activity (TE, p. T37) to elicit student responses.

Answers

MAP MASTER Skills Activity **Identify** Answers will vary: students may find England, Ireland, Scotland and France familiar, and Castile, Aragon, and Holy Roman Empire may be unfamiliar.
Apply Information Merchants traveling from Constantinople to Venice would travel down the coast of the small Greek States past Crete to the Mediterranean Sea, then northward past the coasts of the Byzantine Empire, Serbia, and Hungary to the east and Naples and the Papal States to the west.

Chapter Resources

Teaching Resources
- L2 Vocabulary Development, p. 296
- L2 Skills for Life, p. 289
- L2 Chapter Tests A and B, pp. 301–306

Spanish Support
- L2 Spanish Chapter Summary, p. 44
- L2 Spanish Vocabulary Development, p. 45

Media and Technology
- L1 Student Edition on Audio CD
- L1 Guided Reading Audiotapes, English and Spanish
- L2 Social Studies Skills Tutor CD-ROM
- **Exam*View*® Test Bank CD-ROM**

Discovery CHANNEL **SCHOOL** World Studies Video Program

interactive Textbook

PRENTICE HALL
TeacherEXPRESS™
Plan • Teach • Assess

Objectives

Social Studies

1. Learn when the Middle Ages were and what they were like.
2. Find out how land and power were divided under feudalism.
3. Learn how the manor system worked.
4. Discover what life was like for peasants and serfs.

Reading/Language Arts

Recognize sequence signal words to help in understanding the relationships in time between ideas and events.

Prepare to Read

Build Background Knowledge   **L2**

Ask students to preview the headings and visuals in this section. Tell them to make predictions about what they will learn. Provide a few examples to get students started. Have them engage in a Think-Write-Pair-Share activity (TE, p. T36) to generate a list of predictions. Write their responses on the chalkboard.

Set a Purpose for Reading   **L2**

- Preview the Objectives.

- Read each statement in the *Reading Readiness Guide* aloud. Ask students to mark the statements true or false.

- Have students discuss the statements in pairs or groups of four, then mark their guides again. Use the Numbered Heads participation strategy (TE, p. T36) to call on students to share their group's perspectives.

All in One Medieval Times to Today Teaching Resources, *Reading Readiness Guide,* p. 270

Vocabulary Builder

Preview Key Terms   **L2**

Pronounce each Key Term, then ask the students to say the word with you. Provide a simple explanation such as, "The period known as the Middle Ages was given this title because it falls between ancient times and modern times."

Feudalism and the Manor System

Prepare to Read

Objectives

In this section, you will

1. Learn when the Middle Ages were and what they were like.
2. Find out how land and power were divided under feudalism.
3. Learn how the manor system worked.
4. Discover what life was like for peasants and serfs.

Taking Notes

As you read this section, look for the major features of feudalism. Copy the web diagram below and record your findings in it.

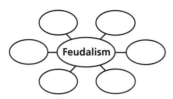

Target Reading Skill

Recognize Sequence Signal Words Noting the order in which important events take place can help you understand how the events relate to one another. Sequence signal words, such as *first, then, began,* and *in [date],* point out relationships in time. Look for such words in this section to help you understand the Middle Ages.

Key Terms

- **knight** (nyt) *n.* a man who received honor and land in exchange for serving a lord as a soldier
- **Middle Ages** (MID ul AY juz) *n.* the years between ancient and modern times
- **medieval** (mee dee EE vul) *adj.* referring to the Middle Ages
- **feudalism** (FYOOD ul iz um) *n.* a system in which land was owned by kings or lords but held by vassals in return for their loyalty
- **manor** (MAN ur) *n.* a large estate, often including farms and a village, ruled by a lord
- **serf** (surf) *n.* a farm worker considered part of the manor on which he or she worked

A knighting ceremony

118 *Medieval Times to Today*

As darkness fell, a young man put on a white tunic and red and black cloaks. Then he walked to the church, where he spent the long night alone, praying. Soon he would no longer be a mere squire, or knight-in-training. He would become a real **knight,** who would receive honor and land in exchange for serving his lord as a soldier.

The next morning, the squire entered the castle courtyard, where knights and ladies had gathered. His lord presented him with his sword, spurs, and shield. The squire knelt. Then he felt the lord's sword lightly tap him on each shoulder. "In the name of God, Saint Michael, and Saint George, I call you a knight," declared the lord. "Be loyal, brave, and true."

A knight was expected to be loyal to the lord who knighted him. His lord was loyal to a more powerful lord or king. Knights and lords protected the less powerful people loyal to them. This system held society together.

Target Reading Skill   **L2**

Recognize Sequence Signal Words Point out the Target Reading Skill. Tell students that recognizing sequence signal words will help them find the relationship between events and ideas.

Model the skill by identifying the signal words in Charlemagne Reunites Western Europe on p. 120 (*in 768, at the time, soon, nearly 50 years, after Charlemagne's death*).

Give students *Recognize Sequence Signal Words*. Have them complete the activity in groups.

All in One Medieval Times to Today Teaching Resources, *Recognize Sequence Signal Words,* p. 285

The Middle Ages

A thousand years ago, scenes like the one you just read about took place throughout Western Europe. These were the times of knights in shining armor, lords and ladies, and castles and cathedrals. These were the **Middle Ages,** the years between ancient times and modern times.

Historians usually say that ancient times lasted until about A.D. 500 and that modern times started about 1500. The period in the middle, the Middle Ages, is also called the **medieval** period. *Medieval* comes from Latin words that mean "middle ages."

The Collapse of the Roman Empire The Middle Ages began with the collapse of the Roman Empire in Western Europe. For centuries, the Roman Empire had provided order and stability in the region. It had spread its culture, the Latin language, and Christianity across the continent. Over time, however, the Roman Empire grew weak. It suffered economic and social troubles. Worse, the Roman Empire also suffered from invasions by peoples from the north.

Bronze plaque of a Lombard warrior

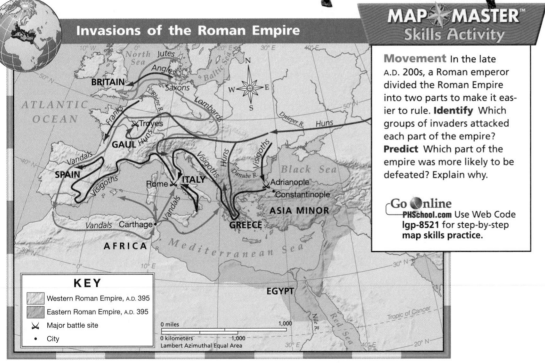

Invasions of the Roman Empire

MAP MASTER™
Skills Activity

Movement In the late A.D. 200s, a Roman emperor divided the Roman Empire into two parts to make it easier to rule. **Identify** Which groups of invaders attacked each part of the empire? **Predict** Which part of the empire was more likely to be defeated? Explain why.

Go Online
PHSchool.com Use Web Code lgp-8521 for step-by-step map skills practice.

KEY
- Western Roman Empire, A.D. 395
- Eastern Roman Empire, A.D. 395
- ✕ Major battle site
- • City

0 miles 1,000
0 kilometers 1,000
Lambert Azimuthal Equal Area

Vocabulary Builder

Use the information below to teach students this section's high-use words.

High-Use Word	Definition and Sample Sentence
promote, p. 120	*v.* to contribute to the growth of The students organized a pep rally to **promote** school pride.
majority, p. 122	*n.* a number greater than half of a total The **majority** of the students in the class enjoyed the extended recess.
interior, p. 123	*n.* the inner part of something The **interior** of the car was much cleaner than the outside of it.

The Middle Ages L2

Guided Instruction

- **Vocabulary Builder** Clarify the high-use word **promote** before reading.

- Read The Middle Ages using the Oral Cloze strategy (TE, p. T33).

- Ask students **When did the Middle Ages begin?** *(about A.D. 500)* **When did they end?** *(about A.D. 1500)*

- Discuss the reasons why the Roman Empire collapsed. *(It suffered economic and social troubles and was invaded by people from the north.)*

Answers

MAP MASTER
Skills Activity **Identify** Visigoths and Huns attacked the Eastern Roman Empire; Visigoths, Huns, Vandals, Franks, Lombards, Saxons, Angles, and Jutes attacked the Western Empire. **Predict** The Western European Empire; according to the map, this region suffered more invasions than the Eastern Roman Empire.

Go Online
PHSchool.com Students may practice their map skills using the interactive online version of this map.

Guided Instruction (continued)

- Ask students **What did Charlemagne accomplish during his reign?** *(He kept Western Europe united, established schools, spread the Christian religion, issued money, and improved the economy.)*

- Ask **Who were the Vikings?** *(skilled sailors and tough warriors who came from northern Europe)*

- Have students compare the collapse of the Roman Empire with the collapse of Charlemagne's empire. *(Invasions by people from the north helped lead to the collapse of both empires.)*

Independent Practice

Assign *Guided Reading and Review.*

All in One **Medieval Times to Today Teaching Resources,** *Guided Reading and Review,* p. 271

Monitor Progress

Circulate and make sure students are correctly answering the questions. Provide assistance as needed.

⟳ Target Reading Skill

Recognize Sequence Signal Words As a follow up, ask students to answer the Target Reading Skill question in the Student Edition. *(began, continued)*

The Emperor Charlemagne
In return for Charlemagne's support of the Church, Pope Leo III crowned him emperor in 800. **Analyze Images** *How does this statue show Charlemagne's greatness and power?*

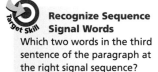

Recognize Sequence Signal Words
Which two words in the third sentence of the paragraph at the right signal sequence?

In wave after wave, the invaders destroyed Roman towns and cut off trade routes. They claimed parts of the empire for themselves. Because these peoples kept their own languages and laws, they broke the bonds that had held the Roman Empire together.

By about A.D. 500, the Roman Empire in Western Europe had completely collapsed. It was replaced by a patchwork of small kingdoms. Reading and writing were in danger of disappearing from Europe because many of the invading groups could not do either.

Charlemagne Reunites Western Europe One of the invading groups was the Franks. They claimed the area called Gaul, which is now France. In fact, the name *France* comes from the word "Franks." In 768, a skilled military leader named Charlemagne (SHAHR luh mayn) became king of the Franks.

At the time, the many small kingdoms of Western Europe were often at war with one another. Charlemagne expanded his kingdom by conquering these weaker kingdoms. Soon, he ruled an empire that stretched across most of Western Europe.

Charlemagne ruled his empire for nearly 50 years. During that time he worked hard to keep Western Europe united. He established schools throughout the land to promote learning and culture. He spread the Christian religion. He issued money and improved the economy. Western Europe had not been so prosperous or so united since the time of the Roman Empire.

After Charlemagne's death, his empire was divided among his three sons. They fought one another, weakening the empire. Other groups also attacked the weakened empire. Perhaps the fiercest attacks were made by the Vikings.

Attacks From the North The Vikings came from the far north of Europe—present-day Denmark, Sweden, and Norway. They were skilled sailors and tough warriors. Their attacks began around 800 and continued for about 300 years. Relying on surprise, the Vikings burned and looted European towns. But they also reopened trade routes to Mediterranean lands and beyond. And they settled in other parts of northern Europe, mixing with the local populations. Even so, the Vikings did not unite these lands into a lasting empire.

✓ Reading Check Why did Charlemagne's empire fall apart?

Answers

Analyze Images Possible answer: The crown shows that Charlemagne was in power and the armor shows his strength.

✓ Reading Check When Charlemagne died, the empire was divided among his three sons who fought one another and weakened the empire. Invasions from outsiders, such as the Vikings, also contributed to the empire's collapse.

Differentiated Instruction

For Less Proficient Readers **L1**
Have students read the section as they listen to the recorded version on the Student Edition on Audio CD. Check for comprehension by pausing the CD and asking students to share their answers to the Reading Checks.

⊙ Chapter 5, Section 1, **Student Edition on Audio CD**

For Gifted and Talented **L3**
Ask students to do Internet or library research to find out more about Charlemagne. Tell them to use what they learn to write a short biography about him. Encourage them to include illustrations and other helpful visuals in their biographies.

Feudalism: A Kind of Government

Charlemagne's empire was gone. Western Europe was again divided into many small kingdoms. Viking attacks were a constant threat. Life was dangerous. The people of Europe had to find a way to defend themselves and to organize their communities. Slowly they worked out a new system of government.

The Feudal System The system that developed was called feudalism. Under **feudalism**, land was owned by kings or lords but held by vassals in return for their loyalty. By about 1000, feudalism was the way of life throughout Western Europe. It would last for hundreds of years.

In medieval Europe, power belonged to those who controlled the land. These landowners were nobles, such as barons and princes. They gave a share of land, called a fief (feef) to each of their vassals, who promised to follow the landowner's laws and to fight for him. A vassal could also be a lord.

Feudal Duties Lords promised to treat their vassals with honor. In addition, the chief duty of lords was to protect their vassals and their lands. If a vassal with young children died, for example, the lord became the children's protector. The lord also asked his vassals' advice before making laws or going to war.

Vassals were expected to raise and lead armies that would fight for their lord. Many of these vassals were knights —professional horse soldiers who led other men into battle. Vassals also appeared at the lord's court when commanded to do so. And they paid taxes, often in the form of crops, to their lords.

✓ **Reading Check** What did lords give vassals in exchange for the vassals' loyalty?

The Manor System

Feudalism was the way medieval Europeans organized power and government. Manorialism was the way they organized their economy. This system was based on the **manor,** a large estate that included farm fields, pastures, and often an entire village. It also included a large house, called the manor house, where the lord, or ruler, of the manor lived.

Links Across The World

Vikings in America The Vikings did not limit their conquests to Europe. They went as far south as North Africa. Viking ships, such as the one shown below, also traveled westward to Greenland and beyond. An Icelandic saga, or story, gives clues about the location of Vinland, a Viking settlement in lands west of Greenland. Historians who have studied these clues and examined ruins in North America think that Vinland was probably in what is now Newfoundland, Canada.

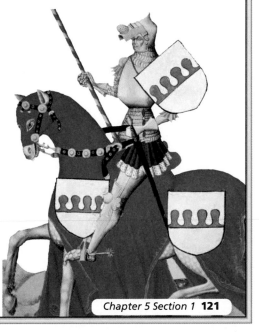

A medieval knight in armor

Links

Read the **Links Across the World** on this page. Ask students **What has led some historians to suggest that Vinland was located in Newfoundland?** *(clues provided in an Icelandic saga and the study of ruins in North America)*

Feudalism: A Kind of Government 🔲L2

Guided Instruction

- Read Feudalism: A Kind of Government with students. As students read, circulate and make sure individuals can answer the Reading Check question.

- Ask students **Who held the power in the feudal system?** *(those who owned land, such as kings, barons, and princes)*

- Ask **Why do you think lords believed it was important to give vassals land and treat them well?** *(Possible answer: They wanted vassals to remain loyal and fight hard for them when necessary.)*

Independent Practice

Ask students to create the Taking Notes graphic organizer on a separate piece of paper. Tell them to fill in the circles with details about feudalism. Briefly model how to choose the correct details.

Monitor Progress

As students fill in the graphic organizer, circulate and make sure individuals are choosing the correct details. Provide assistance as needed.

Answer

✓ **Reading Check** a share of their land

The Manor System L2

Peasants and Serfs L2

Guided Instruction

- **Vocabulary Builder** Clarify the high-use academic words **majority** and **interior** before reading.

- Read The Manor System and Peasants and Serfs together as a class.

- Ask students to explain the difference between the manor system and feudalism. (*Feudalism was the way medieval Europeans organized their government, while the manor system was the way they organized their economy.*)

- Discuss the role of noblewomen in feudal society. (*A noblewoman managed the household, provided medical care, and supervised servants.*)

Independent Practice

Ask students to complete their graphic organizers with the information they have just learned.

Monitor Progress

- Show *Section Reading Support Transparency MT 65* and ask students to check their graphic organizers individually. Go over key concepts and clarify key vocabulary as needed.

  Medieval Times to Today Transparencies, *Section Reading Support Transparency MT 65*

Show students *Feudal Life in the Middle Ages.* Ask **How was society divided under feudalism?** (*It was strictly divided into social classes, including lords and peasants.*)

- Tell students to fill in the last column of the *Reading Readiness Guide.* Probe for what they learned that confirms or invalidates each statement.

  All in One Medieval Times to Today Teaching Resources, *Reading Readiness Guide,* p. 270

Answers

Generalize Possible answer: Noblewomen were educated and were in charge of household functions.

✓ Reading Check They were far from towns, villages, or other manors.

Noblewomen at Home
The larger illustration shows a lady in charge of a dinner where her guests are seated according to rank. A noblewoman sits at her desk in the smaller illustration. **Generalize** *What can you infer about the lives of noblewomen from these illustrations?*

Learn about the knights and castles of the Middle Ages.

Lords and Manors The lord of the manor was typically a vassal of a king or of a more powerful lord. The manor was part of his fief. Most manors were far from towns, villages, and other manors. Therefore, they had to be self-sufficient, or able to supply their own needs. Food, clothing, and other things needed by the people who lived on the manor were made there.

A lord depended on the wealth his manor provided. He ruled over his manor—and the poor people who lived there. He made the rules and acted as judge. He decided who would oversee the farming and other daily work. And he collected taxes from the peasants who lived on the manor.

The Role of Noblewomen Women of the noble classes also played an important part in feudal society. Like the men in her family, a noblewoman went to other noble families for training. Then, she took her place as lady of the household. She managed the household, performed necessary medical tasks, and supervised servants. When her husband or father was away fighting, she often served as "lord of the manor," making important decisions.

✓ Reading Check Why did manors have to be self-sufficient?

Peasants and Serfs

The majority of the people of medieval Europe were not lords, ladies, or knights. They were peasants, a group of people who made their living as farmers and laborers. Their lives were very different from the lives of the nobles.

Peasants were often very poor. They did all of the work on the manors of the Middle Ages. They farmed the lord's fields to raise food for his household. They were only allowed to farm a small strip of land for themselves. Even so, they had to give part of their own harvest to their lord.

Tied to the Manor Most peasants were also serfs. **Serfs** were peasants who were considered to be part of the manor. When a noble was given a manor as part of his fief, its serfs became his. They could not leave the manor, or even get married, without his permission.

Although serfs were tied to manors, they were not quite slaves. A successful serf could save money to buy his freedom and his own plot of land. A serf who escaped to a city and lived there for a year and a day without being caught also became free. Most serfs, however, remained serfs their whole lives.

A Hard Life Medieval peasants worked hard for most of their lives. They farmed their own fields and those of their lord. Men, women, and children were all required to work.

Peasants lived in one-room huts that often had only a single opening for a window. For heating and cooking, they built a fire on the dirt floor. Smoke filled the dark, cramped interior before drifting out of a hole in the roof. Peasants ate mostly simple foods such as black bread, cabbage, and turnips. They rarely ate meat, since the animals of the manor and surrounding land were reserved for their lord. Peasants even suffered when they slept: their mattresses were cloth sacks stuffed with straw.

Peasant Life
Peasant women worked in the fields along with the men. **Contrast** *Use this illustration and those on page 122 to contrast the lives of peasant women and noblewomen.*

✓ **Reading Check** What was life like for medieval peasants?

Section **1** Assessment

Key Terms
Review the key terms at the beginning of this section. Use each term in a sentence that explains its meaning.

Target Reading Skill
Review the text under the heading The Collapse of the Roman Empire. List the words that signal the order of events.

Comprehension and Critical Thinking
1. (a) **Recall** When were the Middle Ages?

(b) Identify Cause and Effect Why did the collapse of the Roman Empire lead to a new age in Western Europe?
2. (a) **Define** What was feudalism?
(b) **Explain** How did the system of feudalism work?
3. (a) **Describe** How was a manor organized?
(b) **Conclude** Why did a manor produce a wide variety of goods?
4. (a) **Explain** What was the relationship of a serf to his or her manor?
(b) **Infer** How and why might a serf become free?

Writing Activity
During the Middle Ages, most poor peasants remained poor their entire lives. Why do you think this was so? Write a paragraph explaining what you think the reason or reasons were.

Go Online
PHSchool.com

For: An activity on feudalism
Visit: PHSchool.com
Web Code: lgd-8501

Chapter 5 Section 1 **123**

Section 1 Assessment

Key Terms
Students' sentences should reflect knowledge of each Key Term.

Target Reading Skill
began, for centuries, over time, by about 500

Comprehension and Critical Thinking
1. (a) from about A.D. 500 to 1500, between ancient times and modern times (b) The empire had broken into many small kingdoms, and other groups began moving into the region.
2. (a) the system of government that existed in Western Europe during the Middle Ages (b) Landowner nobles such as lords and kings held the power. Vassals held the land in return for their loyalty to the nobles. Vassals were expected to raise armies and fight for the nobles when necessary.

3. (a) A manor was a large estate given to a lord as part of his fief. The lord ruled the manor and controlled the peasants who farmed the manor's land. (b) People who lived on a manor had to produce all of the items they needed.

4. (a) A serf was considered to be part of the manor. (b) Serfs could become free by buying their freedom and a plot of land or by running away to a city without being caught for a year and a day.

Chapter 5 Section 1 **123**

Assess and Reteach

Assess Progress   **L2**

Have students complete the Section Assessment. Administer the *Section Quiz*.

All in One **Medieval Times to Today Teaching Resources,** *Section Quiz,* p. 272

Reteach   **L1**

If students need more instruction, have them read this section in the Reading and Vocabulary Study Guide.

📖 Chapter 5, Section 1, **Medieval Times to Today Reading and Vocabulary Study Guide,** pp. 46–48

Extend   **L3**

Assign the *Small Group Activity* in which students will write a documentary about knights in the Middle Ages.

All in One **Medieval Times to Today Teaching Resources,** *Small Group Activity: Writing a Documentary,* pp. 290–293

Answers

Contrast Possible answer: Both classes of women had responsibilities, but peasant women had to perform grueling physical labor.

✓ **Reading Check** Peasants worked hard for most of their lives, lived in one-room huts, slept on uncomfortable hay beds, and ate simple foods.

Writing Activity

Use the *Rubric for Assessing a Writing Assignment* to evaluate students' paragraphs.

All in One **Medieval Times to Today Teaching Resources,** *Rubric for Assessing a Writing Assignment,* p. 297

Go Online
PHSchool.com Typing in the Web code when prompted will bring students directly to detailed instructions for this activity.

Focus On A Medieval Manor

L2

Guided Instruction

- Ask students to read the text and study the art, photos, and captions on these pages.

- Ask students **What kinds of goods were produced on manor estates?** *(grain, bread, fence posts, shingles, planks, linen cloth, shirts, honey, chickens, eggs, cheese, and butter.)* **What were many of these goods used for?** *(Nobles depended on what peasants produce to pay taxes to higher nobles and to the king.)*

- Ask students **How did the people in a medieval manor use the surrounding manor lands?** *(The lands and forests surrounding the peasant houses provided grain, fruits, and vegetables; peasants grazed cattle, sheep, and goats in the fields, and pigs roamed in the forests in search of food; woods provided timber and fuel; nobles hunted in the forests.)*

- As a class, answer the Assessment questions. Allow students to briefly discuss their responses with a partner before sharing their answers with the class.

Focus On
A Medieval Manor

Although peasants and nobles led very different lives, their reliance on the lands of the manor estate bound them together. Peasants worked the land to pay what they owed to their lords. Nobles depended on what the peasants produced so that they could pay taxes to higher nobles and to the king. In addition to cash, taxes were paid in grain, bread, fence posts, shingles and planks, linen cloth, shirts, honey, chickens, eggs, cheese, and butter. All of these goods were produced on the manor estate.

A peasant's house

The Manor Estate Medieval manors included the lord's home, the homes of the peasants and serfs, a mill for grinding grain, and often a chapel or a church. Attached to the manor house, or in a separate building, was a bakery that peasants and serfs would use for baking bread.

Most people in medieval Europe were agricultural workers. The lands and forests surrounding the manor and peasant houses provided grain, fruits, and vegetables. Peasants grazed cattle, sheep, and goats in the manor fields. Their pigs roamed the manor's woodlands in search of food. Woodlands also provided timber for building and fuel. Hunting in the forests was reserved for the nobles.

The illustration on the facing page shows a manor estate of the Middle Ages. At the top of this page is a shield painted with a noble's coat of arms.

124 Medieval Times to Today

Differentiated Instruction

For Special Needs Students   L2
Help reinforce the different parts of a manor by having students draw and label their own picture of a medieval manor. Tell them to use the diagram on p. 125 as a guide, and to label the different buildings in their drawings. Encourage students to be creative, and add animals and people to their drawings. Then have them present their drawings to the class.

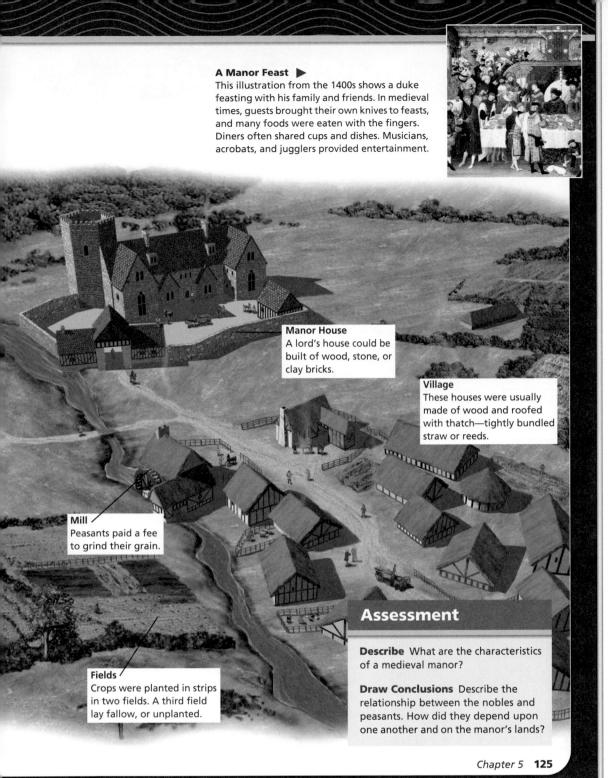

A Manor Feast ▶
This illustration from the 1400s shows a duke feasting with his family and friends. In medieval times, guests brought their own knives to feasts, and many foods were eaten with the fingers. Diners often shared cups and dishes. Musicians, acrobats, and jugglers provided entertainment.

Manor House
A lord's house could be built of wood, stone, or clay bricks.

Village
These houses were usually made of wood and roofed with thatch—tightly bundled straw or reeds.

Mill
Peasants paid a fee to grind their grain.

Fields
Crops were planted in strips in two fields. A third field lay fallow, or unplanted.

Assessment

Describe What are the characteristics of a medieval manor?

Draw Conclusions Describe the relationship between the nobles and peasants. How did they depend upon one another and on the manor's lands?

Independent Practice

Ask students to carefully examine the illustration of a manor feast on this page, and reread its accompanying caption. Then ask students to think about the ways in which meals in their homes today are similar or different. Conduct an Idea Wave (TE, p. T35) to elicit student responses, and then list them on the board.

Answers

Assessment

Describe Medieval manors included the lord's home and homes of the peasants and serfs, a mill, a chapel or church, a bakery, and usually surrounding fields for growing crops, and woodlands.
Draw Conclusions Nobles depended on the peasants to produce goods so that the nobles could use them to pay taxes to higher nobles and the king. Peasants depended on the lands to produce goods that they used to pay what they owed to the nobles.

Objectives

Social Studies

1. Learn why the Roman Catholic Church was so important and powerful during the Middle Ages.
2. Discover the connection between an increase in trade and the growth of towns.
3. Find out what life was like in a medieval town.
4. Understand the role of culture and learning in the Middle Ages.

Reading/Language Arts

Identify the sequence of events to help you understand and remember them.

Prepare to Read

Build Background Knowledge   **L2**

Tell students that in this section they will learn about the role of the Roman Catholic Church in the Middle Ages. Display *Color Transparencies MT 35* and *36*. Ask students to describe what they see and discuss the cathedral's features.

📖 **Medieval Times to Today Transparencies,** *Color Transparency MT 35; Color Transparency MT 36*

Set a Purpose for Reading   **L2**

■ Preview the Objectives.

■ Read each statement in the *Reading Readiness Guide* aloud. Ask students to mark the statements true or false.

■ Have students discuss the statements in pairs or groups of four, then mark their guides again. Use the Numbered Heads participation strategy (TE, p. T36) to call on students to share their group's perspectives.

All in One Medieval Times to Today Teaching Resources, *Reading Readiness Guide,* p. 274

Vocabulary Builder
Preview Key Terms   **L2**

Pronounce each Key Term, then ask the students to say the word with you. Provide a simple explanation such as, "An apprentice works for free in exchange for being trained to learn a certain trade."

Section 2
The Church and the Rise of Cities

Prepare to Read

Objectives

In this section you will

1. Learn why the Roman Catholic Church was so important and powerful during the Middle Ages.
2. Discover the connection between an increase in trade and the growth of towns.
3. Find out what life was like in a medieval town.
4. Understand the role of culture and learning in the Middle Ages.

Taking Notes

As you read this section, think about what caused towns to grow in the Middle Ages and the effects of this growth. Copy the diagram below and record your findings in it.

🎯 Target Reading Skill

Identify Sequence

Noting the order in which significant events occur can help you understand and remember them. You can track the order of events by making a list. Then use signal words and dates in the text to make sure your events are listed in the correct order.

Key Terms

- **clergy** (KLUR jee) *n.* persons with authority to perform religious services
- **excommunication** (eks kuh myoo nih KAY shun) *n.* expelling someone from the Church
- **guild** (gild) *n.* a medieval organization of crafts workers or tradespeople
- **apprentice** (uh PREN tis) *n.* an unpaid person training in a craft or trade
- **chivalry** (SHIV ul ree) *n.* the code of honorable conduct for knights
- **troubadour** (TROO buh dawr) *n.* a traveling poet and musician of the Middle Ages

The cathedral at Chartres, France, still dominates the city.

126 Medieval Times to Today

Tall spires reach toward the heavens. Gorgeous stained-glass windows feature rich colors. Sculptures and carvings of people, plants, and animals seem to be everywhere. Amazing flying buttresses—masses of stonework or brickwork attached to the walls—help hold the building up. What is this building? It is a Gothic cathedral.

Even today, these huge medieval churches dominate towns in many parts of Europe. During the Middle Ages, cathedrals were built not only to glorify God but also to be a credit to their city. Entire communities worked for decades to build the biggest, tallest, most beautiful cathedral.

Once completed, a cathedral served as a house of worship, a gathering place, and even as a religious school. Its beautiful glass windows and sculptures told Bible stories and presented the lives of the saints to a population that could not read or write.

🎯 Target Reading Skill   **L2**

Identify Sequence Point out the Target Reading Skill. Explain that identifying the sequence of events can help you understand and remember them.

Model the skill by reading The Revival of Trade on p. 130 and listing in order the events that led to the revival of trade. (*People felt safe; people traveled to distant places, such as Asia; they brought goods back from Asia;* *Europeans began wanting more of these goods; ancient trade routes came into use again; merchants traveled to trade for these goods.*)

Give students *Identify Sequence*. Have them complete the activity in groups.

All in One Medieval Times to Today Teaching Resources, *Identify Sequence,* p. 286

The Church in the Middle Ages

Most Gothic cathedrals were built in Western Europe between 1100 and 1400. *Gothic* refers to the style of architecture, as you can see in the Eyewitness Technology feature on page 128. A cathedral was the church of a bishop, an important leader of the Roman Catholic Church. During the Middle Ages, nearly all people in Western Europe were Roman Catholic. The Roman Catholic Church had so much influence that it was known simply as "the Church." Why was the Church so powerful? There were many reasons.

Religious and Economic Power During the Middle Ages, life was short and hard for most people. They were comforted by the Christian belief that they would enjoy the rewards of heaven after death if they lived according to Church teachings. The Church also held that if people *didn't* obey those rules, they would be punished after death. The promise of reward combined with the threat of punishment made most people follow the teachings of the Church.

The Church also had great economic power. It gained great wealth by collecting taxes. It also took fiefs from lords in exchange for services performed by **clergy**, or persons with authority to perform religious services. In fact, the Church was the single largest owner of land in Europe during the Middle Ages.

Political Power of the Church The combination of religious and economic power enabled the Church to take on many of the roles that government performs today. It even made laws and set up courts to enforce them. People who did not obey the Church were threatened with being excommunicated. **Excommunication** means being expelled from membership in the Church and participation in Church life. This was a very serious threat. Few people would associate with someone who had been excommunicated.

High Church officials were advisors to kings and lords. The ever-present threat of excommunication gave Church officials great influence in political matters. The Church used its authority to limit feudal warfare. It declared periods of truce, or temporary peace. That was one reason warfare began to decline during the 1100s.

Teaching Tool
This stained glass window in Canterbury Cathedral, England, shows three kings following a star to the birth of Jesus. **Infer** *How might this window have helped medieval people understand Church teachings?*

Instruct

The Church in the Middle Ages ▣2

Guided Instruction

- **Vocabulary Builder** Clarify the high-use words **expel, authority,** and **dedicate** before reading.

- Read The Church in the Middle Ages, using the ReQuest procedure (TE, p. T35).

- Discuss the reasons why most Western Europeans followed the teachings of the Roman Catholic Church. (*Life for people in the Middle Ages was short and hard. They were comforted by the Roman Catholic belief that they would go to heaven if they followed the Church's teachings. They also feared punishment after death for not following the Church's teachings.*)

- Ask **What gave the Church so much political power?** (*the combination of its religious power and the economic power it obtained from collecting taxes and being the single largest landowner in Europe*)

- Ask students to make a prediction about the role of the Roman Catholic Church in daily life during the Middle Ages. (*Possible answer: The Roman Catholic Church probably affected most aspects of people's daily lives because the Church held religious, economic, and political power in Europe.*)

Vocabulary Builder

Use the information below to teach students this section's high-use words.

High-Use Word	Definition and Sample Sentence
expel, p. 127	*v.* to force to leave The principal warned that he would **expel** students who disobeyed school rules.
authority, p. 129	*n.* power, control The general had **authority** over the conquered region.
dedicate, 129	*v.* to devote to the worship of a divine being The priest vowed to **dedicate** his life to God.
prevent, p. 131	*v.* to keep from happening Jay put the food in the freezer to **prevent** it from spoiling.

Answer

Infer Possible answer: The window helped teach people who could not read about the story of Jesus' birth.

Gothic Cathedral

Guided Instruction L2

Read the introductory paragraph aloud as a class and study the diagram and other images. Then have student volunteers take turns reading each caption aloud. Tell students to answer the Analyzing Images question individually. Then allow them to share their answers with their neighbor.

Independent Practice

Have students do Internet or library research to find photos and information about another Gothic cathedral built in the Middle Ages, such as those in Chartres, France, or Canterbury, England. Ask them to write a brief report about the cathedral, including why and when it was built and any other information unique to the cathedral. Tell them to include photos, illustrations, or tracings of the cathedral in their reports.

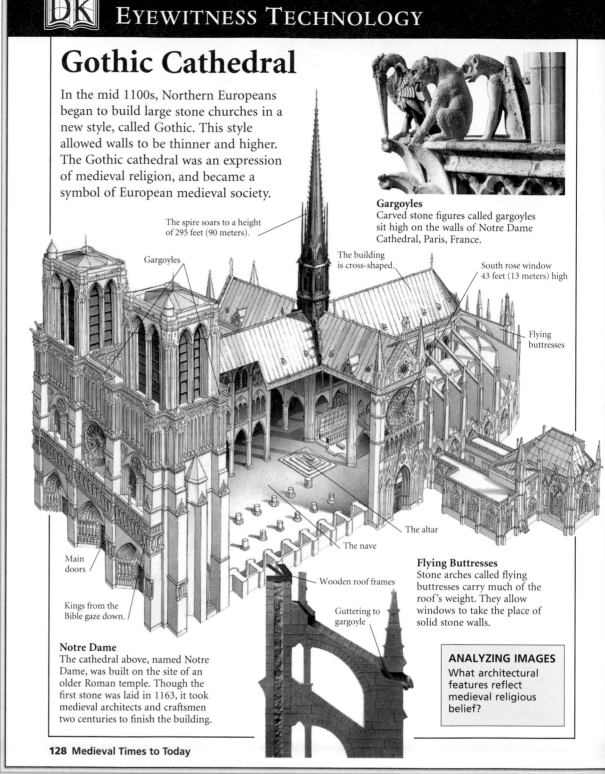

EYEWITNESS TECHNOLOGY

Gothic Cathedral

In the mid 1100s, Northern Europeans began to build large stone churches in a new style, called Gothic. This style allowed walls to be thinner and higher. The Gothic cathedral was an expression of medieval religion, and became a symbol of European medieval society.

Gargoyles
Carved stone figures called gargoyles sit high on the walls of Notre Dame Cathedral, Paris, France.

The spire soars to a height of 295 feet (90 meters).

Gargoyles

The building is cross-shaped.

South rose window 43 feet (13 meters) high

Flying buttresses

Main doors

The altar

The nave

Kings from the Bible gaze down.

Wooden roof frames

Guttering to gargoyle

Flying Buttresses
Stone arches called flying buttresses carry much of the roof's weight. They allow windows to take the place of solid stone walls.

Notre Dame
The cathedral above, named Notre Dame, was built on the site of an older Roman temple. Though the first stone was laid in 1163, it took medieval architects and craftsmen two centuries to finish the building.

ANALYZING IMAGES
What architectural features reflect medieval religious belief?

128 Medieval Times to Today

Differentiated Instruction

For Gifted and Talented L3

Challenge students to make a three-dimensional model of a cathedral using clay, cardboard, or another medium of their choice. Tell them to use the diagram on this page as a guide. Encourage students to research other cathedrals as well for further guidance.

Answer

ANALYZING IMAGES features of the Gothic style of architecture, including soaring spires

Church Organization The Church was highly organized. Almost every village had a priest. A bishop supervised several priests and an archbishop supervised several bishops. Finally, the archbishops were under the authority of the pope. The papacy, or government of the Church, was based in Rome. These areas of Church authority overlapped and crossed the boundaries of kingdoms. Thus, the Church had power in every kingdom, every fief, and every village.

The Church in Everyday Life The medieval Church touched nearly all aspects of life. Think of any major event—the birth of a child, a serious illness, a marriage, or a death. During the Middle Ages, the clergy were almost always in attendance to offer a blessing or to perform a service.

The clergy helped people follow Church rules about how to live. They also listened when people came to church to confess their sins. In the name of God, the clergy then forgave them for the wrongs to which they had confessed.

Monasteries and Convents Some religious men felt that they should dedicate their lives to God by living together in religious communities called monasteries. Religious women, called nuns, lived in similar communities called convents. This form of religious life is called monasticism.

These religious communities developed better ways of growing crops and tending livestock. In this way, the Church helped improve the economy of the Middle Ages, which was based mostly on farming. Monks and nuns also looked after the sick and set up schools. Monks were more educated than most people. Because they copied books from ancient times, they preserved knowledge that otherwise would have been lost. Convents gave women a rare opportunity to become educated.

Scholasticism Some Christian scholars studied ancient Greek texts that said people should use reason to discover truth. However, the Church taught that many ideas must be accepted on faith. These medieval scholars worked out a system that tried to resolve the two philosophies. Called scholasticism, it used reason to support Christian beliefs.

✓ **Reading Check** What were monasteries and convents?

Medieval Wedding
In the Middle Ages, ceremonies such as weddings had to be performed by a priest. **Conclude** How did this requirement increase Church power?

This detail from a medieval manuscript shows a monk copying a manuscript.

Differentiated Instruction

For Less Proficient Readers **L1**
Pair less proficient readers with more proficient students and have them make a table showing the organization of the Roman Catholic Church. Tell them to place the highest ranking official at the top and the lowest ranking at the bottom. Remind them to include a title for their table.

Guided Instruction (continued)
- Ask **Which official had the most authority in the Church?** *(the pope)*

- Have students list the major events for which Roman Catholic clergy offered their services. *(births, deaths, illnesses, and marriages)*

- Ask students **What unique opportunity did convents offer to women?** *(the opportunity to receive an education)*

- Ask students to create a cause and effect chart similar to the one on p. 126 to help them see the relationship between the events explained in Scholasticism. *(Cause: Christian scholars respected Greek texts that said people should use reason to discover truth, while the Church taught that some ideas must be accepted on faith. Effect: Scholars worked out a system called scholasticism that used reason to support Christian beliefs.)*

Independent Practice
Assign *Guided Reading and Review.*

All in One Medieval Times to Today Teaching Resources, *Guided Reading and Review,* p. 275

Monitor Progress
Circulate and make sure students are correctly answering the questions. Provide assistance as needed.

Answers
Conclude It gave the Church power in more aspects of everyday life.

✓ **Reading Check** Monasteries and convents were religious communities where people who wanted to dedicate their lives to God lived and worked. Men lived in monasteries and women lived in convents.

Trade Revives and Towns Grow

Guided Instruction

- Have students read Trade Revives and Towns Grow.

- Ask **Why did people begin to travel more in Western Europe?** *(Feudalism and the Church had stabilized the region, making it a safer place.)* **Explain how this led to the revival of trade.** *(People brought back desirable goods from the places they visited and introduced them to their region. People then began to want more of these goods, leading to the revival of trade for them.)*

- **Discuss the two major reasons for the growth of towns.** *(As trade grew, so did Europe's medieval towns and cities. The possibility of a better life and freedom from serfdom drew many people from the surrounding countryside to the new, growing towns. The growth of these towns' population further increased their prosperity and trade.)*

- Draw students' attention to the map on p. 130. Point out that many of the major trade centers are located on the coast. Ask students to explain why they think this is so. *(Possible answer: It may have been easier for traders to travel by sea to reach meeting places rather than to travel over the often mountainous terrain of Western Europe.)*

Independent Practice

Ask students to create the Taking Notes graphic organizer on a separate piece of paper. Tell them to fill in the first box with the causes of town growth. Briefly model how to record information on the chart.

Monitor Progress

As students fill in the graphic organizer, circulate and make sure individuals are choosing the correct details.

Answers

MAP MASTER Skills Activity **Identify** Cádiz, Córdoba, Toledo, and León; Provins, Troyes, and Var-sur-Aube **Infer** Possible answer: Their locations on or near the coast of the Mediterranean Sea made them easily accessible by boat.

Go Online PHSchool.com Students may practice their map skills using the interactive online version of this map.

Trade Revives and Towns Grow

By about A.D. 1000—the middle of the Middle Ages—feudalism was well established in Europe and the Church was a stabilizing force. Europe was becoming a safer place, and the population was growing.

The Revival of Trade As people felt safer, they began to travel more and learn more about distant places. As you will read in Section 3, the crusaders brought many desirable goods back from Asia. Europeans began to demand such things as spices and cloth that they could get only from Africa and Asia. Ancient trade routes came into use again. European merchants traveled abroad to buy and sell valued goods.

The Growth of Towns At first, local goods were traded in the markets of small villages. As trade grew, so did these markets. Some developed into major trade fairs. You can find these market towns on the map below.

This beautiful bottle from Syria, made in the 1300s, would have been a valued trade item.

MAP MASTER™ Skills Activity

Trade Centers in Europe

Movement As trade increased, towns along major trade routes held trade fairs and became important business centers. **Identify** Name the major trade centers of Castile. Name French towns with trade fairs. **Infer** Why do you think places such as Valencia, Naples, and Rome became important trade centers?

Go Online PHSchool.com Use Web Code lpg-8532 for step-by-step map skills practice.

KEY
- Major trade center
- Towns with major trade fairs
- Border as of 1400

0 miles 500
0 kilometers 500
Lambert Azimuthal Equal Area

Differentiated Instruction

For Advanced Readers   L3

Display *Color Transparency MT 27: Western Europe: Physical-Political*. Ask students to compare the borders of today with the borders from the past shown on the map on p. 130. Tell them to write three quiz questions asking which kingdoms and empires made up modern-day countries.

For example, students could ask **In which modern-day country was the kingdom of Aragon located?** *(Spain)* Have students exchange their quizzes with a partner and answer each others' questions.

Medieval Times to Today Transparencies, *Color Transparency MT 27: Western Europe: Physical-Political*

Traders also gathered at convenient places for travelers, such as river crossings and along highways. They chose important monasteries and fortified places built by nobles. Before long, towns developed in these locations, too.

As trade grew, so did Europe's medieval towns and cities. The possibility of a better life and freedom from serfdom drew many people from the surrounding countryside to the new, growing towns. The growth of these towns' population further increased their prosperity and trade.

✓ Reading Check Why did towns begin to grow?

Shops in a Paris Street
Notice the many kinds of shops in Paris in the early 1500s. Merchants were becoming an important part of society at this time. **Generalize** *What types of goods were available in European cities in the 1500s?*

Life in Towns and Cities

By about 1300, many towns in Western Europe were growing into cities. Paris, with a population greater than 100,000, was one of the largest cities in the world.

The Rise of a Middle Class Town life was not at all like farm or manor life. Towns and cities were not self-sufficient. Instead, their economies were based on the exchange of money for goods and services. A new class of people developed, made up of merchants, traders, and crafts workers. In status, it was between nobles and peasants, and so it was called the middle class.

The Role of Guilds In many towns and cities, the merchants, traders, and crafts workers began to form associations called guilds. A **guild** included all the people who practiced a certain trade or craft. Thus there was a guild of weavers, a guild of grocers, a guild of shoemakers, and so on.

◀ **A shield representing the Guild of Notaries, who prepared and verified documents**

Guilds set prices and prevented outsiders from selling goods in town. They set standards for the quality of their goods. Guild members paid dues. This money was used to help needy members or to support the families of members who had died.

It took a long time to become a member of a guild. Between the ages of about 8 and 14, a boy who wanted to learn a certain trade became an **apprentice**, or unpaid worker being trained in a craft. He lived and worked in the home of a master of that trade for as long as seven years. Then he could become a journeyman, or salaried worker. In time, if guild officials judged that the journeyman's work met their standards, he could join the guild.

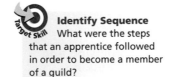

Identify Sequence What were the steps that an apprentice followed in order to become a member of a guild?

Chapter 5 Section 2 **131**

Background: Global Perspectives

Higher Learning The first university in Europe was founded in Bologna, Italy, during the 1000s. Universities had the right to explore all academic subjects without interference from the government or the Church. However, universities paid a price for their freedom—they received no funding from the government or the Church. As a result, university teachers had to charge fees for their services. They also had to be sure they satisfied their students so that they would not leave to attend another university.

Assess and Reteach

Assess Progress `L2`

Have students complete the Section Assessment. Administer the *Section Quiz*.

All in One Medieval Times to Today Teaching Resources, *Section Quiz,* p. 276

Reteach `L1`

If students need more instruction, have them read this section in the Reading and Vocabulary Study Guide.

Chapter 5, Section 2, **Medieval Times to Today Reading and Vocabulary Study Guide,** pp. 49–51

Extend `L3`

Assign the *Enrichment* activity in which students will learn about the history of Vatican City.

All in One Medieval Times to Today Teaching Resources, *Enrichment,* p. 288

Answers

✓ **Reading Check** a disease called the bubonic plague which was spread by fleas and killed one third of Europe's population

✓ **Reading Check** Cities attracted traveling scholars and were centers for learning and art.

Section 2 Assessment

Key Terms
Students' sentences should reflect knowledge of each Key Term.

Target Reading Skill
growth of trade, gathering of traders at convenient places for travelers, overcrowding of manors

Comprehension and Critical Thinking
1. (a) The Church touched nearly all aspects of life, providing services for many major events including births and marriages.
(b) The influence of the Church in everyday life contributed to its religious, political, and economic power.
2. (a) The region became safer, leading to increased travel and increased demand for new goods. **(b)** Possible answer: An ordinary person might have access to a new variety of goods.

3. (a) associations formed by merchants, traders, and crafts workers **(b)** Possible answer: Since consumers knew that guild members' goods met quality standards, they might have preferred to buy goods from a member, increasing the member's business.
4. (a) the code of honorable conduct by which knights were supposed to live **(b)** Possible answer: People probably considered stories of chivalry to be exciting and entertaining.

Writing Activity
Use the *Rubric for Assessing a Writing Assignment* to evaluate students' paragraphs.

All in One Medieval Times to Today Teaching Resources, *Rubric for Assessing a Writing Assignment,* p. 297

Troubadours provided entertainment and preserved traditional tales.

Overcrowding and Disease Medieval towns and cities were extremely crowded. Their lack of sanitation, or procedures for keeping the town clean, bred disease, and the overcrowded conditions meant that disease spread quickly. One disease, the bubonic plague, wiped out one third of Europe's population between 1347 and 1351. Called the Black Death, it was spread by fleas living on the rats that thrived in the unsanitary towns.

✓ **Reading Check** What was the Black Death?

Medieval Culture

Despite its hardships, medieval life was not all a struggle for survival. The growing cities attracted traveling scholars, and young men flocked to cathedral schools. Many of these schools became great centers of learning. Much of the beautiful artwork of the Middle Ages was displayed in churches where many could enjoy it.

Stories, poems, and songs about chivalry were also very popular. **Chivalry** is the code of honorable conduct by which knights were supposed to live. Throughout Western Europe, traveling poets and musicians called **troubadours** went from place to place singing about the brave deeds performed by knights to win the love of a beautiful and worthy woman.

✓ **Reading Check** Describe some advantages of living in a medieval city.

Section 2 Assessment

Key Terms
Review the key terms at the beginning of this section. Use each term in a sentence that explains its meaning.

Target Reading Skill
Identify and list in sequence three events or conditions that led to the growth of towns.

Comprehension and Critical Thinking
1. (a) Recall How was the Church important in everyday life?
(b) Identify Effects How did this importance contribute to the Church's power?
2. (a) List What factors led to the increase in trade in Western Europe?
(b) Infer How might the growth of trade have affected the life of an ordinary person?
3. (a) Define What were guilds?
(b) Draw Conclusions Why would someone join a guild?
4. (a) Explain What was chivalry?
(b) Infer Why was chivalry a popular topic for troubadours?

Writing Activity
During the Middle Ages, children began apprenticeships as early as the age of eight. Do you think that is too young an age to start such work? Write a paragraph that answers this question.

> **Writing Tip** Begin your paragraph with a topic sentence that tells whether or not you think eight years old is too young. Use supporting sentences to give reasons for your position.

Prepare to Read

Objectives
In this section you will
1. Learn about the causes of the Crusades.
2. Find out about the different Crusades and what they accomplished.
3. Discover the effects the Crusades had on life in Europe.

Taking Notes
As you read this section, look for the ways various people or groups contributed to the Crusades. Copy the table below and record your findings in it.

Person or Group	Contribution

🎯 Target Reading Skill

Recognize Sequence Signal Words Signal words point out relationships between ideas or events. This section discusses the Crusades, which took place over many years. To help keep the order of events clear, look for words such as *first, then, finally,* and *in [date]* that signal the order in which the events took place.

Key Terms
- **Holy Land** (HOH lee land) *n.* Jerusalem and parts of the surrounding area where Jesus lived and taught
- **Crusades** (kroo SAYDZ) *n.* a series of military expeditions launched by Christian Europeans to win the Holy Land back from Muslim control
- **Jerusalem** (juh ROOZ uh lum) *n.* a city in the Holy Land, regarded as sacred by Christians, Muslims, and Jews
- **pilgrim** (PIL grum) *n.* a person who journeys to a sacred place

On November 27, 1095, a crowd gathered in the town of Clermont, located in present-day France. They came to hear an urgent message from the pope:

> **❝You common people who have been miserable sinners, become soldiers of Christ! You nobles, do not [quarrel] with one another. Use your arms in a just war! Labor for everlasting reward.❞**
>
> —Pope Urban II

The crowd roared its approval. They shouted, "God wills it!"

Pope Urban II was calling the people of Europe to war. The purpose of this war was to capture the **Holy Land,** a region sacred to Christians because Jesus had lived and taught there. It was a small region on the eastern shore of the Mediterranean Sea known in ancient times as Judea, today part of Israel and the West Bank. Now, said the pope, the Holy Land has fallen to the Muslims. Christians must win it back.

Pope Urban II calling for a war to win back the Holy Land

🎯 Target Reading Skill L2

Recognize Sequence Signal Words Point out the Target Reading Skill. Tell students that recognizing sequence signal words will help them find the relationship between events or ideas.

Model the skill by identifying the signal words in Later Crusades on p. 136 *(then, by 1187).*

Give students *Recognize Sequence Signal Words.* Have them complete the activity in groups.

All in One Medieval Times to Today Teaching Resources, *Recognize Sequence Signal Words,* p. 285

Objectives
Social Studies
1. Learn about the causes of the Crusades.
2. Find out about the different Crusades and what they accomplished.
3. Discover the effects the Crusades had on life in Europe.

Reading/Language Arts
Recognize sequence signal words to help build an understanding of the relationships between ideas and events.

Prepare to Read

Build Background Knowledge L2
In this section, students will learn about the Crusades. Ask students to preview the headings, map, and other visuals in the section. Then tell them to write five questions they would like to have answered that will help them remember important information from the section. Students can use these questions to fill in the second columns of their *Reading Readiness Guides.* Ask students to answer the questions as they read the section.

Set a Purpose for Reading L2
- Preview the Objectives.
- Form students into pairs or groups of four. Distribute the *Reading Readiness Guide.* Ask the students to fill in the first two columns of the chart. Use the Numbered Heads participation strategy (TE, p. T36) to call on students to share one piece of information they already know and one piece of information they want to know.

  All in One Medieval Times to Today Teaching Resources, *Reading Readiness Guide,* p. 278

Vocabulary Builder
Preview Key Terms L2
Pronounce each Key Term, then ask the students to say the word with you. Provide a simple explanation such as, "Pilgrims have traveled to Jerusalem for many centuries because it is considered to be a holy place."

Causes of the Crusades

L2

Guided Instruction

- **Vocabulary Builder** Clarify the high-use words **launch** and **prestige** before reading.

- Read Causes of the Crusades, using the Paragraph Shrinking strategy (TE, p. T34). As students read, circulate and make sure individuals can answer the Reading Check question.

- Ask **What were the Crusades?** *(eight military expeditions started by the Church to capture the Holy Land)* **What city in the Holy Land attracted religious pilgrims?** *(Jerusalem)*

- Ask students to identify the religious groups that considered Jerusalem sacred. *(Christians, Muslims, and Jews)*

- Have students contrast the ways Arab Muslims and Seljuk Turks treated Christian pilgrims. *(Arab Muslims allowed Christian pilgrims to visit Jerusalem, while the Seljuk Turks sometimes attacked pilgrims and eventually closed pilgrimage routes.)*

Embarking on a Crusade
Huge armies of crusader knights sailed to the Holy Land.
Conclude *What was involved in transporting these large armies?*

Many medieval Christians believed that Jerusalem was the center of the world, as this map from the 1200s shows.

134 Medieval Times to Today

Causes of the Crusades

Over the next 200 years, the Church launched eight military expeditions, called the **Crusades,** to capture the Holy Land. The word comes from *crux,* the Latin word for "cross." People who carried the Christian cross into battle against the non-Christian enemy were called crusaders.

Pilgrims to the Holy Land Since about A.D. 200, European Christians had been traveling to **Jerusalem,** a city in the Holy Land regarded as sacred by Christians, Muslims, and Jews. These people were **pilgrims**—people who journey to a sacred place. Nobles and peasants alike made the long and difficult journey. They wanted to visit the places written about in the Bible.

The Rise of the Turks For centuries, Jerusalem had been controlled by Arab Muslims who generally welcomed Christian pilgrims. Then, in the 1000s, the Seljuk Turks (SEL jook turks) took control of the Holy Land. This Muslim group sometimes attacked the Christian pilgrims from Europe. Then they closed the pilgrimage routes to Jerusalem.

At the same time, the Turks were also conquering much of the Byzantine Empire. The Byzantine emperor in Constantinople asked Pope Urban II to send knights to defend his Christian empire. The pope agreed and called on the people of Europe to fight the Muslim Turks.

Vocabulary Builder

Use the information below to teach students this section's high-use words.

High-Use Word	Definition and Sample Sentence
launch, p. 134	*v.* to set in motion The candidate **launched** a campaign to help her win the election.
prestige, p. 135	*n.* a commanding position in people's minds Pat gained **prestige** for himself by consistently earning the highest grades in the class.
advise, p. 136	*v.* to give a recommendation The coach **advised** Jim to swing at a fastball, not a curveball.

Answer

Conclude Possible answer: Many people had to work to load the boats with supplies the large army would need.

Why Go to War? Why did Pope Urban II agree to organize a war against the Muslim Turks? Mainly, he wanted the Holy Land to be under the control of Christians. He wanted Christian pilgrims to be able to visit Jerusalem and other religious sites.

But he also had other reasons. The pope thought a crusade would unite Europeans against a common enemy—the Muslim Turks—and they would stop fighting among themselves. He also hoped to gain power and prestige for himself and the Church.

Some Europeans had other reasons for encouraging the Crusades. They wanted to control not only the Holy Land but also key trade routes between Africa, Asia, and Europe.

✓ **Reading Check** Why did the pope want to conquer the Holy Land?

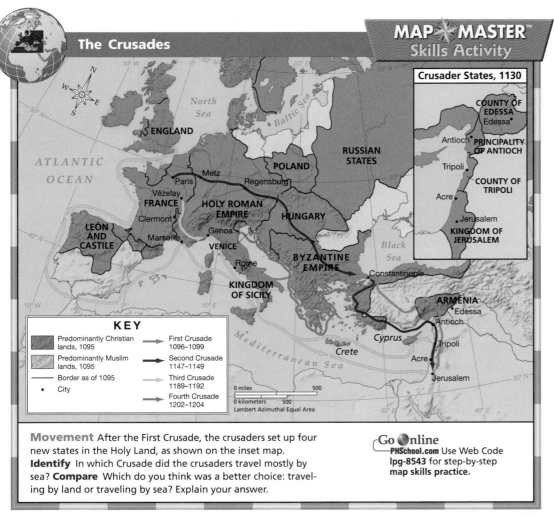

The Crusades

MAP MASTER™ Skills Activity

Crusader States, 1130

- COUNTY OF EDESSA · Edessa
- Antioch · PRINCIPALITY OF ANTIOCH
- Tripoli · COUNTY OF TRIPOLI
- Acre ·
- Jerusalem · KINGDOM OF JERUSALEM

North Sea · Baltic Sea · ENGLAND · ATLANTIC OCEAN · RUSSIAN STATES · POLAND · Metz · Regensburg · Paris · Vézelay · FRANCE · Clermont · HOLY ROMAN EMPIRE · HUNGARY · Genoa · Marseille · LEÓN AND CASTILE · VENICE · Rome · BYZANTINE EMPIRE · Black Sea · KINGDOM OF SICILY · Constantinople · ARMENIA · Edessa · Antioch · Cyprus · Tripoli · Mediterranean Sea · Crete · Acre · Jerusalem

KEY
- Predominantly Christian lands, 1095
- Predominantly Muslim lands, 1095
- Border as of 1095
- · City
- → First Crusade 1096–1099
- → Second Crusade 1147–1149
- → Third Crusade 1189–1192
- → Fourth Crusade 1202–1204

0 miles 500
0 kilometers 500
Lambert Azimuthal Equal Area

Movement After the First Crusade, the crusaders set up four new states in the Holy Land, as shown on the inset map.
Identify In which Crusade did the crusaders travel mostly by sea? **Compare** Which do you think was a better choice: traveling by land or traveling by sea? Explain your answer.

Go Online PHSchool.com Use Web Code lpg-8543 for step-by-step map skills practice.

Chapter 5 Section 3 **135**

Differentiated Instruction

For Special Needs Students L1
If students are having trouble interpreting the map on p. 135, pair them with more proficient students and have them complete Level 2 of the *Analyzing and Interpret-* *ing Special-Purpose Maps* lesson on the Social Studies Skills Tutor CD-ROM.

◉ *Analyzing and Interpreting Special-Purpose Maps*, **Social Studies Skills Tutor CD-ROM**

Guided Instruction (continued)

■ Ask **How did the Turks' attack on the Byzantine Empire help trigger the Crusades?** *(The Byzantine emperor in Constantinople asked Pope Urban II to send knights to help Constantinople defend against an attack by Muslim Turks. Pope Urban II agreed to help and declared war against the Turks, who were also occupying the Holy Land.)*

■ Discuss the three reasons why Pope Urban II wanted to control the Holy Land. *(He wanted Christian pilgrims to be able to visit Jerusalem; he thought that if Europeans united against a common enemy, they would stop fighting each other; he wanted to gain power and prestige for himself and the Church.)*

Independent Practice
Ask students to create the Taking Notes graphic organizer on a blank piece of paper. Then have them fill in the table with information about the people and groups they have just read about. Briefly model how to identify which details to record.

Monitor Progress
As students fill in the graphic organizer, circulate and make sure individuals are filling in the appropriate information. Help students as needed.

Answers

✓ **Reading Check** The Pope wanted to conquer the Holy Land to enable Christian pilgrims to visit Jerusalem. He also hoped that Europeans would unite against a common enemy and stop fighting each other, and he hoped to gain power and prestige for himself and the Church.

MAP MASTER™ Skills Activity **Identify** the Third Crusade **Compare** Some students may think that traveling by sea was easier because at the time of the Crusades, people did not have modern means of transportation for travel by land. Others might suggest that traveling by land might be easier because Crusaders could sometimes take shorter routes.

Go Online PHSchool.com Students may practice their map skills using the interactive online version of this map.

🎯 Target Reading Skill

Recognize Sequence Signal Words As a follow up, ask students to answer the Target Reading Skill question in the Student Edition. *(before; Possible answer: It tells you that the events explained in the next paragraph happened before the events explained in the paragraphs that follow.)*

A Series of Crusades L2

The Results of the Crusades L2

Guided Instruction

■ **Vocabulary Builder** Clarify the high-use word **advise** before reading.

■ Read A Series of Crusades and The Results of the Crusades as a class.

■ Ask students to compare and contrast the First and Second Crusades. *(Both Crusades were launched to gain control of Jerusalem. The First Crusade succeeded while the Second Crusade had little success.)*

■ Have students choose one effect of the Crusades and explain why it was important to Europe. *(Effects include revival of trade, growth of cities, increased use of money, introduction of new ideas and technology.)*

Independent Practice

Ask students to complete their organizers with the information they have just learned.

Monitor Progress

■ Show *Section Reading Support Transparency MT 67* and ask students to check their graphic organizers individually. Go over key concepts and clarify key vocabulary as needed.

📖 **Medieval Times to Today Transparencies,** *Section Reading Support Transparency MT 67*

■ Tell students to fill in the last column of the *Reading Readiness Guide*. Ask them to evaluate if what they learned was what they had expected to learn.

All in One **Medieval Times to Today Teaching Resources,** *Reading Readiness Guide,* p. 278

Answer

✓ Reading Check He said that Jerusalem was as important to Muslims as it was to Christians.

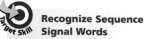
Recognize Sequence Signal Words
What word in the paragraph at the right signals sequence? How does this clue help you understand the next few paragraphs?

A Series of Crusades

The pope's best hope for capturing the Holy Land rested with European lords and their knights. But before these armies could assemble, a band of common people set out for Jerusalem.

Peter the Hermit and the People's Crusade Peter, a small man who wore monk's robes, gathered an "army" of common people. They set out in 1096. When they got to Constantinople, the Byzantine emperor advised them to wait for help from an army of knights from Europe. Peter agreed, but his followers rebelled. His soldiers attacked the Turks, who easily defeated them. Only a small part of his army survived.

Crusaders led by Louis IX of France retake the city of Damietta, near Jerusalem.

The First Crusade At last, the European armies sent by Pope Urban II reached Constantinople. Joined by what remained of Peter's army, the knights fought their way to Jerusalem and captured it in 1099. While taking control of the city, the crusaders killed thousands of its Muslim, Christian, and Jewish inhabitants.

After the capture of Jerusalem, most of the crusaders returned to Europe. Those who stayed in the Holy Land set up four Christian states. The Muslim Turks attacked these kingdoms repeatedly. European Christians then launched more Crusades to keep control of the region.

Later Crusades The Second Crusade had little success. Then a strong Arab Muslim leader rose to power. He was known to the Europeans as Saladin (SAL uh din). By 1187, Saladin had retaken Jerusalem. King Richard I of England tried to persuade Saladin to return the Holy City to the Christians. Saladin refused, saying,

> **❝To us Jerusalem is as precious . . . as it is to you, because it is the place from where our Prophet [Muhammad] made his journey by night to heaven. . . . Do not dream that we will give it up to you. ❞**
>
> *—Saladin*

Even so, Saladin negotiated a treaty with King Richard. He agreed to reopen Jerusalem to Christian pilgrims.

✓ Reading Check Why did Saladin refuse to give up Jerusalem?

Skills for Life — Skills Mini Lesson

Identifying Frame of Reference and Point of View

1. Teach the skill by explaining that point of view is an opinion or perspective on a topic and frame of reference is a person's background. Frame of reference often affects point of view.

2. Help students practice the skill by identifying the topic of the Saladin quote on p. 136 *(control of Jerusalem)* and his point of view on the topic *(He felt that Muslims should control Jerusalem.)*

3. Have students apply the skill by identifying Saladin's frame of reference and how it might have affected his point of view.

The Results of the Crusades

Although crusaders did capture the Holy Land for a while, they were never able to gain firm control of it. Still, the Crusades brought important and lasting changes to Europe.

Increased Trade The European ships that carried crusaders and their supplies to the Holy Land returned with rugs, jewelry, glass, and spices. Soon, these goods were in great demand in Europe. Thus, the Crusades helped revive trade, which in turn led to the growth of towns and cities.

The Crusades also encouraged the use of money in Europe. For much of the Middle Ages, most people bartered, or traded goods for other goods or for land or protection. But the crusaders went far from home, where they needed to *buy* supplies. In that case, it was easier to use money than it was to barter.

New Ideas Returning crusaders also brought new ideas and technology back to Europe. You have read about the advances made by Arabs in medicine, mathematics, and technology. The crusaders helped increase European knowledge of these techniques. Europeans learned how to make better ships and maps—skills that would help them become worldwide explorers.

Medieval Banking
A man deposits gold in a bank.
Synthesize *Why did banking increase after the Crusades?*

✓ **Reading Check** **Describe two effects of the Crusades.**

Section 3 Assessment

Key Terms
Review the key terms at the beginning of this section. Use each term in a sentence that explains its meaning.

Target Reading Skill
Reread the text on page 134 under the heading The Rise of the Turks. What signal words helped you understand the sequence of these events?

Comprehension and Critical Thinking
1. (a) Find Main Ideas What was the chief goal of the crusaders?

(b) Infer Why do you think Pope Urban II called the First Crusade a "just," or honorable, war?
2. (a) Sequence List the events of the First Crusade in order.
(b) Identify Frame of Reference How do you think European Christians viewed the Muslim Turks? How do you think Muslims living in the Holy Land viewed the crusaders?
3. (a) Identify Effects What were the main effects of the Crusades on life in Europe?
(b) Predict What might have happened in Europe if the Crusades had never taken place?

Writing Activity
Suppose that there were European newspapers that published editorials at the time of the Crusades. Write an editorial either in support of or against the First Crusade.

> **Writing Tip** Remember that editorials are persuasive writing. State your position. Then use reasons and facts to convince readers that your opinion is the right one.

Section 3 Assessment

Key Terms
Students' sentences should reflect knowledge of each Key Term.

Target Reading Skill
for centuries, then, in the 1000s, at the same time

Comprehension and Critical Thinking
1. (a) to capture the Holy Land **(b)** Possible answer: He believed that Christians should control the Holy Land and felt that going to war to gain control of it was just.

2. (a) the army of Pope Urban II reaches Constantinople; captures the Holy Land in 1099; sets up four Christian kingdoms
(b) Possible answer: European Christians probably viewed the Muslim Turks as enemies who were trying to control something that was more important to Christians. In turn, Muslim Turks probably viewed European Christians as enemies who were trying to take something that was more important to Muslims.

3. (a) revival of trade, growth of cities, increased use of money, introduction of new ideas and technology **(b)** Possible answers: European cities might not have grown as quickly. Europeans may not have started explorations when they did.

Assess and Reteach

Assess Progress L2
Have students complete the Section Assessment. Administer the *Section Quiz.*

All in One **Medieval Times to Today Teaching Resources,** *Section Quiz,* p. 280

Reteach L1
If students need more instruction, have them read this section in the Reading and Vocabulary Study Guide.

Chapter 5, Section 3, **Medieval Times to Today Reading and Vocabulary Study Guide,** pp. 52–54

Extend L3
Have students work with a partner to complete the *Why Do Wars Begin?*

Go Online
PHSchool.com **For:** Environmental and Global Issues: *Why Do Wars Begin?*
Visit: PHSchool.com
Web Code: lgd-8506

Answers
Synthesize It was easier to use money than to trade goods. This increased the use of money and the need for banking.

✓ **Reading Check** Students should describe two of the following: revival of trade, growth of cities, use of money, and introduction of new ideas and technology.

Writing Activity
Use the *Rubric for Assessing a Newspaper Article* to evaluate students' editorials.

All in One **Medieval Times to Today Teaching Resources,** *Rubric for Assessing a Newspaper Article,* p. 298

Skills for Life

Objective
Learn how to distinguish fact and opinion.

Prepare to Read

Build Background Knowledge L2
Write the following statements on the board: *Geography is the study of people and places. Geography is the best subject.*

Ask students which statement is a fact and which is an opinion. Poll students by asking for a show of hands. Explain that sometimes it is difficult to distinguish facts from opinions, but they will learn the steps for this skill in this lesson.

Instruct

Distinguishing Fact and Opinion L2

Guided Instruction

- Read the steps to distinguishing fact and opinion. Summarize each step and write it on the board.

- Practice the skill by using the steps on p. 139 to distinguish the facts and opinions in the passage about Richard I on p. 138. Identify one fact that tells how much (*He spent most of his reign fighting in the Crusades.*), one that tells what (*He made peace with Saladin.*), one that tells where (*He spent only six months of his reign in England.*), and one that tells when (*Richard died in 1199.*).

- Explain that students can check these facts in an encyclopedia or other reliable reference book or website.

- Help students find two words in the passage that show personal feelings (*loved, admired*). Point out that the statements containing these words cannot be proven true or false. Identify a word that judges (*bravely, great, courage*) and explain that the statements containing these words cannot be proven true or false either.

- Explain that some people could make the argument that the passage helps prove that Richard was a good king, but the passage does not provide enough information to prove that he was a kind king.

Skills for Life — Distinguishing Fact and Opinion

Richard I was born on September 8, 1157. He became king of England in 1189 but spent most of his reign fighting in the Crusades. He led his armies to free the Holy Land. Richard loved to be in the midst of battle and always fought bravely. He spent only six months of his reign in England, but his people loved him anyway. They admired his great courage and called him Richard the Lion-Hearted.

Richard won many battles, but he failed to free the Holy Land. He did make peace with the Muslim leader Saladin, who allowed Christians to visit the holy city of Jerusalem. That was a great accomplishment. Richard died in 1199. He was a good and kind king.

King Richard I of England

Facts are statements that can be proved true. Opinions are personal beliefs or value judgments. You will often need to make your own judgments or decisions based on facts, so you must be able to recognize them.

Learn the Skill
To distinguish fact from opinion, use the following steps:

1. **Look for facts by asking what can be proved true or false.** A fact usually tells who, what, when, where, or how much. A fact can be proved true.

2. **Ask how you could check whether each fact is true.** Could you do your own test by measuring or counting? Could you find information in an encyclopedia or in another reliable reference book?

3. **Look for opinions by identifying personal beliefs or value judgments.** Look for words that signal personal feelings, such as *I think* or *I believe*. Look for words that judge, such as *great* or *brave*, or *should* or *ought to*. An opinion cannot be proved true or false.

4. **Decide whether facts or good reasons support each opinion.** A well-supported opinion can help you make up your own mind—as long as you recognize it as an opinion and not a fact.

Independent Practice
Assign *Skills for Life* and have students complete it individually.

All in One **Medieval Times to Today Teaching Resources,** *Skills for Life,* p. 289

Monitor Progress
As students are completing *Skills for Life,* circulate to make sure students are correctly applying the skill steps. Provide assistance as needed.

Practice the Skill

Read the passage about Richard the Lion-Hearted until you are sure that you understand it. Then reread it for facts and opinions.

1 Identify facts in the paragraph that tell who, what, when, where, and how much.

2 Explain how each fact could be proved true or false.

3 (a) Identify two examples of words that show personal feelings. Can these statements be proved true or false? (b) Now identify one word that signals judgment. Can the statement containing this word be proved true or false?

4 The last sentence in the passage expresses an opinion. Is the opinion well supported with facts and reasons? Explain your answer.

Richard I riding into battle

Burying victims of the plague, 1349

Apply the Skill

Read the passage at the right. List two facts and two opinions from the passage. If you found this passage in a book, how useful would it be as a source for a research paper? Explain your answer.

> The Black Death was the worst thing that happened in medieval Europe. The disease struck quickly. It caused horrible spots and almost certain death. The Black Death eventually killed so many people—more than 25 million—that normal life broke down. There was a labor shortage, and those workers who survived the disease unfairly demanded higher wages. Farmers turned from growing crops to grazing sheep, which required fewer workers. Fear of the disease and economic disruption caused riots all over Europe. That kind of reaction would never happen today.

Assess and Reteach

Assess Progress **L2**
Ask students to do the Apply the Skill activity.

Reteach **L1**
If students are having trouble applying the skill steps, have them review the skill using the Social Studies Skills Tutor CD-ROM.

⊙ *Distinguishing Fact and Opinion*, **Social Studies Skills Tutor CD-ROM**

Extend **L3**
Ask students to write a brief essay about any subject they have studied in this text. Tell them to include three facts and three opinions. Ask them to underline the facts and circle the opinions.

Answer
Apply the Skill

Possible facts: The Black Death struck in Europe during medieval times. The disease struck quickly. It caused spots and almost certain death. It killed more than 25 million people. The disease caused labor shortages, and workers who survived demanded higher wages. Farmers turned from growing crops to grazing sheep. Fear of the disease and economic disruption caused riots all over Europe.

Possible opinions: The Black Death was the worst thing that happened in medieval Europe. Workers' demands for higher wages were unfair. That kind of reaction would never happen today.

Students should explain that they could use some of the facts for a research paper but should take care to not include the opinions. It might also he helpful to check the facts against another source.

Section 4
Step-by-Step Instruction

Objectives

Social Studies

1. Learn about the forces that led to nation building in Europe.
2. Find out about nation building in England.
3. Discover how the Hundred Years' War affected England and France.

Reading/Language Arts

Identify the order of events to help in understanding and remembering them.

Prepare to Read

Build Background Knowledge L2

Ask students to share what they know about how the United States became a nation. Use the Give One, Get One participation strategy (TE, p. T37) to lead a discussion on the causes and effects of the American Revolution and the creation of the United States government. Explain that the building of the United States began hundreds of years after the building of European nations. Ask students to think about the similarities and differences between the building of the United States and the building of European nations as they read.

Set a Purpose for Reading L2

■ Preview the Objectives.

■ Form students into pairs or groups of four. Distribute the *Reading Readiness Guide*. Ask the students to fill in the first two columns of the chart. Use the Numbered Heads participation structure (TE, p. T36) to call on students to share one piece of information they already know and one piece of information they want to know.

All in One Medieval Times to Today Teaching Resources, *Reading Readiness Guide,* p. 282

Vocabulary Builder
Preview Key Terms L2

Pronounce each Key Term, then ask the students to say the word with you. Provide a simple explanation such as, "France is considered to be a nation because the people living there share territory, a government, a language, and a culture."

The Power of Kings

Prepare to Read

Objectives

In this section you will
1. Learn about the forces that led to nation building in Europe.
2. Find out about nation building in England.
3. Discover how the Hundred Years' War affected England and France.

Taking Notes

As you read this section, think about what factors led to nation building in England and France. Copy the table below and record your findings in it.

Nation Building	
England	France
•	•
•	•

Target Reading Skill

Identify Sequence Noting the order of events can help you understand and remember them. Make a sequence chart of events that led to nation building in England. Write the first event in the first box. Then write each additional event in a box. Use arrows to show how one event led to the next.

Key Terms

• **nation** (NAY shun) *n.* a community of people that shares territory and a government

• **Magna Carta** (MAG nuh KAHR tuh) *n.* the "Great Charter," in which the king's power over his nobles was limited, agreed to by King John of England in 1215
• **Model Parliament** (MAHD ul PAHR luh munt) *n.* a council of lords, clergy, and common people that advised the English king on government matters
• **Hundred Years' War** (HUN drud yeerz wawr) *n.* a series of conflicts between England and France, 1337–1453

Pope Gregory VII forgiving King Henry IV

140 *Medieval Times to Today*

For three days, the king waited outside the castle where Pope Gregory VII was staying. Barefoot in the winter cold, the king begged forgiveness. Would the pope forgive King Henry IV?

During the Middle Ages, kings and popes quarreled over who should select bishops. Because bishops were Church officials, popes claimed the right to choose them. Kings wanted this right because bishops often controlled large areas of their kingdoms. They also wanted to play a role in the Church.

In 1077, Henry IV of Germany ruled much of Europe. He had been choosing bishops even though Pope Gregory had ordered him not to. In response, the pope had excommunicated the king and declared that his people no longer had to obey him. However, after putting Henry off for three long, cold days, the pope gave in. He allowed Henry to rejoin the Church.

Pope Gregory had made a serious mistake. In 1081, King Henry invaded Italy, where the pope lived. By 1084, Henry had replaced Pope Gregory with a new pope, who crowned Henry emperor of the Holy Roman Empire. Gregory was sent into exile.

Target Reading Skill L2

Identify Sequence Point out the Target Reading Skill. Explain that identifying the sequence of events can help you understand and remember them.

Model the skill by reading the last two paragraphs on p. 140 and listing in order the events that led to Henry becoming emperor of the Holy Roman Empire. (*In 1077 King Henry ruled much of Europe; he appointed bishops against Pope Gregory's will; the pope*

excommunicated Henry; the pope allowed Henry to rejoin the Church; in 1081, Henry attacked Italy; by 1084 he replaced Pope Gregory with a new pope; the new pope crowned Henry emperor.)

Give students *Identify Sequence.* Have them complete the activity in groups.

All in One Medieval Times to Today Teaching Resources, *Identify Sequence,* p. 286

Nation Building

Henry's success in overthrowing the pope was a hint of things to come. As later kings gained power, they often dared to put their own wishes before those of the Church. They would soon increase their power in other ways as well.

Castle Stronghold
This English castle is protected by walls and water. **Infer** What would be involved in defending this castle from attack?

The Power of Nobles When the 1200s began, Europe was still a feudal society. While kings reigned over kingdoms, the wealthiest lords also had great power. Many saw themselves as nearly the king's equal. In fact, it was not unusual for a noble to have more land, vassals, and knights than his king. But the nobles' power was based on the feudal system. If the feudal system began to decline, so would the nobles' power.

The Decline of Feudalism One reason for the decline of the feudal system was the growth of trade and towns. Kings began to support the new towns in exchange for money. They agreed to protect towns and made laws to help towns grow rich. Then, with the money paid by townspeople, kings hired armies and used them to attack troublesome nobles.

The Crusades also weakened the nobles. Many gave up land to raise money so they could join the Crusades. Other nobles were killed in the Crusades, and kings claimed their land.

The Birth of Nations Over time, kings became more and more powerful. Instead of a patchwork of fiefs ruled by many nobles, large areas of Europe became united under a single king. The kings became strong enough to challenge the Church.

Gradually, these larger kingdoms began to turn into nations. A **nation** is a community of people that shares territory and a government. A common language and culture also often unite the people of a nation. The process of combining smaller communities into a single nation with a national identity and a national government is called nation building.

In the late Middle Ages, the idea of nationhood was taking hold in Europe. A royal marriage united the two largest kingdoms in Spain. In Russia, rulers called tsars were expanding their territory and their power over other nobles. In France, a long line of kings slowly but surely increased royal power. Louis IX, who ruled from 1226 to 1270, was a deeply religious king. He strengthened both Christianity and the central government in his kingdom.

✓ **Reading Check** What is nation building?

Vocabulary Builder

Use the information below to teach students this section's high-use words.

High-Use Word	Definition and Sample Sentence
object, p. 142	*v.* to oppose actively Jill **objects** to the use of animals for medical research.
inspire, p. 143	*v.* to fill with an emotion or attitude that encourages someone to do something The beauty of the Grand Canyon **inspired** Alex to draw a picture of it.

Instruct

Nation Building L2

Guided Instruction

■ Read Nation Building using the Oral Cloze reading strategy (TE, p. T33).

■ Discuss how the decline of feudalism helped lead to the building of nations. (*As feudalism declined, the power of kings increased. Kings used this power to unite smaller, separate kingdoms under their rule. Gradually, these larger kingdoms became nations.*)

■ Ask **What things do the people of a nation share?** (*territory, a government, and often a language and culture*)

■ Ask **How do you think the development of nations affected the power of the Church?** (*Possible answer: It probably decreased the Church's power because kings had become powerful enough to challenge the Church.*)

Independent Practice

Ask students to create the Taking Notes graphic organizer on a separate piece of paper. Tell them to begin filling it in with the information they have just learned. Display *Transparency B11: Chart/Table* and fill in a few of the general factors that led to nation building to get them started.

📖 **Medieval Times to Today Transparencies,** *Transparency B11: Chart/Table*

Monitor Progress

As students fill in the table, circulate and make sure individuals are choosing the correct details. Help students as needed.

Answers

Infer possible answer: preventing invaders from accessing the bridge leading to the entrance

✓ **Reading Check** the process of combining smaller communities into a single nation with a national identity and a national government

⊙ Target Reading Skill

Identify Sequence As a follow up, ask students to answer the Target Reading Skill question in the Student Edition. *(Students' charts should include the following events: William of Normandy conquered England in 1066. As king, he was a strong ruler who made sure to keep more power than the nobles. Kings who followed William—especially Henry I and Henry II—further increased the power of the king.)*

Changes in England L2

Guided Instruction

■ **Vocabulary Builder** Clarify the high-use word **object** before reading.

■ Read Changes in England as a class. As students read, circulate and make sure individuals can answer the Reading Check question.

■ Ask **How did King John anger the people of England?** *(He taxed people heavily, and jailed enemies unjustly.)* **How did he anger the Church?** *(He objected to the appointment of a bishop, and seized Church property.)*

■ Ask students to make a generalization about the effect of the Magna Carta on the people of England. *(Possible answer: The Magna Carta gave people more voice in government and protected some of their basic rights.)*

Independent Practice

Ask students to continue to fill in their tables with the information they have just learned.

Monitor Progress

Circulate and make sure students are correctly filling in the graphic organizer. Provide assistance as needed.

Answers

Synthesize nobles and clergy; these groups received more power

✓**Reading Check** It gave more power to the Great Council. This later became the Model Parliament, which was made up of all types of people, from common people to lords and clergy.

⊙ Identify Sequence
What events described in the paragraph at the right led to increased power of the king? Write these events in a sequence chart.

King John at Runnymede
The Magna Carta marked the beginning of limitations on the power of the king. This engraving shows King John surrounded by English nobles and clergymen. **Synthesize** *How did these groups benefit from the Magna Carta?*

Changes in England

By the 1200s, England was already well on its way to becoming a unified nation. In 1066, William of Normandy, a duke from France, had conquered England in what came to be called the Norman Conquest. As king of England, William the Conqueror was a strong ruler who made sure to keep more power than his nobles. The kings who followed William—especially Henry I and Henry II—further increased the power of the king. Of course, the nobles began to resent this power. King John, a son of Henry II, would soon face their anger.

King John Angers the Nobles When John became king of England in 1199, he quickly moved to increase his wealth and power. He taxed people heavily. He jailed his enemies unjustly and without trial. Even the most powerful nobles were hurt by John's unfair actions.

John also angered Church leaders and clergymen. He seized Church property and tried to block the pope's choice for the chief bishop of England. When this bishop took office, he supported the nobles who opposed the king's actions.

The Magna Carta John was not strong enough to defy the nobles and clergy whom he had angered. With the backing of the bishops, English nobles demanded a meeting with the king. On June 15, 1215, about 2,000 English nobles gathered at Runnymede, a meadow along the Thames River. They presented John with a list of their demands.

John was forced to place the royal seal on the document, and it became law. Called the **Magna Carta** (MAG nuh KAHR tuh), or the "Great Charter," it limited the king's power. The king could no longer jail any freeman without just cause, and he could not raise taxes without consulting his Great Council of lords and clergy.

This council later became the **Model Parliament,** which included common people as well as lords and clergy. Eventually, Parliament evolved into a powerful legislature, or law-making assembly. As it gained power, Parliament also helped unify England. At the same time, however, the Magna Carta also strengthened the power of the king. Because nobles now had a say in government, they were more likely to support what the king did.

✓**Reading Check** How did the Magna Carta help unite England?

Differentiated Instruction

For English Language Learners L2
Pair English language learners with native English speakers to complete the *Guided Reading and Review*. If appropriate, give English language learners *Guided Reading and Review (Spanish)* and ask them to work with their partners to answer the questions in English.

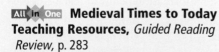 **Medieval Times to Today Teaching Resources,** *Guided Reading Review,* p. 283

📄 **Medieval Times to Today Spanish Support,** *Guided Reading and Review (Spanish),* p. 42

The Hundred Years' War

Despite the growth of nations, Western Europe was not at peace. Now, instead of nobles fighting each other, the emerging nations went to war. One long series of clashes between England and France was called the **Hundred Years' War.** It lasted from 1337 to 1453.

Causes of the War In the 1300s, the borders of England and France were not the ones we know today. As a result of marriage and inheritance, the English king had come to be the lord of many counties in present-day France.

You have read that William the Conqueror, who became king of England in 1066, was also Duke of Normandy in France. The 1152 marriage of King Henry II of England and the French noblewoman Eleanor of Aquitaine brought more French land under English control.

Then, in 1328, the French king died. King Edward III of England, whose mother had been a French princess, claimed to be king of France under feudal law. The French nobles did not agree. Determined to get his way, Edward III invaded France— and began the Hundred Years' War.

There were other causes of the war. Both England and France wanted to control the English Channel, the waterway that separates their countries. Each nation also wanted to control trade in the region and the wealth it brought.

Joan of Arc's Victory The Hundred Years' War dragged on, fought by one king after another. England won most of the battles, but the French continued to fight. However, the tide turned in 1429 when a peasant girl called Joan of Arc took charge of the French forces at the battle of Orléans (awr lay AHN). French troops at Orléans greeted her with hope and curiosity.

Under Joan's command, the French defeated the English at Orléans. She then led her forces to victory in other battles. In 1430, Joan was taken prisoner by allies of the English. England tried Joan for witchcraft. She was convicted and burned at the stake.

The French saw Joan of Arc as a martyr, and her death inspired them to many victories. By 1453, the English had been driven from most of France. With the English troops in retreat, France was on its way to becoming a strong and united nation.

Citizen Heroes

Joan of Arc

The young girl who would become one of France's greatest heroes was the daughter of a tenant farmer. Joan was very religious and believed that she saw heavenly visions. In 1429, when she was only 17, she journeyed to the court of Charles, the heir to the French throne. She convinced him that God had called her to lead the French forces at the battle of Orléans. Charles finally agreed. He gave Joan armor, attendants, horses, and a special banner to carry into battle. You can see that banner in this statue of Joan, which stands in Paris.

Background: Links Across Time

Wars of the Roses From 1455 to 1485 descendants of Edward III fought each other for control of England. The descendants from Lancaster, England, used the white rose as their emblem while the descendants from York, England, used the red rose, causing the civil wars to later be named the Wars of the Roses. Power seesawed between the two families until 1485 when Lancastrian Henry Tudor defeated the last Yorkist ruler and married a York descendant, uniting the two families' claims to the throne. He became Henry VII, founder of the Tudor dynasty which later included the rulers Henry VIII and Elizabeth I.

Citizen Heroes

Read the **Citizen Heroes** text on this page. Ask **Why did Joan of Arc travel to see the heir to the French Throne?** *(She believed that God had told her to lead the French forces at the battle of Orléans, so she went to ask the heir for permission to do so and for the supplies and army she needed.)*

The Hundred Years' War L2

Guided Instruction

- **Vocabulary Builder** Clarify the high-use word **inspire** before reading.

- Read about the causes and effects of the Hundred Years' War.

- Discuss the causes of the Hundred Years' War. *(Edward III claimed to be king of France, but French nobles did not agree. Edward III invaded France to get his way. Also, both England and France wanted to control the English Channel and trade in the region.)*

- Ask students to draw a conclusion about how the Hundred Years' War helped lead to the colonization of North America. *(After the war, the English realized that they must give up their dream for an empire in Europe and eventually began to look toward other lands for trade and conquest.)*

Independent Practice

Ask students to complete the table with information about nation building in France.

Monitor Progress

- Show *Section Reading Support Transparency MT 68* and ask students to check their graphic organizers individually. Go over key concepts and clarify key vocabulary as needed.

  Medieval Times to Today Transparencies, *Section Reading Support Transparency MT 68*

- Tell students to fill in the last column of the *Reading Readiness Guide.* Ask them to evaluate if what they learned was what they had expected to learn.

  All in One Medieval Times to Today Teaching Resources, *Reading Readiness Guide,* p. 282

Assess and Reteach

Assess Progress ⬛L2

Have students complete the Section Assessment. Administer the *Section Quiz*.

 Medieval Times to Today Teaching Resources, *Section Quiz,* p. 284

Reteach ⬛L1

If students need more instruction, have them read this section in the Reading and Vocabulary Study Guide.

📖 Chapter 5, Section 4, **Medieval Times to Today Reading and Vocabulary Study Guide,** pp. 55–57

Extend ⬛L3

Have students begin to work on the *Book Project: The Birth of a Nation.* Tell them that they can choose to research and write about England, France, or another nation they have learned about.

 Medieval Times to Today Teaching Resources, *Book Project: The Birth of a Nation* pp. 83–85

Answers

Analyze Images Possible answer: His stance and ornate clothes suggest that he is a confident and powerful man.

✓ **Reading Check** Students should explain any two of the following: New weapons that were developed during the war increased the importance of soldiers and decreased the importance of knights. The war inspired national feeling. It gave kings more power, but also gave Parliament more power. It helped set the modern boundaries for England and France. It ultimately led England to explore and colonize distant lands.

Section 4 Assessment

Key Terms
Students' sentences should reflect knowledge of each Key Term.

🔿 Target Reading Skill
Students' charts should include the following events: grew up on a farm; had a vision that she should lead the French at Orléans; visited Charles VII in 1429 to get permission to do so; defeated the English; taken prisoner in 1430; was burned at the stake.

144 *Medieval Times to Today*

King Henry VIII
The Tudor monarchs of England, 1485–1603, were very powerful. Yet Henry VIII consulted with Parliament on important issues. **Analyze Images** *How does this portrait show Henry's power and personality?*

The Growing Power of Kings The Hundred Years' War affected the balance of power in England and France. On the battlefield, new weapons such as the longbow and cannon increased the importance of footsoldiers. Armored knights, on the other hand, became less valuable in battle. Feudal castles could not stand up to the firepower of the new cannons. Kings now needed large armies, not small bands of knights, to fight for them.

The Hundred Years' War also led to national feeling. People began to think of themselves as citizens of England or of France, not simply as loyal to their local lords. Kings who had led their nations in battle became more powerful as the influence of nobles declined. On the other hand, the English king had been forced to ask Parliament for more and more money to fund the war. This helped Parliament win "the power of the purse" and increased its power in relation to the king. These two developments helped unify England.

The Hundred Years' War helped set the modern boundaries of England and France. Forced to give up their dream of an empire in Europe, the English began to look to more distant lands for trade and conquest. Leaving feudalism behind, Europe was becoming a continent of nations. And some of these nations, as you will read in Chapter 6, would soon rule much of the world.

✓ **Reading Check** **Explain two effects of the Hundred Years' War.**

✦ Section 4 Assessment

Key Terms
Review the key terms at the beginning of this section. Use each term in a sentence that explains its meaning.

🔿 Target Reading Skill
Reread page 143. Write the events of Joan of Arc's life in a sequence chart.

Comprehension and Critical Thinking
1. (a) Recall How much power did kings have under feudalism?
(b) Identify Cause and Effect Why did feudalism decline, and how did this affect the power of kings?
2. (a) Identify What are two limits on the king's power established by the Magna Carta?
(b) Identify Effects How did the Magna Carta help unify England as a nation?
3. (a) Name Who fought the Hundred Years' War?
(b) Identify Effects How did this war help unify two nations?

Writing Activity
Suppose that you are a French soldier preparing for the battle of Orléans. Describe your reaction to the news that a young peasant girl is your new commander.

For: An activity on the Hundred Years' War
Visit: PHSchool.com
Web Code: lgd-8504

144 Medieval Times to Today

Comprehension and Critical Thinking
1. (a) They reigned over kingdoms but often had the same power as wealthy lords. **(b)** the growth of trade and towns and the weakening of nobles; kings gained more power

2. (a) The king could no longer jail freemen without a trial or raise taxes without consulting the Great Council. **(b)** It gave more power to the Parliament.

3. (a) England and France **(b)** Possible answer: It stirred national pride and helped define the borders of the two countries.

Writing Activity
Use the *Rubric for Assessing a Writing Assignment* to evaluate students' reactions.

Medieval Times to Today Teaching Resources, *Rubric for Assessing a Writing Assignment,* p. 297

Go Online PHSchool.com Typing in the Web code when prompted will bring students directly to detailed instructions for this activity.

Review and Assessment

Lombard warrior

◆ Chapter Summary

Section 1: Feudalism and the Manor System

- The Middle Ages was the period from about A.D. 500 to 1500.
- Feudalism, in which land was owned by nobles but held by vassals in return for loyalty, was the medieval government system.
- The manor system, in which many people lived and worked on large estates owned by lords, was the medieval economic system.
- Most people of the Middle Ages were peasants. Serfs were peasants who were considered part of the manors on which they worked.

Section 2: The Church and the Rise of Cities

- During the Middle Ages, the Roman Catholic Church was a powerful force that touched nearly every aspect of people's lives.
- An increase in trade led to the growth of towns and cities.
- The new middle class organized craft and trade guilds. Medieval towns and cities were crowded and unsanitary.
- Culture and learning were limited to small groups of people. Troubadours brought stories of chivalry from place to place.

Section 3: The Crusades

- The Crusades were a series of wars launched by European Christians to capture the Holy Land from Muslim Turks.
- The First Crusade succeeded in capturing the holy city of Jerusalem.
- Later Crusades were launched to defend the Christian kingdoms in the Holy Land from Muslim Turk attacks.
- The Crusades changed life in Europe: trade increased, towns grew, the use of money increased, and the learning of the Arab world came to Europe.

Section 4: The Power of Kings

- Nation building in Europe began as feudalism declined and kings increased their power.
- The Magna Carta limited the power of the English king but also helped unify England into a nation.
- The Hundred Years' War helped unify both England and France into nations.

◆ Key Terms

Write one or two paragraphs about life in the Middle Ages. Use all of the following terms correctly in your paragraphs.

1. Middle Ages
2. feudalism
3. pilgrim
4. fief
5. manor
6. serf
7. clergy
8. apprentice
9. troubadour
10. Crusades

─ Vocabulary Builder ─

Revisit this chapter's high-use words:

promote	authority	prestige
majority	dedicate	advise
interior	prevent	object
expel	launch	inspire

Ask students to review the definitions they recorded on their *Word Knowledge* worksheets.

All in One Medieval Times to Today Teaching Resources, *Word Knowledge,* p. 287

Consider allowing students to earn extra credit if they use the words in their answers to the questions in the Chapter Review and Assessment. The words must be used correctly and in a natural context to win the extra points.

Chapter 5

Review and Assessment

Review Chapter Content

- Review and revisit the major themes of this chapter by asking students to classify which Guiding Question each bulleted statement in the Chapter Summary answers. Form students into groups and ask them to complete the activity together. Refer to page 1 in the Student Edition for text of Guiding Questions.

- Assign *Vocabulary Development* for students to review Key Terms.

  All in One Medieval Times to Today Teaching Resources, *Vocabulary Development,* p. 296

Answers

Key Terms

1–10. Students' paragraphs should use each Key Term correctly and in the appropriate context.

Review and Assessment

Comprehension and Critical Thinking

11. (a) Lords were powerful landowners. A vassal was given a share of the lord's land in return for the vassal's promise to follow the lord's laws and fight for him. **(b)** Possible answer: A lord might be another lord's vassal.

12. (a) A manor was a large estate that included farms, pastures, the manor house where the lord or ruler lived, and often an entire village. Everything needed by the workers and other people living on a manor was produced on the manor. **(b)** Serfs were people who were considered possessions of the manor. **(c)** Possible answer: The manor system helped keep lords powerful and wealthy. This made it possible for lords to serve as vassals for more powerful lords or kings.

13. (a) the Roman Catholic Church **(b)** Most people followed the Church's teachings; the Church had economic power through collecting taxes and controlling large plots of land; the Church's religious and economic power enabled it to perform many governmental roles.

14. (a) at crossroads for trade, such as river crossings and along roads **(b)** Possible answer: By preventing outsiders from selling goods in their towns, guild members encouraged the production and sale of goods within the town, thus helping it to grow.

15. (a) military expeditions organized for the purpose of capturing the Holy Land **(b)** Possible answer: The Crusades helped Europe because they revived trade, helped the growth of cities, encouraged the use of money, and introduced new ideas and technology to Europe.

16. (a) the combining of communities into a single nation with a national identity and government **(b)** the decline of feudalism and the increase in national pride stirred by the Hundred Years' War

17. (a) a French peasant who led the French to victory over the English at Orléans **(b)** She led the French to military victories over the English. After she was captured and executed, the French saw her as a martyr and her death inspired them to many victories.

Skills Practice

Students should identify the following phrases as opinions: gorgeous stained-glass windows; amazing flying buttresses; beautiful glass windows. Students might suggest that

---

Review and Assessment (continued)

◆ Comprehension and Critical Thinking

11. (a) Recall In the feudal system, what was the role of a lord? Of a vassal?
(b) Synthesize How could one person be both a lord and a vassal at the same time?

12. (a) Describe What was a manor, and how did it meet people's needs?
(b) Explain What was the relationship of serfs to the manor?
(c) Draw Conclusions How did manorialism help support feudalism?

13. (a) Identify What was "the Church" in the Middle Ages?
(b) Draw Conclusions Why was the Church so powerful in the Middle Ages?

14. (a) Recall Where did towns spring up during the Middle Ages?
(b) Synthesize Information How was the growth of medieval towns related to the growth of guilds?

15. (a) Define What were the Crusades?
(b) Draw Conclusions Do you think the Crusades helped or hurt Europe? Explain.

16. (a) Define What is nation building?
(b) Identify Causes What factors led to nation building in Europe in the later Middle Ages?

17. (a) Recall Who was Joan of Arc?
(b) Identify Effects How did she influence the outcome of the Hundred Years' War?

◆ Skills Practice

Distinguishing Fact and Opinion In the Skills for Life activity in this chapter, you learned how to distinguish fact from opinion. Review the steps you followed to learn the skill. Then reread the opening paragraphs of Section 2 of this chapter on page 126. List the facts and opinions in this text. For each opinion, note whether or not you think the opinion is well supported and reliable.

◆ Writing Activity: Science

The bubonic plague—the Black Death that killed so many Europeans during the Middle Ages—still exists today. However, it is not nearly so common or deadly as it once was. Use an encyclopedia and other reliable sources to learn how modern medicine and sanitation prevent and control the disease. Write a brief report titled "The Bubonic Plague in Modern Times."

MAP★MASTER™ Skills Activity

Place Location For each place listed below, write the letter from the map that shows its location.
1. England
2. France
3. Jerusalem
4. Mediterranean Sea
5. Rome
6. Constantinople

Go Online
PHSchool.com Use Web Code lgd-8554 for an interactive map.

Europe and the Holy Land

---

photographs throughout the section support these opinions.

All of the remaining sentences on p. 126 are facts.

Writing Activity: Science

Students' answers will vary, but should reflect what they have learned about the bubonic plague in this section and should reflect the completion of outside research.

Use *Rubric for Assessing a Report* to evaluate students' reports.

All in One Medieval Times to Today Teaching Resources, *Rubric for Assessing a Report,* p. 299

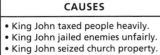

Standardized Test Prep

Test-Taking Tips

Some questions on standardized tests ask you to identify cause and effect. Study the graphic organizer below. Then use the tip to help you answer the sample question.

```
┌─────────────────────────────────────┐
│              CAUSES                  │
│  • King John taxed people heavily.   │
│  • King John jailed enemies unfairly.│
│  • King John seized church property. │
└─────────────────────────────────────┘
                  ↓
┌─────────────────────────────────────┐
│         EVENT: MAGNA CARTA           │
└─────────────────────────────────────┘
                  ↓
┌─────────────────────────────────────┐
│              EFFECTS                 │
│  • King couldn't jail nobles.        │
│  • King couldn't tax without consent.│
│  •                                   │
└─────────────────────────────────────┘
```

TIP Remember that a *cause* is what makes something happen. An *effect* is what happens as a result of something else. Is the question asking for a cause or an effect?

Pick the letter that best answers the question.
What information belongs with the last bullet (•) in the graphic organizer?

A King John clashed with the pope.
B It became law with King John's seal.
C It helped unite England.
D King John seized Church property.

Think It Through The question is asking for an effect: What else happened as a result of the Magna Carta? You can eliminate A and D because both were causes, or events leading up to the Magna Carta. That leaves B and C. The Magna Carta did become law with King John's seal, but that was not an *effect* of the law. The answer is C: the Magna Carta had the effect of helping to unite England.

Practice Questions

Choose the letter of the best answer.

1. Which of the following was a major cause of the growth of towns during the Middle Ages?
   A a decrease in the power of the Church
   B an increase in trade
   C a decrease in Europe's population
   D an increase in the number of manors

2. Which of the following was NOT an effect of the Crusades?
   A The demand for foreign goods increased.
   B Europeans learned new shipbuilding techniques.
   C The use of money became more common.
   D The Holy Land came under permanent European control.

3. The decline of _____ helped the growth of _____.
   A trade, towns
   B feudalism, manorialism
   C Charlemagne's empire, feudalism
   D the Roman Empire, trade

Study the diagram. Then use it to answer the question that follows.

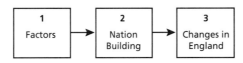

```
┌──────────┐     ┌──────────┐     ┌──────────┐
│    1     │ →   │    2     │ →   │    3     │
│ Factors  │     │  Nation  │     │ Changes  │
│          │     │ Building │     │    in    │
│          │     │          │     │ England  │
└──────────┘     └──────────┘     └──────────┘
```

4. In the diagram,
   A **1** represents a single effect of nation building, and **2** and **3** represent several causes.
   B **1** represents a single cause of **2**, and **2** is a cause of **3**.
   C **2** is a cause of both **1** and **3**.
   D **1** represents several causes of **2**, and **3** represents how nation building affected England.

Use Web Code lga-8504 for a **Chapter 5 self-test.**

Objectives

- Understand why King Arthur's subjects loved him.

- Learn about some of the rules of honor in battle that were part of the code of chivalry.

- Analyze the effectiveness of plot elements such as setting and conflicts.

Prepare to Read

Build Background Knowledge L2

Have students read the title of the story and the text on p. 148 under the heading Background Information. Ask students to recall any stories they have read or movies they have seen about King Arthur, Merlin, or Camelot. Use the Numbered Heads participation strategy (TE, p. T36) to help students share what they know with the rest of the class.

Instruct

Of Swords and Sorcerers L2

Guided Instruction

- Point out that some potentially unfamiliar words are defined for students in the margin. Clarify the meanings of the words before reading.

- Have students read the selection using the Structured Silent Reading strategy (TE, p. T34).

- Ask **Who did Arthur defeat in order to unite his land?** (*twelve kings, including his brother-in-law, King Lot*)

- Ask **Who are Gawain and Mordred?** (*They are Lot's sons; they both become knights at Camelot. Gawain is handsome, strong, and courteous, while Mordred is insincere and thirsts for power.*)

- Ask students to scan the first two paragraphs of the story. Then ask students to describe Arthur based on his actions, information that the author gives about him, and vivid words that the author uses to describe him. (*Answers may include that Arthur is an able leader, courageous in battle, and loved by his people.*)

Literature

Of Swords and Sorcerers:
The Adventures of King Arthur and His Knights
By Margaret Hodges and Margery Evernden

Prepare to Read

Background Information
How should a good and just ruler behave? What traits should a king or queen have? What do you admire in people who lead others?

People have read and enjoyed the stories of King Arthur for hundreds of years. To many, he symbolizes the virtue and justice of a good ruler. According to legend, he was loved and respected by all of his people.

Legends about King Arthur exist in many forms, and stories about him have been written and rewritten in several languages. The following selection is one tale of how Arthur met his friend Pellinore and found his sword, which was named Excalibur.

Objectives
As you read this selection, you will
1. Understand why King Arthur's subjects loved him.
2. Learn about some of the rules of honor in battle that were part of the code of chivalry.

No king before Arthur had been able to unite the realm and rule it. This Arthur did. Lightnings and thunders surrounded him as he fought. In twelve great battles he defeated <u>petty</u> kings who had been constantly at war, laying waste all the land. The last to surrender was Arthur's own brother-in-law, King Lot of Orkney. When Lot laid down his arms and swore <u>fealty</u> to Arthur, he sent his sons to become knights at Camelot.

petty (PET ee) *adj.* unimportant; of low rank

fealty (FEE ul tee) *n.* loyalty to a feudal lord

King Arthur standing with the crowns of 30 kingdoms, in an illustration from 1325

One son was Gawain, handsome and strong, whom Arthur called Gawain the Courteous. Another was Mordred, whose foxy smile and <u>gimlet eyes</u> concealed <u>malice</u> and a thirst for power. Gawain took the vows of knighthood in good faith, but Mordred's vows were insincere, and he soon began listening at the castle doors in hope of ferreting out secrets that might damage the court and someday play into his own hands. He saw that the time to strike had not yet come. The powers of heaven and earth all seemed to be on Arthur's side. The people loved him, and Camelot was in its glory.

Now there came a day when Arthur rode with Merlin seeking adventure, and in a forest they found a knight named Pellinore, seated in a chair, blocking their path.

"Sir, will you let us pass?" said Arthur.

"Not without a fight," replied Pellinore. "Such is my custom."

"I will change your custom," said Arthur.

"I will defend it," said Pellinore. He mounted his horse and took his shield on his arm. Then the two knights rode against each other, and each splintered his spear on the other's shield.

"I have no more spears," said Arthur. "Let us fight with swords."

"Not so," said Pellinore. "I have enough spears. I will lend you one."

Then a squire brought two good spears, and the two knights rode against each other again until those spears were broken.

"You are as good a fighter as ever I met," said Pellinore. "Let us try again."

Two great spears were brought, and this time Pellinore struck Arthur's shield so hard that the king and his horse fell to the earth.

Then Arthur pulled out his sword and said, "I have lost the battle on horseback. Let me try you on foot."

Pellinore thought it unfair to attack from his horse, so he dismounted and came toward Arthur with his sword drawn. Then began such a battle that both were covered with blood. After a while they sat down to rest and fought again until both fell to the ground. Again they fought, and the fight was even. But at last Pellinore struck such a blow that Arthur's sword broke into two pieces. Thereupon the king leaped at Pellinore. He threw him down and pulled off his helmet. But Pellinore was a very big man and strong enough to wrestle Arthur under him and pull off the

gimlet eyes (GIM lit eyez) *n.* eyes having a piercing quality
malice (MAL is) *n.* spite; a desire to damage or hurt someone

Knights in battle, in an illustration by N. C. Wyeth

✓ **Reading Check**
Why did Arthur and Pellinore fight?

Literature **149**

Guided Instruction (continued)

■ Ask students to reread pp.149–150, paying careful attention to the fight between Arthur and Pellinore. Ask **How do Arthur and Pellinore show respect for one another?** *(Pellinore lends Arthur a spear, compliments Arthur's fighting, dismounts his horse to make the battle fairer, and is fearful when he finds that he is fighting the king. Arthur calls Pellinore "Sir" when they first meet, and says Pellinore is the best knight he has ever fought. They allow each other a short rest during the fight.)*

■ Ask **How does Arthur lose his sword?** *(It is destroyed in his fight with Pellinore.)* **How does Merlin help Arthur after the fight?** *(Merlin brings Arthur to a hermit to treat his wound, and takes him to the Lady of the Lake, who gives Arthur a new sword with special powers.)*

■ Ask students to discuss how the setting, or the time and place of the story, is important to the story's plot. *(The story takes place sometime in the Middle Ages in a feudal society. The characters travel on horses; Arthur and Pellinore fight with swords and spears and observe codes of chivalry during their battle. Many of the characters are knights, a type of soldier. A story with similar events would have a very different meaning if it was set in the present.)*

Read Fluently

Partner students and have them choose a paragraph from the selection. Have students take turns reading the paragraph aloud. Ask them to underline words that give them trouble as they read. Then, have them decode the problem words with their partner. Provide assistance as needed. Have them reread the paragraph two more times to improve their reading speed. Remind them to stop at the commas and periods and to read with expression.

Answer

✓ **Reading Check** It was Pellinore's custom not to let anyone pass without fighting him.

Independent Practice

Partner students and have them review Arthur's qualities as a leader. *(bravery, fairness, being a great warrior)* Then ask students to suppose that Arthur can no longer serve as the king of Camelot. Have students write a job description that explains the personal and professional qualifications required of the new king. If students are having trouble organizing their thoughts, give them *Organizing Details* to help them.

All in One **Medieval Times to Today Teaching Resources,** *Organizing Details,* p. 295

Monitor Progress

Circulate to make sure students are communicating their ideas effectively to their partners. Provide assistance as needed.

---

king's helmet. All this time Merlin had watched, silent, but when he saw that Pellinore was about to cut off Arthur's head, he interfered.

"Do not kill this man," he said to Pellinore. "You do not know who he is."

"Why, who is he?" said the knight.

"It is King Arthur," said Merlin.

wrath (rath) *n.* great anger or rage

When he heard this, Pellinore trembled with fear of the royal <u>wrath</u>, for he would not knowingly have fought against the king. Then Merlin cast a spell of sleep on Pellinore so that he fell to the earth as if dead.

"Alas," said Arthur, "you have killed the best knight I ever fought."

"Have no fear," said Merlin. "He will awake in three hours as well as ever he was."

hermit (HUR mit) *n.* a person who lives alone and away from others
salve (sahv) *n.* an oily substance used as medicine on the skin

Then he mounted Pellinore's horse and led Arthur to a <u>hermit</u>, who bound up the king's wounds and healed them with good <u>salves</u>, so that he might ride again and go on his way.

But Arthur said, "I have no sword."

"Never fear," said Merlin. "Not far away is a sword that can be yours." So they rode on until they came to a broad lake of clear water. Far out in the middle of the lake Arthur saw an arm clothed in shining white and holding a noble sword, its golden hilt richly set with jewels.

"Lo," said Merlin, "yonder is the sword Excalibur."

King Arthur claiming Excalibur, in an illustration by N. C. Wyeth

150 Medieval Times to Today

Differentiated Instruction

For English Language Learners **L2**

Have students create flashcards of the words defined in the margin. Students can also include any other words from the story that are unfamiliar to them, using a classroom dictionary to find definitions. Then partner students and have them take turns quizzing each other using their flashcards.

Then they saw a lady floating toward them as if she walked on the water. Her garments were like a mist around her.

"That is the Lady of the Lake," said Merlin. "Within the lake is a rock, and within the rock is a palace, and within the palace lives this lady with many other ladies who serve her. She is called Vivien. Speak to her as a friend, and she will give you that sword."

So, when she had come close, Arthur said to her, "Lady, I wish that sword were mine, for I have no sword."

"It shall be yours," said the lady, and she showed Arthur a little boat lying at the edge of the lake. "Row out to the sword," she said. "Take it with its <u>scabbard</u>." Then she disappeared. Arthur and Merlin rowed out into the lake, and Arthur took the sword from the hand that held it. And the arm and the hand vanished under the water.

Arthur and Merlin rowed to shore and went on their way, and whenever Arthur looked on the sword, he liked it well.

"Which do you like better? asked Merlin. "The sword or the scabbard?"

"I like the sword better," said Arthur.

"The scabbard is worth ten such swords," said Merlin, "for while you wear the scabbard, you will never lose blood, no matter how sorely you are wounded."

So they rode back to Arthur's court, and all his knights marveled when they heard that the king risked his life in single combat as his poor knights did. They said it was merry to be under such a <u>chieftain</u>.

About the Selection

Of Swords and Sorcerers: The Adventures of King Arthur and His Knights was published in 1993. It includes nine episodes in the life of King Arthur.

scabbard (SKAB urd) *n.* a case or cover for a sword or dagger
chieftain (CHEEF tun) *n.* the head of a clan; leader of many people

✓ **Reading Check**

Which did Arthur like better, the sword or the scabbard?

About the Authors

Margaret Hodges, above, was a children's librarian and a storyteller for a children's radio program. She believed in the lasting value of myths. **Margery Evernden** has written children's books, biographies, and plays.

Review and Assessment

Thinking About the Selection

1. (a) Describe How did Arthur and Pellinore fight?
(b) Predict How do you think the fight would have ended if Merlin had not interfered? Why do you think so?
2. (a) Note What did Arthur's knights think when they heard about his fight with Pellinore?
(b) Draw Conclusions What qualities does Arthur demonstrate in this episode that would make him a good ruler?

(c) Predict What kind of a ruler do you think Arthur would be in today's world? Explain your answer.

Writing Activity

Write a Poem or a Story Many characters in myths and legends have objects that protect them or give them special powers, as Arthur's sword and scabbard did for him. Write a poem or a story about a character who receives one such tool. What are its powers? How does it help the character?

Literature **151**

Assess and Reteach

Assess and Progress   L2

Have students answer the assessment questions.

Reteach   L1

If students are having difficulty remembering the plotline of the selection, have them create a chart of the story's major events. Show the blank *Flow Chart Transparency* to help students structure their charts.

📖 **Medieval Times to Today Transparencies,** *Transparency B5: Flow Chart*

Extend   L3

To extend the lesson, have students create a short play based on the selection. Have students form groups and assign each group a responsibility such as creating simple props, writing the story in script form, or playing the roles of the characters. If possible, have students perform their play for another class.

Answer

✓ **Reading Check** Arthur liked the sword better than the scabbard.

Review and Assessment

Thinking About the Selection

1. (a) They fought on horseback with spears and on foot with swords. **(b)** Pellinore probably would have killed Arthur, because Arthur no longer had his sword.

2. (a) They were amazed that Arthur risked his life just as they themselves did, and were happy to have a leader who fought in the same manner they did. **(b)** He is fair-minded, even when facing an enemy in battle. **(c)** Answers will vary, but should be supported from the text. Most students will probably think that Arthur has leadership qualities, such as being courageous and just, that would make him a good ruler in today's world.

Writing Activity

Use the *Rubric for Assessing a Student Poem* or the *Rubric for Assessing a Writing Assignment* to evaluate students' poems or stories.

All in One **Medieval Times to Today Teaching Resources,** *Rubric for Assessing a Student Poem,* p. 300, *Rubric for Assessing a Writing Assignment,* p. 297

6 A New Age in Europe

Chapter Overview

Overview

 Section 1
The Renaissance and Reformation
1. Learn about the Renaissance and why it occurred when and where it did.
2. Find out about Renaissance art and artists.
3. Discover how the Reformation changed religious life in Europe.

 Section 2
The Age of Exploration
1. Discover why Europeans set out to explore the world in the 1400s.
2. Learn how the Portuguese reached India by sailing east and how Columbus reached the Americas by sailing west.
3. Find out how Magellan's expedition sailed all the way around the world.

 Section 3
The Age of Powerful Monarchs
1. Learn about absolute rule in France.
2. Find out why the reign of Queen Elizabeth I was a golden age in England.
3. Discover the accomplishments of strong rulers in Spain and Russia.

Section 4
Conquests in the Americas and Africa
1. Discover how Spanish conquistadors conquered great civilizations in the Americas.
2. Find out why the African slave trade developed and what its effects were.

Leonardo da Vinci: A Renaissance Man
Length: 5 minutes, 7 seconds
Use with Section 1
This video segment explains why Leonardo Da Vinci was the ultimate Renaissance man. The segment introduces Da Vinci as a painter, sculptor, architect, engineer, and scientist, and describes his plans for machines that were far ahead of their time.

Technology Resources

 **Go Online**
PHSchool.com

Students use embedded Web codes to access Internet activities, chapter self-tests, and additional map practice. They may also access Dorling Kindersley's Online Desk Reference to learn more about each country they study.

 **Interactive Textbook**

Use the Interactive Textbook to make content and concepts come alive through animations, videos, and activities that accompany the complete basal text—online and on CD-ROM.

 **PRENTICE HALL TeacherEXPRESS**
Plan • Teach • Assess

Use this complete suite of powerful teaching tools to make planning lessons and administering tests quicker and easier.

Reading and Assessment

Reading and Vocabulary Instruction

⟳ Model the Target Reading Skill

Context Explain to students that they can determine the meanings of unfamiliar words by using context clues in nearby words, phrases, or sentences. To help students understand context, write the following sentences, from p. 160 of the Student Edition, on the board:

In an effort to wipe out heresy, or beliefs that did not conform to Church teachings, the Church strengthened the power of the Inquisition. The Inquisition was a system of church courts that used secret testimony and torture to root out heresy and forced non-Catholics to convert to Catholicism.

Model the skill by thinking about these sentences aloud: "The first sentence contains two words that I am not familiar with: *heresy* and *Inquisition*. I will see if I can determine the meaning of these words from the sentences and words around them. As I read the first sentence, I notice that the word *or* comes after the word *heresy*. This word signals to me that a definition of the word may follow. From this, I can conclude that *heresy* has to do with beliefs that do not conform to Church teachings. I still am not sure what *Inquisition* means, so I will read on. The next sentence tells me exactly what the *Inquisition* was: *a system of church courts that used secret testimony and torture to root out heresy and forced non-Catholics to convert to Catholicism.*"

Use the following worksheets from All-in-One Medieval Times to Today Teaching Resources (pp. 329–330) to support the chapter's Target Reading Skill.

Vocabulary Builder
High-Use Academic Words

Use these steps to teach this chapter's high-use words:

1. Have students rate how well they know each word on their Word Knowledge worksheets (All-in-One Medieval Times to Today Teaching Resources, p. 331).
2. Pronounce each word and ask students to repeat it.
3. Give students a brief definition or sample sentence (provided on TE pp. 155, 162, 171, and 181).
4. Work with students as they fill in the "Definition or Example" column of their Word Knowledge worksheets.

Assessment

Formal Assessment

Test students' understanding of core knowledge and skills.

Chapter Tests A and B, All-in-One Medieval Times to Today Teaching Resources, pp. 351–356

Customize the Chapter Tests to suit your needs.
Exam*View*® Test Bank CD-ROM

Skills Assessment

Assess geographic literacy.

MapMaster Skills, Student Edition, pp. 153, 159, 164–165, 182, 186

Assess reading and comprehension.

Target Reading Skills, Student Edition, pp. 159, 166, 176, 181, and in Section Assessments

Chapter 6 Assessment, Medieval Times to Today Reading and Vocabulary Study Guide, p. 71

Performance Assessment

Assess students' performance on this chapter's Writing Activities using the following rubrics from All-in-One Medieval Times to Today Teaching Resources.

Rubric for Assessing a Writing Assignment, p. 349
Rubric for Assessing a Report, p. 350

Assess students' work through performance tasks.

Small Group Activity: Simulation: Keeping a Ship's Log, All-in-One Medieval Times to Today Teaching Resources, pp. 334–337

Online Assessment

Have students check their own understanding.
Chapter Self-Test

Section 1 The Renaissance and Reformation

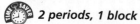 *2 periods, 1 block*

Social Studies Objectives

1. Learn about the Renaissance and why it occurred when and where it did.
2. Find out about Renaissance art and artists.
3. Discover how the Reformation changed religious life in Europe.

Reading/Language Arts Objective

Use context clues, such as definitions and synonyms, to determine the meaning of unfamiliar words.

Prepare to Read	Instructional Resources	Differentiated Instruction
Build Background Knowledge Ask students to preview the section and contrast the Renaissance and the Middle Ages. **Set a Purpose for Reading** Have students begin to fill out the *Reading Readiness Guide*. **Preview Key Terms** Teach the section's Key Terms. **Target Reading Skill** Introduce the section's Target Reading Skill of **using context clues**.	**All in One Medieval Times to Today Teaching Resources** **L2** Reading Readiness Guide, p. 314 **L2** Use Context Clues: Definition and Description, p. 330	**Spanish Reading and Vocabulary Study Guide** **L1** Chapter 6, Section 1, pp. 44–45 ELL

Instruct	Instructional Resources	Differentiated Instruction
The Renaissance Ask questions about city-states and discuss the new attitudes towards art and science that came about in the Renaissance. **The Renaissance Artist** Discuss some of the artists of the Renaissance. **The Protestant Reformation** Ask questions about Martin Luther and the Reformation. **Target Reading Skill** Review **using context clues**.	**All in One Medieval Times to Today Teaching Resources** **L2** Guided Reading and Review, p. 315 **L2** Reading Readiness Guide, p. 314 **Medieval Times to Today Transparencies** **L2** Section Reading Support Transparency MT 69 **World Studies Video Program** **L2** Leonardo da Vinci: A Renaissance Man	**All in One Medieval Times to Today Teaching Resources** **L3** Looking for a Job: A Letter from Leonardo da Vinci, pp. 342–343 AR, GT **L3** Outline Map 14, p. 341 AR, GT **L3** Enrichment, p. 332 AR, GT **Teacher's Edition** **L1** For Special Needs Students, TE p. 157 **L3** For Advanced Readers, TE pp. 157, 159 **L3** For Gifted and Talented, TE p. 159 **Medieval Times to Today Transparencies** **L1** Color Transparency MT 40 ELL, LPR, SN

Assess and Reteach	Instructional Resources	Differentiated Instruction
Assess Progress Evaluate student comprehension with the section assessment and section quiz. **Reteach** Assign the Reading and Vocabulary Study Guide to help struggling students. **Extend** Extend the lesson by assigning an online activity.	**All in One Medieval Times to Today Teaching Resources** **L2** Section Quiz, p. 316 Rubric for Assessing a Writing Assignment, p. 349 **Reading and Vocabulary Study Guide** **L1** Chapter 6, Section 1, pp. 59–61 **PHSchool.com** **L3** **For:** Long-Term Integrated Projects: Modeling World Art **Web Code:** ldg-8606	**Spanish Support** **L2** Section Quiz (Spanish), p. 47 ELL

Key

L1 Basic to Average   **L3** Average to Advanced   **LPR** Less Proficient Readers   **GT** Gifted and Talented

L2 For All Students   **AR** Advanced Readers   **ELL** English Language Learners

     SN Special Needs Students

Section 2 The Age of Exploration

 2 periods, 1 block (includes Focus On A Sailor's Life at Sea)

Social Studies Objectives

1. Discover why Europeans set out to explore the world in the 1400s.
2. Learn how the Portuguese reached India by sailing east and how Columbus reached the Americas by sailing west.
3. Find out how Magellan's expedition sailed all the way around the world.

Reading/Language Arts Objective

Use context clues, such as explanations, to determine the meaning of unfamiliar words.

Prepare to Read	**Instructional Resources**	**Differentiated Instruction**
Build Background Knowledge Ask students to preview the illustrations and list information about some of the explorers in the section. **Set a Purpose for Reading** Have students begin to fill out the *Reading Readiness Guide*. **Preview Key Terms** Teach the section's Key Terms. **Target Reading Skill** Introduce the section's Target Reading Skill of **using context clues**.	**All in One Medieval Times to Today Teaching Resources** L2 Reading Readiness Guide, p. 318 L2 Use Context Clues: Definition and Description, p. 330	**Spanish Reading and Vocabulary Study Guide** L1 Chapter 6, Section 2, pp. 46–47 ELL

Instruct	**Instructional Resources**	**Differentiated Instruction**
Europeans Begin to Explore Discuss the Age of Exploration. **The Portuguese Head East** Discuss the reasons for and the results of the Portuguese sailing east. **Columbus Heads West** Discuss Columbus' expedition to the Americas. **Target Reading Skill** Review **using context clues**. **All the Way Around the World** Ask about Magellan's expedition around the world.	**All in One Medieval Times to Today Teaching Resources** L2 Guided Reading and Review, p. 319 L2 Reading Readiness Guide, p. 318 L2 Journal Entry, p. 102 **Medieval Times to Today Transparencies** L2 Section Reading Support Transparency MT 70	**All in One Medieval Times to Today Teaching Resources** L3 Activity Shop Lab: Making a Compass, pp. 338–339 AR, GT, LPR, SN **Teacher's Edition** L3 For Advanced Readers, TE p. 163 L1 For Less Proficient Readers, TE p. 163 L3 For Gifted and Talented, TE p. 168 **Spanish Support** L1 Guided Reading and Review (Spanish), p. 48 ELL

Assess and Reteach	**Instructional Resources**	**Differentiated Instruction**
Assess Progress Evaluate student comprehension with the section assessment and section quiz. **Reteach** Assign the Reading and Vocabulary Study Guide to help struggling students. **Extend** Extend the lesson by assigning a Small Group Activity.	**All in One Medieval Times to Today Teaching Resources** L2 Section Quiz, p. 320 L3 Small Group Activity: Keeping a Ship's Log, pp. 334–337 Rubric for Assessing a Writing Assignment, p. 349 **Reading and Vocabulary Study Guide** L1 Chapter 6, Section 2, pp. 62–64	**Spanish Support** L2 Section Quiz (Spanish), p. 49 ELL

Key

L1 Basic to Average   L3 Average to Advanced

L2 For All Students

LPR Less Proficient Readers   GT Gifted and Talented

AR Advanced Readers   ELL English Language Learners

SN Special Needs Students

Section 3 The Age of Powerful Monarchs

 3.5 periods, 1.75 blocks (includes Skills for Life)

Social Studies Objectives
1. Learn about absolute rule in France.
2. Find out why the reign of Queen Elizabeth I was a golden age in England.
3. Discover the accomplishments of strong rulers in Spain and Russia.

Reading/Language Arts Objective
Use context clues and your own knowledge to determine the meaning of unfamiliar terms.

Prepare to Read

Build Background Knowledge
Ask students to preview the section and list what they already know about European rulers.

Set a Purpose for Reading
Have students evaluate statements on the *Reading Readiness Guide*.

Preview Key Terms
Teach the section's Key Terms.

Target Reading Skill
Introduce the section's Target Reading Skill of **using context clues**.

Instructional Resources

All in One Medieval Times to Today Teaching Resources
- L2 Reading Readiness Guide, p. 322
- L2 Use Context Clues: General Knowledge, p. 329

Differentiated Instruction

Spanish Reading and Vocabulary Study Guide
- L1 Chapter 6, Section 3, pp. 48–49 ELL

Instruct

Absolute Rule in France
Ask questions about absolute rulers and discuss the role of Richelieu in increasing the power of the king.

A Powerful Queen of England
Discuss the events leading up to Elizabeth I's reign and ask about the accomplishments of the Elizabethan age.

Strong Rulers Unite Spain
Discuss the marriage of Isabella and Ferdinand and its effects on the region of Spain.

Target Reading Skill
Review **using context clues**.

Absolute Rule in Russia
Discuss tsars in Russia.

Instructional Resources

All in One Medieval Times to Today Teaching Resources
- L2 Guided Reading and Review, p. 323
- L2 Reading Readiness Guide, p. 322

Medieval Times to Today Transparencies
- L2 Section Reading Support Transparency MT 71

Differentiated Instruction

All in One Medieval Times to Today Teaching Resources
- L2 Skills for Life, p. 333 AR, GT, LPR, SN

Teacher's Edition
- L1 For Less Proficient Readers, TE p. 172
- L1 For English Language Learners, TE pp. 172, 174
- L3 For Gifted and Talented, TE p. 174
- L1 For Special Needs Students, TE p. 176
- L3 For Advanced Readers, TE p. 176

Medieval Times to Today Transparencies
- L1 Transparency B20: Timeline ELL, LPR, SN

Assess and Reteach

Assess Progress
Evaluate student comprehension with the section assessment and section quiz.

Reteach
Assign the Reading and Vocabulary Study Guide to help struggling students.

Extend
Extend the lesson by having students write plays about events in this section.

Instructional Resources

All in One Medieval Times to Today Teaching Resources
- L2 Section Quiz, p. 324
- L3 Writing Plays, p. 347
  Rubric for Assessing a Writing Assignment, p. 349

Reading and Vocabulary Study Guide
- L1 Chapter 6, Section 3, pp. 65–67

Differentiated Instruction

All in One Medieval Times to Today Teaching Resources
- L3 Reading a Road Map, p. 340 AR, GT

Teacher's Edition
- L1 For Special Needs Students, TE p. 179

Social Studies Skills Tutor CD-ROM
- L1 Analyzing and Interpreting Special Purpose Maps ELL, LPR, SN

Spanish Support
- L2 Section Quiz (Spanish), p. 51 ELL

Key
- L1 Basic to Average   L3 Average to Advanced
- L2 For All Students
- LPR Less Proficient Readers
- AR Advanced Readers
- SN Special Needs Students
- GT Gifted and Talented
- ELL English Language Learners

Section 4 Conquests in the Americas and Africa

 4 periods, 2 blocks (includes Chapter Review and Assessment)

Social Studies Objectives
1. Discover how Spanish conquistadors conquered great civilizations in the Americas.
2. Find out why the African slave trade developed and what its effects were.

Reading/Language Arts Objective
Use context clues in surrounding paragraphs to determine the meaning of unfamiliar words.

Prepare to Read	Instructional Resources	Differentiated Instruction
Build Background Knowledge Ask students to preview the map on p. 182 to determine which countries had empires in the Americas. **Set a Purpose for Reading** Have students begin to fill out the *Reading Readiness Guide*. **Preview Key Terms** Teach the section's Key Terms. **Target Reading Skill** Introduce the section's Target Reading Skill of **using context clues.**	**All in One Medieval Times to Today Teaching Resources** **L2** Reading Readiness Guide, p. 326 **L2** Use Context Clues: Definition and Description, p. 330	**Spanish Reading and Vocabulary Study Guide** **L1** Chapter 6, Section 4, pp. 50–51 ELL

Instruct	Instructional Resources	Differentiated Instruction
Spain's Empire in the Americas Discuss how Spain established an empire in the Americas. **Target Reading Skill** Review **using context clues.** **The African Slave Trade** Ask questions about the African slave trade.	**All in One Medieval Times to Today Teaching Resources** **L2** Guided Reading and Review, p. 327 **L2** Reading Readiness Guide, p. 326 **Medieval Times to Today Transparencies** **L2** Section Reading Support Transparency MT 72	**Teacher's Edition** **L3** For Gifted and Talented, TE p. 182 **L1** For Special Needs Students, TE, p. 179 **Spanish Support** **L2** Guided Reading and Review (Spanish), p. 52 ELL

Assess and Reteach	Instructional Resources	Differentiated Instruction
Assess Progress Evaluate student comprehension with the section assessment and section quiz. **Reteach** Assign the Reading and Vocabulary Study Guide to help struggling students. **Extend** Extend the lesson by assigning a literature reading.	**All in One Medieval Times to Today Teaching Resources** **L2** Section Quiz, p. 328 **L3** The Talking Stone, p. 344–346 Rubric for Assessing a Writing Assignment, p. 349 **L2** Word Knowledge, p. 331 **L2** Vocabulary Development, p. 348 Rubric for Assessing a Report, p. 350 **L2** Chapter Tests A and B, pp. 351–356 **Reading and Vocabulary Study Guide** **L1** Chapter 6, Section 4, pp. 68–70	**Spanish Support** **L2** Section Quiz (Spanish), p. 53 ELL **L2** Chapter Summary (Spanish), p. 54 **L2** Vocabulary Development (Spanish), p. 55

Key
L1 Basic to Average **L3** Average to Advanced
L2 For All Students

LPR Less Proficient Readers
AR Advanced Readers
SN Special Needs Students

GT Gifted and Talented
ELL English Language Learners

Section Lesson Planner

Reading Background

Writing Tips

In this chapter, students will be asked to write paragraphs. To help them create complete and successful paragraphs, ask students to follow these steps when completing this chapter's writing assignments:

- Begin with a topic sentence that tells what the paragraph is about.
- Using transition words or phrases, provide three to five examples that expand on the topic sentence.
- Include a summary sentence.
- Tell students to make sure that their sentences vary in length and structure.

   Model the process by providing students with a topic sentence, followed by three details, and ending with a summary sentence. For example: *There are many reasons why Leonardo Da Vinci has been called a Renaissance man. First of all, he studied nature to learn more about flying. Secondly, Leonardo was a talented artist whose abilities helped him translate the information from his studies into plans for flying machines. He also created one of the most famous Renaissance paintings, the* Mona Lisa. *Leonardo Da Vinci's achievements in the fields of science and art led him to become a symbol of the Renaissance.*

Tips for Using the Oral Cloze Strategy

In this chapter, students will use the Oral Cloze strategy (TE, p. T33) to read the text. To make this strategy effective, preview the selection ahead of time to determine which words you will be leaving out as you read. Try to leave out meaningful words that most students understand. Do not drop very difficult words that most students do not know or cannot read. Prepositions and conjunctions should also be avoided. The following is an example of words that might be dropped, using a selection from p. 155 of the Student Edition. Words to be dropped have been underlined:

   During the Middle Ages, <u>northern</u> Italy, where Leonardo lived, was <u>different</u> from the rest of Western Europe. Most people in northern <u>Europe</u> lived under feudalism. They <u>labored</u> for their lords and depended on their lords for <u>protection</u>.

   You may want to use this technique with the text on the section opener page to engage students' interest. After you have read the first few paragraphs together using the Oral Cloze strategy, have students go back and read the material silently.

World Studies Background

Inside the Human Body

Leonardo Da Vinci's human figure drawings show that he had extensive knowledge of human anatomy. Leonardo developed this knowledge by dissecting and studying cadavers to gain insight into the skeletal and muscular architecture of the human body. Leonardo kept detailed drawings of his study of anatomy. These drawings are considered among the most important accomplishments of Renaissance science.

The Viking Age

Before the European Age of Exploration, there was the Viking Age, during which Scandinavian warriors, known as Vikings, were the world's greatest sailors and shipbuilders. The Vikings set out to explore other lands to trade, find adventure, and escape overpopulation and dissension at home. The Viking Age ended with the introduction of Christianity into Scandinavia and the rise of European states that could defend themselves against Viking invasions.

Infoplease® provides a wealth of useful information for the classroom. You can use this resource to strengthen your background on the subjects covered in this chapter. Have students visit this advertising-free site as a starting point for projects requiring research.

Use Web Code **lgd-8600** for **Infoplease®**.

Learn Vocabulary by Making Choices

Help students build their understanding of Key Terms and high-use words from the chapter by asking them to make choices between correct and incorrect examples of the words. For each word below, read the two examples and ask students to say which example best shows the true meaning of the word.

conform

Example 1: The student did not follow the directions for the writing assignment.
Example 2: The student followed the directions for the writing assignment. *(correct)*

circumnavigate

Example 1: The plane left from New York and flew east around the world until it reached New York again. *(correct)*
Example 2: The flight left from New York and flew east, stopping in London.

emerge

Example 1: The groundhog came out of its hole and saw its shadow. *(correct)*
Example 2: The groundhog went back into its hole after seeing its shadow.

deprive

Example 1: Andrea could not have a cookie because she had not finished her dinner. *(correct)*
Example 2: Bob ate a cookie after finishing his dinner.

Sibling Rivalry

Before Elizabeth became queen of England, she was arrested for alleged treason against her half-sister, Mary, who was queen at the time. Mary I's determination to return England to Roman Catholicism earned her many enemies. In 1554, a group of rebels sought to overthrow Mary I and bring Protestants into power. As heir to the throne, Elizabeth was the prime suspect for plotting against the queen, and she was imprisoned in the Tower of London. Elizabeth was released two months later after an investigation proved her innocence. She became queen after Mary I's death in 1558 and restored Protestantism to England.

Changes Under Peter the Great

Peter the Great's attempts to modernize Russia went beyond his improvements to the army, navy, and industry. After traveling to Western Europe, Peter ordered Russian men to replace their traditional long robes with a Western European style of clothing. He modified the calendar and streamlined the alphabet. Peter the Great also established Russia's first modern hospitals and medical schools.

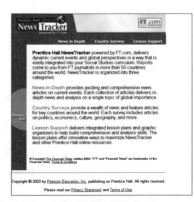

Get in-depth information on topics of global importance with **Prentice Hall Newstracker,** powered by FT.com.

 Use Web Code **lgd-8605** for **Prentice Hall Newstracker.**

Guiding Questions

Remind students about the Guiding Questions introduced at the beginning of the book.

Section 1 relates to **Guiding Question 2** **How did each society's belief system affect its history?** *(Humanism, which focuses on human beings rather than on the divine, influenced the work of Renaissance artists and scholars. Martin Luther's dissatisfaction with the Catholic Church sparked new forms of Christianity.)*

Section 2 relates to **Guiding Question 1** **How did physical geography affect the development of societies around the world?** *(European explorers sailed around Africa and to the west in search of a direct route to Asia, bringing Europeans into contact with people in other lands.)*

Section 3 relates to **Guiding Question 3** **What types of governments were formed in these societies?** *(Many of the nations of Europe had absolute monarchs, or royal rulers with complete authority over the government and the people of the kingdom.)*

Section 4 relates to **Guiding Question 5** **How did each society organize its economic activities?** *(Spain's economy was closely tied with its conquest of the Americas, and the enslavement of Africans was an important factor in the economy of European colonists.)*

Target Reading Skill

In this chapter, students will learn and apply the reading skill of context. Use the following worksheets to help students practice this skill:

AllᴵⁿOne Medieval Times to Today Teaching Resources, *Use Context Clues: General Knowledge,* p. 329; *Use Context Clues: Definition and Description,* p. 330

Differentiated Instruction

The following Teacher's Edition strategies are suitable for students of varying abilities.

Advanced Readers, pp. 157, 159, 163, 176
English Language Learners, pp. 172, 174
Gifted and Talented, pp. 159, 168, 174, 182
Less Proficient Readers, pp. 163, 172
Special Needs Students, pp. 157, 176, 179

Chapter 6

A New Age in Europe

Chapter Preview

This chapter will introduce you to the ideas and events that changed Europe after the Middle Ages. These ideas and events led Europeans to new places and to new ways of looking at themselves and the world.

Section 1
The Renaissance and Reformation

Section 2
The Age of Exploration

Section 3
The Age of Powerful Monarchs

Section 4
Conquests in the Americas and Africa

Target Reading Skill

Context In this chapter you will focus on using context to help you understand unfamiliar words. Context includes the words, phrases, and sentences surrounding a word.

▶ The gardens at the Palace of Versailles, France

152 Medieval Times to Today

Bibliography

For the Teacher
Burke, Peter. *The Italian Renaissance.* Princeton University Press, 1999.
Chadwick, Owen. *The Reformation (Penguin History of the Church 3).* Viking Press, 1990.
Koch, Peter O. *To the Ends of the Earth: The Age of the European Explorers.* McFarland & Company, 2003.

For the Student
L2 Cole, Alison. *Eyewitness: Renaissance.* DK Publishing, 2000.
L2 Flowers, Sarah. *The Age of Exploration (World History).* Lucent Books, 1999.
L3 MacDonald, Fiona. *The Reformation.* Raintree/Steck Vaughn, 2002.

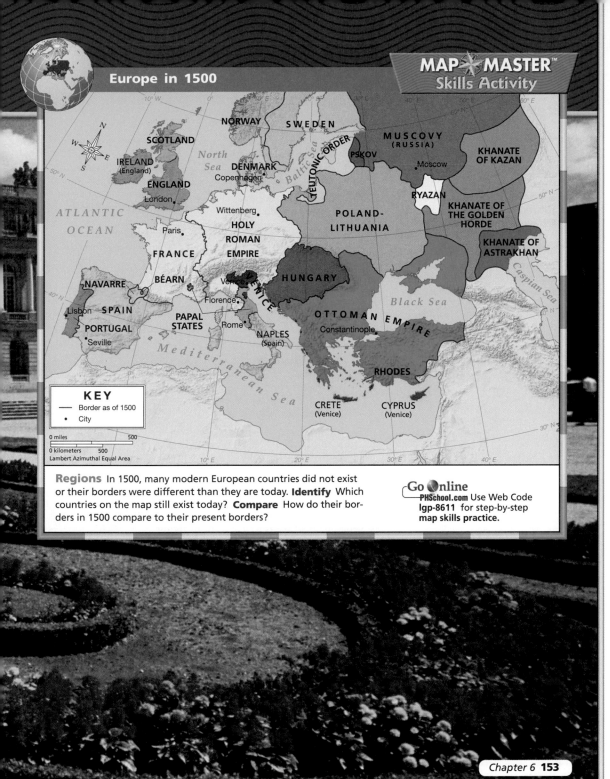

Europe in 1500

NORWAY
SWEDEN
SCOTLAND
North Sea
MUSCOVY (RUSSIA)
PSKOV
Moscow
KHANATE OF KAZAN
IRELAND (England)
DENMARK
Copenhagen
Baltic Sea
TEUTONIC ORDER
ENGLAND
London
ATLANTIC OCEAN
Wittenberg
HOLY ROMAN EMPIRE
POLAND-LITHUANIA
RYAZAN
KHANATE OF THE GOLDEN HORDE
KHANATE OF ASTRAKHAN
Paris
FRANCE
Caspian Sea
NAVARRE
BÉARN
Venice
VENICE
HUNGARY
Black Sea
Florence
SPAIN
Lisbon
PAPAL STATES
Rome
OTTOMAN EMPIRE
PORTUGAL
Seville
NAPLES (Spain)
Constantinople
Mediterranean Sea
RHODES
CRETE (Venice)
CYPRUS (Venice)

KEY
— Border as of 1500
• City

0 miles 500
0 kilometers 500
Lambert Azimuthal Equal Area

Regions In 1500, many modern European countries did not exist or their borders were different than they are today. **Identify** Which countries on the map still exist today? **Compare** How do their borders in 1500 compare to their present borders?

Go **Online**
PHSchool.com Use Web Code lgp-8611 for step-by-step map skills practice.

Chapter 6 **153**

■ Have students look at the map and use their fingers to trace the borders of each country.

■ On the board, create a chart with two columns. Label the first column "Country" and the second column "City." List the countries from the map in the first column. In the second column, place the major cities found on the map next to their corresponding countries.

Go **Online**
PHSchool.com Students may practice their map skills using the interactive online version of this map.

Using the Visual

Reach Into Your Background Draw students' attention to the caption accompanying the picture on pp. 152–153. Ask students to compare the garden at Versailles with other gardens they have seen. Then ask them to share similarities and differences using an Idea Wave. (TE, p. T35)

Answers

MAP ★ MASTER™ Skills Activity **Identify** Although borders have changed, these countries still exist today: Portugal, Spain, France, Norway, Sweden, Denmark, Hungary, Poland, Lithuania, and Russia. England, Scotland, and Northern Ireland today make-up the United Kingdom. **Compare** Students should compare this map with a political map of Europe to determine how the borders of European countries in 1500 compare with their borders today.

Chapter Resources

Teaching Resources
L2 Vocabulary Development, p. 348
L2 Skills for Life, p. 333
L2 Chapter Tests A and B, pp. 351–356

Spanish Support
L2 Spanish Chapter Summary, p. 54
L2 Spanish Vocabulary Development, p. 55

Media and Technology
L1 Student Edition on Audio CD
L1 Guided Reading Audiotapes, English and Spanish
L2 Social Studies Skills Tutor CD-ROM
Exam*View*® Test Bank CD-ROM

Discovery World Studies
CHANNEL Video Program
SCHOOL

interactive
Textbook

PRENTICE HALL
TeacherEXPRESS™
Plan • Teach • Assess

Objectives

Social Studies

1. Learn about the Renaissance and why it occurred when and where it did.
2. Find out about Renaissance art and artists.
3. Discover how the Reformation changed religious life in Europe.

Reading/Language Arts

Use context clues, such as definitions and synonyms, to determine the meaning of unfamiliar words.

Prepare to Read

Build Background Knowledge L2

Tell students that in this section they will learn about the Renaissance. Ask students to quickly preview the headings and visuals in the section with this question in mind: **How was Europe in the Renaissance different from Europe in the Middle Ages?** Provide a few examples to get students started. Ask students to share their thoughts using an Idea Wave (TE, p. T35), and create a class list.

Set a Purpose for Reading L2

- Preview the Objectives.

- Form students into pairs or groups of four. Distribute the *Reading Readiness Guide*. Ask students to fill in the first two columns of the chart. Use the Numbered Heads participation strategy (TE, p. T36) to call on students to share one piece of information they already know and one piece of information they want to know.

   All in One Medieval Times to Today Teaching Resources, *Reading Readiness Guide*, p. 314

Vocabulary Builder
Preview Key Terms L2

Pronounce each Key Term, then ask students to say the word with you. Provide a simple explanation such as, "The Renaissance was a period of renewed interest in learning that began in Europe in the 1300s."

Section 1 The Renaissance and Reformation

Prepare to Read

Objectives
In this section, you will
1. Learn about the Renaissance and why it occurred when and where it did.
2. Find out about Renaissance art and artists.
3. Discover how the Reformation changed religious life in Europe.

Taking Notes
As you read this section, look for the main features of the Renaissance. Copy the diagram below and record your findings in it.

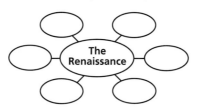

◎ Target Reading Skill
Use Context Clues You can often figure out the meaning of an unfamiliar word by using context clues in nearby words or sentences. One kind of context clue is a synonym, such as the one in italics in the following example: "The wealthy became great patrons, or *supporters*, of the arts."

Key Terms
- **Renaissance** (REN uh sahns) *n.* the period of the rebirth of learning in Europe between about 1300 and 1600

- **humanism** (HYOO muh niz um) *n.* a system of thought that focuses on the nature, ideals, and achievements of human beings, rather than on the divine
- **Reformation** (ref ur MAY shun) *n.* the effort to change or reform the Roman Catholic Church, which led to the establishment of Protestant churches
- **Protestant** (PRAHT us tunt) *adj.* referring to Christian religions that grew out of the Reformation

Have you ever wanted to fly like a bird? Leonardo da Vinci did. This brilliant artist and scientist, who lived about 500 years ago, thought that people could learn to fly. He studied birds and bats as well as winged seeds to learn about flying.

Leonardo never actually built a flying machine. But, as you can see from the drawing at the left, he drew plans for a machine that looks very much like a helicopter. His sketches also included designs for early examples of a parachute and an airplane.

Leonardo was just one of the many gifted Europeans who lived between about 1300 and 1600. This was the time of the **Renaissance**, a period of rebirth of learning in Europe. As you recall, learning was limited during the Middle Ages. The word *Renaissance* means "rebirth," and this period saw a reawakening of interest in art, literature, and science, as well as in the classical civilizations of Greece and Rome.

Leonardo da Vinci's sketch of a flying machine

154 Medieval Times to Today

◎ Target Reading Skill L2

Use Context Clues Point out the Target Reading Skill. Tell students that information surrounding an unfamiliar word can provide clues to the word's meaning.

Model using context clues to find the meaning of *indulgences* in this sentence from p. 158: "Luther especially despised the Church practice of selling indulgences, or pardons for sins." (The word *or* signals that "pardons for sins" is a definition of *indulgences*.)

Give students *Use Context Clues: Definition and Description*. Have them complete the activity in their groups.

   All in One Medieval Times to Today Teaching Resources, *Use Context Clues: Definition and Description*, p. 330

The Renaissance

The Renaissance began in northern Italy. Why did it begin there?

During the Middle Ages, northern Italy, where Leonardo lived, was different from the rest of Western Europe. Most people in northern Europe lived under feudalism. They labored for their lords and depended on their lords for protection. Manors, rather than cities, were the centers of economic life.

The Italian City-States In northern Italy, however, people lived in city-states, or cities that were both cities and independent states. They had their own governments and were not as closely controlled by nobles or the Church. Instead, wealthy families or wealthy merchants held power. These merchants controlled European trade with Asia. Italian merchants bought precious goods such as silk and spices in Muslim trading centers around the Mediterranean Sea. Then they transported these goods throughout Europe, reselling them at high prices. The city of Venice, built on islands in the Adriatic Sea, was a leader in this trade.

Being at the center of this lively international trade exposed the Italian city-states to other cultures and ideas. And because trade brought them wealth, many northern Italians had more time to think, to read, and to create and enjoy art. The wealthy became great patrons, or financial supporters, of scholarship and the arts. By the 1430s, the city of Florence, ruled by the prosperous Medici family, had become a center for the arts. Lorenzo de Medici, called the Magnificent, was a generous and powerful patron of artists, poets, and philosophers.

Links to Government

Machiavelli's *The Prince*
Niccolò Machiavelli (nee koh LOH mahk ee uh VEL ee) was a Florentine diplomat. He drew on his experience of politics and his study of Roman history to write *The Prince*, which he dedicated to Lorenzo de Medici (photo). This book was a guide for gaining and keeping power. Machiavelli said rulers should use whatever methods were necessary to accomplish their goals. He advised rulers that getting results was more important than keeping promises. *The Prince* became famous—and controversial. Today, the term *Machiavellian* still refers to cynical dishonesty in politics.

Renaissance Florence
This 1490 view of Florence shows how the city-state spanned the banks of the Arno River. **Conclude** *How do you think its location on the Arno affected the growth of Florence and life within its borders?*

Vocabulary Builder

Use the information below to teach students this section's high-use words.

High-Use Word	Definition and Sample Sentence
financial, p. 155	*adj.* having to do with the management and use of money Ross makes smart **financial** decisions, so he has saved a lot of money.
perspective, p. 157	*n.* the technique of representing a real object on a flat surface The artist used **perspective** to make the house in his drawing look real.
technology, p. 159	*n.* the use of science to do practical things New medical **technology** can help people live longer, healthier lives.
conform, p. 160	*v.* to be in agreement with Ms. Lee asked that her students **conform** to all of the rules.

Links

Read the **Links to Government** on this page. Ask students **Why does the term Machiavellian refer to cynical dishonesty in politics?** *(because Machiavelli believed that rulers should use whatever methods were necessary to achieve their goals, and that getting results was more important than keeping promises)*

Instruct

The Renaissance   L2

Guided Instruction

- **Vocabulary Builder** Clarify the high-use word **financial** before reading.

- Read The Renaissance using the Oral Cloze strategy (TE, p. T33).

- Ask students **What were city-states?** *(cities that were both cities and independent states with their own governments)*

- Ask **Why do you think the Renaissance began in Italian city-states?** *(Possible answer: Because of their location, city-states were centers for international trade that exposed people to other cultures and ideas. The wealth brought by this trade gave northern Italians more time for intellectual pursuits.)*

Answer

Conclude Trade along the river would have exposed the people of Florence to new cultures and ideas. The quality of life was probably high, because trade brought wealth to the city-state.

- Ask students **What societies did Italian Renaissance scholars and artists study?** *(the ancient societies of Rome and Greece)*

- Ask students **What effect did studying the art and ideas of these ancient cultures have?** *(It inspired curiosity and a new focus on the nature and achievements of individuals, called humanism.)*

- Discuss how the Northern Renaissance developed. *(Cities in northern Europe became prosperous and grew to be centers of intellectual rebirth. Artists and scholars from the north visited Italy and brought ideas of the Italian Renaissance back to their countries.)*

Independent Practice

Ask students to create the Taking Notes graphic organizer on a blank piece of paper. Then have them look for some main features about the Renaissance introduced in this section and record them in the ovals on their organizers. Briefly model how to identify which ideas to record.

Monitor Progress

As students fill in the graphic organizer, circulate and make sure individuals are choosing the correct features. Provide assistance as needed.

A New Realism
Both paintings above were done in Italy. Duccio painted the one on the left around 1311. The painting by Raphael on the right was done about 200 years later. **Compare and Contrast** *What elements make one painting more realistic than the other? Consider the treatment of people, buildings, scenery, and three-dimensional space.*

Old Ideas and New Ideas In the 1300s, the scholars and artists of Italy began to look at life in a new way. First, they looked back—not to the Middle Ages, but to the literature, science, and art of ancient Greece and Rome. Ruins of fine architecture and realistic statues were all around them, especially in the city of Rome. These works inspired study and curiosity as well as a new focus on the achievements of individual people.

Renaissance scholars and artists developed a new focus on the nature, ideals, and achievements of human beings, rather than on the divine. This philosophy is called **humanism.** The ideal of this new era was someone with talent and achievements in many fields, such as Leonardo. Such a person came to be called a Renaissance man.

The Northern Renaissance A rebirth of culture occurred somewhat later in northern Europe. In the early 1400s, artists such as Jan van Eyck developed a distinctive Flemish style of painting. By the 1450s, newly prosperous cities in the north were the center of a Northern Renaissance. Scholars and artists, such as the German artist Albrecht Dürer, traveled to Italy and helped spread the ideas of the Italian Renaissance in the north. By the late 1500s, the Renaissance had reached England, where the plays of William Shakespeare drew large audiences.

✓ **Reading Check** What was the Northern Renaissance?

156 Medieval Times to Today

Background: Links Across Time

The Rise of Vernacular Works Before the invention of the printing press, Christian monks preserved classic literature in the Latin language. During the early Renaissance, Italian writers began to write in the vernacular, or spoken language of the time. Dante Alighieri (1265–1321) wrote the poem *The Divine Comedy*, setting the stage for Italian as a literary language. Francesco Petrarca (1304–1374), known as Petrarch, wrote Italian love poems about a woman named Laura. Giovanni Boccaccio (1313–1375) wrote his well-known collection of prose tales in Italian. The collection is called the *Decameron*, and is one of the most important examples of Italian classical prose.

Answers

Compare and Contrast Raphael's painting appears more realistic because the figures overlap each other, the pattern on the ground becomes smaller as it recedes, and the people in the background are smaller than the people in the foreground.

✓ **Reading Check** the cultural rebirth that occurred later in northern Europe

The Renaissance Artist

Artists of the Middle Ages had not painted people or nature realistically. Their goal had been to celebrate God, the saints, and the Church. In contrast, the artists of the Renaissance studied and copied the more realistic art of ancient Greece and Rome. While they continued to do religious paintings, they often used the architecture and clothing of their own time for these biblical scenes.

In keeping with their interest in individual achievement, these artists also painted realistic portraits of important people of the day—including their patrons. One of the most famous Renaissance paintings, the *Mona Lisa* by Leonardo da Vinci, depicts a woman who was not famous. In fact, to this day, no one is sure who she was.

Art Meets Science To better understand how to portray people, Italian painters and sculptors studied the bones and muscles of the body. Some artists even dissected corpses to learn about anatomy. Renaissance painters also used a new technique called perspective to make objects and landscapes look more realistic. By making distant objects smaller, artists could create scenes that appeared three-dimensional. They also used light and shadow to make objects look solid.

Michelangelo Michelangelo was one of the greatest artists of the Renaissance. He could sculpt marble so that it looked like flowing cloth, rippling muscle, and twisting hair. However, his most famous work is not a sculpture but a series of paintings that cover the ceiling and walls of the Sistine Chapel in Vatican City in Rome. The Vatican is the headquarters of the Roman Catholic Church.

Painting and sculpture were not Michelangelo's only achievements. He was also a poet and an architect. Michelangelo designed the dome of St. Peter's Cathedral in Rome as well as military fortifications for the city of Florence. Like Leonardo, Michelangelo was a Renaissance man.

✓ **Reading Check** Why is Michelangelo called a Renaissance man?

Explore the art and science of Leonardo da Vinci.

Mastery in Marble
In 1499, when he was in his early twenties, Michelangelo carved this statue of the Virgin Mary holding the body of Jesus. **Infer** *What can you infer about Michelangelo from this work of art?*

Chapter 6 Section 1 **157**

Show students *Leonardo da Vinci: A Renaissance Man.* Ask **What are some ideas that da Vinci's notebooks contained?** *(plans for ships, planes, weapons of war, and other machines)*

The Renaissance Artist L2

Guided Instruction

- **Vocabulary Builder** Clarify the high-use word **perspective** before reading.

- Read The Renaissance Artist with students. As students read, circulate and make sure individuals can answer the Reading Check question.

- Ask students **What is one of the most famous paintings of the Renaissance?** *(the* Mona Lisa*)* **Who painted it?** *(Leonardo da Vinci)*

- Ask students **What is Michelangelo's most famous work?** *(a series of paintings that cover the ceiling and walls of the Sistine Chapel in Vatican City in Rome)*

- Discuss how humanism affected art in the Renaissance.*(Humanism led to an interest in creating realistic images of people, including portraits of important figures of the day.)*

Independent Practice

Have students continue to fill in the graphic organizer with details about the Renaissance.

Monitor Progress

As students fill in the graphic organizer, circulate and make sure individuals are choosing the correct details. Provide assistance as needed.

Answers

Infer Michelangelo was an accomplished artist and sculptor who created realistic works of art.

✓ **Reading Check** He was a person with talent in many fields, such as painting, sculpture, poetry, and architecture.

Differentiated Instruction

For Special Needs Students L1
Show a color transparency of one of Michelangelo's paintings in the Sistine Chapel. Ask pairs to consider why the paintings are so famous.

📖 **Medieval Times to Today Transparencies,** *Color Transparency MT 40: Michelangelo, Eritrean Sibyl from the Sistine Chapel*

For Advanced Readers L3
Have students find out more about Leonardo Da Vinci by reading his letter to the Duke of Milan asking for a job. They should then answer the discussion questions in pairs.

All in One Medieval Times to Today Teaching Resources, *Looking for a Job: A Letter from Leonardo da Vinci,* pp. 342–343

The Protestant Reformation

Guided Instruction

- **Vocabulary Builder** Clarify the high-use words **technology** and **conform** before reading.

- Have students read The Protestant Reformation.

- Ask students **Who was Martin Luther?** *(a German monk who challenged the teachings and practices of the Roman Catholic Church)*

- Ask students **Do you think Martin Luther planned to start a new form of Christianity when he nailed his complaints to the church door? Why or why not?** *(Possible answer: Probably not; he was a monk and probably wished to improve the Catholic Church.)*

- Discuss Martin Luther's criticism of the Catholic Church with students. *(Luther believed that people did not need the Church to tell them how to please God. He thought people should be able to read the Bible for themselves. He also disagreed with the Church's practice of selling indulgences.)*

Martin Luther
This modern stained-glass window illustrates the story of Martin Luther nailing his complaints to the church door. **Analyze Images** *What details suggest Luther's dual roles as professor and monk?*

The Protestant Reformation

Michelangelo painted many religious works. His patrons included Lorenzo de Medici as well as two popes. Clearly, the Roman Catholic Church still held great power during the Renaissance. But that power was about to be challenged.

In 1517, only five years after Michelangelo finished the Sistine Chapel, a German monk named Martin Luther began to criticize the Church. Following the custom of the time, he posted a list of his complaints on the door of his church in Wittenberg, Germany. This act is regarded as the beginning of the **Reformation**, an effort to reform, or improve, the Catholic Church. At first, instead of reform, it led to the establishment of new forms of Christianity.

Luther's Beliefs Luther disagreed with many of the teachings and practices of the Roman Catholic Church of the early 1500s. He believed that people did not need popes or other Church officials to tell them what God wanted them to do. In Luther's view, faith in God coupled with common sense, and not obedience to the Church, was the key to a proper Christian life.

Luther also felt that ordinary people could understand the Bible for themselves. He translated the Bible into German so that ordinary people could read it. He was in favor of creating town schools that would teach everyone to read.

Luther especially despised the Church practice of selling indulgences, or pardons for sins. At that time, people were asked to pay money to the Church to be forgiven for their sins. Luther felt that the Church did not have the power to exchange God's forgiveness for money. What's more, the Church often sold indulgences more to raise money than for any truly religious reason.

Luther's Teachings Spread In Germany, priests, nobles, and ordinary people rallied behind Luther's ideas. Some priests agreed with Luther about corruption in the Church. Nobles were eager to limit the Church's overwhelming power. They wanted to collect their own taxes and make their own laws, like the leaders of Italy's city-states.

Answer

Analyze Images The window shows religious symbols, such as crosses, as well as books, which are symbols of education.

 Skills Mini Lesson

Supporting a Position

1. Tell students that to support a position, you should identify reasons supported by evidence, then draw a conclusion.

2. Have students identify reasons why Luther despised indulgences. *(He believed that people did not need the Church to tell them what God wanted them to do. He also thought that the Church had no power to sell God's forgiveness, and that indulgences were sold mostly to make money.)*

3. Have the class debate an issue, such as whether there should be laws against using cell phones while driving. Students should conduct research to support their positions on the issue.

Meanwhile, a revolution in technology had begun in Germany. In the 1400s, the German printer Johann Gutenberg invented the first European printing press using movable type. He printed a Bible in 1455. The development of the European printing press helped spread Luther's writings across Europe. Bibles printed in German became available. By the time Luther died in 1546, most of the people in what is now northern Germany were Lutheran, or followers of Luther's teachings.

Protestant Churches Soon, people in much of northern Europe held views similar to Luther's. They created their own Christian churches, free of Roman Catholic control. These came to be called **Protestant** churches because they grew out of protests against the power and abuses of the Roman Catholic Church. Their members, even today, are called Protestants.

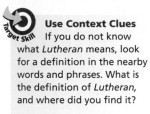

Use Context Clues
If you do not know what *Lutheran* means, look for a definition in the nearby words and phrases. What is the definition of *Lutheran*, and where did you find it?

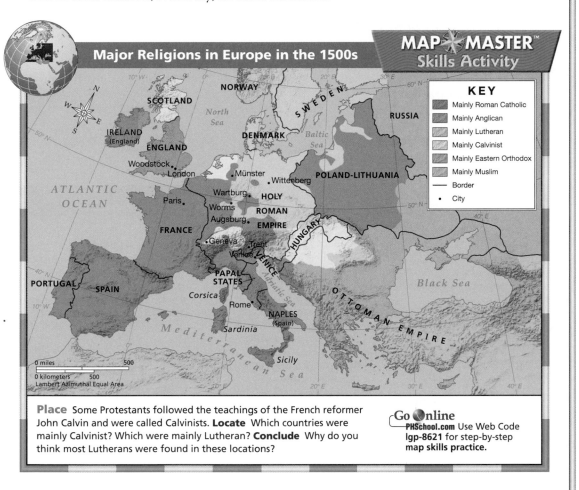

Major Religions in Europe in the 1500s

MAP ★ MASTER™
Skills Activity

KEY
- Mainly Roman Catholic
- Mainly Anglican
- Mainly Lutheran
- Mainly Calvinist
- Mainly Eastern Orthodox
- Mainly Muslim
- — Border
- • City

Place Some Protestants followed the teachings of the French reformer John Calvin and were called Calvinists. **Locate** Which countries were mainly Calvinist? Which were mainly Lutheran? **Conclude** Why do you think most Lutherans were found in these locations?

Go Online
PHSchool.com Use Web Code lgp-8621 for step-by-step map skills practice.

Chapter 6 Section 1 **159**

Target Reading Skill L2

Use Context Clues As a follow up, ask students to answer the Target Reading Skill question in the Student Edition. *(a follower of Luther's teaching; the definition follows the word and is signaled by the word* or*)*

Guided Instruction (continued)

- Ask students **How did Martin Luther's ideas change Europe?** *(They led to people having more direct access to the Bible and to new forms of Christianity.)*

- Ask students **How did Gutenberg's printing press affect the Reformation?** *(Possible answer: Bibles could be printed in German, rather than written by hand in Latin, allowing people to read and interpret the Bible themselves.)*

- Ask students **What was the Catholic Reformation?** *(an attempt to correct abuses in the Catholic Church, while maintaining its basic teachings)*

Independent Practice

Have students complete their graphic organizers by adding main ideas from what they have just read.

Monitor Progress

- Show *Section Reading Support Transparency MT 69* and ask students to check their graphic organizers individually.

  Medieval Times to Today Transparencies, *Section Reading Support Transparency MT 69*

- Tell students to fill in the last column of the *Reading Readiness Guide*. Ask them if they learned what they had expected to learn.

  All in One Medieval Times to Today Teaching Resources, *Reading Readiness Guide*, p. 314

Answers

MAP ★ MASTER™ Skills Activity **Locate** Calvinist: Hungary, Scotland, and parts of the Holy Roman and Ottoman Empires; Lutheran: Sweden, Norway, Denmark, parts of the Holy Roman and Ottoman Empires, Hungary, Poland-Lithuania, and Russia **Conclude** because they are near Germany, where Luther taught

Go Online PHSchool.com Students may practice their map skills using the interactive online version of this map.

Assess and Reteach

Assess Progress `L2`

Have students complete the Section Assessment. Administer the *Section Quiz*.

 Medieval Times to Today Teaching Resources, *Section Quiz*, p. 316

Reteach `L1`

If students need more instruction, have them read this section in the Reading and Vocabulary Study Guide.

📖 Chapter 6, Section 1, **Medieval Times to Today Reading and Vocabulary Study Guide,** pp. 59–61

Extend `L3`

Have students learn more about the art of the Renaissance by completing the project *Modeling World Art*.

Go Online
PHSchool.com

For: Long-Term Integrated Projects: *Modeling World Art*
Visit: PHSchool.com
Web Code: lgd-8606

Answer

✓ Reading Check members of the Society of Jesus who became well-known as teachers and missionaries

Section 1 Assessment

Key Terms

Students' sentences should reflect knowledge of each Key Term.

🎯 Target Reading Skill

The word *or* signals that the definition of the word follows. A *city-state* is both a city and an independent state.

Comprehension and Critical Thinking

1. (a) northern Italy **(b)** Possible answer: In city-states, trade brought wealth and exposure to other cultures and ideas. In turn, wealth allowed people more leisure time. **(c)** Scholars and artists were inspired by the ideas and art of ancient Rome and Greece.

2. (a) Art of the Middle Ages was not realistic and celebrated the divine; Renaissance art was more realistic and focused on the individual.

The opening session of the Council of Trent, 1545

The Catholic Reformation Many Roman Catholics agreed with some criticisms made by Protestants. Instead of turning away from the Church, however, they worked to reform it. As part of this Catholic Reformation, Pope Paul III set up the Council of Trent in 1545. For almost 20 years, it worked to correct the worst abuses of the Church. But it also maintained the basic teachings of the Catholic Church.

The Catholic Reformation also strove to bring Protestants back to the Catholic Church and to make sure that Catholics held strictly to Church teachings. In an effort to wipe out heresy, or beliefs that did not conform to Church teachings, the Church strengthened the power of the Inquisition. The Inquisition was a system of church courts that used secret testimony and torture to root out heresy and force non-Catholics to convert to Catholicism.

At the same time, the effort to reform the Church led to a rebirth of sincere faith among many Catholics. St. Vincent de Paul worked to help the poor people of Paris. Teresa of Avila set up a new order of nuns in Spain. Ignatius of Loyola founded the Society of Jesus. Jesuits, as members of this society are called, were among the best-educated people of Europe at this time. They became well known as teachers and missionaries.

✓ **Reading Check** Who were the Jesuits?

✦ Section 1 Assessment

Key Terms
Review the key terms at the beginning of this section. Use each term in a sentence that explains its meaning.

🎯 **Target Reading Skill**
Find the word *city-states* on page 155. What context clue helps you understand it? What does *city-states* mean?

Comprehension and Critical Thinking
1. (a) Identify Where in Europe did the Renaissance begin?

(b) Identify Causes Why did it begin there?
(c) Analyze How did the Renaissance combine old ideas with new ideas?
2. (a) Compare How was Renaissance art different from the art of the Middle Ages?
(b) Conclude How did Renaissance art represent the new ideas of the age?
3. (a) Define What was the Reformation?
(b) Compare How were the Protestant Reformation and the Catholic Reformation alike? How were they different?

Writing Activity
Write a paragraph explaining how the Renaissance represented a change in the way Europeans viewed the world and themselves. Be sure to include the reason this era is called the Renaissance.

Go Online
PHSchool.com

For: An activity on the Renaissance
Visit: PHSchool.com
Web Code: lgd-8601

(b) Possible answer: Renaissance art reflected humanism by focusing on human beings rather than on the divine.

3. (a) The Reformation was an effort to reform the Catholic Church that led to the establishment of new forms of Christianity.
(b) Possible answer: Alike—Both aimed to reform the Catholic Church. Different—The Protestant Reformation created a group of Christian Churches separate from the Catholic Church; the Catholic Reformation tried to reform the church but keep its teachings.

Writing Activity
Use the *Rubric for Assessing a Writing Assignment* to assess students' paragraphs.

 **Medieval Times to Today Teaching Resources,** *Rubric for Assessing a Writing Assignment,* p. 349

Go Online
PHSchool.com Typing in the Web code when prompted will bring students directly to detailed instructions for this activity.

Section 2 The Age of Exploration

Prepare to Read

Objectives

In this section, you will

1. Discover why Europeans set out to explore the world in the 1400s.
2. Learn how the Portuguese reached India by sailing east and how Columbus reached the Americas by sailing west.
3. Find out how Magellan's expedition sailed all the way around the world.

Taking Notes

As you read this section, look for the major causes and effects of the Age of Exploration. Copy the diagram below and record your findings in it.

Target Reading Skill

Use Context Clues When you come across an unfamiliar word, you can sometimes figure out its meaning from clues in the context. Context refers to the surrounding words and sentences. One type of context clue is an explanation of the term. It may appear either before or after the term. In the following example, the clue is in italics: "The Portuguese developed *a new type of ship* called the caravel."

Key Terms

- **Age of Exploration** (ayj uv eks pluh RAY shun) *n.* the period of European exploration overseas from about 1400 to 1600
- **Cape of Good Hope** (kayp uv good hohp) *n.* the southern tip of Africa
- **Northwest Passage** (nawrth WEST PAS ij) *n.* a sea route through North America
- **Strait of Magellan** (strayt uv muh JEL un) *n.* a waterway near the southern tip of South America
- **circumnavigate** (sur kum NAV ih gayt) *v.* to sail or fly completely around something, such as Earth

Look at the map on this page. It was drawn in the 1470s by an Italian mapmaker. Europe, Asia, and Africa cover the whole map. North America and South America are nowhere to be seen. Why? Because the people in Europe didn't even know that these continents existed.

During the Middle Ages, Europeans had done little exploring beyond their own shores. Except for the Holy Land, they had very little knowledge of, or interest in, other lands. During the Renaissance, however, Europeans became curious about the world around them. This led to an interest in science and technology. It also led to exploration.

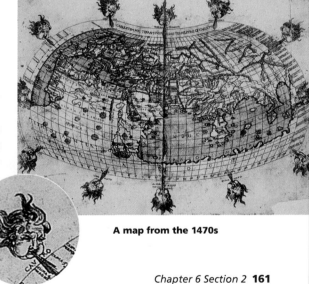

A map from the 1470s

Chapter 6 Section 2 **161**

Target Reading Skill L2

Use Context Clues Point out the Target Reading Skill. Review with students that information surrounding an unknown word can provide clues to the word's meaning.

Model using content clues to find the meaning of *navigator* on p. 163. "He invited mapmakers, shipbuilders, and expert sailors called navigators from all over the

country." *(The words "expert sailors" can help students learn that* navigator *means someone who directs a ship.)*

Give students *Use Context Clues: Definition and Description*. Have them complete the activity in their groups.

All in One Medieval Times to Today Teaching Resources, *Use Context Clues: Definition and Description,* p. 330

Section 2
Step-by-Step Instruction

Objectives

Social Studies

1. Discover why Europeans set out to explore the world in the 1400s.
2. Learn how the Portuguese reached India by sailing east and how Columbus reached the Americas by sailing west.
3. Find out how Magellan's expedition sailed all the way around the world.

Reading/Language Arts

Use context clues, such as explanations, to determine the meaning of unfamiliar words.

Prepare to Read

Build Background Knowledge L2

In this section students will learn about the explorers of the Renaissance. Using the Think-Write-Pair-Share strategy (TE, p. T36), ask students to preview the illustrations and list two of the explorers that they will learn about. Have the pairs share their answers along with any additional information that students may know about these explorers. Write their responses on the board.

Set a Purpose for Reading L2

■ Preview the Objectives.

■ Form students into pairs or groups of four. Distribute the *Reading Readiness Guide.* Ask the students to fill in the first two columns of the chart. Use the Numbered Heads participation strategy (TE, p. T36) to call on students to share one piece of information they already know and one piece of information they want to know.

All in One Medieval Times to Today Teaching Resources, *Reading Readiness Guide,* p. 318

Vocabulary Builder
Preview Key Terms L2

Pronounce each Key Term, then ask students to say the word with you. Provide a simple explanation such as, "European explorers were looking for a Northwest Passage, a water route between the Atlantic and Pacific oceans through North America."

Instruct

Europeans Begin to Explore
■ L2

Guided Instruction

■ **Vocabulary Builder** Clarify the high-use word **capable** before reading.

■ Have students read Europeans Begin to Explore, using the Choral Reading strategy (TE, p. T34).

■ Ask students **What new technology enabled Europeans to explore during the 1400s?** *(advances in sailing technology such as the caravel, the mariner's compass, the astrolabe, and better maps)*

■ Have students study the images on this page. Then ask **When was the magnetic compass invented?** *(in the 1100s)* **What is a compass used for?** *(to show direction)*

■ Ask students **Why did Europeans want to find a new route to Asia?** *(They were tired of paying high prices for goods because the goods passed through the hands of first the Ottomans, then the Italians, on their way to the rest of Europe.)*

Independent Practice

Ask students to create the Taking Notes graphic organizer on a blank piece of paper. Then have them fill in two causes mentioned in this section that led to the Age of Exploration. Briefly model how to find the causes.

Monitor Progress

As students fill in the graphic organizer, circulate and make sure individuals are recording their causes accurately. Provide assistance as needed.

Seafaring Technology

Astrolabes, invented by the Greeks and improved by the Arabs, were used to measure the angles of the sun and stars in order to determine latitude. An Arabian astrolabe is shown at the right. ▶

▲ The magnetic compass was invented in the 1100s. By the 1200s, the needle pivoted on a pin over a card that showed the directions. This Italian mariner's compass is from 1570.

Caravels adopted the triangular lateen sails found on Arab ships. Lateen sails allowed ships to sail into the wind. Some caravels also used traditional European square sails. The watercolor at the right depicts the ships of Columbus. ▶

Europeans Begin to Explore

Driven by curiosity, a desire for trade, and great advances in sailing technology, Europeans soon traveled far beyond their homelands—and all the way around the world. From about 1400 to 1600, Europeans sailed across the vast oceans to explore Asia, Africa, and the Americas. This period is called the **Age of Exploration.** Eventually, Europeans would control much of these lands and change the course of world history.

Technology Opens New Worlds What prompted Europeans to make dozens of dangerous and dramatic voyages during the Age of Exploration? One reason is simply that they could. Before this time, European ships were not capable of such long ocean crossings. By the early 1400s, though, Portuguese shipbuilders had developed a new type of ship called the caravel. Strong, maneuverable, and able to sail against the wind, it was the best sailing vessel of its time.

The Europeans also had two improved navigation tools, the mariner's compass and the astrolabe. Further, they had learned how to make better, more accurate maps. Now they were able to set out on long voyages. But technology alone was not enough to explain why they made those long and hazardous expeditions.

Vocabulary Builder

Use the information below to teach students this section's high-use words.

High-Use Word	Definition and Sample Sentence
capable, p. 162	*adj.* able to do something Matt is **capable** of doing well in his math class.
monarch, p. 165	*n.* a royal ruler of state or country An absolute **monarch** is a ruler who governs with complete power.
emerge, p. 167	*v.* to come out from The train broke down moments after it **emerged** from the tunnel.
dispute, p. 167	*n.* disagreement They did not agree and had a serious **dispute** about the issue.

Trade Inspires Travel By the early 1400s, many Europeans had grown tired of paying high prices to Italian merchants for Asian goods. These merchants, in turn, had paid high prices to the Muslim traders of the Ottoman Empire, which controlled the trade routes between Europe and Asia.

Europeans wanted to gain control of the rich trade with Asia themselves. To do this, they would have to find a new route to Asia—one that did not use the Mediterranean Sea and the land routes controlled by the Ottomans. Two European nations, Portugal and Spain, set out to find a sea route starting from their Atlantic coasts.

✓ **Reading Check** Why did Europeans seek a new route to Asia?

The Portuguese Head East

By the 1400s, the small nation of Portugal was already a strong and successful seafaring power. It had even conquered some territory on the coast of North Africa. The Portuguese wanted to continue exploring the African coast. And they thought that the best sea route to Asia might be one that went east, around the southern tip of Africa.

Prince Henry the Navigator The search for this eastern sea route was led by Prince Henry, the son of Portugal's king. In 1419, he opened a school to encourage exploration. He invited mapmakers, shipbuilders, and expert sailors called navigators from all over the country.

Henry oversaw more than 50 expeditions. Although he did not go exploring himself, his work won him the title of Henry the Navigator. As expeditions pushed farther south along the western coast of Africa, sailors set up trading posts there. They also gathered information on winds, currents, and coastlines.

Henry's Dream Is Fulfilled Henry the Navigator died in 1460, but his dream of an eastern sea route to Asia lived on. In 1488, the Portuguese sea captain Bartolomeu Dias sailed all the way around the southern tip of Africa, which we now call the **Cape of Good Hope.**

Ten years later, Vasco da Gama sailed around the Cape of Good Hope, up Africa's eastern coast, and then across the Indian Ocean to India. He returned with a cargo of spices and precious stones. Soon the Portuguese seized important ports around the Indian Ocean. They had their trade route to Asia.

✓ **Reading Check** Why was Vasco da Gama's voyage important?

Monument to the Explorers
This monument showing Prince Henry at the prow of a ship followed by explorers and other royal patrons is in Lisbon, Portugal. **Analyze Images** *How does the statue suggest Portugal's contributions to the Age of Exploration?*

Guided Instruction

■ Ask students **Why did the Portuguese decide to sail east?** *(They thought that the best sea route to Asia might be one that went east around the southern tip of Africa.)*

■ Ask students **Why do you think Henry the Navigator encouraged so many expeditions?** *(Possible answer: He wanted Portugal to find a trade route to Asia so that Portugal could control its own trade with the continent.)*

Independent Practice

Have students continue filling in their graphic organizers with causes and effects of the Age of Exploration.

Monitor Progress

As students fill in the graphic organizer, circulate and make sure that they are correctly identifying causes and effects.

Answers

✓ **Reading Check** Europeans wanted to control their own trade routes to Asia rather than pay high prices to Italian merchants for goods bought from Muslim traders of the Ottoman Empire.

Analyze Images The statue suggests that Portugal was a key player in the Age of Exploration and initiated many expeditions to foreign lands.

✓ **Reading Check** Vasco da Gama developed a new route to India around Africa and across the Indian Ocean. This enabled Portugal to control ports around the Indian Ocean.

Differentiated Instruction

For Advanced Readers [L3]
Have students learn more about how a compass works by making their own in the *Activity Shop Lab.*

⬛ **Medieval Times to Today Teaching Resources,** *Activity Shop Lab: Making a Compass,* pp. 338–339

For Less Proficient Readers [L1]
Tell students that good readers ask themselves questions as they read. To practice this skill, help less proficient readers turn the blue heads under the red head The Portuguese Head East into questions. *(Who was Prince Henry the Navigator? How was Henry's dream fulfilled?)* Then ask them to note the answers to these questions as they read.

Columbus Heads West L2

Guided Instruction

- **Vocabulary Builder** Clarify the high-use word **monarch** before reading.

- Read Columbus Heads West with students. Point out the map on pp. 164–165 and ask students to trace the route that Christopher Columbus used on his voyage.

- Ask students **Why did Columbus want to sail west?** *(He knew Earth was round and thought that by sailing west he could establish a sea route to Asia for Spain.)*

- Ask students **Why did Spain's Queen Isabella and King Ferdinand agree to finance Columbus' voyage?** *(They knew if they had their own trade route to Asia, Spain would gain great riches.)*

Christopher Columbus

Columbus Heads West

While the Portuguese were exploring to the east, an Italian sea captain named Christopher Columbus became convinced that he could reach Asia by sailing west, across the Atlantic. At that time, educated Europeans knew that the world was round. It made sense to Columbus that a ship sailing west would eventually reach Asia.

Columbus convinced Queen Isabella and King Ferdinand of Spain to pay for an expedition that headed west across the Atlantic. They knew of the great riches to be gained if Spain had a sea route to Asia.

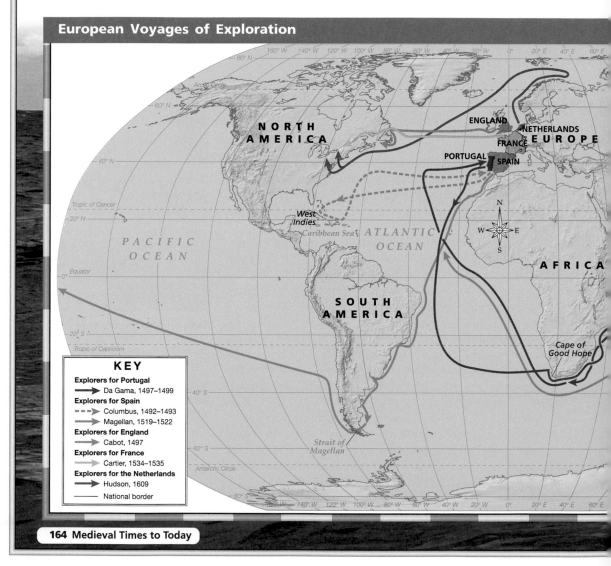

European Voyages of Exploration

KEY

Explorers for Portugal
Da Gama, 1497–1499

Explorers for Spain
Columbus, 1492–1493
Magellan, 1519–1522

Explorers for England
Cabot, 1497

Explorers for France
Cartier, 1534–1535

Explorers for the Netherlands
Hudson, 1609

National border

Background: Links Across Time

Discovering the Americas Though Columbus is widely believed to have been the first European to set eyes on the Americas in 1492, some experts argue the Norse explorer Leif Eriksson arrived centuries earlier. Born in Iceland in about 980 A.D., Leif lived in Greenland until the age of 19, when he traveled to Norway. Icelandic accounts differ on the specifics of his voyage to the Americas; one source says that he was blown off course on his return voyage from Europe, and another tells of Eriksson's crew settling on the coast of present-day North America for the winter. In 1963, a Norwegian expedition uncovered the remnants of a Viking settlement in Newfoundland dating back to A.D. 1000, almost 500 years before Columbus landed.

Columbus Lands in the Americas What neither Columbus nor the Spanish monarchs—nor anyone else—knew was that two huge continents lay between Europe and Asia. So in August 1492, Columbus set sail for Asia—westward across the Atlantic Ocean.

Columbus's expedition included three ships—the *Niña*, the *Pinta*, and the *Santa Maria*—and about 90 sailors. After two months, on October 12, 1492, they landed on a little island in the Caribbean Sea, off the coast of North America. Because he thought he had reached the Indies in Asia, Columbus called the people he found there *Indians*. He claimed the land for Spain.

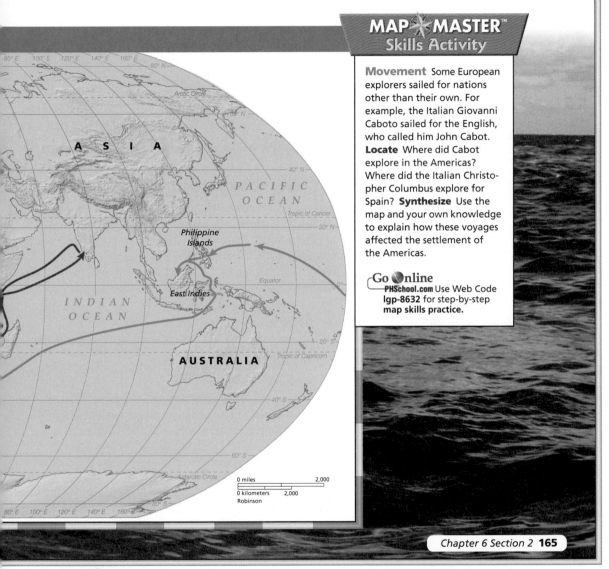

MAP★MASTER™ Skills Activity

Movement Some European explorers sailed for nations other than their own. For example, the Italian Giovanni Caboto sailed for the English, who called him John Cabot. **Locate** Where did Cabot explore in the Americas? Where did the Italian Christopher Columbus explore for Spain? **Synthesize** Use the map and your own knowledge to explain how these voyages affected the settlement of the Americas.

Go Online PHSchool.com Use Web Code **lgp-8632** for step-by-step map skills practice.

0 miles 2,000
0 kilometers 2,000
Robinson

Guided Instruction (continued)

- Ask students **How long did it take Columbus to reach the Americas?** *(about two months)*

- Ask students **Why did Columbus think he had reached the Indies in Asia?** *(Columbus didn't know that the Americas separated Europe from Asia, so he assumed that he must have reached Asia.)*

- Discuss the effects of Columbus reaching the Americas. *(Interest in exploring and claiming land increased. Spain and Portugal set up a Line of Demarcation to try to stop each other from claiming more land than the other. Other explorers, such as John Cabot and Vasco Nuñez de Balboa, led their own expeditions.)*

Independent Practice

Ask students to continue recording the causes and effects of the Age of Exploration on their graphic organizers.

Monitor Progress

As students fill in the graphic organizer, circulate and make sure individuals are correctly recording the causes and effects. Provide assistance as needed.

Skills for Life **Skills Mini Lesson**

Recognizing Bias [L2]

1. To recognize bias, students should consider who is writing and why, and look for facts and opinions in their writing.

2. As a class, analyze this statement by Columbus about indigenous peoples of the Americas: "... they seemed on the whole to me, to be a very poor people."

(The statement is an opinion. These people might not have been considered poor in their own culture.)

3. Have students read and analyze Columbus' *Journal Entry* for more biased statements.

All in One Medieval Times to Today Teaching Resources, *Journal Entry,* p. 102

Answers

MAP★MASTER™ Skills Activity **Locate** Canada; the West Indies **Synthesize** Students should answer that the French and the English influenced the settlements of Canada, and the Spanish influenced the settlements of the West Indies.

Go Online PHSchool.com Students may practice their map skills using the interactive online version of this map.

Use Context Clues As a follow up, ask students to answer the Target Reading Skill question on this page. (*The Line of Demarcation is an imaginary line that determined where Spain and Portugal could settle. Clues: Spain could settle west of the line and Portugal could settle east of the line.*)

All the Way Around the World L2

Guided Instruction

- **Vocabulary Builder** Clarify the high-use words **emerge** and **dispute** before reading.

- Have students read All the Way Around the World.

- Ask students **Who is credited with being the first person to sail around the world?** (*Ferdinand Magellan*)

- Discuss with students why Magellan is considered the first to sail around the world, even though he died before returning to Spain. (*Possible answer: He provided the talent and determination needed to lead the difficult expedition.*)

Independent Practice
Have students complete the graphic organizer.

Monitor Progress

- Show *Section Support Transparency MT 70* and ask students to check their graphic organizers individually. Go over key concepts and clarify key vocabulary as needed.

  📖 **Medieval Times to Today Transparencies,** *Section Reading Support Transparency MT 70*

- Tell students to fill in the last column of the *Reading Readiness Guide*. Ask them to evaluate if what they learned was what they had expected to learn.

  All in One **Medieval Times to Today Teaching Resources,** *Reading Readiness Guide,* p. 318

Answers

Analyze Images The ships in the background, the map, the book, and the scroll probably all represent his accomplishments.

✓ **Reading Check** Europeans still wanted to find alternative routes to Asia. Sailing through North America would result in more profitable trade routes.

⊙ **Use Context Clues** As you read the paragraph at the right, you may not immediately know what the term *Line of Demarcation* refers to. What clues are there in the paragraph? What is the Line of Demarcation?

Ferdinand Magellan
Before 1519, Magellan had already sailed to India, Africa, and Southeast Asia. He had also studied other sailors' reports of winds and currents. **Analyze Images** *How does this painting suggest Magellan's knowledge and accomplishments?*

Exploring the Americas News of Columbus's discovery electrified Europe. Spain and Portugal became rivals. They tried to stop each other from claiming lands in the Americas. In 1494, they signed a treaty that set a Line of Demarcation through the Americas at about 50° W longitude. Spain had the right to settle west of the line. Portugal could do the same east of the line.

England sent the Italian sailor John Cabot across the Atlantic just five years after Columbus's first voyage. He reached what is now Canada. A few years later, his son Sebastian followed. His goal was to find a **Northwest Passage,** a way to sail through North America and then on to Asia. Many other European explorers searched unsuccessfully for a way to continue the western sea route to Asia.

In 1513, a Spanish adventurer named Vasco Nuñez de Balboa led a land expedition across a narrow but hazardous strip of land in Central America. From a mountaintop, he saw a huge ocean to the south, which he claimed for Spain. The Spanish called it the South Sea. Balboa had become the first European to see the Pacific Ocean from the shores of the Americas. The Pacific was the sea that would eventually take Europeans all the way to Asia.

✓ **Reading Check** Why did explorers search for a Northwest Passage?

All the Way Around the World

Even after Columbus reached the Americas, Europeans did not understand how large Earth was. They believed that Japan, which they called Cipango (sih PANG goh), was separated from the Americas by a narrow channel of water. The Portuguese sailor Ferdinand Magellan (FUR duh nand muh JEL un) was eager to cross that channel. But one problem still remained: how to get around the Americas.

Magellan Sets Out With backing from the Spanish king, Magellan set sail in 1519 with five ships. They sailed west to South America and then south along the South American coast. After spending the stormy winter on land, some of the sailors wanted to turn back, but Magellan forced them to continue. Finally, they located a narrow, twisting passage near the tip of South America. Today, it is called the **Strait of Magellan,** in the explorer's honor. It took Magellan 38 days to sail through the strait. Strong currents and fierce winds made the journey difficult. Only three of the five ships made it through.

┌─ **Background: Daily Life** ─────────

A Difficult Journey Magellan's voyage around the world took nearly three years to complete. During this time, the crew faced many storms and tribulations at sea. After six months, two of Magellan's captains led a mutiny, which Magellan was able to overcome. By the time the ships entered the Pacific Ocean more than a year into the journey, the crew was dehydrated, had scurvy, and was eating leather and rat-infested biscuits. When they reached Guam on March 6, 1521, the crew had not eaten fresh food in 99 days.

Sailing the Pacific The three ships emerged from the treacherous strait into the sea that Balboa had sighted. Magellan thought this ocean was much less stormy than the strait, so he called it *pacific*, which means "peaceful."

Magellan and his men had no idea how vast the Pacific Ocean was. Short of food and fresh water, they sailed for three months without sighting any land, except for a few tiny islands. Some men starved to death, while others died of disease. At last, they reached the Philippines. There, tragedy struck: Magellan was killed when he became involved in a local dispute. Thus, the leader of the expedition did not live to return to Spain.

The expedition continued, but only one ship finally made it back to Spain. Of the roughly 250 sailors who had set sail with Magellan, only 18 returned. On September 8, 1522, the survivors reached Seville, where the Spanish hailed them as the first people to **circumnavigate**, or sail around, the world.

An engraving of the *Vittoria*, the only one of Magellan's ships to reach Spain after circumnavigating the globe

✓ **Reading Check** Explain why so few of Magellan's sailors returned to Spain.

Section 2 Assessment

Key Terms
Review the key terms at the beginning of this section. Use each term in a sentence that explains its meaning.

🎯 Target Reading Skill
Find the word *strait* on page 166. What clues in the paragraph help you understand what a strait is? Define *strait*.

Comprehension and Critical Thinking
1. (a) Recall When was the Age of Exploration?

(b) Identify Cause and Effect Why did Europeans set out on overseas voyages during this time?
2. (a) Identify Who was Prince Henry the Navigator?
(b) Conclude How was Prince Henry important to the Age of Exploration?
3. (a) Explain What was Columbus's "mistake"?
(b) Identify Effects Why did Columbus's voyages lead to more exploration?

Writing Activity
Explorers often had difficulty finding financial support for their expeditions. Take the role of either Columbus or Magellan and write a persuasive letter to a monarch asking for support for your voyage.

> **Writing Tip** In your letter, explain why the voyage is important and how it will benefit the monarch. Be sure to use a respectful tone.

Assess Progress L2
Have students complete the Section Assessment. Administer the *Section Quiz*.

📘 **Medieval Times to Today Teaching Resources,** *Section Quiz,* p. 320

Reteach L1
If students need more instruction, have them read this section in the Reading and Vocabulary Study Guide.

📖 Chapter 6, Section 2, **Medieval Times to Today Reading and Vocabulary Study Guide,** pp. 62–64

Extend L3
Have students learn more about life on a ship by completing the small group activity *Keeping a Ship's Log* and having each group read their finished log aloud to the class.

📘 **Medieval Times to Today,** *Small Group Activity: Simulation: Keeping a Ship's Log,* pp. 334–337

Answer

✓ **Reading Check** The men suffered many hardships on their long journey including strong currents, fierce winds, lack of food and fresh water, and disputes.

Writing Activity
Use the *Rubric for Assessing a Writing Assignment* to evaluate students' letters.

📘 **Medieval Times to Today Teaching Resources,** *Rubric for Assessing a Writing Assignment,* p. 349

Section 2 Assessment

Key Terms
Students' sentences should reflect knowledge of each Key Term.

🎯 Target Reading Skill
The text says that Magellan located a narrow, twisting passage that is today called the Strait of Magellan. Therefore, a *strait* must be a narrow, twisting waterway.

Comprehension and Critical Thinking
1. (a) from about 1400 to 1600 **(b)** Europeans were propelled to explore their world by new technology, curiosity, and a desire to find new trade routes. Europeans were tired of paying high prices for Asian goods because the traders of the Ottoman Empire controlled trade routes between Europe and Asia.

2. (a) Prince Henry, the son of Portugal's king, hoped to find an eastern sea route to Asia. **(b)** He encouraged expeditions in search of an eastern sea route to Asia; a route was found almost forty years after his death.

3. (a) When he landed in the Americas, he thought he had reached Asia. **(b)** Columbus had not found a route to Asia, so explorers such as John Cabot, Sebastian Cabot, and Vasco Nuñez began to explore the Americas and search for a Northwest Passage to Asia.

Focus On A Sailor's Life at Sea

Guided Instruction

■ Have students study the text, visuals and captions on pp. 168–169 as a class.

■ Ask students to list the different jobs people had on ships. *(pages, sailor's apprentices, sailors, ship's pilot, master of a ship)*

■ Ask students to discuss why they think so few men became the master of a ship. *(Possible answers: Very few jobs as ship masters were available; it was a difficult job that many men competed for.)*

■ Have students answer the Assessment questions in groups of two or three.

Focus On
A Sailor's Life at Sea

In the 1500s, a life at sea was a hard life. During lengthy voyages of exploration, sailors performed tiring physical labor, suffered from poor nutrition, and endured long stretches of boredom. They were often lonely, surrounded by vast and sometimes violent seas, far from home and family. They ate dried and salted food that was often infested with insects or gnawed by rats. They suffered injuries from their work or from fights with other sailors. Sailors' registries often identified men by their injuries, including crushed fingers and splinters embedded in the flesh.

Onboard a Ship Sailing was often the best job available for poor, uneducated men and orphaned boys who lived near busy ports. Boys as young as seven or eight served as ship's pages until they were about fifteen. A page's duties included scrubbing the ship and turning the sand clocks every half hour to mark the time. Unless they were assigned to specific officers, pages took orders from everyone on board. When they were old enough, pages became sailor's apprentices.

Apprentices were young men training to become sailors. They climbed the rigging in their bare feet to furl, or gather, the sails. They served as lookouts at the top of the masts, rowed smaller boats, and carried heavy cargo.

Sailors might work their way up to other positions, including that of ship's pilot, whose job it was to navigate. A very few men became the master of a ship. The master commanded the ship and was usually part owner of the vessel. The illustration at the right shows a vessel from the 1500s that sailed with about 45 crew members.

Sunken Treasures
This decorated plate and the pottery jug above were recovered from a Venetian shipwreck in the Adriatic Sea. The shipwreck probably occurred in the late 1500s.

Master's or Captain's Cabin
Common sailors slept on deck on straw-filled sacks.

Differentiated Instruction

For Gifted and Talented **L3**
Have students conduct Internet and library research on a topic that interests them related to the life of sailors in the 1500s, such as the technology that allowed ships to travel long distances or the voyages of a particular explorer. Students should create a poster with visuals and text on their topic to present to the class.

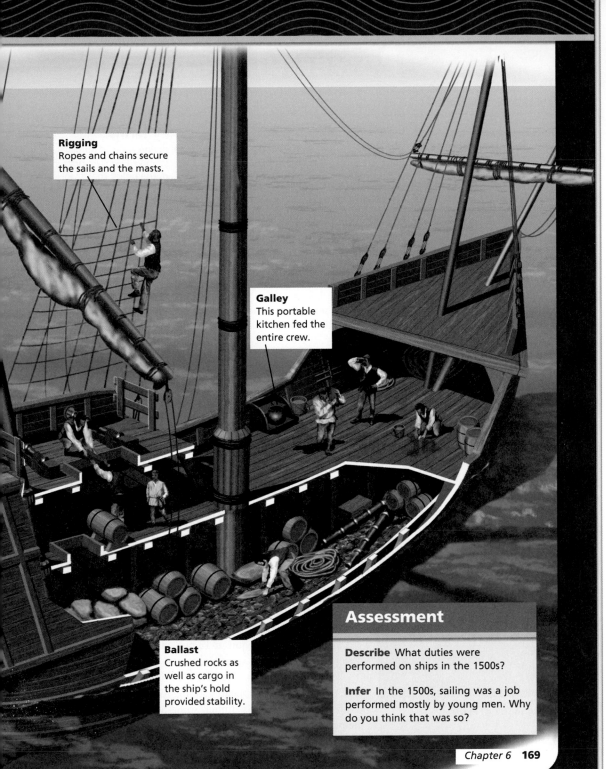

Rigging
Ropes and chains secure the sails and the masts.

Galley
This portable kitchen fed the entire crew.

Ballast
Crushed rocks as well as cargo in the ship's hold provided stability.

Assessment

Describe What duties were performed on ships in the 1500s?

Infer In the 1500s, sailing was a job performed mostly by young men. Why do you think that was so?

Independent Practice

Have students write a short story from the perspective of a page, sailor, or master of a ship using the information on pp. 168–169 as a guide. Students may conduct library or Internet research if they require further information in order to write their stories. Use the *Rubric for Assessing a Writing Assignment* to evaluate students' work.

All in One **Medieval Times to Today Teaching Resources,** *Rubric for Assessing a Writing Assignment,* p. 349

Answers

Assessment

Describe Pages cleaned the ship, turned the sand clocks every half hour, and took orders from everyone on board unless they were assigned to specific officers; sailor's apprentices and sailors climbed the rigging to furl the sails, served as lookouts, rowed smaller boats, and carried cargo; ship's pilots navigated the ship; the master of a ship commanded the ship and usually owned part of the vessel.

Infer Possible answer: Women were probably not allowed to become sailors at that time.

Section 3
Step-by-Step Instruction

Objectives

Social Studies
1. Learn about absolute rule in France.
2. Find out why the reign of Queen Elizabeth I was a golden age in England.
3. Discover the accomplishments of strong rulers in Spain and Russia.

Reading/Language Arts
Use context clues and your own knowledge to determine the meaning of unfamiliar terms.

Prepare to Read

Build Background Knowledge `L2`

In this section students will learn about the powerful rulers of France, England, Spain, and Russia. Using the Think-Write-Pair-Share participation strategy (TE, p. T36), ask students to scan the section for the names of rulers and list what they may already know about these people from books or films. Discuss the pairs' answers as a class. Students may use their lists to fill out the first column of their *Reading Readiness Guides.*

Set a Purpose for Reading `L2`

■ Preview the Objectives.

■ Form students into pairs or groups of four. Distribute the *Reading Readiness Guide.* Ask the students to fill in the first two columns of the chart. Use the Numbered Heads participation strategy (TE, p. T36) to call on students to share one piece of information they already know and one piece of information they want to know.

All in One Medieval Times to Today Teaching Resources, *Reading Readiness Guide,* p. 322

Vocabulary Builder
Preview Key Terms `L2`

Pronounce each Key Term, then ask students to say the word with you. Provide a simple explanation such as, "Versailles is a huge French palace with many rooms that was built for King Louis XIV."

Section 3 — The Age of Powerful Monarchs

Prepare to Read

Objectives
In this section, you will
1. Learn about absolute rule in France.
2. Find out why the reign of Queen Elizabeth I was a golden age in England.
3. Discover the accomplishments of strong rulers in Spain and Russia.

Taking Notes
As you read this section, look for important ideas about absolute monarchs in Europe. Copy the diagram below and record your findings in it.

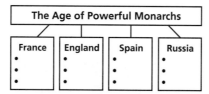

The Age of Powerful Monarchs

France	England	Spain	Russia
•	•	•	•
•	•	•	•
•	•	•	•

 Target Reading Skill
Use Context Clues To understand an unfamiliar term, you can use your own knowledge along with context clues. For example, in the description of a meal below, the term *keeper of the king's china* is in a list of servants. You know that one meaning of *china* is "dishes." This servant is in charge of the king's dishes.

Key Terms
• **divine right of kings** (duh VYN ryt uv kingz) *n.* the belief that the authority of kings comes directly from God
• **absolute monarch** (AB suh loot MAHN urk) *n.* a king or queen with complete authority over the government and people in a kingdom
• **Versailles** (vur SY) *n.* the palace built for the French king Louis XIV
• **Elizabethan Age** (ee liz uh BEE thun ayj) *n.* a golden age of English history when Elizabeth I was queen, 1558–1603
• **tsar** (zahr) *n.* the Russian emperor

King Louis XIV of France

Louis XIV, king of France, was ready for his dinner. He would be dining alone this evening. That did not mean he would be by himself. It meant that he would be the only one who was eating.

Although the meal had just begun, a crowd of servants already surrounded him. It was time for his meat to be brought from the kitchen. Two guards entered first. They were followed by ushers, gentlemen-in-waiting, the keeper of the king's china, and more guards. Somewhere in the crowd were the officers of the food department who actually carried the meat. In all, it required 15 people to bring the meat to King Louis XIV.

Then, when Louis asked for a drink, the chief cupbearer and the gentleman cupbearer sprang into action. Before King Louis XIV finished his dinner, some 500 people would have helped to prepare and serve it.

 Target Reading Skill `L2`

Use Context Clues Point out the Target Reading Skill. Tell students that they can figure out the meaning of an unfamiliar term by considering what they know about words that surround it.

Model using context clues to find the meaning of *tax collector* on p. 176. *(A tax is something that people pay to support a government, and a collector is someone who collects things. Therefore a tax collector is someone who collects taxes from people.)*

Give students *Use Context Clues: General Knowledge.* Have them complete the activity in their groups.

All in One Medieval Times to Today Teaching Resources, *Use Context Clues: General Knowledge,* p. 329

Absolute Rule in France

Why did Louis XIV have so many people waiting on him? What right did he have to this type of service?

Louis XIV was king of France in the 1600s and early 1700s. In Europe at this time, the people did not choose their leaders. They believed that God chose the king. The king's authority came directly from God, and was therefore divine. This belief was called the **divine right of kings.** It seemed logical that a leader chosen by God would be entitled to the best of everything.

Absolute Rule Therefore, it also seemed logical that a leader chosen by God should have more power than anyone else. Louis XIV was an **absolute monarch,** or royal ruler with absolute, or complete, authority over the government and people in his or her kingdom. Absolute monarchs did not share power with nobles, with common people, or with anyone else. From the 1400s to the 1700s, much of Europe was governed by absolute monarchs.

Cardinal Richelieu French kings had not always been absolute monarchs. Over a period of about 150 years, starting in the late 1400s, French kings had gradually taken power away from the nobles. Much of this transfer of power was accomplished not by a king but by a cardinal. (A cardinal is a high official in the Roman Catholic Church.) Cardinal Richelieu served as chief minister to Louis XIV's father, King Louis XIII.

To limit the power of the French nobles, Richelieu allowed wealthy merchants to buy titles of nobility. Then he stripped the nobles of some of their rights. He also started businesses for the French government. These businesses earned a great deal of money for the crown. Altogether, as these changes made the nobles weaker, the king became wealthier and more powerful.

The Power Behind the Throne
The action of the famous novel *The Three Musketeers* unfolds against the backdrop of the secret plots and schemes of Cardinal Richelieu (below). **Conclude** *Why do you think a king might have appointed a cardinal to such an important government post?*

Vocabulary Builder

Use the information below to teach students this section's high-use words.

High-Use Word	Definition and Sample Sentence
authority, p. 171	*n.* the right to do something As team captain, he has the **authority** to lead practice.
logical, p. 171	*adj.* having to do with correct reasoning After Jared's old shoes fell apart, it seemed **logical** to buy new ones.
prosperous, p. 174	*adj.* marked by success She was very **prosperous** because of her ability to handle money.
rebellion, p. 177	*n.* armed fight against those in power During the **rebellion,** the people fought against the government.

Guided Instruction (continued)

- Ask students **How did Louis XIV raise money for his extravagant life at Versailles?** *(He taxed the peasants.)*

- Ask students **Why do you think Louis XIV excused rich nobles from paying many taxes?** *(Possible answer: He wanted to keep them happy so that they wouldn't become a threat to his power.)*

- Discuss with students how taxing the poor to support the rich might create problems. Ask students to predict what might happen if taxation of the poor continued. *(Possible answer: The poor might run out of money, or decide to revolt.)*

Independent Practice

Ask students to create the Taking Notes graphic organizer on a blank piece of paper. Have them record important details about the absolute monarchs of France in the France portion of the graphic organizer. Briefly model how to identify which details to record.

Monitor Progress

As students fill in the graphic organizer, circulate and make sure individuals are choosing appropriate details. Provide assistance as needed.

Answer

Infer Answers will vary. Students might suggest that the people of France would have resented this type of luxury, especially the peasants, who were taxed to help pay for it.

The Splendor of Versailles
These photos show the emblem of the Sun King (inset), the queen's bedroom (below), and the Gallery of Mirrors (bottom).
Infer *How do you think the people of France felt about the luxury shown here? Explain your answer.*

Louis XIV Both Richelieu and Louis XIII died in 1643, and Louis XIV became king. He was the absolute monarch of France for 72 years. King Louis XIV was so powerful that he became known as the Sun King. Just as the sun was the center of the solar system, Louis XIV was the center of the French nation. He went so far as to declare, "I am the state."

The Sun King's Court One way in which Louis showed his power was through his lifestyle. He lived in incredible luxury at **Versailles,** his huge palace outside Paris.

It took 40 years to complete this magnificent estate. At times, as many as 30,000 laborers worked on its construction. Many nobles lived at the palace of Versailles with the king. Having the nobles at Versailles made it easier for Louis to keep them in check. At home on their estates, they might have become a threat to his power. To keep the nobles happy, Louis XIV gave huge parties with fabulous entertainment. For the most part, the king also excused the nobles from paying taxes.

All of this luxury and entertainment was very expensive. To raise the money, the king taxed the peasants. This meant that the poorest and least powerful people in France paid for the luxury of the Sun King's court.

France at War King Louis XIV had more power and wealth than any other person in France. And he wanted France to have more power and wealth than any other nation in Europe.

Differentiated Instruction

For Less Proficient Readers 〔L1〕
If students are having trouble deciphering the Roman numerals in the text, have them list the Roman numerals that they find in the text on a separate sheet of paper. Then ask them to write their corresponding Arabic numerals. Students can refer to this list when reading the text. You may wish to pair students with more proficient readers.

For English Language Learners 〔L1〕
Have English language learners whose native language is Spanish complete the Spanish version of *Guided Reading and Review.*

📄 **Medieval Times to Today Spanish Support,** *Guided Reading and Review (Spanish),* p. 50

To accomplish this goal, he encouraged the growth of industry and supported efforts to build an empire in Asia and in the Americas. Louis also went to war to gain new territories. From 1667 to 1713, France was almost constantly at war with other European countries.

These wars cost huge sums of money, yet they won France little in the way of land or power. By the time King Louis XIV died in 1715, France had huge debts. Even the silverware at Versailles had to be sold to help pay for France's wars.

✓ **Reading Check** Why did King Louis XIV go to war?

A Powerful Queen of England

Nearly a century before King Louis XIV took the throne of France, England already had a powerful monarch ruling over a golden age. This monarch, however, was a woman— Queen Elizabeth I. She became the most powerful and successful ruler England had ever known.

When Elizabeth I became queen in 1558, she found herself in a position of great power. Her grandfather, Henry VII, had ended fighting among local lords. He had made sure that England's monarch would be more powerful than any of the nobles. Her father, Henry VIII, had broken away from the Roman Catholic Church and started a new Protestant church, the Church of England. The English monarch became head of the Church of England and no longer had to share power with the Church based in Rome.

Queen Elizabeth Like her father, Elizabeth was determined and intelligent. She spoke French and Italian, and she could read the classical languages of Greek and Latin. Unlike her father, who had married six times, Elizabeth never married. She knew that if she married, she would lose some of her authority to her husband.

Elizabeth was also wise enough to gain the support of the English people. After she became queen, she often traveled through the English countryside so her people could see her. The English people came to love and admire their queen, whom they called "Good Queen Bess."

Regal Image
Queen Elizabeth was careful about how she appeared to her people during her travels and when she posed for portraits. **Classify** What elements in the painting suggest Elizabeth's power and success?

Background: Links Across Time

The Church of England The Church of England was established when Pope Clement VII would not grant King Henry VIII an annulment from his wife, Catherine of Aragon, who did not give him a male heir. In 1534, Parliament passed an act making the king the head of the English church, separating the church from Rome. After Henry's death, his son Edward VI introduced Protestant reforms to the church. When Edward's half-sister Mary came to power, she reunited the Church of England with Rome. After Mary's death, Elizabeth I reinstated the independent Church of England, but tried to create a doctrine that satisfied both Protestants and Roman Catholics.

Guided Instruction

- **Vocabulary Builder** Clarify the high-use word **prosperous** before reading.

- Read A Powerful Queen of England with students. As students read, circulate and make sure individuals can answer the Reading Check question.

- Help students to put events in order. Ask **What year did Elizabeth become queen of England?** *(1558)* Then ask **Was this before or after Louis XIV became king of France?** *(before; Louis XIV ruled in the late 1600s and early 1700s)*

- Ask students **How did the actions of Elizabeth's father and grandfather influence her reign?** *(Her grandfather, Henry VII, ended fighting among the lords and made sure the monarch would be more powerful than the nobles. Her father, Henry VIII, broke away from the Roman Catholic Church and created his own church. Because of this, the English monarch did not have to share power with the Church in Rome.)*

- Have students discuss why getting married would have lessened Elizabeth's authority. *(Possible answers: Because men were considered more able to rule than women at the time, a husband might have tried to control her decisions. Also, marrying would have caused Elizabeth to lose a powerful negotiating tool.)*

Answers

✓ **Reading Check** to gain new territories

Classify Elizabeth is dressed in ceremonial clothing and has her hand on a globe. A crown sits next to her, and there is a fleet of ships shown on the left.

Links

Read the **Links to Literature** on this page. Ask students **What shape was the Globe Theater?** (*almost round*)

Guided Instruction (continued)

- Ask students **How did Elizabeth I help make England powerful and prosperous?** (*She strengthened England by preventing war between Protestants and Catholics through compromise; she used the possibility of her marriage to foreign kings as one way of preventing war; she supported the British navy and exploration of the Americas.*)

- Ask students **How did the English navy become the most powerful in the world during the Elizabethan Age?** (*With the help of a storm, the English navy's more agile boats enabled England to defeat the Spanish navy in 1588.*)

- Discuss with students how artists often need patrons to succeed. Ask students **How did William Shakespeare benefit from Elizabeth's reign?** (*She loved theater and attended and helped promote his plays.*)

Independent Practice

Ask students to record details about England during the age of absolute monarchs on their graphic organizers.

Monitor Progress

As students fill in the graphic organizer, circulate and make sure individuals are recording the correct ideas. Provide assistance as needed.

Answer

✓**Reading Check** It was a time when England was powerful and prosperous, and when science, art, literature, and theater thrived.

Links to Language Arts

Shakespeare's Globe Theatre
In Elizabethan times, the plays of William Shakespeare were performed in the Globe Theatre, in London. The theater was almost round. Much of it was open to the weather; a thatched roof protected the stage and some of the seats. The least expensive seats weren't seats at all—"groundlings" stood in front of the stage. In the 1990s, a replica of the Globe (photos below) was completed near the site of the original theater. Now modern audiences can see Shakespeare's plays the way they were performed during his lifetime.

The Elizabethan Age Elizabeth's rule, from 1558 to 1603, is called the **Elizabethan Age**. During this time, England grew increasingly powerful and prosperous. Elizabeth strengthened England by using compromise to prevent religious wars between Protestants and the Catholics who were still numerous in England. She made sure that England remained a Protestant nation and that the monarch remained head of the Church of England. However, she also allowed much of Catholic tradition to be practiced in the English church.

At first, Elizabeth avoided war with other European powers. She used the possibility of her marriage with their kings as one way to prevent war. Meanwhile, Elizabeth supported English sea power and exploration in the Americas. The English sea captain Sir Francis Drake sailed around the world. He also delighted Elizabeth by leading attacks on Spanish ships carrying treasure from the Americas. By 1588, Spain had had enough. The Spanish king sent a huge armada, or fleet of ships, to invade England. With the help of a storm that destroyed much of the armada, the lighter English ships defeated the larger, awkward Spanish vessels. Now England had the most powerful navy in the world.

Elizabethan England was not only powerful, it also enjoyed a golden age of science, art, and literature. Elizabeth loved the theater. She often attended and helped promote the plays of William Shakespeare. Today, Shakespeare is regarded as perhaps the greatest writer in the English language. His plays include *Hamlet, King Lear,* and *Romeo and Juliet.*

✓**Reading Check** Why was the Elizabethan Age considered a golden age?

174

Differentiated Instruction

For Gifted and Talented   [L3]
Choose a scene from one of Shakespeare's plays for students to act out for the class. Because many of Shakespeare's plays contain few roles for women, you might select *A Midsummer Night's Dream.*

For English Language Learners   [L1]
Students may have difficulty pronouncing some of the words under the heading The Elizabethan Age such as *prosperous, strengthened, compromise, monarch, exploration, armada,* and *literature.* Encourage students to break these words into smaller parts to help them sound out the pronunciation.

Strong Rulers Unite Spain

Spain, too, came under the control of strong monarchs. When Ferdinand of Aragon and Isabella of Castile married in 1469, their separate kingdoms became one. Together, they ruled almost all of present-day Spain.

Like other European monarchs, King Ferdinand and Queen Isabella worked to limit the power of the nobles. They also used their power to strengthen the Roman Catholic Church throughout Spain. Under their rule, Jews were forced to convert to Catholicism or leave the country. The Moors, North African Muslims who had controlled part of southern Spain since the 700s, were driven out of Spain in 1492. Ferdinand and Isabella also established the Spanish Inquisition, a court that tried and executed people who did not obey the Roman Catholic Church.

The Spanish monarchs also supported voyages of exploration, including those of Christopher Columbus. These voyages eventually led to the creation of a huge Spanish empire in the Americas.

Two Monarchs
Ferdinand and Isabella, shown together on a Spanish coin, ruled Spain jointly. Their Alcazar castle is shown above. **Analyze Images** *What does the coin suggest about their roles as rulers?*

Absolute Rule in Russia

Russia shared many of the religious and political developments of Europe, including the rule of Christian absolute monarchs. But Russia was also different. First of all, not all of Russia is in Europe. Much of it is in Asia. Today, Russia extends all the way from the Pacific coast of Asia to the coasts of the Baltic and the Black seas in Europe.

Background: Links Across Time

The Moors The Moors, a nomadic people of the northern shores of Africa, originally lived in the Roman province Mauretania, in present-day Morocco and Algeria. In the 700s, many of the Moors converted to Islam and joined Arab forces to conquer Spain, where they were powerful for centuries. Gradually Christians regained control of Spain, a process that culminated in the conquest of Granada by King Ferdinand and Queen Isabella in 1492. The Moors were either driven out of the country or forced to convert to Christianity. Many of the converted Moors who remained in Spain, called Moriscos, continued to practice Islam secretly. Despite years of persecution, the skills of Moorish farmers and artisans significantly furthered Spanish agriculture and trade.

Guided Instruction

- Have students read Strong Rulers Unite Spain using the Oral Cloze strategy (TE, p. T33).

- Help students to put events in order. Ask **When did Ferdinand and Isabella marry?** *(1469)* **Was this before or after Elizabeth I came to power in England?** *(before; Elizabeth came to power in 1558)* **Was this before or after Louis XIV came to power in France?** *(before; Louis XIV came to power in 1642)*

- Ask students **What was an immediate effect of the marriage between Ferdinand and Isabella?** *(They united their separate kingdoms and ruled almost all of what is now Spain.)*

- Ask **What were some features of Ferdinand and Isabella's rule?** *(They limited the power of the nobles, supported the Inquisition in Spain, and supported exploration, including those of Columbus.)*

Independent Practice

Ask students to record details from what they have just read about the Spanish monarchs on their graphic organizers.

Monitor Progress

As students fill in the graphic organizer, circulate and make sure individuals are recording appropriate details. Provide assistance as needed.

Answer

Analyze Images The image on the coin suggests that the two monarchs ruled jointly and equally.

Target Reading Skill

Use Context Clues As a follow up, have students answer the Target Reading Skill question in the Student Edition. *(The words "conquered" and "Mongol armies" suggest that the Golden Horde was a Mongol army that took over many lands. The word "horde" implies that this was quite a large army.)*

Absolute Rule in Russia

- **Vocabulary Builder** Clarify the high-use word **rebellion** before reading.

- With students, read Absolute Rule in Russia. As students read, circulate to make sure they can answer the Reading Check question.

- Ask students **How did Russia's leadership change from the 1200s to the 1500s?** *(In the 1230s, Mongols took over much of Russia and ruled it for the next 240 years. Russian groups rebelled against Mongol rule, and by 1505, Prince Ivan of Moscow became ruler of Russia, and Ivan's grandson later became tsar.)*

- Ask students to list Peter the Great's accomplishments. *(He modernized the Russian army and navy, improved farming and industry, expanded Russia's territory and built the city of St. Petersburg.)*

Independent Practice

Have students complete the graphic organizer.

Monitor Progress

- Show *Section Reading Support Transparency MT 71* and ask students to check their graphic organizers individually. Go over key concepts and clarify key vocabulary as needed.

    📖 **Medieval Times to Today Transparencies,** *Section Reading Support Transparency MT 71*

- Tell students to fill in the last column of the *Reading Readiness Guide*. Probe for what they learned that confirms or invalidates each statement.

    All in One Medieval Times to Today Teaching Resources, *Reading Readiness Guide,* p. 322

Answer

Contrast The cathedral in Moscow has rounded spires, and it does not appear to have stained glass windows.

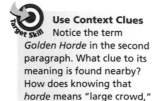

Use Context Clues Notice the term *Golden Horde* in the second paragraph. What clue to its meaning is found nearby? How does knowing that *horde* means "large crowd," or "gang," help you explain *Golden Horde*?

Symbol of Moscow The Cathedral of St. Basil the Blessed, built in the 1550s, shows influences of Byzantine style. **Contrast** *How does this church differ from the Gothic cathedrals shown on pages 126 and 127?*

176 Medieval Times to Today

The Rise of Kiev In the 700s and 800s, Kiev, a city in present-day Ukraine, became an important center of trade. It developed ties to the Byzantine Empire, which sent Christian missionaries to Kiev. In 957, Princess Olga converted to Christianity. Her grandson, Vladimir, expanded the territory ruled by Kiev and also made Orthodox Christianity its official religion. Byzantine arts and architecture influenced the culture of Kiev, which thrived in the 1000s. By the 1200s, however, Kiev had come under the control of invaders.

As you read in Chapter 4, during the early 1200s, the Mongols had conquered much of Asia. In the 1230s, Mongol armies known as the Golden Horde turned west. They took over much of Russia, including Kiev.

Mongol Rule of Russia The Mongols ruled Russia for 240 years. Although they required heavy tribute, the Muslim Mongols allowed Russians to practice Christianity and brought peace to their large empire. However, Mongol rule cut Russia off from Western Europe and many of the advances being made there.

During this period, the princes of Moscow gained power. Moscow was a center of trade, and its princes were the tax collectors for the Mongol rulers. The area they controlled was called Muscovy. Meanwhile, the Russian Orthodox Church made Moscow its headquarters.

Differentiated Instruction

For Special Needs Students L1

Students may have difficulty understanding Absolute Rule in Russia. Ask pairs to create a timeline to clarify the order of events. Show the timeline transparency to guide them.

📖 **Medieval Times to Today Transparencies,** *Transparency B20: Timeline*

For Advanced Readers L3

Ask students to conduct library or Internet research about one of the people that they read about in Section 3. Then have students create a poster about the person, describing what they learned. Encourage students to illustrate their posters and present them to the class.

Russian Rulers Take Power In the 1300s, the leaders of Moscow led other Russian groups in a rebellion against Mongol rule. By 1505, Prince Ivan of Moscow had brought much of Russia under his own control. He then turned to strengthening his power by limiting the power of Russian nobles. Ivan the Great, as he came to be called, declared himself absolute ruler of Russia, "in authority like the highest God." His grandson, Ivan the Terrible, strengthened the monarch's power even more. He was crowned **tsar,** the Russian word for "caesar" or "emperor."

Peter the Great Peter the Great became tsar of Russia in 1682 and ruled for more than 40 years. Peter modernized the Russian army and navy and improved Russian farming and industry by adopting Western European technology. But he also strengthened serfdom, which had already died out in the rest of Europe. Peter expanded Russia's territory, but he could not achieve one of his major goals: a port that would not freeze over in the winter, so that Russia could trade by sea all year.

Like other absolute monarchs, Peter the Great limited the power of the nobles in order to strengthen his own position. Peter also wanted Russia to become more like Western Europe. He built St. Petersburg, a magnificent capital city near the Baltic coast, which he called "a window on the West." The city became a symbol of Peter's power and his desire to make Russia a modern nation.

Peter the Great

√ **Reading Check** What were Peter the Great's accomplishments?

 **Section 3 Assessment**

Key Terms
Review the key terms at the beginning of this section. Use each term in a sentence that explains its meaning.

Target Reading Skill
How do context clues and your own knowledge help you understand *Sun King,* on page 172?

Comprehension and Critical Thinking
1. (a) Summarize How did Cardinal Richelieu increase the power of the French king?

(b) Synthesize How did Louis XIV represent the idea of absolute rule?
2. (a) Describe What was Queen Elizabeth I like?
(b) Identify Causes What did Elizabeth I do to encourage the golden age that bears her name?
3. (a) Recall How did the princes of Moscow gain power in Russia?
(b) Compare How were Ivan the Great and Peter the Great similar? How were they different?

Writing Activity
Write a description of a day at Versailles from the point of view of a noble. Then write a description of how the day might have looked to a French peasant who had the chance to observe it.

For: An activity on Louis XIV
Visit: PHSchool.com
Web Code: lgd-8603

Chapter 6 Section 3 **177**

Objective
Learn how to use route maps.

Prepare to Read

Build Background Knowledge **L2**
Ask students to think about the route they take to school each day. Encourage students to describe the directions for getting to school, and write them on the board. Explain that route maps can also be used to show movement. Have students use the Numbered Heads participation strategy (TE, p. T36) to list things that might be included in a route map. *(Possible answers: beginning and ending locations, indication of the route taken, landmarks)*

Instruct

Using Route Maps **L2**

Guided Instruction
- Read the steps to using route maps as a class and write them on the board.

- Practice the skill by following the steps on p. 179 as a class. Model each step in the activity. Begin by identifying the topic of the map *(Henry Hudson's routes)* and the different elements shown in the key *(the key shows two journeys in two different colors, and labels each with a date)*. Then, interpret the map by tracing Hudson's routes in the order they took place *(first route—began in the Netherlands and ended in England; second route—began in England and ended in North America)*, explain how the last journey ended *(Hudson was abandoned by mutineers.)*, and locate two places on the map that are named after him *(Hudson River, Hudson Bay)*. Finally, draw conclusions from what the map shows *(Hudson did not find a Northwest Passage connecting Europe to Asia, but he reached two major water bodies in North America, both of which were named after him.)*

 **Using Route Maps**

Like many explorers of his time, Henry Hudson hoped to find a short route from Europe to Asia. He made four voyages to look for this Northwest Passage. When his final expedition was stranded by the arctic winter, Hudson's crew mutinied. They put him, his son, and several others into a small boat and cast them adrift. Years later, in the 1630s, another explorer found ruins of a shelter that might have been built by the small group of castaways.

A route map is a type of special-purpose map. In addition to showing location, physical features, and distances, a route map shows movement: how people got from one place to another. Many journeys have played important roles in history, and historical route maps show the paths of such journeys.

Learn the Skill
Use these steps to analyze and interpret a route map.

1. **Read the map title and look at the map to get a general idea of what it shows.** Identify the regions that appear on the map—both physical features and political boundaries. Notice what route or routes the map shows.

2. **Read the key to understand how the map uses symbols, colors, and patterns.** On most route maps, lines show the paths of journeys. Often, each journey is shown in a different color or style (such as a dotted line). Notice how the key identifies the routes and the dates of journeys.

3. **Use the key to interpret the map.** Look for places where the symbols in the key appear on the map. Find the separate routes, their dates, and where each one begins and ends.

4. **Draw conclusions about what the map shows.** Information you discover when you analyze a route map can help you draw conclusions about why a route was chosen or why it was successful or unsuccessful.

◀ **A 1686 map of the Americas**

178 Medieval Times to Today

Independent Practice
Assign *Skills for Life* and have students complete it individually.

All in One Medieval Times to Today Teaching Resources, *Skills for Life,* p. 333

Monitor Progress
As students are completing *Skills for Life,* circulate to make sure individuals are applying the skill steps effectively. Provide assistance as needed.

Practice the Skill

Use the steps below to analyze the route map on this page.

1 What is the topic of the map at the right? What routes does it show?

2 Look at the key. How many journeys does the map show? What colors are the voyages? How do you know when they took place?

3 Trace the routes that Hudson took in order. Where did each journey begin? How did the last journey end? What places on the map bear Hudson's name?

4 You know that Hudson was looking for a Northwest Passage across North America. Did he achieve this goal? What did he accomplish?

The Hudson River today

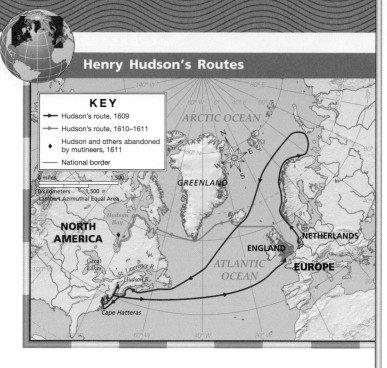

Henry Hudson's Routes

KEY
- → Hudson's route, 1609
- → Hudson's route, 1610–1611
- ◆ Hudson and others abandoned by mutineers, 1611
- — National border

0 miles 1,500
0 kilometers 1,500
Lambert Azimuthal Equal Area

ARCTIC OCEAN
GREENLAND
NORTH AMERICA
Hudson Bay
Great Lakes
St. Lawrence R.
Hudson R.
Cape Hatteras
ATLANTIC OCEAN
NETHERLANDS
ENGLAND
EUROPE

Apply the Skill

Turn to the map named European Voyages of Exploration on pages 164–165. Use the steps in this lesson to draw conclusions about the voyages of the explorers sailing for Portugal and Spain.

Chapter 6 **179**

Assess and Reteach

Assess Progress **L2**
Ask students to do the Apply the Skill activity.

Reteach **L1**
If students are having trouble applying the skill steps, have them review the skill using the interactive Social Studies Skills Tutor CD-ROM.

⊙ *Analyzing and Interpreting Special-Purpose Maps,* **Social Studies Skills Tutor CD-ROM**

Extend **L3**
Have students extend their knowledge of route maps by completing *Reading a Road Map.* Then, have students create their own road maps for a real or hypothetical country. Their maps should include three cities, one principal highway, two other highways, and three main connecting roads. Make sure all the roads are labeled with a name or number and the maps have a title, a key, and a compass rose. Ask students to exchange their maps with a partner and write down the directions for driving from city to city on their partner's map.

All in One Medieval Times to Today Teaching Resources, *Reading a Road Map,* p. 340

Answer
Apply the Skill

Answers will vary, but students should draw conclusions about the voyages of Da Gama, Columbus, and Magellan. (*Possible answer: Explorers from Portugal and Spain sailed both east and west in wide-reaching expeditions around the world.*)

Objectives

Social Studies
1. Discover how Spanish conquistadors conquered great civilizations in the Americas.
2. Find out why the African slave trade developed and what its effects were.

Reading/Language Arts
Use context clues in surrounding paragraphs to determine the meaning of unfamiliar words.

Prepare to Read

Build Background Knowledge L2

Tell students that in this section they will learn about European conquests in the Americas and Africa. Ask students to preview the map on p. 182 with this question in mind: **Which countries had empires in the Americas?** *(Spain and Portugal)* Then have them preview the headings and the rest of the visuals in the chapter.

Set a Purpose for Reading L2
- Preview the Objectives.

- Form students into pairs or groups. Distribute the *Reading Readiness Guide*. Ask students to fill in the first two columns of the chart. Use the Numbered Heads participation strategy (TE, p. T36) to call on students to share one piece of information they already know and one piece of information they want to know.

  All in One **Medieval Times to Today Teaching Resources,** *Reading Readiness Guide,* p. 326

Vocabulary Builder
Preview Key Terms L2

Pronounce each Key Term, then ask the students to say the word with you. Provide a simple explanation such as, "The conquistadors came from Spain and conquered Native American empires during the 1500s."

Prepare to Read

Objectives
In this section, you will
1. Discover how Spanish conquistadors conquered great civilizations in the Americas.
2. Find out why the African slave trade developed and what its effects were.

Taking Notes
As you read this section, look for the important events in the Spanish conquest of the Americas. Copy the timeline below and record your findings on it.

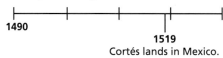

1490 — 1519 — — —

1519
Cortés lands in Mexico.

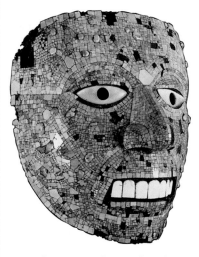

The Aztec god Quetzalcoatl

Target Reading Skill
Use Context Clues When you come across an unfamiliar word, you may have to look for context clues to its meaning in the paragraphs preceding or following the word. For example, to understand the word *withstand* at the bottom of page 182, keep reading to see what happened to the Incan empire.

Key Terms
- **conquistador** (kahn KEES tuh dawr) *n.* a Spanish conqueror in the Americas
- **Hernán Cortés** (hur NAHN kohr TEZ) *n.* the Spanish conquistador who conquered the Aztecs
- **encomienda** (en koh mee EN dah) *n.* a system in which the Spanish king gave Spanish settlers the right to the labor of the Native Americans who lived in a particular area
- **Francisco Pizarro** (frahn SEES koh pea SAHR oh) *n.* the Spanish conquistador who conquered the Incas

You read about the splendid dinner of King Louis XIV in Section 3. About a hundred years before Louis ruled France, another king had sat down to a splendid dinner. Moctezuma was the supreme ruler of the Aztec empire in the Valley of Mexico. Like Louis, Moctezuma was usually the only one who ate at his dinners, which took more than 400 people to serve. After his servants brought the food, Moctezuma looked over the huge selection and chose what he wanted. Then a screen was drawn around him for privacy while his food was served by his personal servants.

Moctezuma was powerful, but the Aztecs believed in gods that were even more powerful. An Aztec legend said that long ago the white-skinned god Quetzalcoatl (ket sahl koh AHT el) had sailed away to the east. The Aztecs believed that someday Quetzalcoatl would return to rule them. In 1519, that seemed to happen. Moctezuma heard about a group of pale-skinned men who had landed on the east coast. He wondered if these men could be Quetzalcoatl and his followers.

180 Medieval Times to Today

Target Reading Skill L2

Use Context Clues Point out the Target Reading Skill. Tell students that information in paragraphs before and after an unknown word can provide clues to its meaning.

Model using context clues to find the meaning of the word *allies* in this sentence from the fifth paragraph on p. 181: "The Spaniards and their Native American allies attacked Tenochtitlán." (*The second paragraph on p. 181 explains that Cortés persuaded Native Americans who hated the Aztecs to fight with him. Therefore, an* ally *must be someone who gives support to another in war.*)

Give students *Use Context Clues: Definition and Description.* Have them complete the activity in their groups.

All in One **Medieval Times to Today Teaching Resources,** *Use Context Clues: Definition and Description,* p. 330

Spain's Empire in the Americas

The leader of the pale-skinned men was not an Aztec god but a Spanish conquistador. A **conquistador** was a Spanish soldier who conquered Native American peoples in the 1500s. Ever since Columbus had brought back reports of new lands, Europeans had dreamed about the riches that might be found there. The Spanish sent expeditions to look for gold and other treasures.

The Conquest of the Aztecs One of these expeditions was led by the conquistador **Hernán Cortés.** Soon after landing in present-day Mexico, Cortés heard about the wealth of the Aztecs. He also heard that many of the local peoples hated the Aztecs, because the Aztecs had conquered them and taxed them heavily. Cortés persuaded some of these groups to help him fight the Aztecs.

A Fateful Meeting
This painting shows the first meeting of Moctezuma and Hernán Cortés. **Analyze Images** What attitude do the two leaders seem to have toward each other? What details support your inference?

Cortés headed for the Aztec capital with 500 soldiers and 16 horses. Aztec spies saw them coming. They had never seen horses before. Moctezuma's spies described the Spanish as "supernatural creatures riding on hornless deer, armed in iron, fearless as gods." When Cortés and his men arrived in Tenochtitlán, the Aztec capital, they were amazed. The city was larger than any European city at the time. As you read in Chapter 3, the Aztecs had developed a very advanced civilization. The Aztec leader Moctezuma welcomed Cortés and his men. He and his advisers were afraid that Cortés might be the returning Quetzalcoatl, so they treated him and his men as honored guests.

In order to gain control of the Aztecs, Cortés kidnapped Moctezuma. The Aztec people soon rebelled. The battle was fierce and bloody. Moctezuma was killed, but the Aztecs drove Cortés and his army out of Tenochtitlán.

Outside the city, Cortés regrouped. The Spaniards and their Native American allies attacked Tenochtitlán. In 1521, the Aztecs finally surrendered. By then, about 240,000 Aztecs had died, and 30,000 of Cortés's allies had been killed. Tenochtitlán and the Aztec empire lay in ruins.

Use Context Clues
How does the description of events both before and after the word *regrouped* help you figure out its meaning? How does the prefix *re-* also help?

Chapter 6 Section 4 **181**

Vocabulary Builder

Use the information below to teach students this section's high-use words.

High-Use Word	Definition and Sample Sentence
network, p. 182	*n.* a system of connected items The computer **network** linked all the work stations to one central computer.
render, p. 183	*v.* to make or cause When I broke my leg, I was **rendered** helpless for weeks.
deprive, p. 184	*v.* to prevent from having or to take away As a punishment, his parents will **deprive** him of the use of his computer for the week.

Chapter 6 Section 4 **181**

Guided Instruction (continued)

- Point out the location of New Spain on the map of the Spanish and Portuguese empires on p. 182. Ask students **How did Cortés make life in New Spain more like that of his home country?** *(He imported European plants and farm animals.)*

- Discuss the fact that people can develop immunities to diseases to which they are exposed. Ask students **Why do you think so many Native Americans died from European diseases?** *(Possible answer: They had never been exposed to these diseases before, and therefore were not immune to them.)*

Independent Practice

Ask students to create the Taking Notes graphic organizer on a blank piece of paper. Then have them fill in the timeline with important events in the Spanish conquest of the Americas.

Monitor Progress

As students fill in the graphic organizer, circulate and make sure individuals are choosing appropriate events for their timelines. Provide assistance as needed.

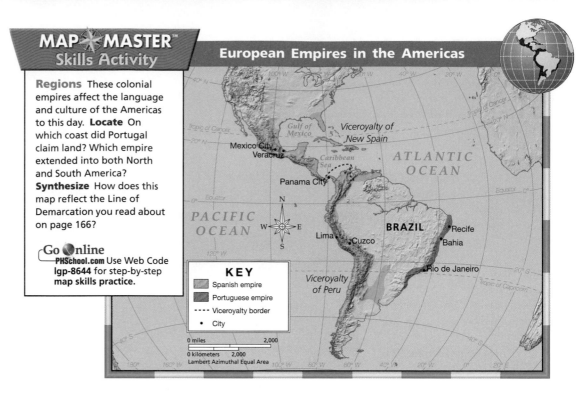

MAP★MASTER™ Skills Activity

European Empires in the Americas

Regions These colonial empires affect the language and culture of the Americas to this day. **Locate** On which coast did Portugal claim land? Which empire extended into both North and South America? **Synthesize** How does this map reflect the Line of Demarcation you read about on page 166?

Go Online
PHSchool.com Use Web Code **lgp-8644** for step-by-step map skills practice.

KEY
- Spanish empire
- Portuguese empire
- - - - Viceroyalty border
- • City

0 miles 2,000
0 kilometers 2,000
Lambert Azimuthal Equal Area

New Spain Cortés took control of the region, which he called New Spain. He built his new capital, Mexico City, on the site of Tenochtitlán.

Cortés tried to make life in New Spain like that in his home country. He imported European plants and farm animals. He also introduced the **encomienda** system, in which the Spanish king gave Spanish settlers the right to the labor of the Native Americans who lived in a particular area. The settlers were expected to convert the Native Americans to Christianity and to treat them well. In reality, the settlers treated them as slaves. Many Native Americans were worked to death, and many others died of European diseases.

The Conquest of the Incas Like the Aztecs, the Incas had built an advanced civilization. Their vast empire covered most of the western coast of South America and was tied together by a well-constructed network of roads and bridges. For all its achievements and power, however, the Incan empire could not withstand the Spanish. In 1531, the conquistador **Francisco Pizarro** led his men into the northern Incan empire. He drove south, and within two years he and his 200 soldiers had conquered an empire of some 12 million people.

182 Medieval Times to Today

Differentiated Instruction

For Gifted and Talented   **L3**
Ask students to compare the map on p. 182 with the current map of North and South America in the Atlas at the end of their books. Have pairs of students figure out which countries today were once part of the Spanish empire, and which were part of the Portuguese empire. Ask pairs to create a chart showing their findings.

Answers

MAP★MASTER™ Skills Activity **Locate** the east coast; the Spanish empire **Synthesize** The Portuguese settled land east of 50° W longitude—the Line of Demarcation—and the Spanish settled land to the west of the line.

How did he do it? First, a war was already raging within the Incan empire. Some of the people rebelling against Incan rule sided with Pizarro. Further, as Cortés had done, Pizarro kidnapped the empire's ruler. Leaderless, the empire was easy prey. Finally, European diseases such as smallpox killed or weakened millions of people in the region.

Effects of Spanish Conquests The Spanish takeover of the Aztec and Incan empires eventually led to Spanish control of most of Central and South America. The riches of gold and silver that Spain brought back to Europe made Spain even more powerful. The large numbers of Spanish settlers changed the course of history in the Americas. And the Spaniards' cruel treatment of the Native Americans—along with the diseases they accidentally brought—devastated the peoples of the Americas.

✓ **Reading Check** How did the Spanish conquest affect the Americas?

The African Slave Trade

Europeans did not limit their conquests to the Americas. They were looking for riches in other lands as well.

You have read that Prince Henry the Navigator helped start trade between Portugal and the west coast of Africa. Soon, British, French, and Dutch ships also sailed to Africa to trade for gold, ivory, and pepper. Then they began to trade for enslaved people as well. One ship brought five enslaved Africans to England in the 1540s. No one would buy them, so they were taken back to Africa. Because it had plenty of cheap labor, Europe did not offer a big market for slavery.

Slavery Comes to the Americas There was a market for slaves in the Americas, however. Spanish and Portuguese settlers in the Americas wanted workers for their plantations and mines. At first they enslaved Native Americans. When many of these slaves died, the Europeans began importing enslaved Africans.

Some historians put the number of Africans taken to the Americas at about 11 million. As many as 2 million may have died on the overcrowded and unsanitary slave ships. Men, women, and children were packed and chained tightly together in the dark holds of the ships. The air was so foul that there was often not enough oxygen to keep a candle burning. "The shrieks of the women, and the groans of the dying, rendered the whole a scene of horror," one survivor recalled.

Chapter 6 Section 4 **183**

This 1846 painting of a Spanish slave ship was done by the British captain who captured the ship and freed the slaves.

The Columbian Exchange The movement of peoples from Africa and Europe to the Americas opened up a global exchange of goods and ideas. Europeans introduced cattle, horses, chickens, goats, and pigs to the Americas. From Africa and Asia, they brought such plants as bananas, coffee, and sugar cane. All became major foods in the Americas. The introduction of food crops such as corn, potatoes, and beans from the Americas made it easier to feed more people in Europe and Africa. Because Columbus's famous voyages made this exchange possible, it is called the Columbian Exchange.

Background: Global Perspectives

Triangular Trade European exploration of the Americas led to the Columbian Exchange and triangular trade routes involving Europe, Africa, and the Americas. In one triangular trade route active in the 1700s, English ships would first sail to Africa to trade manufactured goods or rum for slaves. Next they would sail to the West Indies to sell the slaves and purchase sugar, cocoa, and other products. Finally, they would sail back to England with their new goods. In England, sugar from the West Indies would be processed into rum, which could in turn be traded for slaves on the next journey to Africa, continuing the cycle.

Read the **Links Across the World** on this page. Ask students **What was the Columbian Exchange?** *(the exchange of goods among Europe, Africa, Asia, and the Americas that was created by Columbus's voyages)*

The African Slave Trade L2

Guided Instruction

■ **Vocabulary Builder** Clarify the high-use words **render** and **deprive** before reading.

■ Read The African Slave Trade with students. As students read, circulate and make sure individuals can answer the Reading Check question.

■ **Why did Europeans begin importing enslaved Africans to the Americas?** *(Settlers wanted workers for plantations and mines, and many of the Native Americans they had enslaved had died.)*

■ Ask students **How was slavery damaging to both slaves and slaveholders?** *(Possible answer: because the society that developed was based on injustice and inequality)*

Independent Practice

Have students complete the graphic organizer.

Monitor Progress

■ Show *Section Reading Support Transparency MT 72* and ask students to check their graphic organizers individually.

📖 **Medieval Times to Today Transparencies,** *Section Reading Support Transparency MT 72*

■ Tell students to fill in the last column of the *Reading Readiness Guide.*

All in One **Medieval Times to Today Teaching Resources,** *Reading Readiness Guide,* p. 326

Answer

✓ **Reading Check** The Spanish eventually controlled most of Central and South America. Many Native Americans died of ill treatment and European diseases.

Assess and Reteach

Assess Progress `L2`
Have students complete the Section Assessment. Administer the *Section Quiz*.

AllinOne **Medieval Times to Today Teaching Resources,** *Section Quiz,* p. 328

Reteach `L1`
If students need more instruction, have them read this section in the Reading and Vocabulary Study Guide.

Chapter 6, Section 4, **Medieval Times to Today Reading and Vocabulary Study Guide,** pp. 68–70

Extend `L3`
Have students learn more about the Aztecs by reading *The Talking Stone* and answering the discussion question in groups.

AllinOne **Medieval Times to Today Teaching Resources,** *The Talking Stone,* pp. 344–346

Answer

✓ **Reading Check** Wars were instigated in Africa to capture people to be sold into slavery, and African societies lost many young people. Wars also caused death and destruction.

Section 4 Assessment

Key Terms
Students' sentences should reflect knowledge of each Key Term.

Target Reading Skill
The text says that Pizarro kidnapped the empire's ruler and that European diseases killed many and left others too sick to fight. So in this context, *easy prey* means that the empire was already weakened and easy to attack.

Comprehension and Critical Thinking
1. (a) Hernán Cortés (b) Francisco Pizarro (c) Similar: In both events a Spanish conquistador conquered advanced Native American societies; both conquistadors convinced other Native Americans to fight with them; both kidnapped Native American leaders. Different: The Aztecs initially welcomed Cortés and his men; Cortés conquered the Aztecs ten years before Pizarro conquered the Incas.

The waiting rooms of the House of Slaves on Gorée Island, in present-day Senegal, Africa

Effects of the Slave Trade The slave trade created a disaster, both in the Americas and in Africa. In addition to being deprived of their liberty and taken from their homeland, enslaved Africans suffered terrible brutality. In the Americas, slavery was damaging to both slaves and slaveholders because the society that developed was based on injustice and inequality.

In Africa, groups who were victorious in war had often enslaved the people they conquered. Some of these enslaved people were sold to foreigners. But in the 1500s, the slave trade became big business. As the demand for slaves increased in the Americas, European slave traders lured African groups into wars against their neighbors. These wars guaranteed the traders a steady supply of slaves. Other people were kidnapped in slave raids and sold by African rulers and traders to the Europeans. The captives were exchanged for textiles, metalwork, weapons, and luxury goods.

European settlers wanted Africans who were young, healthy, and strong to work on their plantations in the Americas. The loss of so many young people in their prime was a serious blow to many African societies. Wars also caused death and destruction. These harmful effects of the slave trade lasted for centuries.

✓ **Reading Check** How did the slave trade affect African society?

 Section 4 Assessment

Key Terms
Review the key terms at the beginning of this section. Use each term in a sentence that explains its meaning.

Target Reading Skill
Find the word *prey* in the first paragraph on page 183. Use the text both before and after the word to explain how it is being used in this context.

Comprehension and Critical Thinking
1. (a) Recall Which conquistador conquered the Aztec empire?

(b) Recall Which conquistador conquered the Incan empire?
(c) Compare and Contrast How were these two events similar and different?
2. (a) Explain Why did the Europeans take enslaved Africans to the Americas?
(b) Describe What were conditions like on the ships that brought enslaved Africans to the Americas?
(c) Identify Effects What were two effects of the African slave trade?

Writing Activity
Write two paragraphs, one from the viewpoint of an Aztec soldier defending Tenochtitlán, and the other from the perspective of a Spanish soldier trying to conquer the city.

> **Writing Tip** Think about what the two people might agree on and what they would view differently. Jot down notes or make a chart to help you plan your paragraphs.

2. (a) Spanish and Portuguese settlers wanted workers for their mines and plantations. **(b)** Slave ships were overcrowded and unsanitary. **(c)** Possible answers: Africans were deprived of their freedom and suffered terribly. In the Americas, slavery was damaging to both slaves and slaveholders because it created societies based on injustice and inequality. The market for young, healthy, strong Africans damaged many African societies. Africans were kidnapped in slave raids, and lured into wars against their neighbors by European slave traders.

Writing Activity
Use the *Rubric for Assessing a Writing Assignment* to evaluate students' paragraphs.

AllinOne **Medieval Times to Today Teaching Resources,** *Rubric for Assessing a Writing Assignment,* p. 349

Review and Assessment

◆ Chapter Summary

Section 1: The Renaissance and Reformation

- The Renaissance, a period marked by a rebirth of learning and advances in the arts and sciences, took place in Europe from about 1300 to 1600.
- Renaissance artists used scientific techniques to portray the world around them realistically.
- The Reformation began as an effort to correct abuses of the Roman Catholic Church and resulted in the creation of Protestant churches.

Painting by Raphael

Section 2: The Age of Exploration

- Advances in technology, a desire for trade, and curiosity about the world led Europeans to undertake long sea voyages during the Age of Exploration.
- Encouraged by Prince Henry the Navigator, the Portuguese sailed around Africa to India.
- Christopher Columbus sailed west and landed in the Americas. Many European explorers followed him to these lands.
- Ferdinand Magellan led the first expedition to circumnavigate the world.

Section 3: The Age of Powerful Monarchs

- King Louis XIV, absolute monarch of France for 72 years, lived lavishly and taxed his people heavily.
- Queen Elizabeth I ruled over England during the late 1500s. Her long reign, called the Elizabethan Age, was a golden age for England.
- King Ferdinand and Queen Isabella united Spain and drove non-Christians from the country.
- After being ruled by the Mongols, Russia was governed by tsars, or Russian emperors.

Section 4: Conquests in the Americas and Africa

- Spanish conquistadors conquered the Aztec and Incan empires in the Americas.
- Europeans brought enslaved Africans to the Americas to work on plantations and in mines.

Aztec mask

◆ Key Terms

Each of the statements below contains a key term from the chapter. If the statement is true, write *true*. If it is false, rewrite the statement to make it true.

1. The Renaissance was the effort to reform the Catholic Church.
2. The period marked by a rebirth of learning in Europe was called humanism.
3. The Cape of Good Hope was a sea route through North America.
4. To circumnavigate the world means to sail all the way around it.
5. People who believed in the divine right of kings thought that a king's right to rule came directly from God.
6. A tsar was an absolute ruler of Spain.
7. Encomienda was the capital of the Aztecs.
8. Francisco Pizarro was the conquistador who conquered the Incas.

┌ Vocabulary Builder ─────────────

Revisit this chapter's high-use words:

financial	monarch	prosperous
perspective	emerge	rebellion
technology	dispute	network
conform	authority	render
capable	logical	deprive

Ask students to review the definitions they recorded on their *Word Knowledge* worksheets.

All in One Medieval Times to Today Teaching Resources, *Word Knowledge,* p. 331

Consider allowing students to earn extra credit if they use the words in their answers to the questions in the Chapter Review and Assessment. The words must be used correctly and in a natural context to win the extra points.

Review and Assessment

Review Chapter Content

- Review and revisit the major themes of this chapter by asking students to classify what Guiding Question each bulleted statement in the Chapter Summary answers. Have students copy the Chapter Summary onto a separate piece of paper and write the number of the appropriate Guiding Question next to each statement on the worksheet. Refer to p. 1 in the Student Edition for the text of Guiding Questions.

- Assign *Vocabulary Development* for students to review Key Terms.

  All in One Medieval Times to Today Teaching Resources, *Vocabulary Development,* p. 348

Answers

Key Terms

1. False. The Renaissance was a period of the rebirth of learning in Europe between about 1300 and 1600.
2. False. Humanism was a system of thought that focused on the nature, ideals, and achievements of human beings, rather than on the divine.
3. False. The Cape of Good Hope is the southern tip of Africa.
4. True.
5. True.
6. False. A tsar was an absolute ruler of Russia.
7. False. Encomienda was a system in which the Spanish king gave Spanish settlers land and the labor of Native Americans.
8. True.

Review and Assessment

Comprehension and Critical Thinking

9. (a) There was a renewed interest in art, literature, science, and the classical civilizations of Greece and Rome. **(b)** The Renaissance began in the Italian city-states, where people were exposed to other cultures and ideas through trade. **(c)** Curiosity, a desire for trade, and advances in science and technology led Europeans to exploration.

10. (a) a system of thought that focused on nature, ideals, and the achievements of human beings, rather than on the divine **(b)** They copied the art of ancient Greece and Rome, painted portraits of important people of the day, and used new techniques to create more realistic art.

11. (a) He thought people did not need church officials to tell them what God wanted them do, and that the church should not sell indulgences. **(b)** In Germany, priests, nobles, and people rallied behind Luther's ideas. Many northern Europeans agreed with Luther and created their own churches, independent of Rome.

12. (a) Prince Henry, the son of Portugal's king, hoped to find an eastern sea route to Asia. He encouraged navigation and oversaw many expeditions. **(b)** New technology, curiosity, and a desire to find new trade routes propelled Europeans to explore their world. Europeans were tired of paying high prices for Asian goods because the Ottomans controlled trade routes between Europe and Asia. **(c)** In their search for a route to Asia, Europeans sailed to the Americas. To acquire land and riches, they conquered the peoples of the Americas.

13. (a) Louis XIV **(b)** Possible answer: It showed he was the center of the French nation and the most powerful person in France at the time.

14. (a) It was the prosperous time in England during the rule of Queen Elizabeth I from 1558 to 1603. **(b)** England grew very powerful and prosperous, and it enjoyed a golden age of science, art, and literature. **(c)** Possible answer: She was determined, intelligent, and well-liked by the people. She used compromise to prevent religious wars, and helped to promote the arts and theatre.

15. (a) Herman Cortés, Francisco Pizarro **(b)** Possible answer: They conquered Native Americans, sent Spanish settlers to live there,

tried to convert Native Americans to Christianity, treated Native Americans harshly and as slaves, and accidently spread European diseases, which killed Native Americans. **(c)** Spanish and Portuguese settlers wanted workers for their mines and plantations.

Review and Assessment (continued)

◆ Comprehension and Critical Thinking

9. (a) Describe What changes occurred during the Renaissance?
(b) Identify Causes What caused these changes?
(c) Draw Conclusions How did these changes lead to the Age of Exploration?

10. (a) Define What was humanism?
(b) Explain How did Renaissance artists exhibit humanism in their work?

11. (a) Recall What were Martin Luther's objections to the practices of the Roman Catholic Church?
(b) Conclude Why did the Reformation spread?

12. (a) Identify Who was Henry the Navigator?
(b) Identify Causes Why did Spain and Portugal start making voyages of exploration?
(c) Synthesize How did the Age of Exploration lead to the conquest of Native American peoples?

13. (a) Name What ruler said, "I am the state"?
(b) Explain How did that statement demonstrate the concept of absolute monarchy?

14. (a) Recall When was the Elizabethan Age?
(b) Describe What was the Elizabethan Age like?
(c) Draw Conclusions What qualities and actions made Elizabeth I a successful ruler?

15. (a) Name Which conquistador conquered the Aztecs? The Incas?
(b) Describe How did the Spanish set up an empire in the Americas?
(c) Identify Causes Why did Europeans bring enslaved Africans to the Americas?

◆ Skills Practice

Using Route Maps In the Skills for Life activity in this chapter, you learned how to analyze route maps. Review the steps you followed to learn the skill.

Turn to the map named Invasions of the Roman Empire on page 119. Follow the steps of the skill to analyze the map. Then use the map to draw at least three conclusions about the invasions of the ancient Roman Empire.

◆ Writing Activity: Art

Study some Renaissance paintings that use perspective, such as Raphael's painting on page 156. Then do research to find out how perspective helps artists make their paintings more realistic. Explore how the use of a vanishing point creates the illusion of three-dimensional space. Try drawing your own scene using perspective. Finally, write a brief report explaining how perspective allowed Renaissance artists to create more realistic artwork. Use illustrations if you wish.

Skills Activity

European Empires in the Americas

Place Location For each place listed below, write the letter from the map that shows its location.

1. Atlantic Ocean
2. North America
3. Pacific Ocean
4. Portuguese empire
5. South America
6. Spanish empire

Go Online
PHSchool.com Use Web Code lgp-8654 for an interactive map.

Skills Practice
Students' answers should reflect their knowledge of the five steps for using a route map.

Writing Activity: Art
Use the *Rubric for Assessing a Report* to evaluate students' reports.

All in One **Medieval Times to Today Teaching Resources,** *Rubric for Assessing a Report,* p. 350

Standardized Test Prep

Test-Taking Tips

Some questions on standardized tests ask you to analyze a passage. Read the passage below. Follow the tips to answer the sample question.

> In 1519, Ferdinand Magellan sailed from Spain for South America with five ships. From early in the voyage, he had problems with his crew. After the expedition reached the coast of South America, the crews of three ships refused to sail on. Magellan had to use both skill and force to keep the men from turning back. The ships continued south, searching for a passageway to the other side of South America.

TIP Notice the structure of the passage. Is it organized by cause and effect, by topics, or by chronological order? That will help you determine what may come next.

Pick the letter that best answers the question.

What information would you expect to find in the *next* paragraph of this article?

TIP Use what you already know to help you answer social studies questions.

A what Magellan's childhood was like

B what happened after Magellan reached the Pacific Ocean

C how Magellan's crew got through the Strait of Magellan

D how Magellan died in the Philippines

Think It Through The structure of this passage is chronological, so you can easily rule out A, which happened long before the voyage. You can also rule out D, which happened after Magellan entered the Pacific. That leaves B and C. You can use your knowledge of geography to determine that the passage through the Strait of Magellan would logically come before the crew reached the Pacific Ocean. The correct answer is C.

Practice Questions

Read the passage below. Choose the letter of the best answer to the questions that follow.

> Christopher Columbus led four voyages to the Americas. The first and most famous one began in 1492 and included just three ships. His second voyage, which included 17 ships, founded Nueva Isabela, the first European colony in the Americas. On his third voyage, which left Spain in 1498, Columbus became the first European to visit South America. Columbus's final voyage lasted from 1502 to 1504. He hoped to find a passage through the new lands he had discovered and sail on to Asia, but he never did.

1. During what time period can you infer that Columbus made his second voyage?

   A before 1492
   B between 1498 and 1502
   C between 1492 and 1498
   D after 1504

2. What was significant about Columbus's second voyage to the Americas?

   A He realized he had found a new land.
   B He found a passage through the continent.
   C He began a settlement.
   D He finally reached Asia.

3. What information would you expect to find in the *next* paragraph of this article about Christopher Columbus?

   A what his childhood was like
   B why he founded Nueva Isabela
   C where he landed in South America
   D how he spent his later years

Use Web Code lga-8604 for a **Chapter 6 self-test.**

Assessment Resources

Use *Chapter Tests A and B* to assess students' mastery of the chapter content.

All in One Medieval Times to Today Teaching Resources, *Chapter Tests A and B,* pp. 351–356

Tests are also available on the **ExamView®** **Test Bank CD-ROM.**

ExamView® Test Bank CD-ROM

Overview

 Section 1
The Enlightenment
1. Find out about the Age of Reason and how it grew out of the Renaissance and the Scientific Revolution.
2. Explore the Enlightenment idea of natural rights.
3. Learn how the French thinkers called philosophes contributed to the Enlightenment.

 Section 2
Political Revolutions
1. Learn how a power struggle between English kings and Parliament led to the creation of a limited, constitutional monarchy.
2. Find out how the American Revolution put Enlightenment ideas into practice.
3. Discover how the French Revolution ended the monarchy in France.

 Section 3
The Industrial Revolution
1. Learn about the Industrial Revolution and how it changed the world forever.
2. Identify some serious problems of the Industrial Age.

 Section 4
Nationalism and Imperialism
1. Learn how Napoleon rose to power in France and conquered much of Europe.
2. Understand the growth of nationalism in Europe.
3. Find out how imperialist European nations gained control over much of the world.

Galileo's Telescope
Length: 4 minutes
Use with Section 1
This video segment describes the accomplishments of Galileo. It also explains why he spent the last years of his life in prison as a result of his discoveries.

 # Technology Resources

Students use embedded Web codes to access Internet activities, chapter self-tests, and additional map practice. They may also access Dorling Kindersley's Online Desk Reference to learn more about each country they study.

Use the Interactive Textbook to make content and concepts come alive through animations, videos, and activities that accompany the complete basal text—online and on CD-ROM.

Use this complete suite of powerful teaching tools to make planning lessons and administering tests quicker and easier.

Reading and Assessment

Reading and Vocabulary Instruction

↻ Model the Target Reading Skill

Compare and Contrast Remind students when they compare and contrast, they find the similarities and differences between objects or situations. Model comparing and contrasting using information from Section 1 of the Student Edition. Draw a Venn diagram on the board. Label the left-hand circle "Scientists," the middle circle "Both," and the right-hand circle "Political Thinkers." Tell students that they make comparisons when they find similarities and contrasts when they find differences.

Ask yourself the following questions aloud as you fill in the diagram. "What is the same about the scientists and political thinkers of the Enlightenment? *(Both believed in natural laws, questioned the teachings of the Church, and used reason to come to conclusions.)* What are the differences between the scientists and political thinkers of the Enlightenment? *(scientists: applied the idea of natural laws to science and nature; political thinkers: applied the idea of natural laws to human society)* How can I summarize these comparisons and contrasts? *(The scientists and political thinkers of the Enlightenment questioned the teachings of the Church by believing that natural laws determine how the world works. Both used reason in their thought processes, but applied them to different fields.)*"

Use the following worksheets from All-in-One Medieval Times To Today Teaching Resources (pp. 379–381) to support the chapter's Target Reading Skill.

Vocabulary Builder
High-Use Academic Words

Use these steps to teach this chapter's high-use words:

1. Have students rate how well they know each word on their Word Knowledge worksheets (All-in-One Medieval Times to Today Teaching Resources, p. 382).

2. Pronounce each word and ask students to repeat it.

3. Give students a brief definition or sample sentence (provided on TE pp. 191, 199, 205, and 213).

4. Work with students as they fill in the "Definition or Example" column of their Word Knowledge worksheets.

Assessment

Formal Assessment

Test students' understanding of core knowledge and skills.

Chapter Tests A and B, All-in-One Medieval Times to Today Teaching Resources, pp. 398–403

Customize the Chapter Tests to suit your needs.

Exam*View*® Test Bank CD-ROM

Skills Assessment

Assess geographic literacy.

MapMaster Skills, Student Edition pp. 189, 213, 215, 218

Assess reading and comprehension.

Target Reading Skills, Student Edition, pp. 194, 200, 208, 214, and in Section Assessments

Chapter 7 Assessment, Medieval Times to Today Reading and Vocabulary Study Guide, p. 84

Performance Assessment

Assess students' performance on this chapter's Writing Activities using the following rubrics from All-in-One Medieval Times to Today Teaching Resources.

Rubric for Assessing a Writing Assignment, p. 396

Rubric for Assessing a Journal Entry, p. 397

Assess students' work through performance tasks.

Small Group Activity: Creating a Bulletin Board Display About the Industrial Revolution, All-in-One Medieval Times to Today Teaching Resources, pp. 385–388

Online Assessment

Have students check their own understanding.

Chapter Self-Test

Section 1 The Enlightenment

 3.5 periods, 1.75 blocks (includes Skills for Life)

Social Studies Objectives

1. Find out about the Age of Reason and how it grew out of the Renaissance and the Scientific Revolution.
2. Explore the Enlightenment idea of natural rights.
3. Learn how the French thinkers called philosophes contributed to the Enlightenment.

Reading/Language Arts Objective

Compare and contrast to sort out and analyze information.

Prepare to Read	**Instructional Resources**	**Differentiated Instruction**
Build Background Knowledge Have students preview the headings and visuals and make predictions about what they will learn. **Set a Purpose for Reading** Have students evaluate statements on the *Reading Readiness Guide.* **Preview Key Terms** Teach the section's Key Terms. **Target Reading Skill** Introduce the section's Target Reading Skill of **comparing and contrasting.**	**All in One Medieval Times to Today Teaching Resources** **L2** Reading Readiness Guide, p. 364 **L2** Compare and Contrast, p. 379 **Medieval Times to Today Transparencies** **L2** Color Transparency MT 17: Western Europe: Political **World Studies Video Program** **L2** Galileo's Telescope	**Spanish Reading and Vocabulary Study Guide** **L1** Chapter 7, Section 1, pp. 53–54 ELL

Instruct	**Instructional Resources**	**Differentiated Instruction**
The Age of Reason Compare and contrast the ideas of the Enlightenment and those taught by the Church. **New Political Ideas** Discuss Locke's idea of natural rights. **Target Reading Skill** Review **comparing and contrasting.** **The French Philosophes** Discuss the French thinkers and scientists of the Enlightenment.	**All in One Medieval Times to Today Teaching Resources** **L2** Guided Reading and Review, p. 365 **L2** Reading Readiness Guide, p. 364 **Medieval Times to Today Transparencies** **L2** Section Reading Support Transparency MT 73	**All in One Medieval Times to Today Teaching Resources** **L1** Testing a Theory, p. 391 ELL, LPR, SN **L2** Skills for Life, p. 384 AR, GT, LPR, SN **Teacher's Edition** **L1** For Less Proficient Readers, TE p. 192 **L3** For Advanced Readers, TE p. 192 **L2** For English Language Learners, TE p. 193 **Spanish Support** **L2** Guided Reading and Review (Spanish), p. 56 ELL

Assess and Reteach	**Instructional Resources**	**Differentiated Instruction**
Assess Progress Evaluate student comprehension with the section assessment and section quiz. **Reteach** Assign the Reading and Vocabulary Study Guide to help struggling students. **Extend** Have students write a short play about Galileo's trials.	**All in One Medieval Times to Today Teaching Resources** **L2** Section Quiz, p. 366 **L3** Writing Plays, p. 394 Rubric for Assessing a Writing Assignment, p. 396 **Reading and Vocabulary Study Guide** **L1** Chapter 7, Section 1, pp. 72–74	**All in One Medieval Times to Today Teaching Resources** **L1** Reading a Diagram, p. 389 ELL, LPR, SN **Spanish Support** **L2** Section Quiz (Spanish), p. 57 ELL

Key

L1 Basic to Average	**L3** Average to Advanced	**LPR** Less Proficient Readers	**GT** Gifted and Talented
L2 For All Students		**AR** Advanced Readers	**ELL** English Language Learners
		SN Special Needs Students	

Section 2 Political Revolutions

 *2 periods, 1 block*

Social Studies Objectives

1. Learn how a power struggle between English kings and Parliament led to the creation of a limited, constitutional monarchy.
2. Find out how the American Revolution put Enlightenment ideas into practice.
3. Discover how the French Revolution ended the monarchy in France.

Reading/Language Arts Objective
Compare two situations to see how they are alike.

Prepare to Read	Instructional Resources	Differentiated Instruction
Build Background Knowledge Ask students to survey the visuals in the section and think about how changes in government came about in the 1600s and 1700s. **Set a Purpose for Reading** Have students begin to fill out the *Reading Readiness Guide*. **Preview Key Terms** Teach the section's Key Terms. **Target Reading Skill** Introduce the section's Target Reading Skill of **making comparisons**.	**All in One Medieval Times to Today Teaching Resources** L2 Reading Readiness Guide, p. 368 L2 Make Comparisons, p. 380	**Spanish Reading and Vocabulary Study Guide** L1 Chapter 7, Section 2, pp. 55–56 ELL

Instruct	Instructional Resources	Differentiated Instruction
Changes in England Discuss the government in England from 1603 to 1689. **Target Reading Skill** Review **making comparisons**. **The American Revolution** Discuss the events and ideas that brought about the American Revolution. **The French Revolution** Discuss causes and effects of the French Revolution.	**All in One Medieval Times to Today Teaching Resources** L2 Guided Reading and Review, p. 369 L2 Reading Readiness Guide, p. 368 **Medieval Times to Today Transparencies** L2 Section Reading Support Transparency MT 74	**Spanish Support** L2 Guided Reading and Review (Spanish), p. 58 ELL

Assess and Reteach	Instructional Resources	Differentiated Instruction
Assess Progress Evaluate student comprehension with the section assessment and section quiz. **Reteach** Assign the Reading and Vocabulary Study Guide to help struggling students. **Extend** Have students create posters about citizens' rights during this time period.	**All in One Medieval Times to Today Teaching Resources** L2 Section Quiz, p. 370 Rubric for Assessing a Writing Assignment, p. 396 **Reading and Vocabulary Study Guide** L1 Chapter 7, Section 2, pp. 75–77	**Spanish Support** L2 Section Quiz (Spanish), p. 59 ELL

Key

L1 Basic to Average	**L3** Average to Advanced	**LPR** Less Proficient Readers
L2 For All Students		**AR** Advanced Readers
		SN Special Needs Students

GT Gifted and Talented
ELL English Language Learners

Section 3 The Industrial Revolution

2 periods, 1 block (includes Focus On The Mill Girls)

Social Studies Objectives
1. Learn about the Industrial Revolution and how it changed the world forever.
2. Identify some serious problems of the Industrial Age.

Reading/Language Arts Objective
Contrast two situations to find out how they are different.

Prepare to Read	Instructional Resources	Differentiated Instruction
Build Background Knowledge Have students preview the headings and visuals and think of three questions they would like answered as they read. **Set a Purpose for Reading** Have students evaluate statements on the *Reading Readiness Guide*. **Preview Key Terms** Teach the section's Key Terms. **Target Reading Skill** Introduce the section's Target Reading Skill of **identifying contrasts**.	**All in One Medieval Times to Today Teaching Resources** L2 Reading Readiness Guide, p. 372 L2 Identify Contrasts, p. 381	**Spanish Reading and Vocabulary Study Guide** L1 Chapter 7, Section 3, pp. 57–58 ELL

Instruct	Instructional Resources	Differentiated Instruction
A New Kind of Revolution Discuss the Industrial Revolution. **Eyewitness Technology** Ask students to read and study a diagram about an assembly line, and then research how cars are manufactured today. **Problems of the Industrial Age** Discuss some problems caused by the increase in industry. **Target Reading Skill** Review **identifying contrasts**.	**All in One Medieval Times to Today Teaching Resources** L2 Guided Reading and Review, p. 373 L2 Reading Readiness Guide, p. 372 **Medieval Times to Today Transparencies** L2 Section Reading Support Transparency MT 75	**All in One Medieval Times to Today Teaching Resources** L1 L3 Enrichment, p. 383 AR, GT, ELL, LPR, SN L1 Reading a Line Graph, p. 390 ELL, LPR, SN **Teacher's Edition** L3 For Advanced Readers, TE p. 206 L1 For Special Needs Students, TE p. 206 L1 For Less Proficient Readers, TE p. 208 L3 For Gifted and Talented, TE p. 210 L1 For English Language Learners, TE p. 210 **Spanish Support** L2 Guided Reading and Review (Spanish), p. 60 ELL

Assess and Reteach	Instructional Resources	Differentiated Instruction
Assess Progress Evaluate student comprehension with the section assessment and section quiz. **Reteach** Assign the Reading and Vocabulary Study Guide to help struggling students. **Extend** Extend the lesson by having students complete a Small Group Activity.	**All in One Medieval Times to Today Teaching Resources** L2 Section Quiz, p. 374 L3 Small Group Activity: Creating a Bulletin Board Display About the Industrial Revolution, pp. 385–388 Rubric for Assessing a Journal Entry, p. 397 **Reading and Vocabulary Study Guide** L1 Chapter 7, Section 3, pp. 78–80	**Spanish Support** L2 Section Quiz (Spanish), p. 61 ELL

Key

L1 Basic to Average   L3 Average to Advanced   LPR Less Proficient Readers   GT Gifted and Talented
L2 For All Students   AR Advanced Readers   ELL English Language Learners
     SN Special Needs Students

Section 4 Nationalism and Imperialism

 4 periods, 2 blocks (includes Chapter Review and Assessment)

Social Studies Objectives

1. Learn how Napoleon rose to power in France and conquered much of Europe.
2. Understand the growth of nationalism in Europe.
3. Find out how imperialist European nations gained control over much of the world.

Reading/Language Arts Objective

Compare and contrast to find the similarities and differences between two events or ideas.

Prepare to Read

Build Background Knowledge
Show a transparency to initiate a discussion about colonization in Africa.

Set a Purpose for Reading
Have students evaluate statements on the *Reading Readiness Guide*.

Preview Key Terms
Teach the section's Key Terms.

Target Reading Skill
Introduce the section's Target Reading Skill of **comparing and contrasting**.

Instructional Resources

All in One Medieval Times to Today Teaching Resources
- **L2** Reading Readiness Guide, p. 376
- **L2** Compare and Contrast, p. 379

Medieval Times to Today Transparencies
- **L2** Color Transparency MT 12: Africa: Colonial Rule and Independence

Differentiated Instruction

Spanish Reading and Vocabulary Study Guide
- **L1** Chapter 7, Section 4, pp. 59–60 ELL

Instruct

The Age of Napoleon
Discuss Napoleon's rule of France.

Nationalism
Discuss nationalism and how it affected Napoleon.

Target Reading Skill
Review **comparing and contrasting**.

Imperialism in Africa and Asia
Discuss European colonization in Africa and Asia.

Instructional Resources

All in One Medieval Times to Today Teaching Resources
- **L2** Guided Reading and Review, p. 377
- **L2** Reading Readiness Guide, p. 376

Medieval Times to Today Transparencies
- **L2** Section Reading Support Transparency MT 76

Differentiated Instruction

Teacher's Edition
- **L1** For Less Proficient Readers, TE p. 215

Reading and Vocabulary Study Guide
- **L1** Chapter 7, Section 4, pp. 81–83 ELL, LPR, SN

Spanish Support
- **L2** Guided Reading and Review (Spanish), p. 62 ELL

Assess and Reteach

Assess Progress
Evaluate student comprehension with the section assessment and section quiz.

Reteach
Assign the Reading and Vocabulary Study Guide to help struggling students.

Extend
Extend the lesson by assigning a literature reading.

Instructional Resources

All in One Medieval Times to Today Teaching Resources
- **L2** Section Quiz, p. 378
- **L3** A Letter from Napoleon's Army, pp. 392–393 Rubric for Assessing a Writing Assignment, p. 396
- **L2** Word Knowledge, p. 382
- **L2** Vocabulary Development, p. 395
- **L2** Chapter Tests A and B, pp. 398–403

Reading and Vocabulary Study Guide
- **L1** Chapter 7, Section 4, pp. 81–83

Differentiated Instruction

Spanish Support
- **L2** Section Quiz (Spanish), p. 63 ELL
- **L2** Chapter Summary (Spanish), p. 64 ELL
- **L2** Vocabulary Development (Spanish), p. 65 ELL

Key

L1 Basic to Average	**L3** Average to Advanced	LPR Less Proficient Readers
L2 For All Students		AR Advanced Readers
		SN Special Needs Students

GT Gifted and Talented
ELL English Language Learners

Reading Background

Providing Scaffolding

Providing scaffolding gives students the confidence to analyze and comprehend information. To teach using scaffolding, the teacher gives the students enough support initially, then provides them with less and less as they become more proficient, ultimately leading to students' being able to do tasks on their own. Below are some tips for using scaffolding.

1. Move from teacher-directed to student-directed instruction.
2. Build on what students already know by organizing questions so that they lead students from easier concepts to more difficult ones.
3. Model skills to illustrate the thinking process students should follow.
4. Have students work in groups.
5. For the more difficult tasks, provide additional structures for students, such as templates that they must complete in order to answer the questions.

Read-Cover-Recite-Check

Read-Cover-Recite-Check is a useful strategy for students to retain the information they read. It can be especially effective to help students study for a test. Model the steps for using Read-Cover-Recite-Check to read the paragraph under The Scientific Method on page 193 of the Student Edition.

1. Read the paragraph quickly to grasp the main ideas. (*Think aloud about the main idea: The scientific method was a new way of learning about the world.*)
2. Reread the paragraph, looking for details and key information. (*Think aloud, noting the details: the scientific method involves making predictions or developing theories based on observations, and testing those predictions; logic and mathematics are used to analyze observations; as scientists learn more, old theories are replaced with new ones.*)
3. Cover the paragraph with your hand or a piece of paper.
4. Recall and repeat the information from the paragraph, including the topic and important details. (*Think aloud: Repeat the information from steps 1 and 2.*)
5. Rephrase the paragraph in your own words. (*Scientists came up with the scientific method, a new way of learning. Using this method, scientists make predictions and come up with theories about the world. They try to back up their predictions and theories by conducting experiments and by observation; they examine the results using math and logic. As scientists learn more, they rework their theories to make them more accurate.*)
6. Check to make sure you remembered correctly.

World Studies Background

Newton and Prisms

In addition to his theories about gravity, in the 1600s Isaac Newton came up with an important discovery about light. He conducted experiments using light and prisms, or pieces of glass cut with certain angles. When he passed a beam of light through the prism, a strip of colors that looked like a rainbow came out the other side. If he passed that colored band of light through another prism, it became white light again. These experiments demonstrated that white light is actually a mixture of different colors, and a prism can bend the light to separate the individual colors.

Advances in Technology

Many new processes and inventions helped advance the Industrial Revolution in Britain. The development of the steam-powered engine was crucial. Other inventions made the textile business the key industry in the early years of industrialization. These inventions included John Kay's fly shuttle in 1733, the spinning jenny developed by James Hargreaves and patented in 1770, Richard Arkwright's water frame in 1769, and Edmund Cartwright's power loom patented in 1783. The cotton gin was invented by Eli Whitney in the United States in 1793.

Infoplease® provides a wealth of useful information for the classroom. You can use this resource to strengthen your background on the subjects covered in this chapter. Have students visit this advertising-free site as a starting point for projects requiring research.

Use Web Code **lgd-8700** for **Infoplease®**.

Structured Silent Reading

The key to using the Structured Silent Reading strategy is to give students a reason to read. You can do this by asking a question for students to answer as they read. As students become more comfortable, you can teach them to generate their own questions before reading. End each reading segment with a class discussion to answer questions and make sure everyone understands the main points.

Reading to find answers is a high-level cognitive task. Start by modeling the thought process for students as you read the first paragraph under the heading The American Revolution on p. 201 of the Student Edition to the class. Begin by asking **Why did the British want to tax the American colonists?**

Think aloud: "I'm not sure what a colonist is. I have heard the word *colony* before. I'll read the text to find out what that means so that I can better understand the question. As I scan the paragraph, I see the word *colony* in boldface. That tells me that it is defined in the paragraph. The definition says, *A colony is a territory settled and ruled by a distant nation.* The American colonists must have been people who lived in a territory that was far away from England, but still ruled by the British. The last sentence says, *To help pay for the defense of their faraway colonies, the British wanted to collect taxes from the American colonists.* This reminds me that the colonists were far away from England, and answers my question. The British wanted to tax the colonists so that they would have money to pay for the protection of the territories that they ruled."

The American Revolution at Sea

To combat Britain's sea power during the Revolution, Americans created the Continental Navy and the Marine Corps in 1775. More harmful to the British, however, were attacks by American privateers—private vessels commissioned, but not paid, to attack British ships. To make money, American privateers captured British shipping vessels, stealing the cargo and kidnapping the sailors. By the end of the war privateers are estimated to have captured 1,500 British vessels and more than 12,000 sailors.

The Napoleonic Legend

Napoleon was such an influential figure in France that even after his death, his supporters kept his memory alive by idealizing his life in artwork, songs, and literature. The English poet Lord Byron defended Napoleon's honor in his "Ode to Napoleon Buonaparte," published in 1814. Victor Hugo, a French novelist and poet, wrote "Ode á la Colonne," paying tribute to Napoleon's honor. These works helped contribute to the Napoleonic legend, the glorified story of Napoleon as a great conqueror and important leader in French history.

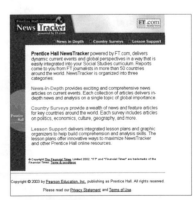

Get in-depth information on topics of global importance with **Prentice Hall Newstracker**, powered by FT.com.

Use Web Code **lgd-8705** for **Prentice Hall Newstracker**.

Guiding Questions

Remind students about the Guiding Questions introduced at the beginning of the book.

Section 1 relates to **Guiding Question 2 How did each society's belief system affect its history?** *(During the Enlightenment, people began to abandon the teachings of the Roman Catholic Church and do their own research to develop new ideas about the physical world.)*

Section 2 relates to **Guiding Question 4 What types of government were formed in these societies?** *(The English Bill of Rights gave more power to Parliament and helped establish a constitutional monarchy in England.)*

Section 3 relates to **Guiding Question 5 How did each society organize its economic activities?** *(During the Industrial Revolution, goods went from being produced by hand to being produced by machine. This allowed them to be produced more quickly and cheaply.)*

Section 4 relates to **Guiding Question 2 How did each society's belief system affect its history?** *(Nationalism, or pride in one's country, contributed to imperialism. Controlling vast territory fueled national pride, which stirred rivalries in which countries wanted to gain more power and wealth than their neighbors.)*

Target Reading Skill

In this chapter, students will learn and apply the reading skill of comparison and contrast. Use the following worksheets to help students practice this skill:

All in One **Medieval Times to Today Teaching Resources,** *Compare and Contrast,* p. 379; *Make Comparisons,* p. 380; *Identify Contrasts,* p. 381

Differentiated Instruction

The following Teacher's Edition strategies are suitable for students of varying abilities.

Advanced Readers, pp. 192, 206
English Language Learners, pp. 193, 210
Gifted and Talented, p. 210
Less Proficient Readers, pp. 192, 208, 215
Special Needs Students, p. 206

Changes in the Western World

Chapter Preview

This chapter will introduce you to important changes that took place primarily in the 1700s and 1800s. They include revolutions in thought, in the way goods were produced, and in the way nations governed themselves at home and conducted themselves around the world.

Section 1
The Enlightenment

Section 2
Political Revolutions

Section 3
The Industrial Revolution

Section 4
Nationalism and Imperialism

 Target Reading Skill

Comparison and Contrast In this chapter you will focus on using comparison and contrast to help you sort out and analyze information.

▶ A Northern Pacific Railroad train, 1900

Bibliography

For the Teacher

Henry, John. *The Scientific Revolution and the Origins of Modern Science.* Palgrave Macmillan, 2002.

Ashton, Thomas S. *The Industrial Revolution, 1760–1830.* Oxford University Press, 1998.

Gengembre, Gerard. *Napoleon: The Immortal Emperor.* Vendome Press, 2003.

For the Student

L1 Collins, Mary. *Industrial Revolution.* Scholastic Library Publishing, 2000.

L2 Murray, Stuart and Dorling Kindersley Publishing. *Eyewitness: American Revolution.* DK Publishing, Inc., 2002.

L3 White, Michael. *Galileo Galilei: Inventor, Astronomer, and Rebel.* Blackbirch Press, 1999.

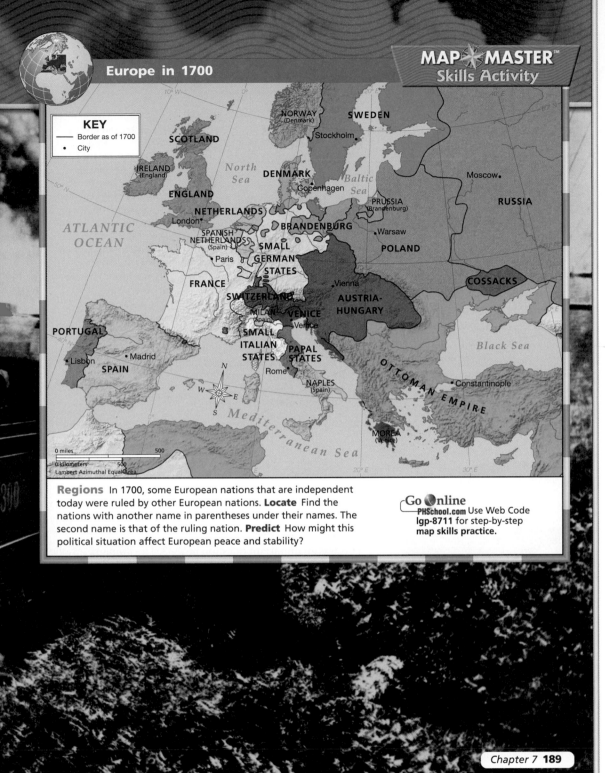

Europe in 1700

KEY
— Border as of 1700
• City

SCOTLAND

IRELAND
(England)

ENGLAND

London •

ATLANTIC
OCEAN

PORTUGAL

• Lisbon   • Madrid

SPAIN

North
Sea

NORWAY
(Denmark)

DENMARK

Copenhagen •

NETHERLANDS

SPANISH
NETHERLANDS
(Spain)

• Paris

FRANCE

SWITZERLAND

MILAN
(Spain)

SMALL
ITALIAN
STATES

SMALL
GERMAN
STATES

BRANDENBURG

• Warsaw

VENICE

• Venice

PAPAL
STATES

Rome •

NAPLES
(Spain)

Mediterranean Sea

SWEDEN

Stockholm •

Baltic
Sea

PRUSSIA
(Brandenburg)

POLAND

Moscow •

RUSSIA

COSSACKS

• Vienna

AUSTRIA-
HUNGARY

Black Sea

OTTOMAN EMPIRE

• Constantinople

MOREA
(Venice)

0 miles   500
0 kilometers   500
Lambert Azimuthal Equal-Area

Regions In 1700, some European nations that are independent today were ruled by other European nations. **Locate** Find the nations with another name in parentheses under their names. The second name is that of the ruling nation. **Predict** How might this political situation affect European peace and stability?

Go Online
PHSchool.com Use Web Code
lgp-8711 for step-by-step
map skills practice.

■ Display *Color Transparency MT 17: Western Europe: Political*. Ask students to compare it to the map on p. 189. Have students make two lists—one list should include the countries that existed in Europe in 1700 and still exist today. The other list should include countries that did not exist in Europe in 1700 but do exist today.

📖 **Medieval Times to Today Transparencies,** *Color Transparency MT 17: Western Europe: Political*

Go Online
PHSchool.com Students may practice their map skills using the interactive online version of this map.

Using the Visual   L2

Reach Into Your Background Point out the photograph on pp. 188–189 and have students read the caption. Ask them to think about how trains are used today. Have students discuss how they think the introduction of railroads in the 1700s might have changed the way people lived and worked.

Answers

 **Locate** Spanish Netherlands, Norway, Milan, Naples, Ireland, Morea, Prussia
Predict It probably made the region less peaceful and stable because the countries may have begun to fight for their independence.

Chapter Resources

Teaching Resources
L2 Vocabulary Development, p. 395
L2 Skills for Life, p. 384
L2 Chapter Tests A and B, pp. 398–403

Spanish Support
L2 Spanish Chapter Summary, p. 64
L2 Spanish Vocabulary Development, p. 65

Media and Technology
L1 Student Edition on Audio CD
L1 Guided Reading Audiotapes, English and Spanish
L2 Social Studies Skills Tutor CD-ROM
Exam*View*® **Test Bank CD-ROM**

Discovery World Studies
CHANNEL SCHOOL Video Program

interactive
Textbook

PRENTICE HALL
TeacherEXPRESS™
Plan • Teach • Assess

Section 1
Step-by-Step Instruction

Objectives

Social Studies

1. Find out about the Age of Reason and how it grew out of the Renaissance and the Scientific Revolution.

2. Explore the Enlightenment idea of natural rights.

3. Learn how the French thinkers called philosophes contributed to the Enlightenment.

Reading/Language Arts

Compare and contrast to sort out and analyze information.

Prepare to Read

Build Background Knowledge L2

Ask students to preview the headings and visuals in this section. Tell them to make predictions about what they will learn. Provide a few examples to get students started. Have them engage in a Think-Write-Pair-Share activity (TE, p. T36) to generate a list of predictions. Write their responses on the board.

Set a Purpose for Reading L2

■ Preview the Objectives.

■ Read each statement in the *Reading Readiness Guide* aloud. Ask students to mark the statements true or false.

■ Have students discuss the statements in pairs or groups of four, then mark their guides again. Use the Numbered Heads participation strategy (TE, p. T36) to call on students to share their group's perspectives.

All in One **Medieval Times to Today Teaching Resources,** *Reading Readiness Guide,* p. 364

Vocabulary Builder

Preview Key Terms L2

Pronounce each Key Term, then ask the students to say the word with you. Provide a simple explanation such as, "During the Scientific Revolution, scientists began to base their ideas about the physical world on what they were able to observe."

Section 1
The Enlightenment

Prepare to Read

Objectives

In this section, you will

1. Find out about the Age of Reason and how it grew out of the Renaissance and the Scientific Revolution.

2. Explore the Enlightenment idea of natural rights.

3. Learn how the French thinkers called philosophes contributed to the Enlightenment.

Taking Notes

As you read this section, look for the achievements of the Enlightenment. Copy the concept web below and record your findings in it.

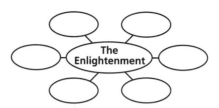

Target Reading Skill

Compare and Contrast Comparing is examining the similarities between things. Contrasting is looking at the differences. These skills can help you sort out and analyze information. As you read this section, compare and contrast Enlightenment ideas with the ideas of earlier time periods.

Key Terms

• **Enlightenment** (en LYT un munt) *n.* a philosophical movement, primarily of the 1700s, that was characterized by reliance on reason and experience

• **Age of Reason** (ayj uv REE zun) *n.* the period of the Enlightenment

• **Scientific Revolution** (sy un TIF ik rev uh LOO shun) *n.* a time when scientists began to rely on observation of the natural world

• **scientific method** (sy un TIF ik METH ud) *n.* a method involving careful observation of nature and, in some sciences, controlled experiments

• **natural rights** (NACH ur ul ryts) *n.* rights that belong to all human beings from birth

• **philosophe** (fee luh ZOHF) *n.* a French thinker of the Enlightenment

Galileo

190 Medieval Times to Today

The whole room was silent. Members of the court leaned forward, waiting for Galileo Galilei (gal uh LEE oh gal uh LAY) to respond to the question. Did the great Italian scientist really believe that Earth moved around the sun?

This was an important question in 1633. The Roman Catholic Church taught that God had made Earth the center of the universe. If that were true, everything—sun, planets, and stars—moved around Earth. But in the 1500s, the Polish astronomer Nicolaus Copernicus (nik uh LAY us koh PUR nih kus) had said that Earth moved around the sun.

Galileo had supported the ideas of Copernicus. Now the Church court was asking Galileo what he really believed. He knew that he could be tortured to death if he disagreed with the Church. So the old man told the court what it wanted to hear—that Earth did not move. Yet, as Galileo was being led away, he is said to have muttered, "Nevertheless, it does move."

Target Reading Skill L2

Compare and Contrast Point out the Target Reading Skill. Tell students that comparing and contrasting ideas will help them to better understand and organize them.

Model the skill by reading the last paragraph on p. 195 with students and comparing and contrasting the *Encyclopedia* with encyclopedias today. *(Both are large volumes containing information on many subjects,* *including arts and science. The* Encyclopedia *contained many articles that expressed opinions, whereas today's encyclopedias contain mostly facts.)*

Give students *Compare and Contrast.* Have them complete the activity in groups.

All in One **Medieval Times to Today Teaching Resources,** *Compare and Contrast,* p. 379

The Age of Reason

As you have read, for hundreds of years the Roman Catholic Church had been the most powerful institution in Europe. The Church told people what to believe about the physical world and how they should behave, based on the Bible and on faith. To protect its power, the Church excommunicated people who questioned its authority or teachings. It also gave the Inquisition, or Church courts, the power to torture, imprison, or condemn to death those who did not strictly obey the Church in thought and deed.

Nevertheless, there were those who questioned Church teachings. Protestants broke away from the Church. The Renaissance encouraged the study of ancient texts and the development of new ideas. As scientists began to make careful observations of nature, they started a revolution in the way people looked at themselves and the world.

A Change in Perspective This revolution in thought was called the **Enlightenment.** It was characterized by reliance on reason and experience rather than on religious teachings and faith. The 1700s, when Enlightenment ideas were the leading ideas in Europe, is called the **Age of Reason.**

Enlightenment thinkers used reason, or logical thought, to shed a new "light" on traditional beliefs. In many cases, they challenged those beliefs. The Enlightenment affected politics, art, literature, science, and religion—almost every field of human thought.

Learn about Galileo, the first scientist to use a telescope.

New World View
This diagram illustrates the view of the universe put forth by Copernicus, who is shown at the left below.
Infer *Compare this diagram to the one on pages M2–M3. How "modern" was Copernicus's view?*

Instruct

The Age of Reason L2

Guided Instruction

■ **Vocabulary Builder** Clarify the high-use words **reject, accurately,** and **method** before reading.

■ Read The Age of Reason using the Paragraph Shrinking strategy (TE, p. T34).

■ Ask students **How was the Church able to protect its power over people's behavior and beliefs?** *(It excommunicated people who questioned its authority and teachings and gave Church courts the power to torture, imprison, or condemn to death those who did not obey the Church in thought and deed.)*

■ Discuss how Enlightenment ideas were different from those taught by the Church. *(Enlightenment ideas were based on reason and experience rather than on religious teachings.)*

Vocabulary Builder

Use the information below to teach students this section's high-use words.

High-Use Word	Definition and Sample Sentence
reject, p. 192	*v.* to refuse to accept Ian's mom **rejected** his request to stay up late.
accurately, p. 192	*adv.* free from error Mia received a good grade for **accurately** completing the math problem.
method, p. 193	*n.* a way of doing something My **method** for preparing eggs produced the tastiest results.
reasonable, p. 193	*adj.* possessing sound judgment Building shelves was a **reasonable** way to make more storage space.

Answer

Infer The diagrams look very similar, because both show the sun as the center of the universe, with planets in orbit around it. Copernicus's view was quite modern.

Read the **Links to Science** on this page. Ask students to restate what Galileo learned from his experiment in their own words. *(Possible answer: An object's weight does not affect the speed at which it falls.)*

Guided Instruction (continued)

- Discuss some of the advances in astronomy that were made during the Scientific Revolution. *(Copernicus discovered that Earth moved around the sun. Kepler calculated the orbits of the planets around the sun. Galileo observed that four moons orbit Jupiter.)*

- Have students create a graphic organizer showing the relationship between the Renaissance, the Scientific Revolution, and the Enlightenment. *(Students may use a cause-and-effect chart or a concept web to show that the Renaissance and the Scientific Revolution led to the Enlightenment.)*

- Ask students to describe the scientific method. *(It involves careful observation of experiments performed under conditions a scientist controls. Mathematics and logic are used to interpret the results.)*

Independent Practice

Ask students to create the Taking Notes graphic organizer on a separate piece of paper. Tell them to fill in the circles with details about the Enlightenment. Briefly model how to choose the correct details.

Monitor Progress

As students fill in the graphic organizer, circulate and make sure individuals are choosing the correct details. Provide assistance as needed.

Links to Science

Galileo and Gravity In addition to studying the heavens, Galileo also experimented with gravity. According to legend, he dropped a light object and a heavy object from a tower at the same time. They landed at the same instant. Even though it seemed logical that a heavier object would fall faster, Galileo concluded—based on his experiment—that the speed of a falling object does not depend on its weight.

The Scientific Revolution Many Enlightenment ideas were rooted in the Scientific Revolution of the 1500s and 1600s. The Scientific Revolution was a time when scientists began to rely on what they could observe for themselves. It was the birth of modern science.

One of these scientists was Nicolaus Copernicus, who put forth the idea that Earth moved around the sun. He published his findings in 1543. At that time, people believed that Earth was the center of the universe and that the sun revolved around it. Both ancient Greek science and the Church supported that view. Many experts rejected Copernicus's theory.

In the late 1500s, however, the Danish astronomer Tycho Brahe (TEE koh BRAH uh) provided evidence to support Copernicus. In the early 1600s, Johannes Kepler (yoh HAHN us KEP lur) used Brahe's data to accurately calculate the orbits of the planets around the sun. Galileo also studied the planets. Using a new scientific tool—the telescope—he was able to observe four moons orbiting around Jupiter.

Milestones in the Scientific Revolution

Scientific Thought
In the early 1600s, Francis Bacon stressed the importance of experiment and observation.

◀ René Descartes said that human reasoning leads to understanding the world.

Medicine
Andreas Vesalius published the first accurate, detailed study of human anatomy in 1543.

◀ In the early 1600s, William Harvey discovered how the blood circulates and how the heart acts as a pump.

Anton van Leeuwenhoek perfected the microscope and in 1684 was the first to accurately describe red blood cells.

Chemistry
In the mid-1600s, Robert Boyle, "the father of chemistry," based his work on experiment and observation. He said that everything is made up of very tiny particles of matter.

Astronomy
In 1543, Nicolaus Copernicus published his theory that Earth and the other planets move around the sun.

▼ In 1609, Galileo used a telescope of his own design to observe the planets.

Differentiated Instruction

For Less Proficient Readers ▪L1▪
Pair these students with more advanced readers to read *Testing a Theory*, in which students will learn about another Enlightenment scientist.

All in One **Medieval Times to Today Teaching Resources,** *Testing a Theory,* p. 391

For Advanced Readers ▪L3▪
Have students choose one of the thinkers or scientists from The Scientific Revolution graphic at the bottom of this page. Tell them to do library or Internet research to learn more about the figure so that they can write a brief biography describing his life and contributions to science.

In England, Isaac Newton developed a theory about why the planets move the way they do. You have probably heard how Newton observed an apple falling from a tree. This observation led him to wonder whether the force that made the apple fall might be the same force that kept the moon in its orbit around Earth. He called that force gravity. He found that gravity also holds Earth and the other planets in their orbits around the sun. In 1687, Newton published a book about the workings of the universe. He said that the natural world follows "natural laws," or rules that can be measured and described mathematically.

The Scientific Method Scientists were developing a new way of learning about the world. This **scientific method** involves careful observation of nature and, in some sciences, controlled experiments. To use the scientific method, scientists make predictions and develop theories based on their observations. Then they test their predictions by doing experiments and by careful observations. Logic and mathematics are used to analyze observations and compare them to the results expected from their theories. As scientists observe and learn more, they replace old theories with new ones that explain the facts better.

✓ **Reading Check** What are natural laws?

New Political Ideas

Scientists were finding out that nature worked according to certain natural laws. Other Enlightenment thinkers declared that there were also natural laws that applied to human society.

John Locke One of these thinkers was the English philosopher John Locke. He said that natural laws govern human behavior. Government, he said, should be based on these natural laws.

Locke believed that people were basically reasonable and good. He argued that people also had **natural rights,** or rights that belonged to all human beings from birth. They included the right to life, the right to liberty, and the right to own property.

According to Locke, people form governments to protect their natural rights. Governments draw the right to rule from the people they govern. Therefore, rulers should govern only as long as they have the support of the people. If a government breaks the agreement by taking away people's rights, the people have the right to change, or even replace, that government.

Newton's Rainbow
Isaac Newton studied optics, or the science of light. Here, he uses a prism to disperse light into a spectrum of colors. **Conclude** *Why do you think Newton conducted this experiment in a dark room?*

Guided Instruction

- **Vocabulary Builder** Clarify the high-use word **reasonable** before reading.

- Read New Political Ideas with students. As students read, circulate and make sure individuals can answer the Reading Check question.

- Ask students **According to Locke, what were people's natural rights?** *(rights that belonged to all humans from birth, including the rights to life, to liberty, and to own property)* Ask **Why did people form governments?** *(to protect their natural rights)*

- Ask **Do you think monarchs supported or rejected Locke's ideas? Explain.** *(Possible answer: Monarchs most likely rejected Locke's ideas because they wanted people to believe they had a divine right to rule so that they could stay in power.)*

Independent Practice

Have students continue to fill in the concept web with political ideas developed during the Enlightenment.

Monitor Progress

Circulate to make sure students are choosing the correct details. Provide assistance as needed.

Differentiated Instruction

For English Language Learners L2
Point out words in the section that have multiple meanings, such as *revolution* (p. 191) and *spoiled* (p. 194). Discuss the possible meanings of each word and then help students use context clues to determine its correct meaning in the sentence in which it appears.

Answers

✓ **Reading Check** the rules that the natural world follows

Conclude Possible answer: It allowed him to see the colors of light clearly without interference from other sources of light.

Compare and Contrast As a follow up, ask students to answer the Target Reading Skill question in the Student Edition. *(Monarchs believed they had a divine right to rule and absolute power. Locke believed rulers should govern with the support of the people and that they should not have absolute power.)*

The French Philosophes [L2]

Guided Instruction

■ Read The French Philosophes together as a class.

■ Ask **Who were the philosophes?** *(a group of French thinkers and scientists who believed that the ideas of the Enlightenment could be used to reform government and society)*

■ Have students choose one philosophe and explain his ideas and contributions. *(Students should list the ideas and contributions of Rousseau, Voltaire, or Diderot.)*

■ Have students compare the ideas of Locke and Rousseau. *(Both believed that people were basically good and that the government should express the will of the people.)*

Independent Practice

Ask students to complete their concept webs with the information they have just learned.

Monitor Progress

■ Show *Section Reading Support Transparency MT 73* and ask students to check their graphic organizers individually. Go over key concepts and clarify key vocabulary as needed.

📖 **Medieval Times to Today Transparencies,** *Section Reading Support Transparency MT 73*

■ Tell students to fill in the last column of their *Reading Readiness Guides*. Probe for what they learned that confirms or invalidates each statement.

All in One Medieval Times to Today Teaching Resources, *Reading Readiness Guide,* p. 364

Answers

✓ **Reading Check** the right to life, the right to liberty, and the right to own property

Infer Possible answer: Their style of dress and wigs suggest that they are in the upper class.

Compare and Contrast What are some differences between Locke's ideas about government and the ideas of absolute monarchs?

Discussing Enlightenment Ideas Voltaire (with arm raised) hosts a gathering of philosophes. **Infer** *What class of French society do these men probably belong to? Explain your answer.*

194 Medieval Times to Today

Locke's Impact Locke's ideas were startling. He was saying that monarchs like those of France, Spain, and Russia did not have a divine right to rule. They should not have absolute power. They could—even *should*—be replaced if they did not meet their responsibilities toward those they ruled. People in many countries read about these new ideas and began to wonder whether their rulers were governing properly. As you will see in Section 2, some people eventually translated Locke's ideas into action.

✓ **Reading Check** What natural rights did Locke describe?

The French Philosophes

Enlightenment ideas were also being explored in France. The **philosophes** (fee luh ZOHF) were a group of French thinkers and scientists who believed that the ideas of the Enlightenment could be used to reform and improve government and society. They spoke out against inequality and injustice. The philosophes distrusted institutions, like most governments and the Church, that did not support freedom of thought.

One of the most important philosophes was Jean Jacques Rousseau (zhahn zhahk roo SOH). Like Locke, Rousseau thought that people were naturally good. He added that imperfect institutions such as the Church and governments corrupted, or spoiled, this natural goodness. In his 1762 book *The Social Contract*, Rousseau argued that governments should express the will of the people and put few limits on people's behavior.

Perhaps the most famous philosophe was Voltaire (vohl TEHR). His essays, plays, and novels exposed many of the abuses of his day. He used his biting wit to attack inequality, injustice, and religious prejudice. Voltaire was a great champion of freedom of speech. He once stated, "I disapprove of what you say, but I will defend to the death your right to say it."

In the mid-1700s, articles by many of the philosophes were collected by Denis Diderot (duh nee DEE duh roh) in the *Encyclopedia*. One purpose of this huge work was to bring together information on all of the arts and sciences. Another purpose was to make this information available to the public. A third goal was to advance the ideas of the Enlightenment. Articles in the *Encyclopedia* attacked slavery, urged education for all, and promoted freedom of expression. They also challenged traditional religions and the divine right of kings. Both the French government and the Catholic Church tried to ban the *Encyclopedia*, but it still was an important influence on Enlightenment thinkers.

Pages from the *Encyclopedia*

✓ **Reading Check** What was the *Encyclopedia*?

Section 1 Assessment

Key Terms
Review the key terms at the beginning of this section. Use each term in a sentence that explains its meaning.

Target Reading Skill
Compare and contrast the view of the universe held by the Church with the view held by Copernicus and Galileo.

Comprehension and Critical Thinking
1. (a) Identify Name two scientists of the Scientific Revolution and describe their contributions.

(b) Contrast How was the scientific method different from the thinking of the Middle Ages?

2. (a) Recall According to John Locke, why do governments exist?
(b) Identify Effects How were Locke's ideas a threat to some governments of the 1700s?
3. (a) Identify Which philosophe wrote *The Social Contract*? Who edited the *Encyclopedia*?
(b) Synthesize Information How did the philosophes contribute to the Enlightenment?

Writing Activity
Suppose you could do a television interview with one of the important thinkers you read about in this section. Write a list of questions you would ask him. Then write a short introduction to your interview.

> **Writing Tip** Capture your viewers' attention by telling how the person on your show changed the world.

Chapter 7 Section 1 **195**

Section 1 Assessment

Key Terms
Students' sentences should reflect knowledge of each Key Term.

Target Reading Skill
The Church believed the sun, planets, and stars revolved around Earth while Copernicus and Galileo believed Earth revolved around the sun.

Comprehension and Critical Thinking
1. (a) Possible answers: Copernicus: Earth revolves around the sun; Brahe: provided evidence to support Copernicus; Kepler: calculated the orbits of planets around the sun; Galileo: Earth revolves around the sun and four moons orbit Jupiter; Newton: explained natural laws and identified gravity

(b) Most thinking during the Middle Ages was based on religion. The scientific method used observation and experiments.

2. (a) to protect people's natural rights
(b) Locke suggested that rulers should be replaced if they took away people's rights or were not supported by the people. Most rulers at the time had absolute power, leading people to wonder whether they were governing properly.

3. (a) Rousseau; Diderot **(b)** They contributed new ideas that could be used to reform society and government to make them better.

Assess and Reteach

Assess Progress ▨L2
Have students complete the Section Assessment. Administer the *Section Quiz*.

📋 **All in One** **Medieval Times to Today Teaching Resources,** *Section Quiz*, p. 366

Reteach ▨L1
If students need more instruction, have them read this section in the Reading and Vocabulary Study Guide.

📖 Chapter 7, Section 1, **Medieval Times to Today Reading and Vocabulary Study Guide,** pp. 72–74

Extend ▨L3
Assign students to groups of four or five to do research to learn more about Galileo's trials. Then have students use the information to write a short play about a portion of the trials. Distribute *Writing Plays* to help them get started. Finally, have groups of students perform their plays in front of the class.

📋 **All in One** **Medieval Times to Today Teaching Resources,** *Writing Plays*, p. 394

Answers

✓ **Reading Check** a huge collection of articles written by many of the philosophes

Writing Activity
Use the *Rubric for Assessing a Writing Assignment* to evaluate students' questions and introductions.

📋 **All in One** **Medieval Times to Today Teaching Resources,** *Rubric for Assessing a Writing Assignment*, p. 396

Objective

Learn how to interpret diagrams.

Prepare to Read

Build Background Knowledge `L2`

Tell students that a diagram presents information with both pictures and words. Ask students to think about diagrams they might see in everyday life, for example, a diagram in a set of instructions that shows how to put together a bicycle. Tell students that they will learn how to interpret such diagrams in this lesson.

Instruct

Interpreting Diagrams `L2`

Guided Instruction

- Read the steps to interpreting diagrams on p. 196 as a class and write them on the board.

- Practice the skill with students by completing the Practice the Skill activity on p. 197 together. First identify the subject of the diagram (*the scientific method*) and the purpose of the diagram (*to show how to use the scientific method*).

- Discuss what the small illustrations mean (*for example, the pencil and paper illustration represents writing down a hypothesis*) and the purpose of the numbers and arrows (*to explain in what order the steps should be completed*). Explain that the captions describe the steps in the process. Explain that the parts of the diagram are related because they are all steps in the process. The diagram is a circle to show that after completing the first six steps, you repeat the process again.

- Ask students to write a brief summary of the diagram in their own words. Circulate and check their summaries to be sure they understand the diagram.

Diagrams present information in both words and pictures. To interpret a diagram, you need to discover what each picture or symbol represents. You must also understand the labels or captions that provide additional information. Finally, you must see how all parts of the diagram—the words, pictures, and symbols—work together to explain how a process works or how something is put together.

Learn the Skill

Use these steps to interpret a diagram.

1. **Look at the title and at the diagram to get a general idea of what it shows.** What is the subject of the diagram? What is its purpose? Does it show how something works or a process for doing something?

2. **Study each part of the diagram, and read the captions or labels that go with each part.** Interpret each picture or symbol. The words will help you understand what each picture or symbol represents.

3. **Notice how each part of the diagram relates to the other parts.** Does the diagram show steps in sequence? If so, notice what happens first, second, and so forth. Does it show details, such as close-ups or cutaways of the inside of something? How do the parts relate to the whole?

4. **Use your understanding of both the pictures and the words to draw a conclusion about the diagram.** Summarize the process or construction shown in the diagram. Think about how using words and pictures *together* helps make the meaning clear.

196 Medieval Times to Today

Independent Practice

Assign *Skills for Life* and have students complete it individually.

All in One Medieval Times to Today Teaching Resources, *Skills for Life,* p. 384

Monitor Progress

As students are completing *Skills for Life,* circulate to make sure individuals are applying the skill steps effectively. Provide assistance as needed.

Practice the Skill

Use the steps on the previous page to interpret the diagram shown at the right.

Francis Bacon (1561–1626), who said that truth is discovered through observation and reason

1 What is the subject of this diagram? What is its purpose?

2 What does each small illustration mean? How do the numbers and arrows help you understand the diagram? Do the captions tell what something is or describe a step in a process?

3 How do the parts of the diagram relate to one another? What does the fact that it is a circle suggest? What does Step Seven mean?

4 Summarize the process shown in the diagram in your own words. Be sure to explain how Step Seven relates to Step One. How does this diagram add to your understanding of the Scientific Revolution?

The Scientific Method

Step One
State the problem.

Step Two
Gather information about the problem.

Step Three
Form a hypothesis, or educated guess.

Step Four
Perform experiments or carry out observations to test the hypothesis.

Step Five
Record and analyze data.

Step Six
State a conclusion.

Step Seven
Repeat the steps.

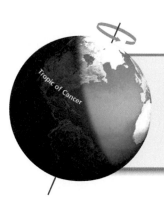

Apply the Skill

Turn to the diagram of the movements of Earth on pages M2–M3 of the MapMaster Skills Handbook. Use the steps of this skill to interpret the large diagram.

Assess and Reteach

Assess Progress [L2]
Ask students to do the Apply the Skill activity.

Reteach [L1]
If students are having trouble applying the skill steps, have them complete *Reading a Diagram* for more practice.

All in One **Medieval Times to Today,** *Reading a Diagram*, p. 389

Extend [L3]
Have students study Inventions Change the World on p. 206 in this chapter. Challenge them to research one of the inventions further and draw a diagram showing how it works.

Answer
Apply the Skill

The subject of the diagram is the movements of Earth. The purpose is to show how Earth's movements affect night and day and the seasons. Each illustration shows Earth at a different position during a different time of year. The arrows show the orbit of Earth. The captions describe what season is caused by Earth's position and why that is so. The parts of the diagram relate to each other because they all show Earth at different points in its orbit during one year. Students' summaries will vary but should explain what season it is in each hemisphere at different points in the year and why. They should also explain how Earth's rotation affects night and day.

Section 2
Step-by-Step Instruction

Objectives

Social Studies
1. Learn how a power struggle between English kings and Parliament led to the creation of a limited, constitutional monarchy.
2. Find out how the American Revolution put Enlightenment ideas into practice.
3. Discover how the French Revolution ended the monarchy in France.

Reading/Language Arts
Compare two situations to see how they are alike.

Prepare to Read

Build Background Knowledge `L2`

Tell students that in this section they will learn how governments in England, North America, and France changed in the 1600s and 1700s. Ask students to scan the visuals in the section with this question in mind: **Did changes in government come about peacefully or through conflict?** Have students explain and discuss their answers. Use the Numbered Heads participation strategy (TE, p. T36) to structure the discussion.

Set a Purpose for Reading `L2`

■ Preview the Objectives.

■ Form students into pairs or groups of four. Distribute the *Reading Readiness Guide*. Ask the students to fill in the first two columns of the chart. Use the Numbered Heads participation strategy (TE, p. T36) to call on students to share one piece of information they already know and one piece of information they want to know.

All in One Medieval Times to Today Teaching Resources, *Reading Readiness Guide,* p. 368

Vocabulary Builder
Preview Key Terms `L2`

Pronounce each Key Term, then ask the students to say the word with you. Provide a simple explanation such as, "A colony is an area governed by another country."

Section 2 Political Revolutions

Prepare to Read

Objectives
In this section, you will
1. Learn how a power struggle between English kings and Parliament led to the creation of a limited, constitutional monarchy.
2. Find out how the American Revolution put Enlightenment ideas into practice.
3. Discover how the French Revolution ended the monarchy in France.

Taking Notes
As you read this section, identify the major changes that took place in England, America, and France in the 1600s and 1700s. Copy the flowchart below and record your findings in it.

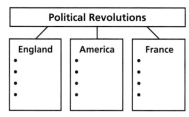

```
              Political Revolutions
        ┌───────────┬───────────┬───────────┐
     England      America      France
      •            •            •
      •            •            •
      •            •            •
      •            •            •
```

Target Reading Skill

Make Comparisons
Comparing two or more situations enables you to see how they are alike. As you read this section, compare the revolutions it describes. Consider their causes and effects as well as the ways they were accomplished.

Key Terms
• **English Civil War** (ING glish SIV ul wawr) *n.* the military clash between forces loyal to King Charles I and the forces of Parliament that overthrew the monarchy

• **English Bill of Rights** (ING glish bil uv rytz) *n.* acts passed by Parliament in 1689 guaranteeing certain rights of English people and limiting the power of the monarch
• **colony** (KAHL uh nee) *n.* territory settled and ruled by a distant country
• **Declaration of Independence** (dek luh RAY shun uv in dee PEN duns) *n.* the document in which the United States announced its independence from Britain
• **Reign of Terror** (rayn uv TEHR ur) *n.* the period (1793–1794) of the French Revolution during which many people were executed for opposing the revolution

As you have read, England enjoyed a golden age under Queen Elizabeth I. Shortly before she died in 1603, Elizabeth told Parliament, "Though God hath raised me high, yet this I count the glory of my crown, that I have reigned with your loves."

Elizabeth I was a very powerful monarch, but she knew that her power was not absolute. As far back as 1215, the Magna Carta had put limits on the power of English rulers. Elizabeth knew that she ruled with the approval of Parliament and the people—and she knew how important that approval was to her success. What she did not know was that the peace and stability of the Elizabethan Age would soon be destroyed by her successors.

Queen Elizabeth I

198 *Medieval Times to Today*

Target Reading Skill `L2`

Make Comparisons Point out the Target Reading Skill. Explain that students can make comparisons to find the similarities between two situations.

Model the skill by reading the last paragraph on p. 202 aloud and asking the following: **How does the Declaration of Independence compare to the Declaration of the Rights of Man?** (*The two documents*

are similar because the Declaration of the Rights of Man echoed the Declaration of Independence.)

Give students *Make Comparisons.* Have them complete the activity in groups.

All in One Medieval Times to Today Teaching Resources, *Make Comparisons,* p. 380

Changes in England

Queen Elizabeth died without children. Her crown went to her cousin, the king of Scotland, James Stuart. Although he had agreed to rule according to English laws and custom, James I believed that he was king by divine right and that his power was absolute.

James, and his son Charles I who ruled after him, clashed with Parliament, the council that had been advising English monarchs since the 1200s. Over the centuries, Parliament had grown in size and power. Divided into the House of Lords and the House of Commons, it had become a true legislature, passing bills that became law with the monarch's approval. Nevertheless, when Parliament would not approve the taxes he wanted, James dissolved, or closed, Parliament.

A Power Struggle Over time, a power struggle developed between the king and Parliament. Both James and Charles often refused to allow Parliament to meet. But when Charles needed money, he summoned Parliament, which could levy taxes. Parliament responded by trying to limit the king's power.

The English Civil War Charles summoned Parliament in 1640, when he needed funds to put down a rebellion in Scotland. This Parliament refused to bow to the king. It tried and executed some of the king's ministers, and declared that it could not be dissolved without its own consent. In response, Charles led troops into the House of Commons. Parliament leaders who escaped raised their own army. Forces loyal to the king fought forces loyal to Parliament in the **English Civil War.**

King Charles I

England at War
In this painting, Oliver Cromwell leads the forces of Parliament during the English Civil War.
Analyze Images *What does the painting reveal about the weapons and tactics of this war?*

Chapter 7 Section 2 **199**

- Ask **Who was Oliver Cromwell?** *(He was the general who led Parliament's army to victory over Charles I. He then ruled England through a committee of Parliament.)*

- Ask students **Why do you think Parliament restored the monarchy?** *(Possible answer: People were probably unhappy with the way Cromwell had ruled, and they hoped that Charles II would rule with respect for Parliament's power.)*

- Discuss how William and Mary gained control of England. *(Parliament invited William and Mary to rescue England from the rule of James II. James fled when William and Mary's armies arrived in England. Parliament then officially offered the throne to William and Mary on the condition that they accept the English Bill of Rights. William and Mary accepted and became the rulers of England in 1689.)*

- Ask **Why did Parliament want William and Mary to accept the English Bill of Rights?** *(Parliament wanted to have more power and rulers to have less power. It also wanted to ensure the rights of English citizens.)*

Independent Practice
Have students create the Taking Notes graphic organizer on a separate piece of paper. Ask them to fill in the England box with the information they have just learned.

Monitor Progress
Circulate and make sure students are correctly filling in the graphic organizer. Provide assistance as needed.

⊙ Target Reading Skill ▫L2

Make Comparisons As a follow up, ask students to answer the Target Reading Skill question in the Student Edition. *(Both governments consisted of monarchs and Parliament.)*

Answers

Predict Possible answer: The people of England may have been expected to follow Puritan ways.

✓ Reading Check It was the document that stated that all laws had to be approved by Parliament, the House of Commons had the power of the purse, and Parliament had to be summoned regularly. It also restated the rights of English citizens.

The king's death warrant, signed by members of Parliament ▶

Led by Oliver Cromwell, a skilled general, the military forces of Parliament were victorious. In 1646, they captured Charles I. Parliament set up a court that tried and convicted the king as "a tyrant . . . and public enemy." Charles I was beheaded in 1649. It was the first time a European monarch had been tried and executed by his own people.

Ruler But Not King
After the English Civil War, Oliver Cromwell was offered the throne but refused to become king.
Predict *What do you think might have happened in England if Cromwell had become king?*

After the war, Parliament abolished, or did away with, the monarchy. Oliver Cromwell ruled England through a committee of Parliament. Cromwell was a Puritan, a member of a Protestant group that wanted to simplify the services of the Church of England and to enforce strictly moral behavior. When he faced challenges to his power, Cromwell took the title Lord Protector and set up military rule.

The Monarchy Is Restored In 1660, just two years after Cromwell's death, Parliament invited the son of King Charles I to return from exile and rule the country. This re-establishment of the monarchy under Charles II is called the Restoration. Charles II was a popular king, but his brother, James II, who became king in 1685, was not. Not only was James Catholic, he also behaved like an absolute monarch.

Parliament's leaders wanted a Protestant king who respected Parliament. In 1688, they invited James's Protestant daughter Mary and her husband, the Dutch prince William of Orange, "to rescue the nation and the religion." When William and Mary's armies landed in England, James fled to France. This bloodless overthrow of James II is called the Glorious Revolution.

Parliament officially offered the throne to William and Mary—with one condition. They had to accept the **English Bill of Rights,** which stated that all laws had to be approved by Parliament and gave the House of Commons the power of the purse—the power to raise and spend money. Parliament had to be summoned regularly. The Bill of Rights also restated the traditional rights of English citizens, such as trial by jury. In 1689, William and Mary agreed, and Britain became a constitutional monarchy, or a government in which the monarch's power is limited by a set of laws.

✓ Reading Check What was the English Bill of Rights?

⊙ Make Comparisons How was England's government before the English Civil War similar to the government established by the Glorious Revolution?

Background: Links Across Time

From England to Great Britain Until 1707, England and Scotland were separate countries. They were, however, ruled by the same monarch. In 1702, Protestant Queen Anne succeeded William and Mary to the throne. Since Anne did not have an heir, the English Parliament passed the Act of Settlement to determine the next Protestant ruler. The Scottish Parliament did not pass a similar law. This concerned England because they did not want Scotland to name its own monarch, who might be Catholic. They saw a union with Scotland as a solution to the problem. In 1707, Scotland and England passed the Act of Union which officially joined the two countries and formed Great Britain.

The American Revolution

By the 1750s, about two million people lived in British colonies in North America. A **colony** is a territory settled and ruled by a distant nation. To help pay for the defense of their faraway colonies, the British wanted to collect taxes from the American colonists.

No Taxation Without Representation Under British law, people could not be taxed unless they had representatives in the Parliament that had voted for the tax. But the colonists had no representatives in Parliament. They complained that by taxing them, the British government was taking away their rights.

As American protests increased, British leaders feared that they were losing control of their colonies. They approved more taxes and stricter laws. Americans grew angrier. Leaders such as Thomas Jefferson and Benjamin Franklin, who admired the Enlightenment ideas of John Locke, started to think about rebelling against British rule. The colonists began to gather weapons and ammunition.

On April 19, 1775, British soldiers marched to Lexington and Concord, towns near Boston, Massachusetts. Their purpose was to take weapons and ammunition away from the Americans. The Americans, however, fought back. The American Revolution had begun.

The Colonies Become the United States In 1776, thirteen North American colonies officially declared their independence from Britain with a document called the **Declaration of Independence.** It was written by Thomas Jefferson. Echoing Locke's ideas, Jefferson stated that governments have power only because the people give it to them. If a government takes away people's rights, the people have a right to change the government or put an end to it.

With the aid of the French, the Americans won their independence in 1781. In 1789, the Constitution became the supreme law of the new nation. It was based largely on the ideas of the Enlightenment and on the traditional rights of English citizens. A written Bill of Rights protecting individual citizens became part of the Constitution.

✓ **Reading Check** What is the Constitution?

Links to
Government

The Declaration of Independence How do these famous words from the Declaration reflect the ideas of the Enlightenment?

"We hold these truths to be self-evident, that all men are created equal, that they are endowed by their Creator with certain unalienable Rights, that among these are Life, Liberty and the pursuit of Happiness. That to secure these rights, Governments are instituted among Men, deriving their just powers from the consent of the governed; That whenever any Form of Government becomes destructive of these ends it is the Right of the People to alter or to abolish it. . . ."

A committee worked with Thomas Jefferson (second from left) on the Declaration of Independence. This pen was used to sign it.

Background: Global Perspectives

Women Leaders Since the times of Elizabeth and Mary, several women have risen to lead nations. Recent female leaders include Indira Gandhi, prime minister of India (1966–1977 and 1980–1984); Golda Meir, prime minister of Israel (1969–1974); Margaret Thatcher, prime minister of Great Britain (1979–1990); Corazon Aquino, president of the Philippines (1986–1992); Benazir Bhutto, prime minister of Pakistan (1988–1990 and 1993–1996); and Megawati Sukarnoputri, who became president of Indonesia in 2001.

Links

Read the **Links to Government** on this page. Ask students to explain how these words reflect the ideas of the Enlightenment. *(They reflect Locke's ideas about natural rights and his idea that the people give the government its power. The people can replace the government if it takes away their rights.)*

The American Revolution ⑿

Guided Instruction
- **Vocabulary Builder** Clarify the high-use word **declare** before reading.

- Read The American Revolution with students. Circulate to make sure students can answer the Reading Check question.

- Ask **What led American colonists to rebel against British rule?** *(They felt that the British were taking away their rights by taxing them when they had no representation in the British Parliament.)*

- Ask students **How was Jefferson influenced by the ideas of the Enlightenment?** *(Jefferson adopted Locke's idea that the government has power only through the support of the people. He also adopted the idea that if the government takes away people's rights, the people have the right to remove it from power. Jefferson included these ideas in the Declaration of Independence.)*

Independent Practice
Have students fill in the America portion of the diagram with the information they have just learned.

Monitor Progress
Circulate and make sure students are choosing the correct details. Provide assistance as needed.

Answer
✓ **Reading Check** the document that serves as the supreme law of the United States and includes a Bill of Rights to protect individual citizens

Read the **Citizen Heroes** on this page. Ask **What did Enlightenment ideas encourage L'Ouverture to do?** (*They encouraged him to lead a rebellion against white masters and end slavery in Haiti.*)

The French Revolution L2

Guided Instruction

- Have students read The French Revolution.

- Ask **Why did Louis XVI help Americans win independence from Britain?** (*He wanted to reduce the power of the British.*)

- Have students compare the causes of both the American and French revolutions. (*Both revolutions began when people in each country felt they were being taxed unfairly by the government.*)

- Discuss the Reign of Terror with students. (*The Committee of Public Safety, led by Robespierre, killed people who were considered to be enemies of the revolution. The Reign of Terror lasted for nearly a year. Eventually, Robespierre was executed and the Reign of Terror soon ended.*)

Independent Practice

Have students compete the graphic organizer by filling in the France box.

Monitor Progress

- Show *Section Reading Support Transparency MT 74* and ask students to check their graphic organizers individually. Go over key concepts and clarify key vocabulary as needed.

  📖 **Medieval Times to Today Transparencies,** *Section Reading Support Transparency MT 74*

- Tell students to fill in the last column of their *Reading Readiness Guides*. Ask them to evaluate if what they learned was what they had expected to learn.

  All in One Medieval Times to Today, *Reading Readiness Guide,* p. 368

Answers

Analyze Images The Bastille was a large prison that held political prisoners. The citizens are probably the figures who are not wearing military uniforms. The uniformed soldiers seem to be retreating from the citizens.

Citizen Heroes ★

Toussaint L'Ouverture

When news of the French Revolution reached the French island colony of Saint-Domingue (san du MAYNG) in the Caribbean Sea, enslaved Africans there were inspired. The ideas of the Enlightenment encouraged them to rebel against their white masters. Their revolt was led by a former slave, Toussaint L'Ouverture (too SAN loo vehr TOOR). He was determined to end slavery on his island. In that, he was successful. However, he was captured by the French in 1802, and died in exile before his goal of an independent nation of Haiti was achieved in 1804.

The French Revolution

King Louis XVI of France had helped the American colonists win their independence. Yet he was no great friend of liberty. He had helped because he wanted to reduce the power of the British. The Americans appreciated the help. The French people did not. They had to pay heavy taxes to support the French army.

France Faces Severe Problems Under the French political system, only the working people paid taxes. Nobles and clergy paid hardly anything. Thus the poorest people carried the heaviest tax burden. As France's debt increased, the French government increased taxes even more. The French people grew resentful and demanded that Louis share power. They used the arguments of Enlightenment thinkers to support their demands.

Adding to France's economic problems, poor harvests in the late 1780s sent food prices soaring. Millions of people were going hungry. Riots broke out as poor people demanded bread. Finally, the king called a meeting of representatives of the three estates, or divisions, of French society—the nobles, the clergy, and the middle class. When these representatives met in 1789, they declared themselves the National Assembly.

The Revolution Begins As food shortages worsened and rumors spread that royal troops were going to occupy the capital, the people of Paris reacted. On July 14, 1789, they attacked the Bastille (bas TEEL), a prison that held political prisoners. To this day, July 14 is celebrated as Bastille Day, the French national holiday.

Rioting continued all over France. Meanwhile, the National Assembly passed laws to make the people of France equal under the law. The Assembly's Declaration of the Rights of Man echoed the American Declaration of Independence. In 1791, the National Assembly produced a constitution setting up a limited monarchy.

202 Medieval Times to Today

The Storming of the Bastille
This painting shows French citizens attacking the Bastille, the building in the left background. **Analyze Images** *Describe the Bastille. Which group is the citizens? Does it look as if they will be successful?*

Skills for Life ⬤ Skills Mini Lesson

Decision Making

1. Tell students that to make a decision they should identify a problem, list possible solutions, evaluate the options, and then choose the best one.

2. Have students practice the skill by identifying the problem that France's people faced and the option they chose to solve the problem.

3. Have students apply the skill by discussing other possible options the French people may have chosen. Ask them to evaluate each option and decide which they thought was best.

European monarchs were horrified. Fearing that the "French plague" would spread and that they would lose their own power, they sent armies to France to help the king. The National Assembly declared war on these foreign powers. When the war began to go badly for France, rioting French citizens stormed the palace and captured the king. A few months later, Louis XVI was executed.

The Reign of Terror A group called the Committee of Public Safety took power to defend France and the revolution. The Committee declared that the constitution was no longer in effect. Maximilien Robespierre (mahk see mee LYAHN ROHBZ pyehr) led the Committee in carrying out what became known as the **Reign of Terror.** For nearly a year, people who were considered enemies of the revolution were executed—perhaps as many as 70 to 80 in a day. No one was safe. As political power shifted, those who had helped to create the constitution were killed as well as those who had fought against it. Finally, Robespierre himself was executed, and the Reign of Terror soon ended.

The French Revolution lasted ten years. It was a time of chaos and tyranny as well as of reform and idealism. The English novelist Charles Dickens called it "the best of times [and] the worst of times." The Revolution would finally end when one of the most powerful leaders in history took control of France in 1799. You will read about him in Section 4.

√ Reading Check What was the Reign of Terror?

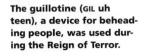

The guillotine (GIL uh teen), a device for beheading people, was used during the Reign of Terror.

Section 2 Assessment

Key Terms
Review the key terms at the beginning of this section. Use each term in a sentence that explains its meaning.

Target Reading Skill
What did the three revolutions described in this section have in common?

Comprehension and Critical Thinking
1. (a) Describe How did James I and Charles I clash with Parliament?

(b) Analyze Information How did the Glorious Revolution show that Parliament had gained more power than the monarch?

2. (a) Identify Cause and Effect What role did taxes play in the American Revolution?

(b) Synthesize Information How did the ideas of John Locke affect the American Revolution?

3. (a) Identify What were two causes of the rioting that began the French Revolution?

(b) Identify Frame of Reference Why did European rulers fear the French Revolution?

Writing Activity
Write a paragraph that answers this question: How was the French Revolution both "the best of times" and "the worst of times"?

> **Writing Tip** Begin by making two lists, one of the benefits of the French Revolution and another of the harm that it caused. You can use the quotation from Dickens as your topic sentence. Support it with details from your list.

Assess Progress [L2]
Have students complete the Section Assessment. Administer the *Section Quiz.*

All in One Medieval Times to Today Teaching Resources, *Section Quiz,* p. 370

Reteach [L1]
If students need more instruction, have them read this section in the Reading and Vocabulary Study Guide.

Chapter 7, Section 2, **Medieval Times to Today Reading and Vocabulary Study Guide,** pp. 75–77

Extend [L3]
Ask students to create a poster persuading people to help fight for citizens' rights during one of the revolutions studied in this section. Encourage students to make the poster appealing by adding catchy slogans and illustrations.

Answers

√ Reading Check the time during which Robespierre led the Committee of Public Safety in killing people who were considered enemies of the revolution

Writing Activity
Use the *Rubric for Assessing a Writing Assignment* to evaluate students' paragraphs.

All in One Medieval Times to Today Teaching Resources, *Rubric for Assessing a Writing Assignment,* p. 396

Section 2 Assessment

Key Terms
Students' sentences should reflect knowledge of each Key Term.

Target Reading Skill
All of the revolutions brought about a change in government, involved some amount of violence, began because people felt their rights were being violated, and incorporated Enlightenment ideas.

Comprehension and Critical Thinking
1. (a) They engaged in a power struggle with Parliament and refused to allow it to meet for long periods of time. **(b)** The monarch was easily defeated without bloodshed and Parliament was able to place the ruler they wanted in power.

2. (a) Americans began to think about rebelling against British rule when they felt they were being unfairly taxed by the British.

(b) Locke's ideas encouraged people like Thomas Jefferson to rebel against the British so that they would have natural rights and a government that served their interests.

3. (a) heavy taxes on the poor and a severe winter that left millions of people starving **(b)** They feared that people in their countries would rebel against their government like the French people had done.

Objectives

Social Studies

1. Learn about the Industrial Revolution and how it changed the world forever.
2. Identify some serious problems of the Industrial Age.

Reading/Language Arts

Contrast two situations to find out how they are different.

Prepare to Read

Build Background Knowledge L2

In this section, students will learn about the Industrial Revolution. Ask students to preview the headings as well as charts and other visuals in the section. Then tell them to write three questions they would like to have answered that will help them remember important information from the section. Ask students to answer the questions as they read the section.

Set a Purpose for Reading L2

- Preview the Objectives.

- Read each statement in the *Reading Readiness Guide* aloud. Ask students to mark the statements true or false.

- Have students discuss the statements in pairs or groups of four, then mark their guides again. Use the Numbered Heads participation strategy (TE, p. T36) to call on students to share their group's perspectives.

  All in One Medieval Times to Today Teaching Resources, *Reading Readiness Guide,* p. 372

Vocabulary Builder
Preview Key Terms L2

Pronounce each Key Term, then ask the students to say the word with you. Provide a simple explanation such as, "During the Industrial Revolution, goods went from being produced by hand to being produced by machines."

Prepare to Read

Objectives

In this section, you will
1. Learn about the Industrial Revolution and how it changed the world forever.
2. Identify some serious problems of the Industrial Age.

Taking Notes

As you read this section, look for the major causes and effects of the Industrial Revolution. Copy the flowchart below and record your findings in it.

CAUSES → EVENT — The Industrial Revolution → EFFECTS

Target Reading Skill

Identify Contrasts When you contrast two situations, you examine how they are different. In this section you will read about a major historical turning point. Keeping track of the various changes caused by the Industrial Revolution will help you understand its significance. As you read, list the differences between life before and during the Industrial Age.

Key Terms

- **Industrial Revolution** (in DUS tree ul rev uh LOO shun) *n.* the change in methods of producing goods—from hand tools at home to machines in factories, 1760s–1860s
- **textile industry** (TEKS tyl IN dus tree) *n.* the making of cloth
- **labor union** (LAY bur YOON yun) *n.* an organization of workers formed to bargain with employers for better pay and working conditions

British factory workers forging an anchor in the early 1800s

H ere are the sights and sounds of a revolution. Look at the painting on this page, and then read the two quotations below.

> **The thunder of the blast deafens you. The ever-brightening flame, flashing up finally as high as fifty feet, blinds you; sparks fall everywhere.**

> **. . . the rumbling growl of rollers, the howls of horrible saws . . . the crashing thunder of falling iron plate, the hoarse coughing of great engines, and the hissing of steam.**
>
> — *visitors to an American factory, around 1900*

What was it like to work in these places? Very different than work had been in previous centuries! The painter of *Forging an Anchor* and the visitors to the American factory were witnessing one of the greatest turning points in human history. This revolution in the way things were made would change the way people lived all around the world.

Target Reading Skill L2

Identify Contrasts Point out the Target Reading Skill. Tell students that contrasting two situations allows them to find out how they are different.

Model the skill by reading The Textile Industry on p. 206 and contrasting the textile industry before and after the invention of the spinning jenny. (*Before the spinning jenny, spinning was done mostly by people working on spinning wheels at home, and it took a long time to make each piece of cloth. As a result, textiles were expensive. The spinning jenny made it possible to produce cloth more quickly and more cheaply. It also moved workers into factories.*)

Give students *Identify Contrasts.* Have them complete the activity in groups.

All in One Medieval Times to Today Teaching Resources, *Identify Contrasts,* p. 381

A New Kind of Revolution

Until the middle of the 1700s, most people lived on farms or in very small towns. Agriculture was the basis of their economies. Most goods that people needed were made by hand, either at home or in small shops.

Then, in only 100 years, this way of life changed in a large part of the world. From about 1760 to about 1860, the way manufactured goods were produced shifted from simple hand tools in homes and shops to complex machines in factories. This change is called the **Industrial Revolution.**

The Industrial Revolution Begins The Industrial Revolution began in Great Britain in the 1760s. At that time, trade from its growing overseas empire was fueling the rapid growth of Britain's economy. British colonies provided both the raw materials needed to manufacture goods and the people to buy the goods once they were produced. British businesspeople became wealthy and had money to invest in new ventures, such as factories.

Factory Production
The Cyclops Steel Works in Sheffield, England, 1853.
Analyze Images Which details in the painting suggest advances in technology and production? Which details suggest possible problems of industrialization?

Vocabulary Builder

Use the information below to teach students this section's high-use words.

High-Use Word	Definition and Sample Sentence
basis, p. 205	*n.* the most important part of something Rice is the **basis** of many families' diets in West Africa.
produce, p. 205	*v.* to make or manufacture The clothing factory **produced** a variety of shirts and sweaters.

Guided Instruction

- **Vocabulary Builder** Clarify the high-use words **basis** and **produce** before reading.

- Read A New Kind of Revolution, using the Oral Cloze strategy (TE, p. T33). As students read, circulate and make sure that individuals can answer the Reading Check question.

- Ask **When did the Industrial Revolution take place?** *(from about 1760 to 1860)* **How did the production of goods change during the Industrial Revolution?** *(Goods were produced by machines in large factories rather than by hand in people's homes and small shops.)*

- Discuss the reasons why the Industrial Revolution began in Britain. *(The British colonies helped Britain's economy grow by providing the raw materials needed to manufacture goods and the people to buy these goods. British business people used their wealth to invest in factories.)*

Answer

Analyze Images The factories and smokestacks suggest advances in technology and production. The smoke stacks also suggest potential problems from these advances, such as air pollution.

Guided Instruction (continued)

- Discuss how the spinning jenny revolutionized the textile industry. (*The spinning jenny allowed one worker to do the work of eight people using spinning wheels. This allowed cloth to be created more quickly and cheaply.*)

- Ask **How were textile machines powered?** (*They were initially powered by flowing water and later powered by steam engines.*)

- Ask students to make a prediction about how the changes in the textile industry might have affected workers. (*Because workers had to begin working in factories rather than in their homes, they probably had less time to spend with their families. Working in factories was probably more dangerous and unhealthy than working at home.*)

- Discuss how the Industrial Revolution improved many people's lives. (*The amount and variety of goods available to people increased. People were able to buy these new goods with the money they made from working in higher-level factory jobs or from selling manufactured goods. Cities grew as more jobs were made available there.*)

Independent Practice

Ask students to create the Taking Notes graphic organizer on a blank piece of paper. Then have them fill in the causes and effects of the Industrial Revolution, about which they have just learned. Briefly model how to identify which details to record.

Monitor Progress

As students fill in the graphic organizer, circulate and make sure individuals are choosing the correct details. Help students as needed.

Inventions Change the World

James Watt is called the Father of the Industrial Revolution because of his improvements to the steam engine in the 1760s.

Samuel F. B. Morse invented the telegraph in the 1830s.

In 1876, Alexander Graham Bell patented the telephone. ▶

Thomas Edison invented many useful devices, including the phonograph in 1877 and the first practical electric light bulb in 1879.

▼ Robert Fulton built the first practical steamboat in 1807 and revolutionized water transportation.

The Textile Industry In the 1760s, the leading industry in Britain was the **textile industry,** or the making of cloth. Spinning and weaving were done mostly by people working in their homes. It took a long time to make each piece of cloth, so textiles were expensive. Only the wealthy had more than one change of clothes.

Several inventions of the 1760s made it possible to produce more cloth more quickly and more cheaply. For example, the spinning jenny allowed one worker to do the work of eight people using spinning wheels. On the other hand, the new textile machines were so big and so fast that they needed more power than one person could supply.

Inventors came up with ways of using flowing water to supply power to these huge machines. They dammed rivers and built mills that used water wheels. Later, steam engines were used to supply power. Britain's large deposits of coal powered these engines. The new textile machines had to be housed in large buildings called factories. Now, in order to work, people had to leave their homes and families and go to the factories. The Industrial Revolution was underway.

The Industrial Revolution Grows Soon other industrial inventions took advantage of the new power supply. Mighty steam-driven hammers forged iron parts for the newly invented farm machines, railroad cars, and engines. Trains powered by steam locomotives, traveling on steel rails, moved people and goods more quickly, cheaply, and reliably. Even agriculture became more like industry, as farmers used new, steam-driven machines to plant, harvest, and process crops.

Effects of the Industrial Revolution The Industrial Revolution spread to other nations in Europe and to the United States, and it affected more than production. It changed people's lives and the structure of society. One change was a huge increase in the amount and variety of goods available to ordinary people. Cities grew as people left their farms and settled near the new factories. Instead of providing for themselves on farms, people bought the things they needed with the money they earned working in factories.

Differentiated Instruction

For Advanced Readers 〔L3〕
Have students complete the *Enrichment* activity individually to learn more about inventions that changed the world.

All in One **Medieval Times to Today Teaching Resources,** *Enrichment,* p. 383

For Special Needs Students 〔L1〕
Have students read the passage in the *Enrichment* activity using the Paragraph Shrinking strategy (TE, p. T34). Then have them work with partners to complete the activity.

All in One **Medieval Times to Today Teaching Resources,** *Enrichment,* p. 383

Assembly Line

The modern age owes much to the work of Henry Ford. He did not invent the automobile. That was done in Germany in 1885. He did not invent the idea of interchangeable parts for making identical products. Nor did he invent the assembly line. But he combined all of these ideas into a process for making affordable cars in huge numbers. This process changed the lives of millions of people throughout the world.

Making Cars
Like the men in this Ford automobile plant, each assembly-line worker has a single task to complete, over and over again. The product moves slowly along a track or conveyor belt.

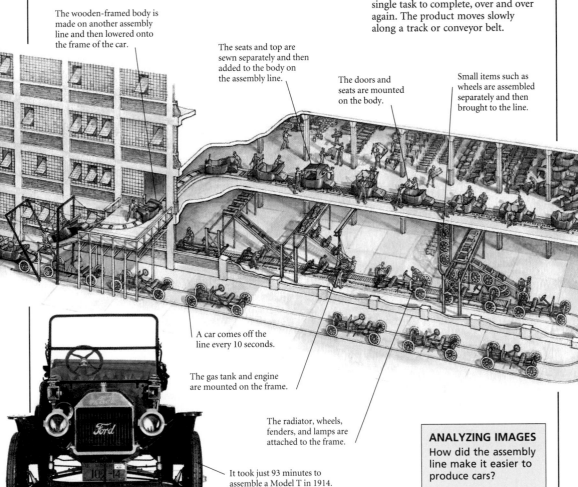

The wooden-framed body is made on another assembly line and then lowered onto the frame of the car.

The seats and top are sewn separately and then added to the body on the assembly line.

The doors and seats are mounted on the body.

Small items such as wheels are assembled separately and then brought to the line.

A car comes off the line every 10 seconds.

The gas tank and engine are mounted on the frame.

The radiator, wheels, fenders, and lamps are attached to the frame.

It took just 93 minutes to assemble a Model T in 1914.

ANALYZING IMAGES
How did the assembly line make it easier to produce cars?

Chapter 7 Section 3 **207**

Assembly Line   L2

Guided Instruction
Read the introductory paragraph aloud as a class and study the diagram and other images. Then have student volunteers take turns reading each caption aloud. Tell students to answer the Analyzing Images question individually.

Independent Practice
Have students do library or Internet research to see how cars are manufactured today. Have them compare and contrast this process with the one Ford developed in the late 1800s. Encourage them to create a graphic organizer, such as a Venn diagram or table, to show the similarities and differences.

Answer
ANALYZING IMAGES Each part of the car was added on as the car made its way down the assembly line. This allowed the car to be created in a faster, more efficient fashion.

Chapter 7 **207**

Problems of the Industrial Age

L2

Guided Instruction

- Read Problems of the Industrial Age as a class.

- Discuss the ways in which the Industrial Revolution made some people's lives harder. (*Factory workers spent long days in noisy and dirty factories; the work was often repetitive and dangerous; they received poor pay; workers who lived in industrial towns had to live in poor housing and an unhealthy environment.*)

- Discuss the purpose of labor unions. (*They helped workers bargain with employers to improve their pay and working conditions.*)

Independent Practice

Have students complete their cause-and-effect charts with the information they have just learned.

Monitor Progress

- Show *Section Reading Support Transparency MT 75* and ask students to check their graphic organizers individually.

  📖 **Medieval Times to Today Transparencies,** *Section Reading Support Transparency MT 75*

- Tell students to fill in the last column of their *Reading Readiness Guides*.

  All in One Medieval Times to Today Teaching Resources, *Reading Readiness Guide,* p. 372

L2

⊙ Target Reading Skill

Identify Contrasts As a follow up, ask students to answer the Target Reading Skill question in the Student Edition. (*People who worked in factories had less time to spend with their families; factory work could be more dangerous.*)

Answers

Graph Skills Identify close to 0 percent; about 40 percent; after 1860 **Conclude** in the late 1800s when the population began to grow rapidly

✔ **Reading Check** Goods were produced faster and more cheaply by machine; people had more money to purchase these goods; people moved from working in their homes to working in factories.

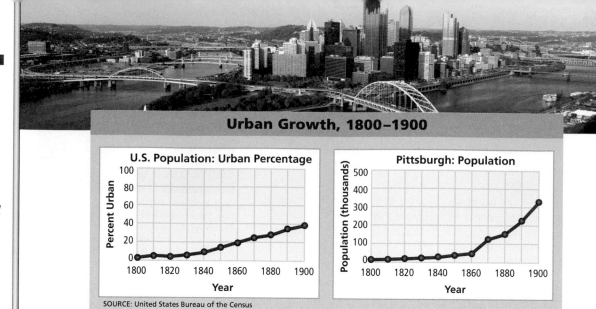

Urban Growth, 1800–1900

U.S. Population: Urban Percentage

Percent Urban (vertical axis): 0, 20, 40, 60, 80, 100
Year (horizontal axis): 1800, 1820, 1840, 1860, 1880, 1900

Pittsburgh: Population

Population (thousands) (vertical axis): 100, 200, 300, 400, 500
Year (horizontal axis): 1800, 1820, 1840, 1860, 1880, 1900

SOURCE: United States Bureau of the Census

■ Graph Skills

The Industrial Revolution caused people to move from farms to cities. Pittsburgh (above) became an important center of steel production. **Identify** What percentage of the United States was urban in 1800? In 1900? When did Pittsburgh's population begin to grow rapidly? **Conclude** When did steel production become important in Pittsburgh?

Identify Contrasts How was factory work different from working at home or in local shops?

208 Medieval Times to Today

The Industrial Revolution also changed society. It created jobs not only for factory workers but also for managers who ran the factories and for merchants who sold the many new goods. These new jobs presented opportunities for more people to move into the middle class. The middle class had the money to purchase many new products that could make people's lives easier.

✔ **Reading Check** What changes did the Industrial Revolution bring?

Problems of the Industrial Age

The Industrial Revolution gave more people than ever before the ability to have comfortable lives. But for many of those who worked in the new factories, life actually became harder.

Work in a Factory People who had produced goods in their homes or in local shops had been able to spend time with their families. Industrial workers, on the other hand, often spent 12 to 14 hours a day, every day, away from home at work in a factory.

Factories were noisy and dirty. The work was mind-numbing: A typical factory worker did the same simple action, over and over, hundreds of times a day. The work could also be dangerous. The large, powerful machines sometimes injured or even killed workers. And factory workers were paid very poorly. Often parents had to put their children to work in a factory just so the family could earn enough money to live.

Differentiated Instruction

For Less Proficient Readers L1
If students are having a difficult time interpreting the line graphs on this page, have them work with a partner to complete

Reading a Line Graph. Circulate to provide assistance as needed.

All in One Medieval Times to Today Teaching Resources, *Reading a Line Graph,* p. 390

Life in Industrial Towns By 1800, in many industrial areas, home offered little relief from the dirt and danger of the factory. Workers lived in small, cramped quarters. Soot from factory smokestacks and trains covered everything, even indoors. Often many families shared a single bathroom or had no indoor plumbing at all.

Garbage piling up in the streets attracted rats and packs of dogs. Dyes and dust from textile mills poisoned the air and water. Diseases swept easily through such cities. Many people died of cholera and typhus. Even minor diseases could be fatal under such conditions.

Workers Fight Back In response to the problems of industrialization, some workers formed **labor unions**. These were organizations that helped workers bargain with employers to improve their pay and working conditions. Factory owners fought against unionization, sometimes with violence. And at first, governments passed laws to keep the unions from becoming powerful. By the late 1800s, however, labor unions were well established. They won shorter hours, better pay, and safer working conditions for their members and for other workers. Eventually, unions became important political forces in many countries.

✓ **Reading Check** What did labor unions fight for?

The Rise of Unions
This illustration is from an 1880s British union membership card. **Conclude** *What types of workers belong to this union, and what issues are important to them?*

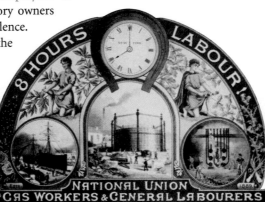

Section 3 Assessment

Key Terms
Review the key terms at the beginning of this section. Use each term in a sentence that explains its meaning.

🎯 **Target Reading Skill**
How was life before the Industrial Revolution different from life in the Industrial Age?

Comprehension and Critical Thinking
1. (a) **Recall** Where and when did the Industrial Revolution begin?

(b) **Identify Causes** Why did it begin in that time and place?
(c) **Synthesize Information** How did the Industrial Revolution change society?
2. (a) **Describe** What was life like for factory workers and their families in the 1700s?
(b) **Identify Cause and Effect** How did these conditions lead to the growth of labor unions?
(c) **Draw Conclusions** Do you think the Industrial Revolution helped or hurt society during the 1800s? Explain your answer.

Writing Activity
Suppose you are a worker in a textile factory in the late 1700s. Write a journal entry describing your workday. You may wish to compare it with your workday when you made cloth at home.

For: An activity on the Industrial Revolution
Visit: PHSchool.com
Web Code: lgd-8703

Assess Progress [L2]
Have students complete the Section Assessment. Administer the *Section Quiz*.

🔲 **Medieval Times to Today Teaching Resources,** *Section Quiz*, p. 374

Reteach [L1]
If students need more instruction, have them read this section in the Reading and Vocabulary Study Guide.

📖 Chapter 7, Section 3, **Medieval Times to Today Reading and Vocabulary Study Guide,** pp. 78–80

Extend [L3]
Have students complete the *Small Group Activity* to learn more about the Industrial Revolution.

🔲 **Medieval Times to Today Teaching Resources,** *Small Group Activity: Creating a Bulletin Board Display About the Industrial Revolution,* pp. 385–388

Answers

Conclude Gas workers belong to this union, and the issue of working long hours is important to them.

✓ **Reading Check** improved pay, shorter hours, and better working conditions

Writing Activity
Use the *Rubric for Assessing a Journal Entry* to evaluate students' journal entries.

🔲 **Medieval Times to Today Teaching Resources,** *Rubric for Assessing a Journal Entry*, p. 397

Go Online PHSchool.com Typing in the Web code when prompted will bring students directly to detailed instructions for this activity.

Section 3 Assessment

Key Terms
Students' sentences should reflect knowledge of each Key Term.

🎯 **Target Reading Skill**
Before the Industrial Revolution, most people lived on farms. Those who manufactured goods did so in their homes or in small shops. After the revolution, more people moved to industrial towns and worked in factories. There were a larger amount and wider variety of goods available to people.

Comprehension and Critical Thinking
1. (a) in Britain; about 1760 (b) At that time, Britain had been gaining wealth from its colonies and business people had the money to invest in factories. (c) It created jobs for factory workers, managers, and merchants. These new jobs allowed more people to move into the middle class.

2. (a) Factory workers worked long days in poor conditions; they performed mind-numbing work and received low pay; families that lived in industrial towns had to deal with cramped quarters, dirty streets, poisonous fumes from factories, and rapidly spreading diseases. (b) Workers formed labor unions to improve their hours, working conditions, and pay. (c) Possible answer: It helped by creating more opportunities.

Focus On
The Mill Girls

L2

Guided Instruction

- Ask students to read the text and study the art, photos, and captions on these pages.

- Have students describe the schedule of the mill workers. *(A factory bell woke them up in the morning, sent them to and from their meals during the day, and told them when to return home at night; mill girls ate and slept at company-owned boarding houses, were required to attend church and observe a 10 P.M. curfew; during their free time they could attend lectures, shop, or read books.)*

- Ask students **Why do you think many native-born women stopped working at the mills?** *(Possible answers: Declining working conditions, lower wages, and having to work faster probably contributed to native-born women wanting to stay at home or find better opportunities.)* **What happened to the mill workforce as these women left?** *(The jobs were filled by new immigrants, including men and children.)*

- As a class, answer the Assessment questions. Allow students to briefly discuss their responses with a partner before sharing their answers with the class.

Focus On
The Mill Girls

In the mid-1800s, they left their family farms—many of them for the first time—to work in textile factories throughout New England. There they worked from dawn until past dark. These young women were known as the mill girls. Although the work was difficult, most mill girls gladly chose factory life over farm life. One mill girl wrote to her sister, "[A]nother pay day has come around. . . . I like [the work] as well as ever and Sarah don't I feel independent of everyone! The thought that I am living on no one is a happy one indeed to me."

Working in a Textile Factory In the mid-1800s, Lowell, Massachusetts, was an important leader in the textile industry. Child labor was used at textile mills during this time, but most laborers at Lowell and similar mill towns were single young women from rural areas. These women, about 15 to 25 years old, usually worked in the mills for about four years.

Workers' lives were strictly regulated. Factory bells woke them up in the morning, sent them to and from meals during the day, and rang them home again at night. The mill girls ate and slept at company-owned boarding-houses and agreed to strict rules, including regular church attendance and a 10 P.M. curfew. During their precious free time they might attend lectures, shop, or read books.

As the textile industry grew, working conditions declined. Factory owners cut wages and made employees work faster. By the 1860s, fewer and fewer native-born women worked at the mills. Instead, they stayed at home or searched for better opportunities.

210 Medieval Times to Today

Differentiated Instruction

For Gifted and Talented **L3**

Have students do research in the library or on the Internet to learn more about Francis Cabot Lowell, founder of the world's first textile mill in Massachusetts. Then have them write a short biographical sketch of Lowell that includes information about his life and accomplishments.

For English Language Learners **L1**

Help students practice their verbal English skills by having them describe aloud to a partner the activities that the women in the art and photograph are performing. Encourage students to make use of the vocabulary on the page, and use words such as *machine*, *loom*, and *weaving* in their descriptions.

Spinning Room ▶
The French Canadian girl at the right worked in the spinning room of a Massachusetts mill, where thread was spun onto bobbins. As fewer native-born women sought work in the mills, the jobs were filled by new immigrants, and increasingly, by immigrant children and men.

Weaving Room
This room was hot, humid, and filled with cotton dust and fumes from oil lamps. The noise made by the looms was deafening.

Power Looms
These machines wove thread into fabric. Loom operators earned more money than the mill girls in most other jobs.

Assessment

Identify Who were the mill girls?

Predict How do you think a farm girl's life changed when she began to work in a textile factory?

Independent Practice
Have students reread the excerpt from a mill girl's letter on p. 210. Then ask them to suppose that they are workers in a mill in the mid-1800s, and have them write a letter to their family or friends back home. Tell students to include details in their letters, such as their daily activities, and how they feel about working in the mill.

Answers

Assessment

Identify young women who left their family farms to work in textile factories in New England

Predict Possible answer: While she may have become and felt more independent, it was probably difficult for a farm girl to leave her family and begin working at a difficult job far from home.

Section 4
Step-by-Step Instruction

Objectives

Social Studies

1. Learn how Napoleon rose to power in France and conquered much of Europe.

2. Understand the growth of nationalism in Europe.

3. Find out how imperialist European nations gained control over much of the world.

Reading/Language Arts

Compare and contrast to find the similarities and differences between two events or ideas.

Prepare to Read

Build Background Knowledge L2

In this section, students will learn about the colonization of Africa and Asia by European nations. Display *Color Transparency MT 15: Africa: Colonial Rule and Independence*. Use the Give One, Get One participation strategy (TE, p. T37) to lead a discussion on how Britain and France might have benefited their colonies in Africa.

📖 **Medieval Times to Today Transparencies,** *Color Transparency MT 12: Africa: Colonial Rule and Independence*

Set a Purpose for Reading L2

■ Preview the Objectives.

■ Read each statement in the *Reading Readiness Guide* aloud. Ask students to mark the statements true or false.

■ Have students discuss the statements in pairs or groups of four, then mark their guides again. Use the Numbered Heads participation strategy (TE, p. T36) to call on students to share their group's perspectives.

All in One Medieval Times to Today Teaching Resources, *Reading Readiness Guide,* p. 376

Vocabulary Builder
Preview Key Terms L2

Pronounce each Key Term, then ask the students to say the word with you. Provide a simple explanation such as, "When Britain colonized parts of Asia and Africa, it was practicing imperialism."

Section 4 — Nationalism and Imperialism

Prepare to Read

Objectives

In this section, you will

1. Learn how Napoleon rose to power in France and conquered much of Europe.
2. Understand the growth of nationalism in Europe.
3. Find out how imperialist European nations gained control over much of the world.

Taking Notes

As you read this section, look for the most important points about European imperialism. Copy the concept web below and record your findings in it.

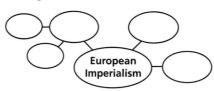

European Imperialism

🎯 Target Reading Skill

Compare and Contrast One way to understand different historical eras is to compare and contrast them, or to identify their similarities and differences. When you compare, you look at the similarities between things. When you contrast, you look at the differences. As you read this section, compare and contrast the Age of Napoleon with the era of European imperialism.

Key Terms

• **Napoleonic Code** (nuh poh lee AHN ik kohd) *n.* the French legal system based on Enlightenment ideas, set up during Napoleon's rule

• **nationalism** (NASH uh nul iz um) *n.* a feeling of pride in one's country and a desire for its independence

• **imperialism** (im PIHR ee ul iz um) *n.* the effort of a nation to create an empire of colonies

---

This 1885 cartoon shows European nations grabbing as much of the world as they can.

It was November 1884. The weather in Berlin was cold and gray. A group of men from Britain, Belgium, France, Germany, Portugal, Spain, and other countries had assembled for a conference. They were not thinking about the gloom of Europe in autumn. They were thinking about Africa. For months, they negotiated, drawing lines on maps of Africa. Finally, they reached an agreement: They had divided up Africa—an entire continent—among themselves.

No one from Africa participated in this conference. Those who did attend were not interested in the African people. The Europeans were interested only in the continent's resources. Their purpose was to avoid conflict with one another about whose nation would control these riches.

How could a few European countries simply take over a huge continent filled with many different cultures and millions of people? To find out, you will have to understand how nationalism and imperialism developed in the 1800s.

🎯 Target Reading Skill L2

Compare and Contrast Point out the Target Reading Skill. Explain that comparing and contrasting can help students identify the similarities and differences between two things.

Model the skill by reading Napoleon's Accomplishments on p. 214 and comparing and contrasting the Napoleonic Code with the United States Constitution. (*Both contained laws and Enlightenment principles, such*

as the equality of citizens before the law. Both provided a basis for a system of laws. Unlike the Code—which was a system of laws—the Constitution was a plan for government.)

Give students *Compare and Contrast*. Have them complete the activity in groups.

All in One Medieval Times to Today Teaching Resources, *Compare and Contrast,* p. 379

MAP MASTER™ Skills Activity

KEY

	French territory
	State under French influence
	French ally, 1812
	Independent European state
✸	Battle site, 1800–1815
→	Route of Napoleon's invasion of Russia
—	Border
•	City

0 miles 500
0 kilometers 500
Lambert Azimuthal Equal Area

Movement By 1812, Napoleon controlled much of Europe, but he wanted to rule Russia as well. **Identify** Where were Napoleon's armies turned back? **Compare** How were Napoleon's ambitions, as shown above, similar to the ambitions of the characters in the cartoon on page 212?

Go Online
PHSchool.com Use Web Code lgd-8724 for step-by-step map skills practice.

Napoleon

The Age of Napoleon

You have read how other European nations invaded France during the French Revolution. At that time, one of the most capable officers in the French army was the young Napoleon Bonaparte. He won victory after victory against the foreign armies, rising quickly from captain to general. Then, in 1799, he took control of the French government. The beginning of Napoleon's rule marked the end of the French Revolution in France but the beginning of its influence on government and culture across Europe.

Chapter 7 Section 4 **213**

Vocabulary Builder

Use the information below to teach students this section's high-use words.

High-Use Word	Definition and Sample Sentence
defend, p. 214	v. to support in the face of opposition José **defended** his decision to join the basketball team despite being the shortest player.
permit, p. 214	v. to allow The teacher **permitted** the children to take a longer recess.
domination, p. 214	n. exercise of power over another Enlightenment ideas weakened the Church's **domination** of people's beliefs.
alliance, p. 214	n. the state of being joined to achieve a common goal Students and teachers formed an **alliance** to help feed the poor.

Instruct

The Age of Napoleon L2

Guided Instruction

■ **Vocabulary Builder** Clarify the high-use words **defend, permit, domination,** and **alliance** before reading.

■ Read The Age of Napoleon, using the Structured Silent Reading strategy (TE, p. T34) and review the map on this page with students.

■ Ask **What marked the end of the French Revolution?** *(the beginning of Napoleon's rule of France)*

■ Discuss the changes Napoleon made to France. *(He created a new system of laws, the Napoleonic Code, that embodied Enlightenment principles. He permitted the Catholic Church to operate freely again and allowed people to practice the religion of their choice. He also expanded French territory by conquering much of Europe.)*

■ Ask **Why do you think European nations formed an alliance to defeat Napoleon?** *(Possible answer: Napoleon controlled so much territory and had such a powerful army that one nation alone could not defeat him.)*

Independent Practice

Assign *Guided Reading and Review.*

⬥ All in One **Medieval Times to Today Teaching Resources,** *Guided Reading and Review*, p. 377

Monitor Progress

As students complete the worksheet, circulate and answer any questions they may have.

Answers

MAP MASTER Skills Activity **Identify** Moscow
Compare Like the people in the cartoon, Napoleon wanted to conquer as many nations as he could.

Go Online
PHSchool.com Students may practice their map skills using the interactive online version of this map.

Nationalism

Guided Instruction

- Read Nationalism as a class. As students read, circulate and make sure individuals can answer the Reading Check question.

- Ask students to define nationalism. *(pride in one's nation and a desire for independence)*

- Ask **How did nationalism help Napoleon?** *(It motivated his armies to win battles and lands for France.)* **How did it later hurt Napoleon?** *(Nationalism inspired the people of the lands he conquered to rebel against him and reclaim their lands.)*

Independent Practice

Have students use their textbooks and other sources to determine when France, England, Spain, Germany, and Italy became nations. Ask them to display the information in a table.

Monitor Progress

Circulate and make sure students are finding the dates and labeling their tables properly.

⟳ Target Reading Skill

Compare and Contrast As a follow up, ask students to answer the Target Reading Skill question in the Student Edition. *(differences; answers will vary but students should be able to clearly express the ideas of the first two sentences)*

Answers

Infer The setting suggests that the French people hold Napoleon in high regard.

✓ **Reading Check** They were forced to retreat because his armies were starving and freezing.

✓ **Reading Check** Germany and Italy

An Emperor's Resting Place
Although he died in exile, Napoleon's remains were brought back to France. His tomb is shown above. To the right is the crown Napoleon wore at his coronation. **Infer** *What does the setting of his tomb suggest about how the French people regard Napoleon?*

⟳ **Compare and Contrast** Notice the word *however* in the last paragraph. Does it signal similarities or differences? State the meaning of the first two sentences in your own words—without using *however*.

Napoleon's Accomplishments Claiming he was defending the ideals of the revolution, Napoleon brought many reforms to France. Perhaps the most important one was reforming French law. The new system of laws, called the **Napoleonic Code,** embodied such Enlightenment principles as equality of all citizens before the law. The Napoleonic Code had far-reaching effects. It became the basis for the legal systems of many European countries that came under French control in the 1800s.

Napoleon made another important change. He permitted the Catholic Church to operate freely again, but he also allowed freedom of worship to followers of other religions.

The Rise and Fall of Napoleon's Empire In 1804, Napoleon convinced the French parliament to name him emperor. He then set out to make Europe a French empire. As you can see on the map on page 213, he almost succeeded. In 1805, however, when Napoleon tried to invade Britain, the French fleet was destroyed at the Battle of Trafalgar. Soon, other nations began to rebel against French domination.

When Russia withdrew from its alliance with France, Napoleon invaded Russia and marched to Moscow. But his freezing, starving armies were forced into a disastrous retreat in 1812. That was the beginning of the end of his power. An alliance of European nations finally defeated Napoleon at Waterloo, Belgium, in 1815.

✓ **Reading Check** What happened to Napoleon's armies in Russia?

Nationalism

Napoleon's armies carried the ideas and the spirit of the French Revolution with them. One of these ideas was **nationalism,** which includes pride in one's own nation and a desire for independence. Pride in France spurred Napoleon's armies to win battles for their nation. However, this spirit of nationalism also led many countries that Napoleon conquered to rebel against French rule.

France, England, and Spain were already nations by the time Napoleon came to power. Much of the rest of Europe, however, was divided into small kingdoms. During the 1800s, many of these kingdoms were unified into nations. Both Germany and Italy became nations in the 1870s.

✓ **Reading Check** Which two nations were formed in the 1870s?

(Skills for Life) Skills Mini Lesson

Synthesizing Information

1. Tell students that they can synthesize two pieces of information by finding similarities and differences between them and drawing a conclusion based on what they have found.

2. Have students practice the skill by finding the similarities and differences between the map on p. 213 and the political map of Europe on p. 256 in the Atlas.

3. Have students apply the skill by drawing a conclusion about how Europe has changed since Napoleon controlled much of the continent in the early 1800s.

Imperialism in Africa and Asia

By the 1800s, some European countries had already claimed land in distant parts of the world. For example, the Spanish, French, English, and Portuguese had established colonies in the Americas. Now, confident of their economic and political strength, they wanted to expand their power even more.

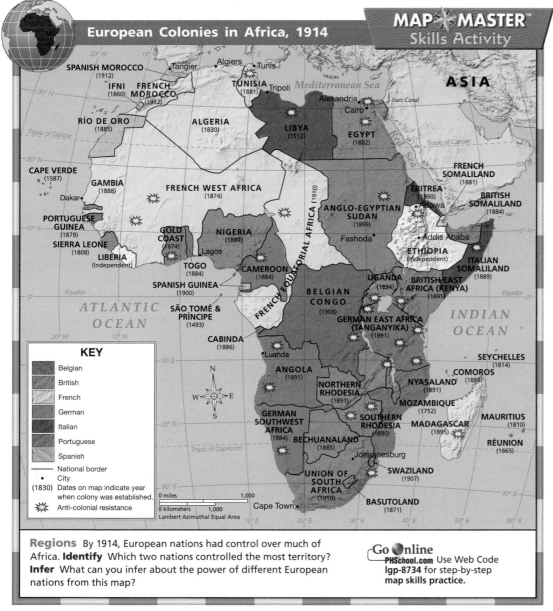

MAP MASTER™
Skills Activity

European Colonies in Africa, 1914

SPANISH MOROCCO (1912)
Tangier · Algiers · Tunis
IFNI (1860)
FRENCH MOROCCO (1912)
TUNISIA (1881) · Tripoli
Mediterranean Sea
ASIA
RÍO DE ORO (1885)
Alexandria
Suez Canal
Cairo
ALGERIA (1830)
LIBYA (1912)
EGYPT (1882)
Red Sea
Tropic of Cancer
CAPE VERDE (1587)
GAMBIA (1888)
FRENCH WEST AFRICA (1874)
FRENCH SOMALILAND (1881)
Dakar
ERITREA (1890)
Adowa
BRITISH SOMALILAND (1884)
PORTUGUESE GUINEA (1879)
ANGLO-EGYPTIAN SUDAN (1899)
SIERRA LEONE (1808)
GOLD COAST (1874)
NIGERIA (1884)
Fashoda
Addis Ababa
LIBERIA (Independent)
Lagos
ETHIOPIA (Independent)
ITALIAN SOMALILAND (1889)
TOGO (1884)
CAMEROON (1884)
UGANDA (1894)
BRITISH EAST AFRICA (KENYA) (1895)
SPANISH GUINEA (1900)
Equator
BELGIAN CONGO (1908)
Equator
ATLANTIC OCEAN
SÃO TOMÉ & PRÍNCIPE (1493)
GERMAN EAST AFRICA (TANGANYIKA) (1891)
INDIAN OCEAN
CABINDA (1886)
Luanda
SEYCHELLES (1814)
ANGOLA (1891)
COMOROS (1886)
NYASALAND (1891)
NORTHERN RHODESIA (1891)
MOZAMBIQUE (1752)
MAURITIUS (1810)
GERMAN SOUTHWEST AFRICA (1884)
SOUTHERN RHODESIA (1890)
MADAGASCAR (1895)
RÉUNION (1665)
BECHUANALAND (1885)
Tropic of Capricorn
Johannesburg
SWAZILAND (1907)
UNION OF SOUTH AFRICA (1910)
BASUTOLAND (1871)
Cape Town

KEY
- Belgian
- British
- French
- German
- Italian
- Portuguese
- Spanish
- — National border
- • City
- (1830) Dates on map indicate year when colony was established.
- ✳ Anti-colonial resistance

0 miles 1,000
0 kilometers 1,000
Lambert Azimuthal Equal Area

Regions By 1914, European nations had control over much of Africa. **Identify** Which two nations controlled the most territory? **Infer** What can you infer about the power of different European nations from this map?

Go Online
PHSchool.com Use Web Code lgp-8734 for step-by-step map skills practice.

Chapter 7 Section 4 **215**

Imperialism in Africa and Asia L2

Guided Instruction

- Read about the European colonization of Asia and Africa in Imperialism in Africa and Asia.

- Discuss the reasons why European nations wanted to expand their overseas territories. (*Their factories needed more raw materials. They needed new markets for their goods.*)

- Draw students' attention to the map. Ask them to name the European countries that had colonies in Africa in 1914. (*Belgium, Britain, France, Germany, Italy, Portugal, and Spain*)

- Discuss the effects that European colonization might have had on the people of Africa and Asia. (*Possible answers: They may have been introduced to some European ways of life; they were not able to participate in government.*)

Independent Practice

Have students create the Taking Notes graphic organizer on a separate piece of paper. Have them fill in information about imperialism.

Monitor Progress

- Show *Section Reading Support Transparency MT 76* and ask students to check their graphic organizers individually.

  📖 **Medieval Times to Today Transparencies,** *Section Reading Support Transparency MT 76*

- Tell students to fill in the last column of their *Reading Readiness Guides.*

  All in One **Medieval Times to Today Teaching Resources,** *Reading Readiness Guide,* p. 376

Answers

MAP MASTER *Skills Activity* **Identify** France and Britain **Infer** The countries that control more African territories, such as Britain and France, were more powerful than countries that controlled fewer colonies.

Go Online
PHSchool.com Students may practice their map skills using the interactive online version of this map.

Assess and Reteach

Assess Progress L2

Have students complete the Section Assessment. Administer the *Section Quiz*.

 Medieval Times to Today Teaching Resources, *Section Quiz*, p. 378

Reteach L1

If students need more instruction, have them read this section in the Reading and Vocabulary Study Guide.

📖 Chapter 7, Section 4, **Medieval Times to Today Reading and Vocabulary Study Guide,** pp. 81–83

Extend L3

Have students read *A Letter from Napoleon's Army* to learn more about the conditions the French soldiers had to deal with as they tried to invade Russia.

 Medieval Times to Today Teaching Resources, *A Letter from Napoleon's Army*, pp. 392–393

Answers

Analyze Images The names of some of the countries that Britain controlled are on the flag.

✔ **Reading Check** France, Russia, Germany, Britain, and Japan

Section 4 Assessment

Key Terms

Students' sentences should reflect knowledge of each Key Term.

🎯 **Target Reading Skill**

Similarities—Both Napoleon and European nations wanted to expand their territories; both were inspired by nationalism; Difference—European nations colonized lands outside of Europe while Napoleon conquered European lands.

Comprehension and Critical Thinking

1. (a) After winning many battles against foreign armies and becoming a general, he took over the French government. **(b)** The legal systems of France and other European countries are based on the Napoleonic Code.

British Imperialism
By 1900, Great Britain controlled about one quarter of the land and people in the world. This flag shows Britain's Queen Victoria. **Analyze Images** How does the flag represent British imperialism?

Effects of Industrialization and Nationalism European factories needed more of the raw materials—cotton, metals, coal, and rubber—that were plentiful in other lands. These factories also needed people to buy their goods. To gain both raw materials and new markets, European countries established colonies in less-industrialized regions of Africa and Asia. Colonies also helped European nations to protect their trade routes. This effort to create an empire of colonies is called **imperialism.**

Nationalism also contributed to imperialism. Controlling vast territory fueled national pride. And pride led to rivalry. Each country wanted more power and greater wealth than its neighbors.

Imperialism Reshapes the World Europeans had a long history of trade with Africa and Asia. In the 1800s, however, European nations colonized nearly all of Africa, as shown on the map on page 215. They also gained control of large areas of Asia. In the 1850s, the British began their rule of India. France, Russia, Germany, Britain, and the Asian nation of Japan divided up large areas of China in the 1890s. The United States, too, became an imperialist power. It claimed Puerto Rico in the Caribbean and the Philippines in the Pacific.

By 1900, the richest and most powerful countries were the imperial powers of Europe. It seemed as though Europe was destined to rule much of the world for a very long time.

✔ **Reading Check** Which nations divided up parts of China?

Section 4 Assessment

Key Terms
Review the key terms at the beginning of this section. Use each term in a sentence that explains its meaning.

🎯 **Target Reading Skill**
Compare and contrast Napoleon's empire-building with later European imperialism.

Comprehension and Critical Thinking
1. (a) Describe How did Napoleon come to power?
(b) Identify Effects What lasting effects did Napoleon have on France and on the rest of Europe?
2. (a) Identify Name the imperialist European powers, and locate their colonies.
(b) Identify Cause and Effect How did industrialization lead to imperialism?

Writing Activity
Write a paragraph answering this question: Was Napoleon a positive or a negative influence on Europe?

For: An activity on the British Empire
Visit: PHSchool.com
Web Code: lgd-8704

Napoleon also helped spread nationalism throughout France and other countries.

2. (a) France, Spain, Italy, Britain, Belgium, Portugal, and Germany had colonies in Africa. Spain, France, Britain, and Portugal had colonies in the Americas. France, Britain, Russia, and Germany had colonies in Asia. **(b)** European nations needed more raw materials to manufacture goods and needed new markets for their goods.

Writing Activity

Use the *Rubric for Assessing a Writing Assignment* to evaluate students' paragraphs.

 Medieval Times to Today Teaching Resources, *Rubric for Assessing a Writing Assignment,* p. 396

Review and Assessment

◆ Chapter Summary

Section 1: The Enlightenment

Galileo

- During the Enlightenment, or Age of Reason, people began to rely on reason and observation rather than on faith and tradition.
- John Locke and other Enlightenment thinkers said that people had natural rights and that governments should protect those rights.
- The French philosophes Rousseau, Voltaire, and Diderot attacked the abuses of their age and favored freedom of speech and limited government.

Section 2: Political Revolutions

- During the 1600s, the English Civil War resulted in the overthrow and execution of the king. Later, a limited constitutional monarchy was established in Britain.
- Britain's American colonies based their successful revolution and new government on Enlightenment ideas.
- The French Revolution, a period of great turmoil and terror, overthrew the monarchy and established the Rights of Man.

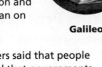

The guillotine

Section 3: The Industrial Revolution

- The Industrial Revolution was the dramatic change from making goods by hand in homes and small shops to producing goods by machine in factories.
- The Industrial Revolution led to poor pay and bad working conditions for factory workers. Labor unions were formed to improve these conditions.

Robert Fulton's steamboat _Clermont_

Section 4: Nationalism and Imperialism

- Napoleon became the leader of France in the early 1800s and conquered most of Europe.
- Feelings of nationalism caused European nations to rebel against French rule and led to the unification of small kingdoms into new nations.
- The desire for raw materials and new markets led the imperialist nations of Europe to take control of large areas of Asia and Africa.

◆ Key Terms

Write one or two paragraphs about important changes of the 1700s and 1800s. Use at least six of the terms below in your paragraphs.

1. Enlightenment
2. labor union
3. imperialism
4. Declaration of Independence
5. Industrial Revolution
6. scientific method
7. Napoleonic Code
8. nationalism

─ Vocabulary Builder ─

Revisit this chapter's high-use words:

reject	restore	defend
accurately	declare	permit
method	basis	domination
reasonable	produce	alliance

Ask students to review the definitions they recorded on their _Word Knowledge_ worksheet.

All in One **Medieval Times to Today Teaching Resources,** _Word Knowledge,_ p. 382

Consider allowing students to earn extra credit if they use the words in their answers to the questions in the Chapter Review and Assessment. The words must be used correctly and in a natural context to win the extra points.

Chapter 7

Review and Assessment

Review Chapter Content

■ Review and revisit the major themes of this chapter by asking students to classify which Guiding Question each bulleted statement in the Chapter Summary answers. Form students into groups and ask them to complete the activity together. Refer to p. 1 in the Student Edition for text of Guiding Questions.

■ Assign _Vocabulary Development_ for students to review Key Terms.

All in One **Medieval Times to Today Teaching Resources,** _Vocabulary Development,_ p. 395

Answers

Key Terms

1–8. Students' paragraphs should use each Key Term correctly and in the appropriate context.

Review and Assessment

Comprehension and Critical Thinking

9. (a) Copernicus and Newton were scientists who developed new ideas about the universe during the Scientific Revolution. **(b)** Copernicus put forth the idea that Earth was not the center of the universe. Newton named gravity and developed a theory about why the planets move the way they do.

10. (a) Locke believed that natural rights were rights that belonged to human beings from birth. These included the right to life, the right to liberty, and the right to own property. **(b)** Possible answer: Locke's ideas were put into practice through both the American and French revolutions.

11. (a) Parliament offered the throne to William and Mary on the condition that they accept the English Bill of Rights, which set up the government as a constitutional monarchy. **(b)** The English Bill of Rights also restated the traditional rights of English citizens, such as trial by jury.

12. (a) working people **(b)** People could be taxed if they had representatives in the Parliament who voted on the tax. **(c)** Citizens in France and in the American colonies rebelled in part because they felt they were being unfairly taxed by the government.

13. (a) to work in factories **(b)** Dangerous working conditions led workers to form labor unions to help them bargain with employers for improvements.

14. (a) He developed the Napoleonic Code which embodied such Enlightenment principles as equality of all citizens before the law. **(b)** Both Napoleon and imperialist nations wanted to expand their territories and both were inspired by nationalism. Imperialist nations colonized lands outside of Europe while Napoleon conquered European lands.

Skills Practice

Students' interpretations should state that the diagram shows automobile production using an assembly line; each caption describes a different step in making an automobile; the images show how the assembly line looks inside the factory. Students may conclude that breaking a complicated process into smaller steps increases efficiency.

Chapter 7 Review and Assessment (continued)

◆ Comprehension and Critical Thinking

9. (a) Identify Who were Nicolaus Copernicus and Isaac Newton?
(b) Synthesize How did they change the way people thought about the universe?

10. (a) Recall Explain John Locke's idea of natural rights.
(b) Identify Effects Describe two events of the 1700s in which Locke's ideas were put into practice.

11. (a) Summarize How did England become a constitutional monarchy?
(b) Conclude How did these events lead to protections for English citizens?

12. (a) Recall Who paid most of the taxes in France before the French Revolution?
(b) Explain Under British law, how could taxes be imposed on citizens?
(c) Compare and Contrast Explain how taxes contributed to both the French and the American revolutions.

13. (a) Explain Why did many people move away from the countryside during the Industrial Revolution?

(b) Identify Causes How did working conditions in factories lead to the formation of labor unions?

14. (a) Recall How did Napoleon reform the legal system of France?
(b) Compare and Contrast How did the efforts of Napoleon to conquer Europe compare with the desire of imperialist nations to establish colonies in Africa and Asia?

◆ Skills Practice

Interpreting Diagrams In the Skills for Life activity in this chapter, you learned how to interpret a diagram. Review the steps of this skill. Then write an interpretation of the diagram in the Eyewitness Technology feature on page 207.

◆ Writing Activity: Math

In this chapter you read that the spinning jenny allowed one worker to do the work of eight workers using spinning wheels. Use your math skills to find out how much more thread could be produced using this new technology or what percentage of time could be saved. Write a letter that manufacturers of the spinning jenny might send to textile companies to persuade them to buy this new machine.

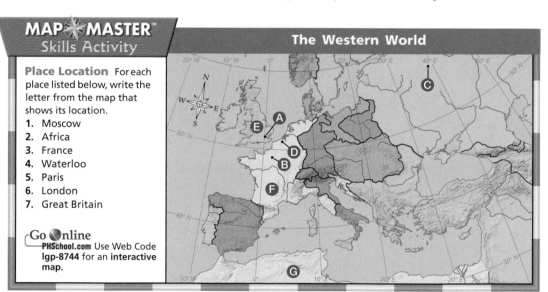

MAP MASTER™ Skills Activity

The Western World

Place Location For each place listed below, write the letter from the map that shows its location.
1. Moscow
2. Africa
3. France
4. Waterloo
5. Paris
6. London
7. Great Britain

Go Online
PHSchool.com Use Web Code lgp-8744 for an interactive map.

Writing Activity: Math
Students' letters will vary, but should state that a worker using a spinning jenny can do eight times the work of a worker without a spinning jenny.

Use *Rubric for Assessing a Writing Assignment* to evaluate students' letters.

All in One Medieval Times to Today Teaching Resources, *Rubric for Assessing a Writing Assignment,* p. 396

Standardized Test Prep

Test-Taking Tips

Some questions on standardized tests ask you to analyze a graphic organizer. Study the concept web below. Then follow the tips to answer the sample question at the right.

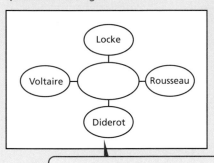

TIP As you review a concept web, notice the kind of information included in each part. Are the entries people, events, dates, or ideas?

Choose the letter that best answers the question.

Which title should go in the center of the concept web?

A Thinkers of the Enlightenment
B Revolution
C Declaration of Independence
D Thomas Jefferson

TIP Try to find the BEST answer, because sometimes more than one answer choice seems possible.

Think It Through A title for the center of a web should be a broad idea that covers the information in all of the outer ovals. You can rule out D because it is too specific: Jefferson is a person like the entries in the outer ovals. B is too general. That leaves A or C. None of these people were directly involved in the Declaration of Independence, but they all had similar ideas. Therefore the answer is A—they were all Enlightenment thinkers.

Practice Questions

Use the concept web below to answer the following questions.

1. Which title should go in the center of the web?
  A Results of the Scientific Revolution
  B Effects of the Industrial Revolution
  C Major Ideas of the Enlightenment
  D Reasons for the Growth of Imperialism

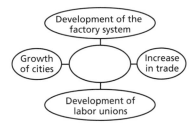

2. According to the web, which is most important?
  A development of labor unions
  B increase in trade
  C growth of cities
  D It is impossible to tell.

3. If you were to add another outer oval to the web, which of the following should it be?
  A increase in the amount of goods produced
  B better working conditions
  C reduction in transportation
  D shrinking of the middle class

PHSchool.com
Use Web Code **lga-8704** for a **Chapter 7 self-test.**

MAP★MASTER
Skills Activity

1. C	**2.** G
3. F	**4.** D
5. B	**6.** A
7. E	

Go Online PHSchool.com Students may practice their map skills using the interactive online version of this map.

Standardized Test Prep

Answers

1. B
2. D
3. A

Go Online PHSchool.com Students may use the Chapter 7 self-test on PHSchool.com to prepare for the Chapter Test.

Assessment Resources

Use *Chapter Tests A and B* to assess students' mastery of chapter content.

All in One **Medieval Times to Today Teaching Resources,** *Chapter Tests A and B,* pp. 398–403

Tests are also available on the **ExamView®** **Test Bank CD-ROM**.

ExamView®Test Bank CD-ROM

Overview

 Section 1

War and Revolution
1. Examine the causes and effects of World War I and the Russian Revolution.
2. Find out about the Great Depression.
3. Discover the ways in which World War II affected the world.

 Section 2

The Postwar World
1. Learn how the Cold War pitted the United States against the Soviet Union.
2. Discover how dozens of former colonies gained independence.

 Section 3

The World Today
1. Learn how modern technology has transformed the world.
2. Explore how migration, trade, and closer economic ties have linked different parts of the world.
3. Consider the new challenges that the world will face during your lifetime.

The Holocaust: In Memory of Millions
Length: 3 minutes, 35 seconds
Use with Section 1
This segment explores what happened to Jewish people during the Holocaust.

Technology Resources

 **Go Online**
PHSchool.com

Students use embedded Web codes to access Internet activities, chapter self-tests, and additional map practice. They may also access Dorling Kindersley's Online Desk Reference to learn more about each country they study.

 **interactive Textbook**

Use the Interactive Textbook to make content and concepts come alive through animations, videos, and activities that accompany the complete basal text—online and on CD-ROM.

PRENTICE HALL
TeacherEXPRESS
Plan · Teach · Assess

Use this complete suite of powerful teaching tools to make planning lessons and administering tests quicker and easier.

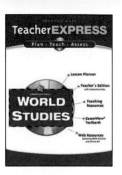

Reading and Assessment

Reading and Vocabulary Instruction

⟳ Model the Target Reading Skill

Word Analysis Explain to students that the meaning of an unfamiliar word can often be determined by focusing on its parts—prefix, suffix, and root. Write this selection from p. 228 on the board:

> *The Cabinet War Rooms also included offices, telephone switchboards, staff dormitories, a mess room where snacks were served, and a transatlantic telephone room—disguised as a bathroom— where Churchill had a direct phone line to Franklin Roosevelt, the President of the United States.*

Model the skill by thinking about this selection aloud: "This selection contains two words that are unfamiliar to me. The first word is *dormitories*. This word begins with *dorm*, which comes from a Latin root meaning 'sleep.' The word ends in *-ies*. This tells me that the word is plural and that *y* was changed to *i* before adding *-es*. Therefore, the suffix of this word is *-ory*, which means 'place of.' I can conclude that *dormitories* are 'places where you sleep.' Another unfamiliar word is *transatlantic*. I see the word *atlantic*, which refers to the Atlantic Ocean. It is preceded by the prefix *trans-*, which means 'across or beyond.' From this I conclude that *transatlantic* means 'across or beyond the Atlantic Ocean.'"

Use the following worksheets from All-in-One Medieval Times to Today Teaching Resources (pp. 421–423) to support the chapter's Target Reading Skill.

Vocabulary Builder
High-Use Academic Words

Use these steps to teach this chapter's high-use words:

1. Have students rate how well they know each word on their Word Knowledge worksheets (All-in-One Medieval Times to Today Teaching Resources, p. 424).

2. Pronounce each word and ask students to repeat it.

3. Give students a brief definition or sample sentence (provided on TE pp. 223, 231, and 239).

4. Work with students as they fill in the "Definition or Example" column of their Word Knowledge worksheets.

Assessment

Formal Assessment

Test students' understanding of core knowledge and skills.

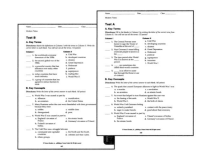

Chapter Tests A and B, and Final Exams A and B, All-in-One Medieval Times to Today Teaching Resources, pp. 440–445, 451–456

Customize the Chapter Tests to suit your needs.

ExamView® Test Bank CD-ROM

Skills Assessment

Assess geographic literacy.

MapMaster Skills, Student Edition, pp. 221, 232, 233, 240, 244

Assess reading and comprehension.

Target Reading Skills, Student Edition, pp. 223, 234, 241, and in Section Assessments

Chapter 8 Assessment, Medieval Times to Today Reading and Vocabulary Study Guide, p. 94

Performance Assessment

Assess students' performance on this chapter's Writing Activities using the following rubrics from All-in-One Medieval Times to Today Teaching Resources.

Rubric for Assessing a Writing Assignment, p. 438

Rubric for Assessing a Journal Entry, p. 439

Assess students' work through performance tasks.

Small Group Activity: Designing World War II Posters, All-in-One Medieval Times to Today Teaching Resources, pp. 427–430

Online Assessment

Have students check their own understanding.

Chapter Self-Test

Test Preparation

Medieval Times to Today Benchmark Test 2 and Outcome Test, AYP Monitoring Assessments, pp. 145–148, 212–217

Medieval Times to Today Practice Tests A, B, and C, Test Prep Workbook, pp. 73–84

Section 1 **War and Revolution**

 2.5 periods, 1.25 blocks (includes Focus On The Cabinet War Rooms)

Social Studies Objectives
1. Examine the causes and effects of World War I and the Russian Revolution.
2. Find out about the Great Depression.
3. Discover the ways in which World War II affected the world.

Reading/Language Arts Objective
Use word parts, including roots and prefixes, to recognize and pronounce unfamiliar words.

Prepare to Read	Instructional Resources	Differentiated Instruction
Build Background Knowledge Discuss the wars and revolutions that occurred during the 1900s. **Set a Purpose for Reading** Have students evaluate statements on the *Reading Readiness Guide.* **Preview Key Terms** Teach the section's Key Terms. **Target Reading Skill** Introduce the section's Target Reading Skill of **using word parts.**	**All in One Medieval Times to Today Teaching Resources** L2 Reading Readiness Guide, p. 410 L2 Use Prefixes and Roots, p. 421	**Spanish Reading and Vocabulary Study Guide** L1 Chapter 8, Section 1, pp. 62–63 ELL

Instruct	Instructional Resources	Differentiated Instruction
World War I Ask questions about World War I. **Target Reading Skill** Review **using word parts.** **The Russian Revolution** Ask about the leaders and discuss the effects of the Russian Revolution. **The Great Depression** Discuss causes and effects of the Great Depression. **World War II** Discuss World War II and the Holocaust.	**All in One Medieval Times to Today Teaching Resources** L2 Guided Reading and Review, p. 411 L2 Reading Readiness Guide, p. 410 **Medieval Times to Today Transparencies** L2 Section Reading Support Transparency MT 77 **World Studies Video Program** L2 The Holocaust: In Memory of Millions	**All in One Medieval Times to Today Teaching Resources** L3 Lenin's Deathbed Words, p. 435 AR, GT L3 Kampf, p. 436 AR, GT **Teacher's Edition** L1 For Less Proficient Readers, TE p. 224 L3 For Advanced Readers, TE p. 224 L1 For English Language Learners, TE pp. 225, 228 L3 For Gifted and Talented, TE p. 228 **Student Edition on Audio CD** L1 Chapter 8, Section 1 ELL, LPR, SN **Spanish Support** L2 Guided Reading and Review (Spanish), p. 66

Assess and Reteach	Instructional Resources	Differentiated Instruction
Assess Progress Evaluate student comprehension with the section assessment and section quiz. **Reteach** Assign the Reading and Vocabulary Study Guide to help struggling students. **Extend** Extend the lesson by assigning a Small Group Activity.	**All in One Medieval Times to Today Teaching Resources** L2 Section Quiz, p. 412 L3 Small Group Activity: Designing World War II Posters, pp. 427–430 Rubric for Assessing a Writing Assignment, p. 438 **Reading and Vocabulary Study Guide** L1 Chapter 8, Section 1, pp. 88–90	**Spanish Support** L2 Section Quiz (Spanish), p. 67 ELL

Key
L1 Basic to Average L3 Average to Advanced
L2 For All Students

LPR Less Proficient Readers
AR Advanced Readers
SN Special Needs Students

GT Gifted and Talented
ELL English Language Learners

Section 2 The Postwar World

 4 periods, 2 blocks (includes Skills for Life)

Social Studies Objectives
1. Learn how the Cold War pitted the United States against the Soviet Union.
2. Discover how dozens of former colonies gained independence.

Reading/Language Arts Objective
Recognize word origins to determine the meaning of unfamiliar words.

Prepare to Read

Build Background Knowledge
Ask students to preview the section and list three people who lived during the decades following World War II.

Set a Purpose for Reading
Have students evaluate statements on the *Reading Readiness Guide.*

Preview Key Terms
Teach the section's Key Terms.

Target Reading Skill
Introduce the section's Target Reading Skill of **recognizing word origins.**

Instructional Resources

All in One Medieval Times to Today Teaching Resources
- **L2** Reading Readiness Guide, p. 414
- **L2** Recognize Word Origins, p. 422

Differentiated Instruction

Spanish Reading and Vocabulary Study Guide
- **L1** Chapter 8, Section 2, pp. 64–65 ELL

Instruct

The Cold War
Discuss the events leading up to the Cold War and the fall of the Soviet Union.

A New Era of Independence
Discuss European colonies.

Target Reading Skill
Review **recognizing word origins.**

Instructional Resources

All in One Medieval Times to Today Teaching Resources
- **L2** Guided Reading and Review, p. 415
- **L2** Reading Readiness Guide, p. 414

Medieval Times to Today Transparencies
- **L2** Section Reading Support Transparency MT 78

Differentiated Instruction

All in One Medieval Times to Today Teaching Resources
- **L3** Activity Shop Interdisciplinary: History Quiz Wizards, pp. 431–432 AR, GT
- **L2** Skills for Life, p. 426 AR, GT, LPR, SN

Teacher's Edition
- **L3** For Advanced Readers, TE p. 233
- **L1** For Special Needs Students, TE p. 233

Spanish Support
- **L2** Guided Reading and Review (Spanish), p. 68 ELL

Assess and Reteach

Assess Progress
Evaluate student comprehension with the section assessment and section quiz.

Reteach
Assign the Reading and Vocabulary Study Guide to help struggling students.

Extend
To extend the lesson, have students write a research paper.

Instructional Resources

All in One Medieval Times to Today Teaching Resources
- **L2** Section Quiz, p. 416
    Rubric for Assessing a Writing Assignment, p. 438

Reading and Vocabulary Study Guide
- **L1** Chapter 8, Section 2, pp. 88–90

Differentiated Instruction

All in One Medieval Times to Today Teaching Resources
- **L3** Reading a Line Graph, p. 433 AR, GT

Teacher's Edition
- **L1** For Special Needs Students, TE p. 237

Social Studies Skills Tutor CD-ROM
- **L1** Analyzing Graphic Data ELL, LPR, SN

Spanish Support
- **L2** Section Quiz (Spanish), p. 69 ELL

Key

L1 Basic to Average	**L3** Average to Advanced	
L2 For All Students		
	LPR Less Proficient Readers	GT Gifted and Talented
	AR Advanced Readers	ELL English Language Learners
	SN Special Needs Students	

Section 3 **The World Today**

 4.5 periods, 2.25 blocks (includes Chapter Review and Assessment)

Social Studies Objectives
1. Learn how modern technology has transformed the world.
2. Explore how migration, trade, and closer economic ties have linked different parts of the world.
3. Consider the new challenges that the world will face during your lifetime.

Reading/Language Arts Objective
Use word parts such as roots and suffixes to recognize and pronounce unfamiliar words.

Prepare to Read	**Instructional Resources**	**Differentiated Instruction**
Build Background Knowledge Have students preview the section and discuss what the headings and visuals show about the world today. **Set a Purpose for Reading** Have students evaluate statements on the *Reading Readiness Guide.* **Preview Key Terms** Teach the section's Key Terms. **Target Reading Skill** Introduce the section's Target Reading Skill of **using word parts.**	**All in One Medieval Times to Today Teaching Resources** **L2** Reading Readiness Guide, p. 418 **L2** Use Roots and Suffixes, p. 423	**Spanish Reading and Vocabulary Study Guide** **L1** Chapter 8, Section 3, pp. 66–67 ELL

Instruct	**Instructional Resources**	**Differentiated Instruction**
The Advance of Technology Discuss how modern technology has affected people's lives. **A Smaller World** Discuss how new technologies have affected business. **Target Reading Skill** Review **using word parts.** **New Challenges** Discuss some challenges that the world faces today.	**All in One Medieval Times to Today Teaching Resources** **L2** Guided Reading and Review, p. 419 **L2** Reading Readiness Guide, p. 418 **Medieval Times to Today Transparencies** **L2** Section Reading Support Transparency MT 79	**All in One Medieval Times to Today Teaching Resources** **L1** Reading a Cartogram, p. 434 ELL, LPR, SN **Teacher's Edition** **L1** For Less Proficient Readers, TE p. 240 **L3** For Gifted and Talented, TE p. 240 **Spanish Support** **L2** Guided Reading and Review (Spanish), p. 70 ELL

Assess and Reteach	**Instructional Resources**	**Differentiated Instruction**
Assess Progress Evaluate student comprehension with the section assessment and section quiz. **Reteach** Assign the Reading and Vocabulary Study Guide to help struggling students. **Extend** Extend the lesson by having students create collages.	**All in One Medieval Times to Today Teaching Resources** **L2** Section Quiz, p. 420 Rubric for Assessing a Journal Entry, p. 439 **L2** Word Knowledge, p. 424 **L2** Vocabulary Development, p. 437 Rubric for Assessing a Writing Assignment, p. 438 **L2** Chapter Tests A and B, pp. 440–445 **L2** Final Exams A and B, pp. 451–456 **Reading and Vocabulary Study Guide** **L1** Chapter 8, Section 3, pp. 91–93	**Spanish Support** **L2** Section Quiz (Spanish), p. 71 ELL **L2** Chapter Summary (Spanish), p. 72 ELL **L2** Vocabulary Development (Spanish), p. 73 ELL

Key

L1 Basic to Average   **L3** Average to Advanced

L2 For All Students

LPR Less Proficient Readers
AR Advanced Readers
SN Special Needs Students

GT Gifted and Talented
ELL English Language Learners

Reading Background

Paragraph Structure

Ask students to write each of the following sentences, from the last paragraph on p. 233, on a separate slip of paper.

1. Russia also developed friendlier relations with the United States.
2. The largest and most powerful of these nations, Russia, adopted capitalism.
3. When the communist government fell in 1991, the Soviet Union broke up into several independent nations.

Ask students to rearrange sentences into a well-ordered paragraph. *(The correct order is 3, 2, 1.)* Tell students to look for main ideas, details, and transition words to help them create their paragraphs.

Vocabulary Tips

Help students learn and remember new vocabulary by finding instances of Key Terms and high-use words used outside the classroom. Ask students to look in newspapers and magazines to find examples of the words *dictator, superpower, millennium,* and *terrorism.* Assign students to small groups to share their examples. Then have the groups present three examples to the class.

Author's Craft

Ask students to determine the organizational plan the author has used to present the information in Section 1. For example, is the text organized chronologically or in a compare and contrast structure? Ask students to write down the clues they used to determine the organizational plan. *(Dates are presented in order, which lets readers know that the content is organized chronologically.)*

World Studies Background

The Fourteen Points

The Treaty of Versailles was based on President Woodrow Wilson's Fourteen Points, his proposal for a postwar peace settlement. The Fourteen Points included general provisions for promoting peace and justice in the world, as well as specific provisions to restore the upheaval caused by World War I. By 1918, Germany accepted President Wilson's Fourteen Points as a basis for peace negotiations. However, the final Treaty of Versailles contained much harsher provisions, including the demand that Germany admit guilt for the war.

Victims of the Nazis

In addition to the estimated six million Jews who died in the Holocaust, millions of others were murdered by the Nazis. Ethnic groups considered racially inferior, such as the Roma and Slavs (including Poles and Russians), and mentally and physically handicapped people were killed. Other victims murdered by the Nazis included Jehovah's Witnesses and political opponents.

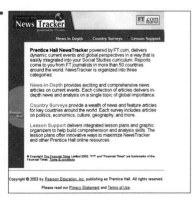

Get in-depth information on topics of global importance with **Prentice Hall Newstracker,** powered by FT.com.

Use Web Code **lgd-8800** for **Prentice Hall Newstracker.**

Guiding Questions

Remind students about the Guiding Questions introduced at the beginning of the book.

Section 1 relates to **Guiding Question** ❷ **How did each society's belief system affect its history?** *(Between 1914 and 1918 World War I was fought between countries who struggled for power against one another; in 1917 Russians fought a revolution to establish communism; Between 1939 and 1945 World War II was fought between Germany, Italy, and Japan, and the United States, Soviet Union, Britain, France, and other allied powers.)*

Section 2 relates to **Guiding Question** ❹ **What types of government were formed in these societies?** *(After World War II, the Soviet Union controlled Eastern Europe and forced the countries there to adopt a communist government; in Africa and Asia many countries that had been under colonial rule gained their independence.)*

Section 3 relates to **Guiding Question** ❺ **How did each society organize its economic activities?** *(Since the mid-1900s, advances in technology have improved transportation and communication around the world, increasing trade among nations.)*

🎯 Target Reading Skill

In this chapter, students will learn and apply the reading skill of Word Analysis. Use the following worksheets to help students practice this skill:

All in One Medieval Times to Today Teaching Resources, *Use Prefixes and Roots,* p. 421; *Recognize Word Origins,* p. 422; *Use Roots and Suffixes;* p. 423

Differentiated Instruction

The following Teacher's Edition strategies are suitable for students of varying abilities.

Advanced Readers, pp. 224, 233
English Language Learners, pp. 225, 228
Gifted and Talented, pp. 228, 240
Less Proficient Readers, pp. 224, 240
Special Needs Students, pp. 233, 237

Modern Times

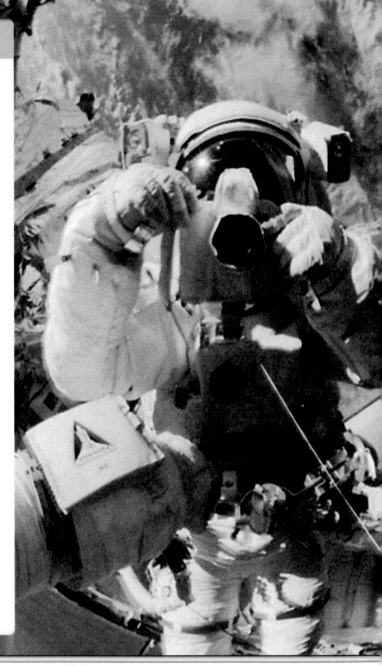

Chapter Preview

This chapter will introduce you to the history of the world from the early 1900s to the present day.

Section 1
War and Revolution

Section 2
The Postwar World

Section 3
The World Today

🎯 **Target Reading Skill**

Word Analysis In this chapter you will focus on looking at parts of unfamiliar words to understand their meaning. Suffixes, prefixes, and roots are parts of a word that can give clues to its meaning.

▶ Astronaut Jeff Wisoff on the Space Shuttle *Discovery* in 2000, with the planet Earth behind him

220 Medieval Times to Today

Bibliography

For the Teacher
Appy, Christian G. *Patriots: The Vietnam War Remembered from All Sides.* Viking Press, 2003.
Dear, Ian, and M.R.D. Foot, Eds. *The Oxford Companion to World War II.* Oxford Press, 2002.
Willmott, H.P. *World War I.* DK Publishing, 2003.

For the Student
L1 Panchyk, Richard. *World War II for Kids: A History with 21 Activities.* Chicago Review Press, 2002.
L2 Adams, Simon. *Eyewitness: World War I (Eyewitness Books).* DK Publishing, 2001.
L3 Damon, Duane. *Headin' for Better Times: The Arts of the Great Depression (People's History).* Lerner Pub Group, 2002.

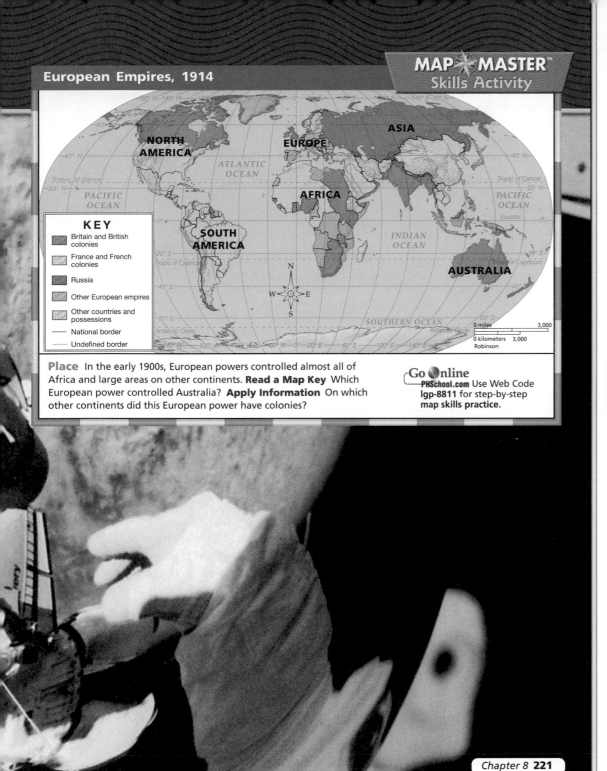

European Empires, 1914

KEY

- Britain and British colonies
- France and French colonies
- Russia
- Other European empires
- Other countries and possessions
- —— National border
- ······ Undefined border

0 miles 3,000
0 kilometers 3,000
Robinson

Place In the early 1900s, European powers controlled almost all of Africa and large areas on other continents. **Read a Map Key** Which European power controlled Australia? **Apply Information** On which other continents did this European power have colonies?

Go Online
PHSchool.com Use Web Code lgp-8811 for step-by-step map skills practice.

- Divide students into three groups, and assign each group one of the following: North and South America; Asia and Australia; or Africa. Using the Atlas in the Student Edition, have students find out which present-day countries on their continent or continents were once under colonial rule. Have students create a chart listing the countries and their colonial rulers.

- Have students do additional research in the library or on the Internet to find out the dates these colonies became independent. They should then add this information to their charts.

Go Online
PHSchool.com Students may practice their map skills using the interactive online version of this map.

Using the Visual L2

Reach Into Your Background Direct students' attention to the photo and caption on pp. 220–221. Ask them to think about the ways space travel has affected society. Then, use the Numbered Heads participation strategy (TE, p. T36) to call on students to share ways that technology has affected their lives.

Answers

MAP MASTER™ Skills Activity **Read a Map Key** Britain
Apply Information North America, South America, Asia, and Africa

---

Chapter Resources

Teaching Resources
- L2 Vocabulary Development, p. 437
- L2 Skills for Life, p. 426
- L2 Chapter Tests A and B, pp. 440–445

Spanish Support
- L2 Spanish Chapter Summary, p. 72
- L2 Spanish Vocabulary Development, p. 73

Media and Technology
- L1 Student Edition on Audio CD
- L1 Guided Reading Audiotapes, English and Spanish
- L2 Social Studies Skills Tutor CD-ROM
- *ExamView Test Bank CD-ROM*

Discovery CHANNEL SCHOOL World Studies Video Program

interactive Textbook

PRENTICE HALL

TeacherEXPRESS™
Plan • Teach • Assess

Objectives

Social Studies

1. Examine the causes and effects of World War I and the Russian Revolution.
2. Find out about the Great Depression.
3. Discover the ways in which World War II affected the world.

Reading/Language Arts

Use word parts, including roots and prefixes, to recognize and pronounce unfamiliar words.

Prepare to Read

Build Background Knowledge L2

Tell students that in this section, they will learn about war and revolution throughout the world in the first half of the 1900s. Using the Think-Write-Pair-Share strategy (TE, p. T36), ask students to preview the headings in the section with this question in mind: **Which revolution and wars occurred during the first half of the 1900s?** *(World War I, the Russian Revolution, World War II)* Have student pairs share any additional information that they know about these events, and list this information on the board.

Set a Purpose for Reading L2

- Preview the Objectives.

- Read each statement in the *Reading Readiness Guide* aloud. Ask students to mark the statements true or false.

  All in One Medieval Times to Today **Teaching Resources,** *Reading Readiness Guide,* p. 410

- Have students discuss the statements in pairs or groups of four, then mark their worksheets again. Use the Numbered Heads participation strategy (TE, p. T36) to call on students to share their group's perspectives.

Vocabulary Builder
Preview Key Terms L2

Pronounce each Key Term, then ask students to say the word with you. Provide a simple explanation such as "A dictator is someone who has complete control over a country."

Prepare to Read

Objectives

In this section you will
1. Examine the causes and effects of World War I and the Russian Revolution.
2. Find out about the Great Depression.
3. Discover the ways in which World War II affected the world.

Taking Notes

As you read this section, look for the main ideas about this time of war and revolution. Copy the table below, and record your findings in it. Add boxes and rows as needed.

War and Revolution	
World War I	• Causes included nationalism, alliances, and militarism. •
The Russian Revolution	• •

⊙ Target Reading Skill

Use Word Parts Sometimes you can break an unfamiliar word into parts to help you recognize and pronounce it. A root is the base of the word and often has meaning by itself. A prefix comes before the root and changes its meaning. In the word surrender, *-render* is the root, meaning "to give." *Sur-* is the prefix, meaning "on" or "over."

Key Terms

- **World War I** (wurld wawr wun) *n.* the first global war of the 1900s (1914–1918)
- **dictator** (DIK tay tur) *n.* an absolute ruler of a country
- **Great Depression** (grayt dee PRESH un) *n.* the worldwide economic downturn of the 1930s
- **World War II** (wurld wawr too) *n.* the second global war of the 1900s (1939–1945)
- **Holocaust** (HAHL uh kawst) *n.* Nazi Germany's mass killing of Jewish people

Cars were an exciting new invention in 1900.

1900 Oldsmobile

I t was New Year's Eve. All over the world, people were about to celebrate the new year. But this was no ordinary New Year's Eve. It was a once-in-a-lifetime event. For the next day would bring not just a new year; it would bring a new century.

One writer summed up the feelings of millions of Americans when he wrote: "1900! The beginning of a new century! When I think of the strides our nation has made in its last century, what great inventions have been made . . . I wonder what will be done in the next hundred years."

This writer had good cause to wonder. Not he, nor anyone else, could possibly have foreseen how much the world would change over the next 100 years. The changes would be dramatic. In some ways, the world would change more in the 1900s than it had in all of recorded history. Sadly, much of this change would come at a terrible cost.

⊙ Target Reading Skill L2

Use Word Parts Point out the Target Reading Skill. Tell students that looking for a root or prefix in an unfamiliar word can help them recognize the word and pronounce it.

Model using word parts to find the meaning of *anticommunists* in the fourth paragraph on p. 224. *(The prefix* anti- *means "against," and the root word is* communist

so anticommunists are people against communism.)

Give students *Use Prefixes and Roots.* Have them complete the activity in their groups.

All in One Medieval Times to Today **Teaching Resources,** *Use Prefixes and Roots,* p. 421

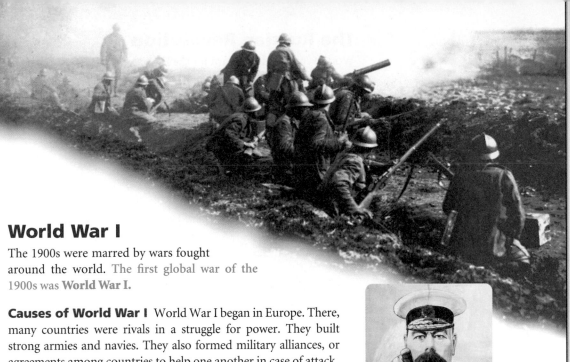

World War I

The 1900s were marred by wars fought around the world. The first global war of the 1900s was **World War I.**

Causes of World War I World War I began in Europe. There, many countries were rivals in a struggle for power. They built strong armies and navies. They also formed military alliances, or agreements among countries to help one another in case of attack.

Rivalries, the military build-up, and the growth of alliances kept tensions high. Europe in the early 1900s was like a gunpowder keg, and one spark could set it off.

The War Begins The spark that set off World War I was the murder in 1914 of Archduke Franz Ferdinand of Austria-Hungary by a Serb. Austria-Hungary declared war on Serbia.

Then the system of alliances caused the war to spread. Alliances linked Russia, France, and Britain with Serbia. These countries were known as the Allied Powers. Later, the United States joined the Allied Powers. They fought the Central Powers, including Germany and Austria-Hungary.

Trench Warfare Soldiers from each side dug lines of muddy trenches to avoid enemy fire. Regularly, soldiers were ordered "over the top" to charge the enemy's trenches. Often, they were cut down by enemy machine-gun fire. Machine guns and poison gas made this war deadlier than any earlier war. More than 8 million soldiers died. Millions of civilians also were killed.

The End of the War In 1918, the Central Powers surrendered. Germany and Austria-Hungary were forced to accept harsh punishments in the Treaty of Versailles (vur SY).

✓ **Reading Check** How many soldiers died in World War I?

World War I Trench Warfare and Recruitment Poster
Some French troops in the photo at the top stand in a trench, while others stand just outside it. The British poster below calls for new recruits. **Analyze Images** *Would the photo at the top be an effective recruitment poster? Explain why or why not.*

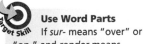

Use Word Parts
If *sur-* means "over" or "on," and *render* means "give," what does *surrender* mean?

Vocabulary Builder

Use the information below to teach students this section's high-use words.

High-Use Word	Definition and Sample Sentence
rivalry, p. 223	*n.* competition The **rivalry** between the two teams made the soccer game more exciting.
opposition, p. 224	*n.* the act of being against something There was great **opposition** by the students to the new school uniforms.
curtail, p. 224	*v.* to reduce He **curtailed** spending to avoid going over the budget.
discontent, p. 226	*n.* lack of satisfaction There was **discontent** among the people who were unhappy with the war.

World War I   L2

Guided Instruction

- **Vocabulary Builder** Clarify the high-use word **rivalry** before reading.

- Read World War I using the Oral Cloze reading strategy (TE, p. T33).

- Discuss the two alliances in World War I. Ask students **Who were the Allied Powers in World War I?** *(those who supported Serbia, including Russia, France, Britain, and the United States)* **Who were the Central Powers?** *(Germany, Austria-Hungary, and the countries that supported them)*

- Ask students **What was the result of these two powers fighting each other?** *(Possible answer: World War I; more than 8 million soldiers killed and millions of civilians killed; the Central Powers surrendered and Germany and Austria-Hungary were forced to accept harsh punishments in the Treaty of Versailles.)*

- Ask **How was World War I more deadly than any earlier wars?** *(New weapons such as machine guns and poison gas were deadlier than weapons used in earlier wars.)*

Independent Practice

Ask students to create the Taking Notes graphic organizer on a blank piece of paper. Then have them fill in more main ideas about World War I in the table. Briefly model how to identify which ideas to record.

Monitor Progress

As students fill in the graphic organizer, circulate and make sure individuals are choosing the correct ideas. Provide assistance as needed.

⊚ Target Reading Skill   L2

Use Word Parts As a follow up, ask students to answer the Target Reading Skill question in the Student Edition. *(to give up, or to give over to something)*

Answers

Analyze Images Possible answers: Yes, because some individuals might want to fight and defend their country; No: some individuals might not want to fight in the trenches.

✓ **Reading Check** more than 8 million

The Russian Revolution L2

Guided Instruction

- **Vocabulary Builder** Clarify the high-use words **opposition** and **curtail** before reading.

- Read The Russian Revolution with students. As students read, circulate and make sure individuals can answer the Reading Check question.

- Ask students **Who led the rebels during the Russian Revolution?** (*Vladimir Lenin*)

- Ask students **What were the effects of the Russian Revolution?** (*The tsar gave up the throne and was later executed with his family; Lenin took control of the Russian government and made peace with Germany; the Russian Empire was renamed the Union of Soviet Socialist Republics, or the Soviet Union.*)

- Discuss with students how communist ideas differed from the reality of communism in the Soviet Union. (*In theory, communism seemed like a fair system in which every citizen would get an equal share of the country's wealth. In reality, members of the Communist Party used the country's wealth to win power for themselves. Lenin and Stalin became dicators.*)

Independent Practice
Have students continue to fill in the Taking Notes graphic organizer by recording main ideas about the Russian Revolution.

Monitor Progress
As students fill in the graphic organizer, circulate and make sure individuals are choosing the correct ideas. Provide assistance as needed.

Answers
Identify Effects They might make daily activities, such as traveling, very dangerous for the people who live there.

✓ Reading Check Hardships resulting from World War I increased opposition to the tsar, who had absolute power.

The Russian Revolution

World War I made life hard for the Russian people. Much of the country's food, fuel, and supplies went for the war effort. This meant that the people at home could not meet basic needs.

Street Battle, St. Petersburg People run for cover at the start of a gun battle during the Russian Revolution in 1917. **Identify Effects** *How might gun battles affect daily life in a city?*

A Russian communist propaganda poster

Overthrowing the Tsar Tsars, or emperors, had ruled Russia for hundreds of years. The tsars were absolute rulers. In the early 1900s, Russians grew more and more unhappy with their government. The hardships of the war increased opposition to the tsar.

In 1917, a revolution forced the tsar, Nicholas II, to give up the throne. Later in the year, rebels led by Vladimir Lenin took control of the government. In 1918, Lenin's government made peace with Germany but executed the tsar and his family. In 1922, the Russian Empire was renamed the Union of Soviet Socialist Republics (USSR), or the Soviet Union.

A Communist Dictatorship Lenin and his followers belonged to the Communist Party. They fought to establish communism, a system in which the government controls most businesses. Communists imposed this system after winning a civil war against anticommunists in 1920. Communists promised everyone an equal share of the country's wealth. Many Russians supported communism because they were tired of living in poverty under the tsars. In theory, communism seemed fair.

In reality, though, communism was brutally unfair. The Communist Party used the country's wealth to support its own power. Lenin became the **dictator**, or absolute ruler, of the Soviet Union. After Lenin's death in 1924, the dictator Joseph Stalin ruled the Soviet Union ruthlessly until 1953. Stalin curtailed people's freedoms. He set up brutal prison camps. He punished anyone who challenged his rule. In all, Stalin was probably responsible for the deaths of more than 10 million of his own people.

✓ Reading Check Why did Russians oppose the tsar?

Differentiated Instruction

For Less Proficient Readers L1
Have students read the section as they listen to the recorded version on the Student Edition on Audio CD. Check for comprehension by pausing the CD and asking students to share their answers to the Reading Checks.

⊙ Chapter 8, Section 1, **Student Edition on Audio CD**

For Advanced Readers L3
Have students find out more about Lenin and Stalin by reading the words of both men in *Lenin's Deathbed Words* and *Kampf.*

All in One Medieval Times to Today Teaching Resources, *Lenin's Deathbed Words,* p. 435; *Kampf,* p. 436

The Great Depression

The end of World War I brought jubilation in the victorious countries. In the United States, people celebrated the growing strength of their country.

The Roaring Twenties The middle and late 1920s were a time of great prosperity in America and other countries. The economy grew rapidly. Some people enjoyed great wealth. During the 1920s, the United States was richer than any other country had ever been. Americans used their wealth to buy many new things. Many people bought cars, electric appliances, and radios for the first time. New art forms, such as jazz music, flourished. The economic boom and the fast-paced lifestyle of the decade earned it the nickname "the Roaring Twenties."

Economic Collapse This prosperity, however, did not last. In 1929, there was a stock market crash, or a sharp drop in the market value of companies owned by investors. The economy of the United States and other countries around the world went from boom to bust. The worldwide economic downturn of the 1930s is known as the Great Depression. The downturn lasted through the 1930s.

The economy during the Great Depression was so weak that about one fourth of the people in America couldn't find a job. Many took to the road, traveling around the country, desperately looking for work. More than a million people became homeless. Many people did not have enough to eat.

America was not alone in its hard times. Almost every country suffered from the economic downturn. The Great Depression continued until countries began to increase the production of goods. Unfortunately, these goods went to fight another world war, which began in 1939.

Graph Skills

The graph below shows the value of economic output per person each year from 1924 to 1940. A drop in output per person occurs when many people lose their jobs. The photo below shows a breadline during the 1930s. **Sequence** In what year was economic output per person lowest? **Infer** How might low output affect people's lives?

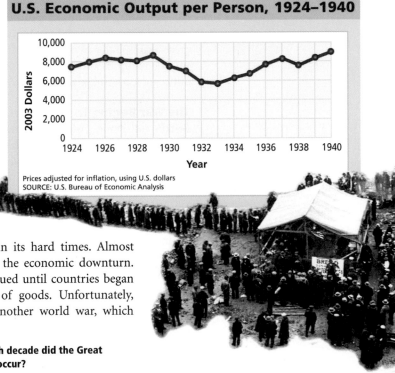

U.S. Economic Output per Person, 1924–1940

Prices adjusted for inflation, using U.S. dollars
SOURCE: U.S. Bureau of Economic Analysis

✔ **Reading Check** During which decade did the Great Depression occur?

The Great Depression [L2]

Guided Instruction

- Read The Great Depression with students and review the graph on this page.

- Have students describe life in the United States during the 1920s. (*The United States was richer than any other country had ever been; people bought goods such as cars, electronic appliances and radios; new art forms such as jazz music flourished.*)

- Ask students **What is a stock market crash?** (*a sharp drop in the value of companies owned by investors*)

- Ask students **What was the Great Depression like in the United States?** (*About one fourth of the population couldn't find a job. People traveled around the country looking for work, and many became homeless and did not have enough to eat.*)

Independent Practice

Have students add a box to the graphic organizer and fill it in with information about the Great Depression.

Monitor Progress

As students add to and fill in the graphic organizer, circulate and make sure individuals are choosing the correct ideas. Provide assistance as needed.

Differentiated Instruction

For English Language Learners [L2]
English language learners whose native language is Spanish will benefit from reading the Spanish version of *Guided Reading and Review* for this section.

📄 Guided Reading and Review (Spanish), **Medieval Times to Today Spanish Support,** p. 66

Answers

Graph Skills Sequence 1933 **Infer** People might not have enough money to buy things they need.

✔ **Reading Check** the 1930s

World War II

Guided Instruction

- **Vocabulary Builder** Clarify the high-use word **discontent** before reading.

- Read World War II with students.

- Ask students **During what year did World War II begin?** *(1939)* **When did the war end in Europe?** *(May 8, 1945)* **When did it end in Japan?** *(September 2, 1945)*

- Ask students **What event drew the United States into World War II?** *(The Japanese attacked Pearl Harbor.)*

- Ask students **What was the Holocaust?** *(Nazi Germany's mass killing of about 6 million Jewish people)*

Independent Practice

Have students complete the graphic organizer by adding boxes and filling them in with main ideas about World War II.

Monitor Progress

- Show *Section Reading Support Transparency MT 77* and ask students to check their graphic organizers individually. Go over key concepts and clarify key vocabulary as needed.

  📖 **Medieval Times to Today Transparencies,** *Section Reading Support Transparency MT 77*

Show *The Holocaust: In Memory of Millions.* Ask **When did the persecution of Jews begin in Germany?** *(in the early 1930s)*

- Tell students to fill in the last column of the *Reading Readiness Guide.* Probe for what they learned that confirms or invalidates each statement.

  Medieval Times to Today Teaching Resources, *Reading Readiness Guide,* p. 410

Answer

Infer Possible answer: Airplanes would allow soldiers to move quickly and to have a better vantage point of the battle than they would from the sea.

World War II Sea Battle
Sailors on the U.S.S. Enterprise ready planes to attack Japanese warships during the Battle of Midway in the Pacific Ocean.
Infer *How would airplanes be useful during a sea battle?*

World War II

The Great Depression hit Germany especially hard. The country was still suffering from the harsh peace treaty of Versailles. The German people felt that they had been unfairly punished for their part in World War I.

Nazi Germany A political leader named Adolf Hitler took advantage of German discontent. He led an organization called the Nazi Party. Hitler and the Nazis promised to make Germany great again. Hitler became the dictator of Germany. Nazi Germany built up its armed forces. Using threats and military force, Hitler took control of lands that bordered Germany.

The War Begins In 1939, Nazi Germany invaded Poland. Britain and France, who had pledged their support to Poland, then declared war on Germany. This was the beginning of **World War II,** the second global war of the 1900s.

Japan and Italy sided with Germany. Like Germany, they had turned to militarism and had invaded other countries. Germany, Japan, and Italy were known as the Axis Powers. Britain, France, and their allies were known as the Allied Powers, or the Allies.

In 1941, Japan attacked American forces at Pearl Harbor, Hawaii. The attack drew the United States into the war on the side of the Allies. Also in 1941, Hitler invaded the Soviet Union. The Soviet Union joined the Allies as well.

The Holocaust The Nazis committed some of the worst horrors of World War II. They tried to destroy entire groups of people, particularly Jews. The Nazis sent Jews and other minorities to concentration camps.

Find out about the Holocaust.

226 Medieval Times to Today

Background: Links Across Place

The Gulag During World War II, some Axis prisoners of war were sent to the Gulag, or a system of Soviet forced-labor camps. With its origins in 1919, these camps lasted until the mid-1950s. Those imprisoned included political dissidents, purged military and Communist Party members, World War II Axis prisoners of war, members of certain ethnic groups, criminals, and many other innocent people. It is believed that 15 to 30 million people died in the Gulag from severe working conditions, harsh climate, starvation, disease, and executions.

In the camps, prisoners were often worked to death, tortured, or simply killed. The Nazis killed about 6 million Jews. Nazi Germany's mass killing of Jewish people is known as the **Holocaust.**

Allied Victories In 1944, the Allies invaded France, which was occupied by Germany. They then attacked Germany from the west. Meanwhile, Soviet forces attacked Germany from the east. As the Allies advanced, they freed people in the brutal Nazi concentration camps. Soon, Allied forces surrounded Germany. The war ended in Europe when Germany surrendered on May 8, 1945.

Despite Germany's surrender, Japan fought on. Allied forces were slowly nearing Japan. U.S. President Harry S Truman believed that invading Japan itself would cost the lives of tens of thousands of Allied soldiers. To end the war quickly, President Truman ordered the first use of a new weapon called the atomic bomb.

The atomic bomb was the most powerful weapon ever used. One bomb could destroy an entire city. The United States dropped atomic bombs on the Japanese cities of Hiroshima and Nagasaki. Over 100,000 people were killed. Faced with this terrible weapon, the Japanese surrendered on September 2, 1945.

World War II was over. The Allied Powers had won the most destructive war in human history. An appalling 55 million people, soldiers and civilians alike, had died in the war.

✓ Reading Check What caused the Japanese to surrender?

Citizen Heroes

Audie Murphy

Audie Murphy was the most decorated American combat soldier of World War II. He received every medal for bravery that the United States awards. He also received medals from Belgium and France. Murphy fought in nine major campaigns in Europe, and he was wounded three times. He killed, captured, or wounded hundreds of enemy soldiers. After the war, he became a movie star. The movie *To Hell and Back* was based on his autobiography.

Section 1 Assessment

Key Terms
Review the key terms at the beginning of this section. Use each term in a sentence that explains its meaning.

Target Reading Skill
Apply your knowledge of the prefix *sur-*. In the fifth sentence under the heading "Allied Victories," on p. 227, what does the word *surrounded* mean?

Comprehension and Critical Thinking
1. (a) Sequence During what years was World War I fought?

(b) Identify Cause and Effect How did World War I help cause the Russian Revolution?
2. (a) Recall When did the Great Depression begin?
(b) Explain How did it affect people's lives?
3. (a) Identify In what year did Japan's surrender end World War II?
(b) Explain What weapon led to Japan's surrender?
(c) Contrast How did this weapon differ from weapons used in the past?

Writing Activity
Based on the events described in this section, write a brief essay describing the role of the United States in defeating Germany and Japan in World War II.

> **Writing Tip** Write at least two versions of your essay. The first version is called a rough draft. Revise it to make your writing clearer. Correct spelling and punctuation errors. Turn in your second or third draft.

Chapter 8 Section 1 **227**

Read **Citizen Heroes** on this page. Ask students **What did the United States award to Audie Murphy?** *(every medal for bravery that the United States awards)*

Assess and Reteach

Assess Progress L2
Have students complete the Section Assessment. Administer the *Section Quiz.*

 All in One **Medieval Times to Today Teaching Resources,** *Section Quiz,* p. 412

Reteach L1
If students need more instruction, have them read this section in the Reading and Vocabulary Study Guide.

 Chapter 8, Section 1, **Medieval Times to Today Reading and Vocabulary Study Guide,** pp. 85–87

Extend L3
Have students learn more about World War II by completing the *Small Group Activity: Designing World War II Posters.*

 All in One **Medieval Times to Today,** *Small Group Activity: Designing World War II Posters,* pp. 427–430

Answers

✓ Reading Check the dropping of the atomic bomb on two Japanese cities

Writing Activity
Use the *Rubric for Assessing a Writing Assignment* to evaluate students' essays.

 All in One **Medieval Times to Today Teaching Resources,** *Rubric for Assessing a Writing Assignment,* p. 438

Section 1 Assessment

Key Terms
Students' sentences should reflect knowledge of each Key Term.

Target Reading Skill
The prefix *sur-* means "above" or "over." *Surround* means to "be on all sides of."

Comprehension and Critical Thinking
1. (a) 1914–1918 **(b)** World War I created hardship for many Russians because they could not meet their basic needs; this caused them to revolt against the tsar.

2. (a) after the stock market crash of 1929 **(b)** About one-fourth of people could not find work and took to the road to find jobs; more than a million became homeless; many did not have enough to eat.

3. (a) 1945 **(b)** the atomic bomb **(c)** It was the most powerful weapon ever used.

Focus On The Cabinet War Rooms

L2

Guided Instruction

- Have students study the text, visuals and captions on pp. 228–229 as a class.

- Discuss how important government members during World War II used the Cabinet War Rooms. Ask students **Why were the Cabinet War Rooms necessary?** *(They protected Churchill and his advisors from heavy bombing by German aircrafts and threats of invasion.)*

- Ask students to discuss how the Cabinet War Rooms were protected from attacks. *(They had concrete, steel beams, heavy timber, and a special ventilation system.)*

- Have students work in small groups to answer the Assessment questions.

Focus On
The Cabinet War Rooms

In May 1940, Great Britain's Prime Minister Winston Churchill entered one of the basement rooms beneath a government building in London and said, "This is the room from which I'll direct the war." The room Churchill spoke of was part of the Cabinet War Rooms, a secret complex of specially equipped and protected underground rooms. During World War II, London suffered heavy bombing by German aircraft and threats of invasion. At such times, Churchill and his advisors met in the Cabinet War Rooms to discuss the war and to plan for their country's defense. Concrete, steel beams, heavy timber, and a special ventilation system protected the rooms from attack.

Map Room Annex Officers prepared military reports in this room.

Underground Headquarters The Map Room, shown at the right, was the most important room in the underground complex. Here, army, air force, and naval officers gathered up-to-date information about the war's progress. These officers, called mapkeepers, prepared regular reports for their superiors and marked ship positions, battle fronts, and supply-line information on maps hung around the room. Some rooms within the complex were used only occasionally, but the Map Room was manned 24 hours a day throughout the war.

The Cabinet War Rooms also included offices, telephone switchboards, staff dormitories, a mess room where snacks were served, and a transatlantic telephone room—disguised as a bathroom—where Churchill had a direct phone line to Franklin Roosevelt, the President of the United States.

Map Room Mapkeepers used pushpins to record allied and enemy movements on wall maps.

228 *Medieval Times to Today*

Differentiated Instruction

For Gifted and Talented L3
Ask students to find out if American President Franklin D. Roosevelt had a war room similar to Churchill's during World War II. Have them create posters based on their findings.

For English Language Learners L1
To better understand the purposes of individual Cabinet War Rooms, ask students to write "Map Room" on a piece of paper and draw a small map symbol next to the words. Then ask them to write the different types of rooms as described in the text and create symbols to represent activities that occurred in each room.

Winston Churchill inspects a bomb crater in London, 1940.

Map Room Exhibit
This is how the Map Room looked while it was in use. Today, the Cabinet War Rooms are a museum.

Telephone switchboard operators in the Cabinet War Rooms, 1945

Prime Minister's Room
This was Winston Churchill's office, from which he made some of his wartime radio broadcasts. Occasionally, he slept here.

Assessment

Describe What were the Cabinet War Rooms?

Infer Why was it important for Churchill and his war advisors to remain safe from enemy attacks?

Independent Practice

Ask students what features they would include in a Cabinet War Room of their own. Have students create a floor map of their own Cabinet War Rooms using the information on pp. 228–229 as a guide. Direct students to label each room. Then ask them to write a sentence next to each room that describes the room's function. Use the *Rubric for Assessing a Writing Assignment* to evaluate students' work.

All in One Medieval Times to Today Teaching Resources, *Rubric for Assessing a Writing Assignment,* p. 438

Background: Links Across Time

Winston Churchill (1874–1965) Beginning his career as a soldier and journalist, Winston Churchill switched to politics and was elected to the British Parliament in 1900 at the age of 26. During World War II, Churchill became Prime Minister. He was known for his inspiring speeches and leadership during the war, in which he encouraged the British to resist the Nazis. In 1953, Churchill was both knighted and awarded the Nobel Peace Prize in Literature for his oratory and writing. In 1963, the United States Congress awarded him honorary U.S. citizenship. He died in 1965 in London at the age of 90.

Answers

Assessment

Describe The Cabinet War Rooms were a secret complex of specially equipped and protected underground rooms. **Infer** Possible answer: They needed a place where they could discuss the war and plan for their country's defense. If Churchill or his war advisors were injured, it could have seriously damaged Great Britain's efforts to win the war.

Section 2
Step-by-Step Instruction

Objectives

Social Studies
1. Learn how the Cold War pitted the United States against the Soviet Union.
2. Discover how dozens of former colonies gained independence.

Reading/Language Arts
Recognize word origins to determine the meaning of unfamiliar words.

Prepare to Read

Build Background Knowledge L2

In this section students will learn about the world in the decades following World War II. Using the Give One, Get One strategy (TE, p. T37), ask students to preview the photos and captions and list three people that lived during this time period. (*Possible answers: George H.W. Bush, Boris Yeltsin, Mohandas Gandhi*) As students share their answers, write their responses on the board. Then have them share any additional information they know about these people with the class.

Set a Purpose for Reading L2
- Preview the Objectives.

- Read each statement in the *Reading Readiness Guide* aloud. Ask students to mark the statements true or false.

  All in One Medieval Times to Today Teaching Resources, *Reading Readiness Guide,* p. 414

- Have students discuss the statements in pairs or groups of four, then mark their worksheets again. Use the Numbered Heads participation strategy (TE, p. T36) to call on students to share their group's perspectives.

Vocabulary Builder
Preview Key Terms L2
Pronounce each Key Term, then ask students to say the word with you. Provide a simple explanation such as, "Developing countries are poor and have little industry, while developed countries are richer and have a greater amount of industry."

Section 2 The Postwar World

Prepare to Read

Objectives
In this section you will
1. Learn how the Cold War pitted the United States against the Soviet Union.
2. Discover how dozens of former colonies gained independence.

Taking Notes
As you read this section, identify important events of the Cold War and the era of independence. Copy the timeline below, add dates as needed, and record events with the dates when they happened.

1945 ——————————————— 1991

Target Reading Skill
Recognize Word Origins The word *decade,* on page 234, contains the root *dec-*, which means "ten" in Latin and Greek. The ending *-ad* or *-ade* refers to a group of elements. As you read, use your knowledge of these word parts to determine the meaning of this word.

Key Terms
- **postwar** (POHST wawr) *adj.* after war; after World War II

- **superpower** (SOO pur pow ur) *n.* a powerful country that has great influence over other countries
- **Cold War** (kohld wawr) *n.* a period of tension between the United States and the Soviet Union from 1945 to 1991
- **developing countries** (dih VEL up ing KUN treez) *n.* poor countries that have little industry
- **developed countries** (dih VEL upt KUN treez) *n.* rich countries that have much industry

Winston Churchill speaking in Fulton, Missouri, in 1946

It was late winter, 1946. Former British Prime Minister Winston Churchill was in the college town of Fulton, Missouri. World War II had ended just a few months before. Churchill was touring a country still jubilant in its victory. The Soviet Union had been an ally of the United States and Britain during the war. But Churchill's words sent chills down people's spines:

> **"[An] iron curtain has descended across the Continent [of Europe]. Behind that line lie all the capitals . . . of Central and Eastern Europe. . . . [A]ll these famous cities and the populations around them . . . are subject . . . to a very high . . . measure of control from Moscow. . . ."**

Churchill meant that the Soviet Union controlled Eastern Europe from its capital in Moscow. He also meant that the Soviet system of government would deprive these people of freedom. It was as if an "iron curtain" now separated these people from the freedoms and democracies of Western Europe and the United States.

World War II was over. Would the **postwar** world, or the world after World War II, bring liberation, or something else?

Target Reading Skill L2

Recognize Word Origins Point out the Target Reading Skill. Review with students that knowing the meaning of roots can help students to figure out unfamiliar words.

Model how to recognize word origins by finding the meaning of *liberation* at the bottom of p. 230. (*The Latin root* liber- *means "free" and the ending* -ion *means "the act of."*

Therefore, liberation *is "the act of becoming free."*)

Give students *Recognize Word Origins.* Have them complete the activity in their groups.

All in One Medieval Times to Today Teaching Resources, *Recognize Word Origins,* p. 422

The Cold War

Although they had cooperated during World War II, the United States and the Soviet Union had different economies and governments. The Soviet Union was a communist country. The government controlled property and businesses. In contrast, the United States was a capitalist country. Under capitalism, individuals, instead of the government, control property and businesses.

Beginning in 1945, the Soviet Union took control of Eastern European countries and forced them to adopt communism. The iron curtain separated those countries from the democratic countries of Western Europe. The Soviet Union wanted to expand its influence and its communist system throughout the world.

Growing Tensions In 1949, two crucial events increased U.S. concerns about the spread of communism. First, communists came to power in China. They were led by Mao Zedong. Second, the Soviets developed an atomic bomb. Before that time, only the United States had had this powerful weapon. The United States adopted a policy of containment, an effort to halt, or contain, the spread of communism.

By 1949, most of the countries of the world were on one of two sides. On one side were capitalist and democratic countries. They were led by the United States. On the other side were communist countries, which were led by the Soviet Union. Both the United States and the Soviet Union were superpowers. A **superpower** is a powerful country that has great influence over other countries.

Superpower Rivalry The period of tension between the United States and the Soviet Union from 1945 to 1991 is called the **Cold War.** It is called a "cold" war because the superpowers did not fight each other directly in a "hot" war. However, the Cold War was a frightening time because both countries built enough nuclear bombs to destroy the world's people.

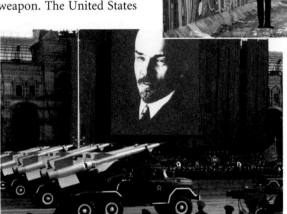

A World Divided
At the top, planes flying above the U.S.S. Eisenhower reflect U.S. air and sea power during the Cold War. At the center, a Soviet soldier guards the Berlin Wall, along the "iron curtain." At the bottom, a parade in Moscow displays Soviet missiles.
Analyze Images *How do these images reflect Cold War tensions?*

Instruct

The Cold War   L2

Guided Instruction

- **Vocabulary Builder** Clarify the high-use words **ally, crucial,** and **collapse** before reading.

- Read The Cold War, using the Choral Reading strategy (TE, p.T34).

- Ask students **How were the Soviet and United States governments different in the mid-1900s?** *(The Soviet Union was a communist country in which the government controlled property and businesses, while the United States was a capitalist country in which individuals controlled properties and businesses.)*

- Ask students **What two events caused the United States to become concerned about the spread of communism?** *(Communists came to power in China, and the Soviets developed an atomic bomb.)*

- Ask students **What was the Cold War?** *(The period of tension between the United States and the Soviet Union from 1945 to 1991.)* **Why was it called a "cold" war?** *(The superpowers did not fight each other directly in a "hot" war.)*

Vocabulary Builder

Use the information below to teach students this section's high-use words.

High-Use Word	Definition and Sample Sentence
ally, p. 230	*n.* a person or country that helps another Britain and the United States were **allies** during World War II.
crucial, p. 231	*adj.* extremely important It is **crucial** that she has proper shoes for running, or she could injure herself.
collapse, p. 233	*v.* to fail suddenly If there is no snow, his ski rental business will **collapse** and have to close.

Answer

Analyze Images The three photos show that the militaries of the Soviet Union and the United States were prepared for war.

Guided Instruction (continued)

- Ask students to name two wars that were a result of the Cold War. *(the Korean War and the Vietnam War)*

- Ask students **What did these two wars have in common?** *(Possible answer: The United States supported and sent troops to the southern parts of each country. Communists supported the northern parts.)*

MAP MASTER™ Skills Activity — **Independence Since 1945**

Place Since 1945, many new nations have gained independence. **Read a Map Key** In which decade did many Eastern European nations gain independence? **Identify Effects** How was the spread of independence in that region connected with the end of the Cold War?

Go Online
PHSchool.com Use Web Code lgp-8821 for step-by-step map skills practice.

ARCTIC OCEAN

Beaufort Sea

Hudson Bay

NORTH AMERICA

ATLANTIC OCEAN

PACIFIC OCEAN

BAHAMAS (1973)
BELIZE (1981)
JAMAICA (1962)
ANTIGUA & BARBUDA (1981)
ST. KITTS & NEVIS (1983)
ST. LUCIA (1979)
ST. VINCENT & THE GRENADINES (1979)
DOMINICA (1978)
BARBADOS (1966)
GRENADA (1974)
TRINIDAD AND TOBAGO (1962)
GUYANA (1966)
SURINAME (1975)

SAMOA (1962)
TONGA (1970)

SOUTH AMERICA

KEY
Decade country gained independence*

Before 1945	1970s
1940s	1980s
1950s	1990s
1960s	2000s

—— National border
- - - Disputed border
*Specific year shown in parentheses on map

Hot Spots in the Cold War The Cold War also resulted in some hot wars. In 1950, communist North Korea invaded noncommunist South Korea. During the Korean War, the United States and other democratic countries sent troops to support South Korea. Communist China supported North Korea. The war ended in 1953 in a stalemate.

In Southeast Asia, Vietnam had split into communist North Vietnam and noncommunist South Vietnam. In the 1960s, the United States sent troops to support South Vietnam and to fight communism in the Vietnam War. Thousands of Americans and millions of Vietnamese died. In 1975, North Vietnam defeated South Vietnam. The whole country became communist.

American soldiers in Vietnam, 1966

232 Medieval Times to Today

Background: Links Across Place

Berlin Wall After World War II, Germany was divided into communist East Germany and democratic West Germany. The city of Berlin, in East Germany, was also divided. Many East Germans tried to flee west, and in 1961 East Germany built the Berlin Wall to prevent East Germans from leaving the country. The Berlin Wall became a symbol of the gulf between eastern and western Europe. About 5,000 East Germans escaped across the wall, about 5,000 were captured, and 191 were killed while trying to cross the wall. In 1989, communism fell in East Germany and the Berlin Wall was torn down, uniting Berlin and Germany more than 40 years after the end of World War II.

Answers

MAP MASTER Skills Activity **Read a Map Key** the 1990s **Identify Effects** The Cold War ended as a result of the collapse of communism in the Soviet Union, allowing many countries in the region to declare their independence.

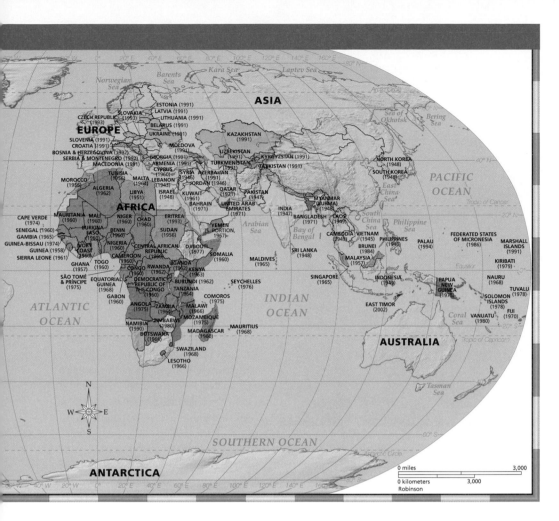

- Remind students that many communist countries began to fall in 1989. Ask students **When did the Soviet government fall?** *(1991)*

- Ask students **What happened as a result of the collapse of the Soviet government?** *(The Soviet Union broke up into independent nations. Russia adopted capitalism and developed friendlier relations with the United States.)*

Independent Practice
Ask students to create the Taking Notes graphic organizer on a blank piece of paper. Then have them fill in the timeline with important events and dates of the Cold War.

Monitor Progress
As students fill in the graphic organizer, circulate and make sure individuals are choosing appropriate events and dates. Provide assistance as needed.

The Cold War Ends The Cold War ended in 1991, when communist rule collapsed in the Soviet Union. Most of Eastern Europe had rejected communism in 1989. Communism ended because Eastern Europeans and Soviet citizens demanded reforms. It also ended because capitalism produced more wealth than communism, and communism could no longer compete.

When the communist government fell in 1991, the Soviet Union broke up into several independent nations. The largest and most powerful of these nations, Russia, adopted capitalism. Russia also developed friendlier relations with the United States.

U.S. President George H. W. Bush with Russian President Boris Yeltsin, 1993, after the Cold War

✓ **Reading Check** Why did the United States send troops to Vietnam?

Differentiated Instruction

For Advanced Readers ▣ L3
Students can learn more about how geography has influenced history, such as America's involvement in the Vietnam War, by completing *Activity Shop Interdisciplinary: History Quiz Wizards.*

All in One Medieval Times to Today, *Activity Shop Interdisciplinary: History Quiz Wizards,* pp. 431–432

For Special Needs Students ▣ L1
Students who learn best visually may benefit from studying the map on pp. 232–233. As students read the text under A New Era of Independence on pp. 234–235, ask them to locate and place their fingers on the areas on the map that are mentioned in the text.

Answer

✓ **Reading Check** to support South Vietnam and fight against communism in the Vietnam War

A New Era of Independence L2

Guided Instruction

- Ask students to read A New Era of Independence. Review the map on pp. 232–233 with students while discussing colonies that obtained their independence.

- Ask students **Which continents had European colonies in 1914?** *(Asia, Africa, and parts of the Americas)* **What happened in these areas when Europeans colonized them?** *(Europeans ruled the colonies; local people had little or no part in their government; local economies were damaged.)*

- Ask students **After World War II, how did Europeans try to keep their colonies?** *(by letting local people take part in the colonial governments)*

- Ask students **Why do you think European powers were reluctant to give up their colonies?** *(Possible answer: Products from these colonies benefited European economies and gave European powers more strength.)*

Independent Practice

Have students complete the timeline by filling in important dates and events in the era of independence.

Monitor Progress

- Show *Section Support Transparency MT 78* and ask students to check their graphic organizers individually. Go over key concepts and clarify key vocabulary as needed.

    📖 **Medieval Times to Today Transparencies,** *Section Reading Support Transparency MT 78*

- Tell students to fill in the last column of the *Reading Readiness Guide.* Probe for what they learned that confirms or invalidates each statement.

    All in One **Medieval Times to Today Teaching Resources,** *Reading Readiness Guide,* p. 414

🎯 Target Reading Skill L2

Recognize Word Origins As a follow up, ask students to answer the Target reading Skill question in the Student Edition. *(ten)*

Answer

Compare People are gathered together, waving flags.

234 *Medieval Times to Today*

A New Era of Independence

The Cold War shaped world events for more than 40 years. However, another major development affected the postwar world. Many new countries, especially in Africa and Asia, gained independence, or freedom from outside control, in the decades following World War II. These countries had been colonies of European nations.

Celebrating Independence
These children in Swaziland are celebrating the second anniversary, in 1970, of their country's independence. **Compare** *How is this celebration like American celebrations on the Fourth of July?*

Recognize Word Origins
Based on the root *dec-*, how many years do you think there are in a *decade?*

The Colonial World In the centuries before World War II, Europeans had colonized much of the world. By 1914, European colonies covered much of Asia and almost all of Africa. There were also European colonies still left in the Americas, particularly in the Caribbean Islands.

When Europeans colonized an area, they did so for their own benefit and not for the people who lived there. Europeans ruled over the colonies, and local people had little or no part in their government. Europeans often damaged local economies. For example, native peoples were forced to grow crops that would benefit the colonizing country instead of crops they could use to feed themselves.

Desire for Independence Colonized peoples resented this treatment. They wanted to end European rule. During World War II, many colonies had helped their colonial rulers, and they wanted to be rewarded. Meanwhile, the United States and other countries had promised that the peoples of the world would be able to choose their own governments after the war. As a result, demands for independence increased after World War II.

New Countries World War II had weakened the European powers. They found it hard to deny these demands for independence. At first, they tried to keep their colonies by letting local people take part in colonial governments. But the colonies demanded full independence.

In the decades after World War II, more than 50 countries gained independence. Most of these countries were in Africa, and many became independent between 1957 and 1965. Some countries won independence peacefully. Others had to fight wars for their independence.

234 Medieval Times to Today

Skills for Life Skills Mini Lesson

Drawing Inferences and Conclusions

1. Teach the skill by pointing out that to draw inferences and conclusions you need to identify what is true, make a logical guess, state inferences in an "if …then" format, use inferences to draw a conclusion, and check the conclusion.

2. Help students practice the skill by making an inference about why Europeans didn't let colonized peoples participate in government.

3. Point out that the inference above may support the conclusion on p. 234 that Europeans colonized an area for their own benefit, and not for the people that lived there. Ask students to find another inference to support this conclusion.

A Global Movement Great movements and great leaders appeared in many colonized countries. India is a good example. Mohandas Gandhi (moh HAHN dus GAHN dee) led this British colony to independence. Gandhi called for civil disobedience—the breaking of a law on purpose in order to protest it. He urged people to protest without using force—to be nonviolent. He helped Indians find ways to reduce their dependence on Britain. India won its independence in 1947.

Challenges for the New Countries Even after the former colonies won independence, they faced serious challenges. Often, their leaders lacked experience in government. Most of the new countries had had their borders drawn by Europeans. They often included people of different ethnic groups who did not get along. Civil wars sometimes resulted.

Poverty was another challenge that the new nations faced. Most of the world's former colonies are **developing countries,** or poor countries with few industries. The United States and the former colonial powers are **developed countries,** which have more wealth and many industries. Developing countries are sometimes also called third-world countries. Some developing countries have managed to improve their economies.

✓ **Reading Check** What is the difference between developing and developed countries?

Indian independence leader Mohandas Gandhi, on the right, at a conference in Simla, India

---

Section 2 Assessment

Key Terms
Review the key terms at the beginning of this section. Use each term in a sentence that explains its meaning.

🎯 Target Reading Skill
Apply your knowledge of the word part *dec-*. What do words such as *decimal* and *decathlon* have in common?

Comprehension and Critical Thinking
1. (a) Identify What was the Cold War?

(b) Explain Which countries did it involve?
(c) Contrast How did it differ from other wars?
2. (a) Recall Which countries gained independence in the decades after World War II?
(b) Describe What problems have they faced?
(c) Draw Conclusions How might they solve those problems?

Writing Activity
Prepare a list of questions about life during the Cold War. Interview a parent or another adult about his or her memories of life during the Cold War. Write down their answers to your questions.

Go Online
PHSchool.com
For: An activity on the end of colonialism
Visit: PHSchool.com
Web Code: lgd-8802

Objective

Learn how to interpret line graphs.

Prepare to Read

Build Background Knowledge L2

Ask students to think about their final grades in social studies during each school year. Do they remember what their grades were last year? Do they think they did or will do better this year? How will they keep track? Tell students that marking their grades on a graph is one way to keep track of their progress over their school career.

Instruct

Interpreting Line Graphs L2

Guided Instruction

■ Read the steps as a class to learn how to interpret a line graph. Then write them on the board.

■ Practice the skill by following the steps on p. 237 as a class. Model each step in the activity. Identify the title of the graph (*Population of Dallas, Texas, 1910–2000*), read the labels and identify the statistics on the graph (*x- axis shows every ten years and y- axis shows the number of people in increments of 100,000*), and interpret the statistics to draw conclusions about the information. (*The graph shows a continued increase in Dallas' population from 1910–2000 with a dramatic increase beginning around 1940.*)

Independent Practice

Assign *Skills for Life* and have students complete it individually.

All in One **Medieval Times to Today,** *Skills for Life*, p. 426

Monitor Progress

As students are completing *Skills for Life*, circulate to make sure individuals are applying the skill steps effectively. Provide assistance as needed.

 Interpreting Line Graphs

Makiko was almost finished with her report on Dallas, Texas. But whenever she tried to write about the number of people living in Dallas at different times in the city's history, it sounded too confusing. Maybe a graph or a diagram would be better. "I could show a population map of the city for each decade, but that's too many different maps," she thought. "Or I could make a table showing the population every 10 years, but that wouldn't show the changes at a glance. I need a graph that will show growth over time."

Downtown Dallas about 1910 (top) and today (directly above)

M akiko needed a line graph, which shows statistics as connected points. The line that connects the points shows a pattern over time.

Learn the Skill

Follow these steps to interpret a line graph:

1 **Read the title.** The title identifies the basic information shown on the graph.

2 **Read the graph labels.** An axis is a line at the side or bottom of a graph. Both the horizontal axis, or *x*-axis, and the vertical axis, or *y*-axis, have labels that give more specific information about the data. Also notice the intervals between the dates or other numbers.

3 **Read the numbers on the graph.** Use the lines on the grid to help you find the *x*- and *y*- values of the points on the graph.

4 **Interpret the numbers and draw conclusions.** Compare data to find similarities, differences, increases, or decreases. Draw a conclusion about what trends, or general changes, are shown by the graph.

236 Medieval Times to Today

Practice the Skill

Use the steps you just learned to read the line graph at the right.

1 Read the title. What is the subject of this graph?

2 Read the labels. What does the *x*-axis show? What does the *y*-axis show? How is each axis divided?

3 In what year was the population of Dallas just over 400,000? Interpret several other points on the graph.

4 What general trend does the line on the graph show? Look more closely to find more specific increases or decreases. For example, when did Dallas's population change the fastest? Write a conclusion of two or three sentences telling what you learned from the graph.

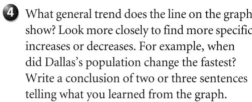

Population of Dallas, Texas, 1910–2000

SOURCE: U.S. Bureau of Labor Statistics

United States Employment, 1900–2000

SOURCE: U.S. Bureau of Labor Statistics

Apply the Skill

The line graph at the left has two lines instead of one. But it works the same way, and you can apply the same steps to interpret it. Write a conclusion of two or three sentences telling what you learned from this graph.

Chapter 8 **237**

Assess and Reteach

Assess Progress   **L2**
Ask students to do the Apply the Skill activity.

Reteach   **L1**
If students have difficulty applying the skill steps, have them review how to analyze graphic data using the interactive Social Studies Skills Tutor CD-ROM.

Analyzing Graphic Data, **Social Studies Skills Tutor CD-ROM**

Extend   **L3**
■ To extend the lesson, ask students to complete *Reading a Line Graph*.

All in One **Medieval Times to Today,** *Reading a Line Graph,* p. 433

■ Ask students to examine how the graph on *Reading a Line Graph* compares to the graphs on p. 237. *(Both show numbers of people on the y-axis and years on the x-axis. The line in the worksheet is curved, while the ones on p. 237 are composed of straight line segments connected by dots.)*

Answer
Apply the Skill

Students' conclusions should note that the graph shows a steady decrease in the percentage of agricultural jobs from 1900 to 2000 and a steady increase in the percentage of nonagricultural jobs during the same time period. Students might also include other details, such as the fact that by 1960, agricultural jobs accounted for less than ten percent of jobs in the United States.

Chapter 8 **237**

Section 3
Step-by-Step Instruction

Objectives

Social Studies

1. Learn how modern technology has transformed the world.
2. Explore how migration, trade, and closer economic ties have linked different parts of the world.
3. Consider the new challenges that the world will face during your lifetime.

Reading/Language Arts

Use word parts such as roots and suffixes to recognize and pronounce unfamiliar words.

Prepare to Read

Build Background Knowledge **L2**

In this section students will learn about advances in technology from the twentieth century to today, and obtain a brief look at the state of the world. Ask students to preview the section's headings, photos, and captions. Then conduct an Idea Wave (TE, p. T37) to have students answer the following question: **What do the headings, photos, and captions tell you about the world today?** Record students' answers on the board.

Set a Purpose for Reading **L2**

■ Preview the Objectives.

■ Read each statement in the *Reading Readiness Guide* aloud. Ask students to mark the statements true or false.

All in One **Medieval Times to Today Teaching Resources,** *Reading Readiness Guide,* p. 418

■ Have students discuss the statements in pairs or groups of four, then mark their worksheets again. Use the Numbered Heads participation strategy (TE, p. T36) to call on students to share their group's perspectives.

Vocabulary Builder
Preview Key Terms **L2**

Pronounce each Key Term, then ask students to say the word with you. Provide a simple explanation such as, "Terrorism is the use of violence to control people through fear."

Section 3 The World Today

Prepare to Read

Objectives

In this section you will

1. Learn how modern technology has transformed the world.
2. Explore how migration, trade, and closer economic ties have linked different parts of the world.
3. Consider the new challenges that the world will face during your lifetime.

Taking Notes

As you read this section, look for facts about the effects of technology, economic links, and new challenges. Copy the diagram below, and record your findings in it.

```
              The World Today
  ┌──────────┬──────────────┬──────────────┐
  │Technology│   Economic   │     New      │
  │          │    Links     │  Challenges  │
  ├──────────┼──────────────┼──────────────┤
  │  •       │  •           │  •           │
  │  •       │  •           │  •           │
  └──────────┴──────────────┴──────────────┘
```

⟳ Target Reading Skill

Use Word Parts When you come across an unfamiliar word, break the word into parts to help you recognize and pronounce it. You may find roots, prefixes, or suffixes. A root is the base of the word that often has meaning by itself. A suffix attaches to the end of a root and changes the root's function or meaning. For example, the word *transportation* combines the root *transport* and the suffix *-ation*, meaning "action" or "process."

Key Terms

• **millennium** (mih LEN ee um) *n.* a period of one thousand years
• **trading bloc** (TRAYD ing blahk) *n.* a group of countries that have agreed to reduce barriers to trade
• **terrorism** (TEHR ur iz um) *n.* the threat or use of violence to cause fear

New Year's fireworks in Paris, France, 2000

238 Medieval Times to Today

It was December 31, 1999. Around the globe people were celebrating the start of a new year, a new decade, and a new century. Above all, they were celebrating a new **millennium,** or a period of one thousand years. Huge parties, parades, and spectacular fireworks displays were held in cities around the world—in fact, most of the world seemed to join in one gigantic festival.

There was only one problem: The new millennium didn't technically begin until the year 2001! But it didn't seem to matter. It was a time for celebrating human accomplishments.

It was a time for reflecting on all the many historical events of the past millennium, events that fill up much of this book. It was a time to think about where those events had led us and to take stock of the state of the world. It was also a time to think about the world's future prospects. For the world of today and the world of the future are the worlds in which you will live. The world of the future is the world that you will help shape.

⟳ Target Reading Skill **L2**

Use Word Parts Point out the Target Reading Skill. Tell students that they can figure out unfamiliar words by looking for roots and suffixes in the word.

Model using word parts to find the meaning of *accomplishments* in the second paragraph on p. 238. Tell students that the root word, *accomplish,* means "to bring about or succeed in reaching a goal." The suffix, *-ment,* means "the act of." Therefore, accomplishment means "the act of accomplishing, or the act of succeeding in reaching a goal."

Give students *Use Roots and Suffixes.* Have them complete the activity in their groups.

All in One **Medieval Times to Today,** *Use Roots and Suffixes,* p. 423

The Advance of Technology

One key process shaping the world to come is the steady development of technology. Until the mid-1800s, there were only two ways to deliver a message from North America to Europe or Asia: in person or on paper. In either case, the message would have taken weeks to reach its destination by sailing ship. Today, information can travel almost instantly via satellite and radio transmission. People can cross oceans in a few hours by plane.

Transportation In 1900, automobiles were a rarity. Today, automobiles are common throughout the world. Huge networks of roads link places that were once isolated. The airplane was developed in the early 1900s. Later in the 1900s, people walked on the moon. Satellites orbiting Earth helped people communicate and study the stars. By the end of the 1900s, space probes had traveled to distant planets.

Communication The first telephones were invented in the late 1800s. Few people could afford telephones, which had to be connected to wires. As the 1900s progressed, radio and then television brought new possibilities for communication. They allowed people to hear and see events thousands of miles away.

The most recent advance in communication has been the development of the Internet. The Internet is a worldwide network of computers. Using electronic mail, or e-mail, people can send and receive information across long distances in a fraction of a second. New handheld devices are making communication much more convenient.

Health and Comfort Since 1900, better ways of understanding and treating diseases have saved millions of lives. Clean water supplies, vaccines to prevent illness, and other medical advances have allowed people to live longer, healthier lives.

✓ **Reading Check** How does information travel between continents today?

Links to
Science

Science Versus Technology
Science and technology are not the same thing. Science is using the scientific method to gain knowledge about the world. Technology is the way people make practical use of knowledge. The NASA technician in the top photo is using technology to monitor the Mars rover shown in the center photo. The rover uses a variety of technologies to conduct science. Its cameras provide images of the surface of Mars (background photo). It also analyzes the composition of Martian rocks and soil.

Chapter 8 Section 3 **239**

Vocabulary Builder

Use the information below to teach students this section's high-use words.

High-Use Word	Definition and Sample Sentence
rarity, p. 239	*n.* something that is uncommon Snow is a **rarity** in the warm southern climate of the United States.
relocate, p. 240	*v.* to move to a new place They decided to **relocate** to a new town.
consumption, p. 241	*n.* the act of using If the **consumption** of oil continues to increase, we may run out of it.

A Smaller World

L2

Guided Instruction

- **Vocabulary Builder** Clarify the high-use word **relocate** before reading.

- Read A Smaller World and review the cartogram on p. 240 with students. As students read, circulate and make sure individuals can answer the Reading Check question.

- Ask students **Why is it easier for people to relocate today?** *(There are improved transportation technologies.)*

- Ask students **Why might people move to a different country to find work?** *(Possible answer: There might not be enough work in their own country, or a job in another country might pay more money.)*

- Ask students **Why do you think an American company might employ workers in another country?** *(Possible answer: It might be cheaper to pay people in other countries to do the work that Americans could do here; the people with the skills to do the work might live in other countries.)*

Independent Practice

Have students continue to record important facts about economic links in their graphic organizers.

Monitor Progress

As students continue to fill in the graphic organizer, circulate and make sure individuals are choosing the correct facts. Provide assistance as needed.

Answers

MAP MASTER Skills Activity **Identify** The countries are not the same size on the cartogram as they are on the map. **Infer** On the map, the size of a country is based on land area, while on the cartogram, it is based on the percentage of world exports the country has.

Go Online PHSchool.com Students may practice their map skills using the interactive online version of this map.

MAP MASTER Skills Activity

The World's Leading Exporters

United Kingdom 4.3%
Sweden 1.3%
Canada 3.9%
Netherlands 3.8%
Russia 1.7%
Republic of Korea 2.5%
United States 10.7%
Germany 9.5%
Belgium 3.3%
Taiwan 2.1%
China 8.2%
Japan 6.5%
Mexico 2.5%
France 5.1%
Philippines 0.6%
Brazil 0.9%
Saudi Arabia 1.1%
India 0.8%
Spain 1.8%
Italy 3.9%
Singapore 1.0%
Malaysia 1.4%
Indonesia 0.9%
South Africa 0.5%
Australia 1.0%

KEY
An area this size represents 0.1% of world exports in 2002.

Movement Each country's size on this cartogram reflects its share of the world's total exports in 2002. **Identify** Compare this cartogram with the map titled European Empires, 1914, on page 221. How are countries' sizes larger or smaller on the cartogram than they are on the map? **Infer** What explains the differences?

Go Online PHSchool.com Use Web Code lgp-8831 for step-by-step map skills practice.

An immigrant from Turkey working in Germany

240 Medieval Times to Today

A Smaller World

Two hundred years ago, when traveling across oceans took weeks or months, people seldom traveled far from home. Their food and clothes came mainly from local sources. Modern technologies have changed all of that.

Migration and Trade Better transportation technologies have helped more people relocate. People tend to go where the jobs are, even when those jobs are in different countries. Millions of people from developing countries have moved to find work in developed countries such as the United States, Canada, and Germany.

Transportation and communication technologies have also increased trade among nations. Someone can now order a product from another country almost instantly via the Internet. That same product can arrive overnight by plane.

Differentiated Instruction

For Less Proficient Readers **L1**

Students may have trouble understanding the cartogram on p. 240. Assign *Reading a Cartogram* for students to complete in pairs.

All in One Medieval Times to Today Teaching Resources, *Reading a Cartogram,* p. 434

For Gifted and Talented **L3**

Ask students to select five countries shown on the cartogram on p. 240. Have students conduct research to create a table showing the products each country exports and to which countries they are exported. Students can create the table in poster form. Display students' posters around the classroom if you wish.

A Global Economy New transportation and communication technologies have made it easier to do business across borders. A company based in the United States may employ engineers in India. It may have a factory in Honduras where its products are actually made. And it may have an office selling those products in Italy. This kind of worldwide business is possible with the help of technologies such as e-mail and air travel.

In some regions, countries have formed **trading blocs,** or groups of countries that have agreed to work together to reduce barriers to trade. Examples include the European Union in Europe and the North American Free Trade Agreement, or NAFTA, linking Canada, the United States, and Mexico.

✔ **Reading Check** What is a trading bloc?

New Challenges

The world today is filled with challenges. The more you know about them, the better you will be prepared to deal with them.

Poverty and Population Poverty is a serious problem in many parts of the world. Almost half of the world's population lives on less than $2.15 a day per person. Hunger and poverty are widespread in parts of Latin America, Africa, and Asia.

In developing countries, populations are growing rapidly. For poor parents, having many children often makes sense. By the time these children reach their teens, they are expected to help support the family. More teenage children can provide more food for the family. As parents get older, having many children helps ensure their security in old age.

However, growing populations burden developing countries. Often there is not enough farmland or enough food for everyone to eat.

The Environment Growing populations in the developing world put stress on the environment. When forests are cut to create more farmland, valuable soil may be washed away and flooding may occur downstream.

In the developed world, the consumption of goods and the use of cars and trucks pollute the air, water, and soil. Heavy use of pesticides and fertilizers on farmland may also cause water pollution. However, using resources more carefully and efficiently can help solve these problems.

> **Target Skill** If *-ation* or *-tion* means "action" or "process," what does *transportation* mean? What does *communication* mean?

Rain Forest Loss in Brazil
Only a few trees remain from a rain forest that was cleared to create pasture for cattle in Brazil. **Identify Causes** *How might growing populations lead to the clearance of rain forests?*

Background: Global Perspectives

Mother Teresa (1910–1997) Born and baptized a Roman Catholic in Albania, Mother Teresa joined the Sisters of Loretto in Ireland in 1928. She was soon sent to India, where she taught for seventeen years. In 1946, she experienced what she believed to be a divine "calling" and devoted herself to caring for the sick and poor. She moved into the slums and founded the Order of the Missionaries of Charity in 1948. She adopted Indian citizenship as well as the sari for her order's habit. She founded a hospice for the terminally ill, centers for the aged and disabled, and a leper colony. In 1979, she received the Nobel Peace Prize for her work.

⊙ Target Reading Skill L2

Use Word Parts As a follow up, ask students to answer the Target Reading Skill questions in the Student Edition. *(the act of transporting, or moving something; the act of communicating, or sharing knowledge)*

New Challenges L2

Guided Instruction
- **Vocabulary Builder** Clarify the high-use word **consumption** before reading.
- Read New Challenges with students.
- Remind students that poverty is widespread throughout many countries. Ask students **How much money does almost half of the world's population live on per day per person?** *(less than $2.15)*
- Ask students **Why did the United States invade Afghanistan in 2001?** *(to topple the Taliban, which was protecting Osama bin Laden, and to capture or kill members of al-Qaeda)*

Independent Practice
Have students complete the graphic organizer by filling in facts about challenges in the world today.

Monitor Progress
- Show *Section Reading Support Transparency MT 79* and ask students to check their graphic organizers individually. Go over key concepts and clarify key vocabulary as needed.

  📖 **Medieval Times to Today Transparencies,** *Section Reading Support Transparency MT 79*

- Tell students to fill in the last column of the *Reading Readiness Guide.* Probe for what they learned that confirms or invalidates each statement.

  All in One **Medieval Times to Today Teaching Resources,** *Reading Readiness Guide,* p. 418

Answers

✔ **Reading Check** a group of countries that have agreed to work together to reduce barriers to trade

Identify Causes As populations grow, they need more land to live on, raise crops, and feed cattle, which might cause more areas of rain forest to be cleared away.

Assess and Reteach

Assess Progress `L2`

Have students complete the Section Assessment. Administer the *Section Quiz.*

All in One **Medieval Times to Today Teaching Resources,** *Section Quiz,* p. 420

Reteach `L1`

If students need more instruction, have them read this section in the Reading and Vocabulary Study Guide.

Chapter 8, Section 3, **Medieval Times to Today Reading and Vocabulary Study Guide,** pp. 91–93

Extend `L3`

Have students work in pairs to create collages of news headlines they feel reflect the world's biggest challenges. Students may use actual news headlines from newspapers and magazines, but also encourage students to create their own headlines about current issues that they believe are important. Post students collages around the classroom, and have each pair share their collage with the class.

Answer

✓ Reading Check Valuable soil may be washed away and flooding may occur downstream.

Section 3 Assessment

Key Terms
Students' sentences should reflect knowledge of each Key Term.

Target Reading Skill
Pollution is the act of polluting, or making something dirty or impure.

Comprehension and Critical Thinking

1. (a) satellites, radio transmission, airplanes, automobiles, space probes, telephones, radios, television, wireless telephones, the Internet **(b)** Possible answers: better transportation, easier and faster communication, better health and comfort, more trade and migration

2. (a) increased **(b)** better and faster transportation and communication technologies

3. (a) Populations are growing rapidly.
(b) Population growth is increasing stress on the environment; use of cars and trucks pollutes the air, water, and soil; heavy use of pesticides and fertilizers causes water pollution.

(c) Possible answer: If there were programs to help the elderly live securely in old age, they might not have as many children; if steps are taken to improve the economies, the need to have many children to support families would decrease.

Writing Activity
Use the *Rubric for Assessing a Journal Entry* to evaluate students' journal entries.

A candlelight vigil in Brooklyn, New York, one year after the September 11 terrorist attacks

Terrorism and War On September 11, 2001, 19 men from a group called al-Qaeda (ahl KY duh) purposely crashed two airliners into the World Trade Center in New York City and another into the Pentagon, near Washington, D.C. A fourth airliner crashed in a field in Pennsylvania. More than 3,000 people in all were killed.

Al-Qaeda is led by Osama bin Laden. Al-Qaeda hopes to achieve political goals by means of **terrorism,** an effort to cause fear through the threat or use of violence. People who practice terrorism are known as terrorists. Al-Qaeda seeks to force the United States to withdraw its troops from the Middle East and end its support for Israel.

In 2001 Osama bin Laden was hiding in Afghanistan under the protection of the brutal Taliban government. With the aid of Afghan rebels, American forces invaded Afghanistan and toppled the Taliban in December 2001. American and Afghan forces captured or killed many members of al-Qaeda.

In 2003, the United States invaded and occupied Iraq, a country in the Middle East. Iraq had been ruled by a cruel dictator, Saddam Hussein. The United States overthrew Hussein and later captured him. Despite the capture of the dictator, Iraq remained unstable in 2004.

The worldwide threat of terrorism continues. However, people around the world share a commitment to make the world safer.

✓ Reading Check What problem can result when forests are cut down?

Section 3 Assessment

Key Terms
Review the key terms at the beginning of this section. Use each term in a sentence that explains its meaning.

Target Reading Skill
Using your knowledge of the suffix *-tion*, give the meaning of the word *pollution,* in the second sentence from the bottom of page 241.

Comprehension and Critical Thinking
1. (a) Identify What are some modern advances in technology?
(b) Identify Effects What is one effect of these advances?
2. (a) Recall Over the past 200 years, have economic ties between countries increased or decreased?
(b) Identify Causes What accounts for this change?
3. (a) Describe How is the population of many developing countries changing?
(b) Explain How is the change in population affecting the environment?
(c) Infer What steps might help to slow the rate of population change in these countries?

Writing Activity
Write a journal entry that describes something you can do—now or when you are an adult—to help meet one of the challenges the world faces.

For: An activity on using the Internet
Visit: PHSchool.com
Web Code: lgd-8803

All in One **Medieval Times to Today Teaching Resources,** *Rubric for Assessing a Journal Entry,* p. 439

Go Online **PHSchool.com** Typing in the Web code when prompted will bring students directly to detailed instructions for this activity.

8 Review and Assessment

◆ Chapter Summary

Section 1: War and Revolution

- Nationalism, a military buildup, and a rigid system of alliances caused World War I, which led in turn to the Russian Revolution.
- The Great Depression was a worldwide economic downturn of the 1930s.
- World War II, fought from 1939 to 1945, left millions dead.

Recruiting poster

Section 2: The Postwar World

- The United States confronted the Soviet Union in the Cold War from 1945 to 1991.
  - Many European colonies became independent countries after World War II.

Soviet missiles

Section 3: The World Today

- New technologies allow quicker communication and transportation as well as better health.
- Migration, trade, and economic alliances have linked different parts of the world.
- Challenges in today's world include poverty, population growth, environmental issues, terrorism, and war.

The Mars rover

◆ Key Terms

Write a paragraph titled The World Since 1900, using all of the following terms correctly in complete sentences.

1. World War I
2. communism
3. Great Depression
4. World War II
5. postwar

6. capitalism
7. Cold War
8. developing countries
9. trading bloc
10. terrorism

Chapter 8 **243**

Vocabulary Builder

Revisit this chapter's high-use words:

rivalry	ally	relocate
opposition	crucial	consumption
curtail	collapse	
discontent	rarity	

Ask students to review the definitions they recorded on their *Word Knowledge* worksheets.

All in One **Medieval Times to Today Teaching Resources,** *Word Knowledge,* p. 424

Consider allowing students to earn extra credit if they use the words in their answers to the questions in the Chapter Review and Assessment. The words must be used correctly and in a natural context to win the extra points.

Review Chapter Content

■ Review and revisit the major themes of this chapter by asking students to classify what Guiding Question each bulleted statement in the Chapter Summary answers. Read the statements in the Chapter Summary aloud, and have students write the number of the Guiding Question on a piece of paper. Refer to p. 1 in the Student Edition for the text of Guiding Questions.

■ Assign *Vocabulary Development* for students to review Key Terms.

All in One **Medieval Times to Today Teaching Resources,** *Vocabulary Development,* p. 437

Answers

Key Terms

1–10. Students' paragraphs will vary, but they should be sure to use all of the Key Terms correctly in complete sentences.

Review and Assessment

Comprehension and Critical Thinking

11. (a) rivalries of countries for power, military build-up, and the growth of alliances **(b)** the assassination of Archduke Franz Ferdinand of Austria-Hungary by a Serb in 1914 **(c)** The formation of alliances caused the war to spread. Russia, France, and Britain were linked with Serbia, while Germany and other countries supported Austria-Hungary. The United States later joined those linked with Serbia.

12. (a) The Axis powers included Japan, Italy, and Germany and the Allied powers included Great Britain, France, the United States, and the Soviet Union. **(b)** German leader Adolf Hitler took control of lands bordering Germany. In 1939 Germany invaded Poland, and Britain and France—who had pledged support to Poland—declared war on Germany. Japan and Italy sided with Germany. The United States entered after the attack by the Japanese on Pearl Harbor, Hawaii. In 1941, the Soviet Union joined the Allies after Hitler invaded the Soviet Union. **(c)** Possible answer: In addition to military deaths, there were many civilian deaths due to the dropping of two atomic bombs on Japan that killed over 100,000 people, and the six million Jews as well as many other minorities who were killed by the Nazis.

13. (a) 1945–1991 **(b)** Possible answer: Eastern Europeans and Soviet citizens demanded reforms, and capitalism in non-communist countries produced more wealth than communism. The Cold War ended when communist rule collapsed in the Soviet Union.

14. (a) in the decades after World War II **(b)** Colonized peoples resented European rule, and since many colonies had helped their rulers in World War II, they wanted to be rewarded. European powers had weakened after World War II, and they found it hard to deny demands for independence.

15. (a) satellites and the Internet **(b)** Possible answer: better and faster transportation and communication, better health and comfort, increased trade, and increased migration **(c)** Economic ties have increased between countries.

Review and Assessment (continued)

◆ Comprehension and Critical Thinking

11. (a) Recall What were three major causes of World War I?
(b) Explain What event led to the actual outbreak of war?
(c) Synthesize Information How did this event pull so many different countries into war?

12. (a) Identify Which major countries fought on each side in World War II?
(b) Explain How did these countries become involved in the war?
(c) Identify Causes and Effects What factors help explain the high death toll in the war?

13. (a) Recall When did the Cold War take place?
(b) Analyze Why did the Soviet Union lose the Cold War?

14. (a) Sequence When did many European colonies gain independence?
(b) Identify Causes Why did those countries gain independence at that time?

15. (a) Identify Which new communication technologies have developed since the mid-1900s?

(b) Describe What are some effects of those new technologies?
(c) Analyze How have those technologies affected economic ties between different parts of the world?

◆ Skills Practice

Interpreting Line Graphs In the Skills for Life activity in this chapter, you learned how to interpret line graphs. Review the steps of this skill.

Now look again at the line graph on page 225, titled U.S. Economic Output per Person, 1924–1940. What does the vertical axis show? What does the horizontal axis show? How does the line change over time? When is it high? When is it low? How does the graph show changes in the economy of the United States?

◆ Writing Activity: Science

There are many challenges facing the world today—poverty, population growth, pollution, and terrorism are some of them. Choose one of these challenges or another one that interests you. Then write a brief essay explaining how science or technology might help solve this problem in the future.

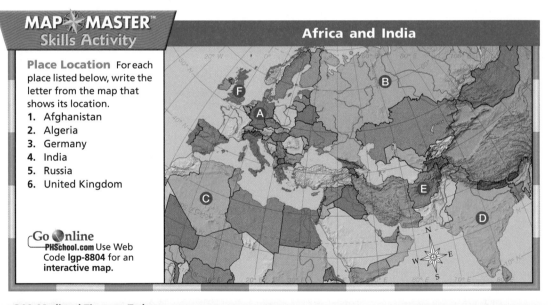

MAP ★ MASTER™
Skills Activity

Place Location For each place listed below, write the letter from the map that shows its location.
1. Afghanistan
2. Algeria
3. Germany
4. India
5. Russia
6. United Kingdom

Go Online
PHSchool.com Use Web Code **lgp-8804** for an interactive map.

Africa and India

Skills Practice

Students' answers should indicate that the vertical axis shows 2003 dollars, the horizontal axis shows years, the line fluctuates up and down over time, and the line is high in 1929 and low in 1933. Students may also observe that the graph indicates that there was generally growth in the economy from 1920 until 1929, a decline in the economy from 1929 until 1933, then a general climb again until 1937.

Writing Activity: Science

Student's answers will vary, but should include information about how science or technology could help to solve one of the challenges in today's world.

Use the *Rubric for Assessing a Writing Assignment* to evaluate students' essays.

All in One Medieval Times to Today Teaching Resources, *Rubric for Assessing a Writing Assignment*, p. 438

Standardized Test Prep

Test-Taking Tips

Some questions on standardized tests ask you to analyze point of view. Read the passage below. Then follow the tips to answer the sample question.

> In 1917, Vladimir Lenin took control of Russia. Hearing about the overthrow of Russia's government, someone said, "It is very good news indeed! Soon, the Russians will leave the world war. That will hurt the Allied Powers and help us."

Choose the letter that best answers the question.

Who might have made this statement?
- **A** a French soldier fighting in the trenches
- **B** a Russian nobleman opposed to the Communists
- **C** a German general fighting in France
- **D** an American soldier in Pearl Harbor after it was bombed

Think It Through You can eliminate D right away: Pearl Harbor was not bombed until 1941. Next, recall what happened when Lenin came to power: Communists gained power. So you can rule out B. Then think about which side would benefit from Lenin's taking Russia out of the war. Russia was an ally of France and Britain, so you can rule out A. French soldiers would not consider this good news. The correct answer is C.

> **TIP** Make sure you understand what the question is asking: Who made the comment that begins with the words "It is very good news indeed"?

> **TIP** Use logic, or good reasoning, to be sure you choose an answer that makes sense.

Practice Questions

Use the tips above and other tips in this book to help you answer the following questions.

1. Which group fought against European colonial rule?
   - **A** American soldiers during World War II
   - **B** African independence leaders during the 1950s
   - **C** members of the Nazi Party in the 1930s
   - **D** American presidents during the 1960s

2. What did the leaders of the Russian Revolution seek to achieve?
   - **A** independence
   - **B** capitalism
   - **C** communism
   - **D** democracy

3. Which of the following has strengthened global economic ties?
   - **A** pollution
   - **B** poverty
   - **C** terrorism
   - **D** e-mail

Read the statement below, and answer the question that follows.

"We must not allow communism to spread."

4. Who would have been most likely to make this statement?
   - **A** an American senator
   - **B** a dictator of the Soviet Union
   - **C** a poor Russian during World War I
   - **D** an Indian protesting British rule

Use Web Code **lga-8801** for a **Chapter 8 self-test.**

Standardized Test Prep

Answers

1. B
2. C
3. D
4. A

Assessment Resources

Teaching Resources
Chapter Tests A and B, pp. 440–455
Final Exams A and B, pp. 451–456

Test Prep Workbook
Medieval Times to Today Study Sheet, pp. 120–123
Medieval Times to Today Practice Tests A, B, and C, pp. 73–84

AYP Monitoring Assessments
Medieval Times to Today Benchmark Test 2, pp. 145–148
Medieval Times to Today Outcome Test, pp. 212–217

Technology
ExamView® Test Bank CD-ROM

Projects

- Students can further explore the Guiding Questions by completing hands-on projects.

- Three pages of structured guidance in All-in-One Medieval Times to Today Teaching Resources support each of the projects described on this page.

  All in One **Medieval Times to Today Teaching Resources,** *Book Project: One Job Through the Ages, pp. 77–79; Book Project: The Birth of a Nation, pp. 83–85*

- There are also two additional projects introduced, explained, and supported in the All-in-One Medieval Times to Today Teaching Resources.

  All in One **Medieval Times to Today Teaching Resources,** *Book Project: Two Tales of One City, pp. 80–82; Book Project: Major Migrations, pp. 86–88*

- Go over the four project suggestions with students.

- Ask each student to select one of the projects, or design his or her own. Work with students to create a project description and a schedule.

- Post project schedules and monitor student progress by asking for progress reports.

- Assess student projects using rubrics from the All-in-One Medieval Times to Today Teaching Resources.

  All in One **Medieval Times to Today Teaching Resources,** *Rubric for Assessing a Student Performance on a Project, p. 89; Rubric for Assessing the Performance of an Entire Group, p. 90; Rubric for Assessing Individual Performance in a Group, p. 91*

 Tell students they can add their completed Book Project as the final item in their portfolios. Assess student portfolios with *Rubric for Assessing a Student Portfolio.*

All in One **Medieval Times to Today Teaching Resources,** *Rubric for Assessing a Student Portfolio, p. 92*

Projects

Create your own projects to learn more about medieval times to today. At the beginning of this book, you were introduced to the **Guiding Questions** for studying the chapters and special features. But you can also find answers to these questions by doing projects on your own or with a group. Use the questions to find topics you want to explore further. Then try the projects described on this page or create your own.

1. **Geography** How did physical geography affect the development of societies around the world?

2. **History** How have societies around the world been shaped by their history?

3. **Culture** What were the belief systems and patterns of daily life in these societies?

4. **Government** What types of government were formed in these societies?

5. **Economics** How did each society organize its economic activities?

Project
RESEARCH THE BIRTH OF A NATION

A Nation Celebration Today there are more than 250 nations in the world. Some are very ancient and others are quite new. Choose one, and research how it became an independent nation. Was it once part of another nation or empire? How did it achieve independence? How did it achieve its modern borders and government? What factors influenced its culture? Write a short history of the nation, including what it is like today. Present your work as part of a class Nation Celebration.

Medieval bakers

Project
CREATE AN EXPANDED TIMELINE

One Job Through the Ages There were no airplane pilots 500 years ago, but there were doctors, carpenters, bakers, and teachers. Learn about one job that has been done at least since the Middle Ages. Find out how different cultures have practiced and changed this job over the course of history. Put major changes, inventions, and individual contributions in a timeline. Then add descriptive paragraphs and illustrations to some of your entries to highlight how the job affected or reflected life at that time.

This Republic Day 2004 parade in New Delhi celebrates the unification of India into a democratic republic on January 26, 1950.

Table of Contents

The World: Political

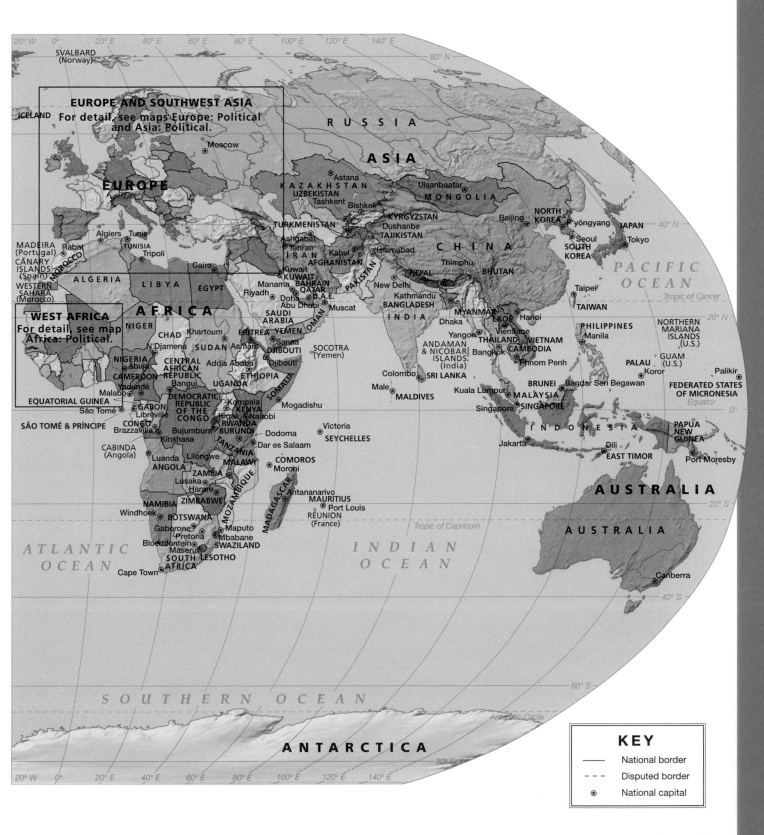

20° W **0°** **20° E** **40° E** **60° E** **80° E** **100° E** **120° E** **140° E**

SVALBARD
(Norway)

80° N

ICELAND

EUROPE AND SOUTHWEST ASIA
For detail, see maps Europe: Political
and Asia: Political.

R U S S I A

Arctic Circle

Moscow

A S I A

EUROPE

⊛ Astana

K A Z A K H S T A N

UZBEKISTAN
⊛ Tashkent Bishkek ⊛

Ulaanbaatar ⊛

M O N G O L I A

40° N

Algiers Tunis

MADEIRA
(Portugal)

TURKMENISTAN

KYRGYZSTAN
Dushanbe
TAJIKISTAN

Beijing ⊛

NORTH
KOREA
P'yŏngyang ⊛ JAPAN

Ashgabat ⊛

CANARY
ISLANDS
(Spain)

TUNISIA
Rabat ⊛
MOROCCO
Tripoli

Tehran ⊛ Kabul ⊛
I R A N
AFGHANISTAN

Islamabad ⊛

C H I N A
Thimphu ⊛

⊛ Seoul
SOUTH
KOREA
⊛ Tokyo

PACIFIC
OCEAN

WESTERN
SAHARA
(Morocco)

ALGERIA

L I B Y A
EGYPT

Cairo ⊛
Kuwait ⊛
KUWAIT
BAHRAIN

NEPAL ⊛

New Delhi ⊛

BHUTAN
Kathmandu ⊛

Taipei ⊛
TAIWAN

Tropic of Cancer

20° N

WEST AFRICA
For detail, see map
Africa: Political.

A F R I C A

NIGER

Manama ⊛
Riyadh ⊛ QATAR
Doha ⊛ U.A.E.
Abu Dhabi ⊛ Muscat ⊛

SAUDI
ARABIA

BANGLADESH
I N D I A
Dhaka ⊛

MYANMAR
LAOS Hanoi ⊛

Yangon ⊛ ⊛ Vientiane
THAILAND VIETNAM

PHILIPPINES
⊛ Manila

NORTHERN
MARIANA
ISLANDS
(U.S.)

CHAD
Khartoum ⊛
ERITREA YEMEN
N'Djamena ⊛
SUDAN
Asmara ⊛
CENTRAL Addis Ababa ⊛
Sanaa ⊛
DJIBOUTI
Djibouti ⊛

SOCOTRA
(Yemen)

ANDAMAN
& NICOBAR
ISLANDS
(India)

Bangkok ⊛
CAMBODIA
⊛ Phnom Penh

PALAU

GUAM
(U.S.)
⊛ Koror

Palikir ⊛

NIGERIA
Abuja ⊛
AFRICAN
REPUBLIC
CAMEROON
Yaoundé ⊛ Bangui ⊛
UGANDA
ETHIOPIA

Colombo ⊛ SRI LANKA
Male ⊛
MALDIVES

Kuala Lumpur ⊛
BRUNEI
⊛ Bandar Seri Begawan
MALAYSIA

FEDERATED STATES
OF MICRONESIA

Equator **0°**

EQUATORIAL GUINEA
Malabo ⊛
São Tomé ⊛

GABON
DEMOCRATIC
REPUBLIC
OF THE
CONGO
Libreville ⊛

Kampala ⊛
KENYA
Kigali ⊛ Nairobi ⊛
RWANDA

SOMALIA

⊛ Mogadishu

Singapore ⊛ SINGAPORE

I N D O N E S I A

Jakarta ⊛

PAPUA
NEW
GUINEA

Dili ⊛
EAST TIMOR

Port Moresby ⊛

SÃO TOMÉ & PRÍNCIPE
CONGO
Brazzaville ⊛
Kinshasa ⊛

Bujumbura ⊛
BURUNDI
TANZANIA
Dodoma ⊛
Dar es Salaam ⊛

Victoria ⊛

SEYCHELLES

CABINDA
(Angola)
Luanda ⊛ Lilongwe ⊛
ANGOLA
MALAWI

COMOROS
⊛ Moroni

A U S T R A L I A

ZAMBIA
Lusaka ⊛
Harare ⊛

MOZAMBIQUE

MADAGASCAR
Antananarivo ⊛
MAURITIUS

NAMIBIA ZIMBABWE
Windhoek ⊛
BOTSWANA
Gaborone ⊛ Maputo ⊛
Pretoria ⊛
Bloemfontein ⊛ Mbabane ⊛
SWAZILAND
SOUTH LESOTHO
Maseru ⊛
Cape Town ⊛ AFRICA

⊛ Port Louis
RÉUNION
(France)

A U S T R A L I A

20° S

Tropic of Capricorn

ATLANTIC
OCEAN

I N D I A N
O C E A N

Canberra ⊛

40° S

60° S

S O U T H E R N   O C E A N

Antarctic Circle

A N T A R C T I C A

80° S

20° W **0°** **20° E** **40° E** **60° E** **80° E** **100° E** **120° E** **140° E**

KEY	
——	National border
– – –	Disputed border
⊛	National capital

The World: Physical

0 miles 2,000
0 kilometers 2,000
Robinson

250 Reference

KEY

ELEVATION

Feet		Meters
More than 13,000		More than 3,960
6,500–13,000		1,980–3,960
1,600–6,500		480–1,980
650–1,600		200–480
0–650		0–200
Below sea level		Below sea level

Ice shelf

Ice cap

——— National border

- - - - Disputed border

EUROPE

ASIA

AFRICA

AUSTRALIA

ANTARCTICA

ATLANTIC OCEAN

INDIAN OCEAN

PACIFIC OCEAN

SOUTHERN OCEAN

Barents Sea

Kara Sea

SIBERIA

CHERSKIY RANGE

KAMCHATKA PENINSULA

Sea of Okhotsk

Iceland

SCANDINAVIA

URAL MOUNTAINS

Ob R.

Yenisey R.

Lena R.

Amur R.

Lake Baikal

Hokkaido

British Isles

North Sea

NORTH EUROPEAN PLAIN

Volga R.

ALTAI MTS.

GOBI

Sea of Japan

Honshu

Aral Sea

BALKAN PENINSULA

Black Sea

CAUCASUS

Caspian Sea

TIAN SHAN

NORTH CHINA PLAIN

IBERIAN PENINSULA

ATLAS MOUNTAINS

Mediterranean Sea

PLATEAU OF IRAN

HINDU KUSH

KUNLUN SHAN

PLATEAU OF TIBET

Hwang R.

Chang R.

East China Sea

Yellow Sea

PACIFIC OCEAN

SAHARA

Niger R.

SAHEL

ARABIAN PENINSULA

Persian Gulf

DECCAN PLATEAU

Bay of Bengal

Taiwan

South China Sea

Philippine Sea

MICRONESIA

Nile R.

Arabian Sea

Philippine Islands

ETHIOPIAN HIGHLANDS

MALAY PENINSULA

Congo R.

Lake Victoria

Sumatra

Borneo

Celebes

New Guinea

MELANESIA

Java Sea

Zambezi R.

Java

Lesser Sunda Islands

Arafura Sea

Coral Sea

Madagascar

AUSTRALIA

GREAT SANDY DESERT

KALAHARI DESERT

GREAT VICTORIA DESERT

GREAT DIVIDING RANGE

Cape of Good Hope

Tropic of Capricorn

Arctic Circle

Antarctic Circle

Tropic of Cancer

Equator

North and South America: Political

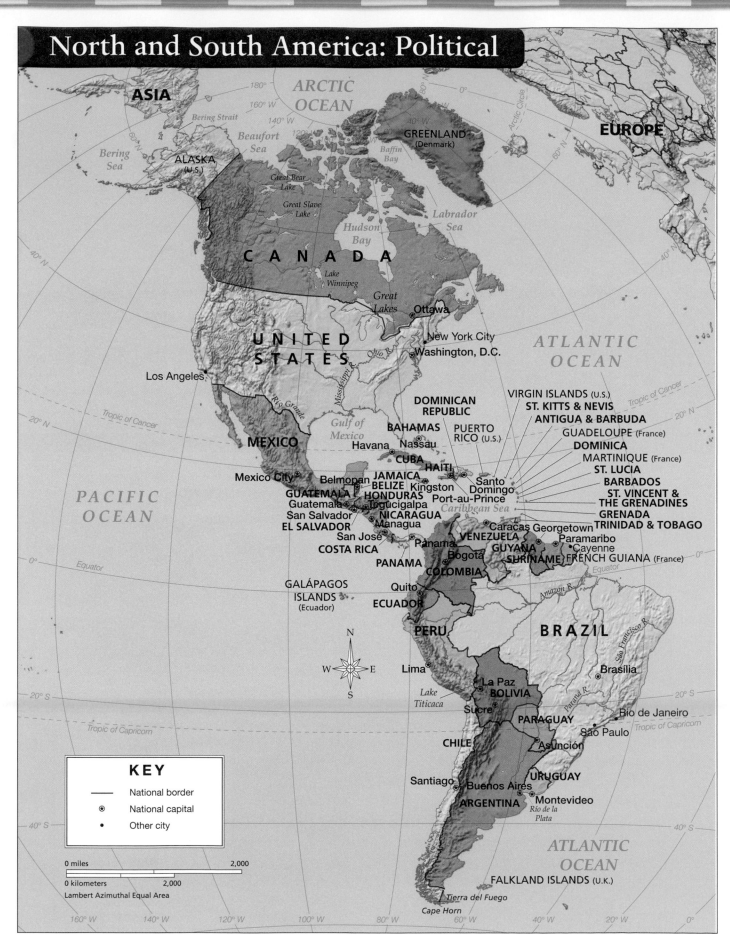

ASIA

ARCTIC OCEAN

EUROPE

Bering Strait

Bering Sea

Beaufort Sea

ALASKA (U.S.)

GREENLAND (Denmark)

Baffin Bay

Great Bear Lake

Great Slave Lake

Labrador Sea

Hudson Bay

CANADA

Lake Winnipeg

Great Lakes

Ottawa

New York City

Washington, D.C.

UNITED STATES

Ohio R.

ATLANTIC OCEAN

Los Angeles

Río Grande

Mississippi R.

Tropic of Cancer

VIRGIN ISLANDS (U.S.)

ST. KITTS & NEVIS

ANTIGUA & BARBUDA

DOMINICAN REPUBLIC

GUADELOUPE (France)

Gulf of Mexico

BAHAMAS

PUERTO RICO (U.S.)

DOMINICA

MARTINIQUE (France)

MEXICO

Havana

Nassau

CUBA

HAITI

ST. LUCIA

BARBADOS

Mexico City

Belmopan

JAMAICA

BELIZE

Kingston

Santo Domingo

Port-au-Prince

ST. VINCENT & THE GRENADINES

GRENADA

GUATEMALA

Guatemala

HONDURAS

Tegucigalpa

Caribbean Sea

TRINIDAD & TOBAGO

San Salvador

NICARAGUA

EL SALVADOR

Managua

Caracas

Georgetown

Paramaribo

PACIFIC OCEAN

San José

Panama

VENEZUELA

GUYANA

Cayenne

COSTA RICA

PANAMA

Bogotá

SURINAME

FRENCH GUIANA (France)

Equator

COLOMBIA

Equator

GALÁPAGOS ISLANDS (Ecuador)

Quito

ECUADOR

Amazon R.

PERU

BRAZIL

São Francisco R.

N

W   E

S

Lima

Brasília

Lake Titicaca

La Paz

BOLIVIA

Sucre

Paraná R.

Rio de Janeiro

PARAGUAY

São Paulo

Tropic of Capricorn

CHILE

Asunción

URUGUAY

Santiago

Buenos Aires

Montevideo

ARGENTINA

Río de la Plata

KEY

—— National border

⊛ National capital

• Other city

0 miles   2,000

0 kilometers   2,000

Lambert Azimuthal Equal Area

ATLANTIC OCEAN

FALKLAND ISLANDS (U.K.)

Tierra del Fuego

Cape Horn

North and South America: Physical

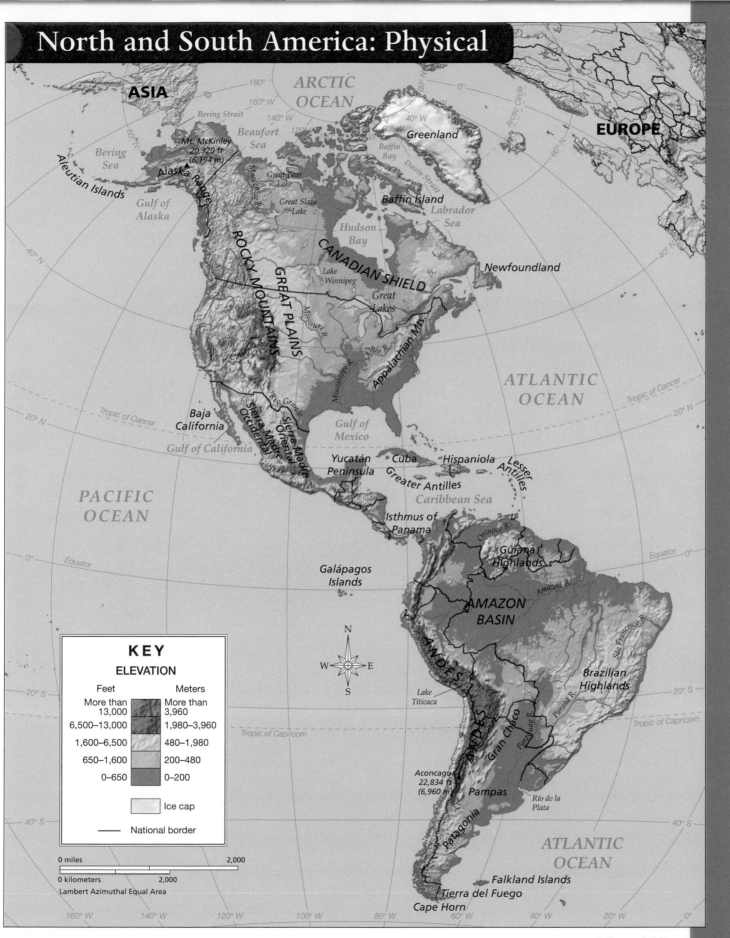

ASIA

ARCTIC OCEAN

EUROPE

Bering Strait

Beaufort Sea

Greenland

Mt. McKinley 20,320 ft (6,194 m)

Bering Sea

Aleutian Islands

Alaska Range

Gulf of Alaska

Great Bear Lake

Mackenzie R.

Great Slave Lake

Baffin Bay

Baffin Island

Davis Strait

Labrador Sea

Hudson Bay

CANADIAN SHIELD

Newfoundland

ROCKY MOUNTAINS

GREAT PLAINS

Lake Winnipeg

Great Lakes

Missouri R.

Ohio R.

Appalachian Mts.

Mississippi R.

Colorado R.

ATLANTIC OCEAN

Tropic of Cancer

Baja California

Río Grande

Sierra Madre Occidental

Sierra Madre Oriental

Gulf of Mexico

Tropic of Cancer

Gulf of California

Yucatán Peninsula

Cuba

Greater Antilles

Hispaniola

Lesser Antilles

PACIFIC OCEAN

Caribbean Sea

Isthmus of Panama

Orinoco R.

Guiana Highlands

Galápagos Islands

AMAZON BASIN

Amazon R.

São Francisco R.

ANDES

Brazilian Highlands

Lake Titicaca

Gran Chaco

Paraguay R.

Paraná R.

Tropic of Capricorn

Aconcagua 22,834 ft (6,960 m)

ANDES

Pampas

Río de la Plata

Patagonia

ATLANTIC OCEAN

Falkland Islands

Tierra del Fuego

Cape Horn

KEY

ELEVATION

Feet	Meters
More than 13,000	More than 3,960
6,500–13,000	1,980–3,960
1,600–6,500	480–1,980
650–1,600	200–480
0–650	0–200

Ice cap

National border

N W E S

0 miles 2,000
0 kilometers 2,000
Lambert Azimuthal Equal Area

Equator

Equator

United States: Political

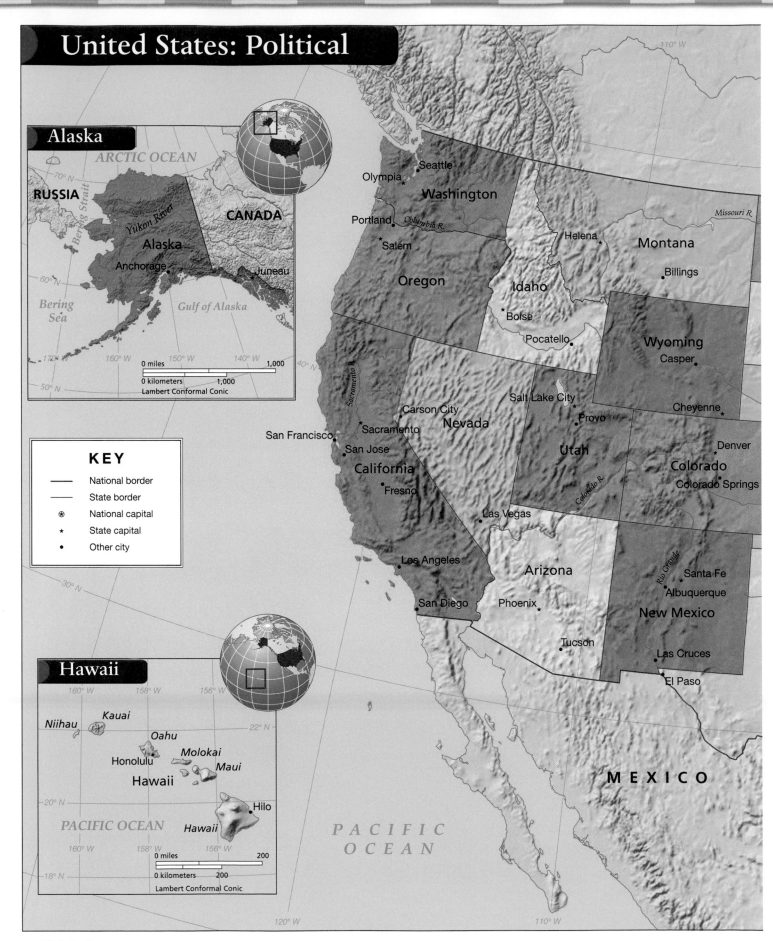

Alaska

ARCTIC OCEAN

70° N

RUSSIA

Bering Strait

CANADA

Yukon River

Alaska

Anchorage

Juneau

Bering Sea

60° N

Gulf of Alaska

170°

160° W

150° W

140° W

40° N

50° N

0 miles   1,000

0 kilometers   1,000

Lambert Conformal Conic

KEY

⎯	National border
⎯	State border
⊛	National capital
★	State capital
•	Other city

Hawaii

160° W   158° W   156° W

Niihau   Kauai

Oahu   22° N

Honolulu   Molokai

Maui

Hawaii

Hilo

PACIFIC OCEAN   Hawaii   20° N

160° W   158° W   156° W

18° N

0 miles   200

0 kilometers   200

Lambert Conformal Conic

110° W

Seattle

Olympia

Washington

Portland   Columbia R.

Salem

Oregon

Helena

Montana

Billings

Missouri R.

Idaho

Boise

Pocatello

Wyoming

Casper

Cheyenne

Carson City

Salt Lake City

Sacramento

Nevada

Provo

San Francisco

San Jose

Utah

Denver

California

Colorado

Colorado Springs

Fresno

Colorado R.

Las Vegas

30° N

Los Angeles

Arizona

Rio Grande

Santa Fe

Albuquerque

San Diego

Phoenix

New Mexico

Tucson

Las Cruces

El Paso

MEXICO

PACIFIC OCEAN

120° W

110° W

CANADA

North Dakota
★ Bismarck
• Fargo

Minnesota

South Dakota
★ Pierre
• Sioux Falls

Minneapolis •
St. Paul ★

Mississippi R.

Wisconsin
• Milwaukee
Madison ★

Lake Superior

Lake Michigan

Michigan
• Grand Rapids
• Lansing
Detroit •

Lake Huron

Lake Erie

Lake Ontario

Maine
★ Augusta
Portland •

Vermont
Montpelier ★

New Hampshire
★ Concord

Albany •
Boston •

New York
• Buffalo

Providence •
Hartford ★
Massachusetts

Rhode Island
Connecticut

Nebraska
• Omaha
★ Lincoln

Iowa
★ Des Moines
• Cedar Rapids

Chicago •

Illinois

Springfield ★

Fort Wayne •

Indiana

Indianapolis ★

Ohio

Columbus ★

Cincinnati •

Ohio R.

Cleveland •
Pittsburgh •

Pennsylvania
Harrisburg ★

Baltimore •

Washington, D.C. ★

West
Virginia

Charleston ★

Frankfort ★

Kentucky

New York City

New Jersey
Trenton ★
Philadelphia •

Delaware
★ Dover
• Annapolis

Maryland

District of Columbia

Richmond ★

Virginia

Norfolk •

Missouri R.

Kansas City •
Jefferson City ★

St. Louis •

Louisville •

Topeka ★

Kansas

Arkansas R.

• Wichita

Missouri

Oklahoma
★ Oklahoma City

Tulsa •

Arkansas

Fort Smith •
Little Rock ★

Memphis •

Mississippi R.

Nashville •

Tennessee

Knoxville •

Tennessee R.

North Carolina

• Charlotte

Raleigh •

South Carolina

Columbia ★

Charleston •

ATLANTIC
OCEAN

Texas

Fort Worth •
Dallas •

Red R.

Shreveport •

Louisiana

Baton Rouge ★

Austin ★

Houston •

San Antonio •

Gulfport •
New Orleans •

Mississippi

Jackson ★

Alabama

Montgomery ★

Birmingham •

Mobile •

Atlanta •

Georgia

Columbus •

Savannah •

Jacksonville •

★ Tallahassee

Florida

Orlando •

Tampa •

Miami •

Gulf of Mexico

N
W — E
S

100° W   90° W   80° W   70° W

50° N

40° N

30° N

90° W   80° W

0 miles   250

0 kilometers   250

Lambert Azimuthal Equal Area

Atlas **255**

Europe: Political

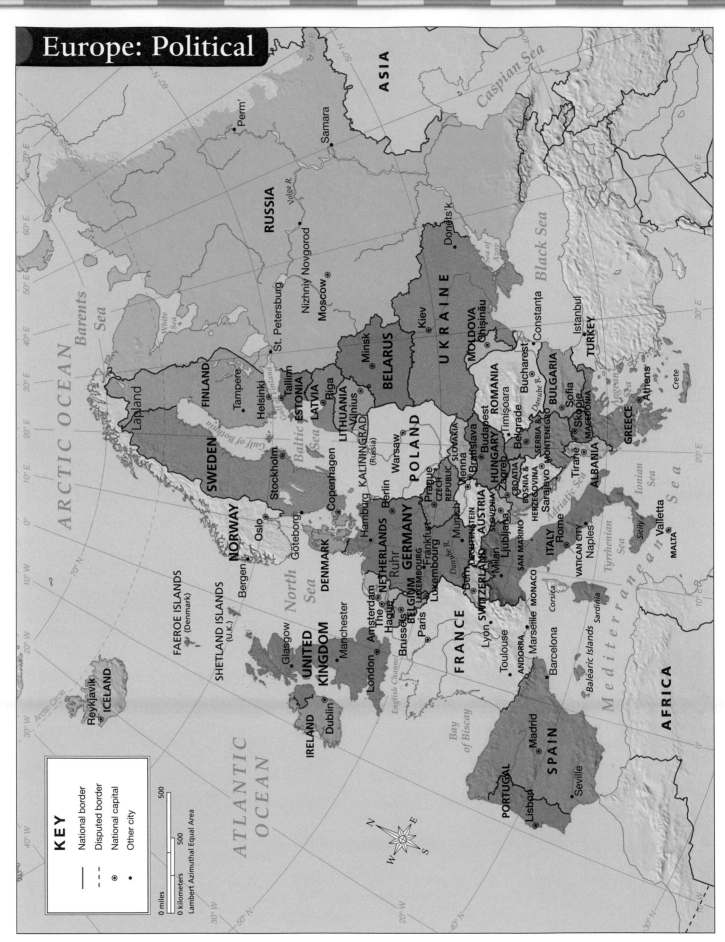

ASIA

Caspian Sea

RUSSIA

• Perm'

• Samara

Volga R.

Barents Sea

Sea of Azov

Nizhniy Novgorod

Moscow ⊛

Black Sea

Donets'k •

St. Petersburg •

White Sea

Kiev •

Constanța •

Istanbul •

U K R A I N E

MOLDOVA

Chişinău •

TURKEY

ARCTIC OCEAN

Minsk ⊛

BELARUS

ROMANIA

Bucharest ⊛

BULGARIA

Sofia ⊛

FINLAND

Tampere •

Helsinki ⊛

Tallinn ⊛

ESTONIA

LATVIA

Riga ⊛

Vilnius ⊛

LITHUANIA

KALININGRAD

(Russia)

Warsaw ⊛

P O L A N D

Timişoara •

Budapest ⊛

SLOVAKIA

Bratislava ⊛

Belgrade ⊛

SERBIA &

MONTENEGRO

Skopje ⊛

MACEDONIA

Tiranë ⊛

ALBANIA

GREECE

Athens ⊛

Aegean Sea

Crete

Lapland

Gulf of Finland

Baltic Sea

Gulf of Bothnia

SWEDEN

Stockholm ⊛

Copenhagen ⊛

Hamburg •

Berlin ⊛

Prague ⊛

CZECH

REPUBLIC

Vienna ⊛

AUSTRIA

SLOVENIA

Ljubljana ⊛

Zagreb ⊛

CROATIA

Sarajevo ⊛

BOSNIA &

HERZEGOVINA

Adriatic Sea

Ionian Sea

NORWAY

Oslo ⊛

Bergen •

Göteborg •

DENMARK

Amsterdam ⊛

The Hague ⊛

NETHERLANDS

BELGIUM

Brussels ⊛

Frankfurt •

GERMANY

LIECHTENSTEIN

Munich •

Danube R.

SWITZERLAND

Bern ⊛

Milan •

SAN MARINO

MONACO

I T A L Y

Rome ⊛

VATICAN CITY

Naples •

Tyrrhenian Sea

Sicily

Valletta ⊛

MALTA

Mediterranean Sea

FAEROE ISLANDS

(Denmark)

SHETLAND ISLANDS

(U.K.)

Glasgow •

UNITED

KINGDOM

Manchester •

London ⊛

LUXEMBOURG

Luxembourg ⊛

Paris ⊛

F R A N C E

Lyon •

Toulouse •

ANDORRA

Marseille •

Corsica

Barcelona •

Balearic Islands

Sardinia

AFRICA

English Channel

Bay of Biscay

North Sea

Reykjavík ⊛

ICELAND

Arctic Circle

IRELAND

Dublin ⊛

ATLANTIC OCEAN

Madrid ⊛

S P A I N

Seville •

PORTUGAL

Lisbon ⊛

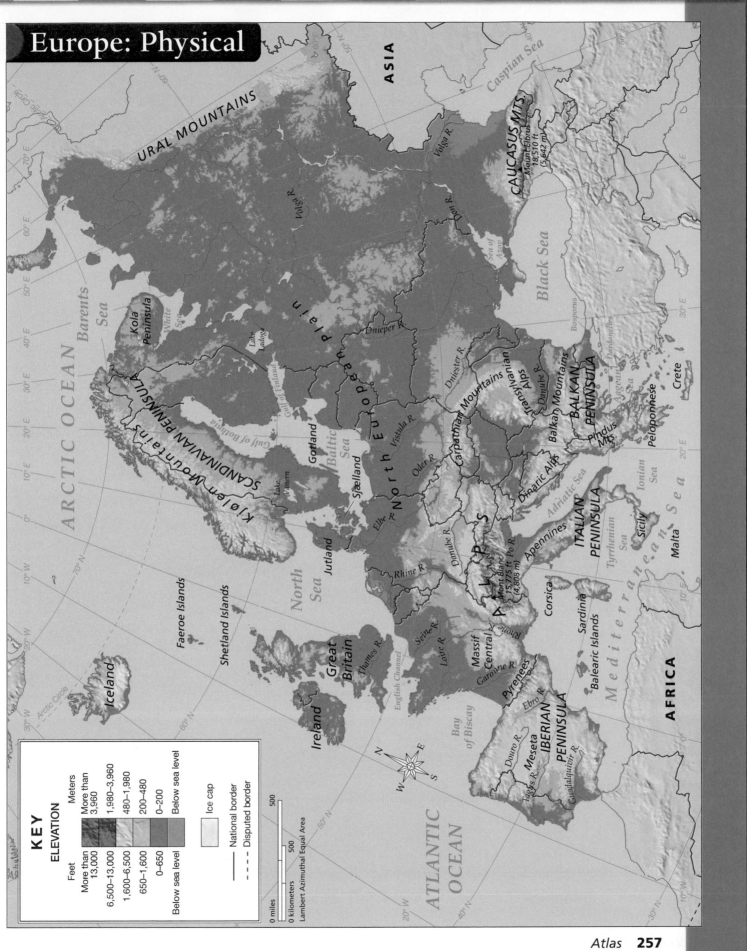

Europe: Physical

ASIA

URAL MOUNTAINS

Caspian Sea

CAUCASUS MTS.

Mount Elbrus
18,510 ft
(5,642 m)

Volga R.

Don R.

Sea of Azov

Black Sea

Barents Sea

ARCTIC OCEAN

Kola Peninsula

White Sea

Lake Ladoga

Dnieper R.

Bosporus

Dardanelles

North European Plain

Dniester R.

Danube R.

Carpathian Mountains

Transylvanian Alps

Balkan Mountains

BALKAN PENINSULA

Aegean Sea

Crete

Gulf of Finland

Gulf of Bothnia

Baltic Sea

Gotland

Sjælland

Vistula R.

Oder R.

Dinaric Alps

Pindus Mts.

Peloponnese

Ionian Sea

SCANDINAVIAN PENINSULA

Kjølen Mountains

Lake Vänern

Elbe R.

Danube R.

ALPS

Mont Blanc
15,775 ft
(4,808 m)

Apennines

ITALIAN PENINSULA

Adriatic Sea

Sicily

Malta

Tyrrhenian Sea

Rhine R.

Po R.

Corsica

Sardinia

Balearic Islands

Mediterranean Sea

North Sea

Jutland

Great Britain

Thames R.

Seine R.

Loire R.

Massif Central

Rhône R.

Garonne R.

Pyrenees

Ebro R.

Douro R.

Meseta

Tagus R.

IBERIAN PENINSULA

Guadalquivir R.

English Channel

Bay of Biscay

Ireland

Faeroe Islands

Shetland Islands

Iceland

Arctic Circle

ATLANTIC OCEAN

AFRICA

KEY

ELEVATION

Feet	Meters
More than 13,000	More than 3,960
6,500–13,000	1,980–3,960
1,600–6,500	480–1,980
650–1,600	200–480
0–650	0–200
Below sea level	Below sea level

Ice cap

National border

--- Disputed border

0 miles 500
0 kilometers 500
Lambert Azimuthal Equal Area

N E S W

Africa: Political

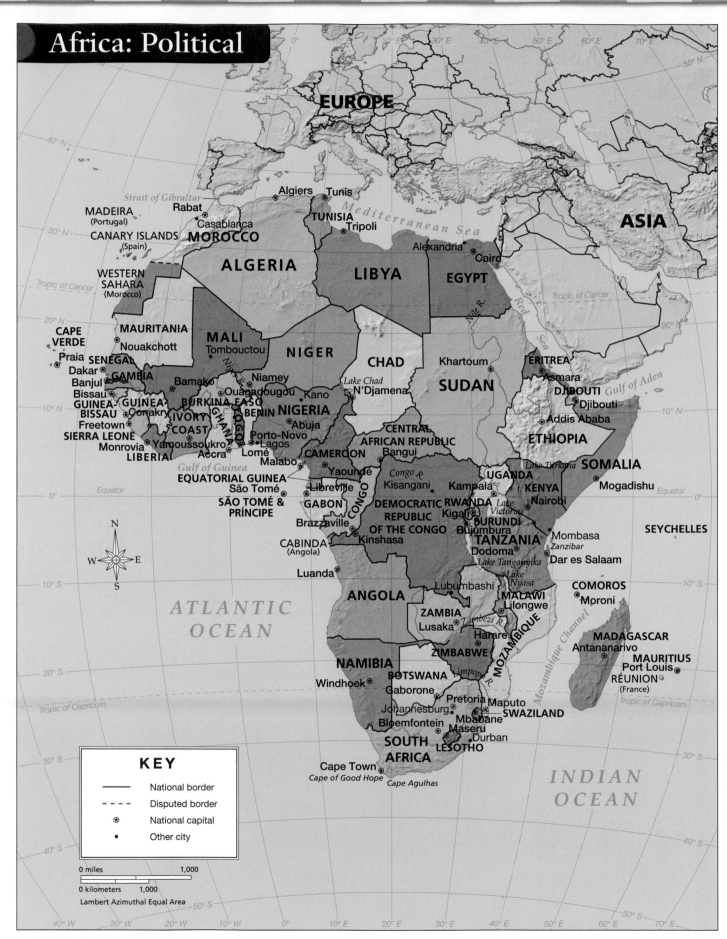

EUROPE

ASIA

Strait of Gibraltar

Mediterranean Sea

Algiers • Tunis
Rabat •
MADEIRA
(Portugal)
Casablanca •
TUNISIA
Tripoli
CANARY ISLANDS
(Spain)
MOROCCO
Alexandria •
Cairo ⊛

ALGERIA
LIBYA
EGYPT

WESTERN
SAHARA
(Morocco)
Tropic of Cancer

Tropic of Cancer

CAPE
VERDE
MAURITANIA
Nouakchott ⊛
MALI
Tombouctou •
NIGER
CHAD
Khartoum ⊛
ERITREA
Asmara ⊛
Praia •
SENEGAL
Dakar ⊛
Bamako ⊛
Niamey ⊛
N'Djamena ⊛
SUDAN
DJIBOUTI
Djibouti ⊛
Banjul ⊛ GAMBIA
Bissau •
Ouagadougou ⊛
Kano •
Lake Chad
GUINEA-
BISSAU
GUINEA
Conakry ⊛
BURKINA FASO
BENIN
NIGERIA
Abuja ⊛
Addis Ababa ⊛
Freetown ⊛
IVORY
COAST
Porto-Novo ⊛
CENTRAL
ETHIOPIA
SIERRA LEONE
Yamoussoukro ⊛
Lagos •
AFRICAN REPUBLIC
Monrovia ⊛
Accra ⊛
Lomé ⊛
Bangui ⊛
LIBERIA
Malabo ⊛
CAMEROON
SOMALIA
Gulf of Guinea
Yaoundé ⊛
Lake Turkana
EQUATORIAL GUINEA
São Tomé ⊛
Congo R.
UGANDA
KENYA
Mogadishu ⊛
SÃO TOMÉ &
PRÍNCIPE
Libreville ⊛
Kisangani •
Kampala ⊛
Nairobi ⊛
Equator
GABON
DEMOCRATIC
RWANDA
Lake
Victoria
REPUBLIC
Kigali ⊛
BURUNDI
SEYCHELLES
Brazzaville ⊛
OF THE CONGO
Bujumbura ⊛
Mombasa •
CABINDA
(Angola)
Kinshasa ⊛
TANZANIA
Zanzibar •
Dodoma ⊛
Dar es Salaam •
Lake Tanganyika
Luanda ⊛
Lake
Nyasa
COMOROS
Moroni ⊛
Lubumbashi •
ANGOLA
MALAWI
Lilongwe ⊛
ATLANTIC
OCEAN
ZAMBIA
Zambezi R.
MOZAMBIQUE
Lusaka ⊛
Harare ⊛
NAMIBIA
ZIMBABWE
MADAGASCAR
Antananarivo ⊛
BOTSWANA
Limpopo R.
MAURITIUS
Port Louis ⊛
Windhoek ⊛
Gaborone ⊛
RÉUNION
(France)
Tropic of Capricorn
Pretoria ⊛ Maputo ⊛
Johannesburg •
SWAZILAND
Bloemfontein •
Mbabane ⊛
Maseru ⊛
• Durban
SOUTH
AFRICA
LESOTHO
Cape Town •
INDIAN
OCEAN
Cape of Good Hope
Cape Agulhas

N
W   E
S

KEY

—————   National border

- - - - -   Disputed border

⊛   National capital

•   Other city

0 miles   1,000
0 kilometers   1,000
Lambert Azimuthal Equal Area

258 Reference

258

Africa: Physical

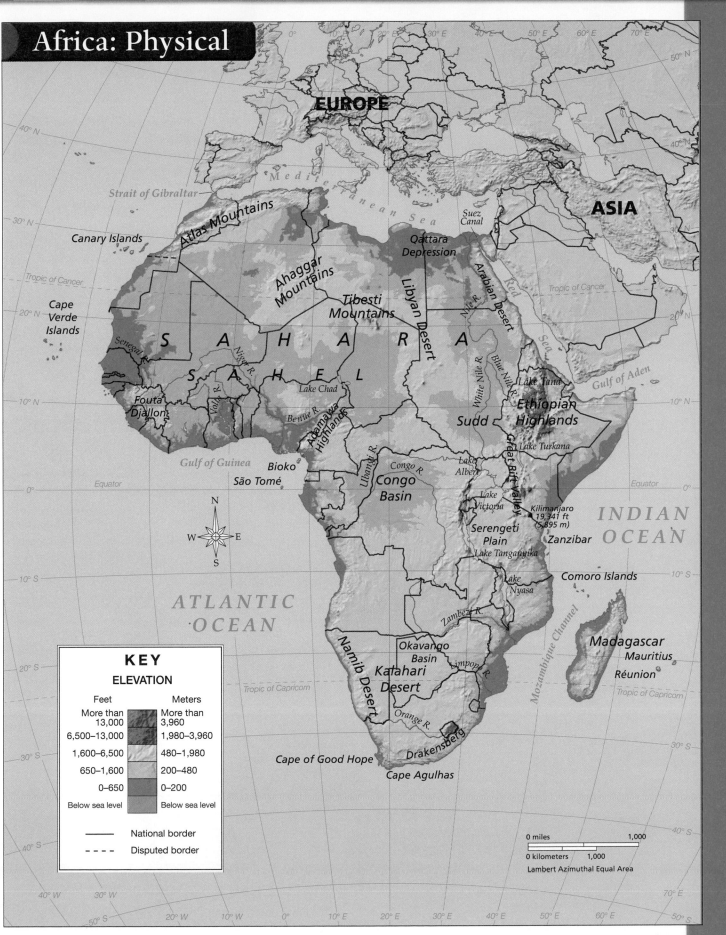

EUROPE

ASIA

Strait of Gibraltar

Mediterranean Sea

Suez Canal

Qattara Depression

Atlas Mountains

Canary Islands

Tropic of Cancer

Cape Verde Islands

Ahaggar Mountains

Tibesti Mountains

Libyan Desert

Arabian Desert

Red Sea

Tropic of Cancer

S A H A R A

Senegal R.

Niger R.

S A H E L

Lake Chad

Nile R.

White Nile R.

Blue Nile R.

Lake Tana

Gulf of Aden

Fouta Djallon

Volta R.

Benue R.

Adamawa Highlands

Ethiopian Highlands

Sudd

Lake Turkana

Gulf of Guinea

Bioko

São Tomé

Ubangi R.

Congo R.

Lake Albert

Great Rift Valley

Equator

Congo Basin

Lake Victoria

Kilimanjaro 19,341 ft (5,895 m)

INDIAN OCEAN

Equator

Serengeti Plain

Zanzibar

Lake Tanganyika

ATLANTIC OCEAN

Lake Nyasa

Comoro Islands

Zambezi R.

Okavango Basin

Limpopo R.

Madagascar

Mauritius

Réunion

Mozambique Channel

Namib Desert

Kalahari Desert

Tropic of Capricorn

Tropic of Capricorn

Orange R.

Cape of Good Hope

Drakensberg

Cape Agulhas

KEY

ELEVATION

Feet		Meters
More than 13,000		More than 3,960
6,500–13,000		1,980–3,960
1,600–6,500		480–1,980
650–1,600		200–480
0–650		0–200
Below sea level		Below sea level

——— National border

- - - - Disputed border

N
W E
S

0 miles 1,000
0 kilometers 1,000

Lambert Azimuthal Equal Area

Asia: Political

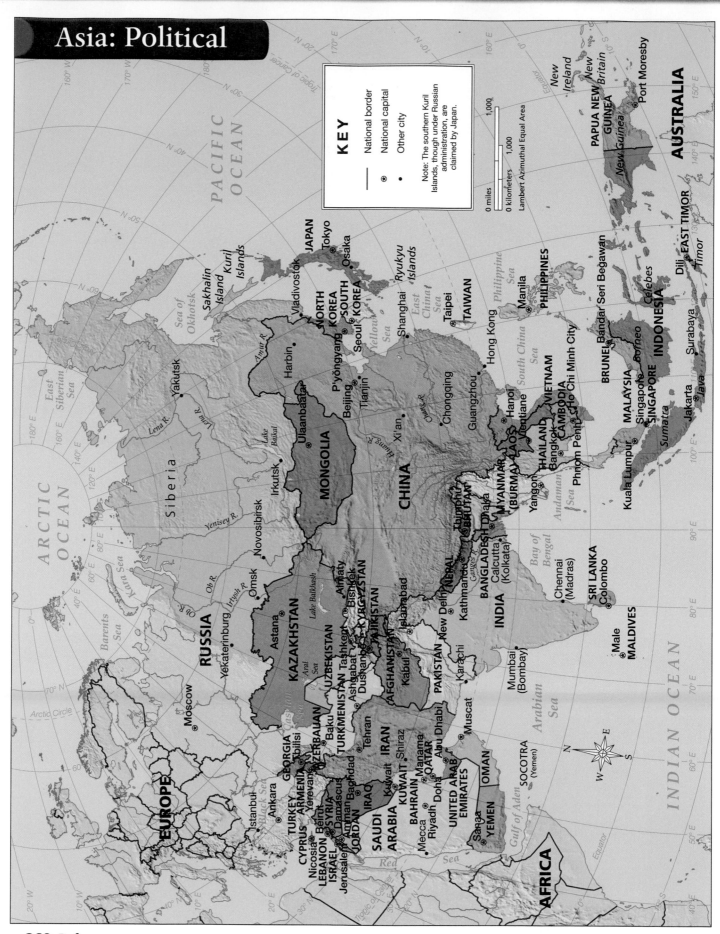

KEY

— National border
⊛ National capital
• Other city

Note: The southern Kuril Islands, though under Russian administration, are claimed by Japan.

0 miles 1,000
0 kilometers 1,000
Lambert Azimuthal Equal Area

ARCTIC OCEAN

PACIFIC OCEAN

INDIAN OCEAN

Arctic Circle

East Siberian Sea

Sea of Okhotsk

Kara Sea

Barents Sea

Siberia

RUSSIA

Moscow ⊛

Yekaterinburg •
Omsk •
Novosibirsk •
Irkutsk •
Yakutsk •

Lena R.
Ob R.
Irtysh R.
Yenisey R.

Sakhalin Island
Kuril Islands

Vladivostok •

Amur R.

Harbin •

MONGOLIA
⊛ Ulaanbaatar

JAPAN
Tokyo ⊛
Osaka •

NORTH KOREA
P'yŏngyang ⊛
SOUTH KOREA
Seoul ⊛

Ryukyu Islands

CHINA

Beijing ⊛
Tianjin •
Xi'an •
Shanghai •
Chongqing •
Guangzhou •

Chang R.
Huang R.

Yellow Sea
East China Sea

Hong Kong •

TAIWAN
Taipei ⊛

Philippine Sea

PHILIPPINES
Manila ⊛

South China Sea

VIETNAM
Hanoi ⊛
Ho Chi Minh City •

LAOS
Vientiane ⊛

THAILAND
Bangkok ⊛

CAMBODIA
Phnom Penh ⊛

MYANMAR (BURMA)
Yangon ⊛

Andaman Sea

BRUNEI
Bandar Seri Begawan ⊛

MALAYSIA
Kuala Lumpur ⊛

SINGAPORE ⊛

INDONESIA
Jakarta ⊛

Borneo
Celebes
Sumatra
Java
Surabaya •

EAST TIMOR
Dili ⊛
Timor

PAPUA NEW GUINEA
Port Moresby ⊛

New Ireland
New Britain
New Guinea

AUSTRALIA

KAZAKHSTAN
Astana ⊛

Aral Sea
Lake Balkhash

UZBEKISTAN
Tashkent ⊛
Almaty •

KYRGYZSTAN
Bishkek ⊛

TAJIKISTAN
Dushanbe ⊛

TURKMENISTAN
Ashgabat ⊛

AFGHANISTAN
Kabul ⊛

PAKISTAN
Islamabad ⊛
Karachi •

NEPAL
Kathmandu ⊛

BHUTAN
Thimphu ⊛

BANGLADESH
Dhaka ⊛

INDIA
New Delhi ⊛
Mumbai (Bombay) •
Calcutta (Kolkata) •
Chennai (Madras) •

Ganges R.
Bay of Bengal

SRI LANKA
Colombo ⊛

MALDIVES
Male ⊛

Arabian Sea

IRAN
Tehran ⊛
Shiraz •

Caspian Sea

AZERBAIJAN
Baku ⊛

GEORGIA
Tbilisi ⊛

ARMENIA
Yerevan ⊛

TURKEY
Ankara ⊛
Istanbul •

Black Sea

CYPRUS
Nicosia ⊛

LEBANON
Beirut ⊛

SYRIA
Damascus ⊛

ISRAEL
Jerusalem ⊛

JORDAN
Amman ⊛

IRAQ
Baghdad ⊛

KUWAIT
Kuwait ⊛

SAUDI ARABIA
Riyadh ⊛
Mecca •

BAHRAIN
Manama ⊛

QATAR
Doha ⊛

UNITED ARAB EMIRATES
Abu Dhabi ⊛

OMAN
Muscat ⊛

YEMEN
Sanaa ⊛

SOCOTRA (Yemen)

Gulf of Aden
Red Sea

EUROPE

AFRICA

N E S W

Asia: Physical

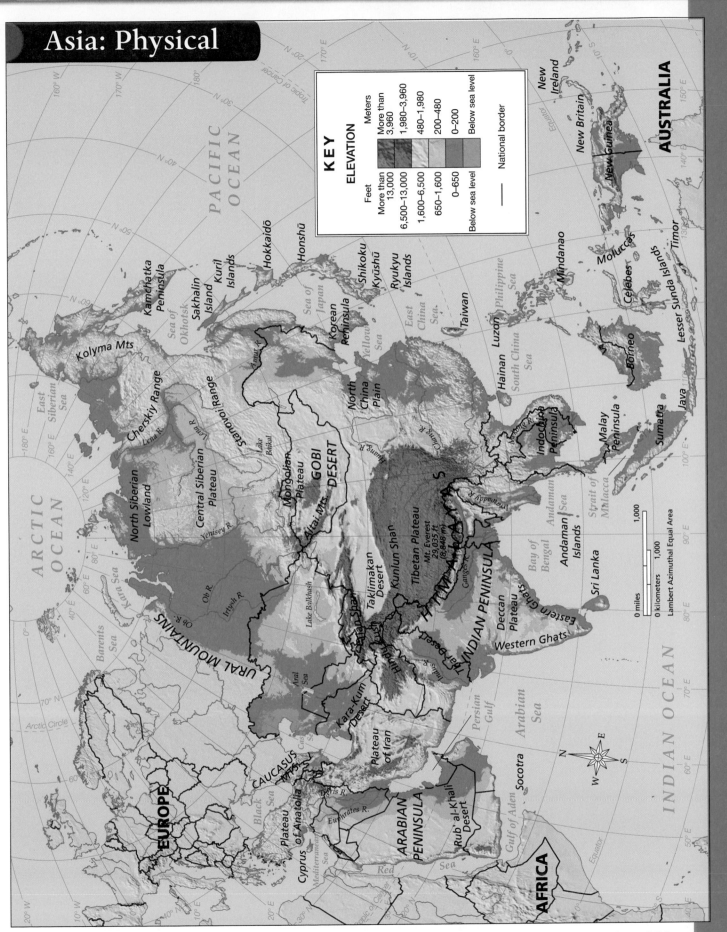

KEY

ELEVATION

Feet	Meters
More than 13,000	More than 3,960
6,500–13,000	1,980–3,960
1,600–6,500	480–1,980
650–1,600	200–480
0–650	0–200
Below sea level	Below sea level

—— National border

PACIFIC OCEAN

AUSTRALIA

New Ireland

New Britain

New Guinea

Equator

Timor

Lesser Sunda Islands

Moluccas

Celebes

Mindanao

Borneo

Java

Sumatra

Philippine Sea

Luzon

Malay Peninsula

Strait of Malacca

Indochina Peninsula

Taiwan

Hainan

South China Sea

East China Sea

Ryukyu Islands

Kyūshū

Shikoku

Honshū

Hokkaidō

Sea of Japan

Korean Peninsula

Yellow Sea

North China Plain

Kuril Islands

Sakhalin Island

Kamchatka Peninsula

Sea of Okhotsk

Kolyma Mts

Cherskiy Range

East Siberian Sea

ARCTIC OCEAN

North Siberian Lowland

Central Siberian Plateau

Lena R.

Lake Baikal

Stanovoi Range

Mongolian Plateau

Altai Mts

GOBI DESERT

Amur R.

Huang R.

Chang R.

Mekong R.

Irrawaddy R.

Tibetan Plateau

Mt. Everest 29,035 ft (8,848 m)

HIMALAYAS

Kunlun Shan

Taklimakan Desert

Tian Shan

Lake Balkhash

Yenisey R.

Ob R.

Irtysh R.

Aral Sea

URAL MOUNTAINS

Ob R.

Kara Sea

Barents Sea

Arctic Circle

EUROPE

Black Sea

CAUCASUS MTS.

Caspian Sea

Plateau of Anatolia

Cyprus

Mediterranean Sea

Tigris R.

Euphrates R.

ARABIAN PENINSULA

Rub' al-Khali Desert

Gulf of Aden

Socotra

Red Sea

AFRICA

Tropic of Cancer

Equator

Hindu Kush

Indus R.

Ganges R.

Thar Desert

INDIAN PENINSULA

Deccan Plateau

Western Ghats

Eastern Ghats

Sri Lanka

Bay of Bengal

Andaman Islands

Andaman Sea

Plateau of Iran

Kara-Kum Desert

Persian Gulf

Arabian Sea

INDIAN OCEAN

1,000

0 miles 1,000

0 kilometers

Lambert Azimuthal Equal Area

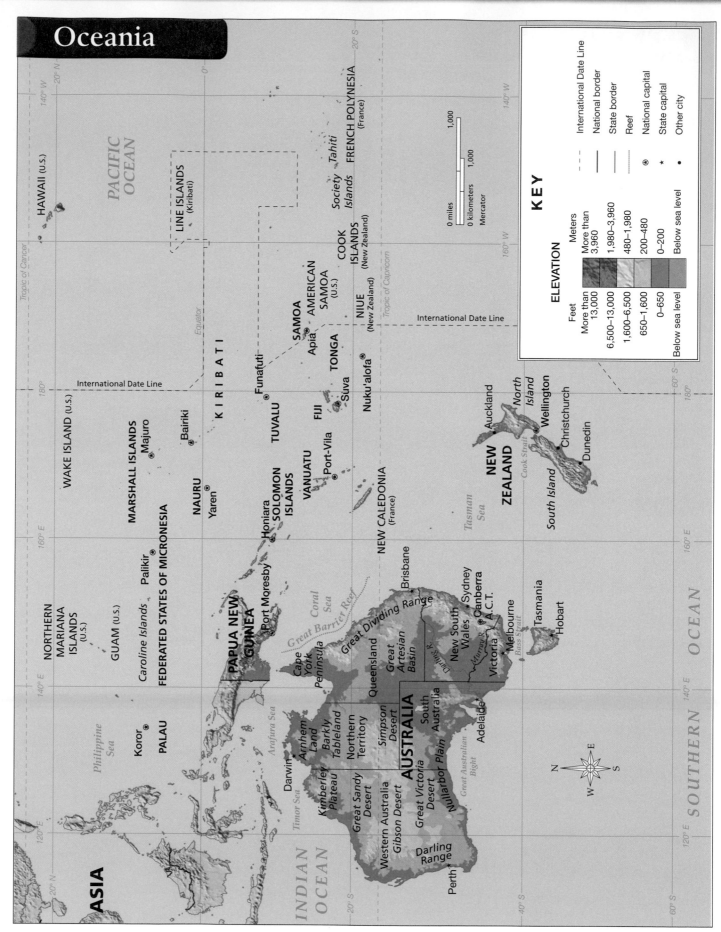

Oceania

KEY

ELEVATION

Feet	Meters
More than 13,000	More than 3,960
6,500–13,000	1,980–3,960
1,600–6,500	480–1,980
650–1,600	200–480
0–650	0–200
Below sea level	Below sea level

International Date Line
National border
State border
Reef
⊛ National capital
★ State capital
• Other city

0 miles 1,000
0 kilometers 1,000
Mercator

ASIA

PACIFIC OCEAN

HAWAII (U.S.)

LINE ISLANDS (Kiribati)

FRENCH POLYNESIA (France)

Society Islands   Tahiti

COOK ISLANDS (New Zealand)

SAMOA
Apia   AMERICAN SAMOA (U.S.)

NIUE (New Zealand)

International Date Line

TONGA
Nuku'alofa

WAKE ISLAND (U.S.)

MARSHALL ISLANDS
Majuro

Bairiki

K I R I B A T I

Funafuti

TUVALU

FIJI
Suva

NAURU
Yaren

VANUATU
Port-Vila

SOLOMON ISLANDS
Honiara

NEW CALEDONIA (France)

NORTHERN MARIANA ISLANDS (U.S.)

GUAM (U.S.)

Caroline Islands   Palikir

FEDERATED STATES OF MICRONESIA

Koror   PALAU

Philippine Sea

PAPUA NEW GUINEA
Port Moresby

Great Coral Sea

Great Barrier Reef

Cape York Peninsula

Arafura Sea

Timor Sea

Darwin

Arnhem Land

Kimberley Plateau

Northern Territory

Barkly Tableland

Simpson Desert

Queensland

Great Artesian Basin

Brisbane

New South Wales   Sydney
Canberra
A.C.T.

Great Dividing Range

AUSTRALIA

South Australia

Western Australia

Great Sandy Desert

Gibson Desert

Great Victoria Desert

Nullarbor Plain

Great Australian Bight

Adelaide

Murray R.

Darling R.

Victoria
Melbourne

Bass Strait

Tasmania
Hobart

Perth

Darling Range

INDIAN OCEAN

SOUTHERN OCEAN

NEW ZEALAND

Auckland

North Island

Wellington

Cook Strait

Christchurch

South Island

Dunedin

Tasman Sea

Tropic of Cancer

Equator

Tropic of Capricorn

International Date Line

N
E
W
S

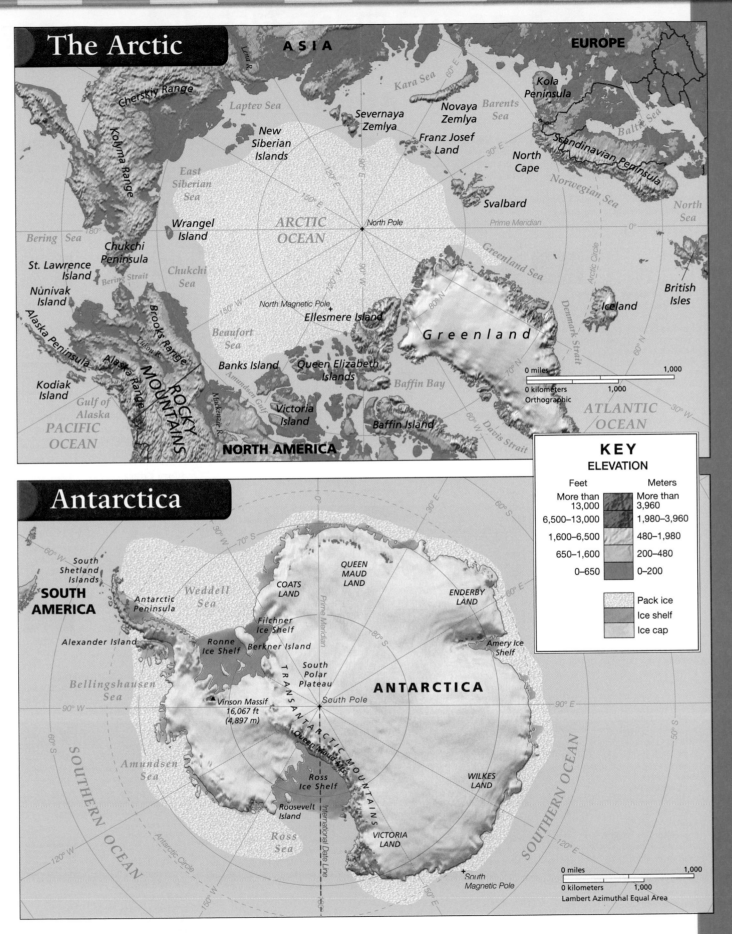

The Arctic

ASIA   EUROPE

Lena R.
Cherskiy Range
Kolyma Range
Laptev Sea
Kara Sea
60° E
Kola Peninsula
Severnaya Zemlya
Novaya Zemlya
Barents Sea
Baltic Sea
New Siberian Islands
Franz Josef Land
30° E
Scandinavian Peninsula
North Cape
East Siberian Sea
120° E
North Sea
90° E
Norwegian Sea
Svalbard
Prime Meridian
0°
Wrangel Island
ARCTIC OCEAN
North Pole
Bering Sea
180°
Chukchi Peninsula
Greenland Sea
Arctic Circle
St. Lawrence Island
Bering Strait
Chukchi Sea
90° W
80° N
British Isles
Nunivak Island
150° W
North Magnetic Pole
Denmark Strait
Iceland
Alaska Peninsula
Brooks Range
Yukon R.
Beaufort Sea
Ellesmere Island
60° N
70° N
Kodiak Island
Alaska Range
ROCKY MOUNTAINS
Banks Island
Amundsen Gulf
Queen Elizabeth Islands
Greenland
Gulf of Alaska
Mackenzie R.
Victoria Island
Baffin Bay
30° W
PACIFIC OCEAN
Baffin Island
Davis Strait
60° N
ATLANTIC OCEAN
NORTH AMERICA
30° W

0 miles   1,000
0 kilometers   1,000
Orthographic

Antarctica

30° W
70° S
Prime Meridian
30° E
60° S
South Shetland Islands
SOUTH AMERICA
60° W
Antarctic Peninsula
Weddell Sea
COATS LAND
QUEEN MAUD LAND
ENDERBY LAND
60° E
Alexander Island
Filchner Ice Shelf
Ronne Ice Shelf
Berkner Island
South Polar Plateau
80° S
Amery Ice Shelf
Bellingshausen Sea
TRANSANTARCTIC MOUNTAINS
ANTARCTICA
90° W
Vinson Massif 16,067 ft (4,897 m)
South Pole
90° E
60° S
Queen Maud Mts.
Amundsen Sea
Ross Ice Shelf
WILKES LAND
Roosevelt Island
International Date Line
SOUTHERN OCEAN
VICTORIA LAND
120° E
SOUTHERN OCEAN
120° W
Ross Sea
Antarctic Circle
50° S
South Magnetic Pole
150° W
150° E

0 miles   1,000
0 kilometers   1,000
Lambert Azimuthal Equal Area

KEY
ELEVATION

Feet	Meters
More than 13,000	More than 3,960
6,500–13,000	1,980–3,960
1,600–6,500	480–1,980
650–1,600	200–480
0–650	0–200

Pack ice
Ice shelf
Ice cap

Country Databank

Africa

Algeria
Capital: Algiers
Population: 32.3 million
Official Languages: Arabic and Tamazight
Land Area: 2,381,740 sq km; 919,590 sq mi
Leading Exports: petroleum, natural gas, petroleum products
Continent: Africa

Angola
Capital: Luanda
Population: 10.6 million
Official Language: Portuguese
Land Area: 1,246,700 sq km; 481,551 sq mi
Leading Exports: crude oil, diamonds, refined petroleum products, gas, coffee, sisal, fish and fish products, timber, cotton
Continent: Africa

Benin
Capital: Porto-Novo
Population: 6.9 million
Official Language: French
Land Area: 110,620 sq km; 42,710 sq mi
Leading Exports: cotton, crude oil, palm products, cocoa
Continent: Africa

Botswana
Capital: Gaborone
Population: 1.6 million
Official Language: English
Land Area: 585,370 sq km; 226,011 sq mi
Leading Exports: diamonds, copper, nickel, soda ash, meat, textiles
Continent: Africa

Burkina Faso
Capital: Ouagadougou
Population: 12.6 million
Official Language: French
Land Area: 273,800 sq km; 105,714 sq mi
Leading Exports: cotton, animal products, gold
Continent: Africa

Burundi
Capital: Bujumbura
Population: 6.4 million
Official Languages: Kirundi and French
Land Area: 25,650 sq km; 9,903 sq mi
Leading Exports: coffee, tea, sugar, cotton, hides
Continent: Africa

Cameroon
Capital: Yaoundé
Population: 16.1 million
Official Languages: English and French
Land Area: 469,440 sq km; 181,251 sqmi
Leading Exports: crude oil and petroleum products, lumber, cocoa, aluminum, coffee, cotton
Continent: Africa

Cape Verde
Capital: Praia
Population: 408,760
Official Language: Portuguese
Land Area: 4,033 sq km; 1,557 sq mi
Leading Exports: fuel, shoes, garments, fish, hides
Location: Atlantic Ocean

Central African Republic
Capital: Bangui
Population: 3.6 million
Official Language: French
Land Area: 622,984 sq km; 240,534 sq mi
Leading Exports: diamonds, timber, cotton, coffee, tobacco
Continent: Africa

Chad
Capital: N'Djamena
Population: 9 million
Official Languages: Arabic and French
Land Area: 1,259,200 sq km; 486,177 sq mi
Leading Exports: cotton, cattle, gum arabic
Continent: Africa

Comoros
Capital: Moroni
Population: 614,382
Official Languages: Arabic, Comoran, and French
Land Area: 2,170 sq km; 838 sq mi
Leading Exports: vanilla, ylang-ylang, cloves, perfume oil, copra
Location: Indian Ocean

Congo, Democratic Republic of the
Capital: Kinshasa
Population: 55.2 million
Official Language: French
Land Area: 2,267,600 sq km; 875,520 sq mi
Leading Exports: diamonds, copper, coffee, cobalt, crude oil
Continent: Africa

Congo, Republic of the
Capital: Brazzaville
Population: 3.3 million
Official Language: French
Land Area: 341,500 sq km; 131,853 sq mi
Leading Exports: petroleum, lumber, sugar, cocoa, coffee, diamonds
Continent: Africa

Djibouti
Capital: Djibouti
Population: 472,810
Official Languages: Arabic and French
Land Area: 22,980 sq km; 8,873 sq mi
Leading Exports: reexports, hides and skins, coffee (in transit)
Continent: Africa

Egypt
Capital: Cairo
Population: 70.7 million
Official Language: Arabic
Land Area: 995,450 sq km; 384,343 sq mi
Leading Exports: crude oil and petroleum products, cotton, textiles, metal products, chemicals
Continent: Africa

Equatorial Guinea
Capital: Malabo
Population: 498,144
Official Languages: Spanish and French
Land Area: 28,050 sq km; 10,830 sq mi
Leading Exports: petroleum, timber, cocoa
Continent: Africa

Eritrea
Capital: Asmara
Population: 4.5 million
Official Language: Tigrinya
Land Area: 121,320 sq km; 46,842 sq mi
Leading Exports: livestock, sorghum, textiles, food, small manufactured goods
Continent: Africa

Ethiopia
Capital: Addis Ababa
Population: 67.7 million
Official Language: Amharic
Land Area: 1,119,683 sq km; 432,310 sq mi
Leading Exports: coffee, qat, gold, leather products, oilseeds
Continent: Africa

Gabon
Capital: Libreville
Population: 1.2 million
Official Language: French
Land Area: 257,667 sq km; 99,489 sq mi
Leading Exports: crude oil, timber, manganese, uranium
Continent: Africa

Gambia
Capital: Banjul
Population: 1.5 million
Official Language: English
Land Area: 10,000 sq km; 3,861 sq mi
Leading Exports: peanuts and peanut products, fish, cotton lint, palm kernels
Continent: Africa

Ghana
Capital: Accra
Population: 20.2 million
Official Language: English
Land Area: 230,940 sq km; 89,166 sq mi
Leading Exports: gold, cocoa, timber, tuna, bauxite, aluminum, manganese ore, diamonds
Continent: Africa

Guinea
Capital: Conakry
Population: 7.8 million
Official Language: French
Land Area: 245,857 sq km; 94,925 sq mi
Leading Exports: bauxite, alumina, gold, diamonds, coffee, fish, agricultural products
Continent: Africa

Guinea-Bissau
Capital: Bissau
Population: 1.4 million
Official Language: Portuguese
Land Area: 28,000 sq km; 10,811 sq mi
Leading Exports: cashew nuts, shrimp, peanuts, palm kernels, lumber
Continent: Africa

Ivory Coast
Capital: Yamoussoukro
Population: 16.8 million
Official Language: French
Land Area: 318,000 sq km; 122,780 sq mi
Leading Exports: cocoa, coffee, timber, petroleum, cotton, bananas, pineapples, palm oil, cotton, fish
Continent: Africa

Kenya
Capital: Nairobi
Population: 31.3 million
Official Languages: Swahili and English
Land Area: 569,250 sq km; 219,787 sq mi
Leading Exports: tea, horticultural products, coffee, petroleum products, fish, cement
Continent: Africa

Lesotho
Capital: Maseru
Population: 2.2 million
Official Languages: Sesotho and English
Land Area: 30,355 sq km; 11,720 sq mi
Leading Exports: manufactured goods (clothing, footwear, road vehicles), wool and mohair, food and live animals
Continent: Africa

Liberia
Capital: Monrovia
Population: 3.3 million
Official Language: English
Land Area: 96,320 sq km; 37,189 sq mi
Leading Exports: rubber, timber, iron, diamonds, cocoa, coffee
Continent: Africa

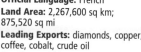

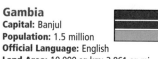

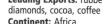

Libya
Capital: Tripoli
Population: 5.4 million
Official Language: Arabic
Land Area: 1,759,540 sq km; 679,358 sq mi
Leading Exports: crude oil, refined petroleum products
Location: Indian

Madagascar
Capital: Antananarivo
Population: 16.5 million
Official Languages: French and Malagasy
Land Area: 581,540 sq km; 224,533 sq mi
Leading Exports: coffee, vanilla, shellfish, sugar, cotton cloth, chromite, petroleum products
Location: Indian Ocean

Malawi
Capital: Lilongwe
Population: 10.7 million
Official Languages: English and Chichewa
Land Area: 94,080 sq km; 36,324 sq mi
Leading Exports: tobacco, tea, sugar, cotton, coffee, peanuts, wood products, apparel
Continent: Africa

Mali
Capital: Bamako
Population: 11.3 million
Official Language: French
Land Area: 1,220,000 sq km; 471,042 sq mi
Leading Exports: cotton, gold, livestock
Continent: Africa

Mauritania
Capital: Nouakchott
Population: 2.8 million
Official Language: Arabic
Land Area: 1,030,400 sq km; 397,837 sq mi
Leading Exports: iron ore, fish and fish products, gold
Continent: Africa

Mauritius
Capital: Port Louis
Population: 1.2 million
Official Language: English
Land Area: 2,030 sq km; 784 sq mi
Leading Exports: clothing and textiles, sugar, cut flowers, molasses
Location: Indian Ocean

Morocco
Capital: Rabat
Population: 31.2 million
Official Language: Arabic
Land Area: 446,300 sq km; 172,316 sq mi
Leading Exports: phosphates and fertilizers, food and beverages, minerals
Continent: Africa

Mozambique
Capital: Maputo
Population: 19.6 million
Official Language: Portuguese
Land Area: 784,090 sq km; 302,737 sq mi
Leading Exports: prawns, cashews, cotton, sugar, citrus, timber, bulk electricity
Continent: Africa

Namibia
Capital: Windhoek
Population: 1.8 million
Official Language: English
Land Area: 825,418 sq km; 318,694 sq mi
Leading Exports: diamonds, copper, gold, zinc, lead, uranium, cattle, processed fish, karakul skins
Continent: Africa

Niger
Capital: Niamey
Population: 11.3 million
Official Language: French
Land Area: 1,226,700 sq km; 489,073 sq mi
Leading Exports: uranium ore, livestock products, cowpeas, onions
Continent: Africa

Nigeria
Capital: Abuja
Population: 129.9 million
Official Language: English
Land Area: 910,768 sq km; 351,648 sq mi
Leading Exports: petroleum and petroleum products, cocoa, rubber
Continent: Africa

Rwanda
Capital: Kigali
Population: 7.4 million
Official Languages: Kinyarwanda, French, and English
Land Area: 24,948 sq km; 9,632 sq mi
Leading Exports: coffee, tea, hides, tin ore
Continent: Africa

São Tomé and Príncipe
Capital: São Tomé
Population: 170,372
Official Language: Portuguese
Land Area: 1,001 sq km; 386 sq mi
Leading Exports: cocoa, copra, coffee, palm oil
Location: Atlantic Ocean

Senegal
Capital: Dakar
Population: 10.6 million
Official Language: French
Land Area: 192,000 sq km; 74,131 sq mi
Leading Exports: fish, groundnuts (peanuts), petroleum products, phosphates, cotton
Continent: Africa

Seychelles
Capital: Victoria
Population: 80,098
Official Languages: English and French
Land Area: 455 sq km; 176 sq mi
Leading Exports: canned tuna, cinnamon bark, copra, petroleum products (reexports)
Location: Indian Ocean

Sierra Leone
Capital: Freetown
Population: 5.6 million
Official Language: English
Land Area: 71,620 sq km; 27,652 sq mi
Leading Exports: diamonds, rutile, cocoa, coffee, fish
Continent: Africa

Somalia
Capital: Mogadishu
Population: 7.8 million
Official Languages: Somali and Arabic
Land Area: 627,337 sq km; 242,215 sq mi
Leading Exports: livestock, bananas, hides, fish, charcoal, scrap metal
Continent: Africa

South Africa
Capital: Cape Town, Pretoria, and Bloemfontein
Population: 43.6 million
Official Languages: Eleven official languages: Afrikaans, English, Ndebele, Pedi, Sotho, Swazi, Tsonga, Tswana, Venda, Xhosa, and Zulu
Land Area: 1,219,912 sq km; 471,008 sq mi
Leading Exports: gold, diamonds, platinum, other metals and minerals, machinery and equipment
Continent: Africa

Sudan
Capital: Khartoum
Population: 37.1 million
Official Language: Arabic
Land Area: 2,376,000 sq km; 917,374 sq mi
Leading Exports: oil and petroleum products, cotton, sesame, livestock, groundnuts, gum arabic, sugar
Continent: Africa

Swaziland
Capital: Mbabane
Population: 1.1 million
Official Languages: English and siSwati
Land Area: 17,20 sq km; 6,642 sq mi
Leading Exports: soft drink concentrates, sugar, wood pulp, cotton yarn, refrigerators, citrus and canned fruit
Continent: Africa

Tanzania
Capital: Dar es Salaam and Dodoma
Population: 37.2 million
Official Languages: Swahili and English
Land Area: 886,037 sq km; 342,099 sq mi
Leading Exports: gold, coffee, cashew nuts, manufactured goods, cotton
Continent: Africa

Togo
Capital: Lomé
Population: 5.2 million
Official Language: French
Land Area: 54,385 sq km; 20,998 sq mi
Leading Exports: cotton, phosphates, coffee, cocoa
Continent: Africa

Tunisia
Capital: Tunis
Population: 9.8 million
Official Language: Arabic
Land Area: 155,360 sq km; 59,984 sq mi
Leading Exports: textiles, mechanical goods, phosphates and chemicals, agricultural products, hydrocarbons
Continent: Africa

Uganda
Capital: Kampala
Population: 24.7 million
Official Language: English
Land Area: 199,710 sq km; 77,108 sq mi
Leading Exports: coffee, fish and fish products, tea, gold, cotton, flowers, horticultural products
Continent: Africa

Zambia
Capital: Lusaka
Population: 10.1 million
Official Language: English
Land Area: 740,724 sq km; 285,994 sq mi
Leading Exports: copper, cobalt, electricity, tobacco, flowers, cotton
Continent: Africa

Zimbabwe
Capital: Harare
Population: 11.3 million
Official Language: English
Land Area: 386,670 sq km; 149,293 sq mi
Leading Exports: tobacco, gold, iron alloys, textiles and clothing
Continent: Africa

Asia and the Pacific

Afghanistan
Capital: Kabul
Population: 27.8 million
Official Languages: Pashtu and Dari
Land Area: 647,500 sq km; 250,000 sq mi
Leading Exports: agricultural products, hand-woven carpets, wool, cotton, hides and pelts, precious and semiprecious gems
Continent: Asia

Armenia
Capital: Yerevan
Population: 3.3 million
Official Language: Armenian
Land Area: 29,400 sq km; 10,965 sq mi
Leading Exports: diamonds, scrap metal, machinery and equipment, brandy, copper ore
Continent: Asia

Australia
Capital: Canberra
Population: 19.6 million
Official Language: English
Land Area: 7,617,930 sq km; 2,941,283 sq mi
Leading Exports: coal, gold, meat, wool, alumina, iron ore, wheat, machinery and transport equipment
Continent: Australia

Azerbaijan
Capital: Baku
Population: 7.8 million
Official Language: Azerbaijani
Land Area: 86,100 sq km; 33,243 sq mi
Leading Exports: oil and gas, machinery, cotton, foodstuffs
Continent: Asia

Bahrain
Capital: Manama
Population: 656,397
Official Language: Arabic
Land Area: 665 sq km; 257 sq mi
Leading Exports: petroleum and petroleum products, aluminum, textiles
Continent: Asia

Bangladesh
Capital: Dhaka
Population: 133.4 million
Official Language: Bengali
Land Area: 133,910 sq km; 51,705 sq mi
Leading Exports: garments, jute and jute goods, leather, frozen fish and seafood
Continent: Asia

Bhutan
Capital: Thimphu
Population: 2.1 million
Official Language: Dzongkha
Land Area: 47,000 sq km; 18,147 sq mi
Leading Exports: electricity, cardamom, gypsum, timber, handicrafts, cement, fruit, precious stones, spices
Continent: Asia

Brunei
Capital: Bandar Seri Begawan
Population: 350,898
Official Language: Malay
Land Area: 5,270 sq km; 2,035 sq mi
Leading Exports: crude oil, natural gas, refined products
Continent: Asia

Cambodia
Capital: Phnom Penh
Population: 12.8 million
Official Language: Khmer
Land Area: 176,520 sq km; 68,154 sq mi
Leading Exports: timber, garments, rubber, rice, fish
Continent: Asia

China
Capital: Beijing
Population: 1.29 billion
Official Languages: Mandarin and Chinese
Land Area: 9,326,410 sq km; 3,600,927 sq mi
Leading Exports: machinery and equipment, textiles and clothing, footwear, toys and sports goods, mineral fuels
Continent: Asia

Cyprus
Capital: Nicosia
Population: 767,314
Official Languages: Greek and Turkish
Land Area: 9,240 sq km; 3,568 sq mi
Leading Exports: citrus, potatoes, grapes, wine, cement, clothing and shoes
Location: Mediterranean Sea

East Timor
Capital: Dili
Population: 952,618
Official Languages: Tetum and Portuguese
Land Area: 15,007 sq km; 5,794 sq mi
Leading Exports: coffee, sandalwood, marble
Continent: Asia

Fiji
Capital: Suva
Population: 856,346
Official Language: English
Land Area: 18,270 sq km; 7,054 sq mi
Leading Exports: sugar, garments, gold, timber, fish, molasses, cocnut oil
Location: Pacific Ocean

Georgia
Capital: Tbilisi
Population: 5 million
Official Languages: Georgian and Abkhazian
Land Area: 69,700 sq km; 26,911 sq mi
Leading Exports: scrap metal, machinery, chemicals, fuel reexports, citrus fruits, tea, wine, other agricultural products
Continent: Asia

India
Capital: New Delhi
Population: 1.05 billion
Official Languages: Hindi and English
Land Area: 2,973,190 sq km; 1,147,949 sq mi
Leading Exports: textile goods, gems and jewelry, engineering goods, chemicals, leather manufactured goods
Continent: Asia

Indonesia
Capital: Jakarta
Population: 231.3 million
Official Language: Bahasa Indonesia
Land Area: 1,826,440 sq km; 705,188 sq mi
Leading Exports: oil and gas, electrical appliances, plywood, textiles, rubber
Continent: Asia

Iran
Capital: Tehran
Population: 66.6 million
Official Language: Farsi
Land Area: 1,636,000 sq km; 631,660 sq mi
Leading Exports: petroleum, carpets, fruits and nuts, iron and steel, chemicals
Continent: Asia

Iraq
Capital: Baghdad
Population: 24.7 million
Official Language: Arabic
Land Area: 432,162 sq km; 166,858 sq mi
Leading Exports: crude oil
Continent: Asia

Israel
Capital: Jerusalem
Population: 6.0 million
Official Language: Hebrew, Arabic
Land Area: 20,330 sq km; 7,849 sq mi
Leading Exports: machinery and equipment, software, cut diamonds, agricultural products, chemicals, textiles and apparel
Continent: Asia

Japan
Capital: Tokyo
Population: 127 million
Official Language: Japanese
Land Area: 374,744 sq km; 144,689 sq mi
Leading Exports: motor vehicles, semiconductors, office machinery, chemicals
Continent: Asia

Jordan
Capital: Amman
Population: 5.3 million
Official Language: Arabic
Land Area: 91,971 sq km; 35,510 sq mi
Leading Exports: phosphates, fertilizers, potash, agricultural products, manufactured goods, pharmaceuticals
Continent: Asia

Kazakhstan
Capital: Astana
Population: 16.7 million
Official Language: Kazakh
Land Area: 2,669,800 sq km; 1,030,810 sq mi
Leading Exports: oil and oil products, ferrous metals, machinery, chemicals, grain, wool, meat, coal
Continent: Asia

Kiribati
Capital: Bairiki (Tarawa Atoll)
Population: 96,335
Official Language: English
Land Area: 811 sq km; 313 sq mi
Leading Exports: copra, coconuts, seaweed, fish
Location: Pacific Ocean

Korea, North
Capital: Pyongyang
Population: 22.3 million
Official Language: Korean
Land Area: 120,410 sq km; 46,490 sq mi
Leading Exports: minerals, metallurgical products, manufactured goods (including armaments), agricultural and fishery products
Continent: Asia

Korea, South
Capital: Seoul
Population: 48.3 million
Official Language: Korean
Land Area: 98,190 sq km; 37,911 sq mi
Leading Exports: electronic products, machinery and equipment, motor vehicles, steel, ships, textiles, clothing, footwear, fish
Continent: Asia

Kuwait
Capital: Kuwait City
Population: 2.1 million
Official Language: Arabic
Land Area: 17,820 sq km; 6,880 sq mi
Leading Exports: oil and refined products, fertilizers
Continent: Asia

Kyrgyzstan
Capital: Bishkek
Population: 4.8 million
Official Languages: Kyrgyz and Russian
Land Area: 191,300 sq km; 73,861 sq mi
Leading Exports: cotton, wool, meat, tobacco, gold, mercury, uranium, hydropower, machinery, shoes
Continent: Asia

Laos
Capital: Vientiane
Population: 5.8 million
Official Language: Lao
Land Area: 230,800 sq km; 89,112 sq mi
Leading Exports: wood products, garments, electricity, coffee, tin
Continent: Asia

Lebanon
Capital: Beirut
Population: 3.7 million
Official Language: Arabic
Land Area: 10,230 sq km; 3,950 sq mi
Leading Exports: foodstuffs and tobacco, textile, chemicals, precious stones, metal and metal products, electrical equipment and products, jewelry, paper and paper products
Continent: Asia

Malaysia
Capital: Kuala Lumpur and Putrajaya
Population: 22.7 million
Official Language: Bahasa Malaysia
Land Area: 328,550 sq km; 126,853 sq mi
Leading Exports: electronic equipment, petroleum and liquefied natural gas, wood and wood products, palm oil, rubber, textiles, chemicals
Continent: Asia

Maldives
Capital: Malé
Population: 320,165
Official Language: Dhivehi (Maldivian)
Land Area: 300 sq km; 116 sq mi
Leading Exports: fish, clothing
Location: Indian Ocean

Marshall Islands
Capital: Majuro
Population: 73,360
Official Languages: Marshallese and English
Land Area: 181.3 sq km; 70 sq mi
Leading Exports: copra cake, coconut oil, handicrafts
Location: Pacific Ocean

Micronesia, Federated States of
Capital: Palikir (Pohnpei Island)
Population: 135,869
Official Language: English
Land Area: 702 sq km; 271 sq mi
Leading Exports: fish, garments, bananas, black pepper
Location: Pacific Ocean

Mongolia
Capital: Ulaanbaatar
Population: 2.6 million
Official Language: Khalkha Mongolian
Land Area: 1,555,400 sq km; 600,540 sq mi
Leading Exports: copper, livestock, animal products, cashmere, wool, hides, fluorspar, other nonferrous metals
Continent: Asia

Myanmar (Burma)
Capital: Rangoon (Yangon)
Population: 42.2 million
Official Language: Burmese (Myanmar)
Land Area: 657,740 sq km; 253,953 sq mi
Leading Exports: apparel, foodstuffs, wood products, precious stones
Continent: Asia

Nauru
Capital: Yaren District
Population: 12,329
Official Language: Nauruan
Land Area: 21 sq km; 8 sq mi
Leading Exports: phosphates
Location: Pacific Ocean

Nepal
Capital: Kathmandu
Population: 25.9 million
Official Language: Nepali
Land Area: 136,800 sq km; 52,818 sq mi
Leading Exports: carpets, clothing, leather goods, jute goods, grain
Continent: Asia

New Zealand
Capital: Wellington
Population: 3.8 million
Official Languages: English and Maori
Land Area: 268,680 sq km; 103,737 sq mi
Leading Exports: dairy products, meat, wood and wood products, fish, machinery
Location: Pacific Ocean

Oman
Capital: Muscat
Population: 2.7 million
Official Language: Arabic
Land Area: 212,460 sq km; 82,030 sq mi
Leading Exports: petroleum, reexports, fish, metals, textiles
Continent: Asia

Pakistan
Capital: Islamabad
Population: 147.7 million
Official Languages: Urdu and English
Land Area: 778,720 sq km; 300,664 sq mi
Leading Exports: textiles (garments, cotton cloth, and yarn), rice, other agricultural products
Continent: Asia

Palau
Capital: Koror
Population: 19,409
Official Languages: English and Palauan
Land Area: 458 sq km; 177 sq mi
Leading Exports: shellfish, tuna, copra, garments
Location: Pacific Ocean

Papua New Guinea
Capital: Port Moresby
Population: 5.2 million
Official Language: English
Land Area: 452,860 sq km; 174,849 sq mi
Leading Exports: oil, gold, copper ore, logs, palm oil, coffee, cocoa, crayfish, prawns
Location: Pacific Ocean

Philippines
Capital: Manila
Population: 84.5 million
Official Languages: Filipino and English
Land Area: 298,170 sq km; 115,123 sq mi
Leading Exports: electronic equipment, machinery and transport equipment, garments, coconut products
Continent: Asia

Qatar
Capital: Doha
Population: 793,341
Official Language: Arabic
Land Area: 11,437 sq km; 4,416 sq mi
Leading Exports: petroleum products, fertilizers, steel
Continent: Asia

Samoa
Capital: Apia
Population: 178,631
Official Languages: Samoan and English
Land Area: 2,934 sq km; 1,133 sq mi
Leading Exports: fish, coconut oil cream, copra, taro, garments, beer
Location: Pacific Ocean

Saudi Arabia
Capital: Riyadh and Jiddah
Population: 23.5 million
Official Language: Arabic
Land Area: 1,960,582 sq km; 756,981 sq mi
Leading Exports: petroleum and petroleum products
Continent: Asia

Singapore
Capital: Singapore
Population: 4.5 million
Official Languages: Malay, English, Mandarin, Chinese, and Tamil
Land Area: 683 sq km; 264 sq mi
Leading Exports: machinery and equipment (including electronics), consumer goods, chemicals, mineral fuels
Continent: Asia

Solomon Islands
Capital: Honiara
Population: 494,786
Official Language: English
Land Area: 27,540 sq km; 10,633 sq mi
Leading Exports: timber, fish, copra, palm oil, cocoa
Location: Pacific Ocean

Sri Lanka
Capital: Colombo
Population: 19.6 million
Official Language: Sinhala, Tamil, and English
Land Area: 64,740 sq km; 24,996 sq mi
Leading Exports: textiles and apparel, tea, diamonds, coconut products, petroleum products
Continent: Asia

Syria
Capital: Damascus
Population: 17.2 million
Official Language: Arabic
Land Area: 184,050 sq km; 71,062 sq mi
Leading Exports: crude oil, textiles, fruits and vegetables, raw cotton
Continent: Asia

Taiwan
Capital: Taipei
Population: 22.5 million
Official Language: Mandarin Chinese
Land Area: 32,260 sq km; 12,456 sq mi
Leading Exports: machinery and electrical equipment, metals, textiles, plastics, chemicals
Continent: Asia

Tajikistan
Capital: Dushanbe
Population: 6.7 million
Official Language: Tajik
Land Area: 142,700 sq km; 55,096 sq mi
Leading Exports: aluminum, electricity, cotton, fruits, vegetables, oil, textiles
Continent: Asia

Thailand
Capital: Bangkok
Population: 62.5 million
Official Language: Thai
Land Area: 511,770 sq km; 197,564 sq mi
Leading Exports: computers, transistors, seafood, clothing, rice
Continent: Asia

Tonga
Capital: Nuku'alofa
Population: 106,137
Official Languages: Tongan and English
Land Area: 718 sq km; 277 sq mi
Leading Exports: squash, fish, vanilla beans, root crops
Location: Pacific Ocean

Turkey
Capital: Ankara
Population: 67.3 million
Official Language: Turkish
Land Area: 770,760 sq km; 297,590 sq mi
Leading Exports: apparel, foodstuffs, textiles, metal manufactured goods, transport equipment
Continent: Asia

Turkmenistan
Capital: Ashgabat
Population: 4.7 million
Official Language: Turkmen
Land Area: 488,100 sq km; 188,455 sq mi
Leading Exports: gas, oil, cotton fiber, textiles
Continent: Asia

Asia and the Pacific (continued)

Tuvalu
Capital: Fongafale
Population: 10,800
Official Language: English
Land Area: 26 sq km; 10 sq mi
Leading Exports: copra, fish
Location: Pacific Ocean

United Arab Emirates
Capital: Abu Dhabi
Population: 2.4 million
Official Language: Arabic
Land Area: 82,880 sq km; 32,000 sq mi
Leading Exports: crude oil, natural gas, reexports, dried fish, dates
Continent: Asia

Uzbekistan
Capital: Tashkent
Population: 25.5 million
Official Language: Uzbek
Land Area: 425,400 sq km; 164,247 sq mi
Leading Exports: cotton, gold, energy products, mineral fertilizers, ferrous metals, textiles, food products, automobiles
Continent: Asia

Vanuatu
Capital: Port-Vila
Population: 196,178
Official Languages: English, French, and Bislama
Land Area: 12,200 sq km; 4,710 sq mi
Leading Exports: copra, kava, beef, cocoa, timber, coffee
Location: Pacific Ocean

Vietnam
Capital: Hanoi
Population: 81.1 million
Official Language: Vietnamese
Land Area: 325,320 sq km; 125,621 sq mi
Leading Exports: crude oil, marine products, rice, coffee, rubber, tea, garments, shoes
Continent: Asia

Yemen
Capital: Sanaa
Population: 18.7 million
Official Language: Arabic
Land Area: 527,970 sq km; 203,849 sq mi
Leading Exports: crude oil, coffee, dried and salted fish
Continent: Asia

Europe and Russia

Albania
Capital: Tiranë
Population: 3.5 million
Official Language: Albanian
Land Area: 27,398 sq km; 10,578 sq mi
Leading Exports: textiles and footwear, asphalt, metals and metallic ores, crude oil, vegetables, fruits, tobacco
Continent: Europe

Andorra
Capital: Andorra la Vella
Population: 68,403
Official Language: Catalan
Land Area: 468 sq km; 181 sq mi
Leading Exports: tobacco products, furniture
Continent: Europe

Austria
Capital: Vienna
Population: 8.2 million
Official Language: German
Land Area: 82,738 sq km; 31,945 sq mi
Leading Exports: machinery and equipment, motor vehicles and parts, paper and paperboard, metal goods, chemicals, iron and steel, textiles, foodstuffs
Continent: Europe

Belarus
Capital: Minsk
Population: 10.3 million
Official Languages: Belarussian and Russian
Land Area: 207,600 sq km; 80,154 sq mi
Leading Exports: machinery and equipment, mineral products, chemicals, textiles, food stuffs, metals
Continent: Europe

Belgium
Capital: Brussels
Population: 10.3 million
Official Languages: Dutch and French
Land Area: 30,230 sq km; 11,172 sq mi
Leading Exports: machinery and equipment, chemicals, metals and metal products
Continent: Europe

Bosnia and Herzegovina
Capital: Sarajevo
Population: 4.0 million
Official Language: Serbo-Croat
Land Area: 51,129 sq km; 19,741 sq mi
Leading Exports: miscellaneous manufactured goods, crude materials
Continent: Europe

Bulgaria
Capital: Sofia
Population: 7.6 million
Official Language: Bulgarian
Land Area: 110,550 sq km; 42,683 sq mi
Leading Exports: clothing, footwear, iron and steel, machinery and equipment, fuels
Continent: Europe

Croatia
Capital: Zagreb
Population: 4.4 million
Official Language: Croatian
Land Area: 56,414 km; 21,781 sq mi
Leading Exports: transport equipment, textiles, chemicals, foodstuffs, fuels
Continent: Europe

Czech Republic
Capital: Prague
Population: 10.3 million
Official Language: Czech
Land Area: 78,276 sq km; 29,836 sq mi
Leading Exports: machinery and transport equipment, intermediate manufactured goods, chemicals, raw materials and fuel
Continent: Europe

Denmark
Capital: Copenhagen
Population: 5.4 million
Official Language: Danish
Land Area: 42,394 sq km; 16,368 sq mi
Leading Exports: machinery and instruments, meat and meat products, dairy products, fish, chemicals, furniture, ships, windmills
Continent: Europe

Estonia
Capital: Tallinn
Population: 1.4 million
Official Language: Estonian
Land Area: 43,211 sq km; 16,684 sq mi
Leading Exports: machinery and equipment, wood products, textiles, food products, metals, chemical products
Continent: Europe

Finland
Capital: Helsinki
Population: 5.2 million
Official Languages: Finnish and Swedish
Land Area: 305,470 sq km; 117,942 sq mi
Leading Exports: machinery and equipment, chemicals, metals, timber, paper, pulp
Continent: Europe

France
Capital: Paris
Population: 59.8 million
Official Language: French
Land Area: 545,630 sq km; 310,668 sq mi
Leading Exports: machinery and transportation equipment, aircraft, plastics, chemicals, pharmaceutical products, iron and steel, beverages
Continent: Europe

Germany
Capital: Berlin
Population: 83 million
Official Language: German
Land Area: 349,223 sq km; 134,835 sq mi
Leading Exports: machinery, vehicles, chemicals, metals and manufactured goods, foodstuffs, textiles
Continent: Europe

Greece
Capital: Athens
Population: 10.6 million
Official Language: Greek
Land Area: 130,800 sq km; 50,502 sq mi
Leading Exports: food and beverages, manufactured goods, petroleum products, chemicals, textiles
Continent: Europe

Hungary
Capital: Budapest
Population: 10.1 million
Official Language: Hungarian
Land Area: 92,340 sq km; 35,652 sq mi
Leading Exports: machinery and equipment, other manufactured goods, food products, raw materials, fuels and electricity
Continent: Europe

Iceland
Capital: Reykjavík
Population: 279,384
Official Language: Icelandic
Land Area: 100,250 sq km; 38,707 sq mi
Leading Exports: fish and fish products, animal products, aluminum, diatomite, ferrosilicon
Location: Atlantic Ocean

Ireland
Capital: Dublin
Population: 3.9 million
Official Languages: Irish Gaelic and English
Land Area: 68,890 sq km; 26,598 sq mi
Leading Exports: machinery and equipment, computers, chemicals, pharmaceuticals, live animals, animal products
Continent: Europe

Italy
Capital: Rome
Population: 57.7 million
Official Language: Italian
Land Area: 294,020 sq km; 113,521 sq mi
Leading Exports: fruits, vegetables, grapes, potatoes, sugar beets, soybeans, grain, olives, beef, diary products, fish
Continent: Europe

Latvia
Capital: Riga
Population: 2.4 million
Official Language: Latvian
Land Area: 63,589 sq km; 24,552 sq mi
Leading Exports: wood and wood products, machinery and equipment, metals, textiles, foodstuffs
Continent: Europe

Liechtenstein
Capital: Vaduz
Population: 32,842
Official Language: German
Land Area: 160 sq km; 62 sq mi
Leading Exports: small specialty machinery, dental products, stamps, hardware, pottery
Continent: Europe

Lithuania
Capital: Vilnius
Population: 3.6 million
Official Language: Lithuanian
Land Area: 65,200 sq km; 25,174 sq mi
Leading Exports: mineral products, textiles and clothing, machinery and equipment, chemicals, wood and wood products, foodstuffs
Continent: Europe

Luxembourg
Capital: Luxembourg
Population: 448,569
Official Language: Luxembourgish, French, and German
Land Area: 2,586 sq km; 998 sq mi
Leading Exports: machinery and equipment, steel products, chemicals, rubber products, glass
Continent: Europe

Macedonia, The Former Yugoslav Republic of
Capital: Skopje
Population: 2.1 million
Official Languages: Macedonian and Albanian
Land Area: 24,856 sq km; 9,597 sq mi
Leading Exports: food, beverages, tobacco, miscellaneous manufactured goods, iron and steel
Continent: Europe

Malta
Capital: Valletta
Population: 397,499
Official Languages: Maltese and English
Land Area: 316 sq km; 122 sq mi
Leading Exports: machinery and transport equipment, manufactured goods
Location: Mediterranean Sea

Moldova
Capital: Chişinău
Population: 4.4 million
Official Language: Moldovan
Land Area: 33,371 sq km; 12,885 sq mi
Leading Exports: foodstuffs, textiles and footwear, machinery
Continent: Europe

Monaco
Capital: Monaco
Population: 31,987
Official Language: French
Land Area: 1.95 sq km; 0.75 sq mi
Leading Exports: no information available
Continent: Europe

Netherlands
Capitals: Amsterdam and The Hague
Population: 16.1 million
Official Language: Dutch
Land Area: 33,883 sq km; 13,082 sq mi
Leading Exports: machinery and equipment, chemicals, fuels, foodstuffs
Continent: Europe

Norway
Capital: Oslo
Population: 4.5 million
Official Language: Norwegian
Land Area: 307,860 sq km; 118,865 sq mi
Leading Exports: petroleum and petroleum products, machinery and equipment, metals, chemicals, ships, fish
Continent: Europe

Poland
Capital: Warsaw
Population: 38.6 million
Official Language: Polish
Land Area: 304,465 sq km; 117,554 sq mi
Leading Exports: machinery and transport equipment, intermediate manufactured goods, miscellaneous manufactured goods, food and live animals
Continent: Europe

Portugal
Capital: Lisbon
Population: 10.1 million
Official Language: Portuguese
Land Area: 91,951 sq km; 35,502 sq mi
Leading Exports: clothing and footwear, machinery, chemicals, cork and paper products, hides
Continent: Europe

Romania
Capital: Bucharest
Population: 22.3 million
Official Language: Romanian
Land Area: 230,340 sq km; 88,934 sq mi
Leading Exports: textiles and footwear, metals and metal products, machinery and equipment, minerals and fuels
Continent: Europe

Russia
Capital: Moscow
Population: 145 million
Official Language: Russian
Land Area: 16,995,800 sq km; 6,592,100 sq mi
Leading Exports: petroleum and petroleum products, natural gas, wood and wood products, metals, chemicals, and a wide variety of civilian and military manufactured goods
Continents: Europe and Asia

San Marino
Capital: San Marino
Population: 27,730
Official Language: Italian
Land Area: 61 sq km; 24 sq mi
Leading Exports: building stone, lime, wood, chestnuts, wheat, wine, baked goods, hides, ceramics
Continent: Europe

Serbia and Montenegro
Capital: Belgrade
Population: 10.7 million
Official Language: Serbo-Croat
Land Area: 102,136 sq km; 39,435 sq mi
Leading Exports: manufactured goods, food and live animals, raw materials
Continent: Europe

Slovakia
Capital: Bratislava
Population: 5.4 million
Official Language: Slovak
Land Area: 48,800 sq km; 18,842 sq mi
Leading Exports: machinery and transport equipment, intermediate manufactured goods, miscellaneous manufactured goods, chemicals
Continent: Europe

Slovenia
Capital: Ljubljana
Population: 1.9 million
Official Language: Slovene
Land Area: 20,151 sq km; 7,780 sq mi
Leading Exports: manufactured goods, machinery and transport equipment, chemicals, food
Continent: Europe

Spain
Capital: Madrid
Population: 40.1 million
Official Languages: Spanish, Galician, Basque, and Catalan
Land Area: 499,542 sq km; 192,873 sq mi
Leading Exports: machinery, motor vehicles, foodstuffs, other consumer goods
Continent: Europe

Sweden
Capital: Stockholm
Population: 8.9 million
Official Language: Swedish
Land Area: 410,934 sq km; 158,662 sq mi
Leading Exports: machinery, motor vehicles, paper products, pulp and wood, iron and steel products, chemicals
Continent: Europe

Switzerland
Capital: Bern
Population: 7.3 million
Official Languages: German, French, and Italian
Land Area: 39,770 sq km; 15,355 sq mi
Leading Exports: machinery, chemicals, metals, watches, agricultural products
Continent: Europe

Ukraine
Capital: Kiev
Population: 48.4 million
Official Language: Ukrainian
Land Area: 603,700 sq km; 233,090 sq mi
Leading Exports: ferrous and nonferrous metals, fuel and petroleum products, machinery and transport equipment, food products
Continent: Europe

United Kingdom
Capital: London
Population: 59.8 million
Official Languages: English and Welsh
Land Area: 241,590 sq km; 93,278 sq mi
Leading Exports: manufactured goods, fuels, chemicals, food, beverages, tobacco
Continent: Europe

Holy See (Vatican City)
Capital: Vatican City
Population: 900
Official Languages: Latin and Italian
Land Area: 0.44 sq km; 0.17 sq mi
Leading Exports: no information available
Continent: Europe

Latin America

Antigua and Barbuda
Capital: Saint John's
Population: 67,448
Official Language: English
Land Area: 442 sq km; 171 sq mi
Leading Exports: petroleum products, manufactured goods, machinery and transport equipment, food and live animals
Location: Caribbean Sea

Argentina
Capital: Buenos Aires
Population: 37.8 million
Official Language: Spanish
Land Area: 2,736,690 sq km; 1,056,636 sq mi
Leading Exports: edible oils, fuels and energy, cereals, feed, motor vehicles
Continent: South America

Bahamas
Capital: Nassau
Population: 300,529
Official Language: English
Land Area: 10,070 sq km; 3,888 sq mi
Leading Exports: fish and crawfish, rum, salt, chemicals, fruit and vegetables
Location: Caribbean Sea

Barbados
Capital: Bridgetown
Population: 276,607
Official Language: English
Land Area: 431 sq km; 166 sq mi
Leading Exports: sugar and molasses, rum, other foods and beverages, chemicals, electrical components, clothing
Location: Caribbean Sea

Belize
Capital: Belmopan
Population: 262,999
Official Language: English
Land Area: 22,806 sq km; 8,805 sq mi
Leading Exports: sugar, bananas, citrus, clothing, fish products, molasses, wood
Continent: North America

Bolivia
Capital: La Paz and Sucre
Population: 8.5 million
Official Language: Spanish, Quechua, and Aymara
Land Area: 1,084,390 sq km; 418,683 sq mi
Leading Exports: soybeans, natural gas, zinc, gold, wood
Continent: South America

Brazil
Capital: Brasília
Population: 176 million
Official Language: Portuguese
Land Area: 8,456,510 sq km; 3,265,059 sq mi
Leading Exports: manufactured goods, iron ore, soybeans, footwear, coffee, autos
Continent: South America

Chile
Capital: Santiago
Population: 15.5 million
Official Language: Spanish
Land Area: 748,800 sq km; 289,112 sq mi
Leading Exports: copper, fish, fruits, paper and pulp, chemicals
Continent: South America

Colombia
Capital: Bogotá
Population: 41 million
Official Language: Spanish
Land Area: 1,038,700 sq km; 401,042 sq mi
Leading Exports: petroleum, coffee, coal, apparel, bananas, cut flowers
Continent: South America

Costa Rica
Capital: San José
Population: 3.8 million
Official Language: Spanish
Land Area: 51,660 sq km; 19,560 sq mi
Leading Exports: coffee, bananas, sugar, pineapples, textiles, electronic components, medical equipment
Continent: North America

Cuba
Capital: Havana
Population: 11.2 million
Official Language: Spanish
Land Area: 110,860 sq km; 42,803 sq mi
Leading Exports: sugar, nickel, tobacco, fish, medical products, citrus, coffee
Location: Caribbean Sea

Dominica
Capital: Roseau
Population: 73,000
Official Language: English
Land Area: 754 sq km; 291 sq mi
Leading Exports: bananas, soap, bay oil, vegetables, grapefruit, oranges
Location: Caribbean Sea

Dominican Republic
Capital: Santo Domingo
Population: 8.7 million
Official Language: Spanish
Land Area: 48,380 sq km; 18,679 sq mi
Leading Exports: ferronickel, sugar, gold, silver, coffee, cocoa, tobacco, meats, consumer goods
Location: Caribbean Sea

Ecuador
Capital: Quito
Population: 13.5 million
Official Language: Spanish
Land Area: 276,840 sq km; 106,888 sq mi
Leading Exports: petroleum, bananas, shrimp, coffee, cocoa, cut flowers, fish
Continent: South America

El Salvador
Capital: San Salvador
Population: 6.4 million
Official Language: Spanish
Land Area: 20,720 sq km; 8,000 sq mi
Leading Exports: offshore assembly exports, coffee, sugar, shrimp, textiles, chemicals, electricity
Continent: North America

Grenada
Capital: Saint George's
Population: 89,211
Official Language: English
Land Area: 344 sq km; 133 sq mi
Leading Exports: bananas, cocoa, nutmeg, fruit and vegetables, clothing, mace
Location: Caribbean Sea

Guatemala
Capital: Guatemala City
Population: 13.3 million
Official Language: Spanish
Land Area: 108,430 sq km; 41,865 sq mi
Leading Exports: coffee, sugar, bananas, fruits and vegetables, cardamom, meat, apparel, petroleum, electricity
Continent: North America

Guyana
Capital: Georgetown
Population: 698,209
Official Language: English
Land Area: 196,850 sq km; 76,004 sq mi
Leading Exports: sugar, gold, bauxite/alumina, rice, shrimp, molasses, rum, timber
Continent: South America

Haiti
Capital: Port-au-Prince
Population: 7.1 million
Official Language: French and French Creole
Land Area: 27,560 sq km; 10,641 sq mi
Leading Exports: manufactured goods, coffee, oils, cocoa
Location: Caribbean Sea

Honduras
Capital: Tegucigalpa
Population: 6.6 million
Official Language: Spanish
Land Area: 111,890 sq km; 43,201 sq mi
Leading Exports: coffee, bananas, shrimp, lobster, meat, zinc, lumber
Continent: North America

Jamaica
Capital: Kingston
Population: 2.7 million
Official Language: English
Land Area: 10,831 sq km; 4,182 sq mi
Leading Exports: alumina, bauxite, sugar, bananas, rum
Location: Caribbean Sea

Mexico
Capital: Mexico City
Population: 103.4 million
Official Language: Spanish
Land Area: 1,923,040 sq km; 742,486 sq mi
Leading Exports: manufactured goods, oil and oil products, silver, fruits, vegetables, coffee, cotton
Continent: North America

Nicaragua
Capital: Managua
Population: 5 million
Official Language: Spanish
Land Area: 120,254 sq km; 46,430 sq mi
Leading Exports: coffee, shrimp and lobster, cotton, tobacco, beef, sugar, bananas, gold
Continent: North America

Panama
Capital: Panama City
Population: 2.9 million
Official Language: Spanish
Land Area: 75,990 sq km; 29,340 sq mi
Leading Exports: bananas, shrimp, sugar, coffee, clothing
Continent: North America

Paraguay
Capital: Asunción
Population: 5.9 million
Official Language: Spanish
Land Area: 397,300 sq km; 153,398 sq mi
Leading Exports: electricity, soybeans, feed, cotton, meat, edible oils
Continent: South America

Peru
Capital: Lima
Population: 28 million
Official Languages: Spanish and Quechua
Land Area: 1,280,000 sq km; 494,208 sq mi
Leading Exports: fish and fish products, gold, copper, zinc, crude petroleum and byproducts, lead, coffee, sugar, cotton
Continent: South America

Saint Kitts and Nevis
Capital: Basseterre
Population: 38,736
Official Language: English
Land Area: 261 sq km; 101 sq mi
Leading Exports: machinery, food, electronics, beverages, tobacco
Location: Caribbean Sea

Saint Lucia
Capital: Castries
Population: 160,145
Official Language: English
Land Area: 606 sq km; 234 sq mi
Leading Exports: bananas, clothing, cocoa, vegetables, fruits, coconut oil
Location: Caribbean Sea

Saint Vincent and the Grenadines
Capital: Kingstown
Population: 116,394
Official Language: English
Land Area: 389 sq km; 150 sq mi
Leading Exports: bananas, eddoes and dasheen, arrowroot starch, tennis racquets
Location: Caribbean Sea

Suriname
Capital: Paramaribo
Population: 436,494
Official Language: Dutch
Land Area: 161,470 sq km; 62,344 sq mi
Leading Exports: alumina, crude oil, lumber, shrimp and fish, rice, bananas
Continent: South America

Trinidad and Tobago
Capital: Port-of-Spain
Population: 1.2 million
Official Language: English
Land Area: 5,128 sq km; 1,980 sq mi
Leading Exports: petroleum and petroleum products, chemicals, steel products, fertilizer, sugar, cocoa, coffee, citrus, flowers
Location: Caribbean Sea

Uruguay
Capital: Montevideo
Population: 3.4 million
Official Language: Spanish
Land Area: 173,620 sq km; 67,100 sq mi
Leading Exports: meat, rice, leather products, wool, vehicles, dairy products
Continent: South America

Venezuela
Capital: Caracas
Population: 24.3 million
Official Language: Spanish
Land Area: 882,050 sq km; 340,560 sq mi
Leading Exports: petroleum, bauxite and aluminum, steel, chemicals, agricultural products, basic manufactured goods
Continent: South America

United States and Canada

Canada
Capital: Ottawa
Population: 31.9 million
Official Languages: English and French
Land Area: 9,220,970 sq km; 3,560,217 sq mi
Leading Exports: motor vehicles and parts, industrial machinery, aircraft, telecommunications equipment, chemicals, plastics, fertilizers, wood pulp, timber, crude petroleum, natural gas, electricity, aluminum
Continent: North America

United States
Capital: Washington, D.C.
Population: 281.4 million
Official Language: English
Land Area: 9,158,960 sq km; 3,536,274 sq mi
Leading Exports: capital goods, automobiles, industrial supplies and raw materials, consumer goods, agricultural products
Continent: North America

SOURCE: CIA World Factbook Online, 2002

Glossary of Geographic Terms

basin
an area that is lower than surrounding land areas; some basins are filled with water

bay
a body of water that is partly surrounded by land and that is connected to a larger body of water

butte
a small, high, flat-topped landform with cliff-like sides

▲ **butte**

canyon
a deep, narrow valley with steep sides; often with a stream flowing through it

cataract
a large waterfall or steep rapids

◀ **cataract**

delta
a plain at the mouth of a river, often triangular in shape, formed where sediment is deposited by flowing water

flood plain
a broad plain on either side of a river, formed where sediment settles during floods

glacier
a huge, slow-moving mass of snow and ice

hill
an area that rises above surrounding land and has a rounded top; lower and usually less steep than a mountain

island
an area of land completely surrounded by water

isthmus
a narrow strip of land that connects two larger areas of land

mesa
a high, flat-topped landform with cliff-like sides; larger than a butte

mountain
a landform that rises steeply at least 2,000 feet (610 meters) above surrounding land; usually wide at the bottom and rising to a narrow peak or ridge

▶ **glacier**

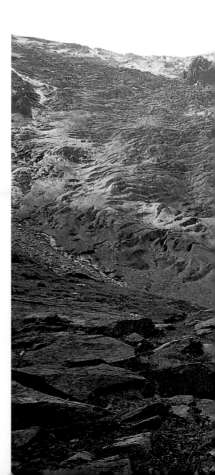

◀ delta

mountain pass
a gap between mountains

peninsula
an area of land almost completely surrounded by water but connected to the mainland

plain
a large area of flat or gently rolling land

plateau
a large, flat area that rises above the surrounding land; at least one side has a steep slope

river mouth
the point where a river enters a lake or sea

strait
a narrow stretch of water that connects two larger bodies of water

tributary
a river or stream that flows into a larger river

valley
a low stretch of land between mountains or hills; land that is drained by a river

volcano
an opening in Earth's surface through which molten rock, ashes, and gases escape from the interior

▶ volcano

Gazetteer

A

Afghanistan (33° N, 65° E) a country in Central Asia where Osama bin Laden's al-Qaeda network was based, p. 242

Africa (10° N, 22° E) the world's second-largest continent, surrounded by the Mediterranean Sea, the Atlantic Ocean, the Indian Ocean, and the Red Sea, pp. 37, 215

Aksum (14°8′ N, 38°43′ E) an ancient town in northern Ethiopia; a powerful kingdom and trade center about A.D. 200–600, p. 53

Andes (20° S, 67° W) a mountain system extending along the western coast of South America, p. 66

Arabian Peninsula (25° N, 45° E) a peninsula in Southwest Asia on which the present-day nations of Saudi Arabia, Yemen, Oman, the United Arab Emirates, Qatar, Bahrain, and Kuwait are located, p. 19

Asia (50° N, 100° E) the world's largest continent, surrounded by the Arctic Ocean, the Pacific Ocean, the Indian Ocean, and Europe, p. 91

Atlantic Ocean (5° S, 25° W) the second-largest ocean, extending from western Europe and Africa to eastern North and South America, p. 164

Austria-Hungary (47° N, 13° E) a former empire in central Europe; the assassination of its archduke in 1914 sparked World War I. p. 223

B

Baghdad (33°30′ N, 44°30′ E) capital city of present-day Iraq; capital of the Muslim empire during Islam's golden age, p. 28

Beijing (40° N, 116° E) capital of present-day China; capital of China under Kublai Khan in the 1200s, p. 96

Benin (6°19′ N, 5°41′ E) a kingdom in the West African rain forest, about 1200 to late 1600s, that was a major cultural and trading center; located in present-day Nigeria, p. 49

Berlin (52°33′ N, 13°30′ E) capital of Germany, p. 212

Bosporus (41°6′ N, 29°4′ E) a narrow strait that separates Europe and Asia and connects the Black Sea with the Sea of Marmara, p. 12

Britain (54° N, 4° W) historically, the island of Great Britain; currently, a term used informally to describe Great Britain or the United Kingdom, p. 205

Byzantium (41°1′ N, 28°58′ E) a city of ancient Greece, later called Constantinople; the site of present-day Istanbul, Turkey, p. 11

C

Cahokia (38°34′ N, 90°11′ W) center of the Mississippian culture which reached its peak about 1100; located in present-day Illinois, p. 81

Canada (60° N, 95° W) a country in North America that joined with Mexico and the United States in the NAFTA agreement, p. 240

Cape of Good Hope (34°24′ S, 18°30′ E) the southern tip of Africa, p. 163

Chaco Canyon (36° N, 108° W) center of the Anasazi culture, located in present-day New Mexico, p. 81

Chang River (32° N, 121° E) the longest river in China and Asia, p. 91

Chang'an (34°15′ N, 108°52′ E) the capital city of China during the Tang dynasty, p. 91

China (35° N, 105° E) a country occupying most of the mainland of East Asia; site of Tang and Song dynasties, p. 91

Constantinople (41°1′ N, 28°58′ E) formerly the ancient city of Byzantium; renamed in A.D. 330 after the Roman emperor Constantine, who made it the new capital of the Eastern Roman, or Byzantine, Empire; now Istanbul, Turkey, p. 10

Cuzco (13°31′ S, 71°59′ W) a city in Peru; the capital city of the Incan empire, p. 64

D

Delhi (28°40′ N, 77°13′ E) the third-largest city in India; capital of medieval India, p. 108

Djenné (13°54' N, 4°33' W) a city in Mali, Africa; an important center of Muslim learning in the kingdoms of Mali and Songhai in the 1300s, p. 46

E

East Africa the eastern region of the continent of Africa, p. 53

England (53° N, 2° W) a country in northwestern Europe; the country where the approval of the Magna Carta in 1215 limited the power of the monarchy, p. 173

Ethiopia (9° N, 39° E) a country in East Africa, officially the People's Republic of Ethiopia; site of an empire ruled by Aksum from about A.D. 100s to 600s, p. 53

Europe (50° N, 28° E) the world's second-smallest continent, a peninsula of the Eurasian landmass bounded by the Arctic Ocean, the Atlantic Ocean, the Mediterranean Sea, and Asia, pp. 12, 119

F

Florence (43°46' N, 11°15' E) a city in central Italy; an important city-state during the Renaissance, p. 155

France (46° N, 2° E) a country in Western Europe; its monarchy was overthrown during the French Revolution. pp. 171, 202

G

Gaul (46° N, 2° E) a region inhabited by the ancient Gauls, including present-day France and parts of Belgium, Germany, and Italy, p. 120

Ghana (8° N, 1° W) a country in West Africa officially known as the Republic of Ghana; a powerful West African kingdom, A.D. 400s–1200s, p. 45

Gobi Desert (43° N, 105° E) a desert in Mongolia and northern China, p. 90

Grand Canal the 1,085-mile (1,747-kilometer) humanmade waterway linking the Chang and Huang rivers in China, p. 92

Great Plains (42° N, 100° W) a mostly flat and grassy region of western North America; home to the Plains Indians, p. 83

Great Serpent Mound (39° N, 83° W) an enormous earthwork built by the Mound Builders; located in present-day Ohio, p. 78

Great Zimbabwe (20°17' S, 30°57' E) a powerful southeast African city, 1100s–1400s, p. 55

Gulf of Mexico (25° N, 90° W) an arm of the Atlantic Ocean in southeastern North America, bordering on eastern Mexico, the southeastern United States, and Cuba, p. 80

H

Himalayas (the) (28° N, 84° E) a mountain system in south central Asia that extends along the border between India and Tibet and through Pakistan, Nepal, and Bhutan, p. 109

Hiroshima (34°30' N, 133° E) a city on the island of Honshu, Japan; the first city on which an atomic bomb was used in warfare, p. 227

Holy Land (32° N, 35° E) a small region on the Mediterranean Sea, which includes parts of modern Israel and Jordan; considered holy by Jews, Christians, and Muslims, p. 133

Huang River (38° N, 118° E) the second-longest river in China, beginning in Tibet and emptying into the Yellow Sea, p. 91

I

Ile-Ife (7°30' N, 4°30' E) the capital of a kingdom in the West African rain forest and a major cultural and trading center, p. 48

Incan empire an empire ruled by the Incas during the 1400s to the 1500s: it stretched along the Andes in South America, p. 64

India (20° N, 77° E) a large country occupying most of the Indian subcontinent in South Asia; site of the Mughal empire, p. 109

Iraq (33° N, 44° E) a country in Southwest Asia; invaded and occupied by the United States in 2003, p. 242

Italy (43° N, 13° E) a boot-shaped country in southern Europe, including the islands of Sicily and Sardinia; birthplace of the Renaissance, p. 155

J

Japan (36° N, 138° E) an island country in the Pacific Ocean off the east coast of Asia; achieved a golden age under the medieval shoguns, p. 101

Jerusalem (31°46' N, 35°14' E) the capital of modern Israel; a holy city for Jews, Christians, and Muslims; a battleground during the Crusades, p. 134

K

Kilwa (9°18' S, 28°25' E) a medieval Islamic city-state on the East African coast; located in present-day Tanzania, pp. 52, 55

Kyoto (35°5' N, 135°45' E) a city in west central Japan; Japan's capital until the late 1800s, p. 102

L

Lowell (42°38' N, 71°19' W) a city in Massachusetts that was an important textile manufacturing center in the 1800s, p. 210

M

Machu Picchu (13°7' S, 72°34' W) a city in the Andes built by the Incas; located near the present-day city of Cuzco in Peru, p. 62

Mali (17° N, 4° W) a country in West Africa, officially the Republic of Mali; a powerful West African trading kingdom from about 1240 to 1500, p. 45

Mecca (21°27' N, 39°49' E) a city in western Saudi Arabia; birthplace of the prophet Muhammad; the holiest Muslim city, p. 20

Medina (41°8' N, 81°52' W) a city in western Saudi Arabia; a city where Muhammad preached, p. 21

Mediterranean Sea (35° N, 20° E) the large sea that separates Europe and Africa, p. 12

Mexico (23° N, 102° W) a country in North America that joined with Canada and the United States in the NAFTA agreement, p. 240

Moscow (55°45' N, 37°35' E) the capital city of modern Russia; capital of Muscovy and of the early Russian tsars, p. 176

Muscovy (55° N, 37° E) an area of present-day Russia that was controlled by the princes of Moscow from the 1300s to the 1500s, p. 176

N

Nagasaki (32°48' N, 129°55' E) a city on the island of Kyushu, Japan; the city on which the second atomic bomb used in warfare was used, p. 227

O

Orléans (47°55' N, 1°54' E) a city in north central France; the site of battles in which Joan of Arc led French forces during the Hundred Years' War, p. 143

P

Pacific Ocean (10° S, 150° W) the largest of the world's oceans; extends from the western Americas to eastern Asia and Australia, pp. 84, 166

Paris (48°52' N, 2°20' E) the capital of France, p. 131

Persia (32° N, 53° E) part of the Muslim empire of medieval times; the region including present-day Iran, p. 26

Peru (10° S, 76° W) a country in northwestern South America; site of the Incan empire, p. 62

Poland (52° N, 19° E) a country in Europe, invaded by Nazi Germany in 1939 to start World War II, p. 226

Portugal (40° N, 8° W) a country in Western Europe; with Spain, occupies the Iberian Peninsula; important sponsor of expeditions during the Age of Exploration, p. 163

R

Rome (41°54' N, 12°29' E) the capital city of Italy; the capital of the ancient Roman Empire; the seat of the Roman Catholic Church, p. 12

Russia (40° N, 84° W) a country in northern Eurasia; ruled by the tsars from the 1500s until 1917, p. 175

S

Sahara (26° N, 13° E) the largest tropical desert in the world, covering almost all of North Africa, p. 37

Silk Road an ancient trade route between China and Europe, p. 90

Songhai (16° N, 0°) a leading kingdom of the West African savanna during the 1400s, p. 47

Soviet Union (40° N, 84° W) officially the Union of Soviet Socialist Republics; the communist nation formed after the Russian Revolution, which included Russia and 14 other republics; adversary of the United States during the Cold War, p. 230

Spain (40° N, 4° W) a country in Western Europe; with Portugal, occupies the Iberian Peninsula; sponsor of Columbus's voyages, pp. 164, 175

St. Petersburg (59°55' N, 30°15' E) large city in Russia; capital city of Peter the Great, p. 177

Strait of Magellan (54° S, 71° W) the channel linking the Atlantic and Pacific oceans near the tip of South America; discovered by Ferdinand Magellan, p. 166

T

Tenochtitlán (19°29' N, 99°9' W) the capital city of the Aztec empire, located on islands in Lake Texcoco, now the site of Mexico City, pp. 70, 181

Tombouctou (16°46' N, 3°1' W) a city in Mali near the Niger River; an important center of trade from the 1400s to the 1600s, p. 50

Turkey (39° N, 35° E) a country located in Southwest Asia, p. 16

U

United States of America (38° N, 97° W) a country in North America; achieved independence from Britain and established a federal republic, p. 201

V

Valley of Mexico (19° N, 99° W) area of present-day Mexico where the Aztec empire flourished from the 1400s to 1521, p. 70

Venice (45° 27' N, 12° 21' E) a major seaport in northern Italy; important Renaissance city-state, p. 155

Versailles (48°48' N, 2°8' E) a city in France; site of the Palace of Versailles built by Louis XIV, p. 172

Vietnam (16° N, 108° E) a country located in Southeast Asia; site of Vietnam War during the Cold War period, p. 232

W

Waterloo (50°43' N, 4°23' E) a village south of Brussels, Belgium, where Napoleon was defeated, p. 214

West Africa the countries in the western region of Africa, p. 44

Wittenberg (51°52' N, 12°39' E) the city in Germany where Martin Luther posted his complaints against the Catholic Church, p. 158

Biographical Dictionary

A

Akbar (AK bahr) (1542–1605) called "the Great;" Mughal emperor of India who expanded the empire, strengthened the government, and granted religious freedom to Hindus, p. 110

B

Babur (BAH bur) (1483–1530) founder of the Mughal dynasty in India and emperor from 1526 to 1530, p. 110

Balboa, Vasco Núñez de (bal BOH uh, VAHS koh NOO nyeth theh) (1475–1519) Spanish explorer who led an expedition across the Isthmus of Panama and became the first European to see the Pacific Ocean from the Americas, p. 166

bin Laden, Osama (bin LAH dun, oh SAH muh) (born 1957) leader of the al-Qaeda terrorist organization that attacked the United States on September 11, 2001, p. 242

Bonaparte, Napoleon (BOH nuh pahrt, nuh POH lee un) (1769–1821) general, consul, and emperor of France; brought reforms to France and extended French rule over much of Europe, p. 213

C

Cabot, John (KAB ut, jahn) (about 1450–1498) Italian sailor sponsored by England, who explored the coast of North America in the 1490s, p. 166

Charlemagne (SHAHR luh mayn) (742–814) king of the Franks who conquered and ruled much of Western Europe; patron of literature and learning, p. 120

Charles I (chahrlz thuh furst) (1600–1649) king during the English Civil War; captured by the Parliamentary forces, tried as a tyrant, and executed, p.199

Churchill, Winston (CHUR chil, WIN stun) (1874–1965) prime minister of Great Britain during World War II, pp. 228, 230

Columbus, Christopher (kuh LUM bus, KRIS tuh fur) (1451–1506) Italian navigator sailing for Spain, who landed in the Americas while looking for a westward sea route from Europe to Asia, p. 164

Constantine (KAHN stun teen) (about A.D. 278–337) emperor of Rome (A.D. 306 to 312) who made Constantinople the imperial capital and encouraged the spread of Christianity, p. 11

Copernicus, Nicolaus (koh PUR nih kus, nik uh LAY us) (1473–1543) Polish astronomer who developed the theory that Earth revolves around the sun, p. 192

Cortés, Hernán (kohr TEZ, hur NAHN) (1485–1547) Spanish conquistador who reached Mexico in 1519, conquered the Aztecs, and won Mexico for Spain, p. 181

Cromwell, Oliver (KRAHM wel, AHL uh vur) (1599–1658) military leader of the forces of Parliament during the English Civil War; ruled England as Lord Protector from 1653 to 1658, p. 200

D

da Gama, Vasco (duh GAM uh, VAHS koh) (about 1469–1524) Portuguese explorer who was the first European to sail around Africa to India, p. 163

da Vinci, Leonardo (duh VIN chee, lee uh NAHR doh) (1452–1519) Italian Renaissance artist, scientist, and inventor; his works include the *Mona Lisa* and *The Last Supper.* p. 154

Dias, Bartolomeu (DEE us, bahr too loo MEE oo) (about 1450–1500) Portuguese explorer; first European to sail around the southern tip of Africa, p. 163

Diderot, Denis (DEE duh roh, duh nee) (1713–1784) French Enlightenment thinker, or philosophe, who edited the *Encyclopedia*, p. 195

E

Elizabeth I (ee LIZ uh buth thuh furst) (1533–1603) queen of England from 1558 to 1603; her reign, called the Elizabethan Age, was a golden age for England. pp. 173, 198

F

Ferdinand II (FUR duh nand thuh SEK und) (1452–1516) Spanish king (1474–1516) who, with his wife Isabella, ruled the first united Spanish kingdom, drove the Muslims from Spain, and sponsored Columbus's voyages, p. 175.

G

Galilei, Galileo (gal uh LAY, gal uh LEE oh) (1564–1642) Italian mathematician, astronomer, and physicist; arrested and tried by the Inquisition for claiming that Earth revolved around the sun, p. 190

Gandhi, Mohandas (GAHN dee, moh HAHN dus) (1869–1948) known as Mahatma (great-souled); led the nonviolent movement that freed India from British rule, p. 235

Gregory VII (GREG uh ree thuh SEV unth) (about 1020–1085) pope from 1073 to 1085; excommunicated Henry IV and then forgave him, and later was deposed by Henry, p. 140

Gutenberg, Johann (GOOT un burg, YOH hahn) (died 1468) German printer who invented movable type and used this technology to print a Bible in 1455, p. 159

H

Harun ar-Rashid (hah ROON ahr rah SHEED) (A.D. 786–809) caliph of Baghdad who ruled during the golden age of the Muslim empire, p. 29

Henry (HEN ree) (1394–1460) prince of Portugal, called Henry the Navigator for sponsoring exploration and trade, p. 163

Henry IV (HEN ree thuh fawrth) (A.D. 1050–1106) king of Germany and emperor of the Holy Roman Empire; excommunicated and then forgiven by Pope Gregory VII, p. 140

Henry VIII (HEN ree thuh ayth) (1491–1547) king of England from 1509 to 1547; separated the English Church from Rome to begin the English Reformation; father of Elizabeth I, pp. 144, 173

Hitler, Adolf (HIT lur, AD awlf) (1889–1945) dictator of Nazi Germany; led military invasions that began World War II; led a campaign of genocide against European Jews, p. 226

Hudson, Henry (HUD sun, HEN ree) (died about 1611) English sailor sponsored by England and the Netherlands; explored parts of the North American coast, p. 178

I

Isabella I (iz uh BEL uh thuh furst) (1451–1504) Spanish queen (1474–1504) who, with her husband Ferdinand, ruled the first united Spanish kingdom, drove the Muslims from Spain, and sponsored Columbus's voyages, p. 175

Ivan the Great (Y vun thuh grayt) (1440–1505) Russian prince who led the rebellion against Mongol rule and became absolute monarch of Russia, p. 177

J

Jefferson, Thomas (JEF ur sun, TAHM us) (1743–1826) statesman, Enlightenment thinker, author of the Declaration of Independence, and third president of the United States (1801–1809), p. 201

Joan of Arc (john uv ahrk) (about 1412–1431) religious peasant girl who led French forces to victory over the English in several battles of the Hundred Years' War; captured by England's allies and executed for witchcraft by the English, p. 143

John (jahn) (1167–1216) king of England (1199–1216); in 1215 was forced to approve the Magna Carta, which limited the power of the king and established the rights of English freemen, p. 142

Justinian (jus TIN ee un) (A.D. 483–565) the greatest Byzantine emperor (527–565), responsible for codifying Roman laws into Justinian's Code, p. 12

K

Kublai Khan (KOO bly kahn) (1215–1294) Mongol emperor who founded the Yuan dynasty in China; encouraged the arts, trade, and religious tolerance, pp. 96, 104

L

Lalibela (lah lee BAY lah) (late 1100s–early 1200s) Christian king of Ethiopia who ordered the construction of churches carved into rock, p. 54

Lenin, Vladimir (LEN in, vlad uh MIHR) (1870–1924) founder of the Russian Communist Party, leader of the Russian Revolution of 1917, and dictator of the Soviet Union (1917–1924), p. 224

Locke, John (lahk, jahn) (1632–1704) English philosopher of the Enlightenment who put forth the idea of natural rights, p. 193

Louis XIV (LOO ee thuh FAWR teenth) (1638–1715) king of France (1643–1715); absolute monarch, called the Sun King, who built Versailles, p. 170

Louis XVI (LOO ee thuh SIKS teenth) (1754–1793) king of France (1774–1792), overthrown and then executed during the French Revolution, p. 202

L'Ouverture, Toussaint (loo vehr TOOR, too SAN) (about 1743–1803) former slave who led the Haitian fight for independence, p. 202

Luther, Martin (LOO thur, MAHRT un) (1483–1546) German monk whose protests against certain abuses of the Roman Catholic Church led to the Protestant Reformation, p. 158

M

Magellan, Ferdinand (muh JEL un, FUR duh nand)) (about 1480–1521) Portuguese explorer who sailed around the tip of South America; his crew was the first to sail all the way around the world. p. 166

Maimonides (my MAHN uh deez) (1135–1204) Spanish-born medieval Jewish philosopher and teacher, p. 30

Mansa Musa (MAHN sah MOO sah) (died about 1332) Muslim king of Mali known for his pilgrimage to Mecca in 1324; encouraged the arts and learning, p. 44

Medici, Lorenzo de (MED uh chee, law REN zoh duh) (1449–1492) ruler of the Renaissance city-state of Florence (1469–1492) and patron of the arts; called "the Magnificent," p. 155

Michelangelo (my kul AN juhl loh) (1475–1564) Italian Renaissance artist, architect, and poet; famous for his sculptures and his painting of the ceiling of the Sistine Chapel, p. 157

Minamoto Yoritomo (mee nah MOH toh yoh ree TOH moh) (1147–1199) founder of the shogunate, a Japanese feudal system that lasted for 700 years, p. 104

Moctezuma (mahk tih ZOO muh) (1466–1520) last emperor of the Aztec empire, conquered and killed by the Spanish, pp. 75, 180

Muhammad (muh HAM ud) (about A.D. 570–632) prophet and founder of Islam; Muslims believe he proclaimed the message of God. p. 18.

N

Newton, Isaac (NOOT un, Y zuk) (1642–1727) English mathematician and scientist who said that the universe obeys certain "laws," such as the law of gravity, p. 193

O

Omar Khayyam (OH mahr ky AHM) (1048–1131) Persian poet, mathematician, and astronomer, p. 26

P

Peter the Great (PEET ur thuh grayt) (1672–1725) tsar, or emperor, of Russia (1682–1725); modernized and westernized Russia; built Saint Petersburg, p. 177

Pizarro, Francisco (pea SAHR oh, frahn SEES koh) (about 1475–1541) Spanish conquistador who conquered the Incan empire and claimed Peru for Spain, pp. 67, 182

Polo, Marco (POH loh, MAHR koh) (1254–1324) Italian traveler who journeyed to China in 1271 and was employed by Kublai Khan for 17 years; his writings sparked European interest in China and increased European-Chinese trade. p. 97

R

Richelieu, Cardinal Armand (RISH loo, KAHRD un ul AHR mund) (1585–1642) cardinal of the Roman Catholic Church and chief minister to King Louis XIII of France; helped establish the absolute power of French monarchs, p. 171

Rousseau, Jean-Jacques (roo SOH, zhahn zhahk) (1712–1778) French Enlightenment thinker, or philosophe, who argued that governments should reflect the will of the people, p. 194

S

Saladin (SAL uh din) (c. 1137–1193) Arab Muslim leader who reconquered Jerusalem during the Crusades but allowed Christian pilgrimages, p. 136

Shah Jahan (shah juh HAHN) (1592–1666) Mughal emperor of India and builder of the Taj Mahal, p. 112

Shakespeare, William (SHAYK spihr, WIL yum) (1564–1616) poet, actor, and playwright of the English Renaissance, who is generally considered the greatest writer in the English language, p. 174

Stalin, Joseph (STAH lin, JOH zuf) (1879–1953) dictator of the Soviet Union (1929–1953) who "purged," or killed, more than 10 million people, p. 224

Sundiata (sun JAH tah) (died 1255) West African king who united the kingdom of Mali, p. 46

T

Tang Taizong (tahng ty ZAWNG) (A.D. 600–649) helped his father establish the Tang dynasty and was emperor from 626 to 649; brought Confucian principles to government, p. 92

Timur (tee MOOR) (1336–1405) Mongol conqueror of northern India, whose empire was based in Samarkand, p. 108

Tokugawa Ieyasu (toh koo GAH wah ee yay AH soo) (1543–1616) founder of the last shogunate in Japan; closed his country off from the rest of the world, p. 104

Toyotomi Hideyoshi (toh yoh TOH mee hee duh YOH shee) (1536–1598) Japanese warrior who united Japan and became its ruler in 1590, p. 104

U

Urban II (UR bun thuh SEK und) (about 1035–1099) pope who began the Crusades, p. 133

V

Voltaire (vohl TEHR) (1694–1778) French Enlightenment thinker, or philosophe, who criticized intolerance and governments that abused their power, p. 195

Glossary

A

absolute monarch (AB suh loot MAHN urk) *n.* a king or queen with complete authority over the government and people in a kingdom, p. 171

Age of Exploration (ayj uv eks pluh RAY shun) *n.* the period of European exploration overseas from about 1400 to 1600, p. 162

Age of Reason (ayj uv REE zun) *n.* the period of the Enlightenment, p. 191

Akbar (AK bahr) *n.* Mughal ruler of India from 1156 to 1605, who encouraged the arts, strengthened the central government, and practiced religious toleration; known as "the Great," p. 110

Aksum (AHK soom) *n.* an important East African center of trade, p. 53

Anasazi (ah nuh SAH zee) *n.* one of the early Native American peoples of the Southwest, p. 81

Andes (AN deez) *n.* a mountain chain of western South America, p. 62

apprentice (uh PREN tis) *n.* an unpaid person training in a craft or trade, p. 131

archipelago (ahr kuh PEL uh goh) *n.* a group or chain of many islands, p. 101

Aztecs (AZ teks) *n.* a people who lived in the Valley of Mexico, p. 70

B

Bantu (BAN too) *n.* a large group of central and southern Africans who speak related languages, p. 36

Benin (beh NEEN) *n.* a kingdom of the West African rain forest, p. 48

C

caliph (KAY lif) *n.* a Muslim ruler, p. 28

Cape of Good Hope (kayp uv good hohp) *n.* the southern tip of Africa, p. 163

capitalism (KAP ut ul iz um) *n.* a system in which individuals control property and business, p. 231

caravan (KA ruh van) *n.* a group of traders traveling together for safety, p. 19

caste system (kast SIS tum) *n.* a Hindu social class system that controlled every aspect of daily life, p. 109

census (SEN sus) *n.* an official count of people in a certain place at a certain time, p. 65

chivalry (SHIV ul ree) *n.* the code of honorable conduct for knights, p. 132

circumnavigate (sur kum NAV ih gayt) *v.* to sail or fly completely around something, such as Earth, p. 167

city-state (SIH tee stayt) *n.* a city that is also a separate, independent state, pp. 55, 155

clan (klan) *n.* a group of families who trace their roots to the same ancestor, p. 40

clergy (KLUR jee) *n.* persons with authority to perform religious services, p. 127

Cold War (kohld wawr) *n.* a period of tension between the United States and the Soviet Union from about 1946 to 1991, p. 231

colony (KAHL uh nee) *n.* territory settled and ruled by a distant country, p. 201

communism (KAHM yoo niz um) *n.* a system in which the government owns most businesses, p. 224

conquistador (kahn KEES tuh dawr) *n.* a Spanish conqueror in the Americas, p. 181

Constantine (KAHN stun teen) *n.* an emperor of the Roman Empire and the founder of Constantinople, p. 11

Constantinople (kahn stan tuh NOH pul) *n.* the capital of the Eastern Roman Empire and later of the Byzantine Empire, p. 10

containment (kun TAYN munt) *n.* the United States policy of trying to halt, or contain, the spread of communism, p. 231

Cortés, Hernán (kohr TEZ, hur NAHN) *n.* Spanish conquistador who conquered the Aztecs, p. 181

Crusades (kroo SAYDZ) *n.* a series of military expeditions launched by Christian Europeans to win the Holy Land back from Muslim control, p. 134

Cuzco (KOOS koh) *n.* the capital city of the Incan empire, located in present-day Peru, p. 64

D

Declaration of Independence (dek luh RAY shun uv in dee PEN duns) *n.* the document in which the United States announced its independence from Britain, p. 201

developed countries (dih VEL upt KUN treez) *n.* industrialized countries, p. 235

developing countries (dih VEL up ing KUN treez) *n.* poorer countries that have little industry, p. 235

dictator (DIK tay tur) *n.* the absolute ruler of a country, p. 224

divine right of kings (duh VYN ryt uv kingz) *n.* the belief that the authority of kings comes directly from God, p. 171

dynasty (DY nus tee) *n.* a series of rulers from the same family, p. 91

E

Elizabethan Age (ee liz uh BEE thun ayj) *n.* a golden age of English history when Elizabeth I was queen, p. 174

encomienda (en koh mee EN dah) *n.* a system in which the Spanish king gave Spanish settlers the right to the labor of the Native Americans who lived in a particular area, p. 182

English Bill of Rights (ING glish bil uv ryts) *n.* the acts passed by Parliament in 1689 guaranteeing certain rights of English people and limiting the power of the monarch, p. 200

English Civil War (ING glish SIV ul wawr) *n.* the military clash between forces loyal to King Charles I and the forces of Parliament that overthrew the monarchy, p. 199

Enlightenment (en LYT un munt) *n.* a philosophical movement, primarily of the 1700s, that was characterized by reliance on reason and experience, p. 191

excommunication (eks kuh myoo nih KAY shun) *n.* expelling someone from the Church, p. 127

F

feudalism (FYOOD ul iz um) *n.* in Europe, a system in which land was owned by kings or lords but held by vassals in return for their loyalty; in Japan, a system in which poor people were legally bound to work for wealthy landowners, pp. 103, 121

G

Ghana (GAH nuh) *n.* the first West African kingdom with an economy based on the gold and salt trade, p. 45

Great Depression (grayt dee PRESH un) *n.* the worldwide economic downturn of the 1930s, p. 225

Great Plains (grayt playnz) *n.* a mostly flat and grassy region of western North America, p. 83

Great Zimbabwe (grayt zim BAHB way) *n.* a powerful East African kingdom, p. 55

guild (gild) *n.* a medieval organization of crafts-workers or tradespeople, p. 131

H

hieroglyphics (HY ur oh GLIF iks) *n.* the signs and symbols that made up the Mayan writing system, p. 72

Holocaust (HAHL uh kawst) *n.* Nazi Germany's mass killing of Jewish people, p. 227

Holy Land (HOH lee land) *n.* Jerusalem and parts of the surrounding area where Jesus lived and taught; an area considered holy by Christians, Muslims, and Jews, p. 133

humanism (HYOO muh niz um) *n.* a system of thought that focused on the nature, ideals, and achievements of human beings, rather than on the divine, p. 156

Hundred Years' War (HUN drud yeerz wawr) *n.* a series of conflicts between England and France, 1337–1453, p. 143

I

Ile-Ife (EE lay EE fay) *n.* the capital of a kingdom of the West African rain forest, p. 48

imperialism (im PIHR ee ul iz um) *n.* the effort of a nation to create an empire of colonies, p. 216

Incas (ING kuhs) *n.* people of a powerful South American empire during the 1400s and 1500s, p. 62

Industrial Revolution (in DUS tree ul rev uh LOO shun) *n.* the change in the methods of producing goods—from hand tools to machines in factories, 1760s–1860s, p. 205

J

Jerusalem (juh ROOZ uh lum) *n.* a city in the Holy Land, regarded as sacred by Christians, Muslims, and Jews, p. 134

Justinian (jus TIN ee un) *n.* one of the greatest Byzantine emperors, p.12

Mosaic of Justinian

Justinian's Code (jus TIN ee unz kohd) *n.* an organized collection and explanation of Roman laws for use by the Byzantine Empire, p. 13

K

Kilwa (KEEL wah) *n.* one of the many trading cities on the East African coast, p. 52

kiva (KEE vuh) *n.* a round room used by the Pueblo people for religious ceremonies, p. 82

knight (nyt) *n.* a man who received honor and land in exchange for serving a lord as a soldier, p. 118

Kublai Khan (KOO bly kahn) *n.* a Mongol emperor of China, p. 96

Kyoto (kee OH toh) *n.* the capital city of medieval Japan, p. 102

L

labor union (LAY bur YOON yun) *n.* an organization of workers formed to bargain with employers for better pay and working conditions, p. 209

M

Magna Carta (MAG nuh KAHR tuh) *n.* the "Great Charter," in which the king's power over his nobles was limited; agreed to by King John of England in 1215, p. 142

maize (mayz) *n.* corn, p. 71

Mali (MAH lee) a rich kingdom of the West African savanna, p. 45

manor (MAN ur) *n.* a large estate, often including farms and a village, ruled by a lord, p. 121

Mansa Musa (MAHN sah MOO sah) *n.* a king of Mali, p. 44

Mayas (MAH yuhs) *n.* a people who established a great civilization in Middle America, p. 71

Mecca (MEK uh) *n.* an Arabian trading center and Muhammad's birthplace, p. 20

medieval (mee dee EE vul) *adj.* referring to the Middle Ages, p. 119

merit system (MEHR it SIS tum) *n.* a system of hiring people based on their abilities, p. 93

Middle Ages (MID ul AY juz) *n.* the years between ancient and modern times, p. 119

migration (my GRAY shun) *n.* the movement from one country or region to settle in another, p. 36

millennium (mih LEN ee um) *n.* a period of one thousand years, p. 238

Model Parliament (MAHD ul PAHR luh munt) *n.* a council of lords, clergy, and common people that advised the English king on government matters, p. 142

mosque (mahsk) *n.* a Muslim house of worship, p. 21

Mound Builders (mownd BIL durz) *n.* Native American groups who built earthen mounds, p. 78

Mughal Empire (MOO gul EM pyr) *n.* a period of Muslim rule of India from the 1500s to the 1700s, p. 110

Muhammad (muh HAM ud) *n.* the prophet and founder of Islam, p. 18

Muslim (MUZ lum) *n.* a follower of Islam, p. 20

N

Napoleonic Code (nuh poh lee AHN ik kohd) *n.* the French legal system based on Enlightenment ideas, set up during Napoleon's rule, p. 214

nation (NAY shun) *n.* a community of people that shares territory and a government, p. 141

nationalism (NASH uh nul iz um) *n.* a feeling of pride in one's country and a desire for its independence, p. 214

natural rights (NACH ur ul ryts) *n.* rights that belong to all human beings from birth, p. 193

nomads (NOH madz) *n.* people with no permanent home, who move from place to place in search of food, water, or pasture, p. 19

Northwest Passage (nawrth WEST PAS ij) *n.* a sea route through North America, p. 166

O

oasis (oh AY sis) *n.* an area of vegetation within a desert, fed by springs and underground water, p. 19

Omar Khayyam (OH mahr ky AHM) *n.* a Muslim poet, mathematician, and astronomer, p. 26

oral history (AWR ul HIS tuh ree) *n.* accounts of the past that people pass down by word of mouth, p. 40

P

philosophes (fee luh ZOHF) *n.* French thinkers of the Enlightenment, p. 194

pilgrim (PIL grum) *n.* a person who journeys to a sacred place, p. 134

Pizarro, Francisco (pea SAHR oh, frahn SEES koh) *n.* Spanish conquistador who conquered the Incas, p. 182

postwar (POHST wawr) *adj.* after a war; after World War II, p. 230

Protestant (PRAHT us tunt) *adj.* referring to Christian religions that grew out of the Reformation, p. 159

pueblo (PWEB loh) *n.* a Native American stone or adobe dwelling, part of a cluster of dwellings built close together, p. 82

Q

quipu (KEE poo) *n.* a group of knotted strings used by the Mayas to record information, p. 65

Quran (koo RAHN) *n.* the holy book of Islam, p. 22

R

Reformation (ref ur MAY shun) *n.* the effort to change or reform the Roman Catholic Church, which led to the establishment of Protestant churches, p. 158

Reign of Terror (rayn uv TEHR ur) *n.* the period (1793–1794) of the French Revolution during which many people were executed for opposing the revolution, p. 203

Renaissance (REN uh sahns) *n.* the period of the rebirth of learning in Europe between about 1300 and 1600, p. 154

S

Sahara (suh HA ruh) *n.* a huge desert stretching across most of North Africa, p. 37

samurai (SAM uh ry) *n.* Japanese warriors, p. 103

savanna (suh VAN uh) *n.* an area of grassland with scattered trees and bushes, p. 37

schism (SIZ um) *n.* a split, particularly in a church or a religion, p. 14

scientific method (sy un TIF ik METH ud) *n.* a method involving careful observation of nature and, in some sciences, controlled experiments, p. 193

Scientific Revolution (sy un TIF ik rev uh LOO shun) *n.* a time when scientists began to rely on observation of the natural world, p. 192

serf (surf) *n.* a farm worker considered part of the manor on which he or she worked, p. 123

shogun (SHOH gun) *n.* the supreme military commander of Japan, p. 104

Silk Road (silk rohd) *n.* a chain of trade routes stretching from China to the Mediterranean Sea, p. 90

Martin Luther, whose actions sparked the Reformation

slash-and-burn agriculture (slash and burn AG rih kul chur) *n.* a farming technique in which trees are cut down and burned to clear and fertilize the land, p. 71

Song (sawng) *n.* a dynasty that ruled China after the Tang, from 960 to 1279, p. 93

Songhai (SAWNG hy) *n.* a powerful kingdom of the West African savanna in the 1400s and 1500s, p. 47

Strait of Magellan (strayt uv muh JEL un) *n.* the channel linking the Atlantic and Pacific oceans near the southern tip of South America, p. 166

Sufis (SOO feez) *n.* a Muslim mystical group that believed they could draw closer to God through prayer, fasting, and a simple life, p. 30

sultan (SUL tun) *n.* a Muslim ruler in India, p. 108

superpower (SOO pur pow ur) *n.* a powerful country that can influence many other countries, p. 231

Swahili (swah HEE lee) *n.* a Bantu language with Arabic words, spoken along the East African coast, p. 55

T

Taj Mahal (tahzh muh HAHL) *n.* a tomb built by Shah Jahan for his wife, p. 112

Tang (tahng) *n.* a dynasty that ruled China for almost 300 years, from the 600s to the 900s, p. 91

Tenochtitlán (teh nawch tee TLAHN) *n.* capital city of the Aztecs, p. 70

terraces (TEHR us iz) *n.* steplike ledges cut into a slope to make land suitable for farming, p. 66

terrorism (TEHR ur iz um) *n.* causing fear through the threat or use of violence as a way to achieve political goals, p. 242

textile industry (TEKS tyl IN dus tree) *n.* the making of cloth, p. 206

A bedroom at Versailles

trading bloc (TRAYD ing blahk) *n.* a group of countries that agrees to reduce barriers to trade, p. 241

troubadour (TROO buh dawr) *n.* a traveling poet and musician of the Middle Ages, p. 132

tsar (zahr) *n.* the Russian emperor, p. 177

V

Versailles (vur SY) *n.* the palace built for the French king Louis XIV, p. 172

W

World War I (wurld wawr wun) *n.* the first major war of the 1900s (1914–1918), p. 223

World War II (wurld wawr too) *n.* the second major war of the 1900s (1939–1945), p. 226

The *m*, *g*, or *p* following some page numbers refers to maps *(m)*, charts, tables, graphs, timelines, or diagrams *(g)*, or pictures *(p)*.

Blue indicates Teacher's Edition entries.

Pittsburgh, Pennsylvania, 208*g*, 208*p*
Pizarro, Francisco, 67, 182–183
Plains Indians, 83
Plateau of Tibet, 89*m*, 91
poetry
 of China, 93, 94
 of Japan, 105
 of Middle Ages, 132
 of Muslim civilization, 28, 30
 Persian, 26, 26*p*
Poland, 117*m*, 226
political cartoons, 212*p*
political geography, 6, 6*m*, 6*p*
pollution, 241
Polo, Marco, 97, 97*p*
popes, 129, 140, 142
population
 of Dallas, Texas, 236–237, 236*p*, 237*g*
 environment and, 241
 of Inca civilization, 64
 during Industrial Revolution, 208*g*
 poverty and, 241
porcelain, 94, 94*p*
Portugal, 55, 117*m*
 in the Age of Exploration, 163, 164*m*, 166
 colonies of, 182*m*, 215, 215*m*
 slave trade and, 183
postal service
 beginnings of, 116*g*
postwar world, 230, 286
potlatch, 84
poverty, 235, 241
The Prince **(Machiavelli),** 155
printing, 95
printing press, 159
propaganda, 224*p*
prophet, 18
Protestant Reformation, 158–160, 158*p*, 159*m*, 160*p*, 174, 191
Pueblo people, 61*m*, 82–83
pueblos, 82
pyramid, 76–77, 76*p*–77*p*

Q

Quecha language, 65
Quetzalcoatl (Aztec god), 74*p*, 180, 180*p*, 181
quipu, 65, 65*p*
Quran, 22, 23*p*

R

radios, 239
railroads, 188*p*, 206
rain forest, 37
 kingdoms of, 48–49, 48*p*, 49*p*
Ramadan, 21
reading skills
 analyze author's purpose, RW1

clarifying meaning, 34
comparison and contrast, 198, 204, 212
distinguish between facts and opinions, RW1
evaluate credibility, RW1
identify cause and effect, 88, 90
identify evidence, RW1
identify implied main idea, 78
identify main ideas, 60, 62
identify sequence, 126, 140, 144
identify supporting details, 70
informational texts, RW1
paraphrase, 44
predict, 18, 22
prepare to read, 180
preview and ask questions, 26
preview and set a purpose, 10
read ahead, 36
reading process, 8
recognize sequence signal words, 118, 133, 137
recognize word origins, 230
reread, 36
sequence, 116
summarize, 52
understand effects, 100
use context clues, 152, 154, 161, 170, 188
use word parts, 222, 238
word analysis, 220
Reformation, 158–160, 158*p*, 159*m*, 160*p*
Reign of Terror, 203, 203*p*
religion
 of Aztecs, 70, 74, 74*p*, 76–77
 Calvinists, 159*m*
 in China, 5*p*, 96
 Church of England, 173, 174
 in Ethiopia, 53–54, 53*p*, 54*p*
 in India, 109, 110, 112
 in Japan, 104, 105
 Lutheran, 159*m*
 Mayan, 72
 Protestant Reformation, 158–160, 158*p*, 159*m*, 160*p*
 Roman Catholic Church, 127, 158–160, 158*p*, 159*m*, 160*p*
 in Russia, 176
 in West Africa, 46
 See also specific religions
Renaissance, 6*m*, 191
 art of, 156, 156*p*, 157, 157*p*, 185*p*
 definition of, 154
 in Italy, 155–156, 155*p*
 Northern, 156
Restoration, 200
Revolutionary War, 201
 at sea, 188*h*
Richard I, King of England (Richard the Lion-Hearted), 136,

138–139, 138*p*, 139*p*
Richelieu, Cardinal, 171, 171*p*
Roaring Twenties, 225
Robespierre, Maximilien, 203
Roman Catholic Church, 14, 17*g*
 Church of England and, 173
 convents, 129
 excommunication, 127, 142
 Inquisition and, 175
 organization of, 129
 popes, 140, 142
 powers of, 127
 and Protestant Reformation, 158–160, 158*p*, 159*m*, 160*p*
 scholasticism, 129
 science and, 190
 women in, 129
 See also Catholic Reformation; religion
Roman Empire, 9*m*, 11, 12, 28
 collapse of, 119–120, 119*m*
 invasions of, 119*m*
Rome, 12, 156
rope bridges, 66*p*
Rousseau, Jean Jacques, 194
route maps, 178–179, 178–179*m*, 186
Rumi, 30
Russia, 6*m*, 175–177, 221*m*
 absolute rule in, 175, 177, 177*p*
 capitalism in, 233
 imperialism of, 216
 religion in, 176
 revolution in, 224, 224*p*
 in World War I, 223
 See also Soviet Union
Russian Orthodox Church, 176
Russian Revolution, 224, 224*p*

S

Sahara, 2*p*, 37, 259*m*
St. Petersburg, 224*p*
St. Peter's Cathedral, 157
Saladin, 136, 281
salt
 value of, 50
salt trade, 45, 45*p*, 51, 59
Samarkand, 108
Samurai warriors, 103–104, 103*p*
satellites, 239
savanna, 37, 45
schism, 14, 23
Scholastic movement, 129
science
 gravity, 192
 iron tools, 58
 in Muslim civilization, 28, 29, 29*p*
 of Persia, 26
 Roman Catholic Church and, 190
 technology and, 239, 239*p*
 writing skills, 86, 114, 146, 244
scientific method, 193, 197*g*, 239

Acknowledgments

Cover Design

Pronk&Associates

Staff Credits

The people who made up *World Studies © 05* team—representing design services, editorial, editorial services, educational technology, marketing, market research, photo research and art development, production services, project office, publishing processes, and rights & permissions—are listed below. Bold type denotes core team members.

Greg Abrom, Ernie Albanese, Rob Aleman, Susan Andariese, **Rachel Avenia-Prol,** Leann Davis Alspaugh, Penny Baker, Barbara Bertell, **Peter Brooks,** Rui Camarinha, John Carle, **Lisa Del Gatto,** Paul Delsignore, Kathy Dempsey, Anne Drowns, Deborah Dukeshire, Marlies Dwyer, **Frederick Fellows,** Paula C. Foye, Lara Fox, Julia Gecha, **Mary Hanisco,** Salena Hastings, Lance Hatch, Kerri Hoar, **Beth Hyslip,** Katharine Ingram, Nancy Jones, John Kingston, Deborah Levheim, **Kathleen Mercandetti,** Art Mkrtchyan, Ken Myett, **Mark O'Malley,** Jen Paley, Ray Parenteau, **Gabriela Pérez Fiato,** Linda Punskovsky, Kirsten Richert, **Lynn Robbins,** Nancy Rogier, Bruce Rolff, Robin Samper, Mildred Schulte, Siri Schwartzman, **Malti Sharma,** Lisa Smith-Ruvalcaba, Roberta Warshaw, Sarah Yezzi

Additional Credits

Jonathan Ambar, Tom Benfatti, Lisa D. Ferrari, Paul Foster, Florrie Gadson, Philip Gagler, Ella Hanna, Jeffrey LaFountain, Karen Mancinelli, Michael McLaughlin, Lesley Pierson, Debi Taffet

DK The DK Designs team who contributed to *World Studies © 05* were as follows:

Hilary Bird, Samantha Borland, Marian Broderick, Richard Czapnik, Nigel Duffield, Heather Dunleavy, Cynthia Frazer, James A. Hall, Lucy Heaver, Rose Horridge, Paul Jackson, Heather Jones, Ian Midson, Marie Ortu, Marie Osborn, Leyla Ostovar, Ralph Pitchford, Ilana Sallick, Pamela Shiels, Andrew Szudek, Amber Tokeley.

DK ## Maps

Maps and globes were created by **DK Cartography**. The team consisted of Tony Chambers, Damien Demaj, Julia Lunn, Ed Merritt, David Roberts, Ann Stephenson, Gail Townsley, Iorwerth Watkins.

Illustrations

Kenneth Batelman: 11; Richard Benson/Dorling Kindersley, 207; KJA-artists.com: 24, 24–25, 50, 50–51, 51, 76, 76–77, 106, 106–107, 124, 124–125, 125, 168, 168–169, 210, 210–211, 228, 228–229; Trevor Johnston: 197; Jill Ort: 10, 18, 26, 90, 100, 108; Jen Paley: 17, 21, 29, 36, 44, 47, 52, 62, 68, 70, 78, 87, 95, 98, 99, 118, 126, 133, 140, 147, 154, 161, 162, 170, 180, 190, 192, 198, 204, 206, 208, 212, 219, 222, 225, 230, 237, 238; XNR Productions: 240

Photos

Cover Photos
tl, Brian Sytnyk/Masterfile Corporation; **tm,** Firstlight/Heatons, **tr,** Robert Marien/MaXx; Chris Ladd/Getty Images, Inc.

Title Page
Chris Ladd/Getty Images, Inc.

Table of Contents
T4, Max Alexander/Robert Harding World Imagery; **T5 t,** Chas Howson/The British Museum, London, UK/Dorling Kindersley; **T5 b both,** Michel Zab/Dorling Kindersley; **T6 t,** Gwalior Fort, Madhya Pradesh, India/Bridgeman Art Library; **T6 b,** Bridgeman Art Library; **T7,** Francis Speckler/EPA/Sipa Photos; **T8,** Sipa Photos; **ix** Morton Beebe/Corbis; **T9,** David Jones/Alamy Images

Professional Development
T35, Royalty-Free/Corbis; **T36,** PhotoDisc/Getty Images, Inc.; **T37,** Comstock

Reading and Writing Handbook
RW Michael Newman/PhotoEdit; **RW1,** Walter Hodges/Getty Images, Inc.; **RW2,** Digital Vision/Getty Images, Inc.; **RW3,** Will Hart/PhotoEdit; **RW5,** Jose Luis Pelaez, Inc./Corbis

MapMaster Skills Handbook
M, James Hall/Dorling Kindersley; **M1,** Mertin Harvey/Gallo Images/Corbis; **M2–3 m,** NASA; **M2–3,** (globes) Planetary Visions; **M5 br,** Barnabas Kindersley/Dorling Kindersley; **M6 tr,** Mike Dunning/Dorling Kindersley; **M10 b,** Bernard and Catherine Desjeux/Corbis; **M11,** Hutchison Library; **M12 b,** Pa Photos; **M13 r,** Panos Pictures; **M14 l,** Macduff Everton/Corbis; **M14 t,** MSCF/NASA; **M15 b,** Ariadne Van Zandbergen/Lonely Planet Images; **M16 l,** Bill Stormont/Corbis; **M16 b,** Pablo Corral/Corbis; **M17 t,** Les Stone/Sygma/Corbis; **M17 b,** W. Perry Conway/Corbis

Guiding Questions
1, Christie's Images/Corbis

World Overview
2 l, Buddy Mays/Corbis; **2 tr,** G. Renner/Robert Harding World Imagery; **3 b,** B.S.P.I./Corbis; **3 t,** Pascal Tournaire/Saola/Getty Images, Inc.; **4 t,** Kevin Fleming/Corbis; **4 b,** Conaculta-Inah-Mex. Authorized reproduction by the Instituto Nacional de Antropologia e Historia; **4 ml,** Piers Cavendish/Impact Photos; **5 t, 5 b,** Ted Spiegel/Corbis; **5 mr,** Lowell Georgia/Corbis; **6 t,** Dorling Kindersley; **6 b,** Ed Simpson/Getty Images, Inc.; **7 t,** Dorling Kindersley; **7 b,** Robert Harding World Imagery; **7 ml,** William J. Hebert/Getty Images, Inc.

Chapter One
8f l, Royalty-Free/Corbis; **8f r,** PhotoDisc/Getty Images, Inc.; **8–9,** Robert Frerck/Woodfin Camp & Associates; **10,** The Granger Collection, New York; **11 t,** Topham/The Image Works; **11 b,** Historical Picture Archive/Corbis; **12 t,** Discovery Channel School; **12 m,** Chas Howson/The British Museum, London, UK/Dorling Kindersley; **12 b,** The Granger Collection, New York; **13,** Robert Frerck/Getty Images, Inc.; **14,** Paul H. Kuiper/Corbis; **15,** Photos12.com-ARJ; **16 t,** Corbis; **16 b,** Jeff Greenberg/The Image Works; **18,** The British Library, London, UK; **19,** Christine Osborne/Agency Worldwide Picture Library/Alamy Images; **20,** Explorer, Paris/SuperStock, Inc.; **21,** Paul Chesley/Stone/Getty Images, Inc.; **22 t,** Latif Reuters New Media, Inc./Corbis; **22 b,** The British Library, London, UK/The Art Archive; **23,** The Granger Collection, New York; **24,** Alan Hills/Dorling Kindersley; **25,** Dorling Kindersley; **26,** Scala/Art Resource, NY; **27,** Archivo Iconografico, S. A./Corbis; **28,** Lauros/Giraudon/Bridgeman Art Library; **29 t, 29 m,** The Granger Collection, New York; **29 b,** Giraudon/Art Resource, NY; **30,** Stuart Cohen/The Image Works; **31 t,** The Granger Collection, New York; **31 b,** Lauros/Giraudon/Bridgeman Art Library

Chapter Two
34f l, Royalty-Free/Corbis; **34f r,** PhotoDisc/Getty Images, Inc.; **34–35,** M. & E. Bernheim/Woodfin Camp & Associates; **36,** Tim Rock/Lonely Planet Images; **37,** Chris Anderson/Aurora Photos; **38–39,** SuperStock, Inc.; **40,** Walter Bibikow/Jon Arnold Images/Alamy Images; **41 all,** Geoff Dann/Dorling Kindersley; **42,** Werner Forman/Art Resource, NY; **43,** Getty Images, Inc.; **44,** The Granger Collection, New York; **45 t,** Nik Wheeler/Corbis; **45 b,** Ariadne Van Zandbergen/Lonely Planet Images; **46,** David Jones/Alamy Images; **47 both,** Werner Forman/Art Resource, NY; **48,** Lars Howlett/Aurora Photos; **49,** Christie's Images/Corbis; **51,** The Art Archive/Musée des Arts Africains et Océaniens/Dagli Orti; **52,** Marc & Evelyne Bernheim/Woodfin Camp & Associates; **53 t,** David Else/Lonely Planet Images; **53 b,** D. Harcourt-Webster/Robert Harding World Imagery; **54 t,** Dave Bartruff/Corbis; **54 b,** Ariadne Van Zandbergen/Lonely Planet Images; **55 t,** Discovery Channel School; **55 b,** Mitch Reardon/Lonely Planet Images; **56,** I. Vanderharst/Robert Harding World Imagery; **57,** Christie's Images/Corbis

Chapter Three
60f l, Royalty-Free/Corbis; **60f r,** PhotoDisc/Getty Images, Inc.; **60–61,** SuperStock, Inc.; **62,** Philippe Colombi/Photodisc Green/ Getty Images, Inc.; **63,** The British Museum, London, UK/Dorling Kindersley; **64,** Anthony Pidgeon/Lonely Planet Images; **65 t,** Charles & Josette Lenars/Corbis; **65 b,** The Granger Collection, New York; **66,** Woodfin Camp & Associates; **67,** The British Museum, London, UK/Dorling Kindersley; **69 both,** The Art Archive/Archaeological Museum Lima/Dagli Orti; **70,** Bodleian Library; **71 t,** Angel Terry/Alamy Images; **71 b,** Robert Fried Photography; **72,** Private Collection/Bridgeman Art Library; **73 t,** Discovery Channel School; **73 b,** Robert Frerck/Getty Images Inc.; **74 both, 75,** Michel Zab/Dorling Kindersley; **77,** Werner Forman/Art Resource, NY; **78,** Werner Forman/Art Resource, NY; **79,** Tony Linck/SuperStock, Inc.; **80 t,** Werner Forman Archive/Art Resource, NY; **80 b,** Richard A. Cooke/Corbis; **81,** Dewitt Jones/Corbis; **82–83 t,** George H. H. Huey Photography, Inc.; **82 b,** David Muench/Corbis; **84,** Peter Gridley/Getty Images, Inc.; **85 l,** David Muench/Corbis; **85 r,** Michel Zab/ Dorling Kindersley

Chapter Four

88f l, Royalty-Free/Corbis; **88f r,** PhotoDisc/Getty Images, Inc.; **88–89,** B. Davis/Woodfin Camp & Associates; **90–91 b,** The British Museum, London, UK/Topham-HIP/The Image Works; **91 t,** Werner Forman/Art Resource, NY; **92,** The Granger Collection, New York; **93,** Honolulu Academy of Arts; **94 l,** The Granger Collection, New York; **94 r,** Alan Hills and Geoff Brightling/The British Museum, London, UK/Dorling Kindersley; **95 tl,** The Art Archive; **95 tr,** ChinaStock; **95 br,** Lawrence Pardes/ The British Library, London, UK/Dorling Kindersley; **96,** Werner Forman/Art Resource, NY; **97 t,** Bettmann/Corbis; **97 b,** Discovery Channel School; **98–99 b,** Anthony Bannister; Gallo Images/Corbis; **99 t,** Burstein Collection/Corbis; **100,** Fitzwilliam Museum, University of Cambridge, UK/Bridgeman Art Library; **101,** Adina Tovy Amsel/Lonely Planet Images; **102,** Akira Nakata/HAGA/The Image Works; **103 t,** Lee Boltin/Boltin Picture Library; **103 b,** Pearson Education U.S. ELT/Scott Foresman; **104,** The Art Archive; **105,** Fujifotos/The Image Works; **106 t,** Victoria & Albert Museum, London, UK/Art Resource, NY; **106 b,** Leeds Museums and Art Galleries (City Museum) UK/Bridgeman Art Library; **108,** The Granger Collection, New York; **109,** John Kelly/Getty Images, Inc.; **110,** The Granger Collection, New York; **111,** Gwalior Fort, Madhya Pradesh, India/Bridgeman Art Library; **112,** David Sutherland/Getty Images Inc.; **113 t,** Bettman/Corbis; **113 b,** Fujifotos/The Image Works

Chapter Five

116g l, Royalty-Free/Corbis; **116g r,** PhotoDisc/Getty Images, Inc.; **116h l,** GeoStock/Getty Images, Inc.; **116h ml,** Comstock; **116h mr,** PhotoDisc/Getty Images, Inc.; **116h r,** SW Productions/Getty Images, Inc.; **116–117,** Steve Vidler/eStock Photography; **118,** Giraudon/Art Resource, NY; **119,** The Art Archive/Bargello Museum Florence, Italy/Dagli Orti; **120,** Gianni Dagli Orti/Corbis; **121 t,** Robin Smith/PhotoLibrary.com; **121 b,** Gianni Dagli Orti/Corbis; **122 tl,** New York Public Library/Art Resource, NY; **122 tr,** The Granger Collection, New York; **122 b,** Discovery Channel School; **123,** Scala/Art Resource, NY; **125,** The Granger Collection, New York; **126,** Adam Woolfitt/Corbis; **127,** The Granger Collection, New York; **128 all,** Dorling Kindersley; **129 t,** The Art Archive/Bibliothèque Municipale Laon/Dagli Orti; **129 b,** The Art Archive/ Bodleian Library Oxford/The Bodleian Library; **130,** The British Museum, London, UK/Topham-HIP/The Image Works; **131 t,** AKG London Lt.; **131 b,** The Art Archive/Museo Civico Bologna/Dagli Orti; **132,** Gianni Dagli Orti/Corbis; **133,** Archivo Iconografico, S. A./Corbis; **134 t,** North Wind Picture Archives; **134 b,** The Granger Collection, New York; **136,** Archivo Iconografico, S. A./Corbis; **137,** Bettmann/Corbis; **138,** Library of Congress; **139 t,** The Granger Collection, New York; **139 b,** Snark/Art Resource, NY; **140,** Scala/Art Resource, NY; **141,** Derek Croucher/Corbis; **142,** ARPL/Topham/The Image Works; **143,** Morton Beebe/Corbis; **144,** Sunday Mirror/Topham/The Image Works; **145,** The Art Archive/Bargello Museum Florence, Italy/Dagli Orti; **148,** The Art Archive/The British Library, London, UK; **149, 150,** Reprinted with permission of Atheneum Books for Young Readers, an imprint of Simon & Schuster Children's Publishing Division from *The Boy's King Arthur* by Sidney Lanier, illustrated by N. C. Wyeth. Copyright 1917 Charles Scribner's Sons; copyright renewed 1954 N. C. Wyeth. **151,** Copyright, Pittsburgh Post-Gazette, V.W.H. Campbell Jr., 2002, all rights reserved. Reprinted with permission.

Chapter Six

152g l, Royalty-Free/Corbis; **152g r,** PhotoDisc/Getty Images, Inc.; **152h l,** GeoStock/Getty Images, Inc.; **152h ml,** Comstock; **152h mr,** PhotoDisc/Getty Images, Inc.; **152h r,** SW Productions/Getty Images, Inc.; **152–153,** Tony Craddock/Getty Images, Inc.; **154, 155 t,** The Granger Collection, New York; **155 b,** Alinari/Art Resource, NY; **156 l,** Erich Lessing/Art Resource, NY; **156 r,** The Art Archive/Galleria Brera Milan/Dagli Orti; **157 t,** Discovery Channel School; **157 b,** Jack Novak/SuperStock, Inc.; **158,** SuperStock, Inc.; **160,** The Art Archive/Museo Tridentino Arte Sacra Trento/Dagli Orti; **161 both,** National Geographic Society Image Collection; **162 t,** Roland et Sabrina Michaud/Woodfin Camp & Associates; **162 m,** The Granger Collection, New York; **162 b,** The Art Archive Museo de la Torre del Oro Seville/Dagli Orti; **163,** Harvery Lloyd/Getty Images, Inc.; **164 t,** Topham/The Image Works; **164–165 b,** Townsend P. Dickinson/The Image Works; **166,** The Art Archive/Marine Museum Lisbon/Dagli Orti; **167,** The Granger Collection, New York; **168 both,** David Lees/Corbis; **170,** Musee du Louvre/Art Resource, NY; **171 t,** Bridgeman Art Library; **171 b,** The Art Archive/Musée du Château de Versailles/Dagli Orti; **172 l,** Cary Wolinsky/IPN; **172 m,** Réunion des Musées Nationaux/Art Resource, NY; **172 r,** Archivo Iconografico, S.A./Corbis; **173,** Topham/The Image Works; **174 t,** Getty Images, Inc.; **174 b,** Charlotte Hindle/Lonely Planet Images; **175 t,** Max Alexander/Robert Harding World Imagery; **175 b,** Archivo

Iconografico/Corbis/Bettmann; **176,** Dallas and John Heaton/Corbis **177,** Leonid Bogdanov/SuperStock, Inc.; **178,** The Art Archive/Maritiem Museum Prins Hendrik Rotterdam/Dagli Orti; **179,** Gabe Palacio/IPN; **180,** Lee Boltin/Boltin Picture Library; **181,** Michel Zabe/Art Resource, NY; **183,** The Granger Collection, New York; **184,** The Art Archive/Dagli Orti; **185 t,** The Art Archive/Galleria Brera Milan/Dagli Orti; **185 b,** Lee Boltin/Boltin Picture Library

Chapter Seven

188g l, Royalty-Free/Corbis; **188g r,** PhotoDisc/Getty Images, Inc.; **188h l,** GeoStock/Getty Images, Inc.; **188h ml,** Comstock; **188h mr,** PhotoDisc/Getty Images, Inc.; **188h r,** SW Productions/Getty Images, Inc.; **188–189,** Bettmann/Corbis; **190,** The Granger Collection, New York; **191 t,** Discovery Channel School; **191 bl,** Paul Almasy/Corbis; **191 br,** The Granger Collection, New York; **192 tl,** The Art Archive/Bibliothèque des Arts Décoratifs Paris/Dagli Orti; **192 bl,** The Granger Collection, New York; **192 br,** James A. Sugar/Corbis; **193, 194,** The Granger Collection, New York; **195 l,** Science Museum, London/Topham-HIP/The Image Works; **195 r,** The Art Archive/ Bibliothèque des Arts Décoratifs Paris/Dagli Orti; **197 l,** Dorling Kindersley; **197 r,** The Granger Collection, NY; **198,** Walker Art Gallery, Liverpool, UK/Bridgeman Art Library; **199 t,** The Granger Collection, NY; **199 b,** Bridgeman Art Library; **200 t,** Stock Montage, Inc.; **200 b, 201 t,** The Granger Collection, New York; **201 b,** Independence National Historical Park; **202,** Topham/The Image Works; **203,** Giroudon/Art Resource, NY; **204,** Bristol City Museum and Art Gallery, UK/Bridgeman Art Library; **205,** Corbis; **206 t,** The Granger Collection, New York; **206 mr,** Bettmann/Corbis; **206 ml,** Dave King/Dorling Kindersley; **206 b, 207 t,** Bettmann/Corbis; **207 b,** Dorling Kindersley; **208,** Joe Sohm/The Image Works; **209,** The Granger Collection, New York; **211,** Bettmann/Corbis; **212,** The Granger Collection, New York; **213,** Austrian Archives/Corbis; **214 t,** Dorling Kindersley; **214 b,** Réunion des Musées Nationaux/Art Resource, NY; **216,** The Art Archive/Bodleian Library Oxford/The Bodleian Library; **217 t,** The Granger Collection, New York; **217 m,** Bettmann/Corbis; **217 b,** Giroudon/Art Resource, NY

Chapter Eight

220f l, Royalty-Free/Corbis; **220f r,** PhotoDisc/Getty Images, Inc.; **220–221,** NASA; **222,** Bettmann/Corbis; **223 t,** Hulton Archive Photos/Getty Images Inc.; **223 b,** Andy Crawford/Imperial War Museum/Dorling Kindersley; **224 t,** Hulton Archive/Getty Images, Inc.; **224 b,** Swim Ink/Corbis; **225,** Bettmann/Corbis; **226 b,** Discovery Channel School; **226 t, 227,** Bettmann/Corbis; **229 all,** The Imperial War Museum; **230,** Topham/The Image Works; **231 t,** Photo by Douglas E. Houser/US Navy/Time Life Pictures/Getty Images, Inc.; **231 m, 231 b,** Peter Turnley/Corbis; **232,** Hulton Archive/Getty Images, Inc.; **233,** Rick Wilking/Corbis; **234,** Jim Pickerell /Stockphoto.com; **235,** Hulton Archive Photos/Getty Images Inc.; **236 t,** From the collections of the Texas/Dallas History and Archives Division, Dallas Public Library; **236 b,** Tim Hursley/SuperStock, Inc.; **238,** Michel Euler/AP/Wide World Photos; **239 t inset,** Francis Speckler/EPA/Sipa Photos; **239 m inset,** Sipa Photos; **239 background,** NASA/JPL/Cornell; **240,** Sean Gallup/Getty Images, Inc.; **241,** Sue Cunningham/Alamy Images; **242,** Rommel Pecson/The Image Works; **243 t,** Dorling Kindersley; **243 bl,** Peter Turnley/Corbis; **243 br,** Sipa Photos

Projects

246 t, The Art Archive/Bodleian Library Oxford/The Bodleian Library; **246 m,** EPA/Harish Taygi/AP/Wide World Photos; **246 b,** Prakash Singh/AFP/Getty Images, Inc.

Reference

247, Migel Angel Muñoz/AGE Fotostock

Glossary of Geographic Terms

272 t, A & L Sinibaldi/Getty Images, Inc.; **272 b,** John Beatty/Getty Images, Inc.; **272–273 b,** Spencer Swanger/Tom Stack & Associates; **273 t,** Hans Strand/Getty Images, Inc; **273 m,** Paul Chesley/Getty Images, Inc.

Biographical Dictionary

278, Austrian Archives/Corbis; **281,** Leonid Bogdanov/SuperStock, Inc.

Glossary

282, The Granger Collection, New York; **283,** Nik Wheeler/Corbis; **284,** The Granger Collection, New York; **285,** The British Museum, London, UK/Dorling Kindersley; **286,** SuperStock, Inc.; **287,** Cary Wolinsky/IPN

Text

Chapter One

26, Excerpt from *The Concise History of Islam and the Origin of Its Empires* by Gregory C. Kozlowski. Copyright © 1991 by The Copley Publishing Group; **30,** Excerpt from